A Pedagogical Design for Human Flourishing

In *A Pedagogical Design for Human Flourishing: Transforming Schools with the McCallister Model*, Cynthia McCallister presents a revolutionary paradigm for education that is practical, conceptually convincing, and grounded in contemporary behavioral science theory. Beginning with the assertion that equality of educational opportunity depends on access to experiences that are sufficiently appropriate and rich to enable the achievement of diverse human potentials, she provides a comprehensive school design for intervention that demonstrates how to achieve it. Grounded in recent advances in learning science, McCallister asserts three necessary conditions for learning: the need for learners to have access to diverse, rich environmental experiences; the need for them to enjoy fundamental freedom and autonomy to direct their own learning; and access to full and free forms of association. In her model, these conditions provide what is necessary for learners to coordinate their minds with others to develop their identities, personalities, and talents. These conditions are animated in concrete procedures that can be adapted to a wide variety of populations in formal, informal, and remote educational settings. The procedures take the form of rules that learners comply with in the exercise of their freedom. When they are followed, the rules provide a grammar for the social norms that govern the moral worlds of learners and compel them to flourish. Tested over two decades in her work as a teacher, scholar, and school reformer in more than 20 NYC public schools, the McCallister Method has delivered an innovative and disruptive approach to schooling that has proven successful in finally transforming low-performing industrial schools into 21st-century learning organizations.

Online support material includes assessments, records, surveys, and more to be used in school design and classroom settings.

Cynthia McCallister is an Associate Professor in the Steinhardt School of Culture, Education, and Human Development at New York University.

"In this work Cynthia McCallister draws from a rich palette of theory and practice, and with a fine bristle brush paints for us a detailed, rigorous, and coherent picture for designing schools as learning cultures. The emphasis on relational process in learning is particularly compelling, and the applicability of the design is impressive."

Kenneth J. Gergen, Ph.D.
Professor Emeritus, Swarthmore College

"Cynthia McCallister's original and widely tested design for classroom learning activities, 'Learning Cultures,' meets the mandates of the school curriculum while allowing learners the freedom necessary for them to take responsibility for their own learning."

David R. Olson, Ph.D.
Professor Emeritus, Ontario Institute for Studies in Education/University of Toronto

"Dr. McCallister has designed an approach to literacy education that is highly effective and generating impressive results at the schools where it has been implemented. In her approach, Learning Cultures, not only do students do more reading and writing, they also learn how to collaborate and provide each other with constructive feedback. For educators and researchers who are looking for ways to enhance literacy and learning in schools this book will be a tremendous resource."

Pedro A. Noguera, Ph.D.
Emery Stoops and Joyce King Stoops Dean, University of Southern California
Rossier School of Education

"As a geneticist interested in education, I didn't expect to like Learning Cultures. Genetics research shows that differences in the schools we have don't make much of a difference in children's achievement. However, I am impressed with Cynthia McCallister's book because it fits so well with my findings on the genetic individuality of children in how well they learn. Based on McCallister's extensive educational experience, Learning Cultures describes practical formats and social norms that give children the freedom they need to discover their appetites and aptitudes."

Robert Plomin, Ph.D.
Medical Research Council Research Professor in Behavioural Genetics at the Institute of Psychiatry, Psychology and Neuroscience, King's College London

"After more than two decades of action research in NYC K-12 schools, Cynthia McCallister now offers an innovative education model based on what is known about how children learn and how schools operate in large, bureaucratic systems. Her whole-school model, proven to raise achievement in multiple NYC schools, holds promise to address the urgent problem of substantive school reform."

Shael Polakow-Suransky, M.Ed.
President, Bank Street College of Education, Former Deputy Chancellor, New York City Department of Education

"Cynthia McCallister has achieved something very rare: a design for educational curricula (and their institutionalization) that is firmly grounded in research and theory from developmental psychology. She grounds her educational proposals in what is scientifically known about the nature of children's learning and cognitive development, especially the important role of cooperative social interaction and classroom culture. This book should be mandatory reading for all educators."

Michael Tomasello, Ph.D.
James F. Bonk Distinguished Professor, Duke University

A Pedagogical Design for Human Flourishing
Transforming Schools with the McCallister Model

Cynthia McCallister

Routledge
Taylor & Francis Group

NEW YORK AND LONDON

Cover image: © SEAN GLADWELL / Getty Images

First published 2022
by Routledge
605 Third Avenue, New York, NY 10158

and by Routledge
4 Park Square, Milton Park, Abingdon, Oxon, OX14 4RN

Routledge is an imprint of the Taylor & Francis Group, an informa business

© 2022 Cynthia McCallister

The right of Cynthia McCallister to be identified as author of this work has been asserted by her in accordance with sections 77 and 78 of the Copyright, Designs and Patents Act 1988.

All rights reserved. No part of this book may be reprinted or reproduced or utilised in any form or by any electronic, mechanical, or other means, now known or hereafter invented, including photocopying and recording, or in any information storage or retrieval system, without permission in writing from the publishers.

Trademark notice: Product or corporate names may be trademarks or registered trademarks, and are used only for identification and explanation without intent to infringe.

Library of Congress Cataloging-in-Publication Data
A catalog record for this title has been requested

ISBN: 978-0-367-45860-7 (hbk)
ISBN: 978-0-367-45859-1 (pbk)
ISBN: 978-1-003-02580-1 (ebk)

Typeset in ITC New Baskerville Std
by KnowledgeWorks Global Ltd.

Access the Support Material: www.routledge.com/9780367458591

To Ed Gordon

Collaborator,

Friend,

Fictive father

And to Monroe, and my children's, children's, children

Contents

Foreword I   ix
Foreword II   xi
Preface   xv
The McCallister Method: A Chronology   xvii
Acknowledgments   xxi

SECTION I
Background   1

1. Schooling the Possible Self: Introduction to a Learner-centered Educational Model   3
2. The Schools We Have   25
3. A Positive Learning Paradigm   42

SECTION II
A Pedagogy for the Self   75

4. The McCallister Method: Program Design   77
5. Sparks: A Learner-facing Personalized Curriculum   88
6. The Cultural Capital Curriculum   115

SECTION III
An Activity Curriculum: The Learning Cultures Formats   129

7. The Learning Environment and the Work Time Format   131
8. Lessons   145
9. The Learning Conference Format   155
10. The Learning Share Format   164
11. The Writing Conference Format   169
12. The Writing Share Format   176

13	The Pretend Play Format	186
14	The Cooperative Unison Reading Format	190
15	The Learning Teams Format	208
16	The Integrative Math Format	219
17	The Language Games Format	225

SECTION IV
The "We" Curriculum: Social Norms — 231

18	Keepers of the Culture: The Social Norms Curriculum	233
19	The Academic and Behavior Intervention Formats	257

SECTION V
The Ecosystem Curriculum — 269

20	Whole-School Transformation: The Ecosystem Design	271
21	The Assessment Program	301
22	The Civil Rights Program	315
23	The Community Education Program	323
24	The Curriculum Program	327
25	The School Culture Program	332
26	The Training Program	335

SECTION VI
Existence Proof — 345

27	There *Are* Learning Cultures	347
28	Transforming a Large NYC High School	363
29	The Urban Assembly's McCallister-Learning Cultures Initiative	378
30	The "Rise of the Phoenix"	388
31	Conclusion: Shapes	418

References	424
Index	437

Access the Support Material: www.routledge.com/9780367458591

Foreword I

It was about 25 years ago that the National Academy of Education invited me to mentor a young professor of literacy who was doing action research in a public Title I school in Northern Manhattan. The questions that framed her research were closely aligned with concerns that had been and remain the focus of my professional career in the production of knowledge, its synthesis, interpretation, and application. How can schools and the practice of pedagogy be designed to ensure every child's right to an education on equitable terms? How can teaching, learning, and assessment practices—the Troika of Pedagogy—be designed to accommodate and harness the variance born of human diversity and to support the achievement of every child's potential? How can the opportunities for educational experience, born of caste like social divisions, interrupt long-established structural systems of social inequity that are built into schooling? How can educational experience equalize the promised intellective and social developmental opportunities and outcomes, despite this variance in the learning persons?

My very ambitious new post-doctoral mentee, Cynthia McCallister, had embraced an assertion I made decades ago: in order to be equitable, educational inputs or treatments need to be appropriate and sufficient to the characteristics and needs of the learning persons, to enable the child to achieve her/his potential. In other words, the influences of all of the phenomena contributing to the child's development need to be appropriate and sufficient to complement, and to overpower the external influences of bias and deprivation born of class/caste, ethnic, language, and religious identity.

Over the course of roughly 25 years, McCallister developed a program of clinical research, in which she self-embedded in more than 20 schools, which intertwined a concern for cultural psychology and cognitive science, and a policy of educational and social equality. In the outcome of this work, Dr. McCallister developed a comprehensive school reform model that has been demonstrated to be effective in reducing the academic achievement gap in a half dozen schools. In the schools where she conducted her research, students' GPAs were not predictable from the social divisions with which the learners identified themselves.

In this book, a deeply thoughtful, especially well-read scholar of pedagogical practice has avoided some of the problematics of customized and individualized design that are born of human diversity and pedagogy. By paying careful attention to the creation of opportunities for the privileging of learners' intentionality; for group determined meaning; for collective problem engagement and solving; for dialogic analysis, she created a pedagogical model sensitive to the interests of learner engagement and multi-learner collaboration.

Philosophically, McCallister situates learning within the social interactions between people, rather than within the heads of individual learners. Problems are defined and solved in the context of collaborative effort and shared rationale. The author justifies her social relational strategies for the design of teaching and learning transactions on what she likes to refer to as *new sciences of the mind* that she employs to inform the development of her pedagogical procedures that stimulate the goals and intentions of learner shared intentionality—meanings, purposes, and objectives born of social exchanges between learners and cooperative effort at arriving at common meanings.

In McCallister's classrooms, learners have freedom of self-expression, movement, thought, and social affiliation, but these freedoms are constrained by the explicit norms that flow from ingroup exchange. The products of such exchanges will be recognized as a function of "normative psychology," and what Rousseau calls "conventional liberties." Learners are at liberty to exercise these freedoms to conform to norms that are made explicit through Rubrics. Rubrics specify the rules that everyone naturally adheres to in their shared social world, as a function of group membership. The rules that are agreed to make sure that learners end up able to know (and be able to do) things that make them intellectively competent in their own eyes, as well as in the eyes of others. Under the impact of social interaction, these conventional liberties are experienced as fundamental freedoms.

McCallister argues that her classroom practices create cultural and social capital—assets or resources that can be used in selected social settings to one's advantage. Embodied cultural capital develops in her program through the learning of personally relevant canonical knowledge, techniques, and modes of intellective exchange. Social capital also develops as learners develop relationships with others through recurrent cycles of self-selected group formation. Knowing how to appropriately present one's self or develop one's argument or to tailor one's language are all examples of social capital that most of us learn in dialogue, one with the other.

The author has named her program of social relational pedagogy Learning Cultures, in part because in practice her transactions are a kind of petri dish designed to facilitate assessment, teaching, and learning as they function to cultivate intellective and social competence. Learning Cultures embeds assessment, teaching, and learning into social transactions where the three processes interact with each other in dialectical transformations. Such integrated forces for epistemic development are indeed Cultures for Learning that catalyze developmental processes in learning persons and result in higher forms of thinking that are targeted/designed (through relational adjudication; mentalizing; perspective shifting; cooperative reasoning). Customization, individualization, and personalization define her model.

Cynthia McCallister's work demonstrates that it is possible to create a system of schooling that is, in James Coleman's (1967) words, adequately "intense" to overcome influences external to school. In other words, she suggests it possible to achieve equity in educational opportunity as indicated by outcomes that do not show disparities between learners who can be identified by the social division with which the learner identifies.

By the middle of the 21st century, the mental energies that we now invest in the storage and recall of information and technique may be freed up by the rapidly increasing capacity of cybernetic technologies to access and make available rationalized data and to apply appropriate techniques. Educated, intellectively competent human beings will find their minds freed to tackle new intellective tasks and to engage problems born of the dialectically relational and contradictory interactions of realities that appear in kaleidoscopic perspectives.

The minds and mindsets required to register and manipulate information of such character will likely be different from the minds that brought us into the 21st century. It is in the anticipation of such realities that McCallister has created what she has dubbed Learning Cultures.

Edmund W. Gordon, Ed.D.

Richard March Hoe, Professor Emeritus of Psychology and Education

John M. Musser, Professor of Psychology, Emeritus, Yale University

Foreword II

Humans are cultural beings. They become human and acquire human abilities and knowledge not as a sole result of their biological endowment, but as result of being treated in a special way by other humans. Since pre-historic times humans have changed and cultivated their physical environment, plants, animals, and objects, but also, perhaps most significantly, themselves. We make each other in constant interaction with each other and our artifacts, using, among other things, our most important artifact, language, in both its spoken and written form.

Indeed, being able to participate in social interaction is a precondition for cognitive development and learning. This is evident with autistic children, whose inability to engage normally with other humans make them severely handicapped linguistically and cognitively. This is compelling evidence that the crucial conditions for symbol formation, language, and thinking is not genetic/biological pre-programming or the sole result of individual activities, as many contemporary psychologists claim, but a learned cultural ability.

This crucial sociocultural aspect of learning is minimized in mainstream psychology and learning theories. Their focus on individual biological aspects has led to simplified models of the mind and, as a result, simplified and inaccurate ideas of education. To be more specific, mainstream contemporary psychology accounts for mental activity, like reading and learning to read, in terms of individual, inner, and private mental processes, which can be divided into atomistic specialized processes. These operate in step-by-step/algorithmic fashion on mental representations or symbols. Mental processes are taken to be computational and instantiated and ideally reduced to brain processes. The mind/brain is seen as an information-processing organ, which, with the right kind of structured input from the teacher, will produce the desired output, in this case reading. Learning literacy practices thus consist in using and/or recombining innate processes, originally dealing with or being part of other information-processing tasks. The activities of literacy are therefore to be based on culture-independent mechanisms. This approach to learning supports the way schooling is set up in most classrooms today.

In a typical classroom of today as well as during the history of Western Civilization, we find teachers presenting material to students, who are supposed to absorb facts and model their behavior and develop skills based on this one-sided interaction. As Professor Cynthia McCallister pointedly puts it, "Teachers act, and students are acted upon." This has been and still is typical of the situation when reading is taught. Of course, most students learn to read even in these situations, but for many it is a painful process and for some a failure altogether. The difficulties and failures are a result of the mainstream individualistic, atomized view of how teaching and learning proceeds.

Learning and cognitive development involve not only typically human biological abilities like various brain processes but also—and crucially—social and cultural interactions and cognitive artifacts. Social interactions and the content of the cognitive culture set the outer limits and possibilities that are relevant for mental activity at any given time and place.

Instead of constituting a branch of biology, as mainstream psychology claims, psychology and educational theory are hybrid sciences involving physiology, primarily neurophysiology, and socio-historical disciplines.

All learning and cognitive changes are the result of various social processes where the form it takes (whether dialogue, lecturing, discussion, etc.) and the content involved are culturally and historically varied. This is the lesson for all learning situations. Neurophysiological enabling conditions are always involved, but these are formed and shaped in symbolic activities, especially in schooling.

Schooling also involves other skills like the ability to ascribe beliefs to others and meta-cognition, the second-order ability to reflect on and criticize one's own and others' cognitive activities both publicly and privately. This involves the awareness of one's own beliefs in relation to the norms and standards set by and agreed to by one's peers, parents as well as teachers or others with institutional authority. Publicly giving and accepting reasons for beliefs, explaining them, acquiring consent for them is an almost universal feature of schooling.

It is such intense norm-infused social interaction which makes learning motivating, enjoyable, and successful. This insight is currently gaining support in the scientific community, but has not yet reached the classroom or teacher education in important ways. Of course there is still much more to learn about how teachers teach and pupils learn—and of what happens in the workshops which schools should become. But a good point from which to start our quest is to recognize that it is a joint venture, in which human biology/brain processes are an enabling conditions, but nothing more. Varying and changing social and cultural practices and traditions is the core of learning, shaping individual biological endowments. Any attempt to escape from this fact, and all the variation and complexity that follows from it, is bound to be futile.

In her impressive work on the acquisition of literacy and academic development, Professor McCallister takes such insights as her steppingstone for her novel approaches to curriculum. These approaches challenge deep-seated theoretical assumptions in philosophy and psychology as well as teaching practices. Committed to recent developments in neuroscience and developmental psychology, she rejects established ideas of cultural independent mechanisms for learning. Humans are biological organisms, but also social beings and moral agents.

Her original, and to some provocative, practices combine recent neurophysiological evidence of how memory, attention, and other cognitive skills function with a well-supported, creative use and management of normative cultural and social interactions. Learning literacy, for her, is a joint venture not based on ability grouping and passive absorption of pre-packed lessons from the teacher, but situations in which students actively choose their own activities, when and how to engage in them, and most importantly, take responsibility for their own learning. It requires the active participation of the individual as well as the guiding of others, not only teachers, but also more importantly fellow students. It is this joint social activity which shapes individual mental skills like memory, attention, and linguistic skills necessary for learning.

This book presents and exemplifies how the classroom is reorganized to emphasize cooperation in literacy and the development of literacy competencies, promoting high achievements both in literacy and in learning strategies. McCallister's model of learning assumes that language primarily is learned through use as a tool to get things done, and reorganize the classroom to reflect this. The book presents concrete and hands-on ways of how the classroom can be redesigned to harness social and cultural processes in ways that support intended outcomes of high learning standards and results. It offers the opportunity for routinized, rule-governed social activities by providing explicit and transparent social norms that afford opportunities for children to practice reading skills in a way that matters to them. The model maximizes the student's engagement and opportunities to communicate with and learn from each other. Assuming literacy is the outcome of participation in various group practices, the Learning Cultures model proposes transparent expectations for students to take ultimate responsibility for the group's and their own learning. It redistributes responsibility from the teacher to the students.

The implementation of McCallister's methods has been highly successful and anyone, whether one shares Professor McCallister's theoretical and scientific commitments or not, should pay attention and read this book. It provides teachers and others concerned about literacy a successful tool to promote literacy in schools and other contexts.

This book gives the reader both the scientific evidence and theoretical underpinnings to her model, and a hands-on accessible guide to implementation of the method. On this level, Professor McCallister practices what she teaches in her workshop, which we call the classroom. Learning and teaching are interactive cooperative endeavors where students are participants and co-creators in changing the material to be learned to suit their own needs and taking responsibility for their own learning.

Christina E. Erneling, Ph.D.
Professor of Psychology, Lund University, Sweden

Preface

Throughout the last 25 years, I have worked in more than 20 K-12 NYC schools to help teachers provide learners with more space to exercise their fundamental freedoms of thought, movement, expression, and association. But these freedoms were tempered by what Rousseau referred to as conventional liberties—freedom to exercise free will while conforming to the academic and social norms of the culture. It is through adhering to these norms that members of a culture develop their own human capital and potential. Over time, I created a *book of rules*—a comprehensive set of universal procedures that learners and adults follow. When learners exercise free will to comply with the norms, they not only achieve what school expects, but develop their personalities and talents in the process.

I have trained thousands of NYC children, hundreds of NYC teachers, and dozens of NYC administrators in my methods, and together we have transformed bureaucratic schools into 21st-century learning organizations, or what Michael Cole (2005) describes as *sustainable gardens*. But my efforts have been situated within the context of the largest bureaucratic labor establishments in the United States, where innovation is metabolized into the system, but gets regurgitated into disfigured replicas of the original. In such settings, innovation does not evolve, but degrades back toward the norms of convention.

My innovations were always provoked by conflicts and problems encountered in practice—situations that drove me off course, and caused me to find a rational way to get back on center. I worked out my solutions in the laboratory of *night science*.

The French biochemist, Francois Jacob (2017), who won the Nobel Prize in Medicine in 1965, distinguished between two types of science: day science emerges from pure logic. It is the science that appears in journals, and reports the ideas that are "allowed to be thought." Night science comes from the subconscious, and appears in dreams and nightmares. It's the kind of thinking Wittgenstein must have been referring to when he said that the best ideas come to us in the *bed*, in the *bath*, or on the *bus*. Night science achieves what Shakespeare described as the imagination bringing forth the *forms* of things unknown in order to give them *shapes*, a *local habitation*, and a *name*.

The McCallister Model is the name. Its shapes—the comprehensive set of procedures I have developed into the *book of rules*—are a product of years of night science. They were woven from seeds of ideas that have come to me on the subway on the way home from a school, or at night, when suddenly connected dots from subconscious ruminations erupt into consciousness as rational solutions to problems of practice linked to theories I'd been reading.

These seeds of innovation were planted early in my life, when, as a child, I attended a Progressive laboratory school on a Midwestern university campus, where teachers taught in the *new way* espoused by John Dewey, and who had learned, so masterfully, how to *let us learn* (Heidegger, 1968). In my classes, we could sit where we pleased, talk freely with peers, create our own projects, and direct our own learning. The fundamental freedoms I experienced as a child gave me the space to become who I am, and I flourished until I was forced by my father to attend a traditional public high school, which he believed was academically superior. There I would spend the next four years of high school imprisoned in classrooms where desks were in rows and students were stripped entirely of their fundamental freedoms. I escaped from school each year for 17 days, which was the maximum number of excused absences allowed to students.

High school was my introduction to institutional oppression, and I disliked the feeling very much. I did not know it at the time, but the name for this form of institution was the *industrial school*. Within 10 years after I graduated from high school, I became a teacher. Though I did not recognize myself as a rights activist at the time, I was intent from the first to ensure that all of my students enjoyed the right to exercise their fundamental freedoms in school. While it was not my original intention, my professional life's work would be devoted toward the goal of dismantling the *industrial school* and replacing it with a humane and democratic form of schooling. Unless children learn to recognize and value the conditions of freedom within society's institutions, they can hardly learn to recognize and take agency to overcome conditions of oppression they encounter in their futures beyond school.

I eventually succeeded to achieve the goals I had set for myself as a researcher decades ago. I used my *book of rules* to work within a large NYC school network to transform six of their low-performing schools into *sustainable gardens*. I wrote this book to present, in precise detail, the technical specifications that were used in these transformations. This *book of rules* provides an approach to education that employs the science of how children learn to satisfy the moral obligation that schools have to provide access to equitable educational opportunities for all children to enact their rights as citizens on equal terms.

My hope is that this book will succeed as a new shape of thinking about schooling. It offers a grammar of rules that others can follow to confer upon children their right to learn and, in the exercise of these rights, to collectively create powerful learning cultures in their own schools.

Cynthia McCallister
Riverside, Connecticut

The McCallister Method: A Chronology

The McCallister Method is the product of a three-decade action research project. The practices and procedures I developed are a compilation of solutions I invented to solve problems that arose in my practice over 30 years as a classroom teacher, teacher educator, literacy scholar, instructional coach, and school reform adviser. Over this period of time I embedded in over 20 high-poverty New York City schools, coached more than 200 teachers and dozens of school administrators in schools to help improve learning outcomes for thousands of children. A chronology of my work in schools is presented below.

The Abraham Lincoln School
  Interned in a 1st-grade classroom where a teacher implemented a progressive, social constructivist curriculum.

Bangor, Maine
Fall, 1986

The Buckley School
  Assistant teacher in a selective Manhattan private school where teachers implemented a traditional curriculum.

New York City, NY
Fall, 1987–Spring, 1988

Lewis Libby School
  Taught in a high-poverty rural school; implemented an original progressive, social constructivist literacy program in grades K-5.

Milford, Maine
Fall, 1988–Spring, 1992

Abraham Lincoln Elementary School
  Conducted field research in a 1st-grade classroom where a teacher implemented a progressive, social constructivist curriculum.

Bangor, Maine
Fall, 1994

University of Maine
  Conducted field research in a college literacy education methods course where a professor, Brenda Power, implemented a social constructivist curriculum (McCallister, 1998).

Orono, Maine
Spring, 1995

W. Haywood Burns School, P.S./I.S. 176, K-8
Developed an original whole-school literacy reform design; provided professional support; conducted field research.

New York City, NY
Fall, 1996–Spring, 1999

New York University, Professional Development
Conducted weekly staff development sessions to support implementation of original whole-school writing program reform. Each day-long session comprised classroom visits, demonstrations, and the facilitation of faculty discussion groups.

P.S. 35 (K-3)
Provided support to implement original whole-school reform design in K-3 writing programs.

Staten Island, NY
Fall, 2007–Spring, 2008

P.S./I.S. 126
Provided support for implementation of original whole-school reform design in Pk-8 reading and writing programs.

New York, NY
Fall, 2007–Spring, 2012

M. 507, Urban Assembly Gateway School for Technology
Provided whole-school reform design and demonstrations for prospective school adoption.

Manhattan, NY
Fall, 2011

P.S. 235 (K-2)
Provided support for implementation of original whole-school reform design in reading and writing programs.

Brooklyn, NY
Fall, 2007–Spring, 2008

P.S. 17, (Grades 3–5)
Provided whole-school reform design in reading programs.

Queens, NY
Spring, 2012

P.S. 143 (Grades K-2)
Provided whole-school reform design and implementation support in reading programs.

Queens, NY
Spring, 2012

P.S. 316 (Grades K-5)
Provided whole-school reform design in reading programs.

Brooklyn, NY
Spring, 2012

H.S. 509, High School for Language and Innovation (9–12, all subjects)
  Provided original comprehensive whole-school transformation program design in all subjects and classrooms; led implementation of Learning Cultures school-wide integrated ESL program in all grades and subjects; led the implementation of Learning Cultures school-wide bureaucratic program design (2013–2015); and provided implementation support in all grades and content subjects.

Bronx, NY
Fall, 2011–Spring, 2015

Education for Tomorrow, Bronx Charter High School
  Led team to develop and submit charter school proposal using Learning Cultures school design to NY State Education Department.

Fall, 2014–Spring, 2015

The Family School, P.S. 443
  Provided original comprehensive whole-school transformation program design and implementation support in grades K-2 reading and writing programs beginning Fall 2011. Grades 3–5 reading and writing programs beginning Fall 2012.

Bronx, NY
Fall, 2011–Spring, 2014

Urban Assembly Academy of Civic Engagement, I.S. 366
  Provided original comprehensive whole-school transformation program design and implementation support in grades 6–8 reading and writing programs.

Bronx, NY
Fall, 2012–Spring, 2013

Urban Assembly Institute for New Technology, I.S. 410
  Provided original comprehensive whole-school transformation program design and implementation support in grades 6–8 reading and writing programs.

New York, NY
Fall, 2012–Spring, 2013

Urban Assembly Institute of Math and Science for Young Women, M.S./H.S. 527
  Provided original comprehensive whole-school transformation program design and implementation support in reading, writing and content subjects in grades 6–12.

Brooklyn, NY
Fall, 2012–Spring, 2015

Paul Robeson School, P.S. 191
  Provided original comprehensive whole-school transformation program design and implementation support in grades K-2 reading programs.

Brooklyn, NY
Spring, 2012

Urban Assembly High School for Green Careers, H.S. 402

Provided original comprehensive whole-school transformation program design in all subjects and classrooms; led the implementation of Learning Cultures school-wide bureaucratic program redesign; and provided implementation support in grades 9–12 in all content subjects.

New York City, NY
Fall, 2013–Spring, 2018

Urban Assembly Unison School, M.S. 351

Co-developed new school proposal based on original whole-school program design, AY 2011–12

Provided original comprehensive whole-school transformation program design in all subjects and classrooms; led the implementation of Learning Cultures school-wide bureaucratic program redesign; and provided implementation support in grades 6–8 in all content subjects.

Brooklyn, NY
Fall, 2013–Spring, 2015

New Hope Academy Charter School

Provided original comprehensive whole-school transformation program design and implementation support in grades K-5 reading and writing programs.

Brooklyn, NY
Fall, 2016–Spring, 2017

Hyde Leadership Charter School

Provided classroom demonstrations of Learning Cultures practices and leadership consultation on comprehensive school reform design.

Hunts Point, Bronx, NY
Spring, 2016

Revolution Fitness Youth Boxing

Developed and assisted in the implementation of an integrated Cooperative Unison Reading literacy program within the summer and after-school boxing programs.

Stamford, CT
Summer, 2015–Fall, 2016

Connections Charter School

Provided original comprehensive whole-school transformation program design and implementation support in grades K-12 in all subjects.

Hilo, Hawaii
Academic Year 2016–2017

Acknowledgments

Many people inspired my thinking throughout the decades of development of my Model. I am forever grateful to have attended Burris Laboratory School, in Muncie, Indiana, where, as a child, I experienced the incredible power of a Progressive curriculum and where I learned not only how to read, write, and do math but also to develop my talents by learning to swim, cook, paint, saw, hammer, sew, sing, and play. During my time at Burris, seeds of inspiration were planted for my future quest to make child-centered education more widely available. I thank Mary Giard, my mentor teacher, in whose first-grade classroom at the Abraham Lincoln School in Bangor, Maine I learned to teach in a way that productively harnessed fundamental freedom and social interaction in ways that enabled learners to achieve academically.

I am especially grateful to the fates that blessed me with the chance to have Edmund W. Gordon as my mentor, friend, and intellectual companion. Through their Scholar Development Program, the Spencer Foundation provided our opportunity to collaborate to improve my research proposal on a problem of pedagogical practice. Ed and I soon found we were working on essentially the same problem—to identify an approach to pedagogy that provides every learner with what they require to function adequately (Gordon & Associates, 1988). When we began work together, Ed had been exploring the educational psychology literature on individualized learning and the interactions between learner attributes and intervention treatments to identify pedagogical strategies that respond effectively to diverse human traits. But he had begun to conclude that the "artificial separateness" of the way this work is reported limits its usefulness as a solution to the problem of a pedagogy for human diversity (Gordon & Associates, 1988). He wrote (1988), "we must be concerned not only with the interactions between attributes and treatments, but also with the interactions within and between attributes and within and between treatments" (p. xix). Ed saw promise in the emerging field of cultural psychology, and so encouraged me to embark on what would be a multi-decade exploration of *culture theory* to address the problem of human adaptation and learning in a way that could, as he wrote, "reconceptualize the interactive multivariant nature of diversity in the behavioral individuality of human learners" (Gordon & Associates, 1988, p. xix).

My NYU colleague, Jerry Bruner, was a continual source of sage advice and encouragement. I owe Jerry credit for the seeds of ideas for several of my key pedagogical innovations to conversations we had in which he offered simple, insightful ways to solve stubborn problems of practice. Just after my arrival at NYU in 1998, Jerry gave me some of the most valuable advice of my career when he urged me, "Watch Tomasello!" For the next 20 years, I read every book Michael Tomasello wrote, incorporating ideas from his *shared intentionality hypothesis* into my model. I thank Mike for being an influential and generous distant mentor. I am grateful to NYU for a grant that enabled a research collaboration with David Olson, who generously shared his expertise as a scholar of literacy and school reform. Having the opportunity to visit classrooms together and to analyze and interpret our observations enabled me to make continual adjustments to protocols so they better align with the theoretical principles that frame the model. I am grateful to Ken Gergen for helping me to understand the development of understanding as a social achievement, and for his generous encouragement through the two decades that I have been applying his theory to my own practice.

I am forever appreciative to Jim Rog, my dear friend and University of Maine professor who introduced me to ethnographic research methods and guided me through my first study to unravel the mystery of play as a context in which my kindergarten students acquired writing literacy.

I am fortunate to have had the opportunity to implement my school reform work within the NYC Department of Education, one of the largest, most diverse, and bureaucratic school districts in the United States. It has served as the perfect laboratory for the study of pedagogy and human individuality. As a mother of three children who collectively attended 10 NYC public schools, I had first-hand experience in grappling with the challenges of traditional industrial schooling from the perspective of a parent, which helped inform the development of my model. I am thankful for the leadership of former NYC Schools Chancellor, Joel Klein, and former Deputy Chancellor, Shael Polakow-Suransky, for their visionary leadership. Through their initiatives, the DOE incentivized innovation and opened space for school leaders to collaborate with innovators.

This book would not have been possible without the opportunities provided to me by the leaders of the schools where I have had the privilege to implement my model. My deepest thanks goes to Lydia Bassett Tyner, former principal of the W. Haywood Burns School in the Inwood section of Manhattan, where I had my first dive into the rip-tide waters of NYC whole-school reform. I would never have had the opportunity to further refine my model if it were not for the principals and school leaders who embraced my ideas and bravely sought to implement them. Thank you to school leaders, Ellen Meltzer, Jennifer Balis, Melissa Garofalo, Kerry Decker, Carlos Romero, Julie Nariman, Pamela Lee, April McKoy, Sandy Mastropaolo, Elsie Capolongo, Emily Paige, Tamika Stewart, Jeff Garrett, Jeff Chetirko, Cameron Berube, Kiri Soares, Kelly DeMonaco, Jennifer Ostrow, Amy Piller, Drew Konkyz, Madeline Young, Luke Jenka, Tara Clark, Sabina McNamara, Shira Wrightman, Yan Wang, Ahmad Mickens, Daphne LaBua, and John Thatcher.

I am grateful to those whose institutional collaborations with the NYC DOE created conditions that enabled my work. Beth Lief was at the helm of New Visions for Public Schools in 1996 when they funded my initial work in NYC at the Haywood Burns School, and she was President of The Carroll and Milton Petrie Foundation when they funded the three-year McCallister-Learning Cultures Initiative at The Urban Assembly. I am grateful to Richard Kahn, founder, and Jon Green, former director, of the NYC school network, The Urban Assembly. Jon and Richard spearheaded the McCallister-Learning Cultures Initiative, allowed me to assist them in their mission "to advance students' economic and social mobility by improving public education." Together, we proved that rapid school transformation could be achieved simultaneously in several failing middle and high schools. Our work shows promise as a way to transform some of the 5,000 schools nationwide that are currently failing to provide children with an education that enables them to function adequately in society. And it provides an example of a "quantum of education" that could be a reference for the criteria of an adequacy-based conceptualization of equality of educational opportunity.

I am forever indebted to Matthew Friberg, my editor at Routledge, who had the courage to embrace a radical new idea and whose support enabled me to bring this project to fruition. I am blessed to have a family who sustains my spirit with their patience, support, and faith in my work. Thank you Packie, Fiona, and Liam for joining me on the long journey to where we now stand.

Cynthia McCallister
Riverside, Connecticut

Section I
Background

1 Schooling the Possible Self

Introduction to a Learner-centered Educational Model

> ...for the longest time there has been nothing but a cry against the established practice without anyone taking it upon himself to propose a better one.
>
> Jean-Jacques Rousseau (in *Emile*, 1979, p. 33)

> It must be considered that there is nothing more difficult to carry out, nor more doubtful of success, nor more dangerous to handle, than to initiate a new order of things.
>
> Niccolò Machiavelli

The McCallister Model: A New Pedagogy for the Possible Self

This book presents a learner-centered, social-constructivist approach to education that is developed with a concern for the nature of the child, what they are capable of learning, and the provision of opportunities that are adequate to enable them to flourish and achieve their potential. The approach is based on the principle that every learner can thrive developmentally and achieve academically if they are provided fundamental freedoms to think, speak, move, and affiliate with others. But these freedoms are not absolute. They are conditional on learners taking responsibility to conform to procedures outlined in a comprehensive curriculum that promotes positive social and academic norms, high achievement, and intellective development. This approach to pedagogy creates the powerful yin-yang conditions of freedom and conformity, or what Rousseau (1920) referred to as *conventional liberties*. Learners exercise conventional liberties to control their own minds and to coordinate their thinking with others. Thus, through a curriculum of responsibility-based self-control (McCallister, 2013f), the McCallister Model shifts the traditional teacher-centered emphasis in pedagogy from a concern for knowledge transfer to a learner-centered emphasis on the exercise of conventional liberties to carry out personal intentions.

The Science of Learning

The McCallister Model is grounded in recent scientific advances in learning and psychological development. Until the cognitive revolution in the 1970s, not much was known about the internal mental mechanisms of the learning process, and little attention was paid to the subjective states of learners in the design of educational methods. But since that time, the field of learning has undergone a veritable Copernican Revolution. A new science of the mind has yielded evidence that human learning is a self-organizing and self-directed process (Kandel, 2007); that higher-order thinking involves most essentially the ability to control one's own mind and to coordinate one's mental states with those of others (Dunbar, 1998; Tomasello, 2019); that culture, the biological human ecological niche, impacts learning and development (Dressler, 2019); and that the capacity for human psychological growth through adaptation and learning is virtually unlimited (Plomin, 2018; Tomasello, 2019). This emerging transactional model of development describes a learning process whereby the person, with their genes, interacting within the environment, takes what she needs to become who she is (Plomin, 2018; Tomasello, 2019). Since genetic influences govern how we react within the social environment, development is defined by our individuality. This paradigm of learning casts the concern for equality of educational opportunity in a new light. Within a transactional paradigm, in which volition drives development, opportunity is created and taken, not given (Plomin, 2018). Rather than a traditional concern for sameness in treatment as the criterion of equality, equitable learning opportunities are those in which learners have autonomy to select from a variety of rich environmental experiences to achieve their potential (Gordon & Associates, 1988; Tucker-Drob, Briley, & Harden, 2013).

Because learning is self-directed, self-identity is the vehicle of development within the McCallister Model. Pedagogy is no longer a matter of the transfer of knowledge from teacher to student, but the provision of access to social systems that enable the learner to manage them-selves and to carry out their own intentions in the company of peers. The McCallister Model is thus a pedagogy for the *self*. The social philosopher George Herbert Mead proposed two forms of self-identity—the "I" and the "Me" (Mead, 1934/1972). The "I" is the agent of action and the driver of volition. The "Me" is the social self, whose identity is informed in interaction, through the mirror of others' perceptions. The "Me" communicates feedback from the social world to the "I," where it is assimilated into the person's intentional states. With age, as our social worlds expand, the "We" self develops, enabling us to coordinate our experience in consonance with widening circles of others who share common values and experiences (Tomasello, 2016, 2019). We draw upon these inter-related, multiple selves as we react and adapt through our experiences within the social environment (see Figure 1.1). Because higher forms of thinking are fundamentally social in nature, equitable learning opportunities are those that support full and free forms of association and ample opportunity to coordinate thinking with others (Dewey, 1916/1944). The scientific framework for learning in pedagogy, called the Positive Learning Paradigm, is presented in Chapter 3.

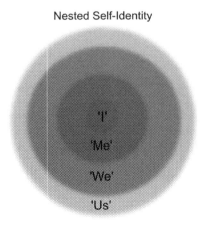

Figure 1.1 Levels of self-identity

Curriculum for the "I"-self, the "Me"-self, and the "We"-self

The McCallister Model incorporates four inter-related curriculum programs that are implemented in the school, which support the development of self. First-level classroom changes are described directly below. These changes involve simple and concrete procedures that are implemented in the same way in every grade level and content subject. The procedures require minimal training or background knowledge, so can be implemented immediately and with ease to quickly transform classrooms. They revolve around both independent and social self-directed activities that stimulate targeted forms of higher-level thinking. When implemented consistently, the practices are orchestrated to generate cohesive cultures for learning.

The McCallister Model also incorporates a bureaucratic curriculum that transforms the industrial school into a cultural niche or ecosystem and freezes first-level changes in classroom practice in place through sustainable systems of distributed leadership. A description of second-level changes follows this section.

Sparks

Since the self directs development, the McCallister Model is organized to delegate responsibility for learning to learners themselves. Sparks is a comprehensive curriculum that supports self-organizing and self-directed learning. It is a personalized, learner-facing academic program that provides a roadmap learners follow to develop academic competencies that align with formal learning standards. This curriculum consists of opportunities for learners to autonomously select rich, engaging learning experiences that suit their interests and proclivities, but which also provide optimal conditions for learning. The activities are *proleptic*, meaning they create opportunities to encounter a skill or concept in the immediate learning situation that will become important to know in the future. The Sparks curriculum provides opportunities for learners to set goals and make and execute plans to meet them. The curriculum enables learners to carry out their own intentions in ways that ensure they achieve academically. Through Sparks, learners discover their interests and passions and develop their talents to meet their potential. This personalized approach to curriculum requires high levels of intellective functioning without the need for teacher-directed lessons. The Sparks curriculum is described in Chapter 5.

The Cultural Capital Curriculum

It is suggested that inequalities in educational outcomes are due to the unequal distribution of human capital in society (Gordon, 1999). Children of privilege are more likely to have acquired embodied cultural capital relevant to academic achievement, which develops over long periods of time with the support of resources from the family (Bourdieu, 1986). For example, children of college-educated parents tend to receive higher levels of out-of-school support for academics, and they are more likely to have opportunities to take part in extracurricular activities that enrich academic development. These experiences are wired into the body in billions of neural connections that serve an adaptive advantage as experiential resources that can be drawn upon in reaction to new situations. The out-of-school influences of socioeconomic status (SES) have a larger influence on educational outcomes than the influences of schooling and teaching (Coleman, United States, & National Center for Education Statistics, 1966), and, as a result, gaps in achievement between high- and low-SES groups persist (NAEP, 2019).

6 *Background*

The Cultural Capital Curriculum is designed to provide learners access to a wide variety of rich environmental experiences that are normally thought of as supplemental to education. Since differential access to rich cultural experiences functions to reproduce educational inequalities, the so-called supplemental enrichment curriculum becomes a central component of the general education curriculum within the McCallister Model. The Cultural Capital curriculum is described in Chapter 6.

Keepers of the Culture: A Curriculum for Civic Engagement

Keepers of the Culture is a school-wide civics curriculum designed to instill values of individual liberty, personal dignity, and collective civility. It centers around the school's Code of Conduct and other rules that establish generative social norms for the school community and promote values of high expectations, respect and tolerance for others, and a sense of mutuality and interdependence. The curriculum includes a comprehensive system of behavioral supports designed to help learners develop self-regulation. The Keepers of the Culture curriculum is described in Chapter 18.

Learning Cultures: A Curriculum of Social Environments

Curriculum is normally thought of as a course of study that encompasses certain topics or subjects. The word *curriculum* is normally used as a noun. But since intellective development is a product of social interaction of a certain kind, the curriculum within the McCallister Model is organized around a number of socially-interactive activities, known as *Formats*. The curriculum of Formats, known as Learning Cultures, consists of activity protocols that provide opportunities for learners to cooperate with peers and adults to solve intellectual challenges that arise from the formal curriculum. Within the McCallister Model, the word *curriculum* now connotes *activity*.

Learning Cultures Formats

The luminary psychologist, Jerome Bruner (1983), coined the term *interaction format* to describe the way in which caregivers arrange predictable, routinized, familiar settings for early speech interactions with young children. Formats are "specialized versions of contexts," such as bedtime stories and mealtime rituals (Bruner, 1983, p. 130). Because they are characterized by properties of order, systematicity, predictability, and recurrence, they provide what Bruner (1983) called a Language Acquisition Support System (LASS)—a constrained situation that provides all the elements needed to communicate effectively (Bruner, 1983). Formats establish contexts that provide children with increasing responsibility to participate with caregivers; and within the pragmatic context of participation, they learn language by using it. By using language over time, children internalize language conventions like new words and grammatical structures. Learning is scaffolded as routines for *developed* competencies are reassembled into new routines to support *developing* competencies. Increasingly higher-order subroutines that develop over time create a social infrastructure to support the co-construction of complex social interactions and discourse (Bruner, 1983). Skills learned in interactive formats can later be "detached" from the context of the format and drawn upon in new situations to communicate with others in conventional ways.

The Learning Cultures Formats are inspired by Bruner's ideas. They are ritual social routines that establish recurrent and predictable environments in which learners practice independence and autonomy, solve problems with others, share perspectives, and develop academically. They are organized to hold learners responsible for conforming to social norms that promote optimal psychological functioning, intellectual development, and academic achievement. The Formats provide learners maximal freedom to move, speak, think, and interact with others, to develop autonomy and independence, engagement and motivation, empathy, and social interdependence. They provide contexts for learners to help each other to read and understand texts, write and complete their own projects, and solve academic problems. Through Formats, the social world provides the framework for learning (Erneling, 2010).

Because Formats are predictable and have continuity, they provide a context for learners to habituate dispositions of independence, responsibility, and cooperation. Within the Formats, learners, rather than teachers, make decisions about what to read, write, and talk about. Because they provide a cooperative context to use skills to solve highly-challenging problems, the Formats promote engagement, motivation, and self-determination. The rules for the Formats are the same for everyone, and easy to learn. Because they are like games that can be played by simple rules, the Formats require little training, are easy to learn by children and adults, and are fun to do.

Reconceptualizing Traditional Learning Zones

The Learning Cultures Formats are derivative of conventional classroom organizational systems, such as one-on-one, small- and large-group lessons and independent work time, but instead of serving as opportunities to group children for didactic instruction and memory activities, the Formats provide environments in which learners can use and develop academic skills through self-directed learning and peer interactions. The Formats target intentional action as opposed to passive submission. Each Format is described in Box 1.1.

Rubrics: Instruments that Pattern the Social World

Bruner's concept of *format* is a continually evolving system of subroutines. In Bruner's thinking, the character of the format changes over time as the competencies of the child develop. The Learning Cultures Formats, on the other hand, are stable over time, and remain characterized by the same consistent routines, regardless of the diverse characteristics of the learners who participate in them. The same Formats are employed universally in every classroom, grade, and course. The principles of systematicity and standardization in response to human diversity might seem counterintuitive. Conventional wisdom dictates that diverse learners require individually-tailored treatments (Gordon & Associates, 1988). Individualization and personalization have been suggested as means to achieve a pedagogy to support human diversity (Gordon & Associates, 1988). But a social construction paradigm challenges this individualist assertion. Within the McCallister Model, the stable social group is understood to be the evolutionary *cultural niche*, which provides the developing person with the relational nutriments needed to nourish the self, and which is essential to survival. Standardized rules for every Format specify the same optimal social conditions for learning that can be applied to a wide variety of populations and situations. Instead of Bruner's notion of the *scaffold*, which is removed when competencies develop, the Formats are a permanent *trellis* around which all learners develop.

To achieve ritualistic standardization, procedures for each Format are specified in an assessment *Rubric*. Rubrics outline procedures and roles that learners and teachers follow in each of the Formats. The Rubrics are like rules for games. Like rules, the language of the Rubrics performs a special linguistic function. They are a certain form of speech act,

> **Box 1.1**
>
> **Summary description of classroom interaction formats of the learning cultures model**
>
> 1. **Lesson Format**: a 10-minute, teacher-directed, whole-group activity at the start of the Activity Block. Lessons typically focus on "academic gossip"—narrative accounts of actual learners' performance of skills outlined in formal learning standards. Lessons are also used to clarify procedures, social norms, and expectations.
> 2. **Work Time Format**: a 40–70-minute period during which time learners have the freedom to pursue their own academic work agenda. Learners can sit wherever in the room they want, collaborate with whomever they wish, and express themselves freely within the parameters of formal behavior expectations.
> 3. **Cooperative Unison Reading Format**: a learner-driven, small-group reading activity in which learners (5 or fewer) follow three rules: (1) read aloud in sync; (2) *breach*, or stop the group if you have a question or something to say; (3) continue reading only after the breach is resolved. Cooperative Unison Reading is further described below.
> 4. **Small-group Lesson Format**: learners with similar needs meet temporarily for targeted assistance.
> 5. **Learning Team Format**: a cooperative approach to learning canonical academic content. Learners work in heterogeneous ability groups chosen by learner team captains. Throughout the course of an academic subject unit they meet together to read, study, and share information as a means to learn standards-based curriculum content.
> 6. **Learning Conference Format**: a one-on-one meeting between a learner and a teacher/assistant focused around a conceptual challenge encountered in the context of the curriculum. The conference provides opportunity for learners to develop self-competence and persistence in meeting high learning challenges.
> 7. **Content Share Format**: a ritual conclusion to the Activity Block, each day two learners share a narrative account of insights about their experience in overcoming an academic challenge in the context of a one-on-one conference with the teacher. The Content Share helps develop a growth mindset in learners.
> 8. **Writing Conference Format**: a one-on-one meeting between a teacher and learner focused around a draft piece of writing that the learner is in the midst of developing. The Conference is organized to help the learner clarify and strengthen what they are trying to achieve and to explore how best to revise the writing to better achieve the purpose.
> 9. **Writing Share Format**: a ritual conclusion to the writing block in Learning Cultures classrooms. Each day the class convenes to hear two learners read a draft of their writing and to provide feedback. The Writing Share helps contribute to a sense of group cohesion, supports learners in developing their academic identity and self-competence, and provides group instruction focused on competencies outlined in learning standards.
> 10. **Academic and Behavior Intervention Formats**: a structured opportunity for a learner to identify personal behaviors that interfere with achievement and well-being, how the behaviors prevent the learner from meeting their responsibilities, and an action plan to replace maladaptive behaviors with generative ones.

known as a *status function declarations* (SFD), which carry *deontic* power and assign a sense of duty to those who use them (Searle, 2010). SFDs, such as game rules, marriage certificates, graduation diplomas, or parking tickets, describe the conditions of a possible world, and by doing so, they bring that world into being (see a sample Rubric in Figure 1.2).

Rubric rules provide the grammar for the academic and social norms that develop within the *learning culture* of the classroom. When they take on their assigned social roles,

learning cultures®

Writing Share Rubric

Rating Scale: (✓-) Needs Immediate Improvement (✓) Making Progress (✓+) Proficient (NA) No opportunity to observe

Procedures

1. A Writing Share Calendar is prepared in advance. Writing Share Calendar is coordinated with Writing Conference to provide writers time after the Conference in order to act on revision goals before presenting again in the Writing Share.
2. The first presenter convenes the audience and establishes collective attention.
3. The presenter identifies the purpose of the writing, the generic form being employed, and the nature of feedback sought.
4. The presenter displays the text on a document camera and reads the text aloud.
5. The presenter solicits feedback from the audience.
6. Feedback is recorded both in a community share notebook and in notes provided to the presenter. The role of recorder should rotate so all students experience the responsibility of taking feedback for others.
7. The second presenter secures collective attention and proceeds to repeat Steps 3-6, above.

Primary Aims

1. To employ writing as a means of taking action to carry out intentions.
2. To develop awareness about the ways writing genres function to perform specific forms of action.
3. To learn to use the conventions of writing genres instrumentally to achieve intentional goals.
4. To provide competence feedback the writer can use in revision to achieve the intended purpose.
5. To concretize the writer's sense of audience and to provide in-the-moment feedback on the impact of the text in relation to the intended responsive understanding.
6. To practice public speaking confidence and competence.
7. To promote a sense of community and collective identity.

1. Presenter   Rating

1a. Convenes the audience and secures collective attention and consideration.
1b. Is prepared to present a short draft that contains sufficient material to elicit audience response in the form of questions, comments, or suggestions.
1c. Identifies the purpose of the text, the generic form employed, and the nature of feedback sought.
1d. Assumes responsibility to facilitate the Share process within a period of 10 minutes. Engages audience members by calling on volunteers for comments. When necessary, follows into comments to seek clarification and elaboration of relevant feedback. Addresses inappropriate or unsupportive comments immediately and decisively and, if necessary, solicits support from peers and/or the guide.

2. Audience   Rating

2a. Is seated in designated group meeting area, facing the presenter, close enough proximity to promote attentive listening and active participation (e.g., eye contact; verbal exchange in the form of dialogue).
2b. Is respectful, promotive, and completely attentive. Participate appropriately through attentive listening. Inappropriate or unsupportive comments are immediately addressed, first by the presenter and/or audience members, then, if necessary, by the teacher. Adheres to rules for large-group discussion (e.g., raise hands to be recognized by the presenter). Refrain from speaking out-of-turn or engaging in off-task behaviors.
2c. Respond to writer's request for feedback in a constructive manner. Provides relevant and specific comments and suggestions that the author can use to improve the draft.

3.	Guide	Rating
3a.	Ensures a safe and comfortable context for students to share writing and receive relevant feedback.	
3b.	Supports the presenter to facilitate the share process within a period of 10 minutes. (The guide is seated in the audience, in close enough proximity to support the presenter to facilitate the share process.)	
3c.	Follows into presenter or audience comments when necessary to help explain or clarify ideas or to request clarification to promote quality feedback.	
3d.	Supports the presenter to ensure audience members adhere to norms for large-group discussion. Immediately and decisively intervenes to support the presenter to address off-task or inappropriate behaviors and non-promotive comments, enabling the presenter to successfully manage the group process. If the presenter is unable to resolve the conflict, the guide intervenes to invoke procedures from the Ladder of Self-regulation.	
3e.	Ensures feedback is recorded for later reference by the presenter.	
4.	Physical Space and Materials	Rating
4a.	Designated group meeting area with flexible theater seating.	
4b.	Projector to display presentation material.	
4c.	Writing Share calendar are posted a week in advance.	
4d.	Community Share Notebook.	

Comments:

Copyright © 2012, 2014, 2015, 2016, 2018, 2020 Cynthia McCallister. All rights reserved. Reproduction and distribution are prohibited without permission from the author.

www.LearningCultures.net

Figure 1.2 Writing Share Rubric

learners are required to perform higher mental operations. For example, the Cooperative Unison Reading Rubric directs learners attune to others' perspectives, to reason cooperatively, to shift and share perspectives, and to be socially promotive. In the process of doing these things, learners exercise their intellect by making assertions, defending positions, defining terms, and making inferences. The Work Time Rubric guides learners' self-directed, autonomous activity, granting them fundamental freedoms of movement and expression they need to learn to manage their minds. By stressing conformity to adaptive norms, the Learning Cultures Formats support learning and development.

RITUAL

Because Formats are standardized and universal, and everyone participates in them on equal terms, they assume a ritual quality within the school community. Ritual is a means through which cultures enact the moral contours of their stable social group and provide a way for members to experience moral collective identity. Ritual-like participation in the Formats functions to create a collective, fully-inclusive life space in which every person, despite their individuality, identifies with others. As forms of ritual, the Formats serve a soul-nourishing function.

RIGHTS

Another way of thinking about the Rubrics is as a body of documented legal rights in a democracy. The rights specified in the Rubrics are universal, and everyone in the learning community enjoys the same rights. The Learning Cultures Rubrics thus provide a way to enact a rights-based education (United Nations Children's Fund/UNESCO, 2007). The curriculum of Rubrics creates a body of documented rights to rich learning experiences that materialize as learners and adults adhere to their terms. Through first- and second-level systems, these rights are granted, exercised, and enforced.

Curriculum Architecture

The Learning Cultures Formats are structured into an architecture of Activity Blocks, which are like subjects or classes in the typical disciplinary domains of reading, writing, math, and content subjects. Activity Blocks are large chunks of time that provide students opportunities to take part in self-initiated activities and Formats. In schools organized by the traditional "egg-crate" design, where learners are grouped into same-age classes, and class schedules are divided into increments devoted to subject study, a school day might include Activity Blocks in Reading, Writing, Math, Social Studies, and Science and Art. In more flexible situations, Activity Blocks can be longer and the use of time can be determined by the learner's individual plan.

Step into a McCallister classroom and you will notice the same routines and procedures in every classroom. The typical egg-crate schedule is structured into an Activity Block of 60–70 minutes. The Block serves as a container in which the Formats are arranged. The Block begins with a brief, whole-class Lesson, during which time teachers present procedural and content lessons. Lessons of no more than 10 minutes in length are designed to be engaging by relating standards-based content to students' interests and experiences.

After the Lesson, learners transition to the Work Time Format, which is typically 40–50 minutes in length. During Work Time, learners enjoy fundamental freedoms of movement, expression, and social affiliation. They can choose their own collaborative partnerships, select activities that align with the curriculum, and practice competencies they have determined to achieve. They plan and design their own projects and set their own goals to complete them.

During Work Time, adults meet one-on-one with students in the Conference Format. Every student has a Conference twice a month to receive individualized attention from adults, assess and reflect on their progress, and plan how to meet their goals.

12 *Background*

The combination of *competence feedback* on their strengths and needs, opportunities to *relate* personally to teachers, and *autonomy* to pursue their intentions provide just the right elements to help learners develop self-determination (Deci & Ryan, 2017).

The Cooperative Unison Reading (CUR) Format (McCallister, 2011a) also occurs during Work Time in reading and content subject classes. CUR is a social constructivist, student-driven method of small-group reading instruction that is played like a game according to three simple rules: (1) read aloud in sync in a voice others can hear; (2) stop the group if you have a question or something to say; (3) be promotive (be nice). Learners choose the texts they wish to read and join reading groups of their choice. New groups form each week, which brings new opportunities for learners to read new texts and to work with a different group of peers.

The Activity Block concludes with the Share Format. Two students take turns sharing a draft of their writing (in the Writing Activity Block) or recounting the experience of resolving an academic challenge (in all other Activity Blocks). Each learner has an opportunity to share twice a month. The Share fosters a sense of relatedness within the learning community (see Activity Block diagram, Figure 1.3 and Appendix 45).

Self-identity and the Curriculum

The Formats offer an environment for multiple facets of self-development. Some of the Formats require independence and autonomy, cultivate individuality, and provide a

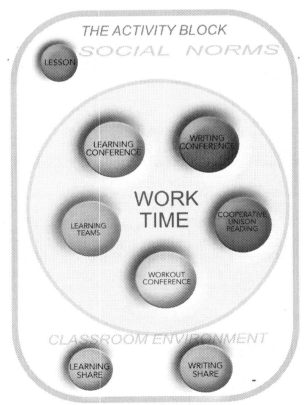

Figure 1.3 Sample Activity Block

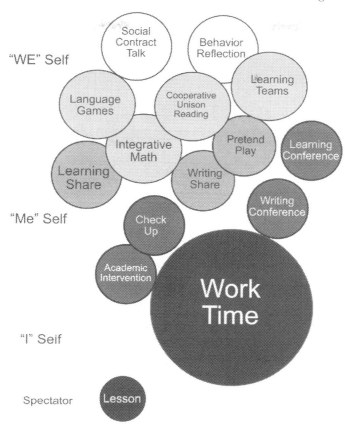

Figure 1.4 Life spaces for the self

context to carry out individual intentions. These Formats nurture the "I" self. Other Formats are organized around cooperative problem-solving activities that foster social cognition, cooperative thinking, collaboration, and higher thinking. These Formats nurture the "Me" self. These Formats stimulate shared intentionality through social interaction and peer-instruction.

In Figure 1.4, the palate of possible Formats are distributed up a continuum from the "I"-oriented Format environments at the bottom of the diagram, to the more "Me"-oriented Formats in the middle, which reference social identity, to the "We"-oriented Formats at the top, which reference collective identity. The more passive self-identity of the spectator in the context of a teacher-directed lesson appears at the bottom of the diagram. The "I"-oriented Formats of Learning and Writing Conferences emphasize self-consciousness and personal awareness. The Formats of Cooperative Unison Reading and Learning Teams are social in nature, and emphasize co-consciousness and mind reading. They provide opportunities to coordinate mental states with others and to self-regulate to group norms.

A Universal Design for Learning

The McCallister Model is a *universal design for learning*.

The instructional systems of the current industrial school, based on sorting and grouping students for leveled instruction, reproduce and reinforce, within the school, patterns

14 *Background*

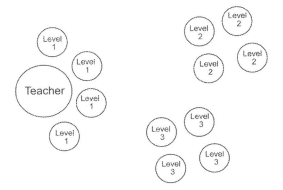

Figure 1.5 Segregated classroom by ability level

of social segregation that exist outside of the school. For example, academic ability is an outcome of embodied social and cultural capital (Bourdieu, 1986). Ability-based grouping practices segregate learners into groups of others who share similar levels of capital. Ability grouping practices impose restrictions on forms of free association that are so essential in a democratic learning culture. Figure 1.5 illustrates segregating grouping patterns based on same-level cognitive abilities.

The U.S. Supreme Court found school segregation to be a violation of the Constitutional right to equal protection under the 14th Amendment. Since ability-based grouping is a form of social segregation, it is prohibited in the McCallister Model. Curricular desegregation is possible when learning is learner-driven and approached as a socially-constructed process as opposed to a process of transfer that can only occur when the learner has adequate background knowledge. Since curriculum within the McCallister Model emphasizes intentionality and personal agency, rather than content transfer, ability groups are not necessary. Learners are not grouped by level for instruction, but instead follow their own initiative to take part in inclusive rituals. Figure 1.6 represents the McCallister classroom in which learners self-select into activities, resulting in inclusive and diverse social groups.

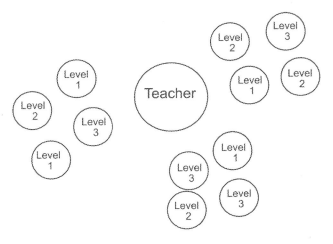

Figure 1.6 Inclusive classroom in which mixed ability groups are formed by learner choice

Second-Order Institutional Changes: An Ecosystem Design for Whole-School Transformation and Sustainability

> His culture provides the raw material of which the individual makes his life. If it is meagre, the individual suffers; if it is rich, the individual has the chance to rise to his opportunity.
>
> Ruth Benedict (1934, p. 252)

The whole-school transformation initiative is engineered through first-level changes to pedagogical practices—those introduced above—and second-level changes to the bureaucratic systems of the school that freeze first-level changes into place. These changes are described in this section.

Second-level changes consist of a comprehensive set of bureaucratic protocols designed to secure and sustain first-level changes and which distribute leadership responsibilities from the principal or school director to teachers. These second-level changes freeze into place a social organization that is fundamentally egalitarian and free from the institutional systems of the industrial school that create social inequality. Second-level changes transform the industrial school into a learning *ecosystem*.

The second-level changes in the McCallister Model are inspired by ideas from the field of evolutionary anthropology. Human beings evolved to exist in stable social groups of about 150 individuals that functioned to accumulate and carry knowledge of relevant cultural practices that were necessary for survival (Boyd, Richerson, & Henrich, 2011; Dunbar, 1998). Egalitarianism was an adaptive advantage, since the group as a whole benefits most through participation of all its members. The "outliers"—those whose unusual thoughts enable them to see reality differently—gave the group an advantage when survival depended on the need to see alternatives and make changes (Dressler, 2019). But through history, as civilization became more complex and resource allocation became more inequitable, human existence became increasingly defined by hierarchical social institutions that function to restrict mobility and opportunity and reinforce social inequality. The so-called "outliers" who are marginalized in modern institutions, such as school—those who lack cultural knowledge and skill relative to others in the culture—are forced into more distal positions within the Euclidean space of culture, and, as a consequence, suffer deleterious effects on physical and mental well-being (Dressler, 2019). Second-level changes are designed to dismantle instructional systems of the industrial school that create structural inequalities and to replace them with a rights-based curriculum that supports an egalitarian institutional ecosystem.

To achieve bureaucratic transformation, a comprehensive distributed leadership agenda is spelled out in programs of *assessment, civil rights, community education, curriculum, school culture,* and *training*. The distributed leadership system enlists staff to carry out responsibilities directly linked to improvements in learning and teaching in the school. Leads are assigned with job descriptions that detail roles and responsibilities and follow a year-long action plan that stages and paces their work (McCallister, 2013e). As leads execute their responsibilities, they activate leadership roles within a system that functions to (1) stage-planned institutional change linked with improvements in teaching and learning; (2) engage the whole school community as participants in the change process; (3) actively monitor and adjust the course of change; and (4) maintain and sustain the momentum of change.

The ecosystem is achieved through the execution of a *Year-long Implementation Guide* that stages and paces the change and transforms the school in less than one year. The Guide specifies tasks to be carried out on a week-by-week basis. Working together, executing the Guide with fidelity, the school leadership and the team of leads replace the traditional school infrastructure and restructure the bureaucracy into a sustainable, decentralized organization that powers its own growth and renewal and supports high achievement. When followed year after year, the Guide creates a self-sustaining, decentralized institutional system of sustainability and renewal; and with each subsequent year the school culture grows more cohesive.[1] The distributed leadership model is briefly described below. The ecosystem design is presented in Chapter 20.

Assessment

Assessment plays an essential role in the educational infrastructure. An Assessment Lead helps implement frequent cycles of formative, curriculum-based assessments, periodic progress monitoring in reading comprehension, and standards-based assessments to state-aligned content curriculum. Data from these assessments provide ongoing evidence of positive changes in student achievement, identify students who are not progressing and need immediate intervention, and provide a source of competence feedback for learners and teachers, helping them know that their efforts are resulting in expected outcomes. The Assessment Program is described in Chapter 21.

Civil Rights

A centralized civil rights program is established to monitor the extent to which the school is upholding its obligation to each learner's right to experiences laid out in the curriculum (McCallister, 2013f). The Civil Rights Lead coordinates an intervention program for learners whose academic or social behaviors prevent them from exercising their rights. The Civil Rights Program is described in Chapter 22.

Community Education

The Community Education Lead organizes school events, develops and implements the school's communications plan, and maintains the school's institutional narrative (McCallister, 2014a). The Community Education Lead takes responsibility to interface with the community. The Community Education Program is described in Chapter 23.

Curriculum

The Curriculum Lead facilitates implementation of the Sparks and Learning Cultures curricula. They maintain quality control by monitoring curriculum materials across grades and subjects and by providing training support in the Formats to learners and adults. The Curriculum Program is described in Chapter 24.

School Culture

Since the social group is the medium of higher-order thinking and intellective development, positive social norms are a defining aspect of a thriving learning culture. The School Culture Lead helps implement this social norms curriculum, known as Keepers of the Culture. Keepers of the Culture is designed to establish a strong sense of civility across the school and to ensure every learner feels the security and safety necessary to exchange their thinking with others. The School Culture Program is described in Chapter 25.

Training

The innovative universal design for learning provided by the Sparks, Learning Cultures, and Keepers of the Culture curriculum models consist of uniform protocols that are implemented similarly in all classrooms. Adults who work with learners at all levels and in every subject take part in the same high-quality training program. McCallister's *Framework for Professional Development* (McCallister, 2008c) provides an approach to collaborative, practice-embedded learning opportunities through peer coaching, lab sites in demonstration classrooms, classroom residencies, workshops, and study groups. The Training Lead takes responsibility for implementing the training program. The Training Program is described in Chapter 26.

Teacher Evaluation

Teacher evaluation is likewise streamlined and simplified. Learning Cultures Rubrics provide the evaluative criteria used to inform teacher evaluation. Administrators use the language of the Format Rubrics to provide constructive and corrective feedback to teachers.

Instructional Accounting

Since equality of educational opportunity for every student depends on their *sufficient* access to participation opportunities within the Formats, a system of Instructional Accounting is instituted in which the school leadership determines Opportunity Targets. Opportunity Targets specify the quantity of Format opportunities learners are entitled to experience annually. These targets are translated into mandates that program the school year into predictable, recurring opportunities, the quantity of which is monitored.

Lateral Cross-School Training

In schools where the McCallister Model is implemented, principals and teachers take part in a lateral, cross-school training program. Participants meet regularly at participating schools on a rotating basis to receive site-based support to implement the McCallister Model practices and to share experiences and expertise.

School Snapshots: Radical Transformation within Microcosms of the Universe of Persistently Failing Schools

I have developed the McCallister Model over the course of 30 years of theoretical research and field-based trials in over 20 urban schools. Chapters 27–30 feature detailed case studies of six of these schools. The section below offers brief snapshots of two of the schools where the McCallister Model was implemented. These interventions are described more fully in Chapters 28 and 30. At both the **High School of Language and Innovation** (HSLI) in the Bronx, beginning in Fall 2011, and at the **Urban Assembly School for Green Careers** (UAGC) on Manhattan's Upper West Side, beginning in Fall 2013, learners had access to the curricula described above.[2] Both schools were a microcosm of the universe of the 5,000 schools nationwide that are considered persistently failing (Duncan, 2009), and which compromise more than 2.5 million students right to an education. Like HSLI and UAGC, these schools reported high dropout rates and low graduation rates, served disproportionately large populations of disadvantaged students, and consistently demonstrated low levels of academic achievement (Education Week, 2004).

18 Background

I began working with the staff of HSLI in Fall 2011, and in Fall 2013, I joined the staff of UAGC to embark on a rapid school transformation initiative. In both settings, I provided training to teachers and principals through monthly school visits where I demonstrated practices in classrooms. Staff in each school also had access to over seven hours of training videos that I created to facilitate training. From 2013 to 2015, staff at both schools took part in the Learning Cultures Initiative's multi-school lateral training program described in Chapter 29.

High School of Language and Innovation

HSLI is one of the small high schools that replaced Christopher Columbus High School, a chronically low-performing school in the Bronx.[3] In 2012, Columbus High School served 749 students with a dropout rate of 19% and a graduation rate of 62%. HSLI is a Title I school, still housed in the Christopher Columbus complex, that serves a population of 81% English language learners (ELLs), 97% of whom live in poverty. HSLI opened in 2011 to its first cohort of 9th graders, adding a new grade each year. In that year, the school began implementing the Learning Cultures model in every grade and subject area.

Learning Cultures was used as the school's comprehensive curriculum model in all grades and subjects beginning in 2011 through Spring 2015, upon graduation of its first cohort. The school staff were new to Learning Cultures in 2011, and I spent the first year demonstrating methods and assisting teachers to learn (and trust) the new paradigm of pedagogy of the model. By the second year, the staff were invested in the McCallister Model and committed to implementing it in all grades and subjects. New teachers were hired with a conditional commitment to the program. In the third and fourth years, the school implemented the second-order changes with fidelity.

In 2015, the first cohort to have had the high school Learning Cultures program for four years graduated at a rate of 73%, outpacing the citywide average by three points and doubling the citywide graduation rate for ELLs. In total, 52% of graduating students were deemed to be "college ready" compared to 35% of students citywide and 19% of students in demographically similar schools. Most remarkably, HSLI's New York City (NYC) Department of Education (DOE) metric score for 4-year college and career readiness was 4.99 on a scale of 0–4.99, equal to that of both the Bronx High School of Science and Stuyvesant High School, two of NYC's highly-selective public magnet schools.[4] The HSLI implementation, in which learners from high levels of economic disadvantage performed on a par academically with learners of economic privilege, offers preliminary evidence that the McCallister Model provides a means to achieve effective equality of educational opportunity.

Urban Assembly School for Green Careers Transformation

Urban Assembly School for Green Careers (UAGC) is a Title I NYC public school on the Upper West Side of Manhattan that serves a population of 395 students who are 25% Black, 71% Hispanic, 23.6% ELLs, 23.8% with IEPs, 15.1% overage, and 83% who live in poverty. UAGC opened in 2009 as one of the small schools that replaced Brandies High School when Brandies was closed under the Bloomberg's small schools reform initiative due to persistent failure. UAGC was proof that small size did not necessarily make a positive difference to school success, as UAGC graduated its first class in 2013 with a 39% graduation rate, placing it at the bottom 1% of high schools citywide on measures of student achievement and other NYC DOE school quality metrics. The school was assigned an "F" on the NYC DOE annual report card in 2012–2013. This is the year that I began what would become a 6-year collaboration with UAGC to employ my comprehensive school transformation design to turn around the school. This effort was part of a network-sponsored project begun in 2011, called the McCallister-Learning Cultures Initiative, in which I was recruited by The Urban Assembly, a nonprofit organization with a mission to advance students' economic and social mobility through public education, to work with six of their low-performing schools to implement my model.

Results from the 2013 environmental survey, in which the school was rated in the categories of academic expectations, safety and respect, communication and engagement, shed light on the problems at hand. According to parents, teachers, and students who took part in the 2012–2013 Learning Environment Survey, the school ranked 0.0% on measures of academic expectations for students, 12.5% on student engagement, 14.3% on safety and respect, and 11.1% on attendance compared to citywide averages. Annual teacher turnover was close to 50% three years running. From 2009 to 2013, the school experimented with several different instructional program designs. In 2012–2013, 39% of the staff reported feeling unsafe working at the school. 100% of staff believed that order and discipline were not maintained and that the behavioral support they needed was not provided.

In 2013, the majority of 9th-grade students at UAGC had failed their 8th grade state math and reading exams in middle school. A nationally norm-referenced assessment of reading comprehension administered in Fall 2013 indicated the average score of students at every grade at the school was below the 3rd-grade level. 0.0% of students met the City's math college readiness standards, and only 34.7% met the City's English college readiness standards. During my initial visits to the school, I observed classroom cultures to be characterized by incivility and social disorder. Usually, when I attempted to demonstrate practices to students and teachers in whole-class and small groups, I was routinely the target of students' vitriolic comments and I struggled to maintain order. Students left classrooms at will, and at any given time large numbers of students were roaming the hallways. It was not surprising to me when teachers reported that they walked the halls with their heads down, afraid of verbal assault, or locked their classroom doors to prevent students from entering. One teacher relayed that she once had to confront students in her class when she discovered them playing the "condom challenge" (snorting a condom in through the nose and taking it out by the mouth). Another teacher reported that boys went shirtless in the hallways on hot days.

After a day of classroom visits with the principal on my first visit to the school, I felt daunted. The HSLI turnaround had been entirely smooth because the school began with a single class of 9th graders and grew by just one grade a year. The gradual phase-in approach created optimal conditions to implement an innovative model while developing a positive school culture. The culture at UAGC was toxic across the entire school of 300 students in grades 9–12. Also, this principal was new to the high school principalship. While she had previously been a principal in PK-8 schools, she was new to the role at the high-school level. On the other hand, this principal had extensive experience with my model. I had worked with her for three years when she recruited me to implement my model in PK-8 reading and writing programs at the Jacob Riis School, a Title I school in Lower Manhattan between 2007 and 2010 where she was principal. She had also worked the previous year as a Coach in the McCallister-Learning Cultures Initiative under my guidance. She possessed a deep knowledge of the model, a proven ability to implement the protocols with fidelity, and a record of accepting my guidance in implementing my model over the previous six years.

20 Background

So while concerned, I also had reasons to feel confident. I had tested my model in at the high school level at HSLI in all subjects, as well as in another high school. Also, in many respects, the challenges at UAGC were fewer. While both HSLI and UAGC were Title I schools, levels of language diversity and economic disadvantage were much higher in HSLI compared to UAGC. On balance, I believed a transformation at UAGC could be accomplished.

Transformation Success

The principal led the staff in implementing the curriculum components of the McCallister Method with skill and precision. Under her impeccable leadership, UAGC increased the graduation rate by more than 10% the first year. In 2016, at the end of the second year of implementation, the school received a "well developed" on its school-wide quality review, a perfect score and one of only a small fraction of schools citywide to receive such a rating. When the principal left the school mid-year in 2016, the assistant principal took the helm to continue implementing planned change. First- and second-order changes continued to be maintained, and achievement continued on a robust trajectory. In 2017, the school graduated its first cohort to have had the Learning Cultures program for four years with graduation a graduation rate of 84%, more than doubling its 2013 graduation rate. The suspension rate in the school dropped from over 200 in 2013–2014 to under 20 in 2016–2017.

The positive impact of the first- and second-order reforms in both HSLI and UAGC can be seen as a direct result of the implementation of the Learning Cultures model under the leadership of capable principals who took the initiative to adopt and implement the program with fidelity.[5] These schools offer a hopeful counter narrative to the conventional wisdom in the comprehensive school reform literature. It is predicted that complex school designs achieve only partial implementation after three to four years, and that it typically takes up to 10 years to turn around a school (Berends, Bodilly, & Kirby, 2002). The UAGC initiative proved to be an historic rapid school transformation, having succeeded in raising graduation rates by 10% in the first year and doubling graduation rates in four years.

Equality of Educational Opportunity

In its historic *Brown v. Board of Education* decision (1954), the U.S. Supreme Court affirmed its commitment to an education on equal terms as a right of all American citizens, and established desegregation as a criterion for equality of educational opportunity (EEO). Since that time, U.S. education policy has sought to reform schools in ways that honor the principle of equality of educational opportunity by ensuring equal access to education irrespective of race, class, language, gender, or ability. But in its Brown decision, while the Court implied a concern for the *effects* of schooling, quality of education as a criterion of equality was obfuscated by a more central concern for desegregation. The psychologist and civil rights leader, Edmund W. Gordon, has argued that while desegregation was beneficial to society in general, it was the wrong strategy to improve equality of educational opportunity for minority and low-income students (Gordon, 2004). Gordon asserts that greater progress toward the achievement of EEO will be realized when education policy shifts its focus toward a concern quality in the effects of schooling and for *sufficiency* and *adequacy* of educational treatments.

The U.S. Supreme Court has signaled its concern for educational adequacy. In *Rodriguez v. San Antonio ISD*, the Court ruled that while education was not a constitutionally-protected right, a certain "quantum of education" that is necessary to teach civic competencies requisite for the exercise of 14th Amendment rights of citizenship could be considered a protection if a case were to come before the Court in which these rights were in question. Education policy has since been concerned to establish criteria for educational adequacy in relation to a "quantum of education." The McCallister Model serves as an example of a "quantum of education." When implemented with fidelity and consistency, the program appears to be sufficiently intense to eliminate gaps in achievement between minority and low socioeconomic status (SES) learners and their higher SES counterparts. The problem of equality of educational opportunity is discussed in Chapter 2.

New Possibilities for Substantive School Reform

U.S. education policy since Brown has been focused on ameliorating the effects of social inequality, evidenced in the achievement gap. The *achievement gap* is the persistent disparity in achievement between minority and low-SES students and their high SES counterparts, which was first documented in the 1966 report, Equality of Educational Opportunity, also known as the Coleman Report (Coleman, United States, & National Center for Education Statistics, 1966), and which still exists today (NAEP, 2019). The Coleman Report, commissioned under the 1964 Civil Rights Act by the U.S. Department of Health, Education and Welfare, revealed that family background, peer influences, and the socioeconomic mix in schools were the most significant factors in academic achievement, and confirmed that educational inputs, such as school facilities and teachers, were of relatively little significance to achievement outcomes. Since that time, U.S. education policy and practice have been unsuccessful in realizing reforms that succeed in closing the achievement gap. The federal Title I program, established in the Johnson administration as part of the War on Poverty, which has been reauthorized every five years since that time, provides compensatory services to economically disadvantaged students. But to date there is no evidence that Title I programs have been shown to be effective (Dynarski & Kainz, 2015) and have not significantly reduced nationwide achievement gaps from 1966 to 2011 (Sousa & Armor, 2016).

Early Title I programs emphasized the provision of remedial instruction to disadvantaged students on an individual basis. But in the 1970s, the U.S. Department of Education created the Comprehensive School Reform (CSR) program with the goal of supporting schools to raise student achievement outcomes by improving school quality and by coordinating every aspect of the school's operation. After mandatory accountability reporting mandated by NCLB legislation revealed the large scale of school failure, federal education policy shifted its emphasis toward a concern for turning around or transforming failing schools. Despite decades of effort and countless billions invested, there are few successful CSR models and there have been virtually no successful turnarounds (Dragoset et al., 2017).

Not only have our school reform efforts since Brown been unsuccessful in raising student achievement in minority and low-income populations, transformation efforts have been costly. For example, the NYC DOE was awarded a $19.8M grant in 2010 to turn around 11 of their chronically low-performing schools (Walz, 2010). Of those funds, the central administration received $6M, the smallest school in the initiative received $757K, and two of the largest schools received $1.8M (Walz, 2010). The most recent price tag for rapid reform initiatives in the NYC DOE was approximately $430K a year in Mayor De Blasio's Renewal Schools Program, which provided 94 schools with $773M worth of extensive social services, teacher training, and an extended learning time, and which ended after 19 months following disappointing outcomes (Zimmerman, 2019).[6] The disappointing outcomes of the Renewal investment are not surprising. As of 2007, there were no known successful turnaround models (Kutash et al., 2010), and even after a decade of effort and billions invested, the turnaround sector has come up empty handed with proven solutions. Not a single school improvement effort funded through Obama's Race to the Top school turnaround initiative was associated with gains in student achievement (Dragoset et al., 2017). And 2017 NAEP results show no impact of Obama-era policy initiatives on student achievement.

Federal school turnaround policy established a new industry sector in education and a growing body of conventional wisdom espoused in the school turnaround literature. The school turnaround literature calls for transformation models that *depart from the norm*, result in *rapid upward trending data* (e.g., achievement, teacher effectiveness, and reduced suspensions), and *make use of data to inform decision making*, and *maintain a persistent focus on results* (Herman et al., 2008). This body of conventional wisdom suggests that every school is unique and requires an individually-tailored reform plan. According to the literature, a plan typically takes a year to develop at a cost of about $300K (Walz, 2010). Former NYC DOE schools chancellor, Richard Carranza, asserted, "The art and craft of school improvement is not a program. You don't pull it off the shelf" (Zimmerman, 2019). This literature also suggests that turnaround leadership expertise is beyond the preparation of all but a limited number of school leaders and the limited capacity of only a few university turnaround preparation programs (Peurach & Neumerski, 2015).

There are currently over 5,000 persistently failing schools nationwide that need to be improved immediately in order to honor more than 2.5 million students' right to an education (Duncan, 2009). Economist Eric Hanushek points out that, at the present rate of change, it will take two-and-a-half centuries for our public schools to close the achievement gap between Black and white students (Hanushek, 2016). But school reform is not just a necessity for failing schools. And the achievement gap is but one problem that school reform needs to address. There is currently a general recognition that all schools need to be transformed to enable all students to meet 21st-century learning demands (Battelle for Kids, 2019; Elmore, 2017, 2018).

The McCallister Model provides a low-cost, universal school transformation design that can be used as a blueprint by any competent leader to guide implementation in a single year with significant achievement gains. The blueprint provides a simple, efficient, and inexpensive way to radically restructure schools by replacing the traditional linear transmission curriculum with a curriculum structured around engaging, learner-directed social practices that turn classrooms into bustling hubs of peer collaboration and rigorous, self-directed inquiry. The same plan can be taken "off the shelf," so to speak, and used in a wide range of settings.

The McCallister Model is simple to implement, involving specific procedures with rules to be followed so that planned change can be secured and sustained. The model provides a coherent system of instruction, assessment, and resources. It provides procedures that support professional collaboration, high expectations for students, and means through which trust between school stakeholders can be established. When the model is brought to scale across a whole school or network, it creates coherent classroom-, school-, and system-level infrastructures.

A Universal Model for Remote Learning

The McCallister Model provides a design for remote education, in which learners can independently (from home) pursue a personalized learning agenda of asynchronous activities through the Sparks curriculum, combined with cloud-based video conferencing activities structured by the protocols of the Learning Cultures curriculum.[7]

Conclusion

The Learning Cultures model answers the current demand for proven school designs that ensure every child's right to an education that adequately supports them to meet their potential, develop their talents, and become prepared to participate socially, economically, and politically in an increasingly global and technological world (e.g., Battelle for Kids, 2019; Education Reimagined, 2015; OECD, 2018). The model provides a fully conceptualized school design for rapid institutional change that can be used in a wide range of situations with diverse learner populations. It provides fully developed instructional and behavioral support programs with clear and simple protocols for implementation. It features an integrated approach to teacher training, professional development, and evaluation. It incorporates a comprehensive, school-wide assessment program that provides continuous streams of data to inform learning, teaching, and institutional decision making. And it includes integrated programs to support academically vulnerable learners, before fully including students with special needs and English language learners in the general education program. In the hands of a skilled leader willing to implement the program according specified standards, the plan can reliably result in an immediate and successful school transformation, turning the traditional industrial school into a self-sustaining, 21st-century learning organization inside the course of a year.

Notes

1. Those interested in reading New York City (NYC) Department of Education reports about the school, written by the leadership of Urban Assembly High School for Green Careers and those who conducted its quality reviews can access public documents through the NYC Department of Education website. School self-reports are available by request through the NYC Department of Education.
2. Both schools retained the egg-crate design of grade- and subject-based classrooms, and the ambitions of the transformation effort were restricted to improvements within the academic curriculum defined by grade and subject domains. Thus, the Cultural Capital Curriculum was not implemented in these cases.
3. The NYC small school initiative under Bloomberg was part of a federal school turnaround initiative spearheaded by the Obama Administration, who invested more than $3 billion to turn around the nation's lowest performing 5% of schools nationwide. A school turnaround involves a change in leadership, replacing at least 50% of staff, and a number of other strategies intended to improve school performance.
4. See the NYC School Quality Guide to find achievement performance data for HSLI, Bronx High School of Science, and Stuyvesant High School.
5. Public reporting documents, such as school quality reviews, comprehensive educational plans, and school budgets record the details of Learning Cultures program implementation and how funds were spent to implement it.
6. I had the opportunity to visit a Renewal school located in Hunts Point in the Bronx. In this school, the Renewal Program offices were located in spaces with windows, and the kindergarten and first-grade classrooms had been re-located to the windowless interior spaces.
7. Urban Assembly High School for Green Careers employs the Formats of Work Time, Unison Reading, and Conferences in their remote learning program (as of Fall, 2020).

Resources

1. Listen to Sir Ken Robinson discuss the traditional educational paradigm and how it has influenced the structure of our current schools. www.ted.com/talks/sir_ken_robinson_changing_education_paradigms. Then watch him discuss how we can bring on a learning revolution: www.ted.com/talks/sir_ken_robinson_bring_on_the_revolution.

2 Read the Universal Declaration of Human Rights with special attention to Article 26, the right to an education. www.ohchr.org/EN/UDHR/Documents/UDHR_Translations/eng.pdf. Then read *A Human Rights-Based Approach to Education for All, a policy and programming framework by UNESCO and UNICEF*, to achieve universal quality education.
3 Read "A transformational vision for education in the U.S.," by Education Reimagined. It explains why our schools need to change and presents criteria that can be used to describe the schools we need in order to create learning cultures. https://education-reimagined.org/wp-content/uploads/2019/01/Vision_Website.pdf.
4 Read *Making Education Brain Science*, by Jenny Anderson to explore similarities and differences in how the Blue School and Learning Cultures each support social-emotional learning. See: www.nytimes.com/2012/04/15/nyregion/at-the-blue-school-kindergarten-curriculum-includes-neurology.html?pagewanted=all.
5 Watch Geoffrey Canada, founder of the Harlem Children's Zone, urges the systemic changes in education in his talk, *Our failing schools. Enough is enough!*
6 Watch Adora Svitak offer her insights about *what adults can learn from kids*. What points of advice does she offer about the need to give students space, autonomy, and responsibility to grapple with real challenges? How do Learning Cultures practices help achieve these aims?
7 Where do good ideas come from? What are the conditions that promote the evolution of good ideas? Think about how we can support these conditions in the classroom.
8 Read *A Permanent Talent Underclass* … to better understand the importance of equity in excellence of educational opportunities.
9 Matthew Taylor explores the meaning of *21st-century Enlightenment*, and presses us to reconsider long-held assumptions about the nature of progress. Some of the ideas presented in this lecture concerning the way people think and learn resonate with Taylor's message. Watch, and see if you can make connections that will help you expand your learning. Share your insights with a colleague.

2 The Schools We Have

> Tradition is as neurotic as any patient; its overgrown fear of deviation from its fortuitous standards conforms to all the usual definitions of the psychopathic.
>
> Ruth Benedict (1934, p. 273)

> I am not interested in preserving the status quo; I want to overthrow it.
>
> Niccolò Machiavelli

The child first comes to school at about the same time they begin to understand the idea of *normal* and can make judgments for themselves about right or wrong, or good or bad (Tomasello, 2019). They are now able to learn about who they are in the eyes of others. They learn expectations for how human beings should treat one other and how they should expect to be treated. They learn the limits of their own sense of possibility and the boundaries of their own power. The school will become the child's primary cultural niche, where they will spend 13,000 hours of their future lives. What kind of schools do we currently have? What do these schools teach children?

It is said that a fish is the last to find water. In other words, awareness of a certain aspect of reality is elusive when there is nothing else to compare it to. This aphorism is fitting to the way most of us think about school. Like the air we breathe, we take for granted that schools are organized into classes of students of the same age or with similar abilities, that classes are led by teachers, and that teaching involves telling students what to do and learn. We take for granted that curriculum is a body of information that is organized into a series of tasks that are systematically taught to achieve a stated objective. Despite the vast abundance of diversity in cultural practices among the world's thousands of cultures, schools from around the globe share an uncanny sameness: desks are lined in rows where students sit facing teachers, recipients of knowledge. They listen, watch, observe, raise hands, and respond to teacher directives. And because much of the traditions and practices of school are so familiar as to be taken-for-granted, they are a challenge to change.

Schools as we know them are creations of culture that came into being as complex societies invented new technologies to improve education for the young. The modern school is a relic of the past, with a reptilian-like resistance to change. It operates on systems based on old technologies that were developed to solve social problems of the past. This chapter attempts to accomplish two objectives. First, it attempts to illustrate how the modern industrial school operates on systems that should now be obsolescent. It presents a survey of several of the most elemental systems of the current industrial school to explain where they came from and the purpose they served. Next, it presents a brief history of the evolution of ideas about the purpose of schooling in a democracy and how these ideas have shaped the course of school reform. The proposal for school reform proposed in this book will begin with a clear understanding of the schools we have and how they need to change.

School as a Relic of History

For most of the time period that modern humans have existed on earth, language has served as a means for members of large social groups of about 150 to communicate in order to survive (Dunbar, 1998). Oral traditions in nomadic hunter-gatherer groups were the vehicle that transmitted cultural knowledge from one generation to the next. Ten thousand years ago, when farming replaced hunting and gathering as the human economic mainstay, human societies became more populous and complex, creating the need for more efficient modes of symbolic communication, and creating conditions that resulted in the invention of writing a little more than 5,500 years ago (Gamble, Gowlett & Dunbar, 2014). Systems of law, trade, and religious practice could now be preserved and transmitted through the written word. The new human technology of writing created a new need to train large numbers of scribes who could read, write, and reproduce texts to meet the administrative needs of the secular and religious systems of early civilization.

Civilization's First Schools

The first evidence of anything resembling what we would today recognize as a school appeared around 3,500 B.C. in Sumer, in ancient Mesopotamia. In temple-like spaces that were used to train scribes, classrooms took the form of stone desks facing forward toward the teacher (Cole, 2005). Cole (2005) points out the striking similarity between the ancient schools of Sumer and modern schools:

> Not only the activities that took place in these schools but the architecture, the organization of activities, and the reigning ideologies within them were in many respects startlingly modern…. The classroom consisted of rows of desks, facing forward to a single location where a teacher stood, guiding them in repetitive practice of the means of writing and the operations that accompanied it.
>
> (p. 200)

Throughout most of written history, knowledge has been viewed as a commodity that can be transferred, and the mind as a receptacle to be filled (Olson, 2003). Classical transmission has been the dominant form of pedagogy employed throughout the history of schools. The aspiring scribes of Sumer learned from teachers through a pedagogy of instructed learning, by memorizing compositions, and then producing written duplicates of them from memory (Delnero, 2012). The pedagogical "technology" of memorization is one of the longest-running traditions in the history of civilization, and still dominates classroom practice. It is estimated that 75–78% of interactions between teachers and students are low-level memory tasks that teach students to memorize and remember content (Elmore, 2018).

As representatives of the state or a religious order, the teacher's role became vested with a kind of moral authority accorded to those in society with the highest status. Teachers were the metaphorical priests within the temple of knowledge.

Compulsory Education and the Aims of the State

Compulsory education, or education required of all people imposed by the government, appeared in Europe in the wake of feudalism, with the rise of the nation state in response to the need for an informed citizenry, as a means to instill national identity, and as a means to create a literate body of clergy and administrators (Olson, 2003). The function of the first public forms of education were to enable individuals to think freely and make up their own minds. Dunbar (personal communication, October 27, 2020) points out that universal education first began in Scotland in the late 16th century to teach basic skills to enable religious participation for the general population, which led to a literacy rate of >75% for the entire adult population (men and women), compared to a 30% literacy rate in England and the rest of Europe. The spirit of free thinking planted seeds for the Edinburgh Enlightenment of the late 18th century and laid the groundwork for modern fields of philosophy, science, political theory, and medicine (Dunbar, personal communication, October 27, 2020).

In the United States, the founding fathers saw a role for compulsory education to prepare citizens to be able to exercise their civic duties. John Adams advocated a system of education in the "national care" that was capable of making knowledge so general as to enable the lower ranks to be raised to the higher (McCullough, 1995). Jefferson (1943) believed education should function to enable the person to exercise their rights as citizens with good judgment and responsibility. Out of concern not to grant too much power to the national government, the founding fathers limited the federal role in education. But constitutions in most of the original 13 colonies established education as a right (Rebell, 2018).

Discipline and Control: The Panopticon

With the disappearance of feudalism and the absolute monarchy, violence as a behavioral deterrent and means of social control gave rise to more rational and scalable means of imposing discipline and order. The social philosopher, Jeremy Bentham, invented an architectural design for prisons, called the *panopticon*. Meaning *view of all*, the panopticon consisted of a circular structure with an observation post at the center and cells built on the periphery. This design embodied efficiency, enabling a single guard to observe and monitor all inmates. The panopticon architectural design was applied to schools and hospitals. Knowing they were being watched, subjects (patients, prisoners, or students) internalized the *eye of authority* to regulate their behavior (Foucault, 1995). Tradition dictates that children in schools are to be seen, and not heard. Viewed as blank slates waiting to receive information from the teacher, social interaction has been viewed as an impediment to learning. If children are to be seen, not heard, the school needed a technology powerful enough to quell the child's boisterous nature. The panopticon served as a form of technology that quelled the boisterous nature of the child, because, as Foucault (1995) writes, the student "is seen, but he does not see; he is an object of information, never a subject in communication" (p. 200). Under the influence of the "eye of power," Foucault (1995) points out, "there is no copying, no noise, no chatter, no waste of time…" (p. 202). Systems of surveillance continue to serve as a means through which learners and teachers are monitored and controlled.

Industrial Schools and the Pedagogy of Efficiency

Efficiency became a dominant concern in education at the turn of the 20th century, as schools faced unprecedented challenges to accommodate a huge influx of students caused by mass migration to cities, child labor laws, and compulsory education requirements in all states by 1918. Secondary school attendance in the United States increased by more than 700% from 1890 to 1918, from 200,000 to 1.5 million students (Tyack, 1974). Technologies from the new field of scientific management were employed in schools to manage students and make instruction more efficient (Taylor, 1911). Within the conception of the school as factory, teachers were seen as technicians on an assembly line where they dispensed knowledge to students on a curriculum conveyor belt (Callahan, 1962).

Linear, Incremental Curriculum

We take for granted that curriculum is a large taxonomy of knowledge that is arranged into an incremental, linear structure for the purpose of systematic teaching. But the linear, incremental curriculum was a new educational technology in the early 20th century adopted to meet the need for instructional methods that were suited to accommodate large numbers of students efficiently.

The influential educationist and professor of education at the University of Chicago, Franklin Bobbitt, believed the curriculum should serve the practical needs of learners by preparing them for the roles they would assume as adults. Bobbitt (1918) advocated a curriculum focused on citizenship, vocational training, and social responsibilities. His vision for a practical, efficient approach to curriculum and teaching was accepted as mainstream in American schools. Bobbit (1918) explained that curriculum design should begin with the identification of the "abilities, attitudes, habits, appreciations, and forms of knowledge that men need," and then turn these competencies into a series of experiences that meet target objectives. Bobbitt (1918) also asserted that the scholastic curriculum should be found in the "shortcomings of children" or their deficits (p. 50). He asserted that whatever competencies are not acquired through indirect experience (e.g., outside of school) should be the focus of directed experiences of the curriculum, which should remediate deficiencies. Bobbitt (1918) wrote, "Only as we list the errors and shortcomings of human performance in each of the fields can we know what to include and to emphasize in the directed curriculum of the schools" (p. 52). The focus of formal instruction for the last 100 years has been organized with the objective of remediating a defect by passing on knowledge through teaching, telling, or demonstrating (Bobbitt, 1918; Olson, 2003).

Ralph Tyler, a professor at the University of Chicago, proposed a rationale for the organization of curriculum (1949) that revolved around 1) the definition of learning objectives; 2) the identification of appropriate learning experiences; 3) the organization of learning experiences; and 4) evaluation of the effectiveness of experiences. Since they progress through the curriculum in a lock-step fashion, it was possible for a supervisor to know at all times where each student was at every point in the curriculum. The Tyler Rationale is still a mainstay of curriculum design in education and is the basis of leveled math and reading programs that emphasize a linear sequence of direct instruction of skills (National Reading Panel (U.S.) and National Institute of Child Health and Human Development (U.S.), 2000).

Within the new field of psychology at beginning of the 20th century, behaviorism had become the dominant theoretical paradigm and dictated methods of curriculum. Behaviorism is the theory that the behavior of organisms can be explained by responses to stimulus in the environment, through operant conditioning, without regard to subjective thoughts, beliefs, or feelings. Within this paradigm, changes in behavior are achieved by altering behavior patterns through conditioning, and reinforcement of associations is achieved through extrinsic rewards (Skinner, 1974; Thorndike, 1898). Edward Thorndike, an influential psychologist who helped develop the field of educational psychology, promoted instructional methods based on association theory and the practice of behavioral reinforcement of observable behaviors through praise. The emphasis in behaviorism for external stimulation squared well with the teacher-centered, transmission-oriented instructional design of mass education.

A Pedagogy of Testing, Sorting, and Group Teaching

The new technology of standardized testing, deriving from the IQ tests invented by French psychologist Alfred Binet, was employed on a large scale to identify deficiencies and measure aptitude in students in order to group them for instruction (Bobbitt, 1918). In 1919, the city of Detroit adopted the "XYZ Plan," whereby all learners were given IQ tests and grouped accordingly—the highest scoring 20% were the "X" group; the middle scoring 60% were the "Y group"; and the lowest performing 20% were the "Z Group" (Courtis, 1925; Kulik, 2004). Students were tested each year for promotion. The *XYZ Plan* became widely adopted across the United States. Though schools eventually stopped using IQ tests as a means by which to group students, achievement and aptitude tests are still used to group students by similar ability for instruction.

The new technology of grouping students by level or ability created a new technology of *whole-group teaching*. Teacher training focused on methods to group students and to provide group instruction. Expansion of the commercial publishing industry and the availability of mass-produced texts made it possible that all students could have access to identical copies of printed materials, increasing the power of group teaching, and securing traditions in practice that make whole-group teaching still prevalent today (Olson, 2003). This form of instruction requires teachers to engage the attention of many learners at once, resulting in a pattern of discourse in which the teacher initiates a discourse sequence with a question ("I"), calls on a learner to respond ("R"), and then evaluates the response ("E"). This "I-R-E discourse" that has become almost universal in schools (Mehan, 1979). The technologies that enabled large, leveled classes, and whole-class teaching meant large numbers of learners could be presented with the same information at the same time. I-R-E discourse is a means of managing the progression of an idea in oral discussion, but it lacks the properties of social discourse that are necessary for the achievement of higher understanding (these properties are described in the next chapter).

Groups are managed by teachers, who transmit a linear curriculum of academic content in increments though group teaching methods. Learners with special needs are isolated from others and form special groups of their own. "Specials" like art, music, and gym are activities considered separate from the core curriculum. The modern industrial school operates on the "Old-World" educational model of "a linear, curriculum-driven 'conveyor belt' that students and schools try (with little success in high-poverty settings) to keep up with" (Calkins et al., 2007). The familiar "egg-crate school," in which students and teachers are compartmentalized in leveled classrooms (Lortie, 1975), is the prevailing archetype of the modern schools.

A Higher Purpose for Public Education

By 1918, compulsory education was mandated in all states, and the industrial school became commonplace in American society (see Figure 2.1, a representation of an industrial school in which classes are organized by groups of learners of similar age or ability). The forces of urbanization and industrialization created urgent demands for schools to organize quickly to teach large numbers of children basic skills, to provide necessary vocational training, and to acculturate immigrant children to the values and traditions of American society. Schools moved quickly to adopt pragmatic and practical systems that addressed immediate problems of overcrowding and socialization. The educational historian, Ellen Lagemann (1989), points out that the industrialists won the debate for the purpose of education in the early 20th century in terms of overall influence on American educational practice and research. John Dewey and the advocates for a child-centered education lost the debate to Edward Thorndike and the advocates of scientific management to determine what our schools would become. But the industrial school had its critics, and debates concerning the purpose of school were ongoing through the

INDUSTRIAL SCHOOL DESIGN

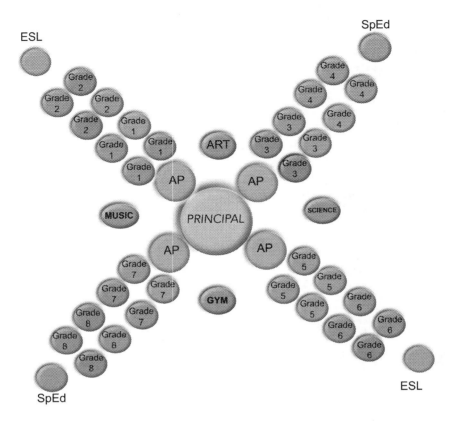

Figure 2.1 Industrial school design

20th century in response to questions about the role of schooling our increasingly diverse, rapidly changing democratic society.

Progressive education philosophers of the early 20th century advocated for an approach to education that is suited to the child's nature and their subjective experiences (Dewey, 1938) and wedded to the democratic values of freedom of will and self-expression (Dewey, 1916/1944; DuBois, 1903). Education was also increasingly seen as a means of self-actualization and of service to the ascendant aims of political enfranchisement (DuBois, 1903).

American society in the early 20th century in the United States was divided into two distinct social worlds: the world of white Americans and the world of African Americans. The prevailing values of efficiency and expediency in mainstream American education also determined the nature of education in the African American community. The last decade of the 19th century saw a spike in violence to Blacks in the South and escalating legal discrimination. Booker T. Washington, the primary voice of the elite Black establishment, proposed what has come to be known as the "Atlanta Compromise." In exchange for basic education and economic opportunity, African Americans would accept the doctrine of separate but equal, forfeit their civil rights, and give up the opportunity of higher education. Washington, a former slave, opposed challenging Jim Crow segregation and legal disenfranchisement directly. Instead, he believed that Blacks would assimilate over time with increased economic wealth and growing status in society. Washington advocated for progress through basic industrial education and entrepreneurship. The "Atlanta Compromise" resulted in a system of education for African Americans that was inferior, and which continues to be the focus of school reform.

Toward a Democratic, Ascendent Education

John Dewey was an American philosopher and school reformer who has been one of the most prominent educational thinkers in American intellectual history. Dewey emphasized the need for education to center education around the learner's interests, experiences, and intentions. He believed that education was a cornerstone of democratic society and saw democratic life as a "mode of associated living, of conjoint communicated experience" (p. 87) that schools had an obligation to foster. Dewey also advocated self-management and self-regulation as a focus of education. According to Dewey (1916/1944), schooling for democracy should enable the learner to renounce external control and cultivate agency and personal development.

Education for the purpose of emancipation and enfranchisement was also a theme in the thinking of W.E.B. DuBois, the American sociologist and civil rights leader. DuBois (1903) saw the value of a classical education as a means of self-assertion and a strategy for assimilation and full political enfranchisement. Like Dewey, DuBois (1903) believed education should serve the interests of personal development and an elevated form of *individualism*. He asserted that struggle for enfranchisement could only be won with an education system that cultivated leadership in the "talented 10%" of the African American community, so that the cause of racial equality and political and economic justice could be advanced through their leadership.

Both Dewey and DuBois emphasized the transcendental power of human experience, and the role of freedom in education. DuBois (1903) wrote:

> …there must come a loftier respect for the sovereign human soul that seeks to know itself and the world about it; that seeks a freedom for expansion and self-development; that will love and hate and labor in its own way, untrammeled alike by old and new… Herein the longing of black men must have respect: the rich and bitter depth of their experience, the unknown treasures of their inner life, the strange rendings of nature they have seen, may give the world new points of view and make their loving, living, and doing precious to all human hearts. And to themselves in these the days that try their souls, the chance to soar in the dim blue air above the smoke is to their finer spirits boon and guerdon for what they lose on earth by being black.
>
> (Chapter VI)

Dewey was critical of the dehumanizing and oppressive consequences of scientific management and industrial education. He wrote extensively on the importance of free will, intention, and personal investment in education. Dewey writes (1916/1944):

> Plato defined a slave as one who accepts from another the purposes which control his conduct. This condition obtains even where there is no slavery in the legal sense. It is found wherever men are engaged in activity which is socially serviceable, but whose service they do not understand and have no personal interest in. Much is said about scientific management of work. It is a narrow view which restricts the science which secures efficiency of operation to movements of the muscles. The chief opportunity for science is the discovery of the relations of a man to his work—including his

relations to others who take part—which will enlist his intelligent interest in what he is doing. Efficiency in production often demands division of labor. But it is reduced to a mechanical routine unless workers see the technical, intellectual, and social relationships involved in what they do, and engage their work because of the motivation furnished by such perceptions. (p. 85)

The Brazilian philosopher and educator, Paolo Freire (1970), was a leading critic of industrial education, and what he called the "banking" approach. The "banking" metaphor views teachers and other school authorities as being responsible for depositing knowledge into the minds of students who are viewed as passive receptacles taking in the content of deposits. Because of the domination-submission dynamic inherent in this banking model, Friere (1970) exposed how education is often employed as an instrument of oppression. As an alternative to the "banking" approach, Freire proposed the development of "critical consciousness" in the oppressed through dialogic education methods that are capable of liberating the individual through instruments of cooperation, organization, unity, and cultural synthesis.

The Modern School Reform Movement

By the middle of the 20th century, American education had developed an extensive infrastructure of systems designed to provide large populations of students with a basic, practical education. But almost as soon as the modern industrial school was established, it became the focus of criticism and calls for reform. The education reform movement in the United States over the last half century has been largely centered on the problem of equality of educational opportunity, which stemmed from the circumstances of our history as a society and our ongoing effort to confront the ugly legacy of slavery.

Civil Rights, Democratic Individualism, and Education

After World War II and the defeat of fascism, and with the rise of a new global political order, the communitarian ethos of public life took a turn toward democratic individualism, with its concern for the political culture of individuality and equal dignity and the civil culture of individual rights (Urbinati, 2015). In this context, education for the purpose of basic training fell short in meeting the higher purpose of self-actualization. In its Universal Declaration of Human Rights (1948), the United Nations embraced a commitment to fundamental rights to freedom, equality and dignity, freedom from slavery, equal protection under the law, freedom of movement, thought, opinion and expression, and peaceful assembly. These values found expression in Article 26 of the Declaration, in which the right to a free and compulsory education based on merit is asserted. The Declaration stipulates that "Education shall be directed to the full development of the human personality and to the strengthening of respect for human rights and fundamental freedoms. It shall promote understanding, tolerance and friendship among all nations, racial or religious groups, and shall further the activities of the United Nations for the maintenance of peace."

After its triumph in World War II with the defeat of fascism and a powerful stand to end genocide, the United States won world domination and implied international leadership. Educational psychologist and civil rights leader Edmund Gordon points out how this new leadership role imposed a moral obligation to lead by example (personal communication, May 24, 2020). Given its position of moral authority on the world stage, the United States could no longer cast a blind eye to apartheid practices at home, and a pathway for political action materialized on the Civil Rights front.

By the mid-20th century, the Civil Rights community had rejected the premise of Booker T. Washington's Atlanta Compromise, and had begun to embrace W.E.B. DuBois' agenda of civic equality, the right to vote, and education according to ability (DuBois, 1903). Given the political landscape, the N.A.A.C.P. (National Association for the Advancement of Colored People) now saw an opportunity to press the cause of civil rights through equality of educational opportunity (EEO) into the courts. The opportunity to bring the question of equality of education to the Supreme Court came in the historic *Brown v. Board of Education* case of 1954, in which the Court ruled that de jure segregation was illegal and established the doctrine of equality of educational opportunity. In its decision, the Court wrote, "In these days, it is doubtful that any child may reasonably be expected to succeed in life if he is denied the opportunity of an education. Such an opportunity, where the state has undertaken to provide it is a right which must be available to all *on equal terms*" (emphasis added). In its ruling, the Court found that racial segregation in schools violated the equal protection clause of the 14th Amendment of the U.S. Constitution. The Court's remedy adjudicated the problem of inequality by attempting to expand access to white educational facilities to Blacks through various plans for school desegregation. And Title IV of the Civil Rights Act (1964) enforced desegregation of public schools.

The Brown decision reflected the justices' concern for the function that free association plays in democratic life. John Dewey (1916/1944) wrote extensively about the relationship between freedom and fluidity of forms of association within democratic society and the functional capacity of its institutions. The justices seemed to be channeling Dewey (1916/1944), who wrote, "A society which makes provision for participation in its good of all its members *on equal terms* and which secures flexible readjustment of its institutions through interaction of the different forms of associated life is in so far democratic" (p. 99) (emphasis added). Equal access to educational opportunity, free from barriers imposed by circumstances of race or other status factors, was established as a primary concern for American education policy. Throughout the next five decades, equal opportunity protections would be extended to students of economic disadvantage, students with disabilities, English learners, non-citizens, and girls.

Equality of Educational Opportunity

Equality of educational opportunity (EEO) has been a concern of U.S. social policy since *Plessy v. Ferguson*, the landmark 1896 U.S. Supreme Court decision that upheld the legality of racial segregation and established the "separate but equal" doctrine. After Plessey, and through the first half of the 20th century, Court action focused on questions having to do with school quality, such as equality of facilities and teacher salaries. In its historic *Brown v. Board of Education* decision of 1954, the Court struck down Plessey and rejected the separate but equal doctrine, asserting that where the state undertakes to provide an opportunity for an education, such an opportunity is a right that must be made available to all *on equal terms*. In its decision, the Court signaled a shift in its definition of the concept of EEO, from an exclusive concern for school *quality* (e.g., equitable teacher pay and school facilities), toward a focus on the equitable *effects* of education.

In Brown, citing evidence of the deleterious effects of segregated schooling on the psychological development of minority children, the Supreme Court identified racial segregation as a source of inequality (Coleman, 1967). So, as Coleman (1967) pointed out, while the Court introduced the *effects* of schooling as an element in the concept of EEO, its decision did not use the effects of schooling as *criterion* of inequality, and so the criterion of effects of schooling was immediately overshadowed by the criterion of racial integration. In other words, education policy that is codified in Supreme Court case law establishes desegregation as the primary criterion of equality, and while the effects of school are a consideration, schooling effects are not criteria by which equality can be judged.

In the wake of Brown, with the passage of the Civil Rights Act of 1964 and the Elementary and Secondary Education Act of 1965, Congress took measures to survey the availability of EEO in U.S. schools. In planning the survey with a concern for equality, Congress made efforts to define the term EEO for the purposes of research design. Five definitions were identified, which concerned both inputs and outputs of schooling (Coleman, 1975). Input-oriented definitions of EEO included differences in global input characteristics such as per pupil expenditure, physical facilities, and library resources; the social and racial student composition of the school; intangible characteristics of the school such as teachers' expectations of students, teacher morale, and the level of interest of the student body in learning. Output-oriented definitions of EEO included equality of results given the same individual input; and equality of results given different individual inputs.

The survey, known as the Coleman Report (1966), found predictable gaps in achievement between black minority groups and their white counterparts, but other findings of the Report shocked the education world. It was previously assumed that school and teacher quality were the primary sources of variance in EEO. But to the surprise of most, the Coleman Report found that school facilities and curriculum accounted for very little variance in achievement and teaching only slightly more. The largest sources of variance in achievement were *family background* and *peer influences*. In other words, the effects on achievement appeared not to arise from factors that the school controls, rather the stimulus arose from student background factors.

The Coleman Report initiated a shift in focus in education policy and practice toward a concern for the "effective equality of opportunity" of schooling, or the "intensity" of school effects relative to inequalities due to out-of-school influences. In addition to the existing concerns for equality in inputs or equality in terms of racial composition, a new standard of equality was introduced via Congress through its survey on EEO, which concerned the consequences of school for students of unequal backgrounds and equality of results given these different inputs (Coleman, 1967). The Report revealed surprising sources of inequality and posed challenging questions about how inequality should be addressed—questions that remain unresolved today.

Adequacy of Opportunity

While the Court established desegregation as a criterion of equality, the Coleman Report (1966) confirmed that biological race was a factor of only minimal influence on academic achievement, suggesting that racial desegregation/integration would prove not to be an educationally appropriate or effective remedy to address inequality in achievement outcomes. Instead, the Coleman Report (1966) found the factors most significant to achievement to be the ethos of the social group, the child's sense of locus of control, and out-of-school supports for academic learning, would be potentially more efficacious approaches to EEO.

Despite its weak relationship to achievement, racial desegregation continues to be pursued as a strategy of choice for EEO in U.S. education policy. Psychologist Edmund W. Gordon challenges this strategy. Gordon (2004) suggests that, while desegregation was beneficial for our society, it was flawed as a strategy to improve the equality of educational opportunity for minority and low-income students. Gordon continues to advocate for criteria for EEO based on the sufficiency and adequacy of educational treatments to the extent they support the individual's fundamental right to social, economic, and political participation. That is, EEO should be determined by the degree to which education has succeeded in supporting the development of civic competencies needed to exercise rights to citizenship.

Evolution of the concept of EEO and its potential to impact education policy has been thwarted in part by ambiguity with regard to the state's obligation to EEO and the absence of objective criteria for its effective achievement. After a right to education on equal terms was decided in Brown, Congress followed suit to determine the availability of EEO and set about implementing a legislative agenda to increase its effectiveness. But the U.S. Supreme Court, with its 1972 *San Antonio School District v. Rodriguez* decision, asserted that, while serving an important function of the state, **education is not a right guaranteed by the Constitution**. The Court did, however, concede that the right to citizenship is a constitutional protection, and that some identifiable "quantum of education" that supports this right *could* be defended if a case were to come before the Court in which such rights were in question (Rebell, 2019). The highest courts in 38 states have now affirmed the primacy of education for civic participation (Rebell, 2019). Pursuit of EEO on the basis of rights to citizenship now holds promise as a strategy to secure constitutionally protected education rights and to more clearly assert the effects of schooling as a criterion of EEO. The McCallister Model, presented in the remainder of this book, serves as an example of a "quantum of education."

Curriculum Reform

The concern for equality of educational opportunity was pursued in the curriculum reform movement of the mid-20th century. It was suggested that advances in curriculum and pedagogy could be employed in ways that could enable education to meet the needs of diverse learners, thereby making EEO more effective (Gordon & Associates, 1988).

In 1959, at the Woods Hole conference, the psychologist Jerome Bruner presented his argument that children of any age could access basic disciplinary ideas as long as they were presented in ways that supported the child's capacity for representational thinking. Bruner proposed a spiral curriculum in which basic disciplinary concepts are recursively revisited with greater complexity (Bruner, 1960). He wrote, "We begin with the hypothesis that any subject can be taught effectively in some intellectually honest form to any child at any stage of development" (p. 33). Bruner, a father of the Cognitive Revolution, incited a curriculum revolution, suggesting that curriculum theory and practice should finally take consideration of the child's subjective experience. Bruner's view, representative of the social constructivists or intentionalist theory of learning, which attends to the learner's beliefs in relation to goals, beliefs, and desires (Olson, 2003), was not shared by mainstream educational researchers who maintained a focus on content and teacher-centered instructional practices that were largely informed by theories of behaviorism and nativism. Nativism is the idea that mental structures are innate, and can be developed through activities designed to stimulate them (Fodor, 1983; Chomsky, 1965). Inter-mental, reductionist perspectives in education research continued to dominate policy on curriculum and instruction throughout the 20th century until today, and behaviorist and nativist learning theories underpin most instructional methodologies that are used in schools.

The curriculum reform movement did very little to change the fundamental nature of the way that students are taught. A study that compared U.S. schools to schools in Japan found huge differences in opportunities to think creatively and apply new knowledge. Students in Japanese schools spend 44% of class time in creative thinking activities, 15% of time applying new knowledge, and 41% of time in repetitive practice; whereas

U.S. students spend 96% of class time in repetitive practice, just 3% applying new knowledge, and only 1% of time in creative thinking activities (Stigler & Hibert, 1999). In a study of more than 1,000 classrooms, by Pianta et al. (2007), researchers found that instruction was consistently undemanding and repetitive, and emphasized mostly basic skills. They found less than 5% of time was spent in cooperative activities or activities that fostered analytic skills. They found the emphasis on skills instruction was greater in early grades, and that low-income students had far fewer opportunities to take part in instruction activities that fostered higher-thinking skills. High-income students spent 53% of time in repetitive practice of basic skills and 47% of time in engaged activities, low-income students spent 91% in repetitive practice of basic skills and only 9% in engaging activities. These studies reveal that instructional methods are a significant contributing factor to lack of social opportunity.

Accountability-based Reform

In the 1983 report, *A Nation at Risk*, the U.S. National Commission on Excellence in education asserted that U.S. schools were falling behind those of other countries, and initiated reforms to include more rigorous high school curricula, higher admissions standards for universities, longer school days and an extended school year, and improvements in the quality of teacher preparation.

The economic consequences of a poorly educated workforce became an increasing concern throughout the 1980s and 1990s. In 1989, the National Governor's Association committed to setting national education goals and initiated the standards and accountability reform agenda. They pressed for the development of common standards that could be used by all states, assessment systems to measure outcomes against standards, and accountability systems to hold schools and teachers to higher standards. Eventually the standards movement resulted in the adoption of the Common Core State Standards (National Governors Association, 2010), a set of explicit college- and career-ready standards for kindergarten through 12th grade in English language arts (ELA)/literacy and mathematics. The standards establish clear indicators for instructional outcomes, but do not provide guidance for inputs, the results being that schooling systems continued to do what they have always done—transmit information didactically—in an effort to improve outcomes. But without changes to inputs, outputs remain constant. This truism has borne out in flat rates of achievement reported by the National Assessment of Educational Progress scores across all grades and subjects over the last few decades.

In 2002, President George W. Bush signed the No Child Left Behind (NCLB) Act (No Child Left Behind, 2002), which mandated math and reading goals, annual testing in ELA and Math from grades 3 through 8, and reports of schools' annual yearly progress (AYP) in meeting achievement expectations. Through NCLB, the Reading First program required schools to use evidence-based practices proposed by The National Reading Panel (National Reading Panel & National Institute of Child Health and Human Development, 2000) in order to receive federal funding. The National Reading Panel (National Reading Panel & National Institute of Child Health and Human Development, 2000) reported a meta-analysis of research on reading to identify programs that showed a significant impact. In their findings, they linked literacy development to five basic sub-skills, namely, rapid naming of letter sounds, segmenting words into phonemes, word identification, word attack (reading nonsense words) and fluency, and recommended systematic and explicit instructional techniques to teach these skills. This has led to the development of programs directed at development of these subskills rather than the more general and traditional goals of learning to read and write meaningful texts (McCallister & Olson, under review). The National Reading Panel's aim—to identify promising practices among existing reading instruction traditions, rather than to explore how new theories about thinking and learning, might inform the invention of more powerful new practices—had the consequence of reinforcing tradition rather than encouraging innovation. The National Reading Panel initiative serves as a fitting example of the kind of reform that is backward-looking, rather than forward-thinking, resulting in public policy based on recommendations for obsolete technologies.

Urgent Reform

The accountability mandates of No Child Left Behind revealed the sobering reality of wide-scale school failure. More than 5,000 schools are considered chronically failing (Duncan, 2009), unable to meet annual progress goals. In order for schools to meet their moral obligation to the rights of these students, the schools they attend *today* need to be successful. The Obama administration embraced school reform with a new sense of urgency and education policy aimed to achieve four goals: to adopt standards and assessments that prepare students to succeed in college, the workplace, and the global economy; to build data systems that measure student growth and success, and inform teachers and principals about how they can improve instruction; to recruit, develop, reward, and retain effective teachers and principals, especially where they are needed most; and to turn around the lowest performing schools (United States Department of Education, 2020b). With passage of the 2009 Race to the Top initiative, $4.35 billion was infused into to state comprehensive school reform (CSR) initiatives.

Race to the Top encouraged school *turnarounds* and *transformations*, which sought dramatic and lasting changes in low-performing schools that could be made rapidly, within the course of *two* years, and that would ready the school for a continued process of transformation into a high-performance organization (Calkins et al., 2007; Kutash et al., 2010).

In response to the mandate for school turnaround, a new school reform industry sector emerged over the last decade, comprised of for-profit service providers, nonprofit NGOs, and university-based turnaround programs aimed at new turnaround consumers. But to date, there are few successful CSR models and no documented examples of successful turnarounds (Dragoset et al., 2017). Peurach and Neumerski (2015) suggest that the very metaphor of transformation is ill-suited to the complex work of building new, complex educational infrastructures in chronically failing schools. In their analysis of Success for All as a CSR strategy, they report that it takes three years to realize achievement gains, seven years (conservatively) to establish a new school-level infrastructure, and a 40-year process to establish a system level infrastructure. Rather than "turnaround" or "transformation," these authors suggest a more fitting metaphor of "building educational infrastructure." They point out the "turnaround" metaphor suggests rapid, radical corrections, when, they argue, more foundational first-order change is necessary to develop foundational systems that support instrumental activities, and that these changes require massive, sustained technical, financial, policy and political support (Peurach & Neumerski, 2015).

Kutash et al. (2010) make the assertion that the work of school turnaround is highly specialized. They write, "Turning around chronically under-performing schools is a different and far more difficult undertaking than school improvement. It should be recognized within education—as it is in other sectors—as a distinct professional discipline that requires specialized experience, training, and support" (p. 4). Peurach & Neumerski (2015) argue that the term *turnaround* belies the complexity of the challenge. Rather than the notion of a simple turnaround—a mere change in direction—a more fitting metaphor for the kind of dramatic and immense cultural changes required in a school transformation might be *the replacement of the school's educational infrastructure* (Peurach & Neumerski, 2015). The educational infrastructure of a school includes its *culture* (teacher professionalism, student motivation, engaged families), *capabilities* (of teachers and leaders), and *structures* (schedules that provide adequate time for instruction, high-quality curriculum and instruction designs), opportunities for teacher learning, and professional development (Peurach & Neumerski, 2015).

Planned change in any organization is difficult. Even in the most simple organizations, change requires *unfreezing, changing,* and then again *freezing* deeply engrained social norms and practices (Cummings, Bridgman, & Brown, 2016). School change is the most daunting of challenges because schools are among society's most conservative and fossilized institutions. Successful school reform involves nothing short of dismantling the existing dysfunctional educational systems and infrastructures, replacing them with those that are designed to be more cohesive, and enacting and securing lasting changes in the systems of schools that prone to fragmentation—achievements that are only rarely achieved (Peurach & Neumerski, 2015; Senge, 2006).

Despite many decades of effort and many billions of dollars invested, school reform has failed to bring about substantive change in schools (Backstrom, 2019). Lack of impact of the last generation of school reform is not surprising in the context of the history of school reform discussed in this chapter. In general, reforms have done little over the last half millennium to alter the form of school aside from providing access to larger numbers of the population, extending the amount of school provided, and expanding the curriculum (Olson, 2003).

Inputs and Outputs: Sizing up Educational Costs and Achievement Trends

Considering the extent of effort and investment in educational improvement and reform, our students have made relatively minimal gains in achievement over the last 50 years. Since the United States has begun keeping track of educational achievement of its students in the National Assessment of Educational Progress (NAEP) in 1971, achievement gains have been relatively flat across all tested age groups. In reading, 9-year-olds have gained only 13 points on a scale of 500, 13-year-olds have gained only 8 points, and 17-year-olds have made no significant gains. In math, since scores were kept in 1973, 9-year-olds gained 25 points, 13-year-olds gained 19 points, and 17-year-olds made no significant gains. Compared to international averages, American students[1] scored 470 in math compared to the global average of 490.[2] In reading literacy, U.S. students scored 497, four points above the global average of 493. Our relatively weak achievement trends are more disappointing considering 67% of our school staff are teachers, higher than the international average of 63%.

Limitations of the effectiveness of our educational interventions also show up in evaluations of Title I programs, the largest program under the Elementary and Secondary Education Act, which provides support to schools that serve students from low-SES homes. As of 2013, there was no evidence that Title I programs have significantly reduced achievement gaps on a nationwide basis since their creation (Sousa & Armor, 2016).

Costs

Anemic achievement trends are particularly disappointing considering the U.S. investment in education reform over the last 70 years. The United States spends $706 billion

Table 2.1 Revenues and expenditures for public elementary and secondary education: school year 2015–2016

Annual revenue and expenditure categories	Amount
Total revenue for U.S. elementary and secondary education	$678.378 billion
Current expenditures³	$596.136 billion
Instruction	$363.048 billion
Salaries and wages	$339.724 billion
Employee benefits	$136.790 billion
Salaries, wages and employee benefits as a percentage of current expenditures	84%

Source: Cornman et al. (2018).

annually on elementary and secondary education, at an average of $13,440 per student for about 56.6 million students (National Center for Education Statistics, 2020). Salaries and benefits account for 84% of the current elementary and secondary expenditures of $569.137 or $476.514 billion annually (see Table 2.1). The cost of extending the school year by 40 days, a common recommendation in the school reform literature, would add another $105.892 billion to expenditures for salaries and benefits.

U.S. investment is significantly higher than the global average of $9,219 (OECD, 2019). In New York City, the largest and most diverse school system in the United States, the cost per student was $25,199 in 2019 (United States Census, 2020). The cost to educate a student rose between 2000–2001 and 2015–2016 by 18%. In addition to public spending, parents spend $117 on classroom supplies and $200 on computers each year (National Retail Federation, 2019).

Dropout Rates

There is also evidence that the schools we have are functioning to turn away a large population of students through high dropout rates and out-of-school suspensions. There are approximately 2 million students between the ages of 16–24 years, or 5.4% of the population, who have not earned a high school credential. Dropouts are disproportionately represented by American Indians/Alaska Natives (10.1%), Hispanics (8.2%), and Blacks (6.5%) (National Center for Education Statistics, 2021). In total, 2.6 million students nationwide received out-of-school suspensions in 2013–2014 (5.3% of all students). Suspension rates are disproportionately high in minority groups. Overall suspensions were 13.7% Black students, 6.7% American Indian/Native Alaskan, 5.3% students two or more races, 4.5% each of Hispanic and Pacific Islander, 3.4% of White students, and 1.1% of Asian students. In total, 17.6% of Black males were suspended, more than twice the percentage for the next group of American Indiana/Alaska Native with a 9.1% suspension rate. In total, 9.6% of Black females were suspended.

The Reproduction of Obsolesce

The last 70 years have seen extensive effort across society to reform schools. But some of the very systems that are the focus of change in on one policy front continue to be reproduced on another front. One of the most powerful forces in maintaining the status quo are laws that secure existing systems in place in the form of teacher contracts.

Teachers are the primary source of labor within the educational system of the industrial school. The extent of the teacher's work is determined by the number of students that can be *managed* effectively for the purpose of providing instruction. Labor union

Table 2.2 Terms of the New York City United Federation of Teachers Contract, High School

New York City United Federation of Teachers Contract Terms

- On Mondays and Tuesdays, the school day can start no earlier than 8:00 a.m. and end no later than 4:00 p.m.[4]
- There are six hours and 57½ minutes is a school day, Monday through Thursday[5]
- The school week is fractured into 25 teaching periods, five professional activity periods, and the remainder in periods to prepare[6]
- The school day can have no fewer than six periods
- The class size is limited to 34 learners[7]
- The curriculum is "a list of content and topics, a scope and sequence, and a list of what students are expected to know and be able to do after studying each topic"[8]
- Professional activities outside of classroom responsibilities is limited to:[9] "(1) Small group instruction (not to exceed 10 students) (2) One-to-one tutoring (3) Advise student activities such as clubs, teams or publications (4) Perform student assessment activities (including portfolios, performance tests, IEPs, ECLAS, etc. (5) Professional development/prepare staff development workshops and demonstration lessons (6) Common planning time (7) Conflict resolution for students (8) Cafeteria duty (9) Schoolyard duty (10) Hallway duty (11) AM bus duty (12) PM bus duty (13) Homeroom (14) Provide inter-disciplinary articulation (15) Develop multicultural curriculum (16) Develop programs to integrate technology into the daily life of the classroom"

Table 2.3 Average class sizes in the United States

Average class in primary self-contained classes	Average class in primary departmentalized classes	Average class in high school self-contained classes	Average class in high school departmentalized classes
21.6	26.2	17.7	24.2

Source: National Center for Educational Statistics (2012).

contracts spell out teachers' rights as laborers within the system. As status function declarations, they create a reality by describing it. So, a useful way to understand the realities of teachers and the scope of work that they do is to refer to their contracts.

The New York City (NYC) United Federation of Teachers (UFT) contract describes conditions of institutional reality that reproduce key systems of the factory school. The contract defines the temporal zones for learning into 25 short periods to be scheduled between the hours of 8:00 and 4:00. It limits the possibilities for what will be learned to a list of sequenced content of limited scope. It restricts the possibilities for what are to be the objectives of education to a list of what students should know and be able to do. And it sets terms on the forms of activity that teaching can take (see Table 2.2).

State laws determine class sizes and length of school year. The average class size for teachers in the United States in 2012 appears in Table 2.3.

Conclusion

The schools we have today have changed very little over 500 years aside from expanding access, increasing length from a few years to a span of nearly 20, and expanding content from basic literacy to a comprehensive education inclusive of a number of different courses (Olson, 2003). The role of the student within the institution of school has also changed very little. The student is still a *blank slate* to be impressed upon, a *receptacle* to be filled, an *inmate* to be controlled, or an *object* on a conveyor belt to be modified. What lessons do our schools teach?

From the minute s/he enters school, the child is deprived of her fundamental freedoms of thought, expression, movement, social affiliation, and self-determination. For most of the 13,000 hours of her future life in school, she will spend every minute of every day following adult directives. She will be told where to sit, when and how to move, when to speak, and what to say. She will be tested, branded with scores, and sorted by status into categories based on her existing abilities. She will be assembled with others into groups for instruction where she will be administered standardized, one-size-fits-all, increments of instruction. She will first be exposed to this degrading existence at a time in her life when she is not able to recognize this kind of treatment as abuse, and will, as a consequence, learn to internalize conditions of oppression as normal. Throughout the hours, days, and years of her experience in the care of the school, she will have learned to obey, comply, and submit.

There is now a consensus that education needs to be personalized, socially-embedded, and self-directed. In addition to teaching basic skills and canonical content subject matter, education needs to foster social awareness, empathy, compassion and altruism, curiosity, creativity, persistence, and self-regulation. Our schools need to prepare young people to be successful in a fast-changing, technologically advanced, globalized world so that they can successfully participate economically, politically, and socially (e.g., Battelle for Kids, 2019; Education Reimagined, 2015; OECD, 2018).

Since the 18th century, there have been calls to reform schools with an emphasis on learning by doing, freedom of experience, self-directed learning, inductive instruction, a focus on self-identity, and social experience (e.g., Dewey, 1938, 1916/1944; Montessori, 1912; Rousseau, 1979). But viable learner-centered educational approaches have not been developed or widely adopted. Over the last 70 years, rather than reinventing new approaches to education, school reform policy has focused on improving access to existing educational systems, improving the quality of curriculum, strengthening accountability measures, improving teacher quality, extending the school day, and lengthening the school year. Perhaps since the substance of schooling has not changed very much over the last century, that is why, despite many decades of effort and many billions of dollars invested, school reform has failed to bring about substantive change in schools (Backstrom, 2019).

The cultural psychologist Michael Cole (2005) points out that society in ancient Sumer, birthplace of the modern school, was known to be one of the most totalitarian societies of all time. He writes, "If the model of education to which it gave rise continues to dominate the world, it bodes ill for us all because that form of education has brought us to the brink of self-extermination" (p. 213). If learning is dependent not only on what teachers teach but also on the degree to which the learner is engaged and willing to learn, it is necessary to replace centuries-old, teacher-centered pedagogical traditions with new ones that cultivate interest, engagement, and intention. This book can be considered a response to the school *turnaround challenge* (Calkins et al., 2007).

Notes

1. NAEP scores are reported on a scale of 0–500.
2. Scores are reported on a scale of 0–1000.
3. Current expenditures include instruction, instruction related, support services, and other elementary/secondary current expenditures, but exclude expenditures on capital outlays, other programs, and interest on long-term debt.
4. NYC UFT Article 7(B)(1)(a).
5. NYC UFT contract Article 6(A)(1)(a).
6. NYC UFT union contract Article 7(B)(4)(a).
7. NYC UFT union contract Article 7(M)(2)(a) and Article 7(M)(2)(d), respectively.
8. NYC UFT union contract Article 7(A)(6)(a).
9. NYC UFT union contract Article 7(A)(6)(a).

3 A Positive Learning Paradigm

> You are what your deepest desire is. As is your desire, so is your intention. As is your intention, so is your will. As is your will, so is your deed. As is your deed, so is your destiny.
>
> Upanishads

> Anything that we have to learn to do we learn by the actual doing of it... We become just by doing just acts, temperate by doing temperate ones, brave by doing brave ones.
>
> Aristotle (Nicomachean Ethics, Book II, p. 91)

Introduction

This chapter presents the Positive Learning Paradigm, a theoretical framework in which learning and development are described with an emphasis on the learner's self-identity and how the self is manifested through the achievement of intentions. The Positive Learning Paradigm is *positive* because it draws from strands of theory in the learning sciences and psychology in order to build a theory for learning in the service of intellective and affirmative academic development (Gordon & Bridglall, 2004), self-assertion, and ascendant development (DuBois, 1903; Douglass, 2005). It is a conceptualization of formal learning that no longer centers around teachers and the content of their lessons, but around the learner and their sense of *self*.

The Positive Learning Paradigm is situated within a moral framework of equality of educational opportunity (EEO) that is committed to access to educational treatment sufficient to adequately prepare its recipients for economic, political, and social participatory competencies necessary for citizenship in a democracy (Gordon, 1972). This Paradigm employs a cognitive model of culture that accounts for the ways in which both biological and sociocultural processes result in the development of target competencies. Based on the principle of self-assertion as a means toward political, social, and economic assimilation (Douglass, 1882; DuBois, 1902; King, 1998; Garvey, 2014), the Paradigm is animated with insights from psychology and philosophy that explain human intention, free will, and transcendent development. It orchestrates scientific insights into a theoretical model for pedagogy in which human cognitive function and cultural competence are augmented through social interaction and contextual variations, providing optimal conditions for learners to take initiative to achieve their potential.

The chapter begins with an exploration of the legal basis for education as a right to experiences that support the development of certain competencies. The chapter then proposes an explanation of the biological and psychological processes that form the basis for learning these competencies. It then situates the project of formal education within a social ontology in which the relationship between individual activity, governed by personal intentions, relates to the structure and functioning of systems and institutions within society, governed by shared intentionality (Searle, 2010). The final section of the chapter situates formal education within a cognitive perspective of culture, and explores how the reciprocal relationship between the person and society, confirmed scientifically, can be applied as a technology for pedagogy designed to instrumentally advance the aims of a rights-based approach to education.

In an ideal democracy, social circumstances are arbitrary factors that do not impair opportunity or life chances. An education system in an ideal democracy minimizes the effects of social inequalities that are external to schooling by increasing the power of the effects of schooling. The Positive Learning Paradigm is an attempt to employ scientific insights about learning that can be applied to pedagogy in an effort to intensify the effects of schooling. This chapter attempts to answer the question: what is the nature of learning opportunities that are sufficiently intense to enable equal educational outcomes, regardless of arbitrary factors?

The Right to an Adequate Education

> In these days, it is doubtful that any child may reasonably be expected to succeed in life if he is denied the opportunity of an education. Such an opportunity, where the state has undertaken to provide it is a right which must be available to all on equal terms.
> U.S. Supreme Court, *Brown v. Board of Education.*

Upon his visit to the United States, the French diplomat and historian Alexis de Tocqueville (1900) observed, "The equality of conditions is the fundamental fact from which all others seem to be derived..." (p. 3). The equality of social conditions is a standard against which American social progress is routinely measured, and perhaps nowhere more assertively than in the arena of American public education since the middle of the 20th century. Chapter 2 described how equality of educational opportunity (EEO) became a central focus of American school reform after the U.S. Supreme Court's Brown decision. In Brown, the Court asserted its fundamental concern for equality of social opportunity. The legal question in Brown concerned the constitutionality of mandatory segregation, and the Court's decision emphasized *desegregation* as the primary criterion for EEO. The Court's primary concern for the elimination of barriers to full and free forms of association obfuscated its parallel concern for the effects of schooling. But in their Rodriguez decision, the Court voiced its continued interest in pursuing a concern for educational adequacy and in considering in the future whether a certain "quantum" of education necessary for citizenship is a constitutional protection. While the Supreme Court has not weighed in on the question of adequacy, the right to a sufficient education incorporated into law in most states and a concern for adequacy is ubiquitous throughout U.S. federal and state education law. For example, Title I of the Elementary and Secondary Education Act (1965), part of President Lyndon Johnson's *War on Poverty*, asserted the school's obligation "to provide all children significant opportunity to receive a fair, equitable, and high-quality education, and to close educational achievement gaps." Congress has reconfirmed its commitment to the moral standard of sufficiency in each reauthorization of the law since its passage, with a concern for equity and with the goal of closing achievement gaps.

Criteria for Equality of Educational Opportunity: Intensity, Adequacy, and Sufficiency

Brown marked a turning point in American education policy with a new concern for educational *quality* (in addition to the traditional concern for educational *access*). In its effort to assess conditions of educational equality in the United States, Congress commissioned the Coleman Report (1966), which identified troubling patterns of inequality of educational outcomes between racial and economic groups. The Report asserted that EEO should be judged by equality of outcomes as opposed to equality of inputs. A focus on outcomes brought new concern for the intensity of effects of educational treatments.

With recognition that out-of-school influences on achievement will always account for some differences in outcomes, the Coleman Report acknowledged that the achievement of EEO can only be *proximal* as opposed to *absolute*. Coleman (1967) advanced the view that proximity is determined not merely by *equality* of inputs, but by the "intensity of the school's influences relative to external divergent influences" (p. 20). Coleman thus introduced a concern for the *power* of the influence of education as a criterion for equal opportunity. Power and intensity of educational treatment thus became a concern for educational research, practice and policy.

An Adequacy-based Definition of Equality of Educational Opportunity

Once patterns of inequality were exposed in the Coleman Report, the American research community got busy trying to make sense of new findings on the state of inequality in the United States and to make recommendations for improving conditions of educational equality in U.S. education. In the proceedings of the Harvard Seminar, On Equality of Educational Opportunity (1972), scholars provided critical analyses, practical applications and implications for the future of equal educational opportunity in America (Mosteller & Moynihan, 1972). One of the seminar faculty participants, Edmund W. Gordon (1972), was commissioned to contribute a paper titled, *Toward Defining Equality of Educational Opportunity*, in which he described the conditions of education that most reasonably approach standards of sufficiency. Gordon identified the school's responsibility to prepare children to participate socially, economically, and politically, and proposed new criteria for EEO based on the extent to which the school adequately satisfies the obligation. Gordon (1972) wrote:

> If the purpose of education in a democratic society is to broaden opportunities for meaningful participation in the mainstream of society through the development of necessary skills and credentials, then education opportunity is unequal unless it serves that purpose for all learners. At any point in the history of a society, the minimum educational goals are defined by the prerequisites for meaningful participation or for economic, social and political survival. The educational experiences can and should enable many persons to go far beyond the development of such survival skills, but it cannot be considered to have provided equality of opportunity unless it enables nearly all to reach the survival or participation level. (pp. 431–432)

Gordon reasoned that, given what children bring to school is unequal, the school's inputs should be unequal and individualized to ensure achievement is equal. In other words, adequacy, by its very definition as a method to respond to diversity in human characteristics, implies the need for differential treatment. Gordon wrote (1972), "To make the opportunity equal, the school would have to develop and use whatever methods, materials, or procedures are required by the special style, special ability, or special background the child may bring" (p. 433). Gordon (1988) has asserted that the sources of human diversity that are the most consequential for academic development are *functional*, and reflect differences in intellect, not differences in *status* (e.g., SES, race, or ethnic origin).

Education policy, through the Brown decision, the Coleman Report, and the ESEA, now emphasized a new concern for educational *quality*. Gordon's proposed definition of EEO emphasized criteria by which judgments about quality education could be made.

To this end, Gordon (1972) proposed four learning domains essential to an adequate education:

- *Mastery of communication skills*: language development, literacy, and numeracy.
- *Problem-solving management of knowledge*: executive regulation in problem formulation and identification, and problem solving.
- *Employment, leisure, and continuing education*: lifelong learning and creative expression.
- *Self-management*: personal, social, and character development. Self-awareness and social awareness. Conflict resolution. Respect for relations the worlds of man and nature.

Gordon's recommendation that schools take responsibility to teach not only academic skills, but social-emotional states and dispositions anticipated future advances in the new science of the mind (Kandel, 2007) that would establish socio-cognitive capacities and emotional states to be integral facets of cognitive functioning. Gordon's adequacy-based definition of EEO has become a global standard for rights-based education (UNESCO, 2007).

Civic Competencies and Democratic Education

Civic competencies are the skills, knowledge, and dispositions necessary to carry out rights and responsibilities as a citizen. These competencies include knowledge, civic skill and agency, deliberation skills, and critical and reflexive use of technology (see Lee, White, & Dong, 2021; Rebell, 2018). The Positive Learning Paradigm provides an explanation of the biological and psychological processes that underlie the civic competencies, described below, as well as competencies in the learning domains proposed by Gordon, above.

- **Knowledge** of history, government, math, science and technical subjects, and culture provide the background necessary to make and hold informed opinions. Knowledge provides the foundation information necessary to understand complex issues. Knowledge also serves as evidence against which false assertions are tested.
- **Civic skill and agency** include the person's sense of moral obligation to participate in civic culture and skills and dispositions that result from participation.
- **Deliberation skills** include the ability to reason with others cooperatively, to shift and share perspectives, to make recursive inferences, to disagree productively, to assess alternative perspectives, to reason critically, to engage in perspective-objective rational analysis.
- **Critical and reflexive use of technology** is the ability to keep abreast of innovations in technology and to use available technology productively for the purposes of social, economic, and political participation.

A Paradigm Shift in Learning

Until the last half century, education practices have been governed by rational-empirical philosophies of cognition. Rationalism and empiricism are two different sides of what has been the coin of the realm in all of philosophy since antiquity. Empiricist theories view the mind as a blank slate, or a *tabula rasa*, as the philosopher John Locke proposed, and suggest that stimulation from the environment is responsible for learning. Behaviorism is an example of empiricism. Rationalism, also known as nativism, suggests that *a priori* knowledge is responsible for cognition. These structures, described as mental modules, consist of many special-purpose mechanisms that developed through evolution to solve narrow, specialized problems (Boyd, Richerson, & Henrich, 2011; Chomsky, 1965; Fodor,

1983). This view suggests that structures in the brain are dedicated to specific kinds of learning and cognitive processing, which are stimulated to develop through interactions in the environment. If the module is not stimulated, it does not develop.

These scientific paradigms have influenced the ways in which our instructional interventions are designed. Typically, researchers propose a hypothesis that a certain independent variable (teaching a certain thing) will cause a desired change in a certain dependent variable (learning a certain thing). These methodologies are based on the assumption that inputs and outputs can be isolated into component parts and manipulated to produce desired behaviors. Scientific rigor leaves no room for the subjectivities of the research subjects (children), unless, of course, a component of subjectivity is a variable of the experimental equation. These methods are ubiquitous in the field of educational research, and a century's worth of scientific findings have reinforced a notion of instruction being "scientifically-based" only when it involves explicit instruction provided by the teacher (e.g., National Reading Panel, 2000).

Recent advances in the new science of the mind have resolved the nature-nurture dualism and provide promising new ways to envision positive learning in schools. Human beings are uniquely social animals. From our first moments of life, our interactions with others shape the way we consciously experience the world. Humans evolved unique mental capacities that enabled them to live in large, complex social groups to cooperate to solve problems and to carry and transmit cumulative cultural information as a means of group survival (Boyd, Richerson, & Henrich, 2011; Dunbar, 1998). Our *social brain* gives us special cognitive and social capacities to read the minds of others, to coordinate our thinking with theirs, and to consciously control our minds and actions (Dunbar, 1998; Tomasello, 2019). The social brain evolved to manipulate information rather than remember it, and to consciously control behavior rather than having behavior be controlled by emotions (Dunbar, 1998). Other advances in learning science reveal that learning is a self-initiated, self-directed process, and that the formation of new memory depends on the organism's selective attention. In other words, the organism cannot make synaptic connections between neurons (new memory) unless it is selectively attending to the phenomenon in question.

Rational-Empirical Learning Paradigm	*Positive Learning Paradigm*
Skills develop as a result of external stimulation to mechanisms within modules in the brain	Learning is self-directed. Memory develops through selective attention and intentional reciprocal interactions in the social environment

Rather than *either-or*, new insights on learning and development propose a *both-and* view of learning. At the biological level, the anatomy of a neural circuit is an example of rationalist a priori knowledge, while changes in neural connections reflect the significance of experience (Kandel, 2007). Tomasello (2019) suggests "a transactional causality in which maturational capacities create the possibility of new kinds of experiences and learning, and then those learning experiences are proximate causes of development" (p. 34). In other words, the capacities exist, then social experiences are had that cause them to develop. Ruth Benedict (1934) suggested this notion nearly a century ago when she asserted that situations determine traits that materialize, then the individual takes in the situation further to develop themselves. Cultural inheritance is as important in human adaptation and development as genetic inheritance (Boyd, Richerson, & Henrich, 2011). Biology, it seems, has finally caught up with anthropology.

This *new science of the mind* offers rich possibilities to reconceptualize the nature of formal learning and inform the development of pedagogical interventions that support it.

Within the transactional paradigm, opportunity is *taken*, not *given* (Plomin, 2018). In other words, genetic influences, which account for more than 50% of psychological traits, are maximized by environmental opportunities in which learners have autonomy to select their own learning environmental experiences (Plomin, 2018; Tucker-Drob, Briley, & Harden, 2013). Based on the power of self-direction in development, equality of educational opportunity to some degree involves adequate access to rich learning environments and freedom to autonomously select environmental experiences that, over time, enable the learner to reach their potential.

The remainder of this chapter presents a paradigm for self-governed learning. This paradigm provides a framework to understand the concept of the mind, how it can be understood from philosophical and biological perspectives, how it works—most particularly, how humans can control their minds to think freely and to coordinate mental states with others—and how the self-directed nature of the human mind enables human beings to carry out their own intentions. The view of learning proposed provides a way to de-center the teacher as the locus of learning through *knowledge transmission* and doing things *to* learners, toward a concern for the cultivation of human potential by transferring responsibility to learners to use their minds most effectively to carry out their own intentions. Based on the assertion that human flourishing and well-being are improved by certain forms of self-regulated thought, it proposes a theoretical framework for the application of positive psychology to the practice of learning in schools.

A Framework for Learning and Equality of Educational Opportunity: Actualizing the Self

The objective of a Positive Learning Paradigm is to provide a framework for learning that is centered around the learner and describes conditions under which learners are supported to carry out their own intentions to achieve their potential. In this framework, the *self* is conceptualized as the agent of development.

Our self-awareness determines how we perceive information from our environment, how we react, and who we ultimately become. Our sense of self seems patently real. But it is really a figment of the imagination in complex organisms like humans. Csikszentmihalyi (1993) provides an explanation of self that explains this complexity. While in simple organisms, the nervous system consists of closed circuits, only a few of which are open at a time and connect to discrete motor responses, the human brain is intricately complex. The way the human brain deals with the otherwise overwhelming sum of information vying for attention is to prioritize the sources coming into it. The executive functions monitor and control information, and, through selective attention, bundles information into manageable chunks. When we consciously reflect on what we see, we assign meanings to our perceptions that really only exist in our imagination. The process of assigning reality to our mental constructions is called *reification*. Csikszentmihalyi's (1993) explanation proposes the self as a reification—a figment of our imagination that we create to organize our experiences.

Since the imagination has the capacity to form new ideas that are not present in the senses, it is a powerful vehicle for self-transformation. With imagination, we can form new ideas about who we are and intend to become. Through autobiographical memory, we can also revise the self's stories of who we have been. A positive learning paradigm, therefore, is concerned with the development of self.

The self might be imagined, but it is nonetheless a product of the biological and social processes that shape development and beckons it forward. In the sections that follow, the concept of self is employed to explain key processes of learning and development and to illustrate how the learning person is able to take responsibility to direct their experiences. George Herbert Mead's (1934/1964) concept of the "I" self and the "Me" self are first used to explain the fundamental biological processes of mental life. Then, the concept of the "We" self is used as a framework to explain how social interactions play a role in the development of the mind.

The I-self

Living organisms respond to stimulus from the environment before becoming aware of it. Most animals lack self-awareness, and never experience any conscious awareness of reality. We share part of our human brain with these lower creatures. The unconscious impulse to act is called the *readiness potential*—an electrical spark in the brain that triggers an action response a split second before we become consciously aware of the action we are performing (Kornhuber & Deecke, 1965). The preconscious impulse to act—the readiness potential—signals an automatic neurological response without coming into awareness. Mead named the preconscious catalyzed action the "I"-self. Mead (1934/1964) explained that the I-self is, "…finding out what we are going to say, what we are going to do, by saying and doing, and in the process, we are continually controlling the process itself" (p. 205). He continues, "We are aware of ourselves, and of what the situation is, but exactly how we will act never gets into experience until after the action takes place" (p. 232).

In other words, our subconscious disposition toward a particular object creates the very possibility of whether or not we have the option to decide to pursue an action directed toward it.

Most reactions to the environment are automatic, and require no thought. They're governed by lower thinking parts of the brain—the part we share with lower animals who lack a conscious self and need only reproduce information from the directions given by their genes to react to the environment (Csikszentmihalyi, 1993). But once an action enters conscious awareness, the "Me"-self is awakened (Mead, 1934/1964).

The Me-self and Conscious Awareness

The father of American psychology, William James (1961), brought attention to the concern for attention in education when he wrote, "The faculty of voluntarily bringing back a wandering attention, over and over again, is the very root of judgment, character, and will. No one is *compos sui* [master of himself] if he have it not. An education which should improve this faculty would be the education *par excellence*. But it is easier to define this ideal than to give practical directions for bringing it about." (p. 424).

Recent advances in neuroscience give evidence of why James might have identified selective attention as being central to the developing mind and the root of intellective and moral development. An understanding of selective attention will explain the way that the volition of the self gets energy.

The biological substance of conscious awareness is *selective attention*. Selective attention is the organism's voluntary reaction to a source of information and the biological form of free will. Selective attention or conscious attention governs perception and memory and has a biological function to unify our sense of conscious awareness (Kandel, 2007). It's a way we tune in to stimuli that are salient or important, and tune out the rest. It is the source of who we will become, since what we pay attention to determines what new memories and behaviors we will form.

Once we become aware of a thing, we become aware of the "Me"-self—the self of awareness (Mead, 1934/1964). The "Me"-self is fundamentally social in nature, and comes into being through interactions in the social world that become embodied capital through the formation of memory structures that give form to the body habitus (Bourdieu, 1986; Mead, 1934/1964). This self carries autobiographical memory that reminds us of the kind of agent we are in the social world, and what knowledge of cultural practices we have experienced.

One function of selective attention is to direct the movement of eyes and hands toward a location (Kandel, Schwartz, & Jessell, 2000). It is an impulse born of intention. Once the "Me" becomes consciously aware of the action we are performing, it either approves or vetoes the action. Self-regulation and the exercise of free will to do something else is the self's means of disapproval. We will discuss the normative psychological processes that govern self-regulation in later sections. Here we will explore the biology of the psychology of the "Me."

In making a new memory, selective attention gives our higher brain the order to signal to the body to make new neural connections (Kandel, 2007). The energy that is needed to forge new connections between neurons depends on the intensity of the energy spent on selective attention. Energy is needed to activate genes to pass information between neurons through neurotransmitters. These transmitters carry "attentional significance" (Kandel, 2007, p. 314), meaning the amount of information they provide depends on salience of stimulus. The human brain evolved these higher powers in the service of survival, so only information worth knowing is remembered. New behaviors manifest relative to the strength of connections between neurons (Kandel, 2007).

Once we select to attend to a thing, we assume a stance of *aboutness* toward it (Searle, 2010). An intention is a sense of "aboutness" in relation to a thing or state of affairs in the world (Searle, 2010). It is what orients our sense of volition in a situation. Since the strength of new learning depends on the energy invested in attention, one's sense of aboutness, or intentionality, defines development.

Intentionality

An *intention* is the mind's capacity to be directed or about a thing in the world (Searle, 2010).[1] To aspire, desire, love, hope, strive, or intend are all intentions. An intention is a *psychological orientation* to a *thing or state of affairs* (Searle, 2010). For example, *Patrick hates reading lessons*. *Hate* is the psychological orientation, and the *reading lesson* is the thing his attitude is directed to.

Our intentions have a mind-to-world fit, which means that, through our psychological orientation, the world as we intend it should be is represented in our intentions (Searle, 2010). A world without reading groups would fit the way Patrick's mind intends the world to be. Since an intention can succeed or fail, it has conditions of satisfaction (Searle, 2010). The psychological orientation of the intention represents how it should be satisfied (Searle, 2010). In order to be satisfied, the intention must function causally to produce the action (Searle, 2010). Hating reading lessons represents conditions which, if satisfied, would create a world in which they did not exist. So, in order to function causally to satisfy Patrick's intention of hating reading groups, the action should result in him avoiding it.

Intentions can be conscious or unconscious. Conscious intentions come in the form of *plans*, or prior intentions, and *actions*, or intentions-in-action (Searle, 2010). We plan changes in our environment through prior intentions, and cause changes in our environment through our intentions-in-action (Searle, 2010). Prior intentions are a state of mind to enact a reality that springs from imagination, desire, or hope. Intentions-in-action are efforts to try to bring this reality into being (Searle, 2010). Patrick hates reading lessons, so he plans to hide in the bathroom this Tuesday at 9:00 reading group. If he doesn't get caught hiding in the bathroom, the situation will function causally to satisfy his intention.

Unconscious intentions come in the form of impulses and dispositions, where they are catalyzed by the *readiness potential*. For example, one morning on his subway ride to school, Patrick doesn't have the will to override his impulse to stay in his seat when the train stops at the station by his school. Patrick's subconscious intentions channel his will to bring about the reality he intends. Of course, Patrick could intentionally change his *I hate reading lessons* intention into an *I will try* intention which, over time, would involve a mind-to-world fit whose conditions of satisfaction meant he would be present in reading lessons and apply effort. If Patrick's intentions to turn away from academic formats, like reading lessons, are continually satisfied throughout his school career, he will miss opportunities to achieve academically.

Intentions-in-action take the form *of basic actions* and *complex actions*. Basic actions are the things you can do intentionally without the need to do some prior thing intentionally (Searle, 2010). Typing on a keyboard or signing your signature are examples. Complex actions are sequences of intentional behavior.

For some, schooling can become a never-ending sequence of complex actions that satisfy the intention to turn away. Some find community in the company of others who are also trying to turn away. A pattern of turn-away intentions could create a continuity of environments that eventually lead to life on the street or a sentence in prison. It is common in school for teachers to respond to the behaviors that result from turn-away intentions as if they represented an internal cognitive deficit that can be corrected through remediation. But if turning away is really a manifestation of the learner's satisfaction of the condition of an intention, a positive learning paradigm dictates we must succeed in assisting the learner to change the psychological content of their intentions.

A positive learning paradigm dictates a pedagogical strategy to intervene at the level of intentions, to recruit the learner to form intentions to do things that help them reach their potential.

In order to have the ability to carry out our intentions and apply intentional states, we need what Searle (2010) refers to as *Background*. For example, I use Background motor and perceptual skills to sign my signature. But, when I was learning to sign my name in cursive, the process was a complex intention-in-action task involving a number of gaps between the planning and trying phases of the activity. These gaps are like leaks in a system that can introduce negative emotions, cause us to want to stop trying, and undermine the ultimate achievement of our intentions. To overcome these gaps, Searle explains, we need *free will* (Searle, 2010). Erica Jong was partially right when she said, "Everyone has talent. What is rare is the courage to follow it to the dark places it leads." But rather than courage, what we really need is *will*. Courage is an emotional response to fear, as the psychological part of an intentional state, its conditions of fit narrow the resources of reaction to brute effort—*to face your fear*. But the word "will" is related etymologically to *wish*. As an intention, will is nourished by the powerful emotions of desire and yearning—attitudes we need to draw from to overcome feelings of doubt, frustration, or despair. It is our ability to exercise rational will to bridge the gaps in intentions within the sequence of complex activities that enable us to achieve our potential and develop our talents.

Complex actions create *an accordion effect,* which is the sequence of basic actions that combine into a complex action whose boundaries are set by the conditions of satisfaction (Searle, 2010). For example, reading the newspaper is a complex intentional action that is part of my daily routine. But without glasses, I can't access my Background. The action of newspaper reading is now more complex with the need for the tool of my spectacles. If I leave them upstairs, which I am sometimes inclined to do, the conditions of satisfaction for my paper reading intention are compromised.

If you understand the powerful force of intentions, you can appreciate just how powerful they can be as a factor in formal learning. Intentionality is the means through which human beings create the worlds they need in order to adapt to their environment in ways that suit their nature and meet their needs. Through intentions, humans direct their minds toward the achievement of possible futures. Intentions are reality-creating means of reacting to the environment.

We are always reacting to stimulation from our environment, and intentions are the biological mechanisms that orient our patterns of response. The thousand trillion connections between neurons in our brain are the physical by-products of what we have selected to pay attention to. More relevant to the moral imperative of the Positive Learning Paradigm, the learner has the power to shape their own mind by choosing what to pay attention to. And since we become what we choose to pay attention to, our intricate memory structures are built from our genetic blueprint and carry expressions of our personality and individuality (Plomin, 2018; Kandel, 2007). Self-reflective consciousness bestows the gift of personal freedom by making it possible to free the self from the command of genes and of culture (Czikszentmihalyi, 1993). The more energy we invest in our own creation, the more we become who we are.

The Activity Arc is a metaphor for the execution of an intentional action (see Figure 3.1; and see Appendix 45 for a full-color image of the Arc). It symbolizes the journey a person takes through the process of beginning and completing any activity. The base of the triangle, which is rendered in blue on the left foot of the Arc, symbolizes the state of existence before embarking on an activity. Red represents the idea of a possible action—a prior or preconscious intention—the motivating spark of energy that ignites an action. The yellow jagged lines represent the sense of self-doubt we sometimes feel when frustration or uncertainty set in. Once the greatest challenges are overcome, we experience feelings of satisfaction and achievement. Green on the descending side of the Arc represents growth and development. Finally, the blue base of the right foot of the Arc symbolizes a changed state of existence after having completed the activity. The Arc represents a fully completed self-initiated activity.

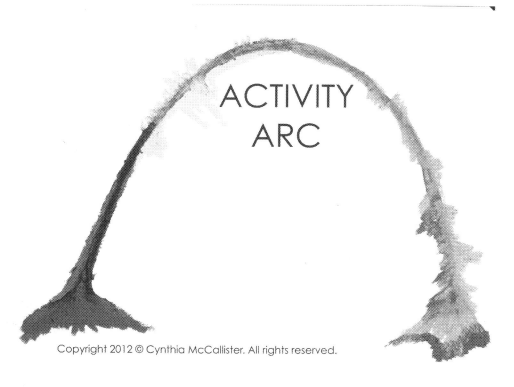

Figure 3.1 The activity arc

Source: McCallister (2011e).

The capacity for conscious thought provides the ability to manage information in consciousness (Csikszentmihalyi, 1993). Integration is a high-level thinking process in which our mind links its various components—the parts that are inside us, in the neurons in our heads and bodies, and the parts that exist in our social experiences (Siegel, 2020). The integration of parts of the mind enables more intricate mental functions to emerge, such as morality, empathy, insight, and intuition. Under stress or in response to threat, integration breaks down and, if it becomes patterned, leads to disordered behavior. Integration supports mental flexibility, creativity, and harmony with others (Siegel, 2020).

Psychic Energy and the Environment

The social psychologist Kurt Lewin drew attention to the relationship between the person and the environment and the field of forces to which the person reacts and adapts. He described the sum of co-existing factors in the environment that shape the person's behavior as the *life space* or *psychological force field* (Lewin, 1943). As we interact within the social environment, we create our own, unique life space for learning that is suited to our individuality (Lewin, 1951). Lewin's famous formula states behavior (B) as a function (F) of the person and their environment (E): $B = f(P,E)$.

Richard Shweder's (1990) person-environment analytic framework is an elaboration of Lewin's equation (see Table 3.1). Shweder explains how volitional impulses are influenced by the intentional states of the self. Shweder's model poses these questions: first, to what extent does the environment support the expression of intentions? Positive environments support or amplify personal intentionality. Negative situations oppose or interfere with intentionality. Second, to what extent does a person exercise agency in a given situation? A situation is active when a person creates or selects their own intentional world, reactive when others create or select an intentional world, and passive when a person finds herself in an intentional world created by others for others or herself. The flow of psychic energy required for new memory to form is most optimal in active-positive environments.

To illustrate Shweder's model, disordered behaviors in learners are usually an outcome of a negative-reactive or negative-passive relationship to the environment. A positive pedagogical response would be to minimize the negative dimensions of the relationship and

Table 3.1 Richard Shweder's person-environment relationship (1990)

Shweder's analytic framework for the person-environment relationship	Active: person creates or selects own intentional world	Reactive: other people create or select intentional world for person	Passive: person finds him/herself in an intentional world created by others for others or themselves
Positive: context supports or amplifies person's intentionality	Positive-active example: child plays make-believe restaurant and serves a playmate pretend pancakes	Positive-reactive example: child plays alphabet concentration during choice time in school	Positive-passive example: children play in neighbor's lawn sprinklers walking home from school
Negative: diminishes, opposes, or interferes with person's intentionality	Negative-active example: child chooses to go to time-out area after losing temper with a classmate	Negative-reactive example: child is assigned to time-out area for disruptive behavior	Negative-passive example: daughter is asked by parents to stay home to watch younger siblings while parents go to dinner

amplify active ones. Providing space to exercise free will and autonomy to more freely use psychic energy in the environment will encourage the development of more active, positive intentions.

Czikszentmihalyi (1993) describes the active-positive person-environment relationship as *flow*. Flow is a condition of optimal psychological functioning, in which the person is engaged in an activity that is sufficiently challenging to encourage the practice of high-level skills (Czikszentmihalyi, 1993). Skills are culturally-valued competencies, and motivations to use them come from social experiences, the nature of which are described in later sections.

Constrained Freedom

> The motive power of all action is in the will of a free creature.
>
> Jean-Jacques Rousseau

Freedom—the ability to act without constraint—provides opportunity for the self to exercise free will. Since activity creates the physical structures of memory, freedom to control one's activity provides a means to control one's own course of development. That is why the basic condition of humanity is to control one's attention freely, and the external control over one's attention against their will is oppression (Csikszentmihalyi, 1993). Dewey pointed out that slavery, the purest form of oppression, is the control of one's conduct by another's purpose. Even when there is no slavery in the legal sense it can still be found when a person is engaged in an activity whose service they don't understand or have personal interest in (1916/1944, p. 85). The traditional activities of schooling are determined by the teacher's purpose, and for some learners can be experienced as psychic oppression. A positive approach to pedagogy grants the learner opportunity for self-determination and broad rights to control their attention freely.

The most optimal psychic states—active-positive intentionality and flow—require basic conditions of autonomy for the exercise of free will. But humans are not free like birds or butterflies. They are social creatures who evolved cognitive capacities to coordinate with others and to comply to social norms. Humans, unlike lower creatures, can only survive by living successfully in the social group and complying to its rules. Left to absolute freedom, the human mind deteriorates. Rousseau (1979) made this assertion when he wrote that the person left alone to absolute freedom would become more monster than others.[2] It is when humans are most free that they are least able to act (Csikszentmihalyi, 1993).

The Positive Learning Paradigm advocates an environment in which learners have maximal freedom to exercise their fundamental freedoms of thought, movement, expression, and social affiliation. But freedoms cannot be absolute; rather, the social learning environment should be organized by activities that invite the learner to exercise free will while also complying with social and academic norms that result in intentional developmental outcomes. Rousseau recognized the pedagogical power of constrained freedom. More than two centuries ago, Rousseau (1979) wrote, "Let him always believe he is the master, and let it always be you who are. There is no subjection so perfect as that which keeps the appearance of freedom. Thus, the will itself is made captive" (p. 120).

Personality

Through conscious awareness, the self controls its own action. Geneticist Robert Plomin (2018) explains, "…we actively perceive, interpret, select, modify, and even create environments correlated with our genetic propensities" (p. 51). Through continuous patterns

> **Box 3.1**
>
> **The Big 5 personality traits**
>
> *Openness*: open-minded, creative, curious, embraces challenge, and adventurous
> *Conscientiousness*: controls impulses, thoughtful, and goal-directed
> *Extroversion*: sociable, assertive, excitable, and emotionally expressive
> *Agreeableness*: caring, empathetic, helpful, kind, generous, trusting, considerate, and compromising
> *Neuroticism*: moody, anxious, worried, easily upset, not resilient, given to negative emotions, and emotional unstable

of activity, the self develops its personality. Because the physical connections between neurons in the brain are created through information in the genes, new behaviors are fundamentally shaped by genetic proclivities. Thus, personality is the expression through behavior of the way the self interacts within the social environment, and the way the genes direct memories to be created.

There are a number of different ways to describe personality. The prevailing view of personality is organized by five main traits, known as the Big 5 personality traits (see Box 3.1) (Cherry, 2020; Roccas et al., 2002). The traits of openness, conscientiousness, extroversion, agreeableness, and neuroticism have been found to be common across populations, and are highly heritable. Genetics account for between 40% and 50% of individual differences between people. That means that our genes account for most of our uniqueness and individuality.

These traits are each caused by hundreds of small genetic effects (Plomin, 2018), and present as a spectrum of behaviors that place the person on a continuum in terms of the strength of the trait. For example, a person can be highly extroverted, highly introverted, or somewhere in between. Through interactions in the environment, personality changes. Stress, for example, can cause cognitive entropy or disorder, and personality traits result in disordered behaviors. Dysregulated openness can lead to recklessness. Dysregulated conscientiousness can lead to a need to control others. Dysregulated agreeableness invites exploitation from others. On the other hand, in optimal functioning, the self can use its awareness and free will to regulate and control behaviors, enabling the person to use the genetic resources of who they are to interact in the environment to thrive and flourish.

The We-self

> The individual in his isolation is nothing; only in and through an absorption of the aims and meaning of organized institutions does he attain true personality.
>
> Dewey (1916/1944, p. 94)

Vygotsky (1978) asserted that "...human learning presupposes a specific social nature and a process by which children grow into the intellectual life of those around them" (p. 88). Through interaction with others, the child learns not just how to think and behave in more conventionally reasoned and normative ways, but also how to access the thinking of others as a way of developing the mind. Vygotsky (1978) speculates about the social conditions necessary for development. He explains, "...learning awakens a variety of internal developmental processes that are able to operate only when the child is interacting with people in his environment and in cooperation with his peers. Once these processes are internalized, they become part of the child's independent developmental achievement" (p. 90). Evolutionary psychologists posit that human beings developed *norm psychology*, an array of psychological adaptations for "inferring, encoding in memory, adhering to, enforcing and redressing violations of the shared behavioral standards of one's community" (Chudek & Henrich, 2011, p. 218). We will now explore these adaptations and consider implications for a positive learning paradigm.

The Development of Shared Intentionality and the Capacity for Mentalizing

One type of thinking that is unique to humans is co-consciousness—the awareness of a phenomenon while, at the same time, being cognizant of another person's awareness of the same thing. Human beings have special biological capacities to share attention with others, to share intentions, and to cooperate socially. These capacities derive from the skills and motivations of *shared intentionality*, or the capacity for *mentalizing, mindreading*, or *theory of mind* (Box 3.2) (Tomasello, 2019).

Box 3.2

Mentalizing

Mentalizing is essentially the ability to recursively understand mental states of others (Lewis et al., 2017). The number of different mind states involved in the process of mentalizing is known as the order of intentionality (Dennett, 1983).

Mentalizing capacities expand with experience, but eventually reach a limit of five orders of intentionality in normal adults, with few able to reach higher orders (Stiller & Dunbar, 2007). Dunbar (2010) points out that an example of sixth-order intentionality is provided in the case of Shakespeare, penning *Othello*, when he "*intends* that the audience *believe* that Iago *wants* Othello to *suppose* that Desdemona *loves* Cassio and he in turn *loves* her" (p. 199). Perhaps, as Robin Dunbar suggests, Shakespeare is considered such a successful playwright because he was able to challenge his audience to their cognitive limit.

In the process of mentalizing, the self uses high levels of psychic energy. The human brain is a massive network of 100 billion neurons that consumes 20% of a person's energy for an organ that is just 2% of their body mass (Herculano-Houzel, 2012). The need to simultaneously handle multiple mental states and to negotiate the relationships between the individuals concerned require enormous neural resources and involve large brain regions, including those known to be associated with theory of mind in the frontal and temporal lobes of the brain (Lewis et al., 2017).

Tasks of higher-order intentionality require more neural effort than non-mentalizing tasks (Lewis et al., 2017). This is because the nature of social decisions needed in more complex social arrangements are more cognitively demanding and require the need for bigger brains (Byrne & Whiten, 1988). And the more complex decisions required to support larger groups are cognitively more demanding (David-Barrett & Dunbar, 2013).

Mentalizing is a two-way street. Human beings have special skills and motivations that *enable* them to coordinate mental states with others; and the act of mentalizing *develops* their cognitive and social abilities. Because mentalizing taxes cognitive capacities to their limits, the self is forced to access high levels of psychic energy from the environment (Lewis et al., 2017).

These powerful mental capacities developed in humans to enable them to carry, distribute, use and transmit cultural knowledge and practices that were essential to their survival (Dunbar, 1998).

> **Box 3.3**
>
> **The Developmental Pathways of Shared Intentionality**
>
> Social cognition
> Prosociality
> Social norms
> Cultural learning
> Communication
> Cooperative thinking
> Collaboration
> Moral identity

The human skills and motivations of shared intentionality give rise to powerful psychological pathways through social interaction These pathways, universal to all human beings, include social cognition, prosociality, social norms, cultural learning, communication, cooperative thinking, collaboration, and moral identity (see Box 3.3) (Source: Tomasello, 2019). But these capacities are so intricate that in order to learn use them, humans require the entire period through childhood to develop their unique *social brain* through interactions with others (Dunbar, 1998; Tomasello, 2019).[3] In this section, we will examine how shared intentionality develops in human children.

The capacity to share reality with others develops in human beings at about nine months of age, when the child is first capable of sharing attention to an object with another person (Tomasello, 1999). The capacity of joint attentional engagement expands the child's psychological field to incorporate the mental landscapes of others. The phenomenon of joint attention forms a referential triangle, or a joint attentional scene, between the child and adult, in which perspectives about an object or state of affairs in the world can be exchanged (Tomasello, 1999). Jerome Bruner (1983) used the term *follow-in* to describe the phenomenon of adult-child interaction whereby the adult follows into a child's focus of attention to interpret the meaning of experience, enhancing the consequences of joint attentional engagement. The quality of joint attentional engagement has been shown to have an impact on language and cognitive development (Tomasello, 1999). For example, in linguistic interactions with their children, mothers who made attempts to follow into the attention of the child had children with larger vocabularies than the children of mothers who used language to direct attention (Tomasello & Farrar, 1986). Children's ability to take part in non-linguistic-mediated joint attentional activities with adults at around one year of age is related to their newly emerging linguistic skills (Tomasello, 1999).

Opportunities to take part in joint attentional interactions with others support the development of *joint intentionality*, which appears at about a year and develops through the juvenile years (Dunbar, 1998; Lewis et al., 2017; Tomasello, 1999, 2019). Joint intentionality is the ability to collaborate with others toward joint goals, to cognitively represent ideas from another perspective, to make recursive inferences (e.g., I think that you think that I feel), and to understand that others have perspectives different from their own (Tomasello, 2014). Tomasello argues that joint intentions enable the child to understand that others are intentional agents with their own beliefs and perspectives, to expand their own perspectives, and to follow into others' attitudes and perceptions in relation to the self (Tomasello, 1999, 2019). The capacity of joint intentions evolved

Table 3.2 The evolution of joint intentionality

Check attention (9–12 months)	Follow attention (11–14 months)	Direct attention (13–15 months)
Joint engagement	Gaze/point follow	Imperative pointing
Social obstacle	Imitative learning	Declarative pointing
Show object	[Social referencing]	[Referential language]

Source: Tomasello (1999).

in human beings so that they could coordinate mental states in order to communicate cooperatively. Joint intentionality is maturational, meaning that it will develop naturally in all infants provided they have access to the context of the social world (Table 3.2) (Tomasello, 2019).

In early humans, social organization was limited to small groups of hunter-gatherers who evolved skills and motivations of *second-personal morality* and *joint intentionality* (Tomasello, 2016). That is, their cognitive capacities allowed them to coordinate mental states with foraging partners. Human cognitive capacities grew in size as humans evolved to exist in larger, more socially-complicated groups (Dunbar, 1998). These capacities come into existence as children approach their third birthday, when they begin to develop the skills and motivations for *shared intentionality* or *collective intentionality* (Tomasello, 2019). Shared intentions make reference to a collective formed by other individuals (Searle, 1983). Shared intentionality is the ability to come together with others interdependently to act as a single agent, while still maintaining individuality, and to coordinate the process through cooperative communication (Tomasello, 2019). With the ability to entertain multiple perspectives and to think objectively, humans are able to resolve conflicting perspectives (Tomasello, 2014, 2019).

Rousseau (1979) said that when the child "begins to be aware of his moral nature, he should study himself in relation to his fellow men" (p. 100). Shared intentionality serves this cause. With shared intentionality, *second-person morality* is now buffeted by *objective morality*, in which the behavior of a person in a group can be judged by the objective criteria of "right" and "wrong" that every member of the group holds. Tomasello (2016) writes, "The self-regulation of 'we>me'; in modern humans therefore took the form of moral self-governance: the individual internalizing the objective values of the group" (p. 146). The child has now entered a world in which there are norms for the way that *we* think and do things. According to Tomasello (2019), "shared intentionality is the executive capacity to normatively self-regulate and to *follow the rules*" (p. 41). It enables children to engage with others collaboratively and cooperatively in group-minded activities, like games (Tomasello, 2016).

Norms

Humans can only survive in the social world because they have an instinctive desire to comply with the norms of their culture. Norms develop out of countless reciprocal, give-and-take interactions with peers and adults (Tomasello, 2009). David Olson (2007) explains that a norm is seeded when a caregiver attempts to hold a child responsible for an action. The child's self-control, or their ability to regulate to what they've learned, represents compliance to a norm. Olson explains that the transfer of responsibility for normative behavior, from adult to child, depends on the child's ability to hold a rule in mind and make causal connections between the rule and their personal action.

> Learners arrive at school with this cognitive ability having internalized only the norms of their family institution. To learn the new academic and social norms of school, learners need opportunities to take part in personally-meaningful situations in which they are motivated to comply. Norms have a powerful sway over us, but they also give us power. Assuming a conscious awareness of norms gives the self the information it can use for intentional action. They provide a grammar for the way that the social organization functions.

After age three, with the understanding that "we do that in this way," children develop a sensitivity to pedagogy and instructed learning. Now able to comply with the norms of their culture, children begin to teach themselves through their perceptions of the perspectives of others (Box 3.4) (Tomasello, 2019).

By the age of four or five, children acquire second-order intentionality, or theory of mind. Theory of mind is the ability to represent the relationship between two or more different epistemic states, which is characterized by the child's ability to understand

---

Box 3.4

The Two Social Worlds of Childhood (Michael Tomasello, 2019)

Children inhabit two distinct mental worlds: the social world of adults and the social world of peers. Prior to age three, joint intentionality constrained the child's mental landscape within the social world of adults. Children trust adults and respect their knowledge and authority. They believe what they say and imitate what they do. They learn from adults through conformity, deference, and respect, but not reasoning. They internalize adult's instruction and executively self-regulate in terms of adult perspectives and standards. Children learn what they should make of their world in the social world of adults.

The new skills and motivations of shared intentionality open up the social worlds of children to their peers. These two social worlds—one of adults and one of peers—afford opportunities to participate and learn in distinctly different ways and nurture different social and cognitive skills (Tomasello, 2019). Now, with opportunities to take part in collaborative, co-equal relationships with their peers, children learn to solve problems cooperatively, to coordinate perspectives, to reason logically, and to negotiate in order to reach reasoned agreements (Tomasello, 2019). Peer collaboration requires competence in mental, social, and cultural coordination. Cooperative problem-solving requires a valuable form of perspective taking that goes beyond the basic alignment of perspectives that is involved in joint intentionality.

These opportunities engender reciprocity, dialogic thinking, and perspective-taking. After age three, children continue to conform to what adults tell them to do and how to think, but rely on peers to learn reasoning, practice mentalizing, exercise moral identity, and practice moral self-governance (Tomasello, 2019).

Special forms of reasoning originate in relationships with peers. Since they do not obligate deference and no point of view dominates, co-equal peer relationships promote true dialogue, collaboration, and communication. Agreements are reached through social construction and through processes of cooperation and negotiation. Therefore, peer relationships serve as the context for moral development. And since moral self-governance is the driving force in development, a positive learning paradigm emphasizes peer pedagogy and the educational importance of the social world of peers.

another person's perspective well enough to detect a false belief (Wimmer & Peerner, 1983). Theory of mind represents second-order intentionality and is a developmental milestone in childhood.

By age seven, children have acquired enough experience in their culture to have internalized a sense of reason and the capacity to govern themselves in order to conform to the norms of their culture. They can be trusted to do things as they should be done (e.g., make food, mind children, and do errands). By now they have acquired the ability to reason based on impartial, objective reasons, and they apply *epistemic vigilance* in their thinking, showing care about what to believe (Tomasello, 2019).

By this time, the brain has reached 90% of its adult size (Tomasello, 2019). Provided they have opportunities to interact with others in their culture, all of the capacities of shared intentionality will continue to develop. They will use the remainder of the juvenile years to develop their unique computational "software" of to read the minds of others, to coordinate mental states, and to consciously control their own minds and actions (Dunbar, 1998; Tomasello, 2019).

Humans' special thinking capacities enable them to conjure mental representations of the physical world. We can reason about these representations reflectively, logically, and inferentially; we can make reflective inferences; and we can think objectively (Tomasello, 2014). Mentalizing expands these capacities. These powerful cognitive capacities—to make cognitive representations, to make recursive inferences about them by accessing the perspectives of others, and to scrutinize thoughts against broader social norms—is what makes human thinking unique (Tomasello, 2014). Biological capacities of shared intentionality make possible infinite forms of higher thinking. We put these capacities to use in social interactions, and through interactions, learn new ways of using our minds. Through the ability to mentalize with others, we are able to mentally represent what we believe to be the perceptions of others and to make recursive inferences, considering mental representations simultaneously from multiple perspectives.

These intricate modes of thought derive from self-regulation. Self-regulation is the culminating capacity in human cognitive and social development. It provides a means for the person to react and adapt to the environment independent of maturation or learning, which accounts for its power to shape personal development (Tomasello, 2019).

Social Construction and the Coordination of Mental States

It might seem that children learn as a result of having been taught. But we now understand that the skills and motivations of shared intentionality (social norms, cultural learning, moral identity, cooperative thinking, collaboration, prosociality, communication, and cooperative thinking) come into being through certain social and communicative interactions with others, not in the form of adult instruction, but through co-constructed cognitive representations with others through cultural experiences (Tomasello, 2019). Therefore, it is necessary to understand the nature of these interactions.

Cooperative understanding requires the maintenance of perspective sharing, and successful communication requires a means to resolve difference or conflict resolution. The back-and-forth mode of coordinated thinking is what Kenneth Gergen (1990) refers to as *relational adjudication*. Just as a judge adjudicates conflict in the courtroom, co-participants in communication resolve differing perspectives through interaction (Gergen, 1990). Relational adjudication is the interpersonal process of resolving or deciding differences in perspectives, which is what human beings are doing in their interactions with others much of the time. Relational adjudication gives rise to new, normative ways of understanding reality.

According to Gergen (1990), the relational connections we share with others are the locus of our understand of reality. The "Me" collects the impressions of reality through interactions with others and gives direction to the "I" as to how these impressions should be interpreted. A *relational nucleus* is formed with others whose perspectives we share. According to Gergen, a relational nucleus is "…a self-sustaining system of coordinated actions in which two or more persons are engaged." (p. 585). Norms for understanding within the relational nucleus become the *evaluative discourse* that we refer to as a standard against which the meaning of reality is judged in future social situations. In conflict, we apply epistemic vigilance. We scrutinize reasons and employ *evaluative discourses* as criteria to adjudicate differences (Gergen, 1990). Over time, we become participants of multiple relational nuclei, and their multiple evaluative discourses become the normative constellation of meanings that we use to navigate the social world.

Relational adjudication is the social equivalent of Piaget's notion of equilibration, in which cognitive disequilibrium is resolved. In equilibration, the person self-regulates from an executive level to reorganize mental contents. In relational adjudication, participants cooperate to regulate the construction of meaning to the executive force of normativity, and the objective social perspectives that govern interchange within the cultural habitus.

Humans have built-in capacities that grease the wheels of social interaction. We adhere to a specific universal set of rules, or maxims for cooperative communication: We are *truthful* in what we say; we provide as much *information* as is necessary; we share relevant information; we are *brief and orderly* (Grice, 1989). But conflicts sometimes arise, and cooperation breaks down. We might have different criteria for truth, we might require different information, or we might need to hear more or less. We employ relational adjudication to resolve social-cognitive dissonance and achieve shared understanding. As we adjudicate differences, we do what we are naturally equipped to do as human beings—we argue cooperatively, shift and share perspectives, and they reason cooperatively (Tomasello, 2014). Meaning is therefore a social achievement—an outcome of mutually-coordinated normative activity (Gergen, 1990). All personal outcomes depend upon the quality of our patterns of interchange with others, and well-being depends to a large degree on the quality of relationships we are able to maintain.

One particularly powerful form of relational adjudication is *perspective-shifting discourse*, in which we shift and share perspectives and reason cooperatively with others to achieve so-called objective or perspective-independent understandings (Box 3.5) (Tomasello, 2019).

Tomasello (2014) asserts that the ever-expanding web of beliefs that results from these kinds of interactions, together with the unique human ability to navigate this web mentally, is foundational to the capacity to engage in individual reasoning and reflective thinking in the context of cultural group standards. If intellective competence and academic ability require multi-contextual competence (Gordon, 1999)—the ability to successfully navigate the multitude of social contexts within our lives—relational adjudication can explain how these abilities are stimulated and develop through interactions with others.

This survey of shared intentionality and psychological development emphasizes the importance of the quality of relationships in learning. Through early interactions, and through opportunities to become mentally attached to caregivers, the child's *mindscape* is formed (Siegel, 2010). The mindscape is the integrated web of meaning and relevance through which reality is experienced. If the child's caregivers are emotionally available, able to calm her when she is in discomfort, and to communicate in a cooperative and

> **Box 3.5**
>
> **Perspective-shifting discourse**
>
> Michael Tomasello (2019) describes a special form of discourse that contributes to objective reasoning. *Perspective-shifting discourse* is a form of communication in which different perspectives or beliefs about an object are highlighted linguistically through *propositional attitude constructions*. These propositions, or assertions, coordinate a subjective attitude (e.g., "I believe") with a potential objective fact (e.g., "he is gone"). This linguistic construction creates a dual level structure from the standpoint that the first level consists of our individual perspectives, and the second the referential, shared perspective that makes it possible to share a common focus. In cases when different perspectives conflict, and only one can align to objective reality, perspective-shifting discourse leads to the distinction between subjectivity (opinion and belief) and objectivity (reality and fact). This mode of discursive thinking inhibits a perspectival point of view. This form of reasoning is the foundation of the capacity to make perspectival-objective recursive inferences—inferences about things that are objective and not connected to any single perspective—and is the foundation of scientific reasoning.

reciprocal manner, the child will begin life securely attached to her caregivers and share mindscapes that help her regulate her emotions in novel situations (to control fight or flight impulses, for example), to trust others, to feel safe, and to use all components of her brain and mind with confidence and security as she begins to engage with others in a broadening range of new situations (Siegel, 2010). Children who are not so well attached have greater difficulty with mental integration. Because humans are exquisitely sensitive to social interactions, attachment relationships are the main way children learn to regulate their own minds (Siegel, 2012).

The opportunity to use psychic energy in mindreading depends on emotional connectedness and feelings of empathy. The psychiatrist Dan Siegel (2010) proposes the concept of *emotionships* as a way of thinking about relationships that provide opportunities to regulate emotionally, to attune to another's perspective, and to resonate with them in shared meaning making. Emotionships are co-equal relationships that foster interpersonal responsiveness and mutual civility. They provide learners a way to diversify their emotion-regulation needs across multiple specialized relationships, resulting in improved states of well-being compared to those who concentrate emotion-regulation needs in fewer, less-specialized relationships (Cheung, Gardner & Anderson, 2015). Emotionships help us negotiate the interior landscapes of our mental lives. A positive learning paradigm supports learners to care for their minds by cultivating emotionships.

The Acquisition of Language and Literacy

> We are speech-act performing animals. We are as much speech-act performing animals as we are animals that move about on two legs, or consume food and water, or inhale the earth's atmosphere. The right to free speech is a natural consequence of the fact that human beings are speech-act performing animals and the characteristic capacity of self-expression is innate to us as a species.
>
> John Searle (2010, p. 189)

For the last 60 years, learning theory has been influenced by the functionalist paradigm of language acquisition. The underlying assumption of this approach is based on a componential logic: higher, more abstract forms of language ability build through mastery of the lower component parts. The progression of the curriculum focuses first on subskills, through memorization and practice, before emphasizing the integrated skills of higher-order thinking (like comprehending extended text). Provided adequate stimulation from the environment, the reasoning goes, language develops naturally and automatically, like any other genetic trait. The functionalist concern for learning focused primarily on the cognitive processes presumed to support the acquisition of verbal language, but did little to explain how higher forms of learning, such as the acquisition of cultural representations encoded in linguistic symbols, were influenced by the way in which language is acquired and learned. Pedagogical applications of both associationism and nativism merely reproduced the linear curriculum models of the factory school, if not with a greater emphasis on reductionism and attention to training component skills.

The first explanations of language acquisition posited that verbal behaviors were learned by simple association (Skinner, 1957). But Chomsky (1957, 1965) argued that complex linguistic structures could not be learned through simple association, and posited instead that humans have innate linguistic capacities, which he believed were located in the brain in the form of what he called a "language acquisition device" (LAD). In his theory of universal grammar, Chomsky reasoned that the LAD held capacities for a universal grammar that enabled people to use language categories and operations in ways that are common across all languages.

Based on functionalist logic, it was thought that language (and linguistic concepts) could be taught through transmission of discrete increments of information organized in a linear curriculum that progressed from an emphasis on basic sub-skills to formal operations. Learning was a matter of doing the activities assigned by the teacher, mostly having to do with memorizing words and phrases. This parts-to-whole, bottom-up approach is entrenched in systems of curriculum and instruction in factory schools. But the functionalist paradigm is now discredited.

A revolution in our understanding of language acquisition overturns both the empiricist's view of associationism and the rationalist's view of nativism. Jerome Bruner (1983) proposed that language is learned by children through use, in everyday, script-like interactions with caregivers (Bruner, 1983). These familiar interaction Formats—what Bruner referred to as the Language Acquisition Support System (LASS)—aid the child by allowing them to learn how to refer to objects, make requests of others, and master the steps in learning to talk (Bruner, 1983). Bruner proposed an inter-mental model of language acquisition, in which the locus of language learning is within social interaction, as opposed to the intra-mental model of language acquisition proposed by Chomsky, in which the locus of language learning is within the LAD, inside the head.

Several decades of research on human language suggest that the ability to use linguistic symbols evolved in humans through their need to cooperate in their activities (Tomasello, 2008). Searle (2010) explains that there is a "ground floor form of collective intentionality that exists prior to the exercise of language and which makes the use of language possible at all" (p. 50). Cooperative linguistic communication depends upon this prelinguistic form of shared intentionality.

Simple linguistic constructions, like words and conventional grammatical devices, are cultural-historical products developed by cultural groups to meet communicative needs (Tomasello, 2008). Searle points out that language involves social commitments that derive from the "social character of the communication situation, the conventional character of the devices used, and the intentionality of speaker meaning" (p. 80). Humans inherit knowledge and skill to use linguistic symbols to provide a Format for shared cognitive representations through cultural practices (Tomasello, 2003). Tomasello elaborates on Bruner's conception of language acquisition as a social process. In what is known as a *usage-based theory of language acquisition*, Tomasello provides a valid explanation for how children learn linguistic symbols and conventions through meaningful social interactions. Tomasello (2003) writes,

> Linguistic acts are social acts that one person intentionally directs to another in order to direct her attention and imagination in particular ways so that she will do, know, or feel what he wants her to. These acts work only if the participants are both equipped with a psychological infrastructure of skills and motivations of shared intentionality evolved for facilitating interactions with others in collaborative activities. Language, or better linguistic communication, is thus not any kind of object, formal or otherwise; rather it is a form of social action constituted by social conventions for achieving social ends, premised on at least some shared understanding and shared purposes among users (p. 343).

A usage-based paradigm of language acquisition argues that language is used for socially pragmatic purposes to accomplish goals. Like all cultural practices, language (and concepts presented in linguistic symbols) is learned through use. According to Tomasello (2003), the usage-based paradigm of language can be described by three principles, described below.

Functionalist: Language is used to express and comprehend communicative intentions. It involves intention reading capacities and is used to direct others' attention to the objects shared in the joint attentional frame (Tomasello, 2003). Children use their knowledge of the function of language—its use in certain ways in specific situations—to make linguistic generalizations. Comprehending communicative intentions that are expressed in linguistic structures, and using linguistic structures to communicate cooperatively with others are central to the language acquisition process.

Construction-based: The most fundamental units of language are whole utterances and constructions as opposed to isolated words. Whole utterances are the fullest embodiment of a person's communicative intentions. Within the context of comprehending broad utterances, the child is able to gain an understanding of the function of isolated words and phrases.

Usage-based: Language structures emerge through language use. As children participate with others, using language to communicate, they hear and store utterances in memory, and then, finding patterns across stored utterances, they are able to construct their own utterances in spontaneous speech that are tailored to specific social purposes. Children learn language through use, as they retrieve stored linguistic expressions from memory and cut and paste them together in cooperative communication.

When we think of language acquisition, we normally think of the process of learning to "talk." But language acquisition is a lifelong process of development. All of the linguistic information that enters our minds depends on our continually-developing language competence.

Literacy Learning as Genre Practice

Literacy and the developed ability to employ reading and writing to access bodies of knowledge is a specialized form of language acquisition that is fundamentally social. The academic disciplines are typically thought of as bodies of knowledge. But disciplines are also bodies of specialized social practices shared by members of scholarly communities. Learning a discipline is as much about learning its social practices as it is about learning its documentary history. It is, therefore, helpful to think of literacy development as a facet of language acquisition.

Prior to the last half century, it was assumed that literacy—the ability to read and write in functional ways—depended on the accumulation of sub-skills or isolated cognitive processes used in reading, math, and writing. But the beliefs regarding what literacy *is* and how it *develops* has evolved significantly over the last several decades. Scholars of literacy now understand that literacy is more like a social condition than the accumulation of purely cognitive skills (Olson, 1994). That is to say that literacy is really a new form of conscious awareness that is an outcome of an individual's experience as a participant in social situations where texts are used and produced.

Through participation, background abilities or skills are developed and stored as memories to be retrieved and used again. Literacy is a social condition, involving a state of conscious awareness about how written language functions, which can only be achieved through interaction with others who enable the learner to gain new perspectives about how symbols are used in conventional ways to represent meaning (Erneling, 2010; Tomasello, 2014; Olson, 2003). This view contrasts the more prevailing understanding that reading and writing competencies are the result of direct instruction of discrete skills.

The use-based paradigm of language acquisition can inform the way opportunities are organized to support formal learning across the span of child development in all facets of the curriculum. In other words, whether learning to decode simple text or decipher a calculus problem, the functionalist, construction-based, and usage-based principles of language learning hold promise to inform the design of learning opportunities within a positive learning paradigm.

A tenet of genre theory suggests that typical forms of response, or genres, are used across different situations, using conventional meanings attached to linguistic elements, like words, sentences, or text devices, to create a token response (Frow, 2006; Searle, 2010). Searle (2010) points out that linguistic symbols are conventions with a standing meaning. Once introduced and learned, they are repeatable devices that can be used, over and over, on different occasions in new situations. Literacy is the achievement of the capacity to use written linguistic symbols generatively, flexibly, and recurrently in new situations.

The common genres of school—reports, essays, stories, and arguments—are often taught as dogma, through the transmission of a sequence of conclusive assertions about how texts should be structured and composed to conform to traditional archetypes. The genres to be *mastered* typically embody the hegemonic values of the dominant culture. In traditional genre study, learners are taught the features of genre as gospel, and practice applying them with paint-by-numbers writing activities or comprehension questions designed to lead to mastery of convention. But in reality, genres defy mastery. They are fluid forms of human creation, imbued with the singular intentions and unique voices of their authors. They are intentionally shaped to respond to the conditions of the life spaces they will occupy. The only way to master a genre is through practice and use (McCallister, 2008).

A positive learning paradigm envisions a more egalitarian, self-determined approach that can be described as Genre Practice (McCallister, 2008a, 2011b). It advocates proficiency of use of linguistic conventions as opposed to mastery. It promotes freedom for learners to make their own choices about the texts they will read and write, and employs the literacy curriculum as a space for learners to make choices for personally-meaningful and pragmatic reasons. In doing so, it creates the possibility that the curriculum will serve the human rights imperative of education, to promote their cultural identities and values, to provide access to diverse sources of information, and to ensure their interests are a primary concern of the curriculum (United Nations Children's Fund/UNESCO, 2007).

When texts are approached pedagogically as forms of action that are performed by authors, learners are able to apply their basic communicative competencies as interpretive. In other words, a literate reader understands their obligation to *listen* to, *cooperate* with, and to *respond* to the voice behind the words on the page. By the same principle, a literate writer is able to anticipate the responsive understanding of their audience and succeeds in deploying writing conventions to achieve intended understanding.

Zone of Proximal Development: Space in the Cultural Niche

The curriculum of traditional factory schools is based on the idea that skills are learned in a progression, and that success in learning a new skill depends on prerequisite knowledge. This skills-based approach created a dilemma for formal pedagogy: if the learner must have prerequisite knowledge and experience in order to understand a concept or skill that needs to be taught, what can teachers do besides wait for them to develop (Cole, 2015)? Vygotsky suggested that it is possible to organize environments to bring about necessary developmental change by creating Zones of Proximal Development (ZPDs) that promote a sequence of learning that is just beginning to develop through the child's social interactions with those more knowledgeable (Cole, 2015; Vygotsky, 1978). Cole explains that interactions within the ZPD stimulate development by inviting learning and beckoning the child to something appealing in the next stage of development (2015).

The ZPD describes two aspects of development. In addition to the child's *actual developmental level*, or the mental functions that exist as a result of already completed development, the level of the child's capability with the assistance of others is even more indicative of mental development than that which can be done independently (Vygotsky, 1978). According to Vygotsky (1978), the ZPD, "...is the distance between the actual developmental level as determined by independent problem-solving and the level of potential development as determined through problem-solving under adult guidance or in collaboration with more capable peers" (p. 86).

The ZPD represents a developmental arc that is defined at one end by what the child can do independently and at the other by what they can do cooperatively with support. The ZPD extends into the child's immediate future in the sense that the child's developmental state, or the biological processes that code and store memories of experience are in reciprocal interaction as experience unfolds. Vygotsky (1978) wrote, "The zone of proximal development defines those functions that have not yet matured but are in the process of maturation, functions that will mature tomorrow but are currently in an embryonic state. ...The actual developmental level characterizes mental development retrospectively, while the zone of proximal development characterizes mental development prospectively" (pp. 86–87).

Vygotsky's well-known concept of the Zone of Proximal Development (ZPD) is commonly used to refer to learning that can potentially unfold given the right circumstances. The ZPD is defined as the "...actual development level as determined by independent problem-solving..." and the level of "...potential development as determined through problem-solving under adult guidance or in collaboration with more capable peers" (1978, p. 86). The ZPD, then, refers to any of the possible developmental outcomes present in a cultural situation in which a learner is engaged. It's an acronym that represents potential.

66 *Background*

Jaan Valsiner, a student of Vygotsky, elaborated the concept of the ZPD in his Zone Theory (1997). According to Valsiner (1997),

> …the developing child is conceptualised in the context of his relationships with the culturally and physically structured environment, where the child's actions upon that environment are guided by assistance from other human beings—parents, siblings, peers, teachers etc. The particular physical structure of the environment of a human child is set up by the activities of other human beings, and modified by them over time.
>
> (p. 76)

Valsiner proposes two 'zones' that are particularly significant influences on development—the Zone of Free Movement (ZFM) and the Zone of Possible Action (ZPA)—each described below.

> *Zone of Free Movement* (ZFM): The ZFM is the cognitive structure of the person-environment relationship that is socially constructed (Valsiner, 1997, pp. 191–92). In a classroom, space is carved up and used in certain ways, usually determined by the teacher. Thus, the classroom environment is created by the teacher. But this environment is the arena of action on the part of the student. The student is the agent of activity within this arena. Thus, the ZFM is created by the student. If you attended high school in classrooms where seats were lined up in rows, your ZFM was confined to the space in which you were permitted to move between the starting and ending bells of class. These boundaries were socially imposed by the teacher. But if, sitting at my desk in my rows in my assigned seat, I decide to draw in my notebook, I am taking agency to determine the boundaries of my ZFM.
>
> According to Valsiiner, the ZFM is both social and cognitive. It is social because others determine its boundaries. But it is cognitive because it's created by the learner when he or she actively determines boundaries (Zittoun et al. 2013).
>
> *Zone of Possible Action* (ZPA): The ZPA are the activities that are promoted within the ZFM. It includes the full range of pursuits and artifacts that are employed to encourage a given range of possible actions. It is defined by those with power, like the teacher, parent, or group leader, but it is mutual in the way it functions. If I place Lincoln Logs on the carpet during choice time, I might be promoting building as an activity. But one of my students might use the logs to symbolize racecars or superheroes and use the Logs differently. Or the high school science teacher might make the internet available to students during work time for the purpose of researching cells, but a student might use the internet instead to go shopping for sneakers.
>
> In my high school classes, teachers stood at the front of the class, lecturing; and by doing so they were promoting a responsive action on the part of students to listen and attend to what was being said. Some kids took part in the action promoted by the teacher, and others didn't. Some listened, took notes, participated. Others drew. Some kids put their heads down and slept through class.

As Valsiner and his colleagues wrote,

> Development is seen as emerging through the activity of a person as she tries to adjust to situations, remembering and anticipating, in interactions with others and the world. All this takes place through constant meaning-making, semiotic attractors emerging from the self-organization of past and present experiences. We literally go

> through the world creating meaning out of anything—or sometimes—out of (seemingly) nothing
>
> (Zittoun et al., 2013, p. 218)

To Valsiner, the concept of the ZPD is a "set of possible next states of the developing system relationship within the environment" (Valsiner, 1997, p. 200). The ZPD depends on what actions are promoted and how the student uses his or her own freedom to engage within the environment. As Valsiner suggests, the three zones converge to create a constellation of possible forms of novel growth. Learning is active and self-directed. As teachers, we need to learn how to work the ZPA so that students achieve their potential. A teacher can direct a course of action, but the learner can respond in any number of ways (acquiesce, ignore, hesitate, resist, object). Unless students feel compelled to take part in the promoted action, learning goals can't be achieved.

"Us": The Cultural Niche

> Beings who are born not only unaware of, but quite indifferent to, the aims and habits of the social group have to be rendered cognizant of them and actively interested. Education, and education alone, spans the gap.
>
> Dewey (1916/1944, p. 3)

Through evolution humans developed cognitive capacities that allowed them to leave behind the ways of life of foraging dyads and to form large social groups. The large social group provided a holder for knowledge of cultural practices needed to survive in diverse environment. Anthropologist Robin Dunbar argues that there is a cognitive limit to the number of persons with whom an individual can maintain stable relationships and understand how each person relates to others, and that there is a correlation between brain size and group size. This number of individuals—called Dunbar's Number—is 150 (Dunbar, 1998).[4] This evolutionary tipping point occurred about 250,000 years ago, when the neocortical processing capacity of humans reached a level needed to support the maintenance of stable, cohesive groups.

In order to maintain a stable group, Dunbar asserts that 42% of group time needs to be devoted to social grooming, an activity in which social animals bond, resolve conflict, and reinforce cultural norms (Dunbar, 2004). In lower animals, social grooming is a one-on-one process, which was no longer possible in large hunter-gatherer groups. Dunbar argues that the human capacity for language evolved as an efficient means of collective social grooming through cooperative communication in the form of free-forming conversation and gossip (Dunbar, 2004). Linguistic communication and the skills of shared intentionality provided effective means to develop and transmit cultural knowledge and practice.

One way of thinking of the human social group is as a *cultural niche*. The cultural niche is a three-dimensional space of meaning created by shared knowledge, contested knowledge, and social practice (Dressler, 2019). Shared, distributed knowledge defines the boundaries of the cultural space.

Human Capital and Social Opportunity

The sum of what we have chosen to remember about our existence within culture is wired into the neurological structure of our brain: the enskulled brain, and the embodied brain. The social practice perspective on development describes socially relevant forms of embodied experience as *human capital*, acquired through experience (Bourdieu, 1977). Embodied cultural capital reflects an investment of time, self-improvement, and sacrifice; and social capital reflects efforts and aptitudes of sociability, institutional membership, the size of the social network, and membership within the "We," with all of its advantages (Bourdieu, 1986).

Dressler (2019) provides a bio-cultural explanation of human capital by explaining the way in which experiences reproduced in behavior reflect varying degrees of shared cultural models. Cultural models are cognitive representations of relevant cultural domains that are organized spheres of discourse (Dressler, 2019). They are a form of human capital. The degree to which the person's experiences reflect dominant cultural models is a measure of their "cultural consonance" (Dressler, 2019). High levels of cultural consonance predict well-being, and low levels predict depressive symptoms (Dressler, 2019).

While hunter-gatherer societies were fundamentally egalitarian, with the development of complex society and unequal resource accumulation, systems of inequality become reproduced in the human cultural niche that today are associated with disparities in social opportunity, and which threaten well-being of society's most distal members (i.e., those who lack cultural consonance) (Dressler, 2019). The biological function of culture to learning invites a renewed commitment to democracy in education. To return to Dewey's (1916/1944) quote in the introduction to this chapter, democratic society makes provision for participation for all its members on equal terms by securing flexible adjustment of its institutions through interaction of the different forms of associated life. The concept of the cultural niche provides a three-dimensional space in which to envision how flexible adjustment and interactions should be supported.

The standard by which judgments about the quality of social life can be made, according to Dewey, concern the extent to which shared interests are numerous and varied, and the extent to which the interplay of forms of association are full and free. Attention to the diversity of shared interests within the community of a school and opportunities to have full and free associations are two ways to strengthen the cultural niche that is the modern school. The school as cultural niche also presents the need for a culture of democratic individualism within the school community, which creates a political culture of equal dignity and a civil culture of rights (Urbinati, 2015). Opportunities to maintain control of psychic energy and to prevent oppression in the form of its external control is a priority for learning.

In the following sections, we will explore sociocultural processes that influence the development of educationally relevant human capital and determine cultural consonance.

Diversity

Schools as factories were designed to sort and treat learners based on deficits. These methods, based on theories of rationalism and empiricism, assume that a specified form of external stimulation will result in predicted outcomes. It is accepted that a normal *dose* will be adequate to promote learning in most subjects. But it is also assumed, even accepted, that the *normal* treatment will not succeed for everyone, and creates the social position of abnormality. By its very structure, a system that operationalizes a process by which some are constructed and treated as *abnormals* produces a whole host of "psychopathetic tragedies" that can never be resolved (Benedict, 1934). Literacy and higher forms of thinking are social conditions that reflect prior social opportunities (Scribner & Cole, 1973; Olson, 1994). Grouping children by ability for instruction reproduces inequalities that are reflected in broader society and exacerbates them (Lleras & Rangel, 2009). These practices create systemic inequalities that prevent learners accessing forms of educationally relevant capital that create true equality of educational opportunity (Gordon, 2014b). These barriers exacerbate social injustices threaten equal opportunity.

Until recently, it was accepted that disordered behaviors were a direct result of genetic disorders. This view stemmed from what is referred to as the OGOD hypothesis: One gene, one disorder (Plomin, 2018). We now know that common disorders are not caused by a single gene, but the result of many DNA differences, each with small effects (Kandel, 2007; Plomin, 2018). Seemingly "abnormal" behaviors are caused by the same genetic differences that appear in the normal distribution (Plomin, 2018). The appearance of abnormality is really the consequence of dysregulation resulting from maladaptive patterns of interaction between the person and the environment. In other words, as geneticist Robert Plomin points out (2018), *abnormal is normal*. The distinction between normal and abnormal is not real. Plomin explains that we cannot cure a disorder, because disorders do not exist. Rather, he suggests, success in treatment should be viewed quantitatively, by the degree to which problems can be alleviated through changes in behavior. The distinction between normal and abnormal is not real. Interventions that target single cognitive functions are based on erroneous logic.

This phenomenon, known as *pleiotropy*, occurs when one gene codes and affects the expression of multiple unrelated characteristics or traits. What we once understood as behavioral disorders are really simply extreme examples of normal behaviors that have been caused by a combination of genetic propensities and environmental factors (Kandel, 2007). For example, a condition such as "dyslexia" is a made-up diagnosis that describes behaviors of people who have reading difficulties; but their behaviors are caused by the same genes responsible for the behaviors of so-called "normal" readers (Plomin, 2018). What we used to think of as abnormal is really just an extreme version of normal (Plomin, 2018). We now realize that we cannot "treat" underlying "disorders" by one-size-fits-all, standardized procedures, because there is no such thing as an underlying genetic behavioral disorder (Kandel, 2007; Plomin, 2018). But we can alleviate difficulties by helping the child replace maladaptive behaviors with adaptive ones.

Within the context of a cultural niche, learners with so-called "abnormal" behavioral disorders—such as ADHD, oppositional defiance disorder, anxiety disorder, or learning disorders—are fully included and have rights to participate in the fullest and freest forms of association in the school where they have opportunities to develop "normal" behaviors by coordinating their minds with others and self-regulating to collective academic social norms.

The brain is "plastic," meaning that it is constantly in a state of growth and change. Disordered and dysregulated thoughts and behaviors can be changed through self-regulation to new practices.

Prolepsis: Creating Opportunities to Learn What Is Expected

An eternal challenge of formal schooling is to engage learners who are alien to the culture to which the goals of schooling have been directed. Within a paradigm of self-directed learning, how can learners be engaged in learning things for which they lack motivational desire or intention to do? The Positive Learning Paradigm answers this question in two parts. First, educationally relevant experiences need to be *proleptic*. Prolepsis is the process of bringing into the present that which will be encountered later. Proleptic experiences provide opportunities to learn ideas and values that will have value in their future, such as those measured in educational output standards (e.g., learning standards and state tests). Second, these experiences need to be educational from the standpoint that they successfully motivate the learner to attend to proleptic content and to assimilate the value of learning it into their intentions. This section will explore how to apply the principle of prolepsis to learning, and the next will explore the principle of motivation.

In order to enable learners to encounter today what will be relevant tomorrow, it is necessary to identify the endpoints of tomorrow. What is the knowledge, skill, and understandings necessary to be had by learners? A plethora of new learning standards have clarified achievement expectations. The Common Core State Standards outline expected competencies in all grades in English language arts (Reading, Writing, Language, and Listening and Speaking), Math, and Social Studies. The Learning Metrics Task Force (LMFT, 2013), convened by UNESCO and the Brookings Institute, proposed a holistic framework for learning that outlines seven domains for all students, from early childhood through secondary, focused on physical well-being, social and emotional learning, culture and the arts, literacy and communication, learning approaches and cognition, numeracy and mathematics, and science and technology.

Proleptic experiences fundamentally emphasize academic abilities. Academic ability includes literacy, numeracy, verbal, and mathematical reasoning, problem-solving in concrete and abstract contexts, inductive and deductive reasoning, the ability to perceive multiple perspectives, skill in using and managing information, and the ability to self-regulate all of these mental operations existentially in social situations (National Study Group for the Affirmative Development of Academic Ability, 2004).

But what is learned is only important relative to who learners become. Intellective competence essentially is "the effective orchestration of affective, cognitive and situative mental processes in the service of sense making and problem solving" (Gordon, 2014a, p. 174). Intellective competence that is especially necessary in technologically advanced societies (National Study Group for the Affirmative Development of Academic Ability, 2004).

Given the fact that learning is self-directed and intentional, it is necessary to appreciate the moral dimensions of learning. To solicit attention toward an object from a learner who is uninterested can only be accomplished through appeal to their sense of obligation to conform to norms that dictate the object must be attended to. To be successful in school, it is necessary for the learner to align their personal intentions to the institutional intentions of the school (Olson, 2003). To that end, the learner must view the self as a member of the moral collective of persons who inhabit the institution of the school. A sense of moral self-identity to the collective creates the possibility that the learner will determine its norms are worth conforming to. Social norms provide desire-independent reasons for engaging in activity. A positive cultural niche is one in which the school is not only responsive to the learner's cultural and personal identity, but one that promotes the learner's ability to access the cultures they wish to become a part of. The curriculum of a positive learning paradigm promotes these culturally promotive practices.

Conformity to institutional norms requires a form of self-regulation that deems the "We" to be greater than the "Me," and which takes the form of moral self-governance (Tomasello, 2019). In such a communal form of life, Tomasello (2016) writes, the sacred refers to the collective practices of the moral community… whereas the profane refers to individuals' self-interested pursuits (p. 132).

If the school is to become a viable cultural niche, what processes of cultural transmission can be employed to ensure all learners have adequate opportunity to learn what is expected? How can intentionally proleptic opportunities be made available to result in the development of educationally relevant human capital? How can the school as an institution come to be perceived by the learner as sacred moral commune, whose collective interests are of greater value than personal interests? Until it is, equality of educational opportunity can hardly be achieved.

Education and Rights

> ...the chance to soar in the dim blue air above the smoke is to their finer spirits boon and guerdon...
>
> W.E.B. DuBois

Educational methods in modern schools are not centered around the *learner's* intentions or subjective experiences. Instead, educational methods center around the *teacher's* intentions. The teacher determines what should be taught and how it should be learned. The teacher-centric view of education is partly explained by the fact that, for most of written history, knowledge has been viewed as a commodity that is transferred from one person to another through classical transmission modes of pedagogy, such as telling or demonstrating.

It is through self-directed social interactions that the person becomes who they are. The Positive Learning Paradigm is based on the assertion that every child has rights to optimal learning experiences that must be granted and enforced through systems of schooling. But rights only exist if they are exercised. The system, therefore, must have means to ensure learners exercise their rights.

The notion of learner' rights is a novel area of concern in education. Education has traditionally served as the formal process through which society transfers knowledge. But a rights-based approach to education invites a reconceptualization of the fundamental nature of education. If the right to exercise one's rights as a citizen depends on competencies learned in school, then the processes of schooling must be structured in the service of supporting children to learn to acquire them through practice. Competencies are learned in activity, as learners conform to the norms of their culture by employing its linguistic and symbolic conventions to participate and achieve goals and intentions. If we accept that children have a right to fundamental freedoms—the right to speak, think, move, and affiliate with others—and if we agree that these rights are absolute and inalienable, then we are obligated to enforce them in school. And if we know that, in the exercise of their freedom, children will conform to the canons of their culture to communicate cooperatively with others, then freedom is an essential condition of curriculum.

In most places, fundamental freedoms are inalienable rights that are considered to be *negative*, meaning that they exist for everyone. Everyone collectively knows they exist, and the exercise of free speech, free movement, or freedom of affiliation does not normally obligate anyone to take action to enforce them. In other words, these freedoms are rights that are not *against* anyone in the sense that they impose an obligation not to interfere (Searle, 2010). Rights that impose an obligation or that are against some person or entity with a corresponding obligation not to interfere can be thought of as *positive rights*. For example, if X has a right to free speech, then Y has an obligation not to interfere with X's right to free speech. The relations can be written quantifiably, expressed in Searle's logical statement (2010):

> X has a right (X speaks freely)
> implies
> Y has an obligation not to interfere with (X speaks freely)

John Searle (2010) identifies the necessary properties of positive rights: "positive rights require more than noninterference" (p. 185). They should state "(1) whom the right is against, (2) what exactly is the content of their obligations to the right bearer, and (3) exactly why the person against whom the right exists is under those obligations" (Searle, 2010, p. 185).

But, due to the conditions of current schooling, learners' fundamental freedoms are persistently and flagrantly violated. Children are restricted from exercising their rights to free speech, movement, thought, and affiliation. They will spend most of the 13,000 hours they spend in school being told what to think, what to say, where to sit, and who to interact with. In order to secure an egalitarian cultural niche as an environment from which the individual can freely and autonomously select their own experiences, negative rights need to be turned into positive ones.

Jeremy Bentham, the 18th-century social philosopher, pointed out that rights are the *children of the law*, and *real rights* come from *real laws*. He points out that *imaginary laws*, like those invented by poets and philosophers, only become *imaginary rights* (in Searle, 2010). A law is defined as a *binding custom or practice of a community*: a *rule of conduct or action prescribed or formally recognized as binding or enforced by a controlling authority*, and the *control brought about by the existence or enforcement of such law* (Merriam-Webster, 2020). Laws gain their deontic power, or their power to impose obligations and to be binding, through the status that they hold in the minds of all of those in the collective group of individuals who use them (Searle, 2010).

Within the Positive Learning Paradigm, our strategy for transforming the autocratic regime of school into a democratic community will be to make what are normally *imaginary* or *negative rights* into *positive* ones by employing the same linguistic device used to write laws. Laws are reality-creating instruments. They are a way of using speech—a speech act—to create a new reality by describing the reality as existing (Searle, 2010). Known as status function declarations, this form of speech act has a status in the social world due to collective intentionality and motivation to conform to shared norms based on the recognition that one's personal welfare is contingent on the general welfare of the group (Searle, 2010).

Applied to our present problem, positive rights for learners might read as follows: learner (X) has a right to move, speak, and affiliate freely (A) during class time. This implies that the teacher (Y) has an obligation not to interfere with the learners right (allowing X to do A).

Responsibility-based Self-Control

Rights only exist when they are exercised. A positive learning paradigm calls attention to the need to approach the teaching of norms pedagogically. While the traditional curriculum of the current school emphasized instructed learning of subject content, a curriculum of social practices requires instruction to explain how the social world of the classroom and school functions, what rules and routines govern activity within them, and how to participate by conforming to social and academic norms.

The "We" self is motivated to comply with norms out of a basic human need to identify and belong to the social group. Aware of expectations, with clarity of norms, the learner is naturally motivated to exercise responsibility-based self-control to comply with expectations. Norm psychology holds promise to help learners to continually develop new and more adaptive patterns of behavior.

Responsibility-based self-control (McCallister, 2013f) is a pedagogical strategy based on the understanding that problematic behaviors or lagging skills in learners are symptoms of maladjustment and lack of appropriate and supportive stimulation from the environment as opposed to an internal defect. By taking responsibility to adhere to positive social and academic norms, learners whose behaviors are disordered, or who are resistant or oppositional to authoritative teaching are usually far more inclined to act in compliance with norms than to submit to teacher directives. A positive learning paradigm employs the strategy of norm psychology to draw dysregulated learners into the orbits of collective social routines where everyone adheres to norms of civility and a strong work ethic.

Conclusion: A Sustaining Theoretical Innovation

Cultural psychologist Michael Cole (1996) proposed the idea of *sustaining innovations* in education—the deliberate creation of new forms of schooling that result in intended outcomes. Cole reasoned that, by identifying what endpoints are desired and intended, cultural experiences can be designed in order to achieve intended outcomes. To illustrate this principle, we will refer to the concept of the mediational triangle, an image derived from Soviet psychology that depicts the process of cultural learning (see Figure 3.2) (Cole, 1996).

In his triangle, the subject (learner) is represented on the left base of the triangle. This point represents the learner before the mediated activity. The outcome of development through a certain experience is represented by the "endpoint," on the right base of the triangle. That is the learner, new memory intact, after having had the learning experience. The social situation in which the experience is set is represented by the light circle containing the triangle. Presuming a person could develop in isolation from culture, the base of the triangle represents the hypothetical *unmediated* course of development. Since every human experience is a social one, this is a suppositional exercise. Given absolute freedom and the possibility of activity unmediated by culture, the mind would not develop any of the capacities made possible through joint and shared intentionality. Humans do not develop in isolation from others. They are social beings and their development is influenced by the interactions they have in their social environments with the people and artifacts of their culture. These mediated experiences are represented as "tools" in the upper point in the triangle.

The Positive Learning Paradigm is a sustaining theoretical innovation. It is a theoretical framework for learning that can be used to inform the development of sustaining innovations in education. The framework prescribes the conditions necessary to support the biological and psychological processes that underlie the acquisition of civic competencies. These processes have been drawn from insights from the natural and behavioral sciences concerned with the new science of the mind (Kandel, 2007). This emerging

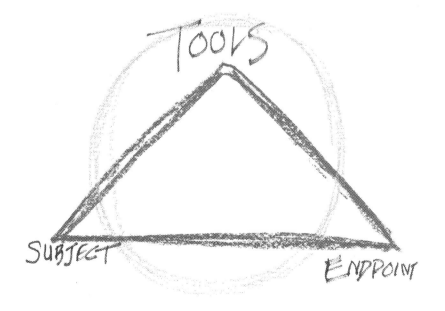

Figure 3.2 Mediational triangle

body of science has affirmed philosophical assertions that have been made by educational philosophers through history (Dewey, 1938; Rousseau, 1979). It has confirmed that higher forms of thinking really *are* social in nature. Humans really do have special cognitive capacities that are tailored to support thinking through social interaction, and our brains are organized in a range of complex ways that enable us to access the mental states of others (Banich & Compton, 2018; Kandel, Schwartz, & Jessell, 2000; Tomasello, 2014, 2019). It has been confirmed that we function most optimally when we feel emotionally comfortable and are able to integrate all the components of our mind (Kandel, 2007; Siegel, 2020). Active engagement really *does* translate into deep learning (Banich & Compton, 2018; Kandel, Schwartz, & Jessell, 2000). We know the relevance and meaning of a situation determines the depth of our memory. Memory is strengthened relative to the salience or strength of stimulation from the environment, and new memory for people, places, and things can *only* develop when we are selectively attending to those things (Kandel, 2007). Freedom really does have a learning advantage. We exercise our will through the freedom we have to inhibit our impulses and take control of our minds to direct our experiences (Kandel, 2007; Searle, 2010). If moral justification never before warranted the need to create schools that center the interests of children, new scientific evidence now makes the case. The new science of self-regulated learning has already had seismic implications in applied practices in psychotherapy, psychiatry, and medicine (Beck, 1996, 2019; Kabat-Zinn, 1991; Siegel, 2010). It is time to apply science to the improvement of education.

This new view of learning challenges traditional notions of equality of educational opportunity as the provision of equal access or the sameness of treatment. Instead of equal access, equality consists in the adequate provision of richly differentiated environments and the freedom to autonomously select environmental experiences that are appropriate and sufficient to enable the achievement of potential in diverse learners (Plomin, 2018; Tucker-Drob, Briley, & Harden, 2013). Learning is the exercise of rights to certain experiences. Within the transactional paradigm presented above, opportunity is not given, but created in the environment and taken by the learner (Plomin, 2018). In other words, biological and sociocultural forces combine to shape a developmental trajectory that is governed by human volition. Genetic influences govern individual proclivities, and the manner in which the individual orients to the social world and takes part in it—their individual and shared intentional states—catalyzes a personalized course of learning that is defined by individuality. To be equitable, opportunities to learn must provide autonomy in the learning process; access to rich, diverse learning environments; ample experience to share intentions and coordinate mental states with others; and support to internalize effective strategies for self-regulation.

In the remainder of this book, the Positive Learning Paradigm is applied to the McCallister, a rights-based model of pedagogical practice.

Notes

1. I refer to John Searle's theory of intentionality and his social philosophy of mind and society.
2. Rousseau's hypothesis was proven in two discoveries of feral children, who, after years of social isolation and neglect, both demonstrated the inability to acquire language, reasoning, and socialization. The "wild child of Aveyron," a French boy who was found living alone in the wilderness in 18th-century France, and "Genie," the American teenager found at age 13 after having spent a decade kept by her parents in captivity and isolation.
3. Human beings' extended period of immaturity needed to develop their mental capacities and to reach 90% adult brain size is six years longer than their nearest primate relative, the chimpanzee, who reaches that milestone at two years of age (Tomasello, 2019).
4. Dunbar's Number is three times greater than chimpanzees (Gamble, Gowlett, & Dunbar, 2014).

Section II
A Pedagogy for the Self

4 The McCallister Method
Program Design

Introduction

The McCallister Model is a pedagogical design premised on the fundamental principle that education should serve to help learners exercise their fundamental freedoms to carry out their own intentions. The Model is a blueprint to transform traditional learning environments into egalitarian communities in which learners exercise freedoms of self-expression, movement, social affiliation, and self-determination to navigate a largely self-organized environment that is structured around self-selected activities. These activities tap into social interaction as a vehicle for higher-order thinking and academic development. They empower learners to exercise intentionality and self-responsibility as means to both reach high learning standards and develop their own individuality and potential. It is a universal design that can be used with diverse learners of all ages, languages, cultures, and exceptionalities. This chapter presents a brief overview of key pedagogical principles of the McCallister Model.

The McCallister Model: A Cultural Habitus for the Cultivation of the *Self*

The McCallister Model practices are structured to exploit self-awareness and social awareness. Within the McCallister Model, self-awareness is the core of the curriculum. The model incorporates a curriculum of self-directed activities and opportunities that help the child learn to manage themselves and regulate to collective academic and social norms. The curriculum cultivates the self, as learners themselves set their own goals and make choices about the activities to pursue in order to meet them.

The model also incorporates social activities and opportunities. Human beings are social animals and can only exist in the company of others; therefore, the stable social group is the evolutionary ecosystem (Dressler, 2019). Within the McCallister Model, the social group is employed as a fundamental aspect of pedagogy. It is the cultural niche in which learners interact to take psychic energy from others to develop their minds and become themselves. Our awareness of what others think about a particular thing is an important aspect of how we think about that thing. Within the McCallister Model, the development of new understanding is approached as a social accomplishment rather than a process of the transfer of knowledge (Gergen, 1990, 2015). The Model, therefore, incorporates a curriculum that establishes norms for civil behavior and optimal social conditions for learning.

A Studio for the Self

If the factory was the inspiration for the industrial school design, the *studio* is the inspiration for the McCallister Model. The word *studio* originates from the Latin word *stadium*, which means *zeal* or *painstaking application* (Study, 2020). Designed to inspire zeal, the McCallister curriculum provides learners with time and space to exercise fundamental freedoms to pursue activities of their choice in order to develop their talents, interests, and competencies. Learning is not a product of transmitted knowledge, but the intentional, passionate, and creative pursuit of a self-determined person.

The *atelier* is a particular kind of studio in which artists produce their work under the guidance of an artistic *master* in a culture of shared aesthetic values. The atelier provides a way to think about formal learning spaces as cohesive cultures in which individual productivity is influenced by collective values and interdependence. Within the classroom-as-atelier, the teacher assumes the role of guide and source of information rather than the more traditional role of foreman (as in the school-as-factory) or guard (as in the school-as-panopticon). The atelier is the supportive cultural niche, providing continuity of ongoing, self-directed practice under inspirational supervision.

Curriculum Components

The McCallister Model incorporates four curriculum components to support self-directed engagement within the social environment.

Sparks

Sparks is a self-directed, personalized curriculum used in all grades and disciplinary subjects to support learners to develop their intellects and identities. It provides structures to help learners make goals and plan how to achieve them. Sparks includes a broad menu of possible activities that learners choose from to meet their goals. The Sparks curriculum is presented in Chapter 5.

Learning Cultures Formats

Learning Cultures is a curriculum of "formats" (Bruner, 1983) or zones of proximal development (Vygotsky, 1978), which provides support to learners to practice autonomy and to interact with others to carry out their own intentions. The Learning Cultures Formats support development of both the "I" self, the "Me" self, and the "We" self. The "I"-self oriented Formats emphasize volition and personal action. The "Me"-self oriented Formats emphasize interactions with others and support mentalizing and cognitive control. These Formats take advantage of the power of peer interaction described in Chapter 3. The "We" formats emphasize moral self-regulation to collective community values. The Learning Cultures Formats are the topic of chapters in Section III of this book.

Rubrics. Social activity within these zones is patterned through procedures outlined in Format Rubrics. The Learning Cultures curriculum is synthesized into a collection of just over a dozen Rubrics that lay out Format procedures, identify educational aims, outline roles and responsibilities that both learners and adults follow, and specify how formal learning standards are used.[1] Rubrics provide a simple a set of rules that learners and adults follow in the context of each Format. The *rules* are written to specify forms of action that stimulate targeted learning processes (e.g., those described in

Chapter 3, in the Positive Learning Paradigm). When they take on the assigned social roles specified within the Rubrics, adults take action to distribute responsibility for learning to learners, and learners take action to assume responsibility for setting and meeting their own learning goals. Sample Rubrics appear at the conclusion of each Format Chapter.

Keepers of the Culture

Keepers of the Culture is a curriculum that secures positive social norms in classrooms and throughout the school. Since social interaction is the vehicle for higher forms of learning, this curriculum specifies activities and procedures that help learners internalize collective norms for civility and personal responsibility. Keepers of the Culture and the social norms curriculum are presented in Section IV.

The Ecosystem Curriculum

The Ecosystem Curriculum is a comprehensive set of school-wide bureaucratic and leadership systems that function to secure and sustain the first-level changes of the McCallister Model. These systems are organized around the domains of Assessment, Civil Rights, Community Education, Curriculum, School Culture, and Training. Leadership responsibilities are distributed to teacher leads, who enact planned changes as they carry out their duties. The Ecosystem Curriculum is outlined in a comprehensive year-long planning guide that coordinates and stages the leadership systems. The Ecosystem Curriculum is presented in Section V.

Learning Zones

The school day in the industrial school is organized into blocks of time dedicated to common school subjects. The curriculum within each class or subject is typically structured into a prescribed sequence of standardized instruction, and group lessons are presented to students who have been sorted by age, ability, or knowledge level for appropriate instruction.

Within the McCallister Model, school design is based on a different model. In the Model, the Activity Block is the blank Canvas for time and space. In schools that are structured by the egg-crate design (a given number of classes for every grade or subject, each with a set number of students), the Activity Block is at least 60–80 minutes in length (see Figure 4.1 for a visual representation of the Formats arranged into a single class period). In educational settings unrestricted by the egg-crate design and in remote learning environments, Activity Blocks can extend to a period that lasts the length of an entire day (see Figure 4.2). Activity Blocks can be dedicated to traditional subjects, like math, science, reading, writing, social studies, and art. But can also serve either a more general or narrow focus. They can be dedicated to a specialized focus of study (e.g., American feminist poetry), or they can be learner-directed, providing zones for learners to pursue personal learning goals.

In the egg-crate environment, the Activity Block usually begins with a lesson of no more than 10 minutes in length that teachers themselves develop based on specific criteria for content and quality. Learners then transition into the Work Time Format, which lasts from 40 to 50 minutes, where learners have opportunities to pursue projects and activities they themselves choose related to the subject of focus. The Learning Cultures curriculum for personalized learning, known as *Sparks*, provides guidelines for the Work

80 *A Pedagogy for the Self*

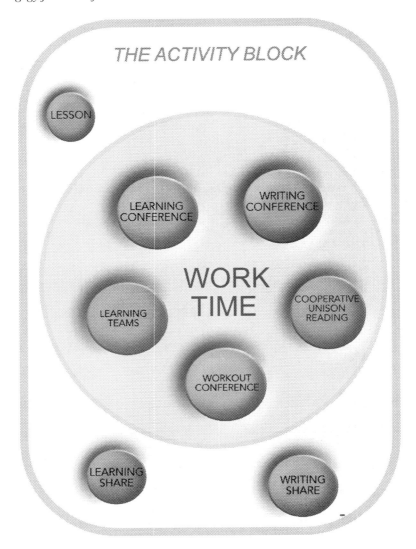

Figure 4.1 The Activity Block, egg-crate design

Time curriculum that ensure the activities learners select will result in the achievement of formal learning standards. The Formats of Cooperative Unison Reading, Learning Teams, Conferences, and Small-group Instruction each take place during Work Time. These activities are problem-based social learning opportunities designed to help learners develop their minds by sharing mental states with others. The Activity Block ends with a large-group Share, which provides the opportunity for learners to individually present their learning projects to classmates for feedback.

Remote Learning

Since the McCallister Methods are organized to support personalized, self-directed learning without the requirement of formal instruction, they are adaptable to remote learning environments. The McCallister Method remote program includes two components. First,

The McCallister Method: Program Design 81

THE WORK TIME ACTIVITY BLOCK

Figure 4.2 The Activity Block, open design

learners adhere to a daily academic Workout Plan comprising specified asynchronous activities from the Sparks curriculum. Guidelines for these activities allow learners to have a role in creating their own curriculum and executing personal learning plans. Second, learners take part in the routine social activities of the Learning Cultures Formats, which provide opportunities to share ideas, collectively solve problems, and co-regulate intellectual activity. Co-regulation supports self-regulatory control, the essence of higher-order thinking. The McCallister Methods are ideally suited to remote learning.

A Curriculum of Rights: Rubrics as Laws

The McCallister Model is a revolutionary curriculum design that employs the construct of a right as an instrument to norm behavior. The Rubrics spell out obligations that both learners and teachers adhere to. They are like laws. When learners and adults conform to obligations, patterned forms of social activity give rise to targeted learning opportunities. The McCallister Model is an example of a new direction in social change, in which norms are employed instrumentally to address social problems (Bicchieri, 2017).

As status function declarations, the Rubrics have a reality-creating power (Searle, 2010). They spell out conditions for optimal learning. They establish new norms by specifying forms of activity that create them. With their reality-creating power, the Rubrics are used for a variety of purposes. The Rubrics are used by learners and adults to guide behavior and to secure and sustain new practices. They are instructional tools that are *taught* to learners so that they understand the aims of the activities, the procedures, and their roles and responsibilities as participants. They are used by teachers pedagogically as a tool for instruction to guide learners how to participate in the Formats. They are used for professional development purposes, as a self-assessment tool for teachers and as a norming tool for staff development. They are used by administrators as a framework for observation and evaluation. They provide language that can be used to provide corrective and constructive feedback to learners and adults in all their uses. The Rubrics are closely aligned with formal learning standards, so the choices that learners make about the activities to engage in, result in their achievement of high learning standards. The Rubrics are also closely aligned to high standards for teacher effectiveness. That means that fidelity of implementation on the teacher's part results in high levels of effective practice. When implemented according to standards outlined in the Rubrics, conventional teacher-directed practices can rapidly be replaced with new learner-directed practices to immediately improve learners' achievement outcomes and well-being. And they are used for the purposes of achieving social justice by ensuring a means by which to guarantee every child has an opportunity to learn and to achieve their potential that is equitable on the basis of being sufficient (Gordon & Nigro, 1988).

Transactional Assessment

Assessment has traditionally been used to measure developed ability. But assessment can also be used transactionally to serve a pedagogical function. Instead of using assessment exclusively to measure or identify learners' or teachers' abilities, the McCallister Model assessments, such as the Rubrics, are used instrumentally to instantiate learning situations that result in planned development. In *transactional assessments,* the assessment probe functions to *catalyze* new learning (Draper, 2009). Transactional assessments can function as a transformational technology used to quickly restructure traditional, teacher-directed classrooms into bustling hubs of peer collaboration and rigorous, self-directed inquiry. This form of technology can be used to effectively change the norms of the culture of an entire school within a period of months. As such, the McCallister Model is an example of how changing norms can be employed as a promising strategy to solve intractable social problems. The Rubrics establish norms to eliminate and replace long-entrenched and problematic pedagogical practices, such as ability-based instructional groups and teacher-directed, didactic lessons, which can be immediately replaced with activities that better support learner autonomy and intentionality.

Genre Practice: A Theory for the Literacy Curriculum

It was once believed that literacy and the higher-order cognitive capacities involved in reading comprehension and writing composition consisted of an accumulation of discrete literacy skills that could be taught through drill and memorization. This view has been discredited in language philosophy and literacy theory, even though it continues to inform mainstream curriculum methods. If knowledge is not a commodity that can be transmitted, but rather an achievement that is an outcome of socially-constructed understanding, how should curriculum be organized? What is the nature of pedagogical practice informed by a theory of social construction?

The traditional conveyor-belt curriculum of the industrial school presents knowledge as a commodity to be transferred. The curriculum assigns teachers the responsibility to *transmit* and students the responsibility to *receive*. These basic obligations define the purpose of the traditional curriculum. Jerome Bruner (1963) made the observation that formal education is responsible for the process of "passing on the knowledge, the skills, the point of view and the heart of a culture" (p. 523). A curriculum for the development of self—one capable of enabling the learner to assume the point of view and heart of their culture—should aspire to higher aims than mere obligation. Bruner was a vocal critic of programmed instruction, which dictates a curriculum that progresses in small, incremental steps, and which is derived, "willy-nilly," from a theory of learning that also views development as incremental and progressing in small steps. Bruner pointed out that humans operate as meaning-makers by taking large "packets" of information and breaking them down into their own increments. Bruner (1963) called for a theory of instruction that focuses on motivation, the factors that predispose a child to learn, and the optimal structuring and sequence of knowledge. He suggested a theory of instruction should be constructed around four problems: "predispositions, structures, sequences, and consequences" (p. 525).

Genre Practice (McCallister, 2008b) is a social constructivist approach to literacy instruction that will be described in this section. It is an approach to literacy education that teaches learners that texts are a form of action performed by writers. The ideas of Genre Practice are inspired by the Literacy Hypothesis—the assertion that literacy is the outcome of participation in social practices of a certain kind (Vygotsky, 1962, 1978; Goody & Watt, 1968; Havelock, 1982, 1991; Ong, 1976; McLuhan, 1962; Olson, 1994; Olson & Torrance, 2009). Genre Practice operates on this logic: if literacy is the outcome of social practices of a certain kind, then learners can be led to take part in certain kinds of social practices that will predictably result in the development of intended literate behaviors.

Genre Practice is also inspired by genre theory (Bakhtin, 1986; Devitt, 2004; Freedman & Medway, 1994; Cope & Kalantzis, 1993). Texts and other forms of symbolic communication are seen as forms of action that are performed by writers/creators to achieve an intended purpose. Genres are the categories that define these creations or cultural models. Genres share common structural elements, which are conventionalized symbols used within the social sphere in which the genre is employed. Learners can more readily 'master' writing forms by learning and using the 'rules' of the genre.

Learning to Employ Texts as Forms of Action

Within the Genre Practice framework, learners are taught, as writers, to employ the medium of composition to carry out their own intentions. They use writing in its many forms and genres (e.g., narrative, information, and argument) to achieve their own goals.

They share their goals and intentions with peers and get feedback on their writing that they assimilate into their intentions and composition revisions. They look for examples of forms of writing in which other authors are seeking to achieve a similar purpose and borrow writing strategies and conventions from these exemplars.

Genre Practice also defines the reading curriculum. In the Cooperative Unison Reading (CUR) Format, learners determine what the text is trying to do and how the author is doing it. As readers, learners are taught to 'listen' to the voice of the person whose writing appears on the page. They assume a relational stance to the text that is determined through a cooperative relationship to the writer in which the reader assumes appropriate attitudes and dispositions. Learners are motivated to read and write through their predispositions as people in relationships with those who they are trying to reach through reading and writing.

Learning Through Use and Activity

Children learn reading and writing Background abilities and dispositions (also known as *skills*) by using reading and writing to communicate with others cooperatively and relationally. They write to communicate goals and intentions to others; and they read to understand others' goals and intentions. They select purposeful reading and writing activities outlined in the Sparks curriculum. They use the Formats of the Writing Conference and Writing Share to receive feedback to improve their writing. They take part in CUR groups to read texts with others to explore issues and ideas of mutual interest. They use CUR as an opportunity to practice ways of listening to the voices of authors who are saying things they are interested in learning about.

Prolepsis

The Genre Practice model shifts the focus in pedagogy from a concern for existing ability (or existing deficits) toward a concern for capability and potential. In this *prospective* approach to pedagogy, it is important to create learning situations that stimulate desired states of development—new capacities that have yet to be internalized through the mechanisms of development through social interaction. *Prolepsis* is the process that instantiates a prospective pedagogical interaction.

Prolepsis is the cultural mechanism that "brings the end to the beginning" (Cole, 1996). A situation is proleptic if it presents a representation of a thing before the thing comes into existence. It anticipates a future need or set of conditions. Genre Practice incorporates the principle of prolepsis into the writing process in several ways. As a baseline, learners are expected to always have a writing agenda that is aimed toward a goal in the future (e.g., to make someone laugh by writing a pun; to invite someone to a birthday party; to wish someone well who is sick; to persuade a parent to extend curfew). Learners write for a purpose, not for the purpose of satisfying the instructional objective of a teacher. Once they establish an intention or sense of *aboutness* in relation to the writing task, they explore the universe of written discourse to find exemplars of other writers' efforts to achieve the same kind of effect. They study the exemplars to determine what features and conventions are used effectively and apply those ideas to their own writing. Learners are expected to examine two exemplars of related generic examples for every formal writing assignment that is submitted for evaluation.

The principle of prolepsis informs the way curriculum activities are structured. In CUR, learners select texts of choice, anticipating how their choices will resonate with the interests and tastes of their peers. Every class is stocked with a wide assortment of grade- and subject-relevant texts, such as children's magazines or discipline-relevant content. The formal curriculum, which is outlined in formal learning standards, is manifested in the activity of the Formats, as learners use written discourse to pursue their goals.

In the Writing Conference, learners meet with an adult to cooperatively analyze the piece and to make determinations about how to improve its effect. They refer to the Common Core Writing Standards to determine how their own writing demonstrates grade-level competencies. The Writing Share provides peer feedback to help the writer determine how their text can be improved to better achieve its purpose.

Mentalizing

Human beings have the unique ability to read others' intentions through a capacity called theory of mind (ToM) (Astington, Harris, & Olson, 1988) or mentalizing (Lewis, Birch, Hall, & Dunbar, 2017). Mindreading enables a person to engage in a process of thinking that involves thinking through the perspective of another person. Mindreading is the most demanding cognitive ability in human beings, requiring high levels of psychic energy, and recruiting neurological processes from multiple components of the brain and mind. Thinking about what others "think" and "mean" necessarily implicates a metalanguage for talking about thought—a language that in turn may be used reflexively, to think about one's own thinking (Olson, 1996). Mentalizing provides a powerful learning context; therefore, it is a process that is targeted in the Rubric assessments.

Most of the "Me"-self oriented Formats are organized to instantiate mindreading by structuring deliberative dialog in situations in which the curriculum has caused learners to experience cognitive disequilibrium. At points of such conflict, learners engage in cooperative reasoning and perspective shifting and sharing to resolve disequilibrium and achieve a higher collective understanding. In other words, the curriculum recruits the human capacities of social referencing and the reconciliation of interpersonal cognitive conflict in the service of the achievement of higher collective understanding. These capacities are fundamental civic competencies and properties of intellective functioning.

In the process of shifting and sharing perspectives, human beings follow-in to the other's focus of attention to help elaborate and extend understanding (Bruner, 1983). Follow-in promotes joint intersubjectivity and clarity of reference of what one is talking about. In traditional teacher-directed instructional Formats, children are expected to follow-in to the object of the teacher's attention with little assurance of mutual understanding. Genre Practice Formats shift the pattern of *follow-in* so that points of confusion raised by the learner are followed-into by teachers and peers. Moreover, in these instances, the number of perspectives engaged in the process of *follow-in* are multiplied by the number of participants involved in the Format. In shifting the locus of follow-in from teacher to learner, the McCallister Model re-centers the curriculum around the subjective perspective of the learner.

The Role of the Adult in Pedagogy

> It is the task of the teacher to educate—to educate for change—to educate through change. To educate for orderly planned revolution. If necessary, educate through more disruptive revolutionary action.
>
> Edmund W. Gordon (2014a, p. 293)

Within a transactive model of pedagogy, in which the learner is supported to take what they need from the environment, the adult (or more experienced peer) assumes a facilitative role within the pedagogical transactions of the Formats. If the word *teacher* is taken to mean someone who performs the specialized labor of knowledge transfer, protocols of the McCallister Model are designed to minimize reliance on teachers. The word *teacher* derives from the word *teach*, which originates from Germanic and Old English words that means *to show, present, or point out* (Teach, 2020). The word *teaching* implies the process of knowledge transfer from an authority (Teaching, 2020). The teacher's role in the industrial school is to efficiently manage the flow of information in the system.

A more appropriate role for the adult within the McCallister environment is that of *guide*. *Guide* means *a person who advises or shows the way to others* (Guide, 2020), and *advise* means *to see, look at, consider, and consult with others* (Advise, 2020). A guide can be a teacher. But a guide can be any adult or "experienced other" (Vygotsky, 1978) who is capable of coaxing the learner forward into a learning experience. In this book, the term *guide* is used to refer to any experienced other who engages with the child in a learning transaction. *Guides* offer guidance to support learners to act with intention and independence. Rather than teaching didactically, the guide is always, as Heidegger (1985) described, *learning to let them learn* (Heidegger, 1985).

In the context of Progressive education traditions, which emphasize learning through imitation and experience, it is the preference for the teacher to assume the role of an enabling guide as opposed to a omniscient authority (Dewey, 1938; Montessori, 1912; Parker, 1900; Rousseau, 1979; Vygotsky, 1978).

The Fourth Pedagogy

The concept of folk pedagogies was conceptualized by Olson and Bruner (1996) as a way to compare different pedagogical approaches. The *first folk pedagogy* supports learning through imitation and experience; the *second folk pedagogy* conceives of learning as the transmission of knowledge from authority to subject; the *third folk pedagogy* views learning as the construction of knowledge; the fourth folk pedagogy views *learning* as a process of sharing intentions and *knowing* as the arrival of agreed-upon understanding. The fourth folk pedagogy supports the achievement of joint intentions between learners, their peers, and teachers in ways that achieve joint understanding of formal learning goals (Olson, 2003).

Progressive approaches have traditionally employed third folk pedagogy methods, which emphasize self-direction and personal meaning, but which have not been successfully employed on a large scale due to their limited effectiveness in ensuring students learn what is expected of the formal curriculum (Olson, 2003). The McCallister Method is an example of the *fourth pedagogy*. It provides systems for learners to engage with others to achieve joint intentions and achieve personal learning goals in ways that enable them to achieve goals outlined in formal learning standards.

Self-organized Learning

The McCallister Model presents an approach that supports self-directed learning and specifications for a way to transform school into a self-organizing learning environment. Individualized learning has been a focus of interest in education for the last 50 years. But until recently there was limited evidence that self-directed learning could result in high levels of achievement.

Indian physicist, Sugata Mitra (2015) found that low-SES children from the urban slums of cities in India who are provided access to high-quality information via internet-connected computer, with only minimal intervention from adults, can achieve the same achievement outcomes as those in elite schools. Mitra and his colleagues found that children, unprompted by adults, took part in peer tutoring, self-organized their learning, underwent desirable behavioral changes, and completed 10% of the curriculum without the need for teachers, regardless of income level or cultural background (Mitra & Rana, 2001). These findings led the investigators to assert that curriculum can be divided into three parts: 1) the part that needs a teacher to deliver subject matter; 2) the part that needs an assistant to support the learner; and 3) the part that needs only resources and a peer group to share knowledge. The McCallister Method provides a systematic way to restructure classrooms in ways that employ primarily Parts 2 and 3. Mitra's findings have led to a global SOLE movement (Mitra, 2015). Mitra admits that he rather serendipitously came upon the phenomenon of self-organized learning, and does not speculate about what psychological or neurological processes might account for learning (Mitra, 2014). But we can assume that some of the phenomena that make SOLEs effective can be accounted for in the processes described in the Positive Learning Paradigm discussed in Chapter 3.

Conclusion

The first- and second-level practices of the McCallister Model incorporate the principles outlined in this chapter. They help create zones for learning in the classroom that provide learners with fundamental freedom to carry out their intentions as they comply with the social and academic norms of the community. They provide a system of social activity in which the principles of Genre Practice and self-directed learning govern learning and academic development.

Note

1. I created the Rubrics at the suggestion of my friend and colleague, Jerry Bruner who, after I shared my concern that even when the teachers I coach commit to making the changes in practice that I demonstrate, invariably resort to old practices. He suggested, "Have you thought about writing indicators?" Since that day, more than a decade ago, I codified by coaching moves—what teachers initially referred to as "Cynthia's way"—into a set of documents that specify the *McCallister Method* of pedagogy. I have revised the Rubrics every two years throughout the last decade based on my interactions with thousands of learners and hundreds of teachers.

5 Sparks
A Learner-facing Personalized Curriculum

> You must be true to yourself. Strong enough to be true to yourself. Brave enough to be strong enough to be true to yourself. Wise enough to be brave enough to be strong enough to shape yourself from what you actually are.
>
> Sylvia Ashton-Warner

Introduction

Sparks is a learner-facing, personalized curriculum that learners themselves follow to create a self-organized learning environment. Activities in the Sparks curriculum provide an agenda that learners use to organize their Work Time priorities. This chapter is presented in two parts. Part I presents an overview of the Sparks program principles and components. Part II presents an inventory of activities.

PART I: THE SPARKS PROGRAM

Once upon a time, people thought that students needed teachers in order to learn what was supposed to be taught in school. In most classrooms, desks are lined up in rows facing the teacher. Teachers are expected to transmit information, and students are expected to listen, memorize, and do what the teacher says. In order to make the process of knowledge transmission more efficient, schools sort learners into groups according to their ability, and teachers provide instruction that is just slightly above the learners' level of independence. Schools have been organized this way for thousands of years.

The Sparks program is based on a new and different logic of learning. Scientists have discovered that learning is self-directed. It happens as a result of a person paying enough attention to a certain thing intensely enough for the body to release chemicals that help form new structures between neurons that carry memory. A teacher can teach a student a fact, but if the student is not paying attention, the fact will not be learned. On the other hand, a learner can come upon the same fact, without the assistance of a teacher, and successfully learn it if they are interested enough. Learning is not teacher-dependent, as once thought, but self-directed. A person only learns what they take responsibility to pay attention to and remember.

Science has proven another important fact about learning. There is literally no upper limit to the space available in the brain to store memories of things that are learned. The only limit to what can be learned is determined by what a person sets their mind to and how well they follow through with their commitments learning commitments.

This means that *you* are responsible for the person you will become. The goals you have and the actions you take to reach them lays down the path that leads to the person you become.

People do not often think about their thinking. Thinking, like breathing, is something that is easily taken for granted. But now that we know that the person's intentions determine what course of action they will take, the experiences that are most significant to learning and academic achievement are those in which the person makes conscious decisions about what they want to achieve and how they will succeed. Thinking about the way you think and act is a way to have control over your destiny. Since you are the master of your thoughts and the creator of your mind, you have the power to control your own learning.

The Sparks program gives you a map you can use to create your own mind. By making choices about what things you choose to do and think about, you literally create your intellect. Sparks is written for you to be a plan you can follow to meet your own learning goals, to become who you want to be, and to meet your personal potential. It's a guide to help you become guardian of your intellect and master of your destiny.

Why Sparks?

This program is called *Sparks* in appreciation of a fascinating scientific fact that explains how organisms react to their environment. All animals develop through a process of reacting and adapting to the environment. Upon sensing some form of stimulation, like noises, visual images, or sensory perceptions, the cells in their bodies give information stored in DNA to respond. The trigger for the impulse to act before conscious awareness kicks in is located deep in the brain. This trigger is called the *readiness potential*. The *readiness potential* was discovered 1964 by Hans Kornhuber and Richard Jung in Freiburg, Germany. These scientists discovered that the brain sends out an electrical signal to direct the body to act a split second before the person becomes aware of their decision to act.

In animals other than humans, this signal causes immediate reaction to external stimulus without reflective thought. But humans are different than most other animals. But human beings are very special animals. They have the ability to sense input from their environment, like all organisms. They have the capacity to think reflectively before they act. In other words, they can override the body's impulse to act. In other words, humans can override the impulses in their bodies to take action in order to decide on a better and different course of action than impulse. They can make plans and exercise self-regulation in order to act in ways that better align with their goals and intentions.

So, for example, when your best friend says something that makes you upset, and your impulse might be to snap back with an angry response, you have the mental power to stop yourself, and say something different. Here is another example. Since our bodies are built to react immediately, sometimes we do things that we *thought* we decided to do, but really just did because the genes in our neuron cells sent signals to our body to act. For example, say you're being lazy, lying in bed on a Saturday morning with the covers over your head. You know you have homework and chores to do before you've planned to meet your friend later. Suddenly, something moves you to jump out of bed. In that split second, it might seem you planned ahead to get out of bed, but what really happened was that your unconscious mind sent an electrical signal from your brain to tell your body to move, and once you began to move, your conscious mind approved the action. It might have seemed like you made a deliberate decision to get up, but that was just your mind playing tricks on you.

This intriguing scientific finding helps us understand how powerful your unconscious attitudes and dispositions are in shaping what you do (and who you become). Sparks is the name for this program because our unconscious intentions—that spark inside us that triggers our actions—is the ignition to the engine of our *self*. Some people live their lives on impulse, responding to the environment without much reflection. On the other end of the continuum, people who are most successful in their lives—people who are happy, have positive relationships with others, succeed in school and work—are those who are able to consciously regulate them*selves*. We can practice *self-habits* on a daily basis and train our brain to do the things that we have planned to do in order to be the person you want to become. Sparks is a way to cultivate your *readiness potential* to meet your true potential.

The Sparks Curriculum

Most curriculum programs in school consist of a list of knowledge, skills, and understandings that are taught by teachers in lessons. Teachers assign students into groups, and teach them things, like math, reading, science, and social studies. The traditional curriculum faces the teacher. Sparks is different. Instead of facing the teacher, the Sparks curriculum faces you. It speaks to you directly, giving suggestions and support to help you make good decisions. Instead of teaching subjects, the curriculum of Sparks teaches the self (*your* self). Of course, it is important for you to learn to read, write, do math, and know science and social studies. But you can easily learn these things, and so much more, when the curriculum is focused on helping you to develop your *self*. Self-direction, self-determination, self-organization, self-competence, and self-regulation are the curriculum of Sparks.

This guide will help you make a plan for your learning that will enable you to flourish. It will help you develop abilities to communicate and cooperate with others; to gain knowledge and skills that are important in the cultures you are a part of; to develop skills in using technology to satisfy the needs you have in order to successfully live your life; and opportunities to spend time doing the things you enjoy and developing your talents and potential. The special curriculum of Sparks is a way of doing school so that you can develop your *possible self*—the self that you have decided you want to become. The Sparks curriculum covers the necessary domains of learning listed in the box below.

Domains of Learning

Physical and emotional well-being
Literacy and symbolic communication
Numeracy and math
Cultural learning (knowledge of history, art, and science)
Technology and scientific inquiry
Recreation, leisure, and talent development
Social cognition (e.g., collaboration and social communication)
Self-regulation (your ability to control your thoughts and emotions)

The Sparks program is organized to help you create your own personal learning agenda that you can follow. The program provides ways that *you*, and not your teacher, make decisions about what to do and learn. This agenda is outlined in a weekly Workout Plan that you create with the help of an adult. Your Workout Plan consists of all the activities you need to complete in order to meet the goals that you have set for the week.

Self-responsibility

The Sparks curriculum will help you make a plan for you to develop yourself, but to succeed, the plan depends on ***self-responsibility***. You have responsibility to make your fullest effort *to achieve academically and to grow personally*. The plan will work if you take responsibility to self-regulate to standards you have identified to help guide your learning journey.

In order to create a Map laying out how to achieve your ambitions, you need to come up with a definition of what your ambitions are and the standards you will follow to reach them. To do this, you will work with an adult who can help you create Curriculum Maps aligned with your goals in foundational academic domains (math, science, social studies, and English language arts).

Learning Cultures®

In order to develop your intellect and to learn what you need in order to succeed academically, you need to have opportunities to take part in special learning activities. First, you need time each day to work on your own learning agenda and to take action to meet your goals. Second, you need time each day to interact with others, to cooperate with them to solve problems, and to exchange perspectives and to reason cooperatively with them in order to expand the way you think about things.

In order to provide you with these essential opportunities to learn, your school uses a program called Learning Cultures®. Learning Cultures is a system of activities that are used to structure time in your day. These opportunities are called Formats. Each Format comes with a set of directions that explain how to participate in the activity. Like games with rules, the Formats are a structured form of play. Learning Cultures is designed so that when you play by the rules of the Formats, you have all the opportunities you need in order to succeed academically and flourish. There are Formats for all of the activities described in Table 5.1.

The Sparks Activity Plan

The Sparks plan is organized into a series of activities that help you identify your goals and develop your learning agenda. The activities help you take stock of who you are as a learner, identify important learning accomplishments, identify your academic ambitions, and make a plan to achieve them. Each activity is described below, with directions for how to complete it. If you follow these activities, you will have all the opportunity you need to meet high learning standards and to achieve your potential.

Activity #1: Create an Outline of the Story of Your Life and Development

Create a timeline of your achievements that represent the *big moments* in your personal history of development. These can be moments of triumph. But they can also be moments of failure, when disappointment or disaster caused you to examine yourself and make positive changes (Table 5.2).

92 *A Pedagogy for the Self*

Table 5.1 Learning Cultures Formats

Work Time: daily blocks of time to carry out activities on your Workout Plan, and to do activities that develop your academic abilities in each of the primary academic subjects of Math, Reading, Writing, and Science/Social Studies.
Cooperative Unison Reading: an opportunity to read a text in a small group to exchange perspectives and reason cooperatively with others. It takes place for 30 minutes, four times weekly.
Integrative Math: a group activity that lets you solve mathematical problems collaboratively with peers. It takes place for 30 minutes, twice weekly.
Learning Conference: an opportunity to solve an academic problem by using and integrating different parts of your mind and your memory and applying critical and logical reasoning. It takes place for 15 minutes, weekly.
Learning Share: an opportunity to share an academic achievement with peers. It takes place monthly.
Writing Conference: an opportunity to receive extensive feedback on a writing project. It takes place twice monthly.
Writing Share: an opportunity to receive peer feedback on a writing project. It takes place monthly.
Learning Teams: an opportunity to cooperate with peers to learn the formal curriculum in academic subjects of science and social studies. It takes place for 30 minutes, four times weekly.
Language Games: an opportunity to learn a new language. It takes place twice weekly, for 60 minutes.
Pretend Play: an opportunity to play with toys and to exercise your imagination. It takes place twice weekly for 30 minutes (for children in Pre-k through 1st grade)

Table 5.2 Personal development timeline

Early childhood, ages 3–5
Middle childhood, ages 6–12
Adolescence, ages 12–21

Activity #2: Develop Your Learning Identity

Now spend time thinking about who you currently are and who you want to become by answering the questions, below. Do this activity with a friend or another person whose opinion you value. Write your responses in your journal.

1. What things do I love to do? What makes me happy?
2. What are two things I know really well or know a lot about?
3. What are two things others think I do really well or know a lot about?
4. What are two things I want to know more about or do better?
5. What are things that someone else I know is really good at doing or knowledgeable about that I would like to know or do, too?
6. What are two ways I work well with others? What are two things that others would say about how I get along with people?
7. What are two personal characteristics that interfere with how well I work with others? What are two things others would say about how well I work with people?
8. What are two things I don't like to do or feel I don't know very much about, but wish I did?
9. What are two things I have been trying that I don't feel confident about or interested in and feel like giving up? Before I decide to give up, are there things I might want try in order to improve?

10. Who are the people in my life who help me become the best person I can be? What opportunities do I need to create in order to spend time with them?
11. What challenges do I want to overcome in order to achieve my goals?
12. What changes in my behavior do I need to make in order to become who I want to be and to achieve my goals and ambitions?
13. What do I want to accomplish in the long term? How will I know I achieved my goals?

>   After two years:
>   After five years:
>   After ten years:

Activity #3: Identify Long-Term Academic Goals

Spend time thinking about the academic goals you want to achieve this year and how to develop an action plan to ensure you meet them. Begin by answering the question: what do I want to accomplish in the short term, after the end of this year in the academic domains of Literacy, Math, Science, Social Studies? See the sample of short-term, year-end goals in the box below.

Sample long-term achievements

Pass the state reading test
Pass the state math test
Improve my reading ability by one grade level by the end of the year/catch up to grade-level standards in reading
Improve my writing fluency by 10 words a minute by the end of the year
Learn the U.S. state history curriculum and pass the state U.S. history test
Apply and gain admission to college
Write a resume and get a job

Activity #4: Create Curriculum Maps to Guide Your Self-Directed Program of Academic Development

The Sparks curriculum helps you create academic plans that are organized make sure you meet high learning standards independently, without having to depend on a teacher to transmit knowledge. This objective is achieved through a process of self-directed learning based on a Curriculum Map that you create from formal learning standards in Math, Science, and Social Studies.

This is how you create your Curriculum Maps. With the assistance of an adult, identify formal learning standards in key academic disciplines that you intend to study this school year. Print copies of the standards in each domain for your grade level, and compile them to create your own Learning Standards Reference Book.

In creating a Curriculum Map, you translate the formal standards into a sequence of actionable goals or questions that can be learned or answered. For example, if you are a 9th-grade student in New York State, you would start with New York State Global History and Geography Standard 9.1 on the Development of Civilization states. The Standards states: "The development of agriculture enabled the rise of the first civilizations, located primarily along river valleys; these complex societies were influenced by geographic conditions, and shared a number of defining political, social, and economic characteristics." To translate this standard into an entry on your Curriculum Map, you translate the statement into an actionable question. You might write: "How did the development of agriculture enable the rise of the first civilizations? How were these complex societies, located primarily along river valleys, influenced by geographic conditions? What defining political, social, and economic characteristics did they share?" You would progress in this fashion until you have translated the entire 9th-grade Global History Standards into a Curriculum Map. Recommended standards are listed in the box below.

Literacy	Common Core State Standards in Reading, Writing, Language, Listening, and Speaking
Math	New York State Next Generation Mathematical Learning Standards for grade-level skills KhanAcademy.com courses at grade level
Science	Next Generation Science Standards at grade level Crashcourse.com KhanAacdemy.com

Social Studies
  Grade 6: Eastern and Western hemispheres, through early human societies
  Grade 7: U.S. History
  Grade 8: U.S. History/Big History
  Grade 9: Global History I
  Grade 10: Global History II
  Grade 11: U.S. History
  Grade 12: Economics and entrepreneurship
	Sources:
	New York State Social Studies Framework, K-8 and 9-12
	Crashcourse.com (Big History; Global History I and II; U.S. History)

Recreation: identify an area in which you are attempting to develop your talent. Identify a source of knowledge you can refer to in developing standards for accomplishment.	

To create a 7th-grade Math Curriculum Map, refer to KhanAcademy.org, 7th-grade math, and translate topic content into questions, as illustrated in the box below.

> **7th-grade Math Curriculum Map, questions derived from KhanAcademy.org.**
>
> What are negative numbers?
> How do you subtract negative numbers?
> How do you add and subtract with negatives on the number line?
> How do you add and subtract integers?
> How do you add and subtract negative fractions?
> How do you add and subtract word problems with negatives?
> What is absolute value?
> What are the properties of addition and subtraction?
> How do you add and subtract negative numbers with variables?

Creating Curriculum Maps for a given subject is a big project. Plan to create Curriculum Maps in teams with your peers so that you can distribute responsibility and combine your efforts.

Once you have created your Curriculum Maps, divide the content into either nine, four-week units or six, six-week units (or other units of time that structure your school's grading period). Your Map will structure your independent learning agenda.

Common Core State Standards (CCSS) in English language arts, for Reading, Writing, Language, and Listening and Speaking, are not mapped in a linear manner in the same way as standards in Math, Science, or Social Studies. Instead, the CCSS English language arts standards are used as a reference for assessment within the context of curriculum activities. For example, you will make reference to the Writing standards in the Writing Conference, when you identify the places in your writing that serve as examples of meeting the standards. You do not need to map ELA standards because the Format protocols specify how they are used.

Activity #5: Create a Daily Learning Regimen

To meet high learning standards by the end of the school year, you will need to challenge yourself to learn a lot each day.

First, make sure you become familiar with the Activity Inventory, which appears at the end of this chapter. The Activity Inventory outlines fun and engaging activities that you can incorporate into your daily work regimen to develop your talents and academic abilities according to your own terms.

Another way you will achieve your potential is by forming new habits and routines that improve your opportunities to learn. In order for the Sparks program to work for you, you need to do the work of creating powerful new routines and work habits. The foundational routines and habits of the Sparks program are described below. But these are just a starting place. As you begin to have more clarity about who you want to become, you will expand the repertoire of activities that are part of your daily regimen.

Play

Develop your passions and potential by spending an hour each day doing something that brings joy, nurtures creativity, and develops talent (cooking, drawing, coding, painting, playing music, dancing, helping others). In other words, take an hour each day to *play*. Spend time every day doing an activity for the sheer pleasure of recreation and enjoyment rather than because you have an obligation to get something done. Mindless surfing of the internet does not count. Plan ahead and make it possible to do something that will allow you to stretch your mind and body into new spaces that develop your talents and potential (e.g., do art, play a new sport, cook a new recipe).

Practice Wellness

Plan to spend 30 minutes a day taking care of your body. Do exercise (run, walk, do calisthenics, yoga, or lift weights). Practice mindfulness (see suggestions in the Activity Inventory). Play soccer or basketball with friends. Whatever you do, have fun while you do it.

Learning Regimen

Make a commitment to learn something new every day. Maintain an agenda of the new things that you need to know and be able to do. Use your daily Work Time to develop

Background and to develop your talents and potential. Practice mathematical operations. Learn to code. Learn to play an instrument. Take care of your body by learning about the science of nutrition and exercise. Constantly revise your plan of action to achieve your goals.

Reading Regimen, for Fluent Readers

It's your responsibility to carve out time each day to read. Plan to read for at least 30 minutes per day. Reading is the most efficient way you gain access to the information that is distributed across cultures, providing a way of taking energy from the environment to expand your mind. The more you read, the more information-energy you absorb, and the more you expand your mental capacities. Daily reading also helps you develop reading fluency, or your ability to effortlessly decode ideas from the text on the page.

It is helpful to know something about the history of reading to appreciate the power you have at your disposal through reading. Before writing was invented about 5,000 years ago, ideas could only be transmitted from one person to the other through direct verbal communication. After the invention of writing, knowledge could now be transmitted beyond immediate context of time and space. Ideas could now be passed efficiently through history, from one generation to the next, and across cultures. Writing opened up new ways for human beings to think and build ideas off of one another. The ability to extend thinking through the medium of writing enabled human beings to develop branches of knowledge that helped to explain the mysteries of the universe and create new technologies to solve problems. Science, philosophy, mathematics, and history were all made possible through the power of writing.

The word **manuscript** means writing by hand (Manu=hand; Script=writing). The invention of the printing press was a giant leap for humanity. Prior to the invention of the printing press, texts had to be written or copied by hand. With the advent of the printing press, it became possible for people to tell long, richly-detailed accounts of their stories and share their view of the world in a new form of text called the *novel*. One of the best ways to get a glimpse of the world from the view of someone else is by reading a novel or autobiography. By reading, you literally alter the way you consciously think about the world. Just like you get to pick your friends, you also get to select who you want to become by read as a way to cultivate your mind.

For most of history, access to knowledge was restricted. Since the invention of writing, literacy—knowing how to read and write—was privilege restricted to the elite in society. Only the children of wealthy families had the opportunity to go to school. Universal, compulsory education was not common until the last century in the United States.

You are among the most fortunate of humans in all of civilization's most fortunate. You have the privilege of a free education that provides social opportunities that you can use to your greatest advantage and to gain control over the circumstances of your life. Not only do you have access to a formal education, you are also living at a time when information is at your fingertips. People of our ancestor's generations had to rely on other people to tell them information or to access it in books that were rare, expensive, and impossible to access without the skills to read. In modern times, in the age of the internet, you can control your own access to knowledge.

Reading is a solemn privilege, so value it. Become ***well read***. People who are well read are informed and knowledgeable as a result of extensive reading. If you want to become well read, what kind of literature do you think you need to read? What do you want to become informed and knowledgeable about?

Reading responsibilities should include the following:

- Keep a reading log. In the log, keep a wish list of the texts you want to read as well as a log of your daily reading activity. Peruse all of the possible text forms in the Genre Inventory.
- Read for fictional novels, magazines, blogs, autobiographies, biographies, short stories, and plays.
- Read two accounts of history from different perspectives.
- Read contemporary works and works from past centuries.
- Read newspapers and articles from informational periodicals. Track weekly national and international stories from at least two different news outlets, each with a different perspective.
- Read for research proposes. Read textbooks, educational websites, and academic papers.
- Reread familiar texts to develop reading fluency. Select from your favorite past Cooperative Unison Reading texts or reread a favorite novel.
- Read poems and song lyrics.
- Read texts you are considering as exemplars for your own writing.
- Read two-faced texts—those that have at least two possible meanings (irony, satire, parody, riddles).
- Read foundational and primary source documents that are of special historical interest.
- At the beginning of every month, take stock of your reading habits and think about how you want to alter them. Review your achievements and outline your ambitions. Evaluate how well you achieved your goals and make goals for your next monthly reading journey.

Reading Regimen, for Emerging Readers

This daily plan provides the emergent reader with a proven routine to develop basic reading skills.

1. *Daily reading.* Read for 20 minutes a day. For 10 minutes, read books that are familiar to you and that you have read before. Keep a special folder for your favorite familiar texts. You can make your own familiar reading books by asking an adult to transcribe a story that you tell them. For the other 10 minutes, read books that are new to you. Make sure to select unfamiliar books that are on your reading level (meaning that you can easily decode at least 9 out of 10 words).
2. *Daily writing.* Write for at least 20 minutes a day. Use the 1,000 Word Card as a reference when you don't know how to spell a word.
3. *Passage puzzles.* Put together a passage puzzle each day. Collect a quote or a passage from a book. Write it on a sentence strip. Cut the strip into individual words. Store the quote in an envelope. Keep a collection of passage puzzles to choose from.
4. Create an alphabet book. Collect a new word each day and illustrate it. (To create your book, use a three-ring binder with tabs for each letter of the alphabet.)
5. Play with letters and words. Using letter tiles, make and break words from the family of "rimes" in Table 5.3. Select a base "rime" and make words by adding letters or letter blends (e.g., b-ack; sm-ack; r-ack). Do two families a day.

Table 5.3 Common word phonograms

-ack	-eat	-ice	-ock	-uck
-ail	-ell	-ick	-oke	-ug
-ain	-est	-ide	-op	-ump
-ake		-ight	-ore	-unk
-ame		-ill	-ot	
-an		-in		
-ank		-ine		
-ap		-ing		
-ash		-ink		
-at		-ip		
-ate		-it		
-aw				
-ay				

Source: Wylie and Durrell (1970).

Writing Regimen

Writing is a form of mindfulness. It creates a kind of healthy tunnel-vision by forcing your mind to think about the topic of your writing. Write every day for at least 30 minutes for the purpose of carrying out your goals and intentions. Daily writing develops writing fluency, which means you can transpose ideas effortlessly onto the page. Writing gives you the power to manage your own thinking and consciousness and to influence the thinking of others. Writing is a skill that can give you power and control over your world.

You can write anything you want, in any genre form, so long as you write for a purpose that you care about. The other expectation for your writing is that you constantly vary the purpose of your writing. Use writing to *inform or explain, to give an opinion or make an argument*, and *to narrate or tell a story*. Constantly rotate across these three purposes. Use the Genre Inventory (Appendix 3, www.routledge.com/9780367458591) to keep track of the written genre forms you write (and read). If you're stuck for a writing topic, see the prompts in the box below for inspiration.

Writing prompts

1. A turn of bad luck that ended up having a silver lining.
2. A time you made a silk purse out of a sow's ear. Or a time you turned lemons into lemonade.
3. Something about the place where you are from that says the most about who you are.
4. The most fun you ever had with your best friend.
5. The time you surprised yourself by how hard you were driven to achieve a lofty goal.
6. A memorable romantic experience (one that you feel comfortable sharing with others).
7. The memory that had the most impact in making you believe in something you care about.
8. Something someone did to make you angry/happy/sad.
9. A time you were frightened.
10. Another story you'd like to tell.

A little writing every day turns into a volume over time. The prolific author, Stephen King, set a daily writing goal of 2,000 words. No matter what, he always wrote 2,000 words a day. For King, day upon day of writing resulted in dozens of published novels.

Writing responsibilities should include the following:

1. Keep a daily writing journal, and never go a day without writing a line. Use your journal to keep lists of goals. Use it to remind yourself of what you are grateful for. Use it to explore what you believe, what you intend to do, and how you feel. Use an online journal app, like Penzu.com, or pick a paper journal with a cover that reflects your identity.
2. If you are seven years of age or older, you should plan to play Genre Practice: draft, revise, and polish an "extended" piece of writing every two weeks using the guidelines, below. These compositions should reflect writing over extended timeframes (for research, reflection, and revision) for a range of discipline-specific tasks, purposes, and audiences (CCSS, Literacy.W.3.10).

Feedback. During the course of your writing process, make sure to share your piece with others for feedback at least *twice* throughout the writing process of assignments you submit to be evaluated for a grade. You should plan to share drafts of these works in Writing Conferences with adults or Writing Shares with your classmates to receive feedback. Incorporate feedback as you revise your piece. Deep, substantive revision is an expectation for each piece of writing you submit. While superficial revision touches the surface blemishes, such as spelling or punctuation errors, deep revision involves major surgery, going deep into the piece and adjusting the bones of its structure to create the species of animal that can perform the task you have in mind. Use the Writing Conference Record to document your intentions as a writer and the feedback you receive.

Exemplars. Collect two pieces of writing that can serve as exemplars in your writing process to imitate and inspire your writing. Study these pieces using the Genre Collection Probes (Appendix 5, www.routledge.com/9780367458591). Ask friends and adults to help you find exemplars if you have trouble finding them on your own, or if you don't know exactly what one is.

Annotate. Create a version of your final draft for annotation. Annotate your piece by analyzing where your writing demonstrates that you achieved a competence outlined in the Common Core Standards for Writing and Language. Also annotate your draft with reference to where you applied feedback to revise the writing. Annotate by hand or use an annotation app, like Diigo.com.

Self-assess. Refer to a reliable set of criteria to assess your writing (e.g., Common Core State Standards for Writing or the 6+1 Trait® Rubrics for writing at http://education-northwest.org/traits/traits-rubrics).

Portfolio. Keep a portfolio of your writing so that you can reflect over time on the range and quality of your writing efforts.

Repeat, and repeat again. Repeat this process every two weeks, and, by the end of the year take pride in how you created more than one-dozen high-quality pieces of writing that enabled you to carry out your own intentions and succeeded in increasing your personal power.

Play Genre Practice

Genre Practice (McCallister, 2008) is the process of using the medium of writing to perform a goal or an action, or to determine the goal or action of an author of a text. When you have something meaningful to say, and a clear idea of how you want your reader to respond thoughtfully, you play Genre Practice by carefully choosing the writing form or genre that is best suited to the achievement of your goal.

Genre Practice is a way to use imitation to develop your writing ability. Plagiarism is the dishonest act of taking of another's work and representing them as your own. Genre Practice is the completely honest act of using a strategy of another writer about how to structure a text in a certain way to accomplish a specific purpose. Genre Practice is the art of imitation in the medium of writing. Honest authors do not take the work of others and represent it as their own. But effective authors are open to inspiration and borrow conventions from others to make their writing more successful.

Genre Practice is inspired by two ideas. A *genre* is a way to describe a certain type or category of text that accomplishes a certain kind of purpose by using a common set of conventions. For example, a riddle is genre. It is a kind of text that is a play on words. It always says one thing, but means something else. To be considered a riddle, a text has to follow a certain set of "rules." For example, a riddle is typically short; it is approached as a puzzle that must not only be read, but in order to succeed as a "user" of the riddle, must also be *solved*. *Practice* is a way that human beings refine and improve their skill. If you were to use Genre Practice to develop your skill as a riddle writer, you would practice writing riddles, for sure. But you would also read examples of riddles, study how they are put together, try out your riddles to see how others respond to them, and revise them. You would continue this form of Genre Practice until you became a renowned riddle writer or until you found something better to do.

Writing forms, like riddles, succeed in accomplishing an action by using conventions that have been handed down through history. For example, school report cards are structured in a particular way because of the information that they present and the way they have been used. Subway or road maps look a certain way because of the conventions developed by map makers and users. Readers aren't just passive decoders of texts. They are *users* who have learned how to p*lay by the rules* of whatever text form or genre they are reading.

In traditional writing programs found in schools, teachers decide which writing forms students will learn. They typically present a lock-step series of activities intended to guide the writer to develop a certain type of writing by executing the teacher's directives. These writing programs emphasize the teacher's intentions, not the learners. These contrived writing activities prevent learning the very phenomenon that enables a writer to succeed: to employ conventional ways of saying things in writing in order to successfully achieve a purpose. Nobody can do that for you. You have to learn to do it yourself. These intricate social competencies cannot be learned by following teacher directives. They cannot be spoon-fed or dispensed in "do now" activities like a daily dose of vitamins. These skills can only be acquired through practice and use. Within the context of the Learning Cultures Formats, you employ Genre Practice as a tool for meaningful self-expression. You take part in frequent cycles of drafting and sharing your writing, receiving feedback, and making constant improvements to what you are trying to do through your writing.

Develop Background

Background is memory of skill, knowledge, and dispositions that are wired into your body's neural circuits. You draw upon this memory in new situations, where it is useful. For example, the sounds that certain letters make, the meaning of familiar words, the knowledge you have of how words are spelled and pronounced, the social etiquette you rely on to get along with others, are all forms of Background. Background is stored in our bodies to help us survive by providing experience resources we need to react immediately and automatically in situations. If you are trying to develop any given ability—like writing, reading, or doing math—having a solid foundation of relevant forms of Background is essential. For example, knowing math facts or how to spell common words means that you will not have to stop and think how to calculate or spell when you are in a situation in which these abilities are needed.

Practice Prolepsis

Prolepsis is the representation of a thing before it exists or occurs. You practice prolepsis when you argue with another person and anticipate their objection ahead of time in order to strengthen your argument. The Sparks and Learning Cultures practices incorporate principles of prolepsis. You gain command of your world by tracking down the formal expectations for the curriculum ahead, using it to create a plan of action.

Make Lists

Lists are a writing genre that describes a future you want to come true. Make lists of the books you want to read, the documentaries you want to watch, the tasks you need to accomplish, the Cooperative Unison Reading texts you want to share with others. Keep your lists in your journal, so you can constantly reflect on them and revise them. You can organize your life by organizing your lists into categories in order of priority and importance. You can use fun list-making software applications, like Listly (http://list.ly/), which lets you post your lists to other social media platforms. Lists are statements of priorities, and reveal something important about who you are.

Develop Language Capacities

Language is an important form of social competence. Languages developed so that people who shared the same culture could communicate and store information to help them survive. Our native language marks us as a member of our native culture. But that does not mean you cannot expand the number of cultures you are able to participate in by expanding your language competencies and learning to use language in new ways.

For example, every national language has a "standard" dialect. This standard is usually determined by the ways language is used by the group of people in the culture with the most power and influence. You can hear the standard dialect when you listen to the national news reports from the most influential news outlets. When you are able to learn to use the "standard" dialect of a language in situations when it works to your advantage, you give yourself opportunity to gain access to power. It's like having a special costume to wear. It is not something you would choose to wear all the time, but it allows you to play a part when you want to. Having multiple dialects, or languages, at your disposal expands the possible social worlds that you can choose to inhabit.

How do you develop a dialect? Just practice. Find time to interact with language users, listen, imitate, and practice until your new language becomes second nature. Train your mouth to say new words with sounds you're not used to making. Pronouncing an unfamiliar word in a different language can feel like a mouth full of marbles. But practice saying it a few times until it rolls off your tongue like a native speaker. Use the Language Games Format with a group of friends, and make the experience of learning a new language fun.

Activity #6: Developing a Weekly Workout Plan to Develop and Achieve Short-Term Academic Goals

Now that you've established some long-term goals, and have made a commitment to habits and routines that will give you opportunities to meet them, the next step is to make short, actionable goals for how to use daily opportunities.

Make a List

To accomplish this, each week you will take stock of the things that you need to complete by the end of the week. This process helps you translate your long-term, aspirational goals into short-term doable ones. You can start by making a list in your journal, like the sample in the box below.

Short-term goals

Write birthday party invitations
Complete a biology experiment
Write a chapter in my history book
Learn five new math skills (to keep pace with the curriculum in Algebra class)
Learn three new vocabulary words
Learn about photosynthesis (for Biology class)
Read three chapters in my novel
Research the causes of the American Revolution (for U.S. History class)
Write a history brief for my Learning Group
Scan two newspapers each day
Write an email to a friend
Clean the fish tank
Finish knitting the hat
Paint a still-life in watercolor
Learn to bake a new recipe
Take a trip to a far-away, distant land via YouTube (create a top-10 destinations and travel to a new one each week)
Spend a couple of hours learning a new language
Learn a new song on a musical instrument/compose a digital music composition

---

Make a Workout Plan

Next, make your weekly Workout Plan (McCallister, 2015). The Plan prompts you to reflect on your progress in activities listed in Table 5.4 and helps you see what you need to do in the main regimen categories described earlier. The Plan helps you meet academic goals and non-academic goals that help you create time in your life to do the things that make you happy and develop your talents (see Appendix 1 (www.routledge.com/9780367458591) and Workout Plan).

Plan Your Agenda in the Formats

Now that you've developed a weekly Workout Plan, consider how you will best use time and opportunity to accomplish your goals. The Learning Cultures program provides

Table 5.4 Workout plan activities

Behavior (the way you conduct yourself)
Mindfulness (the way you control your thinking)
Writing
Reading
Learning
Recreation (the way you develop your talents and interests)
Miscellaneous

opportunities to take part in learning Formats as a context to meet your academic learning goals. Each week you should plan how you intend to utilize the Learning Cultures Formats to your best advantage to achieve your short-term goals. See the Uses of the Learning Cultures Formats in Tables 5.5 and 5.6.

Table 5.5 Uses of the Learning Cultures Formats

Format	*How to plan for it*
Work Time	Plan ahead what activities you need to do in order to achieve your academic goals in each subject.
Cooperative Unison Reading	Think ahead about what texts or ideas you want to have the opportunity to share with others. What text should you select to provide you with the opportunity to share mental states with others in a way that will help you flourish?
Integrative Math	What math concepts do you need support to understand? If you are a group leader, select a problem that will help you develop your thinking in intentional ways. If not, sign up to join a group that will help you learn what you do not yet know.
Learning Conference	Prepare for your Learning Conference by identifying ahead of time something in the curriculum that challenged you and left you with a problem that you cannot solve on your own.
Learning Share	Think about an academic triumph you achieved in a Learning Conference that you believe says something important about you that you want others to know.
Writing Conference	Plan ahead by selecting a piece of writing that you feel challenged to successfully develop and that you think would benefit from if you had strong guidance from another person.
Writing Share	Plan ahead by selecting a piece of writing that you can improve by hearing how others would suggest to change it in order to make it work better.
Learning Teams	Plan time to do the tasks assigned to you by your group. Think about the information that you need to access and which sources can best serve your needs.
Language Games	What language are you trying to learn? What kind of game do you want to play in order to learn it?
Pretend Play	What toy or object do you want to play with? How can you imagine using it as a prop to help you overcome adversity?

Track Your Progress

Some kids dread getting back scores on assessments. But not you! Because, when you follow your Workout Plan, when the scores come back, they just tell you how awesome you are. Yep, if you follow your plan, your Background will develop. Each time you take an assessment, the numbers are going to be proof of your hard effort. Print the Assessment Tracker (see Appendix 2, www.routledge.com/9780367458591) and keep it with your Workout Plan.

Table 5.6 Sample weekly schedule

Time	Monday	Tuesday	Wednesday	Thursday	Friday	Saturday
8:30	Work Time (math)	Work Time (reading)	Work Time (math)	Work Time (reading)	Work Time (math)	Clean room
9:30	Work Time (science)	Work Time (social studies)	Work Time (science)	Work Time (social studies)	Work Time (reading)	Work Time
10:30	Writing Work Time	Writing Work Time	Writing Work Time	Writing Work Time	Writing Conference and Workout Plan for next week	Recreation
11:30	Learning Conference and Workout Plan	Language Games	Cooperative Unison Reading or Learning Teams	Language Games	Cooperative Unison Reading or Learning Teams	Free
12:30	Lunch and Recreation	Lunch and Recreation	Lunch and Recreation	Lunch and Recreation	Lunch and Recreation	Work Time
1:30	Cooperative Unison Reading or Learning Teams	Cooking or science lab	Work Time	Cooperative Unison Reading or Learning Teams	Writing Share	Free
2:30	Recreation	Recreation	Recreation	Recreation	Recreation	Free

Remote applications

The Learning Cultures® Remote educational program is organized to support personalized, self-directed learning in pursuit of intellectual discipline. The Learning Cultures® Remote program includes two components. First, learners adhere to a daily academic Workout Plans comprising independent, self-selected activities they have determined they need to do to meet their short-term academic goals. Second, learners take part in the routine social activities of the Formats. Teachers use the Format protocols to structure their teleconference meetings with learners.

Remote group learning plans are developed using a combination of Format structures and curriculum activities.

Sample Remote Plan I

    8:30–10:00: Work Time
    10:00–10:30: Convene for Cooperative Unison Reading or Learning Teams (small-group Zoom)
    10:30–11:30: Work Time
    11:30: Lunch
    12:00: Walk the dog
    12:30: Learning Conference with a teacher (one-on-one Zoom)
    1:00: Work Time

2:00: Writing Share (large-group Zoom)
2:30: Recreation

Sample Remote Plan II

Each week rotating group leaders take turns selecting classmates to join their Learning Groups of no more than five people. Learning Groups meet each day to share this two-hour agenda (with a break in between). Time before and after Learning Groups is spent in Work Time and Recreation.

Journal share: every person shares an excerpt from their journal (30 minutes)
News gossip: everyone takes part in a conversation about issues in the news (20 minutes)
Learning Conference: each day, one learner shares an academic challenge they cannot resolve, receiving support from the Group to work through the Learning Conference protocol (one student each day for 20 minutes) (Refer to Learning Conference Rubric)
Writing Share: each day one learner shares their writing and receives feedback (one student each day for 20 minutes) (Refer to Writing Share Rubric)
Cooperative Unison Reading: Each day the Learning Group takes part in a Cooperative Unison Reading session (30 minutes) (Refer to Unison Reading Rubric)

Happiness

What is the key to happiness? There are as many answers to this question as there are people in the world. But to end this tome and start you on your journey, I will offer a few good ideas about how you can cultivate your own sense of happiness.

The psychologist Mihaly Csikszentmihalyi (Csik-szent-mi-halyi) urges us to embrace what he calls the *evolutionary self* (1993). An evolutionary self is in control of its own growth. The evolutionary self protects its freedom by preserving its own psychic energy and eliminating forces that drain it.

Csikszentmihalyi (1993) offers a few simple strategies.

- Guard your freedom to control your own mind
- Desire only that which is necessary
- Be satisfied with what makes you unique
- Identify with a source of greater good
- Reflect on your life and identify sources that drain your psychic energy
- Create your own rules to live by.

You alone are in control of your mind. But at any given time, you are surrounded by countless forces that cause you to react and that can cause distraction. Some of these distracting forces are in the immediate environment. Some are in the culture. Some are in your body. Reflect on your life to identify what forces seem to be draining your energy. Are you giving in to impulses that cause you not to be happy with who you are? Does one of your friends take advantage of you? Does your need to have certain possessions that you cannot afford make you feel bad? All of these situations drain psychic energy from your evolutionary *self*. You cannot change others. You cannot change the values of your culture. But you can change yourself and the way you think about things. Change your thinking to preserve your psychic energy.

Find a sense of belonging with social groups whose values you respect and share. Try to find larger meaning in the things that you do. Eliminate people from your close social network who bring you down. Expand your social networks to include people that bring you up. Meet new people who share your values and make new friends to support your self-evolution.

Sparks is a guide you can follow to develop your own happiness. It is not an elixir you can drink every day. It is not a ready-made set of rules you can follow. It is a set of guidelines you can follow to make your own rules that help you to be in control of your life, to make good choices, to do things you care about, to surround yourself with people who bring out your better self, and to control how you use your mind. Doing these things *will* make you happy.

So, to close: follow Sparks. Create rules for yourself. Live by them. And have a good and happy life.

PART II: THE ACTIVITY INVENTORY

This Activity Inventory gives you a menu of possibilities for things you can do during Work Time to develop your talents, interests, and academic abilities. Choose from among these options to make your weekly Workout Plan.

Dispositions

Recipe for Success

Activities that promote high levels of skill with low levels of challenge will help a student approach Work Time in a relaxed and confident state of mind. Encourage the student to create a "recipe for success" or a "warm up" plan by selecting activities from target categories that allow them to practice using skills in contexts that are not too challenging.

One-Minute Meditation

Check the clock. For 60 seconds, focus your attention on your breathing. You can keep your eyes open or closed. When you mind begins to wander, concentrate on your breathing. Once you can control your mind for a minute, add another minute the next time.

Close Observation

Focus on an object that is close to you—a pencil, notebook, or eraser will do. Check the clock. Look at the object for a full minute. Control your mind so that you refrain from thinking about the object. Just look at it.

End-the-distraction

If you're like most people, your mind tunes into some distractions and sticks with them—a voice in the hallway, a siren wailing outside, the chatter of kids in the corner. Try to be in tune with these distractions. But the next time you notice your mind following-into one of these distractions, take note of what it is. Then train your thinking to focus on the sound of your breathing. Focus for 10 breaths to allow your mind to steer clear of the distraction and back to the task at hand.

Count to 5

If you sometimes respond to others with comments that are perceived as negative, try this. Stop yourself from responding immediately. Instead of reacting to their words, think about them. And slowly count to five. Give yourself a chance to think about the response or reaction that will be most helpful to you.

Count to 100

To rescue your mind from distracting or intrusive thoughts, or to stop perseverating over ideas that you can't seem to make go away, close your eyes and count to 100. Each time you say a new number, visualize it in your mind's eye. If you find you lose your train of thought mid-way through counting, you MUST start over. It may take you a dozen times before you make it all the way to 100. But once you do, your mind will be refreshed (Source: this is some wise person's good idea whose name this author has forgotten).

Make a Gratitude List

Write 10 things you are grateful for and explain the reason why. This activity will teach you to see your metaphorical life's *glass* is half full rather than half empty.

Take Stock of What You Believe

Write in your journal every day an answer to these questions: What do you believe? What do you intend or aim for? How do you feel? Over time, you'll strengthen your core sense of who you are, your power to take action in the world, and your understanding of what is important to you.

Refresh Your Body

If you feel like you want to explode, get a "burst pass." Step into the corner or hallway and do a seven-minute workout. You can google "scientific 7" to learn how to get a complete workout in a short period of time by doing just 12 exercises.

Tell the Story from the Other Perspective

Sometimes when you feel strong emotions about what someone else has done to you, try an exercise to shift your perspective. This exercise won't make the problem go away. But it will help you feel differently about it. Tell a once-upon-a-time story about the incident from the perspective of the person who made you feel bad. Tell the story in a way that explains the protagonist's motivations for acting in the way they did.

Banish the "Uglies"

All of us are occasionally cursed by the tendency to obsess or become preoccupied with the things that bother us. Our mind wanders to encircle these "uglies," to replay them, analyze them, *engage* with them. Unless you are disciplined and learn to fight back, the uglies can own you! Whenever an ugly has taken your thinking captive so that you are unable to think thoughts that allow you to grow and be happy, take steps to banish it from your thinking.

1. Catch your mind when it starts to focus on a negative situation or someone who you feel has done you wrong.
2. Tell yourself, "Self, you are allowing yourself to let the person/situation cause you further harm. Don't take the bait!" As if you were reading a part in a book about a nasty character or bad situation, read further. Force your mind into thinking about the next situation or a person who brings out the best in you.
3. If it helps, remove yourself from the situation. Find someone to be with who brings out the "lovelies" in you.

Math Background Skills

Math Facts

The more thoroughly you have memorized your math facts, the quicker and more accurate you will be in solving cognitively challenging math problems. Dedicate whatever time is necessary to memorize all of your math facts. Take a diagnostic assessment to identify which facts you still have not memorized. Make a schedule to master the facts you need to memorize, and stick to your plan.

Math Skills

Background abilities in math allow you to complete tasks quickly and automatically so that you can channel your energy into challenging forms of thinking without wasting time on simple cognitive tasks. Find your skill level on khan.org. Make a work plan so that you master all of the skills that will allow you to bring your background abilities in line with math content at your grade level.

Word Chunking

Collect words that you and your classmates breached over in Cooperative Unison Reading groups. Chunk or divide the word into phonemes. A phoneme is the combination of letters that forms a speech sound (e.g., the word *speech* has four phonemes—"s"; "p"; "ee"; "ch") (four words a day).

Meaning Segment

Collect words that you and your classmates breached over in Cooperative Unison Reading groups. Chunk or divide the word into morphemes. Morphemes are the smallest unit of the word that carries meaning (teaser: word meaning has two morphemes) (four words a day).

Language Sense

Select a quote, rhyme, or poem of choice. Write or have someone write the text in large font. Cut out each word. Practice rereading the text by putting the word pieces back together as you would a puzzle.

Spelling and Sight Word Recognition

Use Word Cards to become a stupendous speller and a quick reader. There is no reason to mis-spell the words you write when you use the Word Card to double-check spelling accuracy of words you're uncertain about. Using the card will help build spelling background abilities. It will also help build sight word recognition for the target words you write and the words you will read as you identify the target word. Encoding (a fancy word for putting speech into writing) words that you use frequently is a way of deepening your memory for accurate word spelling.

Literacy Background: Vocabulary

Word Web

The greater your vocabulary, the more widely you are able to communicate with others across a breadth of social situations. Never miss a chance to not only learn a new word, but to *own it*. When in Cooperative Unison Reading, circle unknown words that you and your group have breached for. Once you discover the pronunciation, say the word together three times (*say it to own it*). During Work Time, create a word web. Write the word in the center of a piece of paper or index card. In the bottom of the space, write the fragment of the sentence in which the word appeared. Then draw "spider legs" from the word leading to as many definitions as you can find.

BBC Wordmaster is a fun game that helps develop vocabulary skills. Students have to supply a correct word to complete a statement. Clues to unknown words are given in the form of dictionary definitions. See:
   http://rentanadviser.com/en/games/bbcwordmaster/default.aspx (daily).

Crossword Puzzles

Finding the word for a thing is usually as tricky as defining the word by the things it can mean. Do crossword puzzles to exercise your mental wires that connect your memories of words to the things they represent.

Keep a Word Collection

Each time you breach a new word, add it to your word book (get one from the teacher or make one from a small notebook that you've alphabetized). Record the word, its pronunciation (you can find the pronunciation key in the dictionary or online), and its meaning.

Genre Practice

Play Genre Practice

Understanding how forms of expression work in different writing genre categories helps you expand your awareness as a reader about how texts work and as a writer about how to use conventions of writing to achieve your purpose as a writer. Use the Writing Genres Inventory to keep track of the writing genre forms you read and write.

Annotating Text Action

Successful reading depends as much on recognizing what a text is trying to do or accomplish as it is reading words accurately or fast. Practice analyzing how texts work to accomplish the aims of their authors. Select a busy text (one that has a lot going on, like the front page of a "subway paper" or the cover of "People Magazine"). With a friend or solo, identify what each text element seems to be doing. Title, subtitle, bi-lines, pictures, icons, and captions are all used by people who want to act on the sensibilities of their readers. What are the "devices" used in the text trying to *DO*? Annotate your text with small post-it notes or number the elements in marker and cross-reference them to a table of explanations on a separate sheet of paper.

Begin a Genre Collection

A *genre* is a category of artistic expression. Forms of creation in a particular category function to *do* things in certain ways using common conventions, or common ways of achieving an effect. Puns, comics, poems, editorials, feature stories, and advertisements are all genres. Create a Genre Collection of texts *do* things in ways that interest you. Each week, select a new text to add to your Genre Collection. Use the Genre Collection Probe (see Appendix 5, www.routledge.com/9780367458591). Follow the Probe to analyze your text. Write a one paragraph synthesis of your reflections. Share your collection with a friend (see Appendix 45 for sample Genre Collections, www.routledge.com/9780367458591).

Analyzing the Action of a Text

Select a *short* text that you consider *super* challenging. Working from the sentence level, analyze each sentence for what the author is trying to *do* in the sentence. Then work at the section level (paragraph, stanza). Once you've analyzed all that the author is trying to do with the sentences in a chunk, think about how they add up to shape the author's larger action or intention. Then work at the whole-text level, analyzing the intentions of the sections. As a whole, what is this text attempting to do? What are the most effective "tools" or "devices" the author used to perform the intended action?

Two-faced Texts

Have you ever heard someone say that a person is "two-faced"? That means that they you can't take them at face value. They say one thing to one person, and turn around and say something else to another. If someone is *two-faced*, you can't trust their action or words unless you are able to read them from *both faces*. Make sense? Texts can behave in the same way when the voice of the text is saying one thing, but meaning something else. You have to be sly to figure out the intended meaning. So practice! Select a "two-faced text"—a text that has a double meaning or that can mean more than one thing. Use the Unison Reading Log to do the following: 1) restate what the text actually says; 2) write what the text is attempting to say (the deeper or second meaning); 3) write how you would say what the text is trying to say, in your own words; and 4) tell why you selected this part of the text to write about (examples: memes, articles from The Onion; riddles, poems; song lyrics; satire/parody; jokes; advertisements).

Gist

Select a high-interest passage or article. Read the first paragraph, and summarize, in 20 words or less, what the author is trying to *do*. Next, read the second paragraph, and do the same thing. Read each subsequent paragraph and repeat the process. When you have read the complete text, summarize in 20 words or less what the author has attempted to do as a whole. Work in teams. Or make GIST-ing a game and work in multiple teams, then compare your summaries.

Analyzing Narrative

The human mind uses narrative thinking to organize and make sense of experience. Analyzing narratives can help you understand how others have made sense of experience. And by learning how others make sense of experience, you develop better ways to develop your own narrative ways of thinking. Use Cynthia's Narrative Worksheet to recount and analyze a personal story or a story from history. Use Jerome Bruner's Narrative Analysis Framework to dive even deeper into story analysis. Analyze your own story as a method to clarify your sense of self-identity, or use the Framework to do a sophisticated analysis of a story from literature or history.

Plan Your Reading Party

Picking a text for your Unison group can provide you with an opportunity to develop sophisticated thinking skills and to practice *mind reading*. It does this by causing you to have to think about a hypothetical group of people and what ideas will challenge or engage them. Selecting a text is the equivalent to deciding what music you will play or food you will serve at your birthday party. Use the Cooperative Unison Reading Text Selection Assignment activity to make your next text selection.

Learning

Breach

Knowing when you don't know something and having the courage and humility to speak up and resolve confusion is one of the marks of genius. Every day, in every class, take responsibility to embrace your confusions. Confusion brings on a mental state of *disequilibrium*, or being thrown off kilter because your current way of thinking about a thing is no longer useful. Confusion is your mind's way of telling you that you need to expand and reorganize your thinking to incorporate new information about the nature of reality. Some of us have the tendency to react to avoid confusion, and our natural tendency to *fight*, *freeze*, or *flee* sets in. The McCallister Method teaches you instead to embrace your confusions as rich opportunities to develop your mind. Each day, in Cooperative Unison Reading, you and others at the table *breach* to voice your confusions and discuss ways to resolve them. Keep a Breach Log to record the confusions you resolved. The Breach Log is a record of the ways you have expanded your mind.

Collective Learning Conference

Take a chance to become much smarter by doubling or tripling your thinking capacity! Identify a cognitive challenge in some curriculum area. Find a friend or two, and try to tackle the challenge through the steps provided in the Learning Conference Record. Make sure to record your thinking and the story of your success!

Audio-books

You are in charge of the person you will become. Your actions today wear a path toward the person you will be tomorrow. If you want to be wise and well informed, you need to be hungry for knowledge. Wide reading is one way you can feed your appetite for knowledge. It's a way of understanding the complex and fascinating world around you. "Read" an audio book every week. Try to read books by authors who will give you different perspectives on the things you are curious and care about (different periods of history; different genres of literature; different racial/cultural perspectives on similar issues; different issues; arguments or conflicts from opposite perspectives). Track down titles you want to read by talking to friends or searching free audio book data based on the internet. Start a list of books you want to read. Check out Librivox.org, audible.com, scribd.com, chirpbooks.com.

Documentary Diet

For all the same reasons books nourish your mind, documentaries do the same. Plan to watch two documentary films each week. Do some research to identify Use the Movie Menu as an initial reference. Explore free documentary sources by going to free documentary websites, and begin to make a priority list of the films you want to watch. Check out Freedocumentaries.org, documentaryhaven.com, Documentary.net, Documentarystorm, Documentary24.com, Documentarylog.com, Documentarytube.com, Science-documentaries.com, Documentaryguide.com.

Get a Library Card

The library is a trove of treasures of knowledge that are free for the taking. Get a library card, and plan to visit the library every two weeks. You can use your library card to sign up for an account at Kanopy.com to watch ad-free, high-quality films and series.

Scale a Comprehension Climbing Wall

Texts come in different forms of complexity. Simple texts communicate simple ideas. They use shorter sentences with common vocabulary words. Complex texts express more complicated ideas. They use longer sentences and less frequently used words. The levels of text complexity are sometimes referred to as Lexile levels (you can learn more about Lexile levels by going to Lexile.com). Just like scaling a wall, the higher you get in levels of complexity, the more challenging it becomes to understand what a text is trying to say. Simple texts are easier to comprehend. But more complex texts offer the chance to have access to more complicated ideas.

Practice reading complex texts. Read your way up a reading wall. Select a NewsELA story. Read the story at its simplest level. What is the story trying to say and do? Then read the next higher level. What more did you learn? Keep reading until you've scaled the wall and reached the story written in the highest level of complexity. Compare what the first story did and compare it to what the last story did. What cognitive strategies did you need to use to understand the more complex texts (e.g., look up words; relate one section of the text to another; research background information; read between the lines or make inferences)? Is there skill you used that you want to apply to your reading regimen?

Prove to Yourself You Are Smarter Than You Thought (and They Thought) You Were

If your score last year on the state test wasn't as high as you think it could be, give it another shot to prove to yourself that you can better your performance with improved effort. Read each question/problem like a sharp-witted detective. Use all your powers of reasoning to fully understand what the text is asking of you, and answer questions as carefully and thoughtfully as you would make a move in a game of chess.

Synchronized Thinking Processes

Daily Writing for Writing Fluency

Writing each and every day, write for at least 30 minutes to develop writing fluency, or the ability to synchronize your skills and apply them to an activity. You can track your writing fluency development over time. Every month or so, time yourself and write as quickly as you can. Write for three minutes. Every word you spell correctly counts as one point. As you develop, your fluency does too. You can compare your writing fluency to the average number of words written correctly in a period of time at each grade level featured in Table 5.7.

Table 5.7 CBM written expression administration norms

Grade	Writing time	Fall	Spring
1	3 minutes	8	14
2	3 minutes	24	31
3	3 minutes	36	36
4	5 minutes	41	46
5	5 minutes	51	67
6–12	7 minutes	44	58

Source: Malecki and Jewell (2003).

Daily Reading for Oral Reading Fluency

Select a text at your grade level. Find a partner to monitor your reading and to check for errors. Set a timer for one minute. Read the text as fast and fluently as possible. Record your score (words read minus number of errors). Compare your score to the grade-level averages in Table 5.8. Set a goal for next time, and practice improving your reading fluency by reading each day for at least 30 minutes.

Table 5.8 Oral reading fluency grade benchmarks

Grade	Correct words per minute, 50th percentile, fall	Correct words per minute, 50th percentile winter	Correct words per minute, 50th percentile spring
1	NA	29	60
2	50	84	100
3	83	97	112
4	94	120	133
5	121	133	146
6	132	145	146
7	131	140	153
8–12	138	146	155

Source: Hasbrouck and Tindal (2017).

Familiar Rereading

Rereading something you have already read will help you build speed and accuracy in reading. Each day, spend time doing some familiar rereading. Select an assortment of texts you want to reread. Keep them in a folder. Read one text each day from the folder (examples: Oral Reading Fluency passages; NewsELA passages; Big History passages; your peers' writing pieces; Unison passages; texts you're reading for your R-Team tasks; your horoscope; your favorite poems or passages from sacred texts).

Audiofiles

Create an audio-file in which you summarize or synthesize information or retell and analyze a narrative. See: https://soundcloud.com/.

Commitment and Discipline

Conference Preparedness

Every couple of weeks you have a Learning Conference with a guide. These Conferences are an important part of your training program. Be aware of the things that confuse you. Take responsibility to collect a breach for your Conference—a question or confusion that arose in your schoolwork that you are unable to resolve.

Maximize Your Time in the Formats

A tutor costs about $100 an hour! The training opportunities you get in school every day are free to you. In the United States, society invests an average of about $140 every day into the education of every child. By the time the average student finishes school, society will have invested about $325,000 in their education. If you make the most out of school, you will have stored powerful experiences into your body, in the neurons in your brain, into memories that will help you to be happy and successful. These memories are what is called *human capital*—the riches you store in your body that you can draw from through life. You need to make sure you make the most out of your experiences. Never again will society invest in you like it did when you were in school. So don't waste your opportunity! Think of ways you can make the most of your time in each Format. Make a plan to use the Formats to support your training program.

Organize Your Research

A mark of stellar scholarship is the ability to make your thinking and research findings transparent and available to others. To this end, you need to practice disciplined inquiry. Keep careful records of your research process by creating an Evidence Record to keep track of the information you find and the sources you use. Date each entry in your notebook.

6 The Cultural Capital Curriculum

...some day, please God, the children should have better nutrition than formal teaching.

Francis Parker (1900, p. 119)

The moment of death may well be distant from that of birth, but life is always too short when this space is poorly filled.

Jean-Jacques Rousseau (1920, p. 211)

To find out what one is fitted to do, and to secure an opportunity to do it, is the key to happiness.

John Dewey

Introduction

Academic achievement is commonly thought to be associated with unequal distribution of certain forms of human capital (Bridglall & Meroe, 2004). After-school arts and recreation activities, travel, access to quality food and nutrition education through informal family experiences, opportunities to participate in music lessons, and cultural arts activities are but a few of the kinds of supplemental educational experiences that enhance academic achievement. Learners from low socioeconomic status (SES) backgrounds typically have much more limited access to these kinds of experiences.

A significant concern for the criteria of equality of educational opportunity is the quality of learning environments and the degree to which these environments provide opportunities for the learning person to flourish. We become who we set our minds to be in the actions we take to carry out our intentions. Self-expression is a vital human liberty because it provides the *self* an environment to enact itself into being. The fullest forms of social opportunity, therefore, are those that provide generous access to rich and diverse environments, and which allow the learner to autonomously select experiences that suit their talents and proclivities. We have attempted to extend self-directed, self-organizing experiences to learners in the context of the academic curriculum. The Sparks curriculum provides the learner with a learner-centered academic program. The Learning Cultures Formats provide a curriculum of social interaction that supports academic development. The Cultural Capital Curriculum incorporates enrichment and so-called supplemental experiences into the school day and places them under the instructional budget, making them legitimate and sanctioned activities of the formal school curriculum.

The Cultural Capital Curriculum is designed to correct structural inequalities by creating opportunities for experiences that provide, as a matter of the formal school curriculum, precisely the kind of rich and enriching learning environments commonly thought to be supplemental to the formal curriculum. The commitment to these experiences is justified by the construct of equality of educational opportunity based on a criterion of adequacy for human flourishing and learning, described in Chapters 2 and 3. Since these forms of supplemental education are known to increase cultural capital, out of a commitment to justice, the formal school curriculum is now expanded to incorporate enrichment and creativity into the general education program. Far from being considered supplemental to the formal curriculum, these forms of learning must BECOME the curriculum.

The Cultural Capital Curriculum expands across five domains.

1 *Individual and cultural expression.* Human beings derive their sense of self-identity through the ways in which they identify with others through social activity. We signal who we are through forms of dress and ornamentation, means of communication and expression (talking, singing, dancing, making art and music), and self-sustenance (eating, drinking, playing, and resting). It is absolutely necessary that the curriculum of school be responsive to and supportive of the learner's cultural identity. But in addition to cultural responsivity, the curriculum should be also be culturally promotive, providing every possible opportunity for learners to explore the boundaries of new cultures and evolve new identities from their interactions within the new cultures they choose to inhabit.

2 *Recreation, enjoyment, and creative expression.* Increasingly, access to a basic education is rejected in recognition of every child's right to a quality education. This right is asserted in the United Nations Declaration of Human Rights, with a commitment to a curriculum that develops the child's personality and talent to the fullest potential. The U.N. framework for a rights-based education advocates the right to recreation, leisure, and play, promotes respect for the natural environment, supports participation in arts and culture, and provides access to knowledge from a diversity of sources (United Nations Children's Fund/UNESCO, 2007, p. 32).

3 *The dignity of work.* Upon the rise of industrialization, various social movements arose to counter the degradation and impoverishment of human existence in the aftermath of industrialization and the mechanization of systems of production. The Arts and Crafts movement in the fine and decorative arts, for example, was an effort to reject the use of machinery in the factory, to regain a sense of coherence of work as a form of activity that was lost through the division of labor in industrialization, and the re-infusion of tradition in material culture. The movement embraced a value for the functionality of everyday objects, the importance of taking pleasure and pride in work, the fundamental dignity of the worker, and expertise as a mode of economic independence. The Cultural Capital Curriculum promotes a sense of dignity in work.

4 *The natural world.* Human beings evolved to be in sync with and survive in the natural world. With the advent of compulsory schooling and the industrial school, the child was suddenly exiled from nature. For many children, being in a state of nature feels almost unnatural. The Cultural Capital Curriculum incorporates opportunities to learn within and from the natural world.

5 *Entrepreneurship.* Rich, varied experiences in multiple domains of culture provide a foundation of experience upon which children can make their lives as adults. These varied experiences can become the basis for vocational opportunities and means by which to participate in the economy. The Cultural Capital Curriculum proposed here presents experiential opportunities in the classroom that connect with industry sectors outside of school. An experientially rich curriculum that provides exposure to modes of living outside of school broadens future opportunity.

Every Day, Every Classroom

A range of activities are incorporated into the general education classroom as a matter of routine practice, and others are incorporated into the school-wide program. These activities fall into the domains of the natural world, games, classroom arts and crafts, the blank canvas curriculum, music, and dance. School-wide programs include sport, culinary arts, media lab, makers space, and the entrepreneur program. The Curriculum also includes "Workshops of Possibility," in which learners themselves determine new topics and activities to incorporate into the curriculum.

The Natural World

A Curriculum of Living Things: Pets

The classroom should be alive with living forms other than children. It is recommended that every community of 50 have four pets (so that each team has the opportunity to care for one animal). Pets promote well-being. They provide forms of physical contact, they promote happiness, relieve depression and anxiety, decrease blood pressure, cholesterol levels, and triglyceride levels, alleviate feelings of loneliness, increase opportunities for socialization, increase opportunities for exercise and outdoor activities, and lower risks of allergies (Centers for Disease Control and Prevention, 2020; Davis, 2020). Through a classroom "pet curriculum," children learn about different forms of animal life, their habits, behaviors, dietary needs, and exercise. Caring for a pet forces a concern for the interaction between animals and the environment, which serves as a foundation of knowledge and moral self-identity that can inform environmental activism in adulthood. The pet industry is a $99.0 billion industry (Box 6.1) (American Pet Products Association, 2020).

A Curriculum of Living Things: Horticulture

The horticulture component of the Cultural Capital Curriculum begins with the cooperative terrarium, which is a sealed container that contains soil and plants. The terrarium is a closed ecological system, which provides the opportunity for children to learn about

---

Box 6.1

Hypoallergenic pets

Birds
Bearded dragons
Fish
Gerbils
Guinea pigs (hairless or not)
Hamster (Syrian hamsters are hypoallergenic)
Lizards, geckos, and iguanas
Mice
Rabbits (Rex rabbits have a low shed count)
Snakes

the water cycle and photosynthesis and practice methods to harness these processes to keep their plants alive. In pairs or groups of three, children work cooperatively to plant and care for their terrarium. Cooperative responsibility in caring for their terrariums forces children to learn and use knowledge in ways that promotes a respect for the natural environment, an aspect of every child's right to a quality education (United Nations Children's Fund/UNESCO, 2007). Horticulture is currently a $13.8 billion industry.

Birding

Bird watching can be both a hobby and a way to participate in what is known as "citizen science" (described below). Birds are everywhere, and birding is a past-time that everyone can participate in. In fact, 47 million Americans are birders (Audubon, 2020). Every school should have several class-size sets of binoculars and copies of bird guides and apps for identifying birds (see Audubon.com). Birding activities include identifying birds by size, color, shape, habitat, behavior, sound, and season. Birding helps build awareness of weather patterns, environmental conditions, animal migration, climate change, and water conservation. It is fun, physically active, and social.

Citizen Science

Every child should have the opportunity to be a citizen scientist. Citizen scientists are amateur scientists who participate in contributing knowledge to the scientific community. Known as participatory monitoring or participatory action research, through a process of systematic observation and reporting, learners have opportunities to participate in advancing scientific research. Being a part of a scientific project relating to the natural world provides the opportunity to develop a respect for the natural environment and a sense of agency in caring for our planet. See Box 6.2 for citizen science websites.

Games

Games are a source of entertainment and play, and can teach skills and strategic thinking. A large menu of game options should be available to children during the daily Recreation Activity Block. Games are a context to learn and apply rules, to develop the ability to apply skills and strategies in situations, and to cooperate with others. Games usually involve an opponent. But we include toys that teach skills under the domain of games. Every classroom should be stocked with an abundance of games to play during Recreation (see Box 6.3).

Box 6.2

Citizen science internet communities

- INaturalist
- eBird
- Zooniverse

> **Box 6.3**
>
> **Game inventory**
>
> > Backgammon
> > Boggle
> > Card games (bridge, poker, and Rummy)
> > Charades
> > Checkers
> > Chess
> > Cribbage
> > Crossword puzzles
> > Dice games (Yahtzee and Poker dice)
> > Dominos
> > Jacks
> > Parcheesi
> > Pictionary
> > Ping pong
> > Scrabble
> > Scattegories
> > Sudoku
> > Tic-tac-toe
> > Yo-yos

Classroom Arts and Crafts

Independent Projects

Art is a form of imaginative expression through the creation of objects using a wide range of media. The classroom should be stocked with ample supplies the learners can use to create art, and simple guidelines that enable them to do art activities independently. Collect images of artwork for learners to refer to for inspiration, and provide them with links to websites to access helpful "how-to" videos. See Box 6.4 for art activities. The art market is a 67.4 billion industry (Artsy, 2020) and the arts industry as a whole adds $754 billion a year to the U.S. economy (Cascone, 2018).

> **Box 6.4**
>
> **Art activities**
>
> > Beading
> > Clay
> > Collage (tissue paper, cloth, photographs, cards, and other miscellaneous objects glued to a dry surface)
> > Coloring (Cray-pas, pastels, and crayons)
> > Crocheting
> > Drawing (charcoal, graphite, and colored pencils)
> > Embroidery

> Fingernail painting
> Knitting
> Makeup and face painting
> Painting (gouache, acrylic, and watercolor)
> Quilting
> Sculptures collage from everyday objects (collect buttons, costume jewelry, thread spools, silverware, toys, and bric-a-brac)
> Wire sculpture

The Blank Canvas Curriculum

School Uniforms

The blank canvas is a metaphor. It represents a new beginning, a space to fill, an invitation to create a unique form of expression. In the spirit of the blank canvas as a space to represent individuality, the school uniform is a project within the Cultural Capital Curriculum that is a game of creativity.

The base of the uniform is white. White anything: white-collared shirts, T-shirts, blouses, and dress shirts all count. White is the canvas of possibility. The shirt is void of color and design so that it can be filled by the hand of the designer. Shirts are the canvas of creation. They can be colored with fabric markers, embroidered, beaded, tie-dyed, inked, or serrated, as long as the expressions that are created do not constitute an infraction of the discipline code (e.g., no offensive, obscene, or denigrating expressions or images). The school uniform curriculum provides an opportunity for learners to display their talents and identities, and provide a way for adults to come to know who children are through their expressive talents. Shirts can be brought from home, but the school purchases white cotton T-shirts in bulk and provides five to each learner free of charge. The school uniform curriculum is an extension of the school's philosophy of self-expression, creativity, and social egalitarianism.

The school uniform policy provides an entry point to the history of dress reform, which stemmed from the women's suffrage movement of the late 19th century in reaction to the restrictive forms of women's couture of the period. The curriculum provides learners with opportunities to liberate themselves from the dictates of fashion and to approach their own wardrobe and habits of dress rationally and with a sense of purpose. The uniform policy reduces the pressure on families to pay for clothing and prevents learners from becoming preoccupied with the need to keep up with new fashion trends. Clothing has always been a medium of human self-expression. The school uniform curriculum provides the opportunity for learners to express themselves through material means with full intention and freedom to create.

Collaborative Art

Determine how many groups need to be formed in order to create teams of three learners. Randomly select names of enough learners to serve as team captains, and guide them in draft in which they take turns selecting from classmates in order to create their artistic team. The team will meet throughout the school year to plan and execute a work of art on a large, blank, pre-stretched 16″ × 24″ canvas. Pieces are sold at the end of the year in the school's auction gala.[1]

Individual Miniature Paintings

Miniature art is a specialized genre with a long history of traditions. Also called "painting in little," the painting size is no larger than a total of 25″, and objects are depicted in miniature. Encourage learners to explore the miniature art movement online and search for inspiration to create their own compositions.

Music and Dance

Music and dance are integrated into the educational program. The music and entertainment industry is worth $717 billion (SelectUSA, 2020).

Dance Time

Once a day, for 10 minutes, learners put down their work, get out of their seats, and dance. Responsibility to create the daily dance playlist revolves through pairs of classmates who take responsibility for hosting Dance Time. Learners post links to the musicians they select and provide a brief profile of the day's Dance Time featured artists.

Open Mic

Once a week, for 30 minutes, the Community holds an "Open Mic" show. Members of the community sign up to perform. On the day of their performance they present a "play bill," which features a brief personal bio and program description featuring background information about their performance.

Personal Play Lists

Every learner compiles a personal playlist of music that captures the essence of who they are. Playlists are limited to 20 pieces, so lists are continually being curated to reflect one's evolving sense of identity.

Curation of Music for Public Space

In teams, learners are continually deliberating about sounds and sources of music to feature on their curated playlists when it comes their turn to provide music for the Boxing Club and the Dining Room.

Electronic Piano

Every Community has its own electronic piano. Each day during Recreation Time, learners have the option to plug in the headphones and practice piano.

Writing Gallery

The Sparks program provides a personalized writing program, in which learners select writing topics and forms of their choice. The Writing Gallery is a social space. It is a physical display of heavy-gage plastic envelopes. Each envelope is an "exhibition space" belonging to a writer, who takes responsibility for curating the space throughout the year and refreshing the collection by adding new pieces as they see fit. The Writing Gallery is located on the corridor wall just outside the classroom, where works are on constant display to the public, as legitimate works of art. Pieces are never graded. The Wall creates an authentic opportunity for writers to engage with their public audience. Encourage learners to take occasional gallery walks to view the fascinating and whimsical forms of writing produced by their peers across the school community and to become inspired. Learners maintain their own "gallery space," by exhibiting a new piece each week.

Workshops of Possibility

The French biologist Francois Jacob coined the term workshops of possibility to describe what he called "night science"—the ideas that emerge from the subconscious and take the form initially through one's sense of intuition and the capacity for imagination. Only later do the ideas hatched in night science turn into the rational outcomes of "day science"—the kind of cold, logical arguments that get published in academic papers. The Workshops of Possibility are opportunities for learners to mess about in night science.

Every school develops a Workshops of Possibility curriculum. Workshops of Possibility are cultural niches that learners themselves develop. Unlike formal instruction, the agenda of Workshops of Possibility originates from children and is overseen by the PTA. The Workshops of Possibility program distributes power to make curriculum decisions into the hands of the people who are the most deeply invested in developing the capacities and potentials of children—the parents themselves. Space and resources are allocated to the Workshop Program so that parents have the means to achieve the ends that learners themselves deem worth pursuing. Workshops of Possibility are a true manifestation of community-based education.

The Student Government works in coordination with the Parent-Teacher Association to implement and maintain 10 Workshops of Possibility in the school. Workshops are high-quality enrichment environments organized around learners' passions and interests. Learners work with guides and parents to develop proposals to present to the student body. Through a democratic election process, Workshops are established. Members of the community are hired to serve as project managers. Project managers undergo requisite training to become a school paraprofessional. They manage project budgets, and work with the administration and PTA to procure resources, maintain equipment and facilities, and supervise learners' independent Work Time activities.

A portion of the instructional budget is reallocated to cover manager salaries, equipment, supplies, seed money, travel, or equipment rental. PTA members volunteer to work in Workshops and chaperone field trips. Workshops are a context to develop passions, talents, and interests. They also provide an important context to develop entrepreneurial skills; therefore, managers are hired with a concern for the degree to which they are active professionally in the area of expertise and the extent to which they can provide mentoring support to learners to develop their talents and explore ways to transform talent into a business enterprise. Workshops provide a cultural niche to explore ways to create value from talent and innovation, to translate creativity into products and services, and to explore the commercially-viable potential of creative endeavors. This program aligns with the goals of the 21st-century

> **Box 6.5**
>
> **Possible workshops of possibility**
>
> Archery
> Baking and cooking
> Biking
> Billiards
> Brass and woodwinds (trombone, saxophone, trumpet, clarinet, and flute)
> Camping/backpacking/hiking
> Coding
> Drama
> Fashion design
> Fencing
> Fooding
> Furniture upholstering and restoration
> Investing
> Machines
> Magic
> Metalworking
> Movie watching
> Percussion
> Photography
> Rock climbing
> Videography
> Strings (viola, violin, and bass)
> Textiles (quilting, sewing/costumes, and weaving)
> Thrifting
> Tiny living
> Travel
> Videography
> Woodworking
> Yoga

Youth Entrepreneurship Act of ESEA. Workshops are semi-permanent, installed for two-year periods at which point they must be put to vote for renewal. See Box 6.5 for a list of possible Workshops of Possibility.

Workshop of Possibility Cycles

Workshops of the Possibility run for a two-year cycle before they are put to vote for another cycle before the student body. In the Workshop election, every learner is given one vote by secret ballot. It is imperative that adults refrain from lobbying learners to support programs, as the decision should be made strictly based on consensus support. Reports of adult lobbying should be handled as a serious infraction of the school's code of honor.

Makers Space

Every school has a Makers Space, which is a permanent Workshop. A Makers Space is a collaborative, creative laboratory where learners can explore their interests using a

> **Box 6.6**
>
> **Top Makers Space materials and supplies**
>
> Arduino
> Batteries
> Cardboard
> Chibitronics
> Copper foil tape
> Cublets
> Dot and Dash
> Engino Brand
> GoldieBlox
> K'NEX
> Keva Structures
> Lego
> Lego Mindstorms
> Makeblock
> MakeyMakey
> Minecraft
> littleBits
> Ozobot
> Playdoh
> Qubits
> RaspberryPi
> Scratch (program and code stories)
> Snap Circuits
> Sphero
> SquishCircuits
> Startup Ecosystem
> Vex Robotics

variety of tools and materials. Makers Spaces are geared to help teach 21st-century learning skills that are useful in the fields of science, technology, engineering, and math (STEM). Maker Spaces provide opportunities to learn coding, robotics, metal, and wood working, 3D printing, and electronics (Box 6.6) (Makerspaces.com, 2020).

Entrepreneur Program

Agency and initiative are qualities that have never been more than they are now to high-school graduates, who will enter a rapidly-changing economic, political, social, and global world. Every learner in grades 9–12 takes part in the Entrepreneur Program, which develops concrete strategies for further education and successful participation in the economy upon graduation. The Entrepreneur Program seeks to support each learner to develop a preliminary life plan that includes postsecondary educational and vocational plans. The Entrepreneur Program includes three goals: 1) to support learners to develop skills and certifications needed to enter the workforce and to embark upon a high-skill career path immediately upon high-school graduation if they so desire; 2) to develop individualized plans to graduate in four years and to develop a postsecondary education plan;

and, 3) to enrich the high-school experience through professional and service-learning opportunities.

The Program begins with an onboarding experience in 9th grade, when learners take a future-planning self-assessment, create an initial career and education plan, and begin to consider distant ambitions. They begin to explore outlooks for occupations in terms of demand and pay rates. While the McCallister Model curriculum is designed to develop talents, interests, and potential, the Entrepreneur Program helps the learner develop strategies to capitalize on talents and interests as a means to create commercial value. Startup business model development is the core focus of the curriculum, providing context to identify key activities and value propositions, customer segments, costs, and revenue streams; to develop a brand essence and marketing strategies; and to develop and test a business model. Learners explore digital "gig economy" platforms, such as Etsy and Fiverr, and refine and use marketable skills as a source of income. Learners apply their developing, smart start-up strategies to post-secondary education planning. They research educational options and financial aid opportunities, and develop and complete a college application by their senior year in high school.

Field learning is integral to the Program, which seeks to build the learner's awareness of work and education opportunities outside of school. Learners identify sites for study (museums, cultural institutions, and events) and organize trips to align with learning standards in history, science, technology, and the arts. Using standards documents as planning tools, learners research opportunities and plan field itineraries. Field learning in Years I and II will be designed to provide foundational experiences in STEM, arts, and history. During Years III and IV, learners will begin working toward CTE endorsements, taking part in internships and/or work opportunities.

The Physical Education Curriculum

The physical education program includes two components: the Boxing program and the Yoga program. Fitness is a $87 billion industry (International Health, Racquet, and Sportsclub Association, 2020), and there were 408K jobs in 2018 in this faster-than-average growing industry (U.S. Bureau of Labor Statistics, 2020). Outdoor recreation is a $427 billion industry (U.S. Bureau of Economic Analysis, 2020).

The Boxing Club

It is recommended that schools develop a Boxing Club as the hub of its integrated athletics program. Boxing is the sport of choice for the school because it a form of competitive, hand-to-hand combat as ancient as schooling itself, dating back to ancient Sumer; it is inexpensive to set up and maintain; it provides a central hub within the school community that is fun, inclusive, and community-oriented; the sport cultivates discipline, self-control, strength, endurance, sportsmanship, coordination, cardiovascular fitness, confidence, and self-esteem. The Boxing Club is a fun place to hang out, supervised by no-nonsense coaches who work with every learner in the school to maintain a physical Workout Plan. In helping to develop Workout Plans, coaches help learners set goals, develop perseverance, endurance, self-discipline, and strength.

Everyone can do boxing, so it is socially inclusive. Most learners will prefer to use the Club as a place to socialize and work out. Some will choose to take part in supervised sparring (with protective gear, of course). And some will choose to step into the ring and compete with others.

The Club is open throughout the day. During school hours, the coaching team works with learners in classrooms to encourage self-regulation to the Format Rubrics. They leverage their relationships with learners to provide extra support, especially to those who exhibit challenging behaviors or have difficulty self-regulating to academic tasks.

Yoga

Yoga is a spiritual and ascetic discipline that emphasizes mind control through breath control, meditation, and bodily postures that are practiced for health, physical well-being, and relaxation. The Yoga Program is a context for learners to meditate and develop mindfulness, and to practice postures or asanas to develop flexibility and muscular strength.

Culinary Arts

The Culinary Arts Program provides learners with the opportunity to take part in the most primordial form of human activity—cooperatively sourcing, preparing, and eating food. Teams of learners rotate on a weekly basis to perform the following tasks: plan menus based on research-based dietary guidelines; source food; solicit bids; prepare and serve meals; clean up; and survey consumer satisfaction. Teams create the dining ambiance by selecting music, lighting, and décor. The cafeteria program features a family-style dining experience, common in the nation's elite private schools, but befitting to everyone.[2] The Culinary Arts Program provides social opportunities to learn about nutrition and health, consumer rights, and strategies to develop food independence for a future in which food instability is becoming a social problem that affects an ever-increasing segment of the population. Every school employs a resident Chef and Culinary Arts Manager to run the Program. The Culinary Arts program aligns to several ESEA food and nutrition program and economics and entrepreneur program allocations. The food marketing system (including food service and food retailing) supplied 1.77 trillion of food in 2019 (United States Department of Agriculture, 2020).[3] FoodTech is one of the largest new business startup sectors and food service jobs employ 5.407 million people in one of the fastest-growing industries (U.S. Bureau of Labor Statistics, 2020).

Media Lab

The Media Lab serves as both a library and a technology hub where learners can receive technical support with computer software applications. Through the McCallister-Genre Practice writing program, learners utilize relevant technologies to produce text forms (e.g., Adobe Suite programs such as InDesign, Photoshop, Illustrator, Animate, Dreamweaver, After Effects, audio software, AutoCAD, and other programs that can be purchased upon learners' requests).

School Hires

To implement the Workshops of Possibility program, the School Newspaper program, the Makers program, Pets, Horticulture, Birding and Citizen Science, Classroom-arts, Boxing Club, Culinary Arts programs, and Workshops of Possibility, the school will need to make a number of non-instructional hires.[4] The school administration should appoint a search committee for each of the positions to include members of the PTA, an adult staff member representative, and a student representative.

Annual Gala

Each year the PTA hosts an annual Gala fundraiser to generate revenue for the Workshop program (in K-8) and for driver's education classes in high school for schools.[5] Learners volunteer to serve on the Gala Program Committee, who develops the program to include entertainment, refreshments, and an inventory of lots to be sold. They develop and implement an advertising plan and produce an auction catalog.

Revising the Programmatic Priorities of Schooling

Traditional schooling has emphasized teacher-directed instruction in academic subjects. The majority of current school budgets funds teachers of academic subjects to the exclusion of enrichment programs. The McCallister Method provides an approach that reduces reliance on the teaching function within the system and successfully transfers responsibility for learning to learners themselves, significantly reducing resources needed for instruction. Reduction in the need for an academic teaching force creates new possibilities for expanding enrichment programs. The traditional school schedule also privileges academic subjects, which is almost wholly devoted to instruction in math, reading, and content subjects with fractional time devoted to art, music, and physical education. Since the learner-driven practices of the McCallister Method intensify the effects of academic learning, learners require less time in the school schedule to meet learning standards, freeing time for recreation, play, and cultural enrichment.

Conclusion

> Give the pupils something to do, not something to learn; and the doing is of such a nature as to demand thinking; learning naturally results.
>
> John Dewey

Progressive educators since Rousseau have honored the relevance of experience and freedom of expression. But in the context of compulsory education, the riches of experiential education have been restricted to children of privilege. The establishments of current schooling have frozen into place structural systems that maintain these inequities. For example, the typical district curriculum is dictated by state mandates that specify the majority of seat time for learners to be spent in academic subjects. Districts purchase commercial curriculum programs that emphasize literacy, numeracy, and traditional content subjects. And Teacher union contracts restrict instructional responsibilities to traditional academic activities.

The Cultural Capital Curriculum has not yet been implemented in a school, unlike the Sparks and Learning Cultures programs. No opportunity has yet appeared. But perhaps now that a quality curriculum is viewed as a fundamental human right, it will not take another century before our schools provide children with experientially rich experiences as a component of the formal school curriculum. The Cultural Capital Curriculum is offered here merely as a North Star to inspire future thinking about the range of content that should be provided in a high-quality curriculum.

Notes

1. The gala is an annual ritual in elite private schools and some selective public schools. The gala is a fundraising event that can be staged in any school, creating an opportunity for learners to plan, publicize, and stage an event to raise funds to support the Workshops of Possibility Curriculum.

2. It is not surprising that our efficiency-oriented industrial schools neglect important life lessons that can be learned through experiences with food, nutrition, and the communal experience of breaking bread together. I once lost out on a job opportunity as a legal assistant in a U.S. Senate office when I was invited to dinner at the Legislative Director's home with a fellow receptionist colleague. I didn't come from a home background where I had any exposure to the dinner party genre of social interaction, and felt uncomfortable. I didn't realize it at the time, but the dinner party was a clandestine job interview, and I wasn't prepared to perform in that context. Years later, as an assistant teacher at the Buckley School, where bankers, former and future presidents and film personalities sent their sons to be educated, we sat every day to dine with the boys in our class. We passed dishes of food while chatting informally and hearing the stories of the lives of our students. The academic curriculum was typical of schools everywhere. But the unofficial dining hall curriculum was a form of privilege that I had never seen in a school before. It gave learners opportunities to engage in the art of conversation and practice dining etiquette. The cafeteria in most public schools is a slop hall that learners avoid once they are old enough. In NYC, beginning in middle school, most children are permitted to leave the school for "out lunch," and taking "school lunch" is a social stigma in some schools. But the "restaurant curriculum," at about $200 per month, is a luxury most families cannot afford. Our public school system invests $23.6435B annually in food service, about $8B more than the amount spent on Title I programs. These educational expenditures could be more used pedagogically.
3. Since food service is a massive industry sector, it is a source of future employment. Culinary arts experiences allow learners to develop a source of cultural capital that is potentially valuable from the standpoint of career readiness.
4. NYC UFT union contract Article 7(A)(6)(a) restrictions concerning legitimate "professional activities" currently preclude teachers from carrying out the responsibilities outlined in the Cultural Capital curriculum.
5. Driving has become a social privilege as schools phase out driver education programs. The school takes responsibility for ensuring every child has the opportunity to learn to drive.

Section III
An Activity Curriculum: The Learning Cultures Formats

7 The Learning Environment and the Work Time Format

> Work which remains permeated with the play attitude is art—in quality if not in conventional designation.
>
> John Dewey (1916/1944, p. 206)

Introduction

Learning is a self-directed, self-organizing, transactional process, and the Work Time Format is a context in which the learner autonomously selects from rich environmental experiences in order to take what they need to become who they are (Plomin, 2019; Tucker-Drob, Briley, & Harden, 2013). Within such a *transactive* paradigm, learning opportunities are understood to be *taken*, rather than *given* (Plomin, 2019). The learner-driven, transactional paradigm replaces the traditional transmission paradigm, and forces a reconceptualization of the fundamental way that learners use time and space in the classroom.

The McCallister Model provides a multi-faceted curriculum that is centered on learners' interests, intentions, and proclivities. Sparks, described in Chapter 5, is the personalized learning program that all learners follow to create short- and long-term learning plans and agendas for individualized learning activities. The Work Time Format and the Learning Cultures Learning Environment provide the spatial and temporal conditions that learners need in order to succeed in meeting the personal goals they have identified for themselves through Sparks. This chapter explains the Work Time Format and the Learning Cultures Learning Environment. Rubrics for each appear at the end of each Format explanation.

The Work Time Format

The Work Time Format is an extended period of time that is programmed into every learner's school day. Work Time provides every learner with fundamental freedoms of thought, movement, expression, and association, so long as they exercise free will in compliance with formal expectations outlined in the Work Time Rubric. They can move about as they see fit, associate with peers of their choice, and express themselves freely. They have maximal freedom to select the activities they need to do in order to meet the goals they have set for themselves in the Workout Plan. These freedoms provide a context for learners to develop work habits and self-responsibility. They also provide a context of continuity of opportunity to carry out their own intentions, develop their talents, and achieve their potential. The primary aim of Work Time is to help learners develop independence and self-determination.

An Activity Curriculum

The Work Time Rubric outlines role, rules, and routines that learners must follow to meet their Work Time obligations (see Work Time Rubric at the end of this chapter). The Rubric specifies how time and materials are used, and makes the expectation that learners will be engaged at all times with projects that they have selected to meet formal curriculum goals.

Every learner's personalized learning plan for Work Time is spelled out in their Workout Plan, discussed in Chapter 5 (see Appendix 1, www.routledge.com/9780367458591). Learners meet the expectations for Work Time as long as they use time, materials, and opportunities in ways that enable them to meet their goals. Over time, as they comply to Work Time expectations, learners internalize dispositions of self-responsibility, self-regulation, persistence, and a positive orientation toward academic goals.

Work Time also serves a democratic function within the school community, creating the conditions necessary for a civil culture of rights and individuality, in which the freest possible forms of association are encouraged.

Timeframe

When the McCallister Model is used in an industrial school infrastructure, in which a teacher is assigned to a class of 30-some students, the daily Work Time block is typically 60–70 minutes in length, and activity choices relate to the subject being taught. In an ecosystem design, where programmatic flexibility is possible, or in remote learning or home-schooling situations, Work Time can last as long several hours, interrupted only by opportunities to take part in other Formats.

Since students pursue activities of their own choice, and not those assigned by someone else, they are motivated to approach Work Time with the same intensity as they approach play or games. During Work Time, students read (during Reading Block), write (during Writing Block), do activities of their choice, freely use space and materials, and freely collaborate with peers.

In addition, Work Time supports socially active, collaborative learning so that students can practice interdependence and cooperation. Students independently select activities that align with their learning goals, following specific procedures for choosing an activity.

Primary Aims of Work Time

1. To provide a context of fundamental freedom (of thought, movement, affiliation, and speech) in which to exercise will in conforming to sanctioned academic and social norms.
2. To provide consistent, ongoing opportunities to autonomously select rich environmental experiences and personally meaningful activities that enable the development of talent and potential.
3. To practice self-organization and self-direction by choosing, creating, and adjusting learning experiences that align with intentions and propensities.
4. To practice persistence, resourcefulness, and to apply self-determination in pursuit of learning goals.
5. To develop autonomy, independence, and self-responsibility in pursuit of learning goals.
6. To cultivate positive emotions and a positive sense of self-identity in relation to formal academic expectations.

7 To take part in intrinsically motivating activities that develop knowledge and background abilities that are of service to future academic achievement.
8 To practice integrating all of the components of the mind—higher cognitive functions, socio-relational processes, emotional self-regulation—in the context of authentic and meaningful academic activities.
9 To experience full immersion and engagement in activities that demand intense, sustained concentration, and which support achievement of socially valued academic goals.

Materials and Learning Environment

The classroom environment contains appropriate cues to support learner independence in negotiating Work Time expectations (e.g., evidence that expectations for Work Time responsibilities have been taught). Digital, print, and material resources pertaining to the curriculum or course subject are available and plentiful. The *Activity Arc* (see Appendix 12, www.routledge.com/9780367458591), a symbolic representation of the execution of a complete intentional activity (McCallister), is posted in the classroom and used as a reference by learners and guides to navigate the completion of activities. Assessment records that are relevant to the learner's achievement trajectory are maintained and accessible to learners and guides; and Conference and Intervention records show evidence of development.

Work Time Procedures

Set up. Children will have been taught Work Time expectations and will know how to responsibly exercise fundamental freedoms within the classroom. They are familiar with the Work Time Rubric. They are aware of learning standards and activity choices that align with curriculum goals of the course. An Activity Inventory for each course or subject outlines a full range of activities that align with the curriculum. Each learner creates their own Workout Plan, the parameters of which are determined by the course expectations and activity options. Adults meet periodically with learners to help them plan and modify their Workout Plan.

1 The learner has maximal freedom to select independent or cooperative activities that align with learning goals and curriculum objectives; they enjoy freedom of movement in the environment (assigned seating is not permitted); and they exercise freedom of expression and social affiliation, interacting freely and promotively with others while maintaining focus on Work Time responsibilities. They adhere to activity protocols and instructions, and take responsibility to access materials and resources needed to meet their Work Time goals. The learner is on-task, non-disruptive and appears engaged, attentive, and focused on work. They take responsibility for self-regulating emotions and behaviors to Work Time expectations, and can articulate consequences for failing to meet personal responsibilities. They are aware of expectations for productivity and achievement, and have goals to ensure success. Their selected activities relate to personal short- and long-term goals and curriculum objectives, and they can defend activity choices.
2 The guide utilizes Work Time as a context for curriculum-embedded assessment and instruction. The adult confers with learners as required for assessment or instructional purposes or when necessary, to encourage self-regulation to Work Time expectations. They monitor learner activity and encourage learner self-regulation to Work Time Format expectations. The guide adheres to expectations to enforce and secure positive social norms (see Social Norms Rubric). Work Time is the context for

other Formats (Cooperative Unison Reading, Learning Conferences, and Writing Conferences), so guides use time productively to tend to their responsibilities.
3   At the conclusion of Work Time, the learner takes responsibility to put away materials and quickly transitions to the next activity.

Discussion

> If education does not afford opportunity for wholesome recreation and train capacity for seeking and finding it, the suppressed instincts find all sorts of illicit outlets, sometimes overt, sometimes confined to indulgence of the imagination. Education has no more serious responsibility than making adequate provision for enjoyment of recreative leisure; not only for the sake of immediate health, but still more if possible for the sake of lasting effect upon habits of mind.
>
> John Dewey (1916/1944, p. 205)

If the Activity Block is the artist's studio, the Work Time Format is the canvas onto which the learner brings their intentions into reality. The curriculum of Work Time unfolds as learners exercise their fundamental freedoms to take responsibility to meet learning goals that they themselves have made in what is called a Workout Plan. The Workout Plan, described in the Sparks curriculum, is the learner's oath to meet their obligation to achieve their goals. Every Workout Plan outlines both the goals learners have made and the activities they have identified in order to meet them. The curriculum materializes as learners use the environment to get what they need in order to satisfy both their own needs and propensities and their obligations to others.

A Home for the Activity Arc

Recall in Chapter 3 the discussion of the Activity Arc—a visual representation of the complete execution of an intentional activity. It is a symbol for intention and agency and a metaphor for self-directed accomplishments. The Arc can represent a small activity, such as the expression of an intention in the form of a sentence, or a larger and more complex activity such as the completion of a research paper. The continuous form of the Arc is deceptive, because in reality the completion of an intentional activity is characterized by gaps—gaps between the reason to act and the decision to act, between the decision and the onset of action, and the gap between action and its continuation to completion (Searle, 2010). These gaps, Searle (2010) points out, are free will. Will must be recruited to forge ahead in the face of challenge, uncertainty, confusion, and lack of confidence. Ongoing opportunities to independently plan, execute, and complete challenging goals provides the right conditions to practice will and to develop the dispositions of tenacity and persistence. The Activity Arc is taught in the form of a lesson, as a reference point for self-regulation; and it is posted in the classroom as a tangible reminder of the power and importance of will.

Development and Curriculum

Work Time gives learners the opportunity to develop the *habitus* in important ways. The *habitus* is the physical embodiment of the way the person perceives their reality. It is the sum of knowledge, habits, and dispositions, coded into the body in memories held in the synaptic connections between the neurons, that influence one's propensities to act, think, and feel. The Work Time curriculum consists of self-selected activities that spring from a combination of *choice* and *obligation*. Learners have the choice to do anything they wish to do, so long as it promotes their previously determined learning goals. This freedom gives learners the fullest possible opportunity to self-organize and self-regulate. The only force that determines what they must do is their moral obligation to the commitments they have made. Work Time is the medium in which the child learns to manage their own mind and to use it to accomplish their goals.

When learners take part in the curriculum activities outlined in their Workout Plan, they create their own situations for learning. The curriculum activities that learners select from are ones that have been designed to target specific psychological processes, such as cultural learning (e.g., learning sanctioned or canonical knowledge), communication (e.g., learning how written language works), cooperative thinking (e.g., learning how to think about things by coordinating mental states with others), and collaboration (e.g., learning how to participate with others to achieve goals). The carefully-designed palate of possible learning activities that learners can select from are *proleptic* in nature—meaning they bring into the present situation opportunities to practice competencies that will be required in future situations. Their design all but eliminates the possibility that learners will waste time and their opportunity to learn.

Self-identity

Work Time provides a zone in which the learner can develop their sense of self. We come to know ourselves and to form our identity through the reflections of the "*I*" or the ego upon our actions and experiences (Mead, 1934/1972). Work Time provides ample space for the "I" self to develop. Because it provides learners with maximal freedom of action, Work Time widens the parameters of possible activity to the broadest extent possible, thereby also widening the resources for the development of self-identity.

Self-regulation

Since the learner spends most of the school day in the Work Time Format, the McCallister Model emphasizes the development of self-management and self-regulation. Self-management necessarily requires the cognitive capacities of self-regulation and the need to recruit and integrate all the components of the mind to achieve goals. Continuity of opportunity to practice cognitive control and self-regulation, over time, gives rise to dispositions of self-sufficiency, persistence, and discipline.

As we learned in Chapter 3, the *readiness potential* is the unconscious spark of intention in all living organisms that triggers a reaction to stimulation in the environment a split second before the organism becomes consciously aware of the action. In other words, we are predisposed to act in certain ways that initially escape conscious attention. We practice self-regulation when we exercise free will to override impulse in order to more appropriately conform to more rational norms. In this cognitive process, a part of our brain—the *cingulate*—detects potential conflict in the environment, and sends a signal to another part of the upper brain—the *dorsolateral prefrontal cortex*—to increase top-down or executive control to resolve the conflict (Banich & Compton, 2018). Ample opportunity to exercise free will to make good choices and comply with norms is a way to practice executive self-regulation.

Over time, the learner's dispositions or underlying intentional states shift and change. They begin to use Work Time as an opportunity to enter a state of *flow* and to be fully immersed in the activities they choose (Csikszentmihalyi, 1990). With continued practice and experience taking part in activities designed to develop competencies, the learner becomes more inclined to want to take part in these activities. The readiness potential now fires the spark of intention to rouse positive learning behaviors. Engagement and motivation increase, and the learner becomes more self-determined. Dispositions of avoidance evolve into dispositions of enthusiasm. Observe Work Time over the course of days, weeks, and months, and you will notice these trends in learners. Trends in engagement and self-regulated learning correlate with positive trends in achievement metrics collected through informal assessments. As learners become more aware of the relationship between effort, engagement, and growth, they become more motivated. Engagement stimulates development, and evidence of development stimulates motivation and engagement.

Talent and Potential

Genetic proclivities are the primary force of development. They are like voices that "whisper" suggestions to the learner to select, modify, and create experiences from the environment that are necessary in order to become who they are meant to be (Plomin, 2018). Work Time is a medium for learners to develop their talents and interests by providing maximal freedom to make choices that suit interests and proclivities. By having opportunities to select activities that promote intellective competencies, learners take an active role in developing their own intellects.

Social Grooming

All social animals take part in what is called *social grooming*, a form of behavior in which animals tend to one another's physical appearance as a means of establishing closeness (e.g., finger grooming by picking insects out of a conspecifics fur). Through evolution, as human social groups grew in size, the one-on-one, time intensive finger grooming was no longer sustainable. Humans needed more efficient ways to groom one another in larger numbers while still reaping the benefits of physical closeness. Gossip became the human solution to large-group social grooming needs (Dunbar, 2004). Gossip satisfies our basic need to establish closeness to others by sharing in the endlessly fascinating, mostly irrelevant details of the minutia of everyday existence. Gossip functions to stimulate positive emotions and enhance well-being. Gossip fosters social connections and stimulates protective hormones that help us stay calm and relaxed. In fact, it is recommended that we humans get a good daily dose of at least 20 minutes of gossip (Dunbar, 2004). Work Time is the perfect environment for gossip. Fundamental freedoms of thought, movement, expression, and association provide the perfect conditions in which the forces of social gravity draw children together for good, healthy gossip as a backdrop to Work Time. So if you happen to overhear a little tête-à-tête during Work Time, let it go. Far from being "off-task," gossip is a sign that learners are doing what they are supposed to do to care for themselves and one another.

Self-regulation

The Work Time environment is a canvass of possibility for the teacher or guide to develop the culture. Just like executive regulation works internally, inside the person, to send down signals from the upper mind to the lower mind to alter behavior, the adult is the executive in the classroom culture, issuing directives to children who are not adhering to agreed-upon collective norms for behavior. So-called misbehaviors are valuable opportunities for children to learn how to self-regulate to expectations. When they occur, the teacher or guide intervenes directly to involve the learner in an opportunity to think about their behavior in relation to the norms and invites them to self-regulate. What might have been thought of as discipline problems in a traditional temple-prison-factory conception of school now becomes a pedagogical opportunity that targets the very highest form of thinking and being—the executive regulation of the mind in response to personal beliefs.

Since most of the activities learners select to do involve some level of social interaction, and since children are still learning to regulate their behavior to expected norms, adults will continually need to monitor and help learners modulate their behaviors. Voice levels should be the focus of a first-day-of-the-year lesson and should be revisited as needed. Some teachers post a voice scale in their classrooms (e.g., 0 for silent, 1 for whispering, 2 for quiet talking, 3 for loud talking, and 4 for playground voices), and refer to the scale when necessary. Make a voice scale for your classroom and teach students to self-regulate to the scale.

Contextualized Instruction and Guidance

Since learners are required to always be actively involved in a self-selected academic activity that relates to the curriculum, Work Time provides a context for *just-in-time* guidance and instruction. Work Time is the context for curriculum-embedded assessment and the instructional Formats of the Learning and Writing Conferences. Because learners are typically highly engaged and focused on intellectual work that aligns with the curriculum, adults can initiate rich pedagogical interactions immediately without the need for the traditional *anticipatory set* or the *lead-in/bridge-in* activities that traditionally serve as the introduction to the teacher-directed skill lesson where it is necessary to capture learner attention and interest.

The Learning Environment

> His culture provides the raw material of which the individual makes his life. If it is meager, the individual suffers, if it is rich, the individual has the chance to rise to his opportunity.
>
> Ruth Benedict

For those of us who grew up going to schools where we sat at desks in rows, or moved our bodies in space according to the dictates of teachers, our use of space was limited to what teachers permitted us to do. Our *personal space* amounted to the area occupied by our body and the desktop and the cubical airspace above the desktop. The remaining space in the classroom belonged to the teacher and was governed through her authority.

This arrangement was justified when it was thought that knowledge could be transmitted from one person into another. This is why formal classroom spaces in schools from the farthest reaches of the globe are organized in the same, predictable ways, with teachers on the stage, the locus of action, and learners, assigned to their seats, being acted upon.

But knowledge is not transmitted in a linear manner. It is a transaction between the learner and the social environment—the product of relational, dynamic, and self-initiated social processes. If Work Time is the zone of proximal development for self-direction, how should classroom space be reorganized to promote the highest possible forms of learning?

Since optimal learning opportunity is contingent on access to rich, diverse environmental experiences, the Learning Environment is an important facet of the curriculum, and it is carefully designed to support learner-driven transactions that are consistent with learners' interests, inclinations, and proclivities, and that also enable them to achieve high learning standards. The Learning Environment Rubric outlines specific conditions and identifies resources that provide learners with access to the experiences they need.

Activities to Organize the Learning Environment

Every aspiring educator holds visions of possibility for students to find activities in their classroom engaging and challenging. But when faced with an empty classroom in the middle of the summer, with polished floors and boxes and chairs piled on desktops, they can seem

138 An Activity Curriculum

overwhelming. Learning environments of the McCallister Method organize the environment to support independence, autonomy, proleptic engagement with cultural representations (curriculum content), and social interaction with emphasis on mentalizing.

1. Copy the Learning Environment Rubric. Use the Rubric as a reference to organize classroom space and materials. Explanations for how the materials and resources are used are explained in the Format chapters.
2. Create a floor plan for your own classroom. Refer to the Primary and High School Floorplans (see Appendices 10 and 11, www.routledge.com/9780367458591) as a guide. Refresh your memory of Vygotsky's Zone of Proximal Development (ZPD) and the Zones of Free Movement (ZFM) and Zones of Possible Action (ZPA) described in Chapter 3. With these zones in mind, envision how space can be maximized. Make sure to include a gathering space for whole-class meetings converging around a Share Chair (a high stool is better in grades 6–12) and a document camera or white board. Distribute round tables for the "Me" Formats of Cooperative Unison Reading, Learning Teams, Table Writing Share, Integrative Math, and Language Tables. Create other workspaces around the room for independent work. Maximize space in the environment for learners to autonomously select what they need to satisfy their learning goals. Limit the adult work space to a small table against the wall so as to maximize space for learners. Before you start moving furniture, share your floor plan with colleagues to get their feedback.
3. Create a Writing Wall in the hallway with a heavy-gage transparent envelope for each learner to display their recent compositions.
4. Create a Genre Exposure display to feature a wide range of texts from different disciplines and social spheres as a reference for learners. Post new writing genre forms after you present them in the weekly Genre Exposure Lesson.
5. Order materials. Refer to the Resources List (see Appendix 34, www.routledge.com/9780367458591).
6. Organize for the Formats. As you read about each of the Formats, make note of the requirements for space, materials, and resources specified in each Rubric.
7. Collaborate with colleagues to *raise the barn*. The Learning Environments in Learning Cultures are a universal design for learning that is consistent across grades and subjects. Since environments are consistent, adults can collaborate to make an efficient and coordinated effort to quickly create rich learning environments across the whole schools. One week prior to school opening, work with colleagues to divvy up the responsibilities so that things to do and get is distributed evenly and the work gets done efficiently. Teachers at the Family School in the Bronx used their "Lunch and Learn" period in the beginning of the year to put together assessment binders. Faculty at High School of Language and Innovation used a professional development day for teachers to work together in classrooms to set up environments. Urban Assembly School for Green Careers uses the week before school as a "Classroom Barn Raising" initiative, when faculty collaborate to help one another prepare their classrooms. Get together with your colleagues and dedicate collective time to supporting one another in creating supportive learning environments for your students.
8. Create classroom signage: the classroom should be full of prompts that students can use to successfully and independently navigate all of the Formats. Create signs and posters to help guide them. (Refer to the Learning Environment Rubric.)
9. Set up inter-classroom observations with colleagues. Use the Learning Environment Rubric to give feedback to one another about what still needs attention.
10. Buy yourself a Conference Stool that you can use to easily slide in next to learners in the Conference Format.

Concluding Thoughts

In her now classic essay, *Dilemmas of a Progressive Black Educator*, Lisa Delpit wrote about the quandary many of us face when we are learning to manage the environments of our classrooms to promote students achievement of learning targets. She wrote:

> ...Many people told me I was a good teacher: I had an open classroom; I had learning stations; I had children write books and stories to share; I provided games and used weaving to teach math and fine motor skills. I threw out all the desks and added carpeted open learning areas. I was doing what I had learned—and it worked. Well, at least it worked for some of the children.
>
> My white students zoomed ahead. They worked hard at the learning stations. They did amazing things with books and writing. My black students played the games; they learned how to weave; and they threw the books around the learning stations. They practiced karate moves on the new carpets. Some of them even learned how to read, but none of them as quickly as my white students. I was doing the same thing for all my kids—what was the problem? (1986, pp. 380–381)

So, what do *you* think? What *was* the problem?

Hopefully by now you are beginning to understand that the alchemy of learning is a concoction of circumstance and personal will. The scientific paradigms available when Delpit wrote this article led teachers to believe that learning was a simple matter creating supportive learning environments and inviting students to do as they wished. This idea was reinforced in child development and teacher education. Rational-empirical learning theories led us to believe that learning was natural given the right environment or provided the right instruction.

But just as the adage goes, *you can bring a horse to water, but you can't make 'em drink*, you can buy new carpets and computers and Lincoln Logs, but kids have intentions all their own. They will use carpets for dances and karate kicks, computers to shop for sneakers, and Lincoln Logs as race cars, because that's what they are inclined to do—even, in a sense, what they're *supposed* to do. It's up to us as their teachers to help them learn otherwise—or other ways. We need help them identify their learning goals and teach them how to use space and social opportunities to achieve their learning goals.

An important part of learning the things that are required is knowing when and how to use them in ways that our culture dictates they are *supposed* to be used. In other words, students come to school from the broadest swaths of the cloth of humanity where they have already learned how to do things with the stuff of their worlds. Some will have had exposure to school-type artifacts. Bedtime story rituals will have helped them learn how to use books in sanctioned ways. But some will not have had the same exposure, and they need to be taught.

Activities

1. Read about the readiness potential, also known in neurology as the *Bereitschaftspotential* potential by the scientists who discovered it. You can read the Wikipedia entry for a well-reported summary. See: http://bit.ly/1EpsGVP.
2. *Students can better meet their goals when time is less structured*: http://bit.ly/1nXI30M.
3. *Can iPads help students learn science?* http://bit.ly/IFPGIp.
4. *Surfing the Web in class? Bad idea*: http://bit.ly/1vjfCkQ.
5. *Daily online testing boosts college performance, reduces achievement gaps...* http://bit.ly/1BmZFwi.
6. You need to like what you do! Read about it: http://nyti.ms/1zokKkg.

Learning Environment Rubric

Rating Scale: (✓·) Needs Immediate Improvement (✓) Making Progress (✓·) Proficient (NA) No opportunity to observe

Procedures

1. The guide continuously tends to the improvement of the classroom environment by delegating responsibility to learners to maintain its physical order and by providing instruction to learners in how to use the environment as a medium for learning.
2. The guide consistently uses the lesson Format throughout the year to review rules, routines and expectations for how the materials and activity opportunities within the classroom environment should be used.
3. The guide uses the Classroom Environment Rubric as a teaching tool to help learners understand expectations and personal responsibilities in relation to how to use and maintain the learning environment.

Primary Aims

1. To serve as an extension of the curriculum, providing a cultural habitus for the learning community.
2. To provide a context for the exercise of fundamental freedoms to speak, move, think and affiliate with others.
3. To provide a psychological field in which the learner can interact and create a unique life space suited to their individuality.
4. To provide a rich environment from which learners can autonomously select experiences that contribute to social opportunity and the achievement of potential.
5. To provide opportunities for action in the environment that align with opportunities for learners to exercise capacities to act.

1. Space   Rating

1a. The classroom is orderly, free of clutter, and organized to facilitate learners' independent access to materials and learning opportunities.
1b. The classroom is organized to promote learners' free movement as they take initiative to work independently or collaboratively.
1c. The classroom is utilized in a manner that evenly distributes activity.
1d. Space is organized to accommodate small-group meetings and individual work time. Rooms are equipped with round tables or desks in clusters.
1e. Space is organized to accommodate a large-group meeting area. In primary classrooms children may convene on the floor on a carpeted space. In middle and secondary classrooms, chairs or stools are used.
1f. The meeting area is equipped with either an easel and chart paper or a whiteboard and document camera so that lesson and share content can be displayed for audience reference.
1g. A seat for the presenter is situated prominently at the head of the meeting area so that the presenter is visible to all audience members. Guides sit in the audience area but in close enough proximity to provide support as needed.
1h. The adult's workstation occupies minimal space in the classroom.
1i. Coats and bookbags are stored in the periphery of the room and do not obstruct areas between desks or tables. Space is allocated for learners to store materials in bins, cubbies, lockers, and/or boxes.
1j. Noise is kept to a minimum (e.g., mechanicals function quietly, squeaky door hinges are oiled, noisy pencil sharpeners are replaced).
1k. The room is well lit by overhead lights. Adequate lighting is necessary to perform academic tasks. Floor and table lamps can be used to soften or supplement, but not replace, overhead lighting.

2.	Environmental Print Displays	Rating
2a.	A voice scale is posted in the room and consistently used as a reference to help learners self-regulate (e.g., Level 0-silent; 1-whisper; 2-quiet talking; 3-public speaking; 4-shouting; 5-screaming).	
2b.	Share and Conference Calendars are posted a month in advance (2 learners per day per Format).	
2c.	Calendars and schedules for Cooperative Unison Reading, Learning Teams and other group Formats are posted a week in advance.	
2d.	Share protocol prompts are posted for reference by presenter during the Share.	
2e.	Writing genre text exemplars are posted for learners' reference (in writing classrooms).	
2f.	A Writing Gallery is prepared with heavy-duty transparent pocket folders labeled for every learner (in writing classrooms).	
2g.	The Social Contract is posted, which outlines specific rights and responsibilities foundational for learning within the school community.	
2h.	Ladder of Self-regulation is posted.	
2i.	Tables are numbered or labeled.	
2j.	Handbook of all Format Rubrics is available for reference by learners and guides.	
2k.	Format procedures and learner/guide roles are excerpted from Rubrics and laminated for reference in spaces in which Formats occur.	
2l.	Group Format sign-up systems are displayed (e.g., CUR sign up displaying each leader's text, sign up form, name clips or sticks; Table Share; Integrative Math; Language Games).	
2m.	Cooperative Unison Reading Leader Schedule is posted (1 per class).	
2n.	Word Cards are available at every table (1000 Word Cards in K-12, and 300 Word Cards in PK-K).	
2o.	Activity Arc poster is posted.	
2p.	Activity Block Poster is posted.	

3.	Resources and Equipment	Rating
3a.	Resources available on every table include word cards, standards indicators, dictionary, and sharpened pencils.	
3b.	Classroom is equipped with digital timers.	
3c.	Classroom library is stocked with books and magazines, or learners have access to handheld devices or laptops.	
3d.	Learning Centers are prepared and equipped with activities that can be autonomously selected by learners to support the full range of competencies expected by the end of the course or grade. Learning Centers in PK-5 classrooms are equipped to support learner-directed activities that support requisite academic background in Reading and Math. Grade 6-12 classrooms are equipped with standards-aligned Curriculum Maps, Unit Questions Guide, standards-aligned resources and reference materials (digital and physical) that learners can use to develop background abilities.	
3e.	Cooperative Unison Reading resource bins, containing a dictionary, white board, dry-erase marker, eraser, atlas and laminated Cooperative Unison Reading Rules and Rubric, are available for each group.	
3f.	A Materials Center is equipped with pens, pencils, markers, Post-it Notes, scissors, scrap paper, copy paper, lined loose-leaf paper, construction paper, glue, tape, index cards, among other resources.	
3g.	A Resource Center is equipped with dictionaries in English and other community languages, atlases, globes, encyclopedias, calculators, rulers, protractors, thesauruses in English and community languages, textbooks, math manipulatives (where relevant), and toys and costumes (where relevant).	

4.	Records	Rating
4a.	Assessment records are well organized, of high quality, and maintained in an accessible location by learners, guides and administrators, and should include: • Standards Checklist binder	

- Lesson binder
- Learning Conference binder
- Writing Conference binder
- Behavior Conference binder
- Guide/teacher Self-Assessment binder
- Responsibility Team documents (Briefs, C-DEEP records, pre- and post-assessment data)

Comments:

learning cultures®

Work Time Rubric

Rating Scale: (✓−) Needs Immediate Improvement   (✓) Making Progress   (✓+) Proficient   (NA) No opportunity to observe

Procedures

1. Learner selects independent or cooperative activities that align with learning goals and curriculum objectives.
2. Learner adheres to Format activity protocols and Work Time expectations.
3. Learner assumes responsibility to access necessary resources.
4. Guides confer with learners when necessary to encourage self-regulation to Work Time expectations.
5. At the conclusion of Work Time, learner takes responsibility to put away materials and quickly transitions to the next activity.

Primary Aims

1. To provide a context of fundamental freedom (of thought, movement, affiliation and speech) in which to exercise will in conforming to sanctioned academic and social norms.
2. To provide consistent, on-going opportunities to autonomously select rich environmental experiences and personally-meaningful activities that enable the development of talent and potential.
3. To practice self-organization and self-direction by choosing, creating and adjusting learning experiences that align with intentions and propensities.
4. To practice persistence, resourcefulness, and to apply self-determination in pursuit of learning goals.
5. To develop autonomy, independence and self-responsibility in pursuit of learning goals.
6. To cultivate positive emotions and a positive sense of self-identity in relation to formal academic expectations.
7. To take part in intrinsically motivating activities that develop knowledge and background abilities that are of service to future academic achievement.
8. To practice integrating all of the components of the mind-higher cognitive functions, socio-relational processes, emotional self-regulation-in the context of authentic and meaningful academic activities.
9. To experience full immersion and engagement in activities that demand intense, sustained concentration, and which support achievement of socially valued academic goals.

1. Learner   Rating

1a. Enjoys freedom of movement in the learning environment (assigned seating is not permitted).
1b. Enjoys freedom of expression, interacting freely and promotively with others.
1c. Is aware of expectations for productivity and achievement, and has goals to ensure success.
1d. Selected activities relate to personal short- and long-term goals and curriculum objectives, and learner can defend activity choices.
1e. Is non-disruptive and appears on-task, engaged, attentive, and focused on work.
1f. Knows how to access the materials and resources needed to meet Work Time goals.
1g. Takes responsibility for self-regulating to Work Time expectations, and can articulate consequences for failing to meet personal responsibilities.

2. Guide   Rating

2a. Teaches behavior expectations for Work Time.
2b. Helps learners develop understanding of formal learning standards and related learning activities.
2c. Participates in small-group and one-on-one meetings with students.
2d. Utilizes Work Time as a context for curriculum-embedded assessment and instruction.

		Rating
2e.	Monitors learner activity and encourages learner self-regulation to Work Time Format expectations.	
3.	**Learning Environment**	
3a.	The classroom environment contains appropriate cues to support learner independence in negotiating Work Time expectations (e.g., evidence that expectations for Work Time responsibilities have been taught).	
3b.	The Activity Arc is posted and used as a reference to guide the completion of activities.	
3c.	Assessment records that are relevant to the learner's achievement trajectory are maintained and accessible to learners and guides. Conference and Intervention records show evidence of development.	
3d.	Digital, print and material resources pertaining to the curriculum or course subject are available and plentiful.	

Comments:

8 Lessons

Description

The Lesson is a 10-minute whole-class team meeting led by a guide. The Lesson Format is a context for formal learning that requires direct instruction or scaffolded assistance, and for the dissemination of information that is pertinent and collectively-relevant to the entire classroom community. As such, lessons typically focus on behavioral expectations, classroom routines, and procedures. The lesson is also an important collective ritual activity that provides the opportunity for learners to practice conventions for participating in large-group discussions.

Primary Aims

> To provide an efficient opportunity for all students to access information or instruction that is collectively beneficial.
> To provide a ritual opportunity to practice civility in the context of group assembly.

Materials

> Projector/document camera
> Lesson artifacts
> Tape or fingernail polish to mark group meeting area boundary
> Document camera/white board
> Half a dozen lightweight stools to facilitate quick convening without having to move desk chairs
> Late Lesson Reflections
> Lesson Rubric
> Enlarged student responsibilities from the lesson Rubric (laminated and posted on the board)
> Electronic timer (display on document camera when in use)
> Standards-aligned lesson archive

Procedures

Set up: Learners will have been previously taught the expectations for participation in the Lesson Format and are familiar with the Lesson Rubric. The teacher prepares lesson material in advance based on the previous assessment of learners' needs. Lesson content

146 *An Activity Curriculum*

should primarily address relevant information that learners cannot access independently. Lessons, therefore, typically focus on guidance relating to behavioral expectations, classroom routines and procedures, and discipline-based content that learners can access independently should not be covered in the lesson. Lesson content aligns with formal learning standards and/or Rubric indicators. Lessons are planned to be no more than 10 minutes in length in order to allow maximum time for learners to work independently during the Work Time Format.

The class will have convened for the lesson on time, sit facing the presenter, within the confines of the group meeting area. Once boundaries are established, no exceptions should be made to allow some students to sit outside the boundary (boundaries can be marked with tape or dots of fingernail polish). Resistant or oppositional students will often use the lesson boundary to test the limits of a teacher's authority, attempting to remain conspicuously outside the circle in a public contest of influence. This behavior should never be permitted, as it secures non-compliance with the norms. Learners need to be seated closely enough to the teacher to promote attentive listening and participation. (Note: circles are discouraged as direct communication/eye contact between teacher and class members is the objective.)

On the first lesson of the year, present the Lesson Rubric (student section) and teach to the lesson expectations. Explain that lessons will be suspended to deal with norm-violating behaviors and will only resume when those behaviors are resolved and everyone is following the lesson Rubric expectations (this procedure is explained in further detail under *norming* in the Discussion section of this chapter). Remind students that they have an obligation to hold their classmates responsible for student expectations. In middle and high schools, where students move from one class to another, it is not necessary to repeat the same procedural lesson for every Format in each class. Teachers should distribute responsibility across classrooms so that, by the end of the first day, every student has been introduced to each Format procedure.

1 The teacher presents the objective of the lesson and makes reference to relevant learning standards, Format Rubric indicators if they are the focus of the lesson, and/or learners' needs. Lesson artifacts are visible to learners (e.g., displayed on a document camera or presentation easel).

   Learners appear engaged and attentive. They participate appropriately by adhering to rules for large-group discussion (e.g., raise hands to be recognized to speak; refrain from speaking without recognition of the facilitator), and provide leadership to peers to adhere to Lesson Format procedures.

2 The lesson is clearly presented, using appropriate, precise, and accurate terms to explain concepts and procedures. The target skill or concept is broken down into discrete components, each of which is accurately described or explained. They monitor for learner understanding and adjust lesson pace accordingly. Suggestions are made to help learners consider how to transfer a skill, competence, or concept to their independent work. The presenter uses appropriate artifacts/examples to successfully explain or clarify concepts or to demonstrate procedures. *Grassroots* lessons are conducted whenever possible, illustrating instructional points with examples from teacher's anecdotes of previous interactional situations. Learners' questions are addressed, but Q&A is not an objective of the lesson.

   The presenter suspends the lesson to address inappropriate or off-task behaviors and non-promotive comments, invoking procedures of the Ladder of Self-regulation if necessary. The Lesson is resumed only when collective attention and positive norms are re-established. (Note: unaddressed negative behaviors are secured as norms.)

3 When the Lesson is concluded, the presenter signals a transition, which should occur in under two minutes.
4 Lesson records document the lesson objective, procedures, artifacts used, and learning standards that were addressed. Lessons content is documented on standards-aligned inventories, which provide evidence of balanced coverage of pertinent learning expectations and standards (skills, understandings, knowledge, procedures, and activity norms). Lesson documents are maintained in an orderly and accessible system so that learners and teachers can access them as needed.

Discussion

The term *lesson* is often interchangeable with the sum total of what a teacher does during the full course of a class period. Whole-group or whole-class teaching was a pedagogical innovation of the early 20th century, when schools were redesigned by principles from scientific management to accommodate or process large numbers of students efficiently (Olson, 2003).

The technologies of IQ and ability testing (Binet) and the new science of the linear curriculum (Bobbit, 1918) enabled large, leveled classes; and whole-class teaching meant large numbers of learners could be presented with the same information at the same time. This form of instruction requires teachers to engage the attention of many learners at once, resulting in a pattern of discourse in which the teacher initiates a discourse sequence with a question ("I"), calls on a learner to respond ("R"), and then evaluates the response ("E"). This "I-R-E discourse" has become almost universal in schools (Mehan, 1979), where whole-group teaching is still a common practice (e.g., Lamov, 2015).

The common dilemma of the traditional, marathon lesson situation is to keep students engaged and on-task. The pedagogical sciences have contrived countless tactics to entice and maintain control of learners' attention during lessons, or to maintain *time on task*. This objective is understandable, since the learner can't make memory of new information about people, places, or things without selectively attending to those things (Kandel, 2007). It is challenging for any person to draw a crowd without something to share that others think is really interesting and an impressive supply of charisma. But school subjects can seem dull to many learners, and only half of people are extroverts—those who are energized by being the center of attention. That means a substantial proportion of the teaching force will find whole-group teaching to be taxing.

Another problem is that time on task does not necessarily mean learning objectives are being met. The kind of thinking necessary for higher forms of learning—to make new connections between different ideas and think creatively—involves active mental coordination, perspective shifting and sharing, and cooperative reasoning between people (Tomasello, 2014). Whole-group teaching does not allow for this kind of active discourse, and the majority of learners remain passive in this Format.

For all of these reasons, the Lesson has a very small role in the Learning Cultures model. It consumes only 10 minutes, or about 10–15% of the Activity Block. It is reserved mostly for procedural lessons that teach learners how to navigate the expectations of their own Work Time learning agendas, cooperative learning activities, and the social expectations of these contexts. The presentation of disciplinary content to the whole class—the aim of the traditional lesson—is unnecessary and even counterproductive if the primary objective is self-directed, personalized learning. The Learning Cultures curriculum rejects the one-size-fits-all paradigm of whole-group teaching. Most knowledge is freely available on the internet. Rather than being told information, learners need to practice how to determine what knowledge they need, and learn how to access, manage,

148 *An Activity Curriculum*

and use the vast universe of information at their fingertips. Cultural learning, or knowledge getting, is the responsibility of the learner during Work Time.

In Learning Cultures classrooms, the lesson is no longer a teacher marathon, but a short sprint. The marathon is now for learners, who practice using Work Time to manage their own minds and meet their learning goals. With their own agenda and their own learning plan, the main lesson of the Activity Block is what learners commit to doing and how they do it for themselves. The traditional concern for time on task is better refocused on creating conditions and time for learners to enter a flow state. Flow state is achieved in activities that are goal-oriented, that offer immediate feedback, and that are sufficiently challenging and require high levels of skill (Csikszentmihalyi, 1990). Work Time activities create the potential for flow, whereas whole-group lessons preclude its existence.

Planning and lesson content: The Learning Cultures model does not adhere to the linear curriculum paradigm in which the same content is taught to all students. One might wonder, where does lesson content come from? Lesson content is usually inspired by guides' observations of what their learners need. These insights generally are derived from interactions in the other Formats. Learners are constantly making smart and impressive cognitive moves through their interactions with others. These moves are documented in Format-embedded assessments. Assessments can be analyzed for what are known as *grassroots lessons* (McCallister, 2011). Lessons are termed "grassroots" because the content, typically derived from teachers' direct interactions with and observations of students, is "harvested" to prepare for whole-group presentation. This method of lesson planning emphasizes the process of taking advantage of competencies that some students already demonstrate in order to expose others to knowledge that they do not yet know. Grassroots lessons recount social situations that are satisfying for other children to hear. The pull of stories of others has a scientific basis. Gossip is a form of social grooming in humans that functions to promote social cohesion (Dunbar, 1998). If presented with information from two different sources—through gossip or through factual accounts—the information contained in gossip is preserved in memory more accurately (Dunbar, 1998).

Grassroots lessons are planned and organized to develop *joint intentions* between with learners. An intention is a resolution that motivates an action. Joint intentions are goal-related commitments that were cooperatively agreed-upon. The reason that joint intentionality is such an important factor in formal learning is because it is only through will and the responsibility one takes to regulate their thinking that new memory is formed through learning. One can only learn what one takes responsibility for (Olson, 2007). Another factor that is important in education is that the learner eventually takes responsibility to learn what the school expects them to learn (Olson, 2003). The meeting of minds between adult and learner needs to be *proleptic* in relation to the forma expectations of school (Cole, 1996). In other words, what they are jointly attending to should be relevant in some way to the curriculum and formal learning standards.

The grassroots lesson methodology is designed both to achieve shared intentionality and to be appropriately proleptic. This is who it works: first, it is important to be familiar with the formal curriculum and related learning standards. What knowledge, understanding, skills, and strategies are learners expected to acquire? Next, peruse assessment records to identify instances in which learners demonstrated target competencies. Cooperative Unison Reading Records, Learning Conference Records, and Writing Conference Records are the best candidates. This process of bringing curriculum content that is an expectation of future achievement into the present moment is an example of *prolepsis* (Cole, 1996). Select scenarios that illustrate the content that is most pertinent to the large majority of students. In planning, turn the scenario into a lesson in which the form of the lesson objective is a narrative relating how the learner grasped and applied the competency. Rather than follow a predetermined sequence of lessons focused on prescribed content, grassroots lessons draw upon professional expertise to determine what content deserves attention in the lesson Format. And by using expertise to analyze the positive outcomes of the learner-guide transaction, expertise is developed.

Another principle to support grassroots lessons was suggested by Montessori, who urged teachers to narrow the focus of their lessons to objects that already command the child's attention and to use the lesson to elaborate on existing understanding. Montessori (1965) explained, "…there shall remain in evidence only the object to which she wishes to call the attention of the child. This brief and simple lesson must be considered by the teacher as an explanation of the object and of the use which the child can make of it…. The teacher shall observe whether the child interests himself in the object, how he is interested in it, for how long, etc." (p. 108). The Learning Cultures approach to lesson planning follows the logic offered by Montessori, stipulating that lessons be brief and relevant to students' existing interests and needs.

Make a habit of cross-referencing your lessons to indicators from the Standards. Over time, fill out your lesson agenda so that all categories and indicators of the standards are covered. It's tempting to teach to the topics that appeal to us, and to stick to what we know well. But in order to honor every child's right to learn, they should have opportunities to access the full range of content represented in the standards. Every time a lesson is taught to the whole class, the lesson date is listed next to the content indicator on the Standards Checklist. A well-distributed, balanced approach to content coverage is achieved in this way. Refer to Box 8.1 (McCallister, 2011, pp. 58–59) to read two teachers' explanations about how grassroots lessons align to learning standards.

Box 8.1

Teachers insights about standards-aligned grassroots lessons

During Unison Reading, I'm constantly thinking, "OK, what's happening here in my group?" and what I noticed that day and "That would be the most beneficial for students the next day. What do they need right now to make them more successful readers?" I think about the four [domains] of reading from the [Cooperative Unison Reading] Record and look at the Cooperative Unison Reading Records and notice the breaches [that students made] and what instructional points will benefit all students in their Unison Reading groups and in their independent reading. I plan lessons directly around the students' needs. Typically, the lesson comes from something that has happened in a Unison Reading group or in an individual conference with students. Being knowledgeable about the standards and being diligent about keeping track of the lessons you've already taught into gives you a better sense of what you haven't taught…

In addition to your knowledge of your students and what's happening daily in your classroom, you also have to be knowledgeable about the grade-level expectations. Using the Standards Checklist is a way that you check in. It holds the teacher accountable. This curriculum is based on accountability. Our students are always holding themselves accountable. The Standards Checklist holds the teacher accountable. It's like your own bookkeeping system. You're using all of the knowledge and experience you have from your students and checking in to make certain that knowledge is also meeting the expectations of the grade. The real purpose of it is that we're giving the students what they need to succeed and move forward.

Ariel Ricciardi, 4th-grade teacher

> "I am amazed at how many of the standards are actually being met through the teaching points that come out of the dialog in Unison Reading. The speaking and listening standards are met every day through Unison Reading, whereas in other Formats of teaching, like guided reading, you don't really focus on that part of the standards. In a transmission kind of curriculum, they're not getting that opportunity to respond to each other. That's not usually what you focus on when you teach reading." Shara Miller, 2nd-grade teacher

Norming: turn problematic behavior into productive conflict: One primary aim of the large-group meeting Formats in Learning Cultures—the Learning Share, the Writing Share, and the Lesson—is to provide an opportunity for learners to take part in a ritual activity that helps develop a sense of collective identity and "we-ness" (Tomasello, 2016). This group identity is an important force in the learner's developing sense of moral identity in relation to the norms of the group. The capacity for moral self-governance to these norms that springs from group identity creates the possibility that the learner will take responsibility to participate in the community in beneficial ways.

The Lesson is an invaluable opportunity for learners to internalize group meeting norms, and provides an opportunity to observe and learn how the presenter manages a group and facilitates its discourse. Since every learner will have the responsibility to lead whole-group meetings in other Formats, it is vitally important that the adult demonstrate how do manage groups successfully.

In schools where a toxic culture has developed, where relationships between and among teachers and learners are characterized by conflict and negativity, and where a sense of hopelessness and powerlessness breeds hostility in the community, the lesson can be initially extremely challenging. Even in the best circumstances, it can be challenging for many learners to remain attentive, even for 10 short minutes. But in classrooms where some children hold resentment toward authority, the Lesson is a stage upon which hostility can play out. For some, the arena of the large group is a tempting place to perform defiance, and create distractions that are, unfortunately, often welcomed by the large group. The focus then becomes on students who have put themselves in the spotlight rather than the teacher. It can seem almost impossible to overcome unruly behaviors, and so teachers ignore them. But there is no such thing as homeostasis in cultures. Every negative behavior that is ignored is an action that serves to secure and strengthen a negative norm; and consistent reinforcement of negative norms will undermine the Lesson Format for the remainder of the year. Since large-group interactions have a powerful influence on the classroom culture as a whole, it is imperative that adults learn to manage them in ways that secure positive norms.

Instead of ignoring negative behaviors, they need to be approached pedagogically, as rich opportunities to learn. The Social Norms Curriculum, described in Chapter 18, Section IV, explains in full detail how a variety of pedagogical Formats are used to address problematic behaviors. One Format, the Ladder of Self-regulation, is used in the classroom whenever there is an instance of problematic behavior. The Ladder of Self-regulation is devised each year after the Social Contract Talk has been given to the whole school (see Chapter 18). The Social Contract Talk outlines each students' rights and responsibilities to learn, and asks students to contribute their suggestions about what should happen in instances of problematic behavior in school.

The Ladder typically involves the following steps: stop the Format. Take note of the time, and explain that the behavior has now begun to take learning time off the clock for others, and is now interfering with their opportunity to learn. Remind the class that their opportunity to learn has a time value: $13,000 is the amount society invests in every child's education per year ($25,000 in New York City). If this sum is divided by the number of minutes in the school year, about 67,000, each minute is worth $0.19 ($0.37 in New York City). Remind the class of their responsibility to encourage their peers to adhere to school procedures (Step 1 on most Ladders). Allow discussion amongst the group, but insist they adhere to expectations of civility. Wait one minute. If the behavior persists, remind the child of their responsibility to group norms (Step 2: a teacher reminder). Tell the child you will suspend the lesson for another. Watch the clock. Then tell the child they will be expected to complete a Behavior Reflection at the conclusion of the Lesson (Step 3). Wait another minute. If the behavior persists, tell the child you will now need to call home (Step 4). Wait another minute. If the behavior persists, tell the child that you will need to make a referral to the principal (Step 5). If the behavior persists after another minute, call the "On Call" teacher (On Call is a system whereby a teacher is at all times assigned to stand by in case they are needed in a classroom to provide behavioral support). This is Step 6. Wait for the On Call teacher to arrive to meet with the student. Allow the group to talk, but hold everyone accountable to adhere to expectations for civility. Problematic behaviors rarely persist to this level. If the child remains uncooperative, call the principal's office to request support. In some schools, the principal will call in support from building security.

When problematic behaviors necessarily become the unplanned focus of the Lesson, it's helpful to embrace circumstances and to recognize it as an authentic opportunity to teach a central lesson of *e pluribus unum*: we join ourselves as a collective through acts of civility toward others and respect for their dignity. When these situations arise, it is important to remain calm. Do not take the behavior personally. View it as an assessment opportunity in which a learner has given evidence of a need for something new to be learned. Stage the intervention slowly enough so that the child has time to respond to your directives by self-regulating their behaviors. Taming an unruly class culture is like training a stallion. You're only in control and making a difference as long as you're in the saddle. But cultures can be trained. Once learners have internalized that rights are like laws, and there's no tolerance for breaking them, they begin to adhere to norms. Also, children learn to covet their Work Time. They realize Work Time cannot begin until the Lesson Format ends; and the Lesson cannot end until the planned agenda is completed; and the Lesson cannot proceed unless every learner *appears engaged and attentive*, as per Lesson Format Rubric criteria 1b. It could take a few weeks, but eventually children begin to insist on *respon-civility* in their peers—the responsibility to be civil. Holding one another accountable, children themselves become keepers of their own school culture. Unexpected social norms lessons are really an ideal context for children to learn moral identity, prosociality, and social norms, in addition to planned Lesson content.

Disruptions from lateness. Lateness is unavoidable in some circumstances. But if late entries become a pattern for some students who dislike the Lesson Format, or an intentional performance to disrupt a class or to gain attention on the part of the late-entering student, procedures should be established to discourage lateness. Their chronic tardiness creates an unacceptable disruption. Allow the late children to only enter the room one-at-a-time. It is sometimes the case that coming into a class late together is a socially-cohesive performance that peers have in the past found entertaining. But negative norms cannot be secured. Again, adhere to the Ladder. Encourage a peer reminder. Then tell the student they will be required to complete a Lesson Late Reflection (see Appendix 13, www.routledge.com/9780367458591). If students enter the classroom late, particularly if this is a habitual behavior, consider having tardy students complete a Late

Lesson Reflection. If necessary, enlist students or a co-teacher to help present lesson content, allowing you to proactively attend to enforcement of the "Late Lesson Reflection." Then adhere to the Ladder.

The Small-group Instruction Format

The Small-group Instruction Format is simply a smaller-scale version of the Lesson Format, and adheres to similar procedures. This Format is a suitable situation for instructed learning and teacher-directed, didactic lesson content. This Format can be used to target a specific competency relevant to the needs of smaller groups of learners. The Format is usually needs- or interest-based, planned to provide extra support in developing a specific background ability. This Format is also a means to provide support requested by students (e.g., Responsibility Teams might request lessons on particular content related to their projects). The Small-group Instruction Rubric should be used to guide implementation and improvement of group instruction procedures. See callout above or go to Section IV (Forms and Records, Rubrics, Small-group Instruction).

learning cultures® — Lesson Rubric

Rating Scale: (✓-) Needs Immediate Improvement (✓) Making Progress (✓+) Proficient (NA) No opportunity to observe

Procedures

1. Lesson content is determined by assessments of learners' needs. Lesson content is balanced between a focus on content, classroom routines and social processes. Lesson content aligns with formal learning standards.
2. The lesson is presented within a period of 10 minutes.
3. Transitions before and after the lesson are executed in a timely manner, under 2 minutes.

Primary Aims

1. To provide an efficient opportunity for all students to access information or instruction that is collectively beneficial.
2. To provide a ritual opportunity to practice civility in the context of group assembly.

1. Learner — Rating

1a. Sits facing the presenter within the confines of the group meeting area.
1b. Appears engaged and attentive.
1c. Participates appropriately by adhering to rules for large-group discussion (e.g., raise hands to be recognized to speak; refrain from speaking without recognition of the facilitator).
1d. Provides leadership to encourage peers to adhere to lesson procedures.

2. Guide — Rating

2a. Prepares lesson material in advance. The purpose or lesson objective is clear and aligns with relevant learning standards, curriculum scope and sequence, and/or learners' needs.
2b. Uses appropriate, precise, and accurate terms to explain concepts. Target skill or concept is broken down into discrete components, each of which is accurately described or explained. Suggestions are made to help learners consider how to transfer a skill, competence or concept to their independent work.
2c. Uses appropriate artifacts/examples to successfully explain or clarify concepts or to demonstrate procedures. *Grassroots* lessons are conducted whenever possible, illustrating instructional points with examples from teacher's anecdotes of previous interactional situations.
2d. Monitors for student understanding and adjusts lesson pace and focus accordingly. Learners' questions are addressed, but Q&A is not an objective of the lesson.
2e. Presents lesson clearly and succinctly under 10 minutes, preserving class time for independent work.
2f. Ensures learners adhere to norms for large-group discussion. Suspends lesson to address inappropriate or off-task behaviors and non-promotive comments, invoking procedures of the Ladder of Self-regulation if necessary. The Lesson is resumed only when collective attention is re-established (Note: Unaddressed negative behaviors become secured as norms).

3. Learning Environment — Rating

3a. Lesson takes place in a designated meeting area. Learners sit closely enough to the presenter to enable attentive listening and participation. (Note: circles are discouraged as direct communication / eye contact between teacher and class members is the objective.)
3b. Lesson artifacts are visible to learners (e.g., displayed on a document camera or presentation easel).

4. Records — Rating

4a. Lesson records document the lesson objective, procedures, artifacts used, and learning standards that were addressed.

		Rating
4b.	Lessons content is documented in standards-aligned inventories, which provide evidence of balanced coverage of pertinent learning expectations and standards (skills, understandings, knowledge, procedures and activity norms).	
4c.	Lesson documents are maintained in an orderly and accessible system so that learners and teachers can access them as needed.	
5.	**Materials**	**Rating**
5a.	Projector/document camera.	
5b.	Lesson artifacts.	
5c.	Document camera/white board.	
5d.	Designated group meeting area with flexible theater seating.	
5e.	Late Lesson Reflections.	
5f.	Lesson Rubric.	
5g.	Enlarged student responsibilities from the lesson rubric (laminated and posted on the board).	
5h.	Electronic timer (display on document camera when in use).	
5i.	Standards-aligned lesson archive.	

Comments:

9 The Learning Conference Format

We only think when confronted with a problem.

John Dewey

Description

The Learning Conference is a 10–15-minute meeting between an individual learner and a guide intended to engage the learner in a problem-solving process focused on resolving a conceptual challenge. At the conclusion of the Conference, the learner recounts the Conference process in a narrative summary. The Learning Conferences takes place in the Work Time Format during the Activity Block in all classes (with the exception of the Writing Activity Block, where the Writing Conference protocol is used instead).

The Conference creates an opportunity to break down a challenge, describe it, resolve it, and generalize new insights to other situations. It provides learners the chance to develop key cognitive processes that play a role in creative thinking, cognitive flexibility, planning, reasoning, problem solving, and self-regulation. The opportunity to retell the problem-solving process as a *triumph narrative* contributes to the development of a core autobiographical memory that is characterized by persistence and a strong sense of agency.

Primary Aims

1. To strengthen self-competence and persistence through a structured opportunity to solve a personally relevant intellectual problem.
2. To use and integrate different components of the mind in support of executive regulation, rational thinking, and creative and strategic problem solving.
3. To develop cognitive control and mental flexibility.
4. To develop a coherent sense of agency within the core identity of the self by recounting a triumph narrative of an intellective achievement.
5. To practice cognitive transfer by speculating about how new knowledge can be applied to other situations.
6. To expand the capacity to resolve cognitive disequilibrium by triangulating thinking.
7. To incorporate situational feedback that can be assimilated into academic intentions.

Materials

> Curriculum material: the learner needs to have planned ahead for the Conference by identifying a "breach" or a point of confusion encountered in the curriculum material and bringing those materials to the Conference.
>
> Learning Conference Record (see Appendix 14, www.routledge.com/9780367458591)
> Learning Conference Rubric (see sample Rubric at the conclusion of this chapter)

Procedures

Set up. A Learning Conference Calendar is prepared ahead of time, indicating which learners are scheduled to meet for a Conference (see Classroom systems, below). The guide moves to the place where the learner is working to conduct the Conference.

The learner will have been previously taught the expectations for participation in the Learning Conference Format and is familiar with the Learning Conference Rubric. The learner is invited to enlist peers in the Conference process. Throughout the Conference, the guide should maintain a facilitative role, allowing the learner to direct the process, following-in to scaffold a self-directed problem-solving process.

The guide begins the dialogue with a quick reference to notes from the previous Conference and invites a conversation about whether the learner feels they have made strides toward meeting past goals.

The Learning Conference Record is used to structure the situation (see Appendix 14, www.routledge.com/9780367458591). The learner is prompted to read each probe and to respond in full utterances. Guides should not read the prompts or speak for the learner. Speech is a form of action, and speaking one's ideas is a strategy to deepen memory.

1. The learner is prepared with curriculum material that presents a challenge that they have tried unsuccessfully to resolve. In response to the probe, *BREACH*, the learner identifies the challenge. The guide records the learner's comments. The learner should not simply talk about or summarize the challenge, but should attempt to engage in the form of action that brings the problem to light. They need to name the elements of the challenge that they understand, and those they are confused by. If they struggle for terms to explain the process, the guide can follow in to extend their thinking.

    The Format teaches learners to integrate their minds and to use their memory in order to think creatively to solve intellectual challenges. Overly general challenges are not appropriate for the conference, such as "didn't do homework," or "isn't prepared." If the learner is unprepared for the Conference, the guide can either prompt the learner to re-engage with curriculum material in order to identify a challenge, or reschedule the Conference to a time when the learner is prepared. In the latter case, assessment notes should indicate that the learner was unprepared, and that the Conference could not take place. The guide should use the opportunity to discuss strategies for better preparation in the future.

2. In response to the probe, *KNOWN*, the learner explores what they already know about the phenomenon that is causing confusion. This probe requires the use of existing conceptual understanding to become a foundation for problem solving. The process of describing the *known* activates existing memory. Existing memory will subsequently become part of new memory when new understandings take the form of new

connections between neurons. Exploring what is known is a way of energizing the neurons that store existing memory.

It is common, when prompted, for learners to *draw a blank* and to say that they do not know anything. In this case, prompt the learner to start from a distant beginning (e.g., *What do you know now that you didn't know when you were in kindergarten? What do you know about this concept that you did not know before you enrolled in this course?*). The guide records the learner's comments.

3 In response to the probe, *UNKNOWN*, the learner attempts to explain their confusion in precise terms. Relating what is known about the problem to what is still not understood establishes the parameters of the problem and focuses the problem-solving effort. In other words, relating the known to the unknown outlines the boundaries of disequilibrium. Using language precisely to explain a problem is a way to cognitively represent the problem as descriptively as possible so it can be fully observed. The guide records the learner's comments.

Words. Words often escape us when we attempt to talk about what we do not know. The more we know, the more we have to say. Language is used instrumentally in the Conference to develop new understanding. Guides should follow into the learner's need for support to use words precisely.

The social world as a reference. In general, our thinking about most complex ideas is preceded by encounters with versions of these ideas in the social world. It is sometimes helpful to prompt the learner to consider how the concept at hand might be handled in the familiar context of Cooperative Unison Reading (e.g., how do you think your peers might resolve the breach?).

Enactive and iconic representations. Lack of understanding of certain symbols and how they are used to express ideas is a common focus of confusion in the Conference. By their very definition, symbols are detached from the particulars of situations. To develop an understanding of the meaning of a symbol, it is sometimes helpful to scale back from the symbolic modes of representation to the iconic or enactive modes of representation (see Bruner, 1963). That is, if symbols are not understood, assist the learner to represent the ideas through tangible forms of action, what Bruner called *enactive* representations (e.g., manipulatives or objects), or through pictures, or what Bruner called *iconic* forms of representation (diagrams and drawings).

4 In response to the probe, *RESOLUTION*, the learner attempts to resolve the challenge by relating and elaborating on what is known to what is unknown. Often by this point in the Conference, the learner has already resolved the problem simply by activating and accessing existing memory and thinking creatively about what they do and do not know. But if they have not solved the problem, prompt the learner to quickly recount the gist of what they have said. If they are still unable to solve the problem, encourage the learner to involve others (peers or guide) in the resolution process. Participants should be directed not to solve the problem, but to guide the learner's self-directed effort. Ideas that are underdeveloped, illogical, wrong, or contradictory, provide opportunities for learning. Discussion, directed by the learner and not the guide, continues until the confusion is resolved. The guide records the learner's comments.

5 Once the challenge is resolved, in response to the probe, *NARRATIVE*, the learner retells the problem-solving experience in a sequential narrative. The guide can use the prompt, "Now tell a once-upon-a-time triumph story about how you conquered this challenge." The guide records the learner's comments. Invariably, new content is learned in the Conference. But this new knowledge *of* a thing is much less relevant than the knowledge learned about *how* it was learned. So, the learner should be

supported to narrate a story that emphasizes the learning *process* as much as the *product* of learning. The guide records the learner's comments. A sample triumph narrative might sound something like this:

"Once upon a time, I was confused by the concept of photosynthesis. I knew that plants turned sunlight into energy. I knew they had something called chlorophyll. But I didn't understand what, exactly, chlorophyll did to make energy from light. I looked up on livescience.com to find out about oxygenic photosynthesis. That's where energy from light causes takes electrons from water to carbon dioxide. This process releases oxygen into the air and turns carbon dioxide into carbohydrates, a form of sugar. The thing I learned is that it is that it's not hard to learn a complex idea when you can find a source of information that presents it in a simple way. My goal is that from now on, when I don't understand something, I'm going to search until I find an answer that is easy for me to understand."

6 In response to the probe, *TAKE AWAY/COMMITMENT*, the learner identifies the "take-away" or *moral* of the story by explaining how the new knowledge can be applied in future situations. Every story has a moral, or a lesson. In this step in the Conference, the learner states the lesson and makes a commitment to applying it in future.

Transfer. Lessons are only effective when they cause change in behavior. An important aspect of learning how to learn is the ability to generalize a new insight, or to be able to think about how it applies to other situations, and to then actually apply it in future situations. The ability to apply knowledge learned in one context to another is known as *transfer*. In this step, prompt the child to verbalize a concrete goal that they will endeavor to apply the next time a similar problematic situation arises. Help them make their goal in the form of a promise or commitment in their own words.

Promise. Then have the student sign or initial the promise. This symbolic gesture has a concrete benefit. The guide records the learner's comments. Research shows that people are more inclined to achieve goals or change behavior when they have made a public promise to do so (Olson, 2007). Connecting the story moral, or lesson, with the commitment to apply or transfer it to new situations, is the mechanism of learning in the *TAKE AWAY/COMMITMENT* probe.

7 The learner prepares to share their Conference story during the Learning Share scheduled at the end of the Activity Block.

Discussion

The central aim of the Conference is not to gain more knowledge or to memorize content, but to help learners learn how to learn. It is designed to create a curriculum-embedded opportunity for the learner to encounter cognitive dissonance in the form of a conceptual challenge, and to stimulate capacities of executive regulation to resolve the challenge and reorganize information in the mind. This process functions to integrate disparate parts of the mind—the higher executive functions, core memory, and sociocultural processes that relate to the problem at hand. The Conference also contributes to emotional self-regulation and the development of persistence dispositions, since it requires learners to regulate emotions in the context of a situation that might normally signal a *fight, flight,* or *freeze* responsive reaction.

The Learning Conference creates a situation that might normally be considered by the teacher as being ripe for didactic instruction. It might appear that the learner might requires *instructed learning*. But self-directed problem solving is the aim of the Conference. The pedagogical emphasis in the Conference situation is support for the learner to integrate their thinking and use their memory to resolve dissonance, not to learn a new skill or acquire new knowledge. Confusion is the medium for learning, and the purpose of the Conference is defeated when the teacher solves the problem at hand.

Disequilibrium

Disequilibrium is a state of imbalance between the organism and the environment, meaning that the learner is confronted with unexpected stimulation from the environment and is forced to react to resolve the dissonance. A whole host of factors come into play in the state of disequilibrium. The capacity for emotional self-regulation determines whether the learner will fight, flee, freeze, or function. The learner's autobiographical memory influences whether the person views him or herself as capable of overcoming challenge and determines persistence and commitment. The capacity to make new connections between disparate ideas in order to solve problems presents a need for creative thinking. Capacities for executive regulation of the mind are stimulated as the person determines how to plan a solution to a problem, to channel attention productively, to hold and use various sources of information in memory (working memory), to toggle attention flexibly between different properties of the problem (task flexibility), to resist or inhibit impulses that impede the problem-solving process (inhibitory control), to reason logically and thoughtfully to make progress in solving the problem, and to regulate emotions to remain in a state of mindfulness so that all aspects of the mind function optimally. In short, the state of disequilibrium creates a potentially rich learning situation.

Concrete Feedback

The Learning Conference helps reinforce an incremental theory of intelligence or a growth mindset about learning (Dweck, 2013). People with a growth mindset believe intelligence is malleable and can be developed with targeted effort. Opportunities to take responsibility to dissect a challenge and to identify strategies to overcome it, over time, helps the learner develop experiences that prove intellect can be improved through effort.

Conferences that focus on general dispositions and behaviors, such as lack of engagement or motivation, lack of motivation, or lack of preparation, do not provide adequately specific feedback to aid in making changes to behavior. The Conference should generate explicit feedback that relates to concrete behaviors that impact the outcome of effort.

Self-Direction

The Conference is only successful when the learner makes the moves to complete the activity arc, not when the guide makes the moves for the learner. Teachers might be inclined to use the Conference as to show, demonstrate, or tell. But *teaching* is not the purpose of the Conference.

Intrinsic Motivation

The Conference provides an opportunity for the learner to develop intrinsic motivation in the form of self-determination. The Learning Conference situation provides what Deci and Ryan (2012) describe as the *nutriments* of self-determination: autonomy, competence feedback, and relatedness. The Conference provides the learner with an autonomous opportunity to work through a problem; it provides ample competence feedback; and locates the activity in a socially-embedded situation, providing the learner with a sense of relatedness to others.

Identity and Self-Perceptions

Our sense of self-competence about a thing influences our motivation to do the thing. The more we perceive ourselves as competent, and the more we perceive that others see us as competent, the more effort we invest in improving our competence. If we see ourselves as incompetent, not only do we invest less effort, we usually invest significant effort in avoiding the task. Self-perceptions are malleable. We are constantly using feedback from our environment to assimilate into our sense of *aboutness* toward the world and who we are within it. The psychologist Carol Dweck (2013) applied this concept to her research on self-theories of intelligence. Dweck asserts that individuals typically fall on a continuum when it comes to their own intelligence mindsets. On the one hand, some people believe intelligence is innate and fixed. They believe their effort has little bearing on outcomes. Since they believe effort has little influence on outcomes, destiny is fixed, or pre-determined. They invest effort in how they appear to others. On the other end of the spectrum are those with growth mindsets. They believe that effort to learn and training determine success. People with growth mindsets naturally have a stronger sense of agency and responsibility in learning.

The more we can help learners understand that they have agency and can control their destiny as learners, the more successful they will be in school. The more they learn what things they can do to improve their competencies, the more targeted their efforts at improvement can become; and the more clearly they understand their competencies, the more motivated and self-determined they will become.

Classroom Systems

The Learning Conference is an assessment, but it is also a curriculum of social activity. Several points should be considered in program-wide implementation.

Rubric as a Tool

The Learning Conference Rubric should be used to guide the implementation of the Learning Conference program. It should be used as an instructional tool to help learners understand Conference procedures, the overall purpose, and their role within the Format. It can be used as a professional development tool so that teachers can refine their practice. Administrators can use the Rubric as a tool for teacher observation and evaluation.

Rights and Opportunities to Learn

In order to ensure and enforce the right to a Learning Conference on a regular basis, a set number of Conferences are determined every year for every course or Activity Block. In a typical 60–80-minute Block, two Conferences should be conducted. If two Conferences are conducted every one of 170 instructional days in the school year (total school days minus days for field trips, testing, and other non-instructional activities), assessment records should yield 340 Conferences per year. The school administration should conduct periodic "opportunity checks" of assessment data throughout the school year to ensure that all learners have equitable access to the Formats. This *instructional accounting* system enacts the principle of equality of opportunity to learn based on sufficiency and adequacy (Gordon & Nigro, 1988).

Recordkeeping

Learning Conference records provide evidence that the curriculum has been implemented and that students have had sufficient opportunity to receive individualized guidance (i.e., evidence of twice monthly conferences in elementary grades, once monthly in middle/high school grades, and double Conference opportunities for low-achieving students). They should also provide evidence of opportunities to practice cognitive functions and positive learning dispositions in the context of authentic problem-solving situations. Records should be accessible to all teachers and administrators and to learners themselves. Records can be kept in Conference binders or maintained digitally. Conference notes should be neat, legible, easily interpreted, dated, and chronologically sequenced.

Activities

1. Listen to Adele Diamond, the developmental cognitive neuroscience, talk about the cognitive functions known as executive functions. Her insights are relevant to all of the Learning Cultures Formats, but especially the Learning Conference. Understanding executive functions will help reveal the power of learning conferences. Once you listen to the podcast, list the cognitive functions that learning Conferences support. http://bit.ly/1kKiWAp.
2. Kenney's podcast featuring Malcolm Gladwell, *How the weak can become strong*, explores the patterns and power of disruptive new ideas. Gladwell speculates about how those who are willing to break conventions and defy traditions bring new creative ideas into being. Think about the ideas presented in the podcast—how to turn disadvantage into advantage—in relation to the ideas presented in this chapter. When you converse with learners about their needs, think about Gladwell's message—that human weaknesses are the birth of tremendous strengths. See: http://bit.ly/1Epl85q.
3. Listen to author J.K. Rowling give her commencement speech at Harvard entitled, "The fringe benefits of failure." Think about how Rowling's lessons relate to those we hope to teach students through our interactions in Conferences. See: http://bit.ly/1EpldpR.
4. Watch Diana Laufenberg's TED talk, *How to learn? From mistakes*. What has Laufenberg learned about teaching? How do Conferences mirror these insights? See: http://bit.ly/1zIbLgI.
5. Read this interview with Carol Dweck to learn more about the theory of mindset and why it is such an important factor in learning. See: http://bit.ly/1kqLChy and http://bit.ly/1oaaghF.

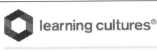 **Learning Conference Rubric**

Rating Scale: (✓-) Needs Immediate Improvement (✓) Making Progress (✓+) Proficient (NA) No opportunity to observe

Procedures

1. Referencing curriculum material, the learner identifies a challenge that they have tried unsuccessfully to resolve.
2. The learner explains what she or he knows or can do in reference to the problem.
3. The learner explains existing confusion or uncertainty in relation to the challenge.
4. The learner attempts to resolve the challenge by relating what is known to what is unknown. Learners are encouraged to involve others (peers or guide) in the resolution process. Learners' explanations reveal ideas that are under-developed, illogical, wrong or contradictory, providing an agenda for learning. The guide maintains a facilitative role, allowing the learner to direct the process. The guide follows into learner's comments, scaffolding a self-directed problem-solving process. Discussion, directed by the learner and not the guide, continues until the confusion is resolved.
5. The learner retells the problem-solving experience in a sequential narrative.
6. The learner identifies the 'take-away' of the story and explains how new insights will be applied to future situations.

Primary Aims

1. To strengthen self-competence and persistence through a structured opportunity to solve a personally relevant intellectual problem.
2. To use and integrate different components of the mind in support of executive regulation, rational thinking, and creative and strategic problem solving.
3. To develop cognitive control and mental flexibility.
4. To expand the capacity to resolve cognitive disequilibrium by triangulating thinking in the company of a guide in relation to a structured problem-solving protocol.
5. To incorporate situational feedback from a problem-solving process that can be assimilated into academic intentions.
6. To practice cognitive transfer by speculating about how new knowledge can be applied to other situations.
7. To develop a coherent sense of agency within the core identity of the self by recounting a triumph narrative of an intellective achievement.

1. Learner   Rating

1a. Is prepared with curriculum material that presents a conceptual challenge, which they have tried unsuccessfully to resolve. Lacking such a sample, the learner is considered unprepared and the Conference rescheduled.
1b. Remains the primary agent in the problem-solving process.
1c. In working through a challenge, demonstrates initiative, resourcefulness, persistence, creativity, cognitive flexibility, and critical thinking.
1d. Can articulate how the new understanding might be applied in other situations.
1e. Is able to retell the Conference experience in a coherent narrative.
1f. The learner is able to identify the focus of new learning and explain how it could be applied in other situations.

2. Guide   Rating

2a. Conducts the Conference at a table where learner is working (e.g., the learner is not called to the teacher's workplace station.)

2b. Supports the learner to take initiative to engage in a self-regulated problem-solving process to resolve a conceptual challenge. The adult guides, but does not direct the process or solve the problem for the learner.

2c. Encourages learner to engage others in the problem-solving process.

2d. If the learner identifies a non-specific or overly-general challenge (e.g., lack of preparation or poor work habits), redirects the learner and supports them to identify a specific conceptual challenge they have encountered in the curriculum material.

2e. Lacking appropriate vocabulary to explain a concept, provides the learner with precise terminology to accurately represent the challenge at hand.

2f. Supports the learner to demonstrate understanding through a retelling of the problem-solving process, ending with a take-away that can be applied as a goal in new situations.

2g. Ensures the conference takes place within a period of approximately 10-15 minutes.

3. Records   Rating

3a. Indicate that each learner has had a Learning Conference opportunity twice per month.

3b. Provide evidence of opportunities to practice learning dispositions in the context of curriculum-embedded, problem-solving situations.

3c. Convey a progression of growth over time, as challenges are overcome, goals are achieved, and needs become strengths.

3d. Records are dated, chronologically sequenced, neat, legible, and easily interpreted.

Comments:

10 The Learning Share Format

Description

The Learning Share is the concluding ritual of the Activity Block. It is a 10-minute whole-class presentation by two learners who, earlier in the period, each had a Learning Conference with a guide. It provides the opportunity for the learner to retell the Learning Conference experience in which they overcame a conceptual challenge encountered in curriculum work. The Share provides "a chance to be smart," as one 2nd-grade learner explained. By recounting a challenge, how they planned and executed a solution, and how they intend to apply learning in future situations provides the opportunity to reinforce self-competence.

Primary Aims

1. To strengthen memory of new learning by recounting the problem-solving process.
2. To develop public speaking confidence and competence.
3. Through recitation of a problem-solving self-narrative, to develop a coherent sense of agency in one's core identity.

Materials

Document camera
Learning Conference Record (see Appendix 14, www.routledge.com/9780367458591)
Learning Conference Rubric (see Conference Rubric at the conclusion of Chapter 9)

Procedures

Set up. The Share takes place in an intimate and comfortable meeting space equipped with a presenter station (e.g., podium or table equipped with AV equipment). The teacher will have signaled a transition to the Learning Share Format. Learners will have been previously taught the expectations for participation in the Learning Share Format and are familiar with the Learning Share Rubric. A Learning Share Calendar is prepared in advance, which is coordinated with the Learning Conference Calendar. Two learners have been scheduled in advance to share an account of the learning experience documented earlier in the period in the Learning Conference Format. The Learning Conference and Learning Share Calendars are coordinated so that the same learners take part in both Formats on the same day. The class will have convened in the classroom meeting area.

1. At the conclusion of Work Time, the first presenter convenes the class and establishes collective attention (saying something like, "I'd like to begin the Share. Could I have your attention?"). The audience is seated in the designated meeting area, facing the presenter, in close enough proximity to promote attentive listening and active participation. The audience is respectful, promotive, and completely attentive.

    Children have been previously taught the procedures for the Learning Share, and are fully aware that there is zero-tolerance for ridicule, disrespect, or inattention toward the presenter.
2. The presenter displays Learning Conference artifacts on the document camera (curriculum material), recounts a narrative account of how they overcame the challenge, shares learning goals, and identifies how new insights might be applied in future situations.

    The Learning Share is intended to be a brief report of personal academic competencies that can be described in several minutes. It is not a venue for dialog or discussion. Questions that from peers can be answered, but Q&A is encouraged.
3. The first presenter concludes their turn with a ritual closing, "Thank you for listening to my share." And the audience responds, "Thank you for sharing."
4. The second presenter repeats the steps above.

Discussion

The Learning Share serves as a stage to recite an accomplishment and provides the opportunity to develop agentic autobiographical memory.

Responsibility

Participation in the Learning Share Format is a right that is guaranteed, granted, and enforced. Some introverted learners are initially reluctant to share before the large group. But the Share is a responsibility. It is not optional. It is a pedagogically powerful Format and it is every learner's right to benefit from it, regardless as to whether or not they feel inclined. In order to support avoidant learners, refer to the Discipline Code, which specifies that every child must follow school procedures. Point out that the Share is a school procedure that must be followed. The Code, like other laws, provide desire-independent sources of motivation to comply. If the child is timid or insecure, a guide or peer can stand with the child in the Share and, with permission, speak for the child. When procedures are follows, over time, every learner participates in the Share.

Vicarious Learning

The Learning Share provides a context for imitative and vicarious learning by providing a daily opportunity to learn how peers have resolved intellectual challenges.

Speaking and Listening

The Share supports the development of listening and speaking competencies. Public speaking competence is an important life skill. The Share provides opportunities to practice speaking and listening standards, such as: *presenting information and supporting evidence, conveying a clear and distinct perspective and a line of reasoning that listeners can follow; adapt speech appropriately to a variety of contexts; demonstrate command of formal English; make strategic use of digital media in presentations* (National Governors Association Center for Best Practices, Council of Chief State School Officers, 2010).

Cultural Learning

Since the Share focuses on the problem-solving process contextualized in curriculum material, the Format provides a brief lesson on subject content. The daily Learning Share Format essentially provides two short lessons on curriculum topics relevant to the whole class.

Positive Group Norms

The Learning Share has a powerful norming function within the classroom community. Each day, two learners assume a place on the stage and make a public statement about themselves, to which the community bears witness. Since the audience is completely responsive and attentive (as per expectations outlined in the Learning Share Rubric), behaviors of responsiveness and attentiveness stimulate empathetic pathways, helping to secure a collective sense of relatedness and camaraderie. The Share develops the soul of the social group. It contributes to group cohesion, provides a way for each learner to perform their identity to peers, and provides opportunities for cultural learning.

learning cultures®

Learning Share Rubric

Rating Scale: (✓⁻) Needs immediate improvement (✓) Making Progress (✓⁺) Proficient (NA) No opportunity to observe

Procedures

1. A Learning Share Calendar is prepared in advance so that at least two learners share each day.
2. At the conclusion of the Activity Block, two learners are scheduled to report a summary of their Learning Conference.
3. The first presenter convenes the class and establishes collective attention.
4. The presenter displays learning conference artifacts on the document camera, recounts a narrative account of how the challenge was resolved, shares learning goals, and identifies how new learning might be applied in novel situations. (Note: Audience questions may be taken, but the share protocol does not include a formal Q&A component).
5. The second presenter secures collective attention and proceeds to repeat Step 4, above.

Primary Aims

1. To strengthen memory of new learning by recounting the problem-solving process.
2. To develop public speaking confidence and competence.
3. Through recitation of a problem-solving self-narrative, to develop a coherent sense of agency in one's core identity.

1. Presenter   Rating

1a. Convenes the audience and secures collective attention and consideration.

1b. Is clear and succinct in presentation of an account of a learning challenge that was encountered and resolved. The challenge is identified, the resolution is provided with a precise explanation of what was learned, and a goal about how the insight will be applied to new situations is offered. The share is approximately three minutes in length with minimal exchange between presenter and audience.

1c. Is prepared with notes/artifacts that illustrate the challenge and its resolution.

1d. Uses appropriate, precise, and accurate terms to describe learning.

2. Audience   Rating

2a. Is seated in designated meeting area, facing the presenter, close enough to enable attentive listening and active participation.

2b. Is respectful, promotive, and completely attentive. Participate appropriately through attentive listening and meaningful response. Inappropriate or unsupportive comments are immediately and decisively addressed, first by the presenter and/or audience members, then, if necessary, by the guide. Adheres to rules for large-group discussion (e.g., hands raised to speak; audience refrains from speaking out of turn or without recognition of the facilitator).

2c. Offers feedback in a constructive manner.

3. Guide   Rating

3a. Ensures a safe and comfortable context for presenters to share accounts of their learning.

3b. Supports presenter to independently manage the presentation process within a period of 5 minutes.

3c. Immediately and decisively intervenes to support the presenter to address inappropriate or non-promotive comments, enabling the presenter to successfully manage the group process.

3d. Follows into presenter comments when necessary to help explain or clarify ideas.

3e. Supports the presenter to ensure audience members adhere to norms for large-group discussion. Supports presenter to address inappropriate comments or off-task behaviors.

4. Physical Space	Rating

4a. Designated group meeting area with flexible theater seating.
4b. Projector to display presentation material.
4c. Learning Conference and Learning Share calendars are posted a week in advance.

Comments:

11 The Writing Conference Format

Description

The writing curriculum provides a powerful means through which children learn to carry out their own intentions. Learners are empowered to write texts for their own purposes, on topics of their choice, and in forms/genres that they select to suit their goals. The Writing Conference provides a source of individualized guidance that is contextualized within the learner's personal writing agenda. It is a 10–15-minute meeting between a learner and a guide, which provides the learner with feedback used to revise writing in order to better achieve its intended purpose.

Primary Aims

1. To employ writing as a means of taking action to carry out intentions.
2. To understand and be able to employ the features of writing genres as means to carry out intentions.
3. To focus the project of writing on the achievement of a particular responsive understanding in the audience/reader.
4. To provide competence feedback that can be used to revise writing in order to achieve its intended purpose.

Materials

Writing Conference Record (see Appendix 15, www.routledge.com/9780367458591)
Draft of student writing
Writing Standards Checklist or Rubric
Text exemplar(s)
Writing Conference Rubric (see Writing Conference Rubric at the conclusion of this chapter)

Procedures

Set it up. The teacher/guide moves to the place where the writer is working to conduct the Conference. Learning is situation-dependent, so the act of moving to the writer preserves the integrity of the situation. The writer will have been previously taught the expectations for participation in the Writing Conference Format and is familiar with the Writing Conference Rubric.

The guide announces the **purpose** of the meeting. The writer is invited to enlist peers in the Conference process for the purpose of moral support and additional feedback.

The Writing Conference Record is used to structure the Conference situation. Throughout the Conference, the guide assumes a facilitative role, prompting and supporting the writer to direct the process. The Conference discourse promotes the development of metalinguistic and metacognitive capacities, or the abilities to think about, analyze, and control written language. Therefore, the writer should speak in full utterances in response to the Record prompts. The guide should not speak for the writer, but can follow into comments.

The writer should be prepared for the Conference with a draft of writing. The writing *must* be in a draft form. Since the purpose of the Conference is to receive feedback that will advance the writing process, polished, final drafts are not shared in Conferences.

The writer is expected to collect one or two text exemplars to refer to in the context of the Conference. An exemplar is a formal or informal published form of writing that has relevance to the writer's current purpose. The exemplar presents an example of writing that succeeds in achieving a purpose shared by the writer (see the Written Genres Inventory in Appendix 3 for examples of possible writing forms, www.routledge.com/9780367458591). The writer might as yet be uncertain about the form their writing should take. If this is the case, the Conference can function to help the writer determine the purpose and identify possible generic forms to employ.

A copy of writing standards or a writing Rubric should be available as a reference. The Writing Conference Record prompts both the guide and learner to identify how the writing demonstrates that learning standards have been met. Since this process provides competence feedback, it serves to motivate self-determination (Deci & Ryan, 2012). This process is also *proleptic*. As previously described in Chapter 3, *prolepsis* is the anticipation of something before it exists. Standards explicitly outline expectations for end-of-grade achievements. Referencing the standards brings these expectations into the present situation.

1. The writer sets up the Writing Conference by announcing their *purpose*, or what they are attempting to *achieve* in their writing. They relate what *genre* or representational form they intend the writing to take. If they have one, they share an example of a published exemplar they are *emulating*. They explain how they want the *reader* to *respond*. If it is difficult for the writer to identify the reader's intended responsive understanding, it is helpful to ask what kind of *emotional expression* they hope to see on their reader's face and, in general terms, what a text would need to do to provoke it (e.g., "I want my reader to look surprised, so I need to include details that are unexpected"). The guide records the student's response.
2. The writer reads the draft aloud. The Conference needs to take place in a period of 10–15 minutes. So, if the writer is working on a longer piece, they should plan in advance which portion they want to share in the Conference.
3. The next part of the Conference should focus on how the writing succeeds in achieving its intended purpose. The writer identifies a specific sentence or passage in the text where the writing achieves its intended purpose, and explains how. The guide records the writer's comments, then offers feedback to the writer's point.
4. The Conference then focuses on how the writing could be revised to better achieve the intended purpose. The writer identifies a point in the text where the writing does not achieve its intended purpose, and explains why. The writer then explains how the writing could be revised to more successfully achieve the intended purpose. The guide records the writers comments, and offers feedback to the points made. The guide

(and peers) then identifies where the writing could be revised to be more effective, and offers a revision strategy. The guide records suggestions on the Record.
5 Making reference to formal writing standards (e.g., from the Common Core State Standards), the writer and guide identify places in the text where formal writing standards have been achieved and, using precise terms from the standards, indicates how (see sample Writing Standards Checklist, Appendix 16, www.routledge.com/9780367458591). The guide records comments on the Record.
6 The writer and guide reference the text exemplar, noting features that could be adapted to the writer's text.
7 The writer identifies a general take-away from the Conference. They state their goal for next steps in the form of a commitment. The guide records the commitment. The writer reads the commitment aloud, then signs the Conference Record, indicating their intention to follow through on their promise.
8 The writer is provided notes from the Conference, which they use to inform the revision process.

Discussion

The Writing Conference is contextualized within the Writing Activity Block, and provides the learner with the opportunity to discuss the purpose of their writing, to explore how writing content and conventions are employed to achieve the intended purpose, and to devise a plan of action. These practices provide a number of advantages.

Executive Functions

Writing is a cognitively challenging activity that many learners find exceedingly difficult. First, it requires the conceptualization of an end-product by thinking inferentially about how it will achieve a desired social effect, and abstractly about how it should be structured to achieve its purpose. The writing process itself is cognitively demanding. The learner is required to plan and execute a complex sequence of goals; to stay on task in pursuing simultaneous goals; to maintain attention and focus; to self-monitor and self-regulate thoughts and emotions; to re-evaluate and modify strategies; and to inhibit behaviors that impede the achievement of goals. The Conference protocol breaks down the complex process of writing into concrete components in which the learner can practice control of these functions.

The "Social Plane" and Mental Coordination

The Writing Conference establishes a social situation that stimulates the cooperative conditions involved in the writing process. It provides an opportunity for writers to test how their writing functions to influence others, and the extent to which the writing functions to achieve the intended goal. The Writing Conferences establishes a social plane (Vygotsky, 1978), which provides an opportunity *today* to take a course of action that will result in development *tomorrow*.

Classroom Systems

The Writing Conference is both an instruction/assessment opportunity as well as a curriculum of social activity. Several points should be considered in program-wide implementation.

Rights and Opportunities to Learn

In order to ensure and enforce the right to a Learning Conference on a regular basis, a set number of Conferences are determined every year for the Writing Activity Block. In a typical 60–80-minute Block, two Conferences should be conducted each day, yielding approximately 340 Conferences per year. The school administration should conduct periodic data or "opportunity checks" throughout the school year to monitor that the quantity and quality of Conference opportunities to learn are guaranteed for every student.

Teachers should create a master Conference Calendar in advance, which should be posted in the classroom so that the writers can prepare in advance. The Writing Conference Calendar should be coordinated with the Writing Share Calendar so that a period of at least a week separates the learner's opportunity to participate in each Format. The delay between the Writing Conference and Share provides time to apply feedback.

Recordkeeping

Writing Conference records provide evidence that the curriculum has been implemented and that learners have had sufficient opportunity to receive individualized guidance (i.e., evidence of twice monthly conferences in elementary grades, once monthly in middle/high school grades, and double Conference opportunities for low-achieving students). Records should be accessible to all teachers and administrators and to learners themselves. Records can be kept in Conference binders or maintained digitally. Records should Conference notes should be neat, legible, easily interpreted, dated, and chronologically sequenced.

Writing Conference Record

learning cultures®

Name: _____   Subject: _____

Intent: Prompt learner to identify purpose/intent (e.g., to describe, explain, convince, inform) and means of expression (writing form/genre). What responsive understanding or action is the writer seeking from the reader?	Strengths: Prompt the learner to identify where in the writing intended meaning was achieved and how. Point out where you believe they achieved intended meaning and how their writing functioned to do so.	Needs/Challenges: Prompt the learner to identify where assistance is needed in clarifying intended meaning and why. Respond accordingly with support. Point out where you believe the writing could be revised to clarify intended meaning.
Date:		
Learning Standard: Record aligning standard.	Exemplar: Prompt learner to share exemplar and explain how it serves as a model. Share your own insights about this exemplar or another.	Learning Standard: Record aligning standard.
Goal/Action: Prompt learner to articulate an action plan to achieve communicative intent and reader's desired responsive understanding. Then follow in to assist learner in developing a goal/action plan. Have learner read goal aloud before signing the Form.		Student Signature:

Intent:	Strengths:	Needs/Challenges:
Date:		
Learning Standard: Record aligning standard.	Exemplar: Prompt learner to share exemplar and explain how it serves as a model. Share your own insights about this exemplar or another.	Learning Standard: Record aligning standard.
Goal/Action:		Student Signature:

© 2014, 2016, 2020 Cynthia McCallister. All Rights Reserved. Reproduction and distribution is prohibited without permission from the author.

www.LearningCultures.net

learning cultures®

Writing Conference Rubric

Rating Scale: (✓-) Needs Immediate Improvement (✓) Making Progress (✓+) Proficient (NA) No opportunity to observe

Procedures

1. The teacher meets with the learner at a location where the learner is working.
2. The learner is welcomed to invite peers sitting nearby to participate in the Conference.
3. The Writing Conference Record is used to structure a dialogic interaction between the learner and guide about the text being shared.
4. The learner identifies the intended purpose of the writing, the generic form they are using to achieve their purpose, and the intended response or understanding they seek in the reader.
5. The learner reads the draft.
6. The learner identifies a place in the text where they believe they achieved the intended purpose and explains how.
7. The audience (guide and peers) identify a place in the text where they believe the writer achieved the intended purpose and explain why.
8. The learner identifies a place in the text where the writing could be revised to strengthen the intended effect and explains how.
9. The teacher and peers identify a place in the text where the writing could be revised to strengthen the intended effect and explain how.
10. Making reference to formal learning standards, the teacher and learner identify places in the text where standards are achieved and, using precise terminology from the standards, indicate how.
11. The learner is provided with notes from the Conference that can be referenced during the revision process.
12. The student makes a commitment to improve the writing and signs the Conference Record.

Primary Aims

1. To employ writing as a means of taking action to carry out intentions.
2. To understand and be able to employ the features of text genres to be employed in the writing process as means to carry out intentions.
3. To focus the project of writing on the achievement of a particular responsive understanding in the audience/reader.
4. To provide competence feedback that can be used to revise writing in order to achieve their purpose.

1. Learner   Rating

1a. Is prepared to share a thoughtfully chosen draft of written work in progress in the form of a short draft or segment of a longer piece, allowing a discussion within a period of 15 minutes.
1b. Is prepared with a text exemplar that they have selected to emulate (only for children ages seven and older).
1c. Takes initiative to direct the Conference according to the Conference Record protocol.
1d. Identifies purpose, generic form, and how the reader is intended to understand and respond to the text.
1e. Identifies how elements of composition function to achieve desired intent.
1f. Identifies how writing could be revised to better achieve desired intent.
1g. Is able to state an actionable goal based on insights generated through the Conference process.

Rating

2.	Guide	
2a.	Moves to the location where the learner is working. Establishes a safe and comfortable context in which the learner can share writing and receive feedback.	
2b.	Supports the learner to facilitate the Conference, based on the protocol of Writing Conference Record (e.g., learner identifies purpose; learner, then guide, identifies how writing functions to achieve purpose; learner, then guide, identifies how writing could be improved to achieve purpose; guide identifies how composition aligns with formal learning standards; learner makes a commitment to revise).	
2c.	Follows into ambiguous comments by prompting clarification to promote quality feedback.	
2d.	Supports learner to execute the Conference within a period of 15 minutes.	

3.	Materials	Rating
3a.	Writing Conference Record and Rubric, draft of learner's writing, text exemplar(s), Writing standards.	

4.	Records	Rating
4a.	Provide evidence that students have sufficient opportunity to receive individualized instruction. (Evidence of twice monthly conferences in elementary grades, once monthly in middle/high school grades, and double Conference opportunities for low-achieving students).	
4b.	Conference notes are neat, legible, easily interpreted, dated, and chronologically sequenced.	

Comments:

Copyright © 2012, 2014, 2015, 2016, 2018, 2020 Cynthia McCallister. All rights reserved. Reproduction and distribution are prohibited without permission from the author.

www.LearningCultures.net

12 The Writing Share Format

Description

The Writing Share is the concluding ritual of the Writing Activity Block. It is a 20-minute whole-group presentation by two writers who have the opportunity to share their writing. In turn, each writer displays their text, introduces the purpose of their writing, the generic form used, and response they seek in their reader. After sharing their writing, they solicit feedback from the audience, which is later used in the revision process.

Primary Aims

1. To employ writing as a means of taking action to carry out intentions.
2. To develop awareness about the ways writing genres function to perform specific forms of action.
3. To learn to use the conventions of writing genres instrumentally to achieve intentional goals.
4. To provide competence feedback that can be used in the revision process to achieve the intended purpose.
5. To concretize the writer's sense of audience and to provide in-the-moment feedback about the impact of the text.
6. To practice public speaking confidence and competence.
7. To promote a sense of community and collective identity.

Materials

Projector/document camera
Writer's text draft
Writing Share Record Notebook (for recording feedback to author)
Writing Share Rubric (see Writing Share Rubric, which appears at the end of this chapter)

Procedures

Set up. A Writing Share Calendar is prepared in advance, and turns are coordinated with the Writing Conference schedule to provide writers time between Format opportunities to act on revision goals.

The teacher signals a transition from Work Time to the Share Format. Learners convene in the classroom meeting area. Learners will have been previously taught the expectations for participation in the Writing Share Format and are familiar with the Writing Share Rubric. Two writers have been scheduled in advance and they have prepared for the Writing Share by selecting a draft that is in process, which contains sufficient material to elicit audience response in the form of questions, comments, or suggestions. The draft should be about a page in length, or a portion of a longer piece of writing. Each Share is allotted 10 minutes, so the draft selected should be short enough to be read in a period of five minutes, leaving adequate time for comments. The writers present in turn.

1. At the conclusion of Work Time, the first writer convenes their classmates and establishes their collective attention (saying something like, "I'd like to begin the Share. Could I have your attention?"). The audience is seated in designated meeting area, facing the presenter, in close enough proximity to promote attentive listening and active participation. The audience is respectful, promotive, and completely attentive.

    Learners have been previously taught the procedures for the Writing Share, and are fully aware that there is zero-tolerance for ridicule, disrespect, or inattention toward the presenter.

    The presenter *sets up* the Share by explaining the purpose of the writing, or what they are trying to do or achieve, what genre form they intend the writing to take, and how they intend the reader to respond (e.g., "I'm writing a comic strip that is supposed to be funny, and I want my reader to laugh."). The writer displays a draft piece of writing, preferably on a screen from a projector.

    It is expected that presenters independently facilitate the Writing Share by adhering to procedures and managing the audience without dependence on the adult. To this end, procedural prompts should be posted at the presenter's station that can be followed to structure the Writing Share Format and to manage the audience (see Box 12.1). Prompts can be laminated on a card or affixed to the document camera or presentation podium.

2. The writer reads the text aloud, then solicits feedback, calling on peers of their choice. Writers should be encouraged to ask for the type of feedback that would be most helpful in achieving their purpose. Audience members respond with feedback in a constructive manner and provide relevant and specific comments and suggestions that the writer can use to improve the draft.

    Audience members participate appropriately through attentive listening. Inappropriate or unsupportive comments are immediately addressed, first by the

---

Box 12.1

Writing Share prompts for the presenter

1. Secure the attention of the audience (Say: I'd like to begin. Can I have your attention?).
2. State your purpose, your intended genre form, and the way you want your audience to respond.
3. Display your writing.
4. Read your draft.
5. Ask for feedback about how your piece works to accomplish your goal or how it can be improved.
6. Thank your audience (Say: Thank you for listening to my share).

presenter and/or audience members, then, if necessary, by the teacher. The audience members adhere to rules for large-group discussion (e.g., raise hands to be recognized by the presenter), and refrain from speaking out-of-turn or engaging in off-task behavior.

In classrooms in which positive, prosocial norms have not yet been established, peer comments might occasionally be inappropriate or unsupportive. These comments must be immediately and decisively addressed; otherwise, they contribute to securing negative norms. It is important for the presenter to first address the behavior. They might need prompting and support from the guide (e.g., "Do you want to remind Sean of his responsibility to be supportive and promotive?"). If inappropriate behaviors continue, the Ladder of Self-regulation should be used (see Chapter 18).

When it is useful, the presenter should follow into peer comments to seek clarification and elaboration. Since a goal of the Writing Share is to gain insight about how others view a piece of writing, some level of dialog might be necessary to successfully exchange mental states. However, norms for group presentations can become mechanical and easily fall into the *pro forma* rut of the repetition of *call-response, call-response*. The discourse of the Writing Share should strive for dialogic interchange instead, and should sound something more like: *call-response-question-elaborate, call-response-question-elaborate*. For example, if a writer receives feedback for a general suggestion, such as, "you should include more details in your birthday party invitation that will make your guests really want to come to your party," instead of saying *thank you* and calling on another peer, the writer might ask for specific feedback about how to apply the suggestion.

Only the presenter, and not the teacher or guide, has the authority to call for comments. This is because the aim of the Writing Share is to provide a context for the writer to gain insights from others about how their writing works and ways to make it work better. The writer, therefore, has to successfully coordinate their thinking with the thinking of others in strategically useful ways. By controlling the floor, the presenter is able to control the source of their own feedback. Aside from following up on audience comments that might benefit from clarification, guides should refrain from offering their comments and suggestions until peers have had the opportunity to give remarks. If they have comments, guides should adhere to established rules by raising their hand and waiting to be called upon. Adhering to collective norms reinforces and secures them, while breaking rules erodes them.

The guide should record feedback in a Community Writing Share Notebook for the writer's later reference. Children 11 years of age or older generally assume responsibility to record feedback. If learners take responsibility for taking notes, the role of recorder should rotate so all students experience the responsibility of taking feedback for others.

3 The first presenter concludes their turn with a ritual closing, "Thank you for listening to my share." And the audience responds, "Thank you for sharing."
4 The second presenter repeats the steps above.

Discussion

The Writing Share is the soul of the writing curriculum. It is a daily, ritual celebration of human creativity and self-assertion. The Share is also a daily lesson in community building. It provides a chance for children to get to become familiar with one another, and plants seeds of friendship and fellowship.

Social Learning

Human beings have the remarkable capacity to learn through the thoughts and behaviors of others. The Writing Share is a powerful opportunity for a writer to get feedback from peers. But it is also a powerful opportunity for audience members to learn how others use writing purposefully and how they apply skill and knowledge in the writing process. Children's natural curiosity for one another creates a situation in which learners are motivated to hear what their peers are writing.

The Writing Share establishes the Vygotskian *social plane* for collective thinking, which intensifies the support the writer receives in making inferences about the mental state of their intended audience, in conceptualizing the most useful linguistic conventions to communicate the intended meaning, and to plan a course of action and establish goals to complete it (Vygotsky, 1978). This intense inter-mental experience becomes internalized as intra-mental cognitive functions, which are called upon in future situations.

The Share provides a context for learners to take part in using "meta language" (Olson, 1994) to talk about texts from a reflective stance, allowing abstract ideas or tacit, taken-for-granted knowledge to be exposed, brought to the surface, and made usable. Meta language is integral to *metacognitive* and *metalinguistic awareness*—the awareness of how one thinks or how language works.

Writing Instruction

The Writing Share Rubric assigns responsibility to audience members to give useful feedback to the writer. Learners are aware of their obligation to provide critical feedback, and engage in the Writing Share with seriousness and a sense of responsibility. They are generous in their effort to help peers achieve their aims as writers, and offer concrete suggestions and strategies that function as a source of powerful instruction. Corrective feedback intended to improve the writing is proleptic from the standpoint that it aligns with formal writing standards that spell out the qualities of effective writing. Exposure to standards-aligned corrective feedback is a lesson in its own right.

Sharing as a Responsibility

Because the Writing Share is a pedagogically powerful Format, it is a right that is guaranteed and enforced. Every child is guaranteed a certain number of opportunities to share each year, and accountability is distributed to ensure that this right is exercised. Learners have a **responsibility** to share their work with the large group. The Share is a community obligation, and it is **not optional**. Age is not a barrier to the Share opportunity. Even young children (ages 5–6) can perform the simple role expectations of the Share.

Some children are initially timid and reluctant to share. In these cases, the child is reminded that sharing is an expectation of the school's formal program and a procedure that everyone has responsibility to follow (the Discipline Code specifies that every student has a responsibility to adhere to school procedures, and the Share is a required procedure). Sometimes a sense of obligation is just enough motivation to act. But invariably a small proportion of children with severe social anxiety might experience a fight, flight, or freeze reaction to the anxiety of sharing. It is important to provide adequate support to these children to help them overcome their anxiety and participate as expected. There are a few strategies that help. First, help the learner rely on the Writing Share Prompts to guide their participation. The Prompts take some of the cognitive load off of the executive functions in the existential moment (such as initiating an action, sequencing and planning, and maintaining a task set) so that the learner can invest optimum energy in emotional regulation (Banich & Compton, 2018). Shy presenters can also enlist a peer to stand with them for the Writing Share for moral support. In severe cases of social anxiety, especially the first share, it helpful to offer the option to have another person stand in for the child entirely, presenting the writing and taking feedback. After having scaffolded support the first time, even the most shy children overcome their fear and develop not only confidence and courage to stand before their peers, but a sense of pride and satisfaction (Box 12.2).

Box 12.2

Supporting children with social anxiety

In a 6th-grade classroom in New York City, it was the first time to share for a child who had been diagnosed with an anxiety disorder. As his turn approached, he fled the room. In his absence, the teacher read the piece of writing he was working on and solicited feedback from his peers. Upon his return, while feedback was still in progress, the student was invited to sit in the Share Chair and hear comments about his writing. Later in the day, the child boasted to his special education teacher that he had shared. At home that night, he reported to his parents that he had had the best day ever at school.

Motivation

The Share experience is a natural source of intense motivation. It provides what Deci and Ryan (2012) describe as the *nutriments* of self-determination: autonomy, competence feedback, and relatedness. Writers have full autonomy in determining what to share and who to select as sources of feedback. They receive effective feedback that is specific, immediate, and actionable. And they experience a sense of connection and relatedness to others through a collective ritual activity.

Classroom Systems

Rights and Opportunities to Learn

Participation in the Writing Share Format is a right that is guaranteed, granted, and enforced. A Writing Share Calendar is prepared in advance, and posted in every classroom so that the writers can prepare for their turns in advance. In a typical Writing Activity Block, two Writing Shares are scheduled each day, yielding approximately 340 Writing Shares per year. This number, divided by the total number of learners in the cohort, will determine how many sharing opportunities each is guaranteed per academic year. Ideally, each learner should have two opportunities to present every month. The administration should conduct periodic "opportunity checks" of Writing Share data to monitor the quantity and quality of Share opportunities. The Writing Conference Calendar should be coordinated with the Writing Share Calendar so that a period of at least a week separates the learner's opportunity to participate in each Format, providing time for the writer to act on feedback.

Space

Every Share should take place in an intimate and comfortable meeting space equipped with a presenter station (e.g., podium or table equipped with AV equipment).

Writing Table Share Format

The Writing Share is both an enjoyable experience and a powerful vehicle for literacy development. In order to increase the quantity of opportunities learners have to share, a Table Writing Share program can be incorporated into the Writing Block. In the Writing Table Share Format, one student shares a piece of writing with an audience of up to five students. A system is established for learners to sign up to share and to be audience members, and a calendar is created.

The procedures for the writing table share are as follows: the author convenes the group in specified meeting area and establishes collective attention. The author either distributes photocopies of text or will have distributed copies of a text ahead of time so that group members can read them in advance. The author announces the purpose of the writing and the type of feedback sought. One participant offers to take written notes of group feedback. The author reads the text aloud then invites feedback. Share takes place in a period of 10–15 minutes, and time is balanced evenly between reading and discussion. Since it affords the opportunity for advance reading, the Writing Table Share Format allows longer texts to be shared.

Writing Share Rubric

Rating Scale: (✓-) Needs Immediate Improvement (✓) Making Progress (✓+) Proficient (NA) No opportunity to observe

Procedures

1. A Writing Share Calendar is prepared in advance. Writing Share Calendar is coordinated with Writing Conference to provide writers time after the Conference in order to act on revision goals before presenting again in the Writing Share.
2. The first presenter convenes the audience and establishes collective attention.
3. The presenter identifies the purpose of the writing, the generic form being employed, and the nature of feedback sought.
4. The presenter displays the text on a document camera and reads the text aloud.
5. The presenter solicits feedback from the audience.
6. Feedback is recorded both in a community share notebook and in notes provided to the presenter. The role of recorder should rotate so all students experience the responsibility of taking feedback for others.
7. The second presenter secures collective attention and proceeds to repeat Steps 3-6, above.

Primary Aims

1. To employ writing as a means of taking action to carry out intentions.
2. To develop awareness about the ways writing genres function to perform specific forms of action.
3. To learn to use the conventions of writing genres instrumentally to achieve intentional goals.
4. To provide competence feedback the writer can use in revision to achieve the intended purpose.
5. To concretize the writer's sense of audience and to provide in-the-moment feedback on the impact of the text in relation to the intended responsive understanding.
6. To practice public speaking confidence and competence.
7. To promote a sense of community and collective identity.

1. Presenter — Rating

1a. Convenes the audience and secures collective attention and consideration.
1b. Is prepared to present a short draft that contains sufficient material to elicit audience response in the form of questions, comments, or suggestions.
1c. Identifies the purpose of the text, the generic form employed, and the nature of feedback sought.
1d. Assumes responsibility to facilitate the Share process within a period of 10 minutes. Engages audience members by calling on volunteers for comments. When necessary, follows into comments to seek clarification and elaboration of relevant feedback. Addresses inappropriate or unsupportive comments immediately and decisively and, if necessary, solicits support from peers and/or the guide.

2. Audience — Rating

2a. Is seated in designated group meeting area, facing the presenter, close enough proximity to promote attentive listening and active participation (e.g., eye contact; verbal exchange in the form of dialogue).
2b. Is respectful, promotive, and completely attentive. Participate appropriately through attentive listening. Inappropriate or unsupportive comments are immediately addressed, first by the presenter and/or audience members, then, if necessary, by the teacher. Adheres to rules for large-group discussion (e.g., raise hands to be recognized by the presenter). Refrain from speaking out-of-turn or engaging in off-task behaviors.

2c. Respond to writer's request for feedback in a constructive manner. Provides relevant and specific comments and suggestions that the author can use to improve the draft.

3. Guide — Rating

3a. Ensures a safe and comfortable context for students to share writing and receive relevant feedback.

3b. Supports the presenter to facilitate the share process within a period of 10 minutes. (The guide is seated in the audience, in close enough proximity to support the presenter to facilitate the share process.)

3c. Follows into presenter or audience comments when necessary to help explain or clarify ideas or to request clarification to promote quality feedback.

3d. Supports the presenter to ensure audience members adhere to norms for large-group discussion. Immediately and decisively intervenes to support the presenter to address off-task or inappropriate behaviors and non-promotive comments, enabling the presenter to successfully manage the group process. If the presenter is unable to resolve the conflict, the guide intervenes to invoke procedures from the Ladder of Self-regulation.

3e. Ensures feedback is recorded for later reference by the presenter.

4. Physical Space and Materials — Rating

4a. Designated group meeting area with flexible theater seating.

4b. Projector to display presentation material.

4c. Writing Share calendar are posted a week in advance.

4d. Community Share Notebook.

Comments:

184 *An Activity Curriculum*

Writing Table Share Rubric

Rating Scale: (✓-) Needs Immediate Improvement (✓) Making Progress (✓+) Proficient (NA) No opportunity to observe

Procedures

1. Copies of the text are distributed to participants prior to the Table Share (optional). The presenter convenes the audience and establishes collective attention.
2. The presenter identifies the purpose of the writing, the generic form being employed, and the nature of feedback sought.
3. The presenter shares copies of the text and reads the text aloud.
4. The presenter solicits feedback from the audience.
5. Feedback is recorded both and provided to the presenter. The role of recorder should rotate so all students experience the responsibility of taking feedback for others.
6. The next presenter secures collective attention and proceeds to repeat Steps 3-6, above.

Primary Aims

1. To employ writing as a means of taking action to carry out intentions.
2. To develop awareness about the ways writing genres function to perform specific forms of action.
3. To learn to use the conventions of writing genres instrumentally to achieve intentional goals.
4. To provide competence feedback the writer can use in revision to achieve the intended purpose.
5. To concretize the writer's sense of audience and to provide in-the-moment feedback on the impact of the text in relation to the intended responsive understanding.

1. Learner — Rating

1a. Convenes the audience and secures collective attention and consideration.

1b. Is prepared to present a draft in process that contains sufficient material to elicit audience response in the form of questions, comments, or suggestions.

1c. Identifies the purpose of the text, the generic form employed, and the nature of feedback sought.

1d. Assumes responsibility to facilitate the Share process within a period of 10 minutes. Engages audience members by calling on volunteers for comments. When necessary, follows into comments to seek clarification and elaboration of relevant feedback. Addresses inappropriate or unsupportive comments immediately and decisively and, if necessary, solicits support from peers and/or the guide.

2. Audience — Rating

2a. Is seated in designated meeting area in close enough proximity to promote attentive listening and active participation (e.g., eye contact; verbal exchange in the form of dialogue).

2b. Is respectful, promotive, and completely attentive. Participate appropriately through attentive listening. Inappropriate or unsupportive comments are immediately addressed, first by the presenter and/or audience members, then, if necessary, by the guide. Adheres to rules for large-group discussion (e.g., raise hands to be recognized by the presenter). Refrains from speaking out-of-turn or engaging in off-task behaviors.

2c. Respond to writer's request for feedback in a constructive manner. Provides relevant and specific comments and suggestions that the author can use to improve the draft.

3. Guide — Rating

3a. Allows learners to facilitate their own groups. Holds learners accountable to procedures and supports their effort to manage group working processes.

3b. Observes informally and provides instruction to guide and support the process when necessary.

3c. Intervenes to correct maladaptive behaviors and to secure prosocial behaviors.

3d. Provides guidance to support learners in identifying resources that can be used in the research process.

4.	Space and Materials	Rating

4a. A system is established for learners to take responsibility to sign up to both share and participate as audience members. Learners refer to a Table Share Calendar that is posted in the classroom.

4b. The Table Share takes place in a designated meeting area. Group members sit facing one another, close enough to promote overall attentive listening and participation.

4c. Participants are provided copies of the writer's draft, prepared in advance.

4d. Tabletops are cleared of clutter and materials that are not related to the Table Share.

5.	Records	Rating

5a. An appointed recorder provides the author with written feedback.

Comments:

13 The Pretend Play Format

Description

The Pretend Play Format creates an imaginary situation in which the child is empowered to take agency and triumph over a negative force (e.g., a "bad guy" or a "bully"). Using a play prop as an artifact, the child imagines the narrative situation in which they perform a triumph. In groups of two or three, each child tells their story in turn. Children can then exchange props and act out their peers' stories.

Primary Aims

1. To take part in an imaginative or pretend play activity in order to support self-efficacy, a positive and empowered view of the self, resilience, creativity, autonomy, and self-direction.
2. To provide opportunities to interact cooperatively with peers and to develop interdependence and collaboration skills.
3. To play for the sake of pleasure and recreation, and to exploit the context of play to develop creativity and the executive functions (planning, task initiation, selective attention, inhibitory response, and emotional self-regulation).

Materials

Pretend play props

Procedures

Set it up. Children's first Pretend Play experience should be introduced with guided instruction about how to handle materials, how to follow procedures, and how to use time and space in the classroom. To that end, learners will have been previously taught the expectations for participation in the Pretend Play Format and are familiar with the Pretend Play Rubric. An abundant assortment of costumes, hats, wigs, eye glasses, gloves, beads and costume jewelry, coats, stuffed animals, dolls, figurines, toy cars, and vehicles are available.

1. Children organize themselves into pairs or groups of three. They each select a playtime artifact of their choice. A stock of play props should be plentiful. Props are the

artifacts of imagined possibility, and so a multiplicity of choices expands the parameters of possibility. Children should be shown how to handle artifacts with care.
2 The imagination is like an enchanted world of possibility that enables a person to transcend the mundane and restrictive conditions of everyday reality. We cross a threshold between these two worlds when we entertain our imagination to envision ourselves through a prism of different possibilities. To make this transformative process tangible, we use the metaphor of the caterpillar and the butterfly. The caterpillar weaves itself a silky cocoon where inside it transforms into a new form of being, taking shape as a butterfly.

In order to help learners embody the experience of this transformation into their charmed imaginary character, they are instructed to clutch their artifact to their heart, and squeeze themselves into a *body cocoon*. For the next few minutes, they remain in that state while they imagine themselves in a pretend story situation. In a voice directed to themselves, they whisper a triumph narrative: they are a powerful character confronted with a formidable challenge, such as a "bad guy" or "evil villain." They imagine the conflict rising to a climax in which they prevail and triumph over adversity. They become an empowered character who demonstrates strength and agency.
3 The children emerge from their *cocoons*. They take turns telling their stories to one another.
4 The children take turns acting out the imaginary situation.
5 The children are encouraged to think about their stories as topics to write about during Writing Work Time (but should not be required to write about them).

Discussion

Since imagination is the space where the self explores possibility, Pretend Play is a powerful context for self-development.

Autobiographical Memory and Agency

The Pretend Play protocol catalyzes a situation in which the child can experience feelings of resilience, tenacity, triumph over hardship, and persistence. These agentic lived experiences, played and practiced with continuity over time, nourish the development of a coherent core autobiographical memory that is characterized by personal agency and focused moral identity.

Cooperation

The Pretend Play activity is socially-embedded, stimulating pathways of social-cognition (empathy and imitation). The play context is congenial and emotionally comforting, and, through play, children are open to the experience of learning through hearing their peers' imaginary narratives.

Creativity

Confronted with a problem of their own invention to solve, the child has the opportunity to invent a creative solution. In sharing their stories with others, children have opportunities to consider their peers' creative solutions to problems, thus expanding their own creative sense of possibility.

Recreation

Recreation provides a core source of energy needed for survival and well being. That is why recreation is a basic human right (United Nations Children's Fund/UNESCO, 2007). Pretend play carves out space for recreation, and provides a context for pleasure, entertainment, amusement, joy, and fun.

Problem Solving

The problem-solving requirement of the Pretend Play situation stimulates the executive functions of task initiation, planning, selective attention, inhibitory response, and emotional self-regulation.

Management

Adults utilize the Pretend Play Format as a context for assessment. They effectively monitor and manage the activity. Problems that arise are quickly resolved as teachers respond appropriately to disruptive behaviors and refrain from interrupting the whole class to address isolated problematic behaviors. Expectations for students' independent responsibilities should be posted throughout the room with evidence they have been taught and revisited. The physical arrangement of the room should facilitate movement and collaboration, and space should be fully utilized for Pretend Play activities.

learning cultures

Pretend Play Rubric

Rating Scale: (✓) Needs Immediate Improvement   (✓) Making Progress   (✓) Proficient   (NA) No opportunity to observe

Procedures

1. Learners work in groups of two or three.
2. Each learner independently selects a play-time artifact of their choice according to their interests.
3. The learner clutches the artifact and squeezes into a *body cocoon*. In that state, they imagine themselves in a pretend story situation. They are a powerful character confronted with a formidable challenge, such as a 'bad guy' or 'evil villain.' They imagine the conflict rising to a climax in which they prevail and triumph over adversity. They become an empowered character who demonstrates strength and agency.
4. Learners emerge from their cocoon, and take turns relating their story to others.
5. Learners take turns playing out the imaginary situation.
6. Learners are encouraged to think about their stories as content for their compositions during Writing Work Time (but should not be required to write about them).

Primary Aims

1. To take part in an imaginative or pretend play activity in order to support self-efficacy, a positive and empowered view of the self, resilience, creativity, autonomy, and self-direction.
2. To provide opportunities to interact cooperatively with peers and to develop collaboration skills.
3. To play for the sake of pleasure and recreation, and to exploit the context of play to develop creativity and the executive functions (planning, task initiation, selective attention, inhibitory response, and emotional self-regulation).

1. Learner   Rating

1a. Moves freely about the room.
1b. Interacts cooperatively with peers.
1c. Demonstrates awareness of expectations for Pretend Play activity: takes responsibility to follow Ladder of Self-regulation; is on-task and non-disruptive; appears engaged, attentive, and focused on activity; shows consideration and support to others; handles Pretend Play artifacts responsibly and with care.
1d. Can situate their character and artifact within an imagined situation. Can explain how their imagined character changes and develops agency through the course of the imagined situation.

2. Guide   Rating

2a. Utilizes Pretend Play as a context for student assessment.
2b. Effectively monitors and manages the activity. Problems that arise are quickly resolved. Responds appropriately to disruptive behaviors, and refrains from interrupting the whole class to address isolated problematic behaviors.

3. Physical Space and Materials   Rating

3a. Expectations for students' independent responsibilities are posted throughout the room with evidence they have been taught and revisited.
3b. Physical arrangement of the room facilitates movement and collaboration, and space is fully utilized for Pretend Play activities.
3c. Pretend Play props are plentiful. An abundant assortment of costumes, hats, wigs, eye-glasses, gloves, beads and costume jewelry, coats, stuffed animals, dolls, figurines, toy cars and vehicles provide options for the imaginative transformation of self in the context of pretend play.

Comments:

Copyright © 2015, 2016, 2018, 2020 Cynthia McCallister. All rights reserved. Reproduction and distribution are prohibited without permission from the author.

www.LearningCultures.net

14 The Cooperative Unison Reading Format

> Once you learn to read, you will be forever free.
>
> Frederick Douglass

Description

Cooperative Unison Reading (CUR) is a learner-directed format for small-group reading instruction.[1] In a group of no more than five, learners gather together to read a text they have selected.[2] They follow a protocol structured by three simple rules: 1) read aloud in sync, in a voice others can hear; 2) *breach*,[3] or stop the group if you have a question or something to say; and 3) be promotive (be helpful and nice to your peers). These simple rules are universal conventions that learners of any age, language, or ability can use to coordinate mental states with others in order to exchange perspectives about ideas that arise from the group reading situation. CUR depends on the human capacity of Theory of Mind—the ability to read the minds of others. CUR groups are re-formed each week, when a new cadre of group leaders selects a short grade-level text to share with their peers. Learners sign up to read texts in the group of their choice.

The practice of CUR achieves multiple learning advantages: it holds learners responsible to be mindful of their own thinking in the process of reading and to be aware of points of confusion; it creates a method by which points of confusion in the reading process are resolved when they arise, explicitly and immediately within the reading process; it eliminates the tradition of sorting learners by same ability for group instruction, a practice proven to be detrimental to minority students' academic achievement (Lleras & Rangel, 2011); it dramatically increases the quantity of individual texts each learner reads in the context of instructional groups each year (typically learners will read at least 30–40 texts a year in the CUR reading program); and it dramatically increases the number of social groups learners take part in each year, providing a means through which learners can develop social capital.

CUR reconceptualizes the traditional teacher-directed, skills-based, ability-group reading lesson into a cooperative, learner-driven, game-like activity. In traditional reading lessons, children learn the skills that they are taught. In CUR, children learn to read by learning from others new ways to think about ideas represented in texts. CUR is both a method for the practice of small-group reading instruction and a classroom-wide program of instruction that is the core component of the school-wide K-12 literacy program. In the reading program, learners are provided at least 60 minutes per week to participate in CUR in elementary, and preferably two hours per week in middle and high school. Once learners have internalized the rules of CUR, it is used as a routine reading practice in the context of other Formats, such as Learning Teams, Language Games, and Integrative Math.

Primary Aims

> 1 To practice cooperation by working with others to solve problems.
> 2 To practice executive self-regulation by conforming to group norms.
> 3 To practice cognitive control and mental coordination by shifting and sharing perspectives and reasoning cooperatively with others in order to achieve collective understanding.
> 4 To expand comprehension of a text through a process of social triangulation, attuning to and resonating with others' thoughts, feelings, and emotions.
> 5 To develop new knowledge, literacy skills, and cognitive competencies.
> 6 To practice reading comprehension as the act of understanding an author's intentions.
> 7 To develop social cognition and stimulate capacities to understand and empathize with others.
> 8 To practice emotional self-regulation.
> 9 To practice democratic, civil discourse by resolving disagreements through non-judgmental deliberation and consensual agreement.

Materials

> At least four round tables serve as designated meeting that are expansively positioned to fill the classroom, minimizing noise distractions (the CUR Format occurs simultaneously with other Formats during Work Time). Tables are labeled with numbers or letters (to facilitate efficient group meeting procedures).
>
>   Texts (digital or physical), selected by learners
>   Cooperative Unison Reading Record for in-the-midst note-taking by the guide (see Appendix 17)
>   Cooperative Unison Reading Log, to be filled in by learners *after* the conclusion of the session (see Appendix 19)
>   Cooperative Unison Reading Rules (see Appendix 20)
>   Cooperative Unison Reading Rubric (see the Cooperative Unison Reading Rubric at the end of this chapter)
>   Cooperative Unison Reading Text Selection Assignment (to be completed by group leaders) (see Appendix 9)
>   Electronic timer
>   Materials bin for each table (Contents: dictionary, atlas, white board, dry-erase marker, eraser, laminated CUR Rules, and Rubric)
>
> See www.routledge.com/9780367458591 for mentioned Appendices.

Format Procedures

Set up. Learners will have been previously taught the expectations for participation in the Cooperative Unison Reading Format and are familiar with the Cooperative Unison Reading Rubric and Cooperative Unison Reading Rules.[4]

1 The group convenes quickly and sits facing one another, close enough so that whisper reading is audible, and peers' texts can be easily reached and referenced. The group leader will have come prepared with copies of the text, a materials bin (containing

a dictionary, atlas, white board, dry-erase marker, eraser, and Cooperative Unison Reading Rubric and Cooperative Unison Reading Rules). Tabletop is cleared of clutter except for text copies, Unison Reading Rules, a whiteboard, and dry-erase marker. Materials bin is stored on the floor.

2 The first few minutes of the group's session is spent either orienting to the author's purpose or determining a reading stance if it's a new text, or recapping the main points if it's a text discussed in a previous session. Learners approach the text as a form of action on the part of the author, attending to author's purpose and text conventions are employed to achieve intent. Once the group decides where it will begin reading, the group leader assumes responsibility for initiating this discussion by saying something like, "Put your finger on the word, 'The.' Ready, set, read." This is the only time the group leader takes leadership initiative. All group decisions are collective.

3 Once they begin reading, learners adhere to Cooperative Unison Reading Rules by 1) reading aloud in sync in a voice others can hear; 2) breaching or stopping the group with questions or comments; and 3) being promotive (being nice and promoting others' learning) (see Appendix 20, www.routledge.com/9780367458591, Cooperative Unison Reading Rules). Learners cooperate and contribute evenly to resolve confusions as they arise and to offer comments appropriately. Most times learners themselves can resolve confusions raised in the breach—we call this *closing the breach*. But when they are unable to do so, the guide follows in to support learners to take action to solve the problem independently. After resolving a confusion or *breach*, the group resumes reading at the beginning of the sentence in which the breach occurred in order to read the sentence with full meaning intact.

Group cohesion. Learners maintain cohesive groups by participating in productive discussions and interacting responsively through verbal and non-verbal communication (e.g., attending to facial expressions, showing eye contact, following into others' comments, sharing and shifting perspectives, and reasoning cooperatively). They approach the text mindfully by triangulating attention to the text with attention to the mental states of others. They are non-judgmental of others, and they are open-minded to ideas as they arise.

CUR as a rule game. Learners approach CUR in the spirit of a rule game to be "played" cooperatively, in the spirit of fun.

Distributed leadership and even participation. No single learner dominates, and passive learners are supported to contribute. The group leader does not dominate the process or play the role of *teacher*, but participates on equal terms with other group members.

Resources. Learners utilize resources and technology appropriately. They are resourceful in their attempts to resolve questions, readily using resources such as globes, research texts, and smartphones or tablets to access information on the internet. Use context clues before referring to a dictionary to find meanings of unknown words.

Productive breaching. When groups are functioning well and learners are readily breaching, they will breach as many as a half dozen times in a single CUR session. This rate of breaching amounts to more than 700 opportunities over the year to resolve problems with others. Problems that arise in the *breach* focus on both global meaning as well as Background knowledge, providing a student-driven approach to skills instruction (e.g., National Reading Panel, 2000).

Process check. An occasional process check is useful to help learners reflect on their group's functioning. Asking, "Can we stop for a minute and think about what we're doing. If you take a look at the Unison Reading Record, you will see that the conversation isn't well balanced in our group. What's happening? What can you do to help the conversation be more balanced?"

4 In the concluding two minutes of the session, the group debriefs, reflecting on strengths, needs, and goals for the next meeting. Learners complete CUR logs and CUR text selection assignments on a weekly basis, but wait until the session concludes to begin work.
5 The group leader collects materials. Group members quickly transition to other Work Time activities (transition times are under two minutes).

The role of the guide. The role of the adult or *more experienced other* (Vygotsky, 1978) in the CUR situation is the *guide on the side.* They encourage CUR to be conducted as a rule game that learners can play independently, and play the role of referee, breaching to stop the game when rules are broken, and encouraging group members to correct behavior. Learners who are new to CUR might need the teacher to breach relatively frequently until rules are internalized and become behavior norms. The guide refrains from directing learner behavior and never takes over the CUR Format to teach didactically. In CUR, teaching is no longer equated with *telling.* Instead, the guide *facilitates* learners' coordinated interactions. The guide should manage the Format schedule, using an electronic timer to signal transitions so as not to interrupt *flow* with the sound of their voice.

The power of CUR Rules. As we have discussed previously, game rules have a kind of status function. They establish relevance to particular conditions of the social environment and have a deontic power to hold participants responsible to their obligations to agreed-upon conventions for behavior (Searle, 2010; Tomasello, 2009). The Rules of CUR are designed to engage participants in cognitive activities that promote metacognitive and metalinguistic awareness and stimulate social cognition. As just described, CUR revolves around three simple rules:

1 Read in sync with others in a voice they can hear;
2 Breach, or stop the group when you have a question or something to say; and,
3 Be promotive and supportive of group members.

These rules are applied in CUR sessions for children of all ages, kindergarten through college. The **first rule**—that all group members read aloud, audibly, the same words at the same time—creates the phenomenon of a shared experience that makes the ideas expressed in a text simultaneously tangible to all participants so that they can coordinate their thinking with others. Oral reading also provides opportunities to practice reading fluency and skills or background abilities in context.

With the exception of children who do not yet speak the language of the text being read, everyone is expected to read loudly enough to be heard by everyone else in the group. Children who are not yet fluent in the language of the table or the text being read can "read in the wake" of the group, echoing their peers' voices as they track the text. Guides participate in the reading process and adhere to the rules, but they read in a whisper so as to attend to learners' voices. If a group member stops reading, they are breaking Rule #1, and the CUR game should stops to address the underlying cause. Usually when someone stops reading it is because they are confused by some aspect of the text. Avoidant or oppositional attitudes can also be a cause for the learner to withdrawal from the activity. In either case, the group needs to work together to come to a solution so the group can resume synchronized reading.

The **second rule**—to breach or stop the group with questions or comments—creates a way for group members to share their states of cognitive dissonance so that others can follow-into confusions and help resolve them. Until learners internalize their responsibility to actively interrogate points of confusion, the guide should actively seek to establish new norms. In instances when there is an apparent confusion and the group stops reading in sync, the referee/guide might say something like, "It's your job to stop the group when you're confused. Nobody at the table knew what that word was, but I was the only one to stop the group. Next time you need to take responsibility for stopping the group when you come to something you don't know." Points of concern that arise from cognitive dissonance become a kind of existential curriculum, providing a *just-in-time* pedagogy that ensures each person's questions are resolved and everyone fully understands the text. Discussions that attempt to resolve breaches necessarily turn to aspects of written language, such as letter, word, and syntactic properties, as well as to issues of meaning and understanding—factors considered to be basic reading skills known to be correlated with reading competence (National Reading Panel, 2000). This rule promotes conceptual development because it forces learners to reconcile incompatible perspectives of others, sharing inferences, and resolve differences to achieve a collective understanding (Gergen, 1990, 2015; Tomasello, 2019). This form of thinking—self-regulating perceptions and actions from an executive level—is the definition of intelligent thought (Tomasello, 2019).

"Be promotive" is the **third rule**, and the golden rule. It requires learners to treat others as they wish to be treated, and thereby secures prosocial norms. These conditions create a conceptual habitus of the environment that naturally tailors participation to meet each child's competence level (Bruner, 1983; Tomasello, 1999). Learners are taught to recognize any form of unkind or disrespectful behavior, whether they be words or facial expressions, as *violations of Rule #3*. The opportunity to practice compassionate behavior on a daily basis in reading groups has a stabilizing influence on the classroom culture as a whole. Since others' perspectives are seen to be a key to deepen understanding about how texts work and what they mean, the social dimensions of the group reading experience are emphasized on a par with content. In fact, others' perspectives are a prerequisite to the acquisition of skills. This rule emphasizes the need to be empathetic. In the spirit of supportive collaboration, participants naturally adhere to universal maxims that structure cooperative conversation in human beings by ensuring their own contributions are truthful, informative, relevant, and direct (Grice, 1989).

An environment of social safety fosters positive emotions, creates a context in which everyone feels free to express their ideas, and derives satisfaction from the social experience. Promotive group norms foster behaviors in which empathetic pathways are stimulated, enabling learners to attune to one another, to resonate to others' perspectives, and to share mental states (Siegel, 2020). The positive and accepting emotional climate in CUR eliminates the feelings of being negatively judged that some low-functioning readers experience in deficit-based, leveled reading instruction.

Some children who dislike group reading instruction (which, in my experience are typically those who have spent their school years in low ability groups) are reluctant to buy into the CUR program. and might even exhibit defiance. In these situations, negative behaviors violate Rule #3 of the *game*, and the rule breaker is held accountable, preferably by teammates. In highly toxic middle- and high-school cultures, it can take weeks consistently adjudicating infractions of Rule #3 before positive norms are secured in classrooms and across the school. Until learners internalize the norms of the rules of CUR, it might initially be the guide who does all or most of the breaching when rules are broken. But over time, the guide's interruptions should be minimal. Minor social conflict, miscommunication, or inconsideration for the group are all behaviors that break Rule #3. Social behaviors are as consequential to learning as instruction of skills. So negative behaviors are *followed-into* as a legitimate instructional concern.

With these three rules in place, any group of children has the means to function independently to read and interpret a text.

Program Procedures

CUR is a school-wide literacy program that involves a number of consistent systems that are implemented in every classroom. These systems are described below. A comprehensive program description is featured in the book, *Unison Reading: Socially-inclusive Group Instruction for Equity and Achievement* (McCallister, 2011a).

Set up

CUR takes place during Work Time. The classroom environment is prepared with four or more small, round tables dispersed apart, throughout the room. Tables are labeled with numbers or letters (to facilitate efficient group meeting procedures).

Grouping

The classroom implementation of the CUR program is organized so that each week 20% of the class assumes the role of group leader. Group leaders choose short grade-level texts they are interested in reading with others, such as magazine articles or blog posts,[5] which are posted publicly several days prior to the first group meeting. Groups are formed when peers sign up to read the texts that most interest them. Each week group leaders rotate, so that every child has an opportunity to be a leader and to select a text of their choice. Leadership opportunities are not contingent upon "good" behavior. Learners are given the freedom to join groups based on social motivations and interests—on what they want to learn about and whose minds they want to coordinate with. This policy of inclusiveness eliminates the problematic practice of grouping children by skill deficit for instruction, which is disproportionately deleterious to minority children (Lleras & Rangel, 2009). It also eliminates the costly practice of assessing and leveling learners.

A schedule should be created indicating deadlines for text selection and group sign-up. Sign-up procedures should be staged so that opportunities to be in the first subgroup to sign up for a new text alternate. The top limit of CUR is five group members. This number aligns with the top limit of the order of intentionality that human beings are capable of (see the discussion of orders of intentionality discussed in Chapter 3). Breach-resolving requires simultaneously coordinating the mental states of several individuals, creating the need to cope with high orders of intentionality, or the number of separate minds involved in the task (Dunbar, 1998). Higher-order intentionality tasks have been shown to be more cognitively more demanding than independent tasks by drawing on greater neural resources across larger numbers of brain regions, especially those associated with theory of mind, the frontal and temporal lobes (Lewis, Birch, Hall, & Dunbar, 2017). Groups *close* once the fifth member has signed up. Popular texts close quickly, and learners are routinely expected to practice tolerance and open mindedness by participate in groups that do not reflect their social preferences or topical interests. Daily CUR practice stimulates higher cognitive functions.

Complete freedom to associate in groups of choice can result in cliques that threaten the classroom culture. Since groups are limited to five participants, and *first-in-line* sign up opportunities rotate, so learners are always being exposed to new personal perspectives and ideas.

Text Selection

The process of selecting a text as a group leader is a powerful comprehension activity. Learners should be encouraged to think ahead about the kinds of ideas they want to share with others, whose minds they want to access, and what text will best help them achieve their intentions. In other words, text selection is a powerful comprehension activity. One 4th grader once told me his text collection strategy: "Well, me and D'Andre don't like each other. I like history, and he likes sports, so I pick things to read about history and he picks sports, and we're never in the same group." Children learn to use grouping procedures as much to create their own social capital in the classroom as to be exposed to new ideas. Assign the Text Collection Activity is used to support the text selection process (see Appendix 9, www.routledge.com/9780367458591).

> What types of texts are good candidates for CUR? A text should be short enough to be closely read, in full, inside an hour to 90 minutes. Aside from these two rules, anything goes. Short feature short stories, comics, book reviews, gossip columns, game reviews, obituaries, and feature articles on politics, entertainment, sports, and the arts are all options. In subject classes, encyclopedia entries, editorials, speeches, and sections from textbooks are good possibilities. Functional texts are also good possibilities: greeting cards, ticket stubs, restaurant menus, invitations, billboard ads, and subway advertisements.

Text Preparation

A system for photocopying print texts should be organized centrally so that: a) the office staff is prepared to support the clerical demands of the CUR program; or b) photocopiers are dispersed in classrooms so that teachers themselves can photocopy texts (e.g., one photocopier per grade). iPads and electronic texts can be used in place of photocopied texts.

Group Schedules

The weekly group schedule remains consistent throughout the year. The schedule is created by calculating the number of groups needed by dividing the class evenly into subgroups of no more than five. For example, six groups would be required for a class of 26 students; and in a class of 32 students, seven groups would be needed. A sample schedule for a five-week day appears below. Schedules should also be created for four- and three-day vacation weeks.

	Monday	Tuesday	Wednesday	Thursday	Friday
10 minutes	Lesson	Lesson	Lesson	Lesson	Lesson
20 minutes	CUR A Group	CUR C Group	CUR B and D Groups	CUR C and D Group	CUR B and D Groups
20 minutes	CUR C and B Groups	CUR A and D Groups	CUR C Group	CUR A and B Groups	CUR A Group
10 minutes	Share	Share	Share	Share	Share
	Procedural agenda: next week's leaders identify text choice and complete Text Selection Assignment	Procedural agenda: print selections are photocopied	Procedural agenda: next week's leaders post new text selections		Procedural agenda: text sign up Learners complete CUR Logs

Groups meet several times over the course of the week—typically twice with an adult and twice independently. And the whole process begins again the following week. Each week creates a new opportunity for learners to work with a different group of peers and to access new perspectives on topics that arise from the formal curriculum.

Assessment

Using the Cooperative Unison Reading Record, monitor the activities of learners and record the discussions that occur (see Appendix 17, www.routledge.com/9780367458591). The Record is formatted to that discussions that occur as a result of following into a breach can be recorded sequentially.

When a child breaches, the teacher codes the type of breach in the first column (SP/G/C/D), writes #1 in the child's column and records his/her comments. When another child follows into Child #1's comments, the teacher writes a #2 in the appropriate column, and records comments, and so on until the turns in conversation following the breach are complete. Notes of conversations capture the sequence of learning that takes place as children make moves to follow into one another's thoughts and take action resolve differences in perspectives by creating shared understandings. These normatively acceptable understandings—those representing a more general objective perspective as opposed to a perspective associated with an individual—are a defining aspect of intelligent thought (Tomasello, 2019). Transcripts of dialogue indicate what problems occur and how they are resolved, and document skills that were discussed as a matter of solving problems that arose.

The top section of the Record contains a classification framework that can be referenced to identify the nature of the problem that is resolved in the breach. This framework is organized into the domains of Social Processes (the things participants do to coordinate mental states and cooperate); Genre (features of the text having to do with the forms of action it is performing); Comprehension (the strategies used to make meaning of the text); and Decoding (the strategies used to decipher text). The domains serve as an analytic and mnemonic function, as a reference for guides to identify the strategies being used in the collective meaning-making process of CUR. Once a breach is made, the guide determines the instructional focus and records it in the far-right column on the Record. Accumulated Records provide evidence of learning aligned with formal standards.

The Record has several other important uses. It can be an *instructional tool* used to show learners patterns of action and participation in their group. It can be a *curriculum-planning resource* when teachers examine their records for content that is relevant to the majority of students in the classroom and warrants re-teaching in the Lesson Format as a *grassroots lesson*.

The CUR assessments provide evidence of opportunities to learn, and, in accordance with the instructional accounting system within the McCallister Model, Records are archived and monitored. Opportunity targets are set at the beginning of the year to determine how many CUR sessions should occur throughout the year. The administration conducts Instructional Accounting tallies periodically throughout the year to ensure opportunity to learn targets in the CUR program are being met. Therefore, it is important that records are dated, chronologically sequenced, neat, legible, easily interpreted, and accessible.

Sample Cooperative Unison Reading Records taken in grades 1, 5, and 8 are featured (see Appendices 21–23, www.routledge.com/9780367458591). Referring to each Record, analyze the discourse that unfolds after each breach on every line. Refer to Chapter 3, and review the social interchange concepts of relational adjudication and perspective-shifting discourse to identify precisely how each group develops a collective representation of the ideas raised.

Cooperative Unison Reading Log

After each CUR cycle, have learners complete a Cooperative Unison Reading Log. The Log is a comprehension activity that prompts the learner to reflect on the group experience, the meaning-making experience, and word learning (see CUR Log in the Appendix 19, www.routledge.com/9780367458591).

Test Genre Exposure

The McCallister Model curricula are never suspended for the purpose of test preparation activities. The Formats continue to operate normally in the days and weeks leading up to the State exam. However, since it is important that learners have opportunities to understand how formal standardized tests behave as a writing genres, and to learn how to "cooperate" with these texts, two weeks prior to the State test in Math and ELA (grades 3–8), the normal Cooperative Unison Reading program is used as a context for test genre exposure. Group leaders for these weeks select "retired" state tests from the State Education website. (If your state does not archive past tests, visit the NY State Education department website, where previous years' tests are archived by grade and subject.)

Learners should be encouraged to use their "genre practice" savvy to determine what the test is trying to do and how they should respond. This practice helps learners practice "listening" to the voice behind the test to determine what it is asking of them, trying to ask of them and how to cooperate, react, or respond. The McCallister Model curriculum components are sufficient preparation for the state test, and there is no more to be done to prepare for the test than to take part in two brief weeks of Test Genre Exposure.

Discussion

> Unison reading…is one of our most powerful learning Formats. We attribute our increased graduation rate to this particular Format. We also attribute our rising regents (state test) pass rates to this Format. It is our single most powerful Format and you will see it happening in every single class that our students take whether in person or remote, whether in the fall of 2020, or in the spring of 2023, or 2029. It is a very, very wonderful learning Format.
>
> Daphne LaBua, Assistant Principal,
> Urban Assembly School for Green Careers (2020)

Conventional small-group reading instruction is typically organized by reading level or ability and students are provided a pre-determined instructional plan based on teacher assessments (or assumptions) about which skills and competencies require attention. Several problems arise in this form of teacher-directed instruction. First, the teacher assumes total responsibility for determining what points in a text deserve attention. In actual fact, reading is a self-organizing process contingent on selective attention to cues that have salience for the reader that are deemed relevant to the author's intent. Second, this approach is based on an overly cognitive view of reading and assumes that the process of learning to read equates with the mechanical accumulation of skills. This view defies current conceptions of literacy as a self-organizing, socially motivated process through which skills and background abilities develop *as a result of practice and social participation*, and in which the reader's intentions govern every aspect of how they interact with a text. Third, the routines of skill-based grouping minimize student agency and autonomy in the learning process, limiting the potential for motivation and engagement (Deci & Ryan, 1985). Fourth, leveled groups function to stratify the classroom, preventing interaction of students between groups. Ability groups have been shown to be detrimental to minority students (Lleras & Rangel, 2011). In the following section, we will explore some of the ways that CUR breaks the traditional mold of group reading instruction.

Democracy

Dewey (1916/1944) asserted that a democracy is "a mode of associated living, of conjoint communicated experience" (p. 87), and that a society is democratic to the extent that it promotes the fullest possible freedom of interaction of all of its members. Traditional reading groups based on ability function to segregate the social world of the classroom based on ability status. CUR provides a means to create more democratic and inclusive classroom social worlds. Learners self-select into groups that are socially inclusive, formed on the basis of interest and fairness—everyone taking a turn—rather than on the basis of the more traditional segregating grounds of ability, disability, and language background. The CUR program also provides a means through which obligations to a human rights-based education can be achieved. It provides a way for children to develop their talents; exercise fundamental freedoms of thought, expression, and social affiliation; learn tolerance and friendship; to exercise cultural identity and personal values; access information from a variety of sources; prioritize children's interests; and give them opportunities to exercise their rights (United Nations Children's Fund/UNESCO, 2007). Every day, in CUR, learners practice the poses of democratic citizenship and exercise their basic human rights.

Executive Regulation

Executive regulation involves the self-regulation of the brain's executive functions, such as inhibitory response, planning, working memory, cognitive control, attention switching, and conscious decision making. But executive regulation is also a part of a higher mental process that Piaget identified as *equilibration*, when the person resolves disequilibrium by reorganizing, at an executive level, the components of the mind in order to re-establish coherence and consistency in cognitive functioning (Tomasello, 2019). The resolution of every breach is an instance of equilibration.

Relational Adjudication

Relational adjudication is the social equivalent of equilibration. In the context of CUR, the process of relational adjudication supports participants to resolve confusions by reasoning cooperatively and shifting and sharing perspectives, and in doing so, by making reference to objective knowledge. These processes build up capacities for objective reasoning, and thus support intellective and academic development.

Self-responsibility

Instructional programs that focus on reading as a mechanical set of skills often neglect the more general goal of learning to read—to cooperate socially with the author of a text

Genre Practice

CUR is a context in which learners hone their skills in *Genre Practice*. CUR prompts learners to approach texts as forms of action, and to "listen" to the author to determine what he or she is attempting to say or do. In this context, learners gain practice in critically analyzing how writing genres "behave" and function. And because they have opportunity to analyze a different text/genre each week, they have ample opportunity to learn how texts function based on the author's purpose and the social circumstance in which the text performs its function. Through Genre Practice in the context of CUR, learners not only learn the features of texts and how to interpret them, they also learn about the social worlds in which these writing genres operate. CUR is a culturally promotive pedagogical practice since it dramatically expands the quantity of social and cultural worlds that learners have opportunity to explore.

Participation on the Social Plane

Cooperative Unison Reading (CUR) is a concrete example of what Vygotsky referred to a social plane. The social plane provides a context for activity that enables the learner to practice competencies that they are just beginning to learn, *in advance of development* (Vygotsky, 1978). It allows them to do things today, with others, that they will be able to do independently in the future (Vygotsky, 1978).

Deep Learning

The practice of CUR promotes self-determination and high levels of volition (executive regulation; self-responsibility; follow-in to others' intentions), all the while supporting attention to text content and opportunities to triangulate meanings with others. In a state of intense, volitional engagement, when learners are expending large amounts of psychic energy in the task at hand, knowledge and skills are learned more deeply. Heightened levels of involvement stimulate *selective attention* to instructional points that are being discussed, a necessary condition for the formation of long-term memory (Kandel, 2007). Selective attention in these situations recruits a whole range of cognitive capacities that evolved in human beings to coordinate problem-solving social behavior such as *initiation of behavior, goal setting*, and *planning, working memory, emotional* and *cognitive self-regulation, inhibition,* and *initiation of behavior* (Banich & Compton, 2018). When they coordinate their minds with others, social-cognitive capacities are stimulated, such as Theory-of-mind (ToM), or the capacity to cognitively represent others' mental states and intentions; social cognition, or the capacity to read social cues in others' responses; empathy, or the capacity to feel the way others feel; and imitation, or the capacity to carry out an action that is observed in another person (Banich & Compton, 2018). Motivation and engagement are heightened because the CUR Format provides the "nutriments" of self-determination: learners have *autonomy* in joining groups and exercising fundamental freedoms of thought, movement, expression, and affiliation; they experience feelings of *relatedness* to others through the group experience; and they receive continuous competence feedback through the opportunity to resolve problems that arise in the group process (Deci & Ryan, 2012).

By distributing responsibility from the adult to the learner for attending to points of confusion and challenge within a text, the CUR procedures help guarantee that instructional discourse is more closely attuned to the actual developmental needs that learners themselves identify. Repairing the *breach* by themselves assures that the relevant learning occurs even in the absence of explicit instruction by the teacher. The result is a kind of *just in time* pedagogy; the teaching that occurs instrumentally and pragmatically in the context of the activity itself to solve a problem rather than as an explicit exercise from an activity's reduced component. Thus, CUR allows the learner to learn through their own problem-solving ability and to develop independent problem-solving skills.

Coordinating Mental States

As groups take action to solve problems, they necessarily engage in *relational adjudication* (Gergen, 1990, 2015) or perspective-shifting discourse (Lohman & Tomasello, 2003), the interpersonal process of resolving or deciding conflicts between perspective. When disagreements arise, disequilibrium is resolved as learners exchange perspectives and reason cooperatively to resolve them. In CUR, cooperative discourse is the engine of learning, as opposed the process of transmission of skills. Since the texts learners select reflect the ideas and values of the canons of the broader culture (Benedict, 1934), and since learners have freedom to think and react to these bodies of knowledge of their own will, they have opportunities to actively coordinate their beliefs to normative and objective cultural models. Through these experiences, learners broaden their own evaluative discourses, or frameworks for making judgments in future situations (Gergen, 1990, 2015). This ever-expanding web of beliefs frames one's capacity to engage in rational and reflective thinking within a broader context of cultural group standards (Tomasello, 2014).

Purposeful social discourse provides opportunities to share intentions with others, stimulating cognitive skills and motivations of social cognition, cooperative thinking, communication, cultural learning, collaboration, prosociality, social norms, and moral identity (Tomasello, 2019). In addition to providing a context in which traditional academic skills are learned, participation in CUR stimulates targeted forms of higher-level learning that align with 21st-century learning standards, such as social awareness, self-regulation, resilience, self-direction, collaboration, persistence, problem solving, critical decision making, flexibility, and creativity (Learning Metrics Task Force (LMTF), 2013; Organisation for Economic Co-operation and Development (OECD), 2018).

Identity Building

Learners build their identity by directing their own learning experiences by selecting into groups that allow them to learn about topics of interest shared with people they care to associate with. Over the course of the year, every child has the opportunity to read at least 40 different texts in 40 different social groups. Learners become agents of the creation of their own identities. They use CUR to develop their own talents and expertise and to expand their own social networks.

In one 4th-grade classroom, a boy was among the last to sign up, finding the only remaining slot in an all-girl group whose text selection was an advice column on training bras. Initially upset, within days he had become an integrated and productive member of the group, and the experience no doubt expanded his capacity to empathize with others who are different from him in fundamental ways. Children learn to use and appreciate the freedom to venture into groups that allow them to cross what would otherwise be exclusive social boundaries of culture, class, race, language, and gender. Through a continuous process of sharing minds and becoming closely acquainted with the *Other*, one expands who they are.

Social Capital

Social capital is the accumulation of resources linked to a network of institutionalized relationships that derive a benefit to the person (Bourdieu, 1986). One way in which ability-grouping practices for instruction of the industrial school create structural inequalities is through differential opportunities to develop social capital by restricting opportunities to associate with others. The CUR program provides an institutional system to support learners to develop their own social capital through self-selected membership in groups.

Mindful Reading

Cooperative Unison Reading is a method of *mindful reading*. Mindful reading is the overall effort to bring the focus of one's attention and awareness to the present moment through a form of hypervigilance and, with conscious effort, to observe the contents of one's attention without judgment. Mindful reading emphasizes the need to inhibit the impulse to react or evaluate. It trains the mind to be aware of the process of creating meaning, as if *bearing witness* to one's own thinking process. It is an approach to reading that encourages open-minded listening and non-judgmental engagement with the author of a text. Mindful reading leads to more empathetic listening and meaningful interpersonal exchanges.

Embracing Confusion and Uncertainty

Reading accuracy is the primary aim of traditional reading instruction. In reading groups focused on skill development, learners read texts aloud and, upon error, are corrected. Correction without competence feedback contributes to a *fixed mindset* in which the learner believes their reading abilities cannot be changed (Dweck, 2013). Continued exposure to negative stimulus in the context of reading instruction gives rise to all sorts of disordered behaviors that we see in learners in schools that present in the form of dyslexia. In CUR, oral reading is not a performance aimed at perfection. Instead of being avoided, cognitive dissonance is an invitation to shift into "we-mode" and share mindscapes (Tomasello, 2009).

Dismantling Curricular Segregation

Traditional methods of group reading instruction in school involve sorting students by reading level or ability for standardized instruction. Leveled groups are then provided a pre-determined instructional plan based on teacher assessments or assumptions about which skills and competencies students in each group need to learn. These practices lead to institutional segregation based on age and ability (Cole, 2005), and create the conditions for what Dewey (1916/1944) described as an "undesirable society" that sets up internal and external barriers to "free intercourse and communication of experience" (p. 99). This is why ability groups have been shown to be detrimental to minority students' achievement (Lleras & Rangel, 2009). CUR eliminates the practice of ability- and level-based reading groups. Rejecting the traditional view that reading proficiency is an outcome of knowledge transmission and can be taught through a systematic process of direct explicit instruction of increments of knowledge and skill (National Reading Panel,

2000), CUR rests on the premise that knowledge and so-called reading "skills" are really cooperative social achievements, acquired in the form of shared normative ways of thinking (e.g., we all *agree* that "R" makes the /R/ sound, and our belief directs our behavior). The more diversity in perspectives within a group, the greater resources the group has to solve problems.

Social Grooming

Social grooming satisfies the psychological needs of social animals to interact and be cared for by others. In human beings, social grooming takes the form of verbal grooming (Dunbar, 1998). Joking, teasing, gossiping, and *just messin'* are forms of talk that satisfy the basic human need to feel positively connected with others, enhancing feelings of security and emotional well-being. Verbal grooming lives in the life space of the CUR Format. CUR interactions are peppered with soothing speech acts that indulge the need to groom and be groomed by others—through laughter, gossip, and repartee.

Transfer

Once learners have mastered the rudimentary procedures of CUR, it can be employed as a social tool in any situation where reading and text interpretation benefit from perspective-sharing and cooperative reasoning. For example, learners use CUR in the context of other Formats, such as Learning Teams, Integrative Math, and Academic and Behavior Interventions, enlisting the support of others to read texts to solve problem.

The Power of Discourse

Read through the Cooperative Unison Reading Records for grades 1, 5, and 8 (see Appendices 21–23, www.routledge.com/9780367458591). Consider the processes of relational adjudication (Gergen, 1990) and perspective-shifting discourse (Tomasello, 2019) discussed in Chapter 3, and identify where in the transcripts these processes are illustrated. Consider the capacities of shared intentionality, the infrastructure for group-minded activities like CUR. Think about how instances of joint attentional engagement represented in the transcripts show evidence of the phenomenon of *follow-in* described in Chapter 3. Through patterns of relational adjudication, particularly through perspective-shifting discourse, and through the phenomenon of follow-in, what cultural representations do you observe learners to be wrestling with? What Background skills do they appear to be building? What are the literacy lessons that emerge from these examples of peer pedagogy?

Notes

1. In the context of CUR, human diversity is a resource. Differences in experience, ability, language, personal and cultural identities are resources that can be shared with others to help them expand their thinking. Thus, there are no restrictions to group membership, other than the rule that no more than five can join a group.
2. Theory of Mind emerges in human children at just around the same time they come to school, at age four or five. It is advisable that children ages four and five take part in CUR in groups of no more than three until they become practiced in coordinating mental states with others in the context of group reading.
3. *Breach* used in this context means to break into the author's turn of speech at the very moment in time that disequilibrium occurs. In order to do this effectively—to identify the slightest confusion in one's thinking about what a writer is attempting to say at the moment the

confusion arises—necessarily requires a state of hypervigilance. The disposition of hypervigilance in relation to the author's intent during the act of reading is the very definition of comprehension.
4. I recommend introducing the Format of Cooperative Unison Reading to a class of students in a fishbowl Format. Conduct a focus group of three or four learners while the rest of the class encircles the group to observe. Allow learners to take turns participating in the process to enable as many as possible to experience the Format. Learners of all ages routinely remain engaged in the fishbowl for 40–50 minutes, and the class can be quickly "trained" in the method inside of a single class period.
5. All but for subscriptions to print and digital media, CUR essentially eliminates the costs associated with curriculum materials and remediation programs.

Activities

1. Read: Researchers show power of mirror neuron system in learning, language understanding (2013): https://www.sciencedaily.com/releases/2013/12/131219142317.htm.
2. Read: Study shows 'readability' scores largely inaccurate (2014): https://www.sciencedaily.com/releases/2014/01/140108102449.htm.
3. Read: More challenging content in kindergarten boosts later performance (2014): https://www.sciencedaily.com/releases/2014/03/140319093753.htm. and doing share the same cognitive pathways: http://bit.ly/1FuoIPn.
4. Read: Sound and vision: Visual cortex processes auditory information, too (2014). https://www.sciencedaily.com/releases/2014/05/140525155316.htm.
5. Read: Comprehending Comprehension (2013). https://www.sciencedaily.com/releases/2013/11/131106101610.htm.
6. Listen to NYU Associate Professor Michael Kiefer discuss the nature of attention and how it is taxed in the reading process. http://www.voiceofliteracy.org/posts/54427.

learning cultures®

Cooperative Unison Reading Rubric

Rating Scale: (✓-) Needs Immediate Improvement (✓) Making Progress (✓+) Proficient (NA) No opportunity to observe

Classroom Procedures

1. A system is established for group leaders to make and post text selections that are short enough to be read in a week. Group leadership rotates on a weekly basis so that all students consistently experience the leadership role. Leadership is not contingent on 'good' behavior.
2. A system is established for learners to sign up for texts of their choice. Sign-up turns rotate so learners have fair opportunities to select 'first-choice' texts. Turns are not contingent upon 'good' behavior.
3. Learners complete Cooperative Unison Reading logs and text selection assignments outside of CUR meetings.

Group Procedures

1. Learners meet in designated groups, convening quickly and coming to the meeting prepared. Groups meet at a small table, seated facing one another, closely enough so that low voices are audible and peers' texts can be easily reached and referenced.
2. Group leaders take responsibility for materials, bringing copies of texts and a materials bin to a designated meeting location (materials bin contains a white board, marker, Cooperative Unison Reading Rules and Rubric, dictionary/atlas or tablet). The tabletop is cleared except for white board, eraser, texts, and CUR Rules. Materials bin is stored under the table.
3. Learners first discuss the text globally, inferring the author's purpose, intent, and the desired responsive understanding in the reader. They determine their reading stance and sense of purpose.
4. Learners collectively determine a place in the text to begin reading, and the group leader initiates the reading process (Typically directing members to put their finger under the first word to be read and counting down to begin the reading process).
5. Learners adhere to Cooperative Unison Reading Rules by reading aloud in sync in a voice others can hear, breaching or stopping the group with questions or comments, and being promotive (e.g., being nice and promoting others' learning). They use Rules to efficiently coordinate behaviors, participate in well-paced discussions, and communicate effectively in order to develop collective understanding.
6. Learners cooperate and contribute evenly to resolve confusions as they arise and offer comments appropriately. After resolving a mid-sentence breach, the group resumes reading at the beginning of the sentence in order to read with meaning intact.
7. Learners debrief during the final few minutes of the session, identifying accomplishments and goals for the next meeting. Completion of reading logs and other writing tasks are postponed until after the session concludes.
8. Group leader collects materials. Group members quickly transition to other Work Time activities within a period of two minutes.

Primary Aims

1. To practice cooperation by working with others to solve problems.
2. To practice executive self-regulation by conforming to group norms.
3. To practice cognitive control and mental coordination by shifting and sharing perspectives and reasoning cooperatively with others in order to achieve collective understanding.
4. To expand comprehension of a text through a process of social triangulation, attuning to and resonating with others' thoughts, feelings, and emotions.
5. To develop new knowledge, literacy skills and cognitive competencies.
6. To practice reading comprehension as the act of understanding an author's intentions.
7. To develop social cognition and stimulate capacities to understand and empathize with others.
8. To practice emotional self-regulation.

9. To practice democratic, civil discourse by resolving disagreements through non-judgmental deliberation and consensual agreement.

1.	Learner	Rating
1a.	Is promotive, respectful, and completely attentive to group members.	
1b.	Participates in Cooperative Unison Reading by 'playing' by the Rules: 1) Read aloud in sync; 2) Stop the group with questions or comments; 3) Promote others' learning.	
1c.	Takes responsibility to participate equally in productive discussions. Passive learners strive to be active; and assertive learners strive to encourage others to contribute. (Note: the group leader does not dominate, but participates on equal terms with others).	
1d.	Demonstrates cooperative behavior through appropriate verbal and non-verbal communication (e.g., attends to facial expressions, makes eye contact, follows into others' comments).	
1e.	Attunes to others' perspectives with flexibility, shares and shifts perspectives, and reasons cooperatively. Remains open-minded and resonates with others' ideas.	
1f.	Approaches the text as a form of action, attending to literary, linguistic, and stylistic features in relation the author's purpose and intent. Makes the attempt to *listen* to what the author is saying.	
1g.	Utilizes resources appropriately and resourcefully (e.g., uses context clues before referring to a dictionary or reference materials).	
1h.	After a breach is resolved, rereads from the beginning of the sentence in order to hear the sentence intact with full meaning.	

2.	Guide	Rating
2a.	Encourages learners to approach Cooperative Unison Reading as a rule game. Supports learners to use Cooperative Unison Reading Rules to govern the group reading process.	
2b.	Acts as referee, breaching when rules are broken. Before explaining or suggesting alternative behaviors, prompts learners to identify the rule in question, relate it to the problematic behavior, and proceed according to the Rules. Developing groups will involve frequent calls by the referee until 'players' have internalized rules.	
2c.	Supports learners in approaching text as a form of action derived from the author's intentions. Supports learners to follow into what the author is doing, as well as what the text is saying. Encourages cooperative participation with the author of a text.	
2d.	Supports learners to approach reading as a mindful practice, centered on non-judgmental reflection of one's thinking in relation to the thinking of others.	
2e.	Encourages learner agency and interdependence by allowing learners to manage the group process. Serves in a facilitative capacity, enabling learners to initiate and lead discussions. Refrains from directing learner behavior or teaching content didactically. When learners are unable to independently resolve a question, follows into discussion to allow maximal autonomy to learners and to enable them to facilitate their own resolution.	

3.	Physical Space and Materials	Rating
3a.	Four round tables serve as designated meeting locations. Tables are positioned to be distributed as far from one another as possible, minimizing noise distractions (The CUR Format occurs simultaneously with other Formats during Work Time, so sources of ambient noise should be distributed across classroom space). Tables are labeled with numbers or letters (to facilitate efficient group meeting procedures). Tabletop is cleared of clutter except for text copies, Unison Reading Rules, a whiteboard and dry-erase marker.	
3b.	Materials bin for each table, which contains a dictionary, atlas, white board, dry-erase marker, eraser, and Cooperative Unison Reading Rubric and Cooperative Unison Reading Rules.	
3c.	Cooperative Unison Reading Record for in-the-midst note-taking by the guide.	
3d.	Cooperative Unison Reading Log, to be filled in by learners *after* the conclusion of the session.	
3e.	Cooperative Unison Reading Analysis Form.	
3f.	Cooperative Unison Reading Rubric.	

3g. Cooperative Unison Reading Text Selection Assignment (to be completed by group leaders).

3h. Electronic timer (to indicate the end of the session to avoid teachers from interrupting Work Time with distracting directives).

4. Recordkeeping   Rating

4a. Cooperative Unison Reading Records demonstrate teacher facility in recording summaries of learner discourse, coding breaches under appropriate reading domains and correctly identifying instructional points that emerge from discussion.

4b. Records show evidence that learners have received sufficient group reading opportunities over time to constitute equality of educational opportunity. Targets are met for weekly teacher-facilitated and independent Cooperative Unison Reading group sessions (e.g., four sessions per week and at least 80 minutes per week).

4c. Records indicate meaningful interaction and evenly-distributed dialogue and deliberation over a full range of instructional points. Records show evidence that learners actively coordinate mental states, following into peer comments.

4d. Records are dated, chronologically sequenced, neat, legible, and easily interpreted.

4e. Learners' CUR logs and Text Selection Assignments are consistently used and archived for reference.

Comments:

15 The Learning Teams Format

Description

Within a tournament structure, Learning Teams (L-Teams) provide a context of interdependence and shared accountability in which a small group of diversely abled team members work cooperatively to learn curriculum-based content knowledge in preparation for an end-of-unit post-test. Competition cycles are built around units of study that are organized based on the state curriculum. Units of study are book-ended by a diagnostic pre-test and a summative post-test. After the pre-test, learners work together to analyze state test questions and content standards in order to determine content that must be learned, distribute responsibility to study and research content, share findings with team members, and assess the team's collective achievement in meeting learning standards through comparison of collective scores of pre- and post-tests. Competitions between Learning Teams establish which team makes the greatest gains.

Learning Teams are a way to value, nurture, and track academic and social growth. The team structure creates an environment where students are responsible for their classmates' learning as well as their own, thus providing a mechanism for creating peer-to-peer accountability for academic performance in every content area. Learning Teams also provide a way to learn formal curriculum content without reliance on teacher-directed instruction.

Teams are selected through a draft in which team captains take turns choosing members from the class roster. Within a tournament structure, with the goal of achieving the highest mean score on a post-test, teams of learners compete by preparing to take a unit assessment. Teams follow preparation procedures that enable them to successfully execute a long-range plan to research and learn required content. At the end of the unit, the team with the highest mean score wins the tournament. Learners are also administered a social assessment through which they give feedback to their teammates on how to improve social-cognitive capacities of *cooperation, discipline, effort, emotional self-regulation*, and their *sense of purpose*. Note: L-Teams are developmentally appropriate in upper elementary through high school/college classes.

Primary Aims

1 To structure and organize learner-facing, standards-aligned, discipline-based units.
2 To practice responsibility for making and meeting formal learning goals.
3 To structure incremental accomplishments toward the achievement of long-term learning goals.
4 To utilize the team structure as a context to practice mutuality, interdependence, shared responsibility, and shared accountability.

5 To utilize the team structure to instill intrinsic motivation and proactive intentions in relation to formal learning objectives.
6 To develop social cognition and stimulate capacities to understand and empathize with others.
7 To develop new knowledge, literacy skills, and cognitive competencies.
8 To practice cognitive control and mental coordination by shifting and sharing perspectives and reasoning cooperatively with others in order to achieve collective understanding.
9 To practice executive self-regulation by conforming to group norms.

Materials

Pre- and Post-tests
Unit Questions Guide (created from unit curriculum)
GIST Form Study Guide (see Appendix 26)
C-DEEP Survey and Self-assessment (see Appendices 27 and 28)
Evidence Record (see Appendix 24)
Personal Learning Responsibilities Form (see Appendix 25)
Research Archive
Curriculum Map (created from subject/discipline state standards)
Research briefs (created by learners)
Dice (physical or digital)
Class list

See www.routledge.com/9780367458591 for mentioned Appendices.

Procedures

Set up. Learners will have been previously taught the expectations for participation in the Learning Teams Format and are familiar with the Learning Teams Rubric. Teachers create a **content pre-test** covering a sampling of questions from a specified section of curriculum that will be covered over the span of the tournament cycle and which will serve as the scope of the unit/game to be given on the first day of the unit. The content pre-test can be created from questions from previous year's state tests, end-of-chapter questions, content from online sources (e.g., Khan Academy), or questions generated from the state curriculum. Teachers also create a **Unit Questions Guide**, a list of 50 questions representing a balanced scope of the curriculum to be covered during the unit. Questions can be derived from previous state exams, curriculum scope and sequence outlines, end-of-chapter textbook questions, or online sources (e.g., Khan Academy). Where possible, teachers should collaborate in subject teams to distribute the workload. Units are organized into six- to nine-week cycles. Teachers create a **Curriculum Map** document comprising the entire breadth of state learning standards that make up the yearly course curriculum organized into equal parts that align with the school's ranking periods (see Appendix 16, Writing Standards Checklist grade 7 for an illustration of the use of formal standards as assessments, www.routledge.com/9780367458591).

1 *Drafts.* On the second day of the unit, teams of no more than five are formed. From a class list, teachers appoint pairs of learners to serve as team captains. For the initial tournament cycle, teachers select learners who have earned the respect of their peers, regardless of their teachers' perceptions of them, and will be capable of providing

leadership to their peers throughout the tournament process. After the first championship cycle, leadership opportunities should be distributed and rotated so that every learner is eventually a captain. Leadership has an integrative influence on the mind, and it is a powerful learning opportunity that should be made fairly available.

When teachers meet with team captains to conduct a "draft" process to select teams from a class list, they meet outside of the classroom to prevent embarrassment to children who are selected last. To determine the selection process, each team tosses the dice. For the first round of selections, the team with the highest outcome selects first, and the team with the lowest outcome selects last. For the next round, the process is reversed, with the team who had the lowest outcome selecting first. This process is repeated until all learners have been assigned to a team (e.g., in a class of 30, six pairs of co-captains would select from the remaining 24 peers). Teachers advise team captains to deliberate the merits of potential team members in relation to a strategy for winning the competition (e.g., selecting peers who are conscientious, helpful, intelligent, come to class).

2 *Pre-test.* The pre-test is administered, and learners are each given their individual scores privately. Mean team scores are calculated and publicized. Once teams begin to meet, teachers work with learners to help them analyze their assessment results to identify wrong answers, indicating content to be learned.

3 *Research process.* Once teams are selected, the games begin! Teams meet together as they deem necessary to engage in a comprehensive process of cooperative research and knowledge sharing in order to prepare for the end-of-tournament post-test. The team shares responsibility to ensure each group member learns enough to successfully answer a set of curriculum-aligned questions in the post-test.

The preparation process is organized by a **Unit Questions Guide**. Teams also add questions that were answered incorrectly from the pre-test onto the Unit Questions Guide.

Teams create a unit schedule in order to pace coverage of the Unit Questions Guide and to complete it two weeks before the post-test to allow sufficient time preparation. Learners divide the total number of test questions by the number of weeks allotted for preparation. They also determine how many questions they will analyze each week.

Using the **GIST Study Guide**, the team begins analyzing each question by reading it in Unison and determining the concept or skill being assessed. The purpose of this analysis is to determine what concept(s) the group needs to study, not to determine the correct answer. The concept(s) is recorded in the GIST column on the left side of the Guide, and the corresponding question number is listed in the middle row under the corresponding column. The GIST Study Guide will become an outline of what the learners must study in order to successfully answer the questions on the Unit Questions Handout. The objective of this step is not to answer questions, but to determine what *confusions* must be clarified *in order* to answer the questions (see Box 15.1).

As each question is analyzed, teams determine who is responsible for learning the content, and record their initials in the right column of the Guide. As teams identify concepts to be learned, responsibility is evenly delegated to team members to independently **research** the concept or knowledge they were assigned. Teams together determine how many questions each team member will research each week in order to complete the study guide one week prior to the post-test. In a hypothetical test of 50 questions, each learner should be delegated 10 items to research. Covering 5 questions a day, the group should finish test analysis in 10 days.

Each team member goes on a research "scavenger hunt" to find the information they need to explain the concept or skill they have been assigned to research. Each learner should keep an **Evidence Record** listing the concept/skill and the sources accessed.

> **Box 15.1**
>
> **"GISTING" a state test question**
>
> **Example**
>
> A question from a hypothetical Unit Questions Guide will be used here to illustrate the process. For example, question #4 on the New York State History Regents exam of 2003 was:
> Question #4: The main criticism of the Articles of Confederation was that they failed to
>
> 1. Allow for the admission of new states
> 2. Prevent the development of military rule
> 3. Provide adequate powers for the central government
> 4. Prevent the development of military rule
>
> In unison, learners would have read the question and identified its GIST, or content focus. In this case, the GIST is "The main criticism of the Articles of Confederation." But learners might also have a more basic question, such as, *what were the Articles of Confederation?*
> The Regents question example given above—"What were criticisms of the Articles of Confederation?"—would have been flipped into a study guide question such as, "Identify the primary criticisms of the Articles of Confederation."
> The student who was assigned this question might have accessed videos on YouTube or read excerpts from a history textbook to learn content. Then they might have written a brief that looked something like this:
> *One of the primary weaknesses of the Articles of Confederation was the inability of Congress to raise funds and regulate trade.*
>
> Source: http://memory.loc.gov/ammem/collections/continental/defects.html

They are also expected to share their research agenda with someone from home and get support from that person in finding resources to answer the question (this step is an organic way to involve families in the learner's academic life). The **Personal Learning Form** is used to document this process.

Once they have done their research, they write a 200-word brief, embedding hyperlinks to relevant web content. Briefs are *comprehensible* summaries of research findings that are easily accessible to teammates. (Chicken-scratched notes or piles of printed Google searches are not acceptable.) Learners need to take responsibility to do research and write briefs using class time efficiently, but they should also plan to use out-of-school time to work independently and communicate with teammates via teleconference. Teams devise a way to share briefs, and each team member compiles all their own briefs and those of their teammates into a **Research Archive** that they can reference for test preparation (e.g., Google docs and hyperlinks to sources).

4. *Ground rules for understanding.* Working together as a group, team members make sure that every person fully understands every question or piece of information that comes before the group. In other words, each team member needs to support all of their teammates in understanding the material covered. The group should develop an accountability system to ensure that all members understand pertinent information. The group needs to be especially considerate of non-English speakers' needs to access content in their first/native language.

5 *Social assessment.* Once groups have worked together for a period of at least three days, each student fills out either a **C-DEEP Survey** or a **Learning Teams Peer Assessment** to give social feedback to their teammates and to receive feedback themselves. As each learner receives C-DEEP data from their teammates, they fill out their own **C-DEEP Personal Assessment** and calculate their average scores for each assessment category. Social assessment results are not shared publicly so as to avoid shaming or embarrassing students, and they are not collected by teachers. The team merges their scores to determine their team average in each assessment category. Team captains collect the team averages and submit them to the teacher for the record. Teachers should report *group* means on social assessments to the class.

The social assessments provide feedback to learners in the categories of *cooperation, discipline, effort, emotional self-regulation,* and *sense of purpose.* After analyzing their assessment results, each learner determines their highest and lowest scores. Each team member solicits suggestions from teammates about how to change their behaviors and improve their lowest social assessment scores. And team members provide one another with concrete, actionable suggestions to improve their performance and raise social assessment scores. The main purpose of the social assessment process within the L-Team Format is to provide learners with social data about themselves, together with actionable, corrective feedback, so that they can make efforts to improve behavior in the context of cooperative group endeavors. Once they have reviewed their C-DEEP pre-assessment results, each group member shares a goal for social-emotional development during the unit. The social assessments exist primarily as a form of competence feedback for learners. While it is important for teachers to access the mean social assessment data so that they can make group norms public to the class, C-DEEP data management is not a teacher responsibility.

6 *Check-in quiz.* The teacher administers a check-point quiz mid-way through the unit and provides individual and team scores. The teacher coaches learners how to use scores as feedback, helping them analyze errors and relearn content.

7 *Group goal setting.* With both insights from social assessments and data from the check-in quiz, teams now spend time strategizing their group process, determining strengths, needs, and goals for the remainder of the unit.

8 Once the team has completed the research process, they turn their attention to the sections of the Curriculum Map document that expands the range of content covered in the unit. The team works together to analyze each indicator of the standards to determine if there are additional concepts that need to be researched in order to fully understand the content covered in the unit. They follow the same procedures, adding the knowledge or skill from the standards to the GIST form, the standards indicator number in the middle, and the initials of the researcher on the right.

9 *Answering questions.* Once the research cycle has concluded, all questions on the Unit Questions Guide have been analyzed, and each person has reported their research, the group re-convenes to now *answer* the questions on the Guide. If the process was successful overall, there will be few lingering questions or confusions. If there are still questions that cannot be answered, the team repeats the research process accordingly.

10 *Social assessment.* One week before the post-test, learners once again complete the C-DEEP social assessment and provide feedback to their teammates. Each learner analyzes their own results, determines highest and lowest scores, and compares their pre- and post- C-DEEP assessment scores. Teams merge their scores to determine mean gains in each category. Teammates share feedback for future improvement.

11 Learners spend the remaining time before the post-test preparing, using their Research Archive to prepare for the post-test.
12 The teacher creates a unit post-test or utilizes one from an existing source (e.g., retired state exams or online test items). The post-test is administered on the last week of the unit. Mean scores are calculated and publicized, and individual scores are given privately to individual learners (individual scores are not publicly posted).
13 *"The winners are..."* Teachers announce the final team scores and tournament winners. The team with the highest mean score wins the championship. Teams are given time in the final period of the unit to conduct a post-game analysis of their performance to determine strengths, needs, and goals for future improvement.

Discussion

A primary aim of formal schooling is to help learners accept responsibility for aligning their thoughts and actions (i.e., personal intentions) with those of the school (Olson, 2003). David Olson (2003) asserts that part of this responsibility includes the ability and inclination to interpret archival resources that make up disciplinary knowledge, including the rules, norms, and standards of the discipline, and to view these achievements as attainable and worthwhile. This, Olson suggests, consists in the capacity to appraise one's own intentions in relation to institutional or the collective intentions of the school.

Traditionally, curriculum is organized into the linear arrangement of domains of knowledge onto a curriculum conveyor belt, where increments of information are administered to students in standardized doses, like medicine, regardless of the child's feelings or attitudes about the content to be learned.

L-Teams are the proverbial *spoonful of sugar* that helps the medicine go down. They contextualize the canons of the disciplines into a game-like structure in which learners get to take part in caring relationships and try their hardest to support the collective welfare of the group. In this context, learners develop positive orientations to canonical knowledge sources.

Learning and motivation of shared intentionality

L-Teams are strategically designed to require teammates to take part in perspective-shifting discourse in the process of deliberations. Perspective-shifting discourse is the linguistic processes that enable human beings to access insights from others (Tomasello, 2014). Learners systematically analyze curriculum standards or questions, first by deliberating about what knowledge, understanding, or skills the group needs in order to answer the question, and then by using the information acquired to deliberate about how to answer the question. This process necessarily involves recursive inferences, or the process of thinking about what I am thinking about by thinking about how another person thinks about what I am thinking about. The processes of cooperative reasoning and perspective sharing through recursive inferences, triangulated against objective sources of knowledge, creates opportunities for learners to develop what Tomasello (2019) refers to as perspectival-objective representations, or the ability to understand something from a perspective that is objective or detached from any single person's perspective. This, Tomasello (2019) points out, is the basis of all scientific thinking. Motivational states stimulated in L-Teams shift from the need to "get the right answer" toward a moral need to cooperate promotively with others to obtain what the group needs to succeed—an intrinsically meaningful rationale for investment in the effort of learning.

214   *An Activity Curriculum*

Critical Consciousness

The process of analyzing high-stakes exam questions provides an opportunity for learners to gain insight into what sources of knowledge the institution of school deems most important for young people to learn. Through a systematic encounter with the hegemonic viewpoint, in a medium of dialog and deliberation, learners have the opportunity to develop critical consciousness.

Prolepsis

What learners are able to do cooperatively *today*, on the social plane with the assistance of others, they will be able to do independently *tomorrow* (Vygotsky, 1978). L-Teams help learners organize their minds in ways that will transfer positively in future academic situations. Learning Teams are structured to take advantage of the phenomenon of *prolepsis*, described in Chapter 3. In the process of prolepsis, one anticipates a future act by encountering it in the present. *Proleptic* learning opportunities help students anticipate future challenges in order to prepare, and to gain skill and confidence. Through each L-Teams tournament cycle, the learner will have experienced success in independently (and interdependently) mastering a range of learning expectations from the formal curriculum that will be the focus of a future assessments. L-Teams bring challenges that will be encountered in the future into the present in order to prepare.

A Framework for Discipline-Based Curriculum

L-Teams can serve as the spine of the curriculum in content subjects. Implemented in cycles throughout the entire school year that cover the full breadth of the formal curriculum, they provide a vehicle to ensure every learner has the opportunity to learn what is expected.

Curriculum Extensions and Integration

The L-Teams curriculum can be extended and integrated into other curriculum areas. For example: 1) Topics of interest that arise in the L-team process can become seeds for research and writing projects in the Reading Work Time Format and the Writing Work Time Format. These seeds can evolve into essays, position statements, biographical profiles, historical narratives, and scientific explanations. 2) Research briefs can be turned into entries in the class research encyclopedia,[1] which serve as a resource for the whole classroom community. 3) Teams can host "movie nights," selecting a documentary or series of videos on topics relating to the unit, providing a post-viewing Q&A to explore issues relevant to the curriculum.

Peer Accountability

Some children may be inclined to use Learning Teams as a camouflage for inactivity and off-task behavior. "Free-riding" is not acceptable. Team members should know that they will be responsible for ensuring that their teammates adhere to Format procedures. If a member fails to live up to their responsibilities, the group should adhere to the Ladder of Self-regulation: issue a reminder, then a warning, then ask the learner to leave the group. Teachers/guides also adhere to the Ladder of Self-regulation. If teams do not adhere to procedures, or if they demonstrate off-task behavior, they will be given a warning by the teacher, and then asked to disband. It is the responsibility of each group member to enforce positive norms and to ensure participants are actively involved and contributing at all times.

Supporting ELLs and Students with Special Needs

It's imperative that teams support the needs of ELLs. ELLs will need time and opportunity to access information in their native language and to translate it into English for their teammates. It might be necessary for teams to consider accommodations for their ELL peers, such as reducing the expected number of research items and briefs required.

Social Cognition and Moral Self-Governance

Group interdependence instills a sense of social motivation to support group achievement and stimulates the cognitive capacities (Tomasello, 2016) of collective intentions and commitments, the sense of there being a right and wrong way of doing things; collective commitments, and self-governing behavior to adhere to the rules.

Integrated Technology

L-Teams provide a context for technology and technological literacy to be woven into the curriculum. Learners use technology to access knowledge, to organize it, and to communicate it to others. A wide range of forms of technology are useful in the L-Team curriculum, such as social bookmarking platforms, pdf writing software, digital archiving technologies, and teleconferencing technologies.

Note

1. Each class can compile an Encyclopedia containing every learners' research briefs.

Activities

The effectiveness of the pre- and post-test. Learn why the pre-/post-test system is effective. Read some possible reasons in the New York Times article, "Why Flunking Exams is Actually a Good Thing." https://www.nytimes.com/2014/09/07/magazine/why-flunking-exams-is-actually-a-good-thing.html.

Learning Teams Rubric

Rating Scale: (✓-) Needs Immediate improvement (✓) Making Progress (✓+) Proficient (NA) No opportunity to observe

Procedures

1. *Preparations.* Units are organized into typical six- or nine-week cycles. Teachers create a **pre-test** covering a specified section of curriculum content that will be covered over the span of the tournament and which will serve as the scope of the unit/game. Teachers derive test questions from retired state assessments, Khan Academy questions, or state curriculum standards indicators that have been reworded into questions. Teachers also create a **Unit Questions Handout**, comprised of 50 questions that span the most salient content covered in the unit. Teachers create a **Curriculum Guide** comprising the entire breadth of state learning standards that make up the course curriculum for the year. This is done by downloading the state curriculum or scope and sequence of the formal curriculum, and translating it onto a document that is accessible to students as a point of reference.

2. *Drafts.* On the first day of the unit, teams of no more than five are formed through a draft in which pairs of learners, who serve as co-captains. In the first Learning Team cycle, co-captains are learners who have earned the respect of their peers, regardless of their teachers' perceptions, and will be capable of leadership in the game. After the first championship cycle, leadership opportunities should be distributed and rotated so that every learner is eventually a captain since leadership is has an integrative influence on the mind, and it's a powerful learning opportunity. Co-captains select team members from a class list. Before making draft selections, teams of co-captains should deliberate the merits of potential team members in relation to a strategy for winning the competition (e.g., selecting peers who are conscientious, helpful, insightful). To determine the selection process, each team tosses the dice. For the first round of selections, the team with the highest outcome selects first, and the team with the lowest outcome selects last. For the next round, the process is reversed, with the team who had the lowest outcome electing first (snake draft). This pattern is repeated until everyone has been selected from a class list of peers (e.g., in a class of 30, six pairs of co-captains would select from the remaining 24 peers). The selection process is conducted outside the classroom, away from their classmates.

3. *Pre-test.* On the second day of the unit, the pre-test is administered, and learners are each given their individual scores privately. Mean team scores are calculated and publicized. Teachers work with teams to help them analyze their assessment results and determine learning priorities.

4. *Research.* The research process begins when teams refer to the Unit Questions Guide to plan how to pace their work in order to finish researching one week prior to the post-test. Students divide the total number of Guide questions by the number of weeks allotted preparation (preparation ends one week prior to the post-test to allow sufficient time for post-test preparation).

   Using the GIST Form, learners analyze each pre-test question by reading it in Unison and determining the concept or skill being measured. The objective of this step is not to answer questions, but to determine what *confusions* must be clarified *in order* to answer the questions (see Box 15.1). List the concept or skill in the left column and the question number in the middle column. As teams identify concepts to be learned, they evenly delegate responsibility to team members to conduct independent research to resolve confusions. As each question is analyzed, determine who in the group is responsible for learning the content, and record their initials in the right column. Teams together determine how many questions each team member will research each week in order to complete the study guide at least one week prior to the post-test (in a six-week unit, teams will have 4.5 weeks to analyze all test questions and standards indicators, so they should spend time the first week planning a pacing calendar for their work). In a hypothetical test of 50 questions, each learner should be delegated 10 content items to research. Covering 5 questions a day, the group should finish test analysis in 10 days.

   Each person in the group independently takes responsibility to research the concepts and skills assigned to them, and to write a 200-word brief for each, including hyperlinks to helpful web content. Research can be conducted during Work Time or as homework. The learner keeps an Evidence Record of sources used in their research. They also share their research process with someone outside of school, using the Personal Learning Form.

Teams devise a way to share briefs (e.g., Google docs and hyperlinks to sources). Learners consolidate all their research briefs—their own and those received from teammates—into their personal Research Archive.

5. *C-DEEP pre-assessment.* After teams have worked together for a period of one week, administer a C-DEEP social assessment. The CDEEP assesses *cooperation, discipline, effort, emotional self-regulation,* and *sense of purpose*). Each team member receives C-DEEP data from each of their teammates. After analyzing their assessment results, each learner determines their highest and lowest scores. Each learner solicits suggestions from teammates about how to change their behaviors and improve their lowest social assessment scores. C-DEEP results are not shared publicly so as to avoid shaming or embarrassing students, and they are not collected by teachers.

6. *Check-in quiz.* The teacher administers a check-point quiz mid-way through the unit and provides individual and team scores. The teacher coaches learners on how to use scores as feedback, helping them analyze errors and relearn content.

7. *Group goal setting.* With both insights from social assessments and data from the check-in quiz, teams now spend time strategizing their group process, determining strengths, needs and goals for the remainder of the unit.

8. *Curriculum review.* Once the team has completed the research process, they turn their attention to the sections of the Curriculum Map document that span the range of content covered in the unit. The team works together to analyze each indicator of the standards to determine if there are additional concepts that they need to research in order to fully understand the content covered in the unit. They follow the same procedures, adding the knowledge or skill from the standards to the GIST form, the standards indicator number in the middle, and the initials of the researcher on the right.

9. *Answering questions.* Once the team has completed the analysis of questions, they now take time to answer the questions on the GIST Study Guide. If there are still questions that cannot be answered, repeat the research process accordingly.

10. *C-DEEP post assessment.* One week before the post-test, administer a C-DEEP social assessment. Each learner analyzes their results, determines highest and lowest scores, and compares pre- and post- C-DEEP assessment scores. Teammates share feedback for future improvement.

11. *Preparation.* Learners use the week before the post-test to study and prepare. Teammates should share study strategies, and the teacher should provide whole-class guidance and support to scaffold the study process.

12. *Post-test.* The teacher creates a unit post-test or utilizes one from an existing source (e.g., retired state exams or online test items). The post-test is administered the last week of the unit. Mean scores are calculated and publicized, and individual scores are given privately to individual learners (individual scores are not publicly posted). The team with the highest mean score is declared the winner.

13. *Debrief.* Teams are given time in the final period of the unit to conduct a post-game analysis of their performance to determine strengths, needs, and goals for future improvement.

Primary Aims

1. To structure and organize learner-facing, standards-aligned, discipline-based units.
2. To practice responsibility for making and meeting formal learning goals.
3. To structure incremental accomplishments toward the achievement of long-term learning goals.
4. To utilize the team structure as a context to practice mutuality, interdependence, shared responsibility and shared accountability.
5. To utilize the team structure to instill intrinsic motivation and proactive intentions in relation to formal learning objectives.
6. To develop social cognition and stimulate capacities to understand and empathize with others.
7. To develop new knowledge, literacy skills and cognitive competencies.
8. To practice cognitive control and mental coordination by shifting and sharing perspectives and reasoning cooperatively with others in order to achieve collective understanding.
9. To practice executive self-regulation by conforming to group norms.

1.	Learner	Rating
1a.	Is promotive, respectful, and completely attentive to group members.	
1b.	Demonstrates cooperative behavior through appropriate verbal and non-verbal communication (e.g., attends to facial expressions, makes eye contact, follows into others' comments).	
1c.	Attunes to others' perspectives with flexibility, shares and shifts perspectives, and reasons cooperatively. Remains open-minded and resonates with others' ideas.	
1d.	Is on task, adheres to Learning Team procedures. (Teams are permitted to meet only so long as members adhere to procedures.)	
1e.	Assumes responsibility for helping to manage the group process.	
1f.	Adheres to Cooperative Unison Reading Rules when referencing a text.	
1g.	Takes initiative and is resourceful.	
1h.	Completes and submits assigned *briefs* in a timely manner. Briefs are relevant, complete and comprehensible.	

2.	Guide	Rating
2a.	Conducts on-going assessment of each team's progress in meeting learning goals.	
2b.	Holds learners accountable for taking responsibility to adhere to Learning Team procedures.	
2c.	Intervenes when necessary to provide appropriate behavioral or instructional guidance.	

3.	Records and Materials	Rating
3a.	Pre and Post-tests.	
3b.	Unit Questions Guide.	
3c.	GIST Form Study Guide.	
3d.	C-DEEP Survey and Self-assessment.	
3e.	Personal Learning Form.	
3f.	Research Archive.	
3g.	Curriculum Map (created from subject/discipline state standards).	
3h.	Research briefs (created by learners).	
3i.	Dice (physical or digital).	
3j.	Class list.	

Comments:

Copyright © 2014, 2015, 2016, 2018, 2020 Cynthia McCallister. All rights reserved. Reproduction and distribution are prohibited without permission from the author.   www.LearningCultures.net

16 The Integrative Math Format

Description

The Integrative Math Format provides an opportunity for a small group of five or fewer learners to work cooperatively to solve a mathematical word problem. The method provides a way to deepen understanding of mathematical concepts by representing them in increasingly abstract modes of representation. Using the protocol of Cooperative Unison Reading, the group starts reading at the beginning of a word problem, and they breach, or stop the process when they encounter a concept within a sentence that can be represented enactively, or through *action*, with the use of physical objects, like manipulatives. They then represent the concept iconically, through *pictures*. Finally, they represent the concept symbolically, through *numbers and other symbols*. This process functions to integrate multiple components of the mind and to optimize thinking in the service of deep learning. Using these procedures, applying these three modes of representation, the group proceeds through the word problem until it is finished and solved.

Primary Aims

1. To integrate the mind to unite diverse systems of memory in the service of learning mathematical concepts, providing an opportunity for deep learning.
2. To practice cognitive control and mental coordination by shifting and sharing perspectives and reasoning cooperatively with others in order to achieve collective understanding.
3. To apply enactive, iconic, and symbolic modes of understanding to an abstract problem, cultivating adaptive habits of mind that can be applied in future situations.
4. To practice cooperation by working with others.
5. To practice emotional self-regulation.
6. To develop social cognition and stimulate capacities to understand and empathize with others.
7. To practice emotional self-regulation.

Materials

> Grade-level math word problem
> Cooperative Unison Reading Rules (see Appendix 20)
> Math manipulatives (Cuisenaire® Rods, Algebra Tiles, Unifix Cubes, Base Ten Blocks, and Unifix Cubes)
> White boards or scrap paper
> Pencils and markers or crayons
> Small, round table
>
> See www.routledge.com/9780367458591 for mentioned Appendices.

Procedures

Set up. Learners will have been previously taught the expectations for participation in the Integrative Math Format and are familiar with the Integrative Math Rubric. Working in a group of five or fewer, learners select a mathematics word problem at their grade level or from their subject curriculum. Learners are seated at a small round table, in close enough proximity to share materials. Learners are promotive, respectful, and completely attentive to group members. They remain on-task throughout the Integrative Math session, following specified procedures for completing group tasks, and assuming responsibility for managing the group process according to procedures, below.

The guide allows learners the opportunity to facilitate their own groups, manage the group work process, and hold themselves accountable to procedures. They observe informally and provide instruction to guide and support the process when necessary. When necessary, the guide intervenes to correct maladaptive behaviors and to secure prosocial behaviors. The guide also provides guidance to support learners to identify resources that can be used in the research process.

Integrative Math provides an optimal context for imitative learning. Learners are encouraged to borrow good ideas from others in this activity. They are assured that they will hear others say things they wish they had said, or hear others say things that they intended to say. It is important to stress the idea that thinking about things in ways that others think about them is a catalyst for creativity. So, in the Integrative Math activity, it is accepted, even encouraged, to borrow others' good ideas.

1. Using the protocol of Cooperative Unison Reading, learners read the word problem until they come to a point of confusion, when they breach, mid-sentence if necessary, to resolve the confusion.
2. Learners translate the concept encountered in the breach into a form of action, using manipulatives, if possible. This step represents the *enactive* mode of representation (representing an idea through physical objects), in which each learner creates a physical representation of the concept. Learners are reminded to observe others and borrow their thinking. When everyone has had a chance to create an enactive representation of the concept, each person explains what they did. After everyone has had an opportunity to explain, the group collectively identifies the best example of an enactive mode of representation.

    This step enhances thinking and deep learning because it takes an experience that was stored through muscle memory, or that was handled mostly by the right side of the brain (the part that uses context to understand) and integrates the functions of the left side of the brain (the one that uses words) to explain the problem. In other words,

this step of the activity integrates two different systems of the mind and strengthens learning.
3 Next, learners translate their enactive representations iconic representations, or images of the concept in the form of a picture or diagram. Learners use paper and crayons or the white boards and markers to now draw or diagram the concept. The guide should remind learners that imitation is the highest form of flattery, and encourage them to borrow liberally from others' thinking. For example, if one thinks they're bad at drawing, they should be urged to observe and imitate the drawings of others. Learners take turns explaining their iconic representation. Once everyone has explained their picture or diagram, the group collectively identifies the best example of an iconic mode of representation.
4 Next, learners translate the iconic representation into a symbolic representation. They take the picture they drew, or borrow someone else's, and translate it into mathematical symbols. Learners can discuss ideas with others, and borrow ideas from them, but everyone has to write their own symbolic representation using familiar mathematical symbols. Once everyone has explained their symbolic representation, they collectively identify the best example of a symbolic mode of representation.
5 Following the rules of Cooperative Unison Reading, the group rereads the sentence, from the beginning, in its entirety.
6 The group continues reading the word problem, repeating Steps 1–5, until the word problem is completed or the session concludes.

Discussion

Integrative Math is a Format that targets the process of mental integration—how our minds function to unite diverse systems of our memory—to solve problems. The practice is inspired by Jerome Bruner's (1966) theory of Modes of Representation, an explanation of how our minds represent knowledge. The practice is also inspired by Dan Siegel's approach to integration of the brain, or the linkage of different components of the mind (Siegel, 2020). Bruner proposes a way of understanding the components of thinking about knowledge, and Siegel presents a way of understanding how they become integrated and result in a coherent mind and brain.

Bruner's Modes of Representation

In his theory of *modes of representation*, Jerome Bruner (1963, 1966) asserts that human beings represent knowledge in three different modes or three parallel systems of processing information. The first is the *enactive mode of representation*, in which we think about things through our actions and we store memories of them through action. Enactive memory is stored in our bodies and our muscles as well as in our minds. This mode of representation dominates between the ages of 0 and 1, when infants and toddlers use sensory motor capacities to taste, touch, and feel their way into a new world of unfamiliar phenomena. The maturation of the mind and the ability to think through images soon frees the child from the need to understand things through action.

At the next level of abstraction, in the iconic mode of representation, knowledge is represented through iconic symbols, or symbols that resemble the object in question. Knowledge is represented through mental images that mirror the properties of the phenomenon. After the ages of two to three, children rely less on enactive modes of representation and more on iconic modes of representation.

Beginning at the age of six, children can now represent ideas through symbols, such as words or mathematical symbols. Symbolic thinking frees the mind to think about things that are not tied to the immediate here and now of situations. It enables abstract reasoning. Bruner (1963) writes, "It is this capacity to put things into a symbol system with rules for manipulating, for decomposing and recomposing and transforming and turning symbols on their heads that makes it possible to explore things not present, not picturable, and indeed not in existence" (p. 530). The invention of codes and symbols has freed human thinking from the constraints of the *here and now* of situations, creating the conditions necessary for development of the fields of mathematics, science, and history.

These three modes of representation are mental resources that we use throughout our lives to represent knowledge in our thinking. Just as young children must take action on a thing to understand it, or envision it as an image, early in the mastery of a subject the learner may need to represent ideas in terms of what they do with them and how they envision them before they can understand them through symbols (Bruner, 1963). In other words, people cannot use symbols to represent ideas unless they have a solid enough grasp of the idea to envision it.

Bruner thought that learners of almost any age could tackle most conceptual problems if the material were arranged in the appropriate sequence, moving through these different modes of representation. Bruner explains, "You create a structure, not by starting off with the highest brow symbolic version, but by giving it in the muscles, then in imagery and then giving it in language, with its tools for manipulation. The basic task is to orchestrate the three kinds of representation so that we can lead the child from doing, to imaging what he has done, and finally to symbolization" (p. 530).

Integration

Integration links the various components of the mind—the parts of the mind that are inside of us, in our heads and bodies, and the parts of the mind that exist in our relationships with others (Siegel, 2020). The Integrative Math Format creates a situation in which integrative functions of the mind are utilized.

Zone of Proximal Development

The Integrative Math Format establishes a social plane that provides learners opportunities to incorporate new concepts into memory. The fully integrative experience of thinking through an abstract problem in a way that links all parts of the brain, the mind, and the social world, becomes a template for future thinking.

Integrative Math Rubric

Rating Scale: (✓-) Needs Immediate Improvement (✓) Making Progress (✓+) Proficient (NA) No opportunity to observe

Procedures

1. Five or fewer learners meet to read a mathematics word problem they have selected.
2. Using the protocol of Cooperative Unison Reading, begin reading the word problem. Breach, mid-sentence if necessary, to resolve confusions that may arise. Resume reading after the breach is resolved.
3. The group identifies the first point in the word problem when a concept arises that can be translated into an *enactive* mode of representation (representing an idea through physical objects). Each person creates an enactive representation using manipulatives. Group members are encouraged to borrow ideas from others. Each person explains their enactive representation. The group collectively identifies the best example of an enactive mode of representation.
4. Every learner then translates their enactive representation into an iconic mode of representation, or a picture. Each group member explains their iconic representation. The group collectively identifies the best example of an iconic mode of representation.
5. Every learner puts their iconic representation into a symbolic representation, using familiar mathematical symbols. Every learner explains their symbolic representation. The group collectively identifies the best example of a symbolic mode of representation.
6. The sentence in which the breach occurred is now read from the beginning.
7. Repeat Steps 2-7. above until the word problem is completed or the session concludes.

Primary Aims

1. To integrate the mind to unite diverse systems of memory in the service of learning mathematical concepts, providing an opportunity for deep learning.
2. To practice cognitive control and mental coordination by shifting and sharing perspectives and reasoning cooperatively with others in order to achieve collective understanding.
3. To apply enactive, iconic and symbolic modes of understanding to an abstract problem, cultivating adaptive habits of mind that can be applied in future situations.
4. To practice cooperation by working with others.
5. To practice emotional self-regulation.
6. To develop social cognition and stimulate capacities to understand and empathize with others.
7. To practice emotional self-regulation.

1. Learner   Rating

1a. Is promotive, respectful, and completely attentive to group members.
1b. Remains on task during Integrative Math sessions.
1c. Follows specified procedures for joining groups and completing group tasks.
1d. Assumes responsibility for managing the group process as outlined in procedures, above.
1e. Adheres to Cooperative Unison Reading protocols when collectively reading a text.

2. Guide   Rating

2a. Allow learners the opportunity to facilitate their own groups, manage the groupwork process, and hold themselves accountable to procedures.
2b. Observes informally and provides instruction to guide and support the process when necessary.
2c. Intervenes to correct maladaptive behaviors and to secure prosocial behaviors.

2d.	Provides guidance to support learners in identifying resources that can be used in the research process.	
3.	**Materials**	**Rating**
3a.	Grade-level math word problem.	
3b.	Math manipulatives (Cuisenaire rods, Algebra Tiles, Unifix Cubes, Base Ten Blocks, Unifix Cubes).	
3c.	White boards or scrap paper.	
3d.	Pencils and markers or crayons.	
3e.	Small, round tables.	

Comments:

17 The Language Games Format

Description

A group of no more than five students take part in an activity designed to support language learning. A group leader has selected a game to be played or an activity to be learned in a target language, which becomes the *language of the table*. Players have had the opportunity to sign up to learn the game or do the activity of their choice as a means to learn the target language. Players sit together at a small round table. The group leader facilitates the meeting by giving a series of instructions, or directives, to help players learn the game or activity. Upon each directive, group members restate the directive in the language of the table, execute the action, restate it again, and write it down in the language of the table. This procedure is repeated until the game has been learned. Players can use any language or combination of non-verbal means of communication, so long as they translate every utterance into the language of the table. Language Games applies a usage-based theory of language acquisition to pedagogical practice (Tomasello, 2003).

Primary Aims

1. To develop competence in a non-native language through the functional use of language to achieve goals.
2. To practice cooperation by working with others.
3. To practice cognitive control and mental coordination by shifting and sharing perspectives and reasoning cooperatively with others in order to achieve collective understanding.
4. To practice emotional self-regulation.
5. To develop social cognition and stimulate capacities to understand and empathize with others.

Materials

Language Games notebook (one per participant)
Materials needed to play the game of the table (e.g., cards, die, board games)
Dictionary—physical or digital
White boards or scrap paper
Pencils and markers or crayons
Small, round tables

Procedures

Set up. Language Games are based on a set of ground rules and classroom systems that are taught to learners in advance of the Game. Language Games are an established, recursive classroom routine in which new languages are learned through consistent and systematic practice of the activity. Most often the game is used in the ESL program as a means to teach English, but it can also be used to teach any language in the foreign language classroom.

Each week, a new group of leaders selects a game to be played or an activity to learn in a target language. Leaders make an effort to identify a game or activity that is, above all, *fun*. They post their game choice and indicate the language of the table. Peers sign up to play a game of choice. Each game can include no more than five players. Groups meet at a small round table.

Players will have been previously taught the expectations for participation in the Language Games Format and are familiar with the Language Games Rubric. Players are promotive, respectful, and completely attentive to group mates. They remain on-task during Language Games sessions. They follow specified procedures for joining groups and completing group tasks. And they assume responsibility for managing the group process as outlined in the Language Games Rubric.

Guides serve a facilitative function within the program. They allow players to facilitate their own groups, and they hold learners accountable to adhering to formal procedures. They observe informally, provide instruction to guide and support the learning process when necessary, and intervene to correct maladaptive behaviors and to secure prosocial behaviors.

The leader begins by explaining how to do the activity, providing a series of instructions, or directives, to guide the activity. The leader can use any language or means of communication to explain the directives. They can use drawings, hand signals, gestures, or eye contact. But whatever means chosen, the directive must eventually be delivered in the language of the table. Players, too, are allowed to use their own language to communicate, but must translate every utterance into the target language or the language of the table.

1. The Game begins when the group leader issues the first directive, or instruction, in the language of the table, writes the directive on a white board, and demonstrates the directive in action.
2. Upon hearing and observing the directive, each group member repeats the directive in the language of the table at least three times (or until they are able to say the utterance fluently).
3. Group members execute the action. The guide provides assistance, as necessary. Players are allowed to use their native language as means of communication, but must translate any utterance into the language of the table. The group leader or guide may provide translation assistance, or players can use digital translation apps.
4. Group members write the directive in their Language Games notebook. Once everyone has written the directive, the group reads it aloud, adhering to the rules of Cooperative Unison Reading.
5. Procedures 1–4 are repeated for each procedural directive until the game or activity has been learned.

Discussion

Language Games creates a functional rationale for using a new language in an activity that integrates the diverse systems of the mind. The practice is founded on a usage-based theory of language acquisition (Tomasello, 2003), which asserts that a language is a set of linguistic social conventions that are learned through use for functional purposes. Humans' unique language abilities are interwoven with other cognitive capacities, such as intention reading and pattern finding (Tomasello, 2003). Language is learned for purposeful reasons in order to share intentional states with others.

A Usage-based Alternative to Traditional Language Instruction

Language Games provides an alternative to traditional, bottom-up, skills-oriented, or functionalist approach to language instruction (see Chapter 3 for a discussion of approaches to language instruction). It contextualizes the principles of a usage-based theory of language learning into a game-like situation in which learners use a new language for a functional purpose. The game-like context lends an element of fun to the activity, harnessing positive emotional states to enhance learning. Other means of non-verbal communication are employed organically to facilitate cooperative understanding, such as gesturing, drawing, eye contact, and laughter.

In Language Games, players are focused on the overall intention of trying to learn something new and fun, and less concerned for using language correctly. This feature distinguishes Language Games from more traditional, formalist approaches to language instruction, in which accuracy is very important from the beginning. With function as a priority, players integrate snippets of conventional linguistic conventions provided by the group leader into their own language system, through use. In Language Games, players are doing something practical, and using newly-learned words and grammatical constructions pragmatically, to represent ideas that are relevant to the overarching purpose.

Integration

Integration links the various components of the mind—the parts of the mind that are inside of us, in our heads and bodies, and the parts of the mind that exist in our relationships with others (Siegel, 2020). Language Games require players to use both sides of the brain—the left side and right side—and the top of the brain, in the skull, and the bottom of the brain, which extends through the neurons in the lower body. The right brain helps read the facial expressions and make eye contact with others, to read drawings, and to receive information. The left brain helps in the process of writing and reading, using language, and thinking logically. Taking part in the activities of the game incorporate language learning experience into implicit memory systems, deepening learning. Integrating multiple components of the mind promotes its optimal functioning optimally.

 **Language Games Rubric**

Rating Scale: (✓-) Needs Immediate Improvement   (✓) Making Progress   (✓+) Proficient   (NA) No opportunity to observe

Procedures

1. A system is established for group leaders to make and display game selections in a designated language.
2. A system is established for learners to sign up for games of their choice in languages of their choice. Sign-up turns rotate so students have fair opportunities to select 'first-choice' games. Turns are not contingent upon 'good' behavior.
3. Learners meet in designated groups around a small, round table, convening quickly and coming to the meeting prepared.
4. In a step-by-step process, the leader takes initiative to teach others at the table how play the game or do the activity. Each step of the instructions is called a *directive*. The leader should use any communicative means necessary to ensure others understand and can perform the directive (e.g., language, drawing, gestures, pantomime, eye contact).
5. The Game begins when the group leader issues the first directive, or instruction, in the language of the table, and executes the action called for in the directive.
6. Upon hearing the directive, group members repeat the directive in the language of the table, at least three times, or until it slithers easily off the tongue.
7. Group members execute the action. They take responsibility to thoroughly understand and perform the task identified in the directive, using whatever means of communication necessary to understand how to execute the directive, but they must translate every utterance into the language of the table. The group leader provides procedural and/or language support and competence feedback in any language or means of communication, as long as comments are eventually stated in the language of the table.
8. The group leader writes the directive on a white board or in a Language Games notebook, then enlists the group to read the directive in sync.
9. Group members write the directive in their own Language Games notebook.
10. Once everyone has written the directive, the group reads the directive aloud, adhering to the rules of Cooperative Unison Reading.
11. Steps 5-10 are repeated until the game or activity is finished or the session concludes.

Primary Aims

1. To develop competence in a non-native language through the functional use of language to achieve goals.
2. To practice cooperation by working with others.
3. To practice cognitive control and mental coordination by shifting and sharing perspectives and reasoning cooperatively with others in order to achieve collective understanding.
4. To practice emotional self-regulation.
5. To develop social cognition and stimulate capacities to understand and empathize with others.

1.	Learner	Rating
1a.	Is promotive, respectful, and completely attentive to group members.	
1b.	Demonstrates cooperative behavior through appropriate verbal and non-verbal communication (e.g., attends to facial expressions, makes eye contact, follows into others' comments).	
1c.	Attunes to others' perspectives with flexibility, shares and shifts perspectives, and reasons cooperatively. Remains open-minded and resonates with others' ideas.	
1d.	Remains on task and adheres to Language Games protocols.	
1e.	Assumes responsibility for helping to manage the group process.	

2.	Guide			Rating

2a. Allows learners to facilitate their own groups. Holds learners accountable to procedures and supports their effort to manage the group processes.
2b. Intervenes when necessary to provide appropriate behavioral or instructional guidance.
2c. Observes informally and provides instruction to guide and support the process when necessary.
2d. Intervenes to correct maladaptive behaviors and to secure prosocial behaviors.
2e. Provides guidance to support learners in identifying resources that can be used in the research process.

3.	Materials	Rating

3a. Materials needed to play the game of the table.
3b. Dictionary-physical or digital.
3c. White boards or scrap paper.
3d. Pencils and markers or crayons.
3e. Small, round tables.

Comments:

Section IV
The "We" Curriculum: Social Norms

18 Keepers of the Culture
The Social Norms Curriculum

> The rule of law is better than the rule of any one individual.
>
> Aristotle

Introduction

The Keepers of the Culture (KoC) curriculum is designed to instill in learners a sense of group belonging and group identity, to provide a system of accountability and means through which learners and adults can comply with positive social and academic norms, and to establish a system of social organization that is learner-driven.

The We-Ness Principle

Group identity—the sense of what Tomasello describes as "we-ness"—comes about through participation in group-minded activities governed by informal *ground rules* for collective practices (Tomasello, 2009, 2016). The KoC curriculum strives to instill a sense of "we-ness" in learners. Tomasello (2009) writes, "In communal life the sacred refers to the collective practices of the moral community…whereas the profane refers to individuals' self-interested pursuits" (p. 132). In the McCallister Model, group identity and the sense of being a member of the "we" is a pedagogical aim. Group identity provides the moral imperative to conform with group norms, and *conformity* to the rules for curriculum practices is the vehicle for learning.

Knowledge of information that is important to the group and competence to apply this knowledge in practice secures one's position in the group (Dressler, 2019). Those in the group whose relatively high levels of knowledge and skill are in consonance with the values of the culture experience higher levels of well-being than those whose relative lack of knowledge and skill position them more distally (Dressler, 2019). Bringing all learners into a position of consonance by ensuring they have opportunities to learn the knowledge and skill deemed to be of value in school is a moral imperative of the McCallister Model. All human beings share the need for being part of the *we*. Everyone thrives on a sense of connectedness and relatedness to others. KoC protocols function to help learners view collective pedagogical practices (i.e., the Formats) as sacred forms of communal life that warrant commitment. A sense of "we-ness" is a necessity because it provides motivation for learners to adhere to social and academic norms.

KoC recommends a set of practices that function to seed, secure, and sustain positive academic and social norms within the school. The practices of KoC hold learners accountable to meeting their responsibilities as members of the community. By supporting moral self-identity and moral self-governance, KoC practices support cognitive and social development.

Democratic Individualism

KoC is instrumental in creating egalitarian conditions in the school. These systems distribute power and responsibility to learners themselves. Through these systems, learners assume a primary role in managing and norming the social practices of the school. KoC institutes a system of school governance in the tradition of democratic individualism, which emphasizes both the equal dignity of individuals and a school culture of individuality that positively supports human flourishing (Urbinati, 2015). These systems enable learners to be *keepers of their own culture.*

The Social Contract

> Man is born free, and everywhere he is in chains.
>
> Jean-Jacques Rousseau

The Social Contract is a philosophical theory of the Enlightenment that explains the give-and-take nature of citizenship. Under the Social Contract, every member of a society forfeits some personal freedom in exchange for protections, benefits, and affordances provided by the state. The Social Contract solves a basic problem of human social organization, identified by Rousseau, which is to "…find a form of association that will bring the whole common force to bear on defending and protecting each associate's person and goods, and doing this in such a way that each of them, while uniting himself with all, still obeys only himself and remains as free as before." Rousseau referred to the freedoms afforded by the Social Contract as "conventional liberties." The KoC curriculum applies a version of the Social Contract to schooling. The fundamental freedoms that are outlined in the Format Rubrics are "conventional liberties," because they outline the ways in which learners must conform to the rules for activities.

Cultural Respon-civility

Human beings are social creatures, and all higher-order thinking is fundamentally social in nature (Vygotsky, 1978). Because the social world is the laboratory of human existence and becoming, it is imperative that classroom and school cultures be characterized by civility, respect, interdependence, and mutuality. To this end, the McCallister Model encourages the cultivation of *respon-civility*—responsibility to the treatment of others with civility.

The "responsible" part of *respon-civility* recognizes the need for every person to take responsibility to adhere to norms for decency and respect for others. The "civility" part of *respon-civility* recognizes the need for civility in a culture of individual dignity. Civility depends on the existence of objective morality within the communal group. That is, the group's sense of "we-ness" is cemented through compliance to a code for moral behavior that is objectively shared. KoC practices make the code transparent, and make behavioral norms explicit. In KoC, adults have responsibility to secure norms that ensure every learner's right to dignity and respect. In McCallister classrooms, adults take responsibility to help learners understand that their own personal self-interests depend on the interests of the larger group and this is culturally *respon-civil* practice.

Social Norms

Like the air we breathe, social norms are the taken-for-granted medium of human co-existence. We have internalized the norms of our familiar social worlds so deeply that they enable us to conduct ourselves on "auto-pilot," so to speak. Social norms dictate how we speak, what we say, and how we act. People adhere to group norms out of an intrinsic need to belong to the group. Since successful social participation is a taken-for-granted source of psychic comfort that we depend upon for survival, our ability to conform to social norms is an adaptive developmental advantage. Human children develop the capacity to conform to rules around their third birthday (Tomasello, 2009). Tomasello explains, "True social norms based on reciprocity emerge in the late preschool period, as children lose their egocentrism and begin to see others and themselves as coequal autonomous agents. ...Not only do children actively follow social norms, but from almost as early as they follow them they also participate in enforcing them" (p. 36). This inclination comes from the child's sense of personal identification with the group and their appreciation for a sense of "we-ness" that is rooted in the social-emotional capacities of human beings (Tomasello, 2009).

We cooperate to do specific things in certain kinds of situations because that is the way our culture says we should do them. As our social circles widen, so does the constellation of norms that structure our social reality. Human social institutions, like schools, are built upon an infrastructure of collective intentionality that is expressed in institutional facts or assertions, called *status function declarations* (Searle, 2010). Status function declarations (SFDs) are things like report cards, achievement tests, the state curriculum, and teacher contracts. Teachers follow the state curriculum and children and parents accept report card results because of their motivation to conform to institutional norms.

Instrumental Status Function Declarations

SFDs are a powerful influence on behavior because they create a state of motivation that is built upon a sense of obligation (Searle, 2010). Searle (2010) points out that an obligation does not begin as a desire, but becomes the ground of a desire to perform an action that fulfills an obligation. I may not desire to submit a report on time, but my desire to fulfill an obligation to do so provides the motivation I need to succeed in meeting an expectation.

The social reality of school is structured by countless SFDs that govern behavior. Making change in an archaic institution like school is challenging because norms are firmly secured by a kaleidoscopic constellation of institutional facts, or SFDs, with deep roots in tradition that dictate behavior and beliefs. But SFDs are used instrumentally and strategically in the McCallister Model as a technology that is powerful enough to re-describe the institutional reality of school and change deeply-engrained behavioral norms (Bicchieri, 2017). The Format Rubrics, for example, create new social realities in the classroom by describing pedagogical situations that are not constrained by tradition, but informed by scientific insights about learning. The theory-of-change within the McCallister Model employs SFDs and the person's intrinsic need-to-conform to normative expectations to meet one's obligations as mechanisms of change.

Background

Our ability to cooperate with others within the networks of our stable social groups depends on Background (Searle, 2010). Background is the sum of the cognitive capacities (skills, knowledge, and understanding) and dispositions that become coded in memory through experiences in which these abilities and dispositions are demanded. For example, a child learns in a given social situation that the symbol 'B' is pronounced 'Bee' and makes the 'buh' sound in words like 'Bill.' This information is initially arbitrary, but assumes a normative, objective meaning in social situations where it gets remembered because it is relevant. Background is the "abilities, capacities, dispositions, and ways of doing things, and general know-how that enable us to carry out our intentions and apply our intentional states generally" (Searle, 2010, p. 31). In their interactions with others, people rely on the expectation that others share requisite Background to coordinate behavior (Searle, 2010).

In traditional schooling, the curriculum of knowledge, skills, and understanding is presented in increments to learners through a pedagogy of transmission. The curriculum of the McCallister Model establishes interactions in the social world to be the primary body of the curriculum. Intellective abilities develop as learners accumulate forms of Background in Formats specifically designed to bring them about.

Teaching Norms

Norms develop through social experience. They are borne from reciprocal, give-and-take interactions that enable learners to internalize the values of their cultures (Tomasello, 2009). The child's expanding capacity for self-control, or their ability to self-regulate to normative values is a defining characteristic of human psychological development (Tomasello, 2016, 2019). The cultural psychologist David Olson (2007) has proposed a developmental process that explains how a child comes to internalize a norm. A norm takes form when a caregiver attempts to hold a child responsible for an action, the reason for which is based on a normative standard rather than a personal one. The transfer of responsibility for normative behavior from adult to child depends on the ability of the child to hold a rule in mind and to make causal connection between the rule and personal action. Personal responsibility is thus a central concern of pedagogy within the McCallister Model.

By the time they come to school, children have learned to regulate their thoughts and behaviors to the norms of their culture. The world of school introduces a whole new universe of social norms that must be learned. Depending on the values and practices of the social worlds of their primary families, children will have acquired Background that helps or hinders their ability to internalize new norms. The willingness to take responsibility to conform to new norms will determine the child's learning trajectory in school.

Of course, norms have always been a feature of formal education. Learners are not strangers to the understanding that there are rules in school that should be followed. In autocratic classrooms, rules are simple: sit where assigned; speak only when directed; do what you are told. Most learners are able to adhere to these norms with minimal formal instruction. Those who do not internalize these norms are typically punished or disciplined. Traditionally, teaching has been a matter of the management of learner behavior through rules that restrict freedom. But if deep learning depends on the conditions of freedom and autonomy to conform to new norms, rules of submission are counterproductive. Rules that specify conditions of freedom are necessary instead. Rules that specify freedom are called *rights*.

The McCallister Model is a curriculum of rights, which offer a certain amount of autonomy to exercise free will. But rights exist only if they are exercised. If these rights are not granted and enforced, norms will develop by default along the patterns of tradition. That is why *teaching* within the McCallister Model is largely a matter of holding learners responsible for following the rules.

We are normally accustomed to thinking about norms as subterranean forces that govern behavior. But within the McCallister Model, teaching into norms involves a process of making them visible. For example, when a learner is not adhering to the behavioral expectations outlined in the Rubric, it is evidence that the expectation has not been internalized as an obligation. This is the teacher's cue to hold the learner accountable to holding the rule in mind by applying it to new action. Just like rules for a game, norms develop through practice.

Some learners initially refuse to play by the rules. Some will have learned that school is a game of "me versus authority"—a contest where winning depends on showing up the teacher and saving face in front of peers. Typically, learners who refuse to play by the rules are typed and treated as oppositional, avoidant, or diagnosed with a behavioral disability. But within the McCallister Model, when a teacher is if faced with challenging behavior, they respond by holding the learner responsible for playing by the rules. Oppositional and defiant learners especially need to learn the lesson that school is now a fair game, and everyone plays by the rules. Just like teaching anything else, when we teach into a norm, we lift it up for a moment of joint attention and provide the opportunity for a learner to grasp the new meaning of a thing.

Responsibility-based Self-control

Responsibility-based Self-control (RbSc) (McCallister, 2013f) is a pedagogical principle based on the understanding that problematic behaviors or lagging skills are symptoms of social maladjustment or lack of appropriate and supportive stimulation from the environment as opposed to an internal defect. Holding learners responsible to adhere to positive social and academic norms is a more productive pedagogical strategy than forcing avoidant learners to submit to teacher directives. Provided they hold the perspective that We>Me (we is greater than me) and that they are aware of expectations, the learner is naturally motivated to exercise RbSc to comply with expectations. RbSc is an example of *norm psychology* and an approach to the solution of intractable social problems through changing norms (Bicchieri, 2017).

"Discipline": Rethinking Traditional Assumptions

The teacher's primary role in the industrial school is knowledge transmission technician, concerned with control and efficiency. They control the flow of knowledge in the classroom through systems of behavioral management and the application of rewards as incentives to positive behavior and punishments as deterrents.

Many conventional behavior programs are based on the view that human behavior is controlled by extrinsic stimulation. B.F. Skinner's *operant conditioning* forms the basis of many conventional approaches to school discipline. These practices are familiar to almost anyone who has attended formal schooling. Positive behaviors are reinforced through the introduction of "appetitive" stimulus (a.k.a. "rewards"), and negative behaviors are discouraged through punishment by either introduction of a "noxious" stimulus (write *I'm sorry* 100 times) or removal of a positive stimulus (recess detention). Moving cards up and down on a behavior scale or giving and taking points away for behavior has the effect of externalizing motivation to the cards or points; these are both forms of operant conditioning.

But recent evidence in learning sciences has proven that the development of new memory is not controlled by external stimuli but, rather, is controlled through selective attention on the part of the subject (Kandel, 2007). Learning requires willful action. Moreover, extrinsic rewards diminish intrinsic motivation, often by causing *over-justification*, or motivation for the reward itself rather than the reinforced behavior (Tomasello, 2009). Rewards for participation and good behavior—like stickers, candy, or points—should never be used because they undermine the cultivation of learner intentionality.

The issue of punishment is more complicated. Evidence suggests that punishment for non-cooperators through social sanctions does, in fact, help to stabilize cooperation within the group (Tomasello, 2009). Social sanctions, as opposed to punishment as retribution, are effective because they appeal to the person's need to be held in positive regard by the social group. Behavior is motivated by social acceptance, not fear of detention or missing recess. Since they are effective, social sanctions are used in the Keepers of the Culture program (described in Ladder of Self-regulation, below).

The High Costs of Punitive Discipline

There is a high cost to harsh discipline. In a study by the Center for Civil Rights Remedies at UCLS, researchers found that California 10th-grade suspension in the period of the investigation resulted in 10,000 additional high school dropouts. The study found that each dropout is responsible for $163,000 in lost tax revenue and $364,000 in other costs, such as health care and criminal justice. The national total of 67,000 additional dropouts due to suspensions predicts a total cost of $35 billion. If these findings reflect the costs associated with 10th-grade dropouts over a single year, then the costs exceed $100 billion when that figure is multiplied with cohorts from additional years.

Stand-alone programs for behavioral support in schools are also costly. The Positive Behavioral Support System (PBIS) is estimated to costs $33,794 per school, or $50 per learner, with costs associated with training, coaching, and monitoring (Johnson, 2018).

Keepers of the Culture: Curriculum Practices

A comprehensive set of pedagogical practices are employed to implement the Keepers of the Culture curriculum as the school's system of behavioral supports. They are described, below.

Discipline Code as Curriculum

The KoC curriculum employs the Discipline Code as a pedagogical tool. In an education model based on rights to certain experiences, it is necessary for learners to understand their rights and responsibilities. The school discipline code outlines learners' educational rights, personal responsibilities, and behaviors that are prohibited in the school, which serves as the basis of the Social Contract. The New York City Discipline Code is exemplary (New York City Department of Education, 2019). Sections of the NYC DOE's Discipline Code that are pedagogically relevant to the Keepers of the Culture curriculum—learners' rights, responsibilities, and behavior infractions—are presented at the end of this chapter.

Social Norms Onboarding

Every learner takes part in a social norms orientation, in which they have opportunity to become familiar with formal behavioral expectations of the curriculum (the Sparks curriculum, the Learning Cultures Formats, and the school's Discipline Code). Learners who are new to the McCallister Model are introduced to the Formats in through classroom demonstrations and introduction to the Format Rubrics.

The Social Contract Talk: Establishing a Positive School-Wide Culture

At the beginning of the school year, a "Social Contract Talk" is presented to all learners. The Talk outlines each learner's educational rights and responsibilities. It presents education in an historical context as the achievement of civil rights for children. The Talk invites learners to consider the kinds of behaviors that interfere with learning, and offer insights about the appropriate consequences for those whose behaviors interfere with others' rights to learn. The Talk is a presentation designed to help learners understand and appreciate their education as a valuable right, and to understand how to exercise their rights responsibly (McCallister, 2013f). The Social Contract Talk is a rite of passage into the school's democratic community. The Social Contract Talk protocol is presented below:

1 Discuss free, compulsory education as both a human and a civil right that has been achieved through a history of social struggle and sacrifice. Because school is compulsory, some take these rights for granted. Throughout most of history, education was reserved for only the privileged. And through time, in most human cultures, children have been treated as small adults, and have been expected to assume adult responsibilities from a young age. Most children through the course of human civilization were born into slavery or servitude, and were prohibited from learning literacy. For example, in our country, it was a crime to teach slaves to read or write. While the Emancipation Proclamation in 1863 ended legal slavery, Jim Crow laws prohibited Black children from attending white schools. And Black schools were inferior to white schools.

Discuss the labor rights movement. In the early 20th century, laws restricted employment of children and exploitation of child workers. By 1918, education was made compulsory in every state in the U.S.

Discuss the global commitment to education and human rights. World War II ended fascism and genocide in Europe. The United Nations, an outcome of World War II, was founded as an international organization dedicated to global peace, security, friendship, and cooperation between all nations. In 1948, the United Nations passed the Universal Declaration of Human Rights. In Article 26 of the Declaration, states:

(1) Everyone has the right to education. Education shall be free, at least in the elementary and fundamental stages. Elementary education shall be compulsory. Technical and professional education shall be made generally available and higher education shall be equally accessible to all on the basis of merit.
(2) Education shall be directed to the full development of the human personality and to the strengthening of respect for human rights and fundamental freedoms. It shall promote understanding, tolerance, and friendship among all nations, racial or religious groups, and shall further the activities of the United Nations for the maintenance of peace.
(3) Parents have a prior right to choose the kind of education that shall be given to their children.

Education is discussed within the context of the Civil Rights movement, when the right to a free public education was expanded to minorities and other traditionally disenfranchised groups. The U.S. Supreme Court's *Brown v. Board of Education* decision, asserted the right to an education on equal terms; the Americans with

Disabilities Act extended equal education protection to people with disabilities; the Supreme Court's *Lau v. Nichols* decision prohibited discrimination based on language; Title I of the Elementary and Secondary Education Act extended special protections to children who live in poverty; and the Equality Act prohibited discrimination based on gender identity.

Discuss how the achievement of education as a human right is still a struggle in most parts of the world. Many children still live under conditions of slavery and child workers continue to be abused.

2 Discuss education as an investment that society makes in its youth. In the United States, the average annual spending per year on every child is $13,440 (National Center for Education Statistics, 2020), significantly more than the global average of $9,219 (OECD, 2019). In New York City in 2019, $25,091 was spent on every child (United States Census, 2020), over $350,000 dollars in every learner over the course of their schooling. One incredulous Brooklyn 8th grader pointed out the fact that that sum was enough to buy a Maserati. Learners are reminded that there will never be a time in their lives again when they will be the recipient of such a large investment.

Explain the value of time. Divide the total sum invested by years, days, hours, and minutes, so that learners can calculate the real cost of lost opportunities. Learners spend about 67,000 minutes per year in school, each worth a nationwide average of $0.19 and $0.35 in New York City. Explain the fact that each learner has a responsibility to determine how she or he will make the most potential out of this investment. We point out that, when children do not meet their obligations and adhere to expectations, they are taking valuable learning opportunities from others.

3 Discuss the economic benefits of an education and share data about education and predicted lifetime earnings. Give learners an opportunity to reflect on these data. A person who drops out of high school will earn nearly three times less over their lifetime than a person with a graduate degree. These data reflect the economic benefits of an education. They also reflect economic gender inequality. Ramifications of these data are discussed. A boy who does not graduate from high school will earn $410,000 less over his lifetime than a boy who graduates; and a girl who does not graduate from high school will earn $290,000 less than a girl who graduates (keeping in mind that a girl who graduates will earn $740,000 less over the course of her lifetime than a boy who graduates).

Sex	Less than high school	High school graduate	Some college	Bachelor's degree	Graduate degree
Male	1.13	1.54	1.76	2.43	3.05
Female	0.51	0.80	1.01	1.43	1.86

Lifetime gross earnings in millions (Tamborini, Kim, & Sakamoto, 2015)

4 Explain that the right of education comes with responsibility. Discuss the philosophy of the Social Contract and how individuals relinquish certain freedoms to derive benefits of membership in the social collective. Explain how the Rubrics confer fundamental freedoms for learners to control their own minds and bodies, but freedoms are *conventional liberties* that come with obligations to take responsibility to adhere to norms.

5 Reference the New York City Code of Discipline. Most children know the Code, also referred to as the "Blue Book" in New York City, as the book principals refer to when kids get in trouble. But in the Social Contract Talk, the Code is presented as

a venerable document that outlines each learners' rights and responsibilities. It is the Constitution of our Social Contract that applies to everyone—children, parents, teachers, and administrators.

Discuss the difference between negative rights and positive rights. Negative rights are absolute and, to be exercised, mean that others merely need to leave the right-holder alone (Searle, 2010). In our society, for example, most people have the right to free expression, thought, movement, and assembly. These rights are not against anyone. In other words, nobody has to do anything special to ensure these rights are protected besides leave the person alone.

Positive rights, on the other hand, impose an obligation on those the rights are against, meaning that certain actions have to be performed by certain people in order for rights to be protected (Searle, 2010). Because of the ways our schools have been structured, traditionally they have restricted children's fundamental freedoms of thought, movement, expression, and social affiliation—rights that are considered to be negative or absolute rights in our society. In order to correct these human rights abuses, we use the Rubrics to turn negative rights into positive rights that everyone has an obligation to take action to protect. Explain how the Rubrics outline rules that function to provide every learner with maximal opportunity to exercise fundamental freedoms of thought, movement, expression, and social affiliation, and that, by meeting obligations outlined, every person has the opportunity to remain in what we refer to as a *circle of freedom*.

Referring to the Code, in Unison, read each right (see NYC DOE Discipline Code, Student Rights and Responsibilities as end matter in this chapter). Learners of every age are intrinsically concerned with their rights. One 2nd grader in a South Bronx school, after reading in unison with the principal one of his rights, looked at her with an expression of empathetic concern in realizing the school was not upholding its obligation to one of his rights to an education, and said, "Ya'll are gonna get fired!" Since learners are the best enforcers of their own rights to learn, it is important that they know their rights.

Then, in unison, read each responsibility. The Code of Discipline outlines two significant responsibilities that we spend extra time discussing. The first is that every learner attend school regularly and punctually and make every effort to achieve in all areas of their education (Responsibility #1). The other is that each child should provide leadership to encourage fellow learners to adhere to school procedures (Responsibility #23). Make a point to help learners understand that the official procedures of our school include those outlined in the Learning Cultures Format Rubrics, and that it's an expectation for all learners to follow the procedures. These procedures provide a context for every child to enjoy maximal freedom. Explain how helping peers adhere to the procedures is a way of keeping them in the *circle of freedom*. Once learners experience difficulties self-regulating to the procedures, they're at risk of losing these freedoms.

6   Discuss what kinds of behaviors interfere with the rights and responsibilities just discussed. Ask learners to reflect on the kinds of things children do that interfere with other children's right to learn. Make a list. Refer to the NYC DOE Discipline Code Infractions (see Appendix 44, www.routledge.com/9780367458591), and point out that these activities are prohibited. A copy of the Infractions should be posted in classrooms.

Then ask: what should happen when a child breaks a rule or does not meet their obligation? Lead learners in a discussion of appropriate responses to infractions of behavior expectations, and help them create a list of *progressive responses* that can be used in every classroom. Encourage learners to suggest an order in which the responses should happen. This list is revised by the administration, then translated into a Ladder of Self-regulation that is posted in every class.

Talk logistics. All learners should have the opportunity to hear the Social Contract Talk the first week of school (the principal or deans can give the talk in each class, or children can convene in the auditorium to hear the talk together). When everyone has heard the same message—that they have responsibility for their learning and will be expected to live up to their responsibilities—positive social norms are more easily and quickly secured because every child who breaks a rule will do so having heard that non-cooperation is a violation of the Social Contract, and takes from their peers' opportunity to learn.

The Talk can be made accessible digitally or in text form. The Social Contract Talk should be on the onboarding checklist for new learners to ensure that every learner has heard the talk.

Impact of the Talk

The Social Contract Talk is like a magic personal agency potion to some children who have never viewed their education as someone else's considerable investment in *them*. And few have ever viewed the disruptive antics of classmates as being of any personal consequence—or as someone else diminishing an investment society has made in them. The more common mindsets of *'don't tattle', 'stop snitchin,'* or *'mind your own business and I'll mind mine'*, prevail in schools. If the Talk is done well, it can be a tool to help shift these mindsets. And since there is no place for self-interest within the context of the sacred moral collective of the Social Contract, these mindsets *do* need to be shifted. The Talk helps prove the point that the act of enforcing positive norms in the community is not an option, but an expectation for *doing the right thing* as opposed to selling out. The Talk also makes public knowledge of the fact that learners who disrupt others learning are, literally, robbing others of their right to learn.

The Talk helps learners become vigilant about their rights and more willing to both adhere to and enforce the norms of the curriculum. And for those who are the habitual rule offenders—those who are characteristically disruptive, defiant, or disrespectful—the Talk puts them on notice that their behaviors are not simply an act of opposition to the teacher, but a violation of the rights of their classmates to learn. This awareness seems to have a significant impact on many learners who would otherwise continue to show challenging behaviors.

The Social Contract Talk will budge the classroom culture somewhat, provided positive social norms are secured through adequate follow through when children fail to meet their responsibilities. But there will be those few who continue to act out or remain alarmingly passive and unwilling to invest effort in their own education. For those learners, a Behavior or Academic Intervention is the next line of response.

Ladder of Self-regulation

A Ladder of Self-regulation is developed as a set of rules to be used in every classroom. These rules are derived from recommendations solicited from learners during the Social Contract Talk about which sanctions should result from behavior infractions. "Rungs" on the Ladder proceed progressively, and typically include the following:

1 Peer Reminder;
2 Teacher Reminder;

3 Move Seat;
4 Behavior Reflection;
5 Behavior Conference;
6 Call home;
7 "On Call" support (explained below);
8 Principal Referral.

The Ladder is posted in every classroom. It is used to structure adult and peer responses to behavior problems as they arise. The Ladder substitutes for the ubiquitous "classroom rules" typically created by teachers, one classroom at a time. This eliminates the need for learners to norm their behaviors to the different rules of multiple teachers in middle and high school (see Appendix 31 for a sample Ladder of Self-regulation, www.routledge.com/9780367458591).

Adults should hold themselves accountable approaching classroom discipline as a pedagogical process rather than a punitive one. Since social norms are an integral facet of the curriculum, and because they need to be taught explicitly in order to be internalized, the Ladder is a powerful pedagogical tool. Behavior infractions are seen as valuable opportunities for learners to exercise moral self-regulation and cognitive control—the cognitive tools to shape the self.

Adults should follow these guidelines: be attentive to the classroom life space and vigilant for disruptions. When behavior challenges arise, they should be embraced and welcomed as learning opportunities. The adult should suspend the activity they are involved in, and address the problematic behavior directly. They should move to the location where the behavior is occurring (shouting or yelling only serves to violate the positive social norms you are trying so hard to secure). The adult should encourage a peer to offer a directive to correct the problematic behavior. The learner should be given time to re-regulate behavior before moving up to the next rung on the Ladder.

Once learners have come to value Work Time as an opportunity to exercise their fundamental freedoms, the requirement to move seats is a powerful deterrent to non-normative behavior. Freedoms are worth protecting, and incentivize children to govern their behaviors to classroom social norms.

Using the Ladder, By Cynthia

One day, while visiting New Hope Charter School in Canarsie, Brooklyn, I spent the morning with "Stanford," the 4th-grade class notorious for their challenging behaviors. I had planned to teach them Cooperative Unison Reading in a "fish bowl" Format. But behavior was such a problem that we never got so far as reorganizing the furniture for the fishbowl. Instruction of any kind was impossible. By the end of the period, all of the learners ignored me and channeled all of their attention toward one another—fighting, squabbling, laughing, and acting completely unruly. At the end of class, I sent for the backup from the administration in order to teach an important lesson.

The minute the dean of school culture arrived, the class immediately quieted. I explained to the class that it troubled me that a whole period passed without the opportunity for any of them to learn what I had planned. And it troubled me even more that it appeared they relied upon an external authority figure to regulate their behavior. I told them I was disappointed to see that they seemed to lack the ability to control themselves from within.

The next time I visited Stamford, Tamika, the principal, joined me and the teachers. We determined that behavior was too much of a problem to launch into an instructional Format that day, and that we should instead focus on teaching Social Norms. I chose the Lesson Format as the instructional context. The daily "Lesson" within each "Activity Block," or school subject, is a chance for learners to come together as a group to convene in the classroom meeting area. It gives learners the chance to learn about their right to peaceful assembly by practicing it.

Article 20 of the United Nations Declaration of Human Rights outlines the right to freedom of assembly and association. School is a context in which this freedom can come to be appreciated. The opportunity to convene as a group, and to abide by the "laws" outlined in the Format Rubrics give learners opportunities to learn how to participate in group discussions by doing things like attending to the speaker and signaling the wish to be recognized to speak appropriately.

The ability to self-regulate to norms for peaceful assembly means children do not have to be controlled externally by others. Opportunities to experience freedom of assembly fosters the Background needed to internalize the norms of freedom from repression and domination. In a sense, the Lesson is an important opportunity to learn self-regulation as a way to achieve self-determination and personal emancipation.

So today, when they convened, I set about teaching the class the Lesson Rubric and the Ladder of Self-regulation. I first taught them about cultural respon-civility—we all have to show consideration and respect for everyone else's cultural heritage and personal identity; we have to take responsibility to be civil to one another, and to honor every person's right to dignity. I made a point to speak my words compassionately, matter-of-factly, and in a measured cadence in an attempt to beckon their interest and attention.

I anticipated mischief from Victor and Isaac (pseudonyms), and I was mindful in my intentions to respond to them with compassionate firmness. I was ready at their first missteps. Before the contagion of their entertaining antics could spread to their peers, I gave them each reminders and time to self-regulate before moving them each up the next rung on the Ladder.

One learner threw a marker at the wall after she was asked to move her seat as a consequence of failing to self-regulate to my reminder to join the class in the meeting area and to, in compliance with Rubric criteria, "appear engaged and attentive." The teachers and I had to work hard to work the room. With sweat dripping from my brow, I continued to suspend my content lesson in order to address problematic behaviors as they arose.

Each time one of the children I'd assigned to "time out" areas in the periphery of the room attempted to leave their seat, I pursued them back into place. I addressed misbehaviors of Victor and Isaac as they erupted, who, by the end of the lesson, had worked their way up the Ladder. They each moved seats, earned a Behavior Reflection, a Behavior Conference with a teacher, a call home, and a trip to the principal's office (from which place their parents were called and they were eventually sent home).

By the end of class, only 13 of 19 children remained in the meeting area. But they were assembled peacefully, all adhering to the "laws" of the Lesson Rubric, each demonstrating that had internalized their responsibility to appear engaged and attentive. I had achieved my goal. The majority of learners in "Stanford" experienced a functional group meeting in which everyone adhered to democratic discourse procedures.

In the upcoming weeks, their teachers will use the Lesson Rubric criteria and the Ladder of Self-regulation as the cultural trellis to train learners to self-regulate the norms for peaceful assembly.

The Behavior Reflection and Behavior Conference

Every school's Ladder of Self-regulation should include two rungs—the Behavior Reflection and the Behavior Conference. When learners have demonstrated that they are not able to self-regulate to positive social norms, typically after they have been reminded by peers and an adult, and after they have moved their seats, a Behavior Reflection is the next step. Learners move to a quiet place and fill out the form (see Appendix 30, Behavior Reflection, and Behavior Conference Record, www.routledge.com/9780367458591).

If the opportunity to reflect on problematic behaviors and commit to changed behavior does not result in successful re-regulation, a Behavior Conference with an adult is in order. Often when a Behavior Conference is necessary, adults in the classroom are involved in facilitating Formats and cannot abandon their responsibility without compromising other children's opportunities to learn. In the cases such as these, On-call support can conduct the Behavior Conference or assume responsibility for the Format in action so that the teacher or guide can conduct the Behavior Conference.

Back-up/On-call

Occasionally a teacher requires additional adult support to address behavioral challenges that arise in the classroom. This happens when learners do not comply with the terms of the Ladder of Self-regulation and immediate support is needed to maintain classroom activities while also addressing the problematic behavior. To address this problem, an "On-call" system is instituted, in which a teacher or paraprofessional is continually available to teachers in classrooms when behavioral support is needed.

On-call team members are assigned to respond to behavior incidents that occur in the classroom. Every problematic behavior incident needs to be appropriately resolved so that positive norms are secured. Usually, in classrooms with strong learning cultures, behavioral challenges are minor and minimal. But in more toxic school cultures, where negative social norms threaten to overwhelm efforts to secure new norms, teachers often need back-up support in addressing behaviors. This is especially critical in the beginning of the school year, when positive norms have not yet been secured and behavior problems arise more frequently. All of the adults in the school should have the support they need to establish positive learning cultures. The On-call system helps insure this happens. When a learner's problematic behavior escalates to the point it requires sustained attention, and the classroom teacher is unable to provide it, the On-call is called.

The On-call desk is staffed throughout the day by deans, assistant principals, teachers, or paraprofessionals. Those assigned to On-call take incoming calls from teachers who need back-up support. A record of responses is kept, and the data that accumulates is used to identify patterns in a) teachers' need for external classroom support, and b) learners' disruptive or passive behaviors. Teachers who over-use the system are provided professional development to learn how to better utilize the Ladder of Self-regulation. Learners whose behaviors result in multiple principal referrals (more than five in one week) require a Behavior Intervention referral.

Hallway Discipline

In many schools, hallways are typically unmonitored, and chaos reigns. Hallways and bathrooms are seen by some learners as spaces for escape from the classroom. Therefore, hallways and bathrooms are approached as cultural spaces in which positive norms are proactively secured. To that end, the School Culture Lead (described in Chapter 25) works with the school administration to devise the Hallway Monitoring System. Staff make routine rounds to address problematic behaviors and clear the hallways and bathrooms, which will have become hiding spaces for those flee in distressing classroom situations.[1] Staff should circulate on a regular basis. The Ladder of Self-regulation is used to address impermissible behaviors. Hallway infractions that make their way up the Ladder to a Behavior Conference should be recorded centrally so that patterns can be identified.

Academic and Behavior Intervention

The Learning Cultures Formats together with the Keepers of the Culture behavior program provide a universal design for learning for all learners of all abilities and languages. Most learners will develop at a typical pace given their willingness to regulate to normative expectations outlined in the Format Rubrics. However, some children, due to academic or behavior problems, will require a Second-Tier intervention. Interventions are conducted with learners who habitually fail to meet their responsibilities to learn. The Behavior Intervention and Academic Intervention are protocols that help learners gain insight into their own behaviors in relation to community norms and take responsibility for their behavior. Children who fail to make progress academically receive an Academic Intervention and children who exhibit chronic behavior problems receive a Behavior Intervention.

The Academic intervention is typically used for learners who have been identified through the Assessment and Code Blue school-wide systems to be at risk of failing to make typical developmental progress. The Behavior Intervention is typically used for learners who have come to attention through the school-wide systems for learner behavior administered by the School Culture Lead and the central leadership (e.g., principal referral).

Initial Intervention meetings typically involve the principal, teachers, and sometimes peers and family members in a supportive discussion in which the learner can identify problematic behaviors and determine how they interfere with their obligation to adhere to the Social Contract. Learners make a commitment to change, and, with support, identify and make a promise to new behaviors. The Intervention is repeated as needed until problematic behaviors are resolved.

Both the Academic and Behavior Intervention protocols require learners to make an action plan in the form of a "Promise Card" that they keep on their person for reference by their teachers in instances when they are needed.

Keepers Corps

Students who have been nominated by their classmates to be capable of upholding every learner's right to learn join the Keepers Corps. Keepers are trained to conduct Interventions with their peers and to demonstrate how to appropriately participate in the Formats. The Keepers Corps is a learner assembly comprised of 5% of learners from every grade-level cohort who have been nominated by their peers based on the criteria of responsibility, compassionate, leadership, and moral integrity. The School Culture Lead works with the McCallister Project Team to train and supervise Corps members (a process described in Chapter 26), who take responsibility to conduct Behavior and Academic Interventions. Another group of grade-level representatives works with the Training Lead to take responsibility to train their peers in the "Me" Formats of Cooperative Unison Reading, Integrative Math, Language Games, and Learning Teams. Keepers Corps has been incorporated into the bureaucratic DNA of schools where the McCallister Model was implemented, resulting in dramatic declines in suspensions and improved rates in achievement. The positive effects at Urban Assembly School for Green Careers are described in Chapter 32.

The Two Tiers of Keepers of the Culture

Educational interventions are often categorized using a *tier* structure. The term *tier* is borrowed from the medical science and applied to education. Referred to as a schoolwide

Table 18.1 Alignment between tiers of a multi-tiered behavioral support program and the keepers of the culture social norms curriculum

Tiers of intervention process	McCallister Method tiered practices
Tier I: all learners receive the same treatment. Access is universal	First-level classroom activity Formats; behavioral responses specified in the classroom-based Ladder of Self-regulation; Sparks curriculum
Tier II: increased intervention in response to needs. Supports are designed to meet targeted needs	Behavior and Academic Interventions and follow-up meetings
Tier III: intensive, individualized attention to target skill deficits, remediate problems, and prevent more severe problems	Referral to special education, counseling, mentoring, mental health support services, Pupil Personnel Team, principal suspension (PPT)

multi-tiered system of supports (MTSS), it is a design to provide social, emotional, academic, and behavioral supports of necessary intensity (RTI Action Network, 2020). Tier I refers to the baseline treatment that every person receives. Tier II and III interventions are more intensive treatments for those who do not favorably respond to Tier I treatment.

The routine activities of the Sparks curriculum and the Learning Cultures Formats are the first tier of the McCallister Method. This tier provides all learners access to social, emotional, and academic opportunities that support development. For those who do not respond to the Tier I experiences, the Tier II practices of Keepers of the Culture—the Academic and Behavior Interventions—are employed. See Table 18.1 for the alignment between traditional multi-tier processes and McCallister Method practices. Then see Table 18.2 for an alignment between the NYC Department of Education behavioral supports and interventions and the Keepers of the Culture social norms curriculum.

The Social Norms Rubric

The Social Norms Rubric outlines the procedures of the Keepers of the Culture social norms curriculum that should be followed in every school. See the Rubric at the end of the chapter.

Freedom's Paradox

There is a paradox to freedom in the classroom. The cultural archetype of the typical classroom casts the teacher as authority who asserts control over others. In these settings, the acquisition of knowledge is entangled with the requirement of obedience. Teachers typically make the rules and learners obey them. In authoritarian regimes, rules can be minimal: do not speak; do what you are told. They are easy to enforce, and easy to understand. But the greater the number of positive rights that need protection, the more important it is that obligations to these rights are made transparent. And in situations in which freedoms have had to be earned or achieved, they need to be guarded and protected so that they are not eroded by the forces of tradition, convention, or the norms of oppositional subgroups within the school.

Within the McCallister Model, Format rules are constraints that disentangle learning from obedience, enabling learners to enjoy freedom and independence and to exercise agency toward meeting learning goals. The Format rules function like black letter law. Just as laws protect citizens' positive rights in a democracy, the rules of the Formats help ensure consistent and high-quality learning experiences. The more freedoms there are

Table 18.2 Alignment between New York City Department of Education discipline code/supports and intervention options (2019a, b) and Keepers of the Culture social norms curriculum

NYC Department of Education Supports and Intervention Options (NYC DOE Discipline Code, 2019)	Keepers of the Culture Progressive Ladder of Support Disciplinary Responses
Collaborative problem solving: "When a student engages in challenging behavior, a trained school staff member can use the collaborative problem-solving process to identify the specific issues that are precipitating the behavior, articulate the adult concerns about the behavior, and engage the student in a collaborative process to address the underlying reasons for the behavior and decide upon a plan of action that is both realistic and mutually acceptable to both" (p. 15)	Format activities, which require social cognition, communication, prosociality, social norms, moral identity, cooperative thinking, and collaboration. Formats provide a context for collaborative negotiation of interpersonal conflict. Format activities prohibit aggression, bullying, or harassment.
Conflict resolution "Conflict resolution facilitates resolutions between two or more disputants. Using the collaborative negotiation process, students actively listen and talk through an issue or conflict directly with those with whom they disagree to arrive at a mutually satisfactory resolution" (p. 15)	Breaching and resolving conflict through relational adjudication (cooperative reasoning, perspective shifting, and sharing)
Development of individual behavioral contract: "The student meets with teachers to create a written contract that includes objectives and the specific performance tasks that the student will accomplish to meet those objectives. The contract is signed by the student and teacher and, where appropriate, by the parent" (p. 15)	Sparks Workout Plan; Behavior and/or Academic Intervention
Guidance conference: "Principals and teachers may request a guidance conference with the student and, where appropriate, with the parent. The purpose of the conference is to review the behavior, find solutions to the problem and address academic, personal, and social issues that might have caused or contributed to the behavior" (p. 15)	Behavior Conference with a teacher; Academic and Behavior Intervention
Individualized support plan (ISP): "An ISP is a written plan to support students who have been the victim or the initiator of bullying, harassment, intimidation, discrimination, and other aggressive behaviors. It contains, among other things, interventions and supports for the student and provisions for designated school staff to consult with the student and/or their parents, at specified times, to determine whether the behavior has improved. It is useful in student cases warranting a more targeted approach and/or involving regular monitoring" (p. 16)	Behavior Conference Record, Behavior Intervention Contract, and Promise Card
Parent outreach: "School staff should keep parents informed of their child's behavior and enlist parents as partners in addressing areas of concern. Outreach to parents can include, but is not limited to, a phone call and/or written communication" (p. 16)	"Call Home"—a rung on the Ladder of Self-regulation
Social-emotional learning: "Equipping students with skills to manage emotions, set positive goals, show empathy for others, and establish positive relationships, social emotional learning helps students make responsible and constructive decisions" (p. 16)	Classroom activity Formats, which promote social cognition, communication, cooperative thinking, collaboration, prosociality, social norms, and moral identity; Ladder of Self-regulation as a universal progressive discipline intervention; Academic and Behavior Intervention Formats

to protect, the more rules are necessary to protect them. Freedom without norms that pattern and organize social behavior easily deteriorates to chaos. You can think of rules on a continuum with freedom. On one extreme there are few rules, but few freedoms, and on the other extreme there are many freedoms, which, in order to be protected, are spelled out in rules.

Activities

1. Listen to *"New Baboon"* and *"New Nice"* on the podcast entitled, *"New Normal?"* What insights from the podcast resonate with what you have learned in this lecture? See: http://www.radiolab.org/story/91693-new-normal/
2. Listen to Dan Pink talk about, *Drive: The surprising truth about what motivates us.* Think about how the principles in Pink's talk relate to the way in which the norms of the McCallister Model aim to support student learning. See: http://www.youtube.com/watch?v=u6XAPnuFjJc&feature=relmfu
3. *Classroom focus on social skills can lead to academic gains...* http://www.sciencedaily.com/releases/2014/03/140306095522.htm
4. *Victims want to change, not just punish, offenders...* http://www.sciencedaily.com/releases/2014/05/140514153229.htm
5. *Evolution: Social exclusion leads to cooperation...* http://www.sciencedaily.com/releases/2012/12/121205084425.htm
6. *How cooperation is maintained in human societies: Punishment...* http://www.sciencedaily.com/releases/2010/05/100501013529.htm
7. *High school put downs make it hard for students to learn...* http://www.sciencedaily.com/releases/2009/09/090901105142.htm
8. *Cooperation learned through practice, according to a mathematical model...* http://www.sciencedaily.com/releases/2014/05/140529142315.htm
9. *Generosity leads to evolutionary success...* http://www.sciencedaily.com/releases/2013/09/130902162716.htm
10. *Gossip, ostracism may have hidden group benefits...* http://www.sciencedaily.com/releases/2014/01/140127193852.htm

NYC Department of Education Citywide Behavioral Expectations to Support Student Learning, Grades K-5 and 6–12 (2019)

K-12 Student Bill of Rights and Responsibilities

I Right to a Free, Public School Education

1. Attend school and receive a free, public school education from kindergarten to age 21 or receipt of a high school diploma, whichever comes first, as provided by law; students who have been determined to be Multiple Language Learners are entitled to bilingual education or English as a second language program as provided by law; students with disabilities who have been determined to be in need of special education are entitled to a free, appropriate, public education from age 3 until age 21, as provided by law;
2. Be in a safe and supportive learning environment, free from discrimination, harassment, bullying, and bigotry, and to file a complaint if they feel that they are subject to this behavior (see Chancellor's Regulations A-830, A-831, A-832, A-420, and A-421);

3. Receive courtesy and respect from others regardless of actual or perceived age, race, creed, color, gender, gender identity (including the right of students to use bathrooms and locker rooms in accordance with their gender identity and to be addressed by the name and pronouns consistent with their gender identity), gender expression, religion, national origin, citizenship/immigration status, weight, sexual orientation, physical and/or emotional condition, disability, marital status, and political beliefs;
4. Receive a written copy of the school's policies and procedures, including the Citywide Behavioral Expectations for Supporting Student Learning (including the Discipline Code) and the New York City Department of Education (NYCDOE) Student Bill of Rights and Responsibilities, early in the school year or upon admission to the school during the school year;
5. Be informed about diploma requirements, including courses and examinations and information on assistance to meet those requirements;
6. Be informed about required health, cognitive, and language screening examinations;
7. Be informed about courses and programs that are available in the school and the opportunity to have input in the selection of elective courses;
8. Receive professional instruction;
9. Know the grading criteria for each subject area and/or course offered by the school and to receive grades for schoolwork completed based on established criteria;
10. Be informed of educational progress and receive periodic evaluations both informally and through formal progress reports;
11. Be notified in a timely manner of the possibility of being held over in the grade or of failing a course;
12. Be notified of the right of appeal regarding holdover or failing grades;
13. Confidentiality in the handling of student records maintained by the school system;
14. Request or by parental request to have their contact information withheld from institutions of higher learning and/or military recruiters. (To protect the rights of students and parents to determine how student information is released to the military, schools that administer the Armed Services Vocational Aptitude Battery (ASVAB) will not release student scores to military recruiters unless both the parent and the student provide written consent.)
15. Receive guidance, counseling, and advice for personal, social, educational, career, and vocational development.

II Right to Freedom of Expression and Person

1. Organize, promote, and participate in a representative form of student government;
2. Organize, promote, and participate in student organizations, social and educational clubs or teams and political, religious, and philosophical groups consistent with the requirements of the Equal Access Act;
3. Representation on appropriate school-wide committees that influence the educational process, with voting rights where applicable;
4. Publish school newspapers and school newsletters reflecting the life of the school and expressing student concerns and points of view consistent with responsible journalistic methods and subject to reasonable regulations based on legitimate pedagogical concerns;
5. Circulate, including through electronic circulation, newspapers, literature, or political leaflets on school property, subject to reasonable guidelines established by the school regarding time, place, and manner of distribution, except where such material is libelous, obscene, commercial, or materially disrupts the school, causes substantial disorder, or invades the rights of others;

6 Wear political or other types of buttons, badges, or armbands, except where such material is libelous, obscene, or materially disrupts the school, causes substantial disorder, or invades the rights of others;
7 Post bulletin board notices within the school or on the school website subject to reasonable guidelines established by the school, except where such notices are libelous, obscene, commercial, or materially disrupt the school, cause substantial disorder, or invade the rights of others;
8 Determine their own dress within the parameters of the NYCDOE policy on school uniforms and consistent with religious expression, except where such dress is dangerous or interferes with the learning and teaching process;
9 Be secure in their persons and belongings and to carry in the school building personal possessions which are appropriate for use on the premises;
10 Be free from unreasonable or indiscriminate searches, including body searches;
11 Be free from corporal punishment and verbal abuse (as per Chancellor's Regulations A-420 and A-421);
12 Decline to participate in the Pledge of Allegiance or stand for the pledge.

III Right to Due Process

1 Be provided with the Discipline Code and rules and regulations of the school;
2 Know what is appropriate behavior and know which behaviors may result in disciplinary responses;
3 Be counseled by members of the professional staff in matters related to their behavior as it affects their education and welfare in the school;
4 Know possible dispositions and outcomes for specific offenses;
5 Due process with respect to disciplinary responses for alleged violations of school regulations for which they may be suspended or removed from class by their teachers; students with disabilities or who are "presumed to have a disability" have the right to certain protections under the Individuals with Disabilities Education Act (IDEA);
6 Due process of law in instances of disciplinary responses for alleged violations of school regulations for which they may be suspended or removed from class by their teachers; students with disabilities or who are "presumed to have a disability" have the right to certain protections under IDEA.
7 Know the procedures for appealing the actions and decisions of school officials with respect to their rights and responsibilities as set forth in this document;
8 Be accompanied by a parent and/or representative at conferences and hearings;
9 The presence of school staff in situations where there may be police involvement.

IV Additional Rights of Students Age 18 and Over

The federal Family Educational Rights and Privacy Act ("FERPA") gives students who have reached 18 years of age certain rights with respect to the student's education records.

Students age 18 and over have the right to request, inspect, and review their own education records within 45 days of the day the New York City Department of Education (NYCDOE) receives the student's request, in accordance with the procedures set forth in Chancellor's Regulation A-820.

Students age 18 and over have the right to request that their own education records be changed when they believe they are inaccurate, misleading, or otherwise in violation of their privacy rights under FERPA, in accordance with the procedures set forth in Chancellor's Regulation A-820.

Students age 18 and over have the right to provide written consent before personally identifiable information in their own education records is disclosed, except in certain cases when FERPA allows disclosure without consent, including the following:

V Student Responsibilities

Responsible behavior by each student supports the rights set forth in this document. Violation of some of these responsibilities may lead, in accordance with the Discipline Code (https://www.schools.nyc.gov/DCode), to disciplinary measures. Full acceptance of responsibility with the exercise of rights will provide students with greater opportunity to serve themselves and society. Students have a responsibility to:

1. attend school regularly and punctually and make every effort to achieve in all areas of their education;
2. be prepared for class with appropriate materials and properly maintain textbooks and other school equipment;
3. follow school regulations regarding entering and leaving the classroom and school building;
4. help maintain a school environment free of weapons, illegal drugs, controlled substances, and alcohol;
5. behave in a manner that contributes to a safe learning environment and which does not violate other students' right to learn;
6. share information with school officials regarding matters which may endanger the health and welfare of members of the school community;
7. respect the dignity and equality of others and refrain from conduct which denies or impinges on the rights of others;
8. show respect for school property and respect the property of others, both private and public;
9. be polite, courteous, and respectful toward others regardless of actual or perceived age, race, creed, color, gender, gender identity, gender expression, religion, national origin, weight, citizenship/immigration status, sexual orientation, physical and/or emotional condition, disability, marital status, and political beliefs, and refrain from making slurs based on these criteria;
10. behave in a polite, truthful, and cooperative manner toward students and school staff;
11. promote good human relations and build bridges of understanding among the members of the school community;
12. use non-confrontational methods to resolve conflicts;
13. participate and vote in student government elections;
14. provide positive leadership by making student government a meaningful forum to encourage maximum involvement;
15. work with school staff in developing broad extracurricular programs in order to represent the range of physical, social, and cultural interests and needs of students;
16. observe ethical codes of responsible journalism;
17. refrain from obscene and defamatory communication in speech, writing, and other modes of expression, including electronic expression, in their interactions with the school community;
18. express themselves in speech, writing, and other modes of expression, including electronic expression in a manner which promotes cooperation and does not interfere with the educational process;
19. assemble in a peaceful manner and respect the decision of students who do not wish to participate;

20 bring to school only those personal possessions which are safe and do not interfere with the learning environment;
21 adhere to the guidelines established for dress and activities in the school gymnasium, physical education classes, laboratories, and shops;
22 be familiar with the school Discipline Code (https://www.schools.nyc.gov/DCode) and abide by school rules and regulations;
23 provide leadership to encourage fellow students to follow established school policies and practices; and
24 keep parents informed of school-related matters, including progress in school, social and educational events, and ensure that parents receive communications that are provided by school staff to students for transmittal to their parents.

Note

1. This practice was originally inspired by my son, for whom I received a call from the truancy officer in the spring of his sophomore year, who told me he had been absent from school 24 times. I told her that was impossible, since I saw him off to school every day. It is an abdication of the school's moral obligation to ensure every learner's opportunity to learn, and that requires a means to intervene in maladaptive patterns of avoidance.

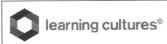

Classroom Social Norms Rubric

Rating Scale: (✓-) Needs Immediate Improvement (✓) Making Progress (✓-) Proficient (NA) No opportunity to observe

Procedures

1. **Instruction:** The School Culture Guide schedules lessons at the start of the school year and periodically throughout the year to review rules, routines, and expectations for general classroom conduct and expectations outlined in each of the Format Rubrics. The Social Norms Rubric is used as a teaching tool to help learners understand expectations and personal responsibilities. The guide reflects on a weekly basis about which norms should be reinforced in routines and social process lessons.

   The Social Contract and Progressive Disciplinary Response: At the beginning of the year, a Ladder of Self-regulation is developed. This process begins with the Social Contract Talk, which outlines the history of education as a right and an opportunity, rights and responsibilities of members of the school community, categories of behaviors that constitute infractions of the Contract, and discussion of disciplinary responses to Contract infringement. The Talk is presented to all learners. Learners provide suggestions for ways that misbehavior should be addressed. With input from learners, the leadership team creates the Ladder of Self-regulation, which is posted in every classroom. The Ladder sets out conditions to be followed in situations where terms of the Social Contract are violated (e.g., 1st step: verbal warning; 2nd step: move seats; 3rd step: isolated work time; 4th step: Behavior Conference with guide; 5th step: after-school detention; 6th step: call home; 7th step: principal referral). A Behavior Conference with the guide is included in the Ladder of Self-regulation, requiring the learner and guide to complete a Behavior Conference Record. Guides make a coordinated effort at the beginning of the year to teach the Ladder as a tool for self-regulation. The Ladder is used throughout the year as a tool to help learners regulate their behavior.

   On-Call: An "On-call" system of back-up support is organized to support classroom guides when they face highly challenging behaviors. The adult on-call provides support to the classroom guide to either address problematic behaviors or to relieve the guide to address the problematic behavior.

   Interventions: If a learner habitually fails to meet responsibilities to learn and to support the learning of classmates, an Intervention is conducted in which learners reflect on problematic behaviors, make a commitment to positive behaviors, and sign a contract (a 'Promise Card'). Learners are provided with laminated copies of their Promise Card and are instructed to bring it to every class. A school-wide system of recording and tracking interventions is created. All guides have access to a roster of learners who have had interventions, and should refer to promise cards when problems arise in class.

Primary Aims

1. Through positive emotional relationships with peers and guides, learners have opportunity to develop higher order thinking, regulate emotions and behavior, develop self-awareness, and experience a positive sense of well-being. Classroom social norms are a medium through which relationships develop. As an important aspect of curriculum, social norms are treated as material to be taught, learned and applied in social interaction. Learning is most successful when learners are able to internalize positive social norms and to participate successfully in a variety of roles as members of the classroom community. The Learning Cultures Formats, structured to support positive social interactions, provide an ecosystem in which positive social norms are learned and applied. Through the successful implementation of the Formats, the classroom provides a universal behavior support system with opportunities for both academic and social emotional learning. This ecosystem supports high achievement and guards against behavioral and disciplinary problems. When implemented successfully, the Learning Cultures Formats provide a Tier I approach to instruction and classroom discipline.

1. Learner   Rating

1a. Learners enjoy maximal freedom of expression and movement within the classroom to use space, associate with peers of their choice, and exercise choice and autonomy in making decisions about curriculum tasks. Learners demonstrate awareness of Format rules by adhering to them.

1b. Learners have been introduced to the Format rubrics and demonstrate awareness of their responsibilities and roles within each Format. Copies of all Format rubrics are available for learner reference.

1c. Learners have been introduced to the Social Contract and demonstrate awareness of their rights and responsibilities to learn and of their responsibility to support the learning of others. Learners adhere to the Social Contract and respond appropriately to behavioral feedback by guides and peers. Learners actively enforce sanctioned procedures when infractions to the Social Contract occur.

1d. Learners who are required to complete a Behavior Conference Record are able to successfully reflect on challenges and possible resolutions.

1e. Learners demonstrate that they have internalized positive social norms through reciprocal interactions with peers, which are characterized by respect and consideration.

2. Guide   Rating

2a. Disruptions are addressed immediately and directly in a non-disruptive manner through efficient execution of the Ladder of Self-Regulation. When behavior infractions occur, the guide accurately identifies the person(s) responsible and quickly addresses the disruptive behavior with an appropriate response from the Ladder of Self-regulation. The process is repeated as many times as necessary, each time issuing a new condition. 'On-Call' support is enlisted when necessary. (Note: Since learning depends on sustained, selective attention and high engagement, the guide should never disrupt the whole class in order to address problematic behaviors of particular learners.)

2b. The guide employs effective strategies to support learners' emotional and behavioral self-regulatory capacities. After responding to an infraction, the guide provides sufficient opportunity for the learner to think about and change behavior before responding again. Responses are made strategically as a means to raise learner self-awareness and to help learners regain self-control and re-regulate behavior or emotions.

2c. When addressing problematic behaviors, the guide uses precise terms, derived from the Social 2d. Contract and/or Format rubrics, to reinforce learners' awareness of rules, boundaries, and expectations.

2d. When warranted, the guide provides a Behavior Conference Record to learners whose behavior warrants a conference.

2e. Guide's interactions and responses with learners strengthen intrinsic motivation and self-regulation. 2f. Extrinsic rewards, such as stickers, points or rewards are never used as they compromise intrinsic motivation.

3. Climate   Rating

3a. The learning environment is supportive. Learner interactions evidence traits of empathy, cooperation, courtesy and respect.

3b. The learning environment is safe. A zero-tolerance policy for words or gestures that could be interpreted by any member of the classroom community as threatening, discriminating, bullying, harassing, or bigoted is enforced by all members of the classroom community.

4. Expectations and Norms   Rating

4a. The classroom environment provides adequate cues to support learners to self-regulate to rules and procedures previously taught. The environment shows evidence of previous instruction relating to expectations and learners' responsibilities.

4b. Transitions between classroom activities are quiet, quick, and efficient (target 2-minute maximum in primary classrooms, 1-minute maximum in upper elementary through high school).

4c. A Ladder of Self-regulation is posted in the classroom and used consistently to secure positive behavioral norms.

5. Environment   Rating

5a. Space in the classroom is provided for learners who need to retreat to a secluded area to regain self-control or to re-channel negative emotions.

5b. Areas in the classroom that are potential conflict *hot spots* are minimized or eliminated through ground rules for using space and taking part in classroom activities (e.g., learners abide by rules for taking turns or sharing).
5c. Ladders of Self-regulation are posted in every classroom.
5d. The Social Contract Talk is documented and made available for learner reference.
5e. The school Discipline Code is available for learner reference.

6.	Records	Rating

6a. Behavior Conference Records show evidence that the learner has, a) gained understanding of why behaviors were problematic in relation to classroom social norms; b) considered new, positive behaviors; and, c) made a commitment to change behaviors by signing a contract/promise card.
6b. Academic and Behavior Intervention records are archived, systematically organized, and accessible to staff.
6c. Promise Cards are archived, systematically organized and accessible to staff.

Comments:

19 The Academic and Behavior Intervention Formats

Abnormal is normal.

Robert Plomin

Description

The Learning Cultures Formats provide a Tier I curriculum framework that is a universal design for all learners. Within the context of the Formats, and provided learners self-regulate to the expectations outlined in the Rubrics, most will develop at a typical pace of academic development. However, in cases in which the learner's patterns of behavior are distorted—exhibited as academic or behavioral difficulties—learners require Tier II supports. McCallister Model Tier II system of support consists of the Intervention. This chapter describes both the Academic Intervention and the Behavior Intervention. The Academic Intervention is typically used for learners who have been identified through the Assessment and Code Blue school-wide systems to be at risk of failing to make typical developmental progress. The Behavior Intervention is typically used for learners who have come to attention through the school-wide systems for student behavior administered by the School Culture Lead and the central leadership (e.g., principal referral).

The Intervention is a meeting between a learner and a guide (teacher, administrator, peer mentor) that results in a personal learning plan. It is utilized when a student exhibits high levels of passivity or avoidance toward learning (in the case of the Academic Intervention) or is not able to assume responsibility to make and meet learning goals (see Appendix 43 for a sample intervention, www.routledge.com/9780367458591).

An **Academic Intervention** is warranted when a learner:

- Habitually fails to complete academic tasks;
- Persistently fails to submit homework in a timely manner;
- Fails to demonstrate achievement growth;
- Is frequently absent or late to class;
- Uses class time unproductively;
- Lacks focus or initiative toward academic goals;
- Lacks awareness of or seriousness to the relationship between academic performance and life opportunity.

A **Behavior Intervention** is warranted when a learner:

- Habitually fails to complete academic tasks;
- Is persistently disrespectful or verbally rude;

- Persists in exhibiting uncooperative or noncompliant behaviors;
- Is disruptive to the point of interfering with others' learning;
- Is habitually disobedient or oppositional toward teacher's authority or classroom rules;
- Exhibits behaviors that are aggressive or potentially harmful or injurious.

Primary Aims of the Intervention

1. To assist the learner in understanding their behavior in reference to objective norms for community conduct.
2. To gain insight about strategies for normative self-regulation.
3. To gain insight into distorted or maladaptive behaviors and to entertain possibilities for more adaptive behaviors.
4. To make the processes transparent that support successful participation with others in the routines and rituals of the community, particularly those of service to future academic achievement.
5. To promote an experience of positive emotional interdependence and shared empathy to enhance feelings of belonging and well-being.
6. To plan a self-directed personal growth plan centered on collectively informed strategies that align with normative community behavioral conduct and academic achievement.

Materials

Academic Intervention Protocol and Behavior Contract (see Appendix 32, www.routledge.com/9780367458591)

or

Behavior Intervention Protocol and Behavior Contract (see Appendix 33)
Academic or Behavior Intervention Rubric (see end-of-chapter sample)
Progress monitoring assessment results (Degrees of Reading Power® scores, scores of curriculum-based measures (CBM) in math, reading and writing fluency, and CBM national norms for reference)
Course grades/transcript
State assessment scores

See www.routledge.com/9780367458591 for mentioned Appendices.

Participants

An Intervention is scheduled between the learner and a group of participants who, together, represent legitimate authority from the perspective of the learner (e.g., a family member, the principal, teachers, friends). Highly resistant or avoidant learners might require attendance of a school administrator, parent, or counselor. A group of peers trained in the protocol (e.g., Keepers Corps) will likely hold legitimate authority in the eyes of learners who are receptive to the Format or those who previously have taken part in the Intervention process.

Procedures

Set up. A facilitator is identified. The facilitator adheres to the Format procedures outlined in the Intervention Protocol throughout the course of the meeting (see Appendix 43, Intervention Protocol-Academic, and Intervention Protocol-Behavior, www.routledge.com/9780367458591). The facilitator should:

- remain objective;
- encourage the learner to take an active role in the proceedings;
- invite others to provide helpful input;
- contain the dialog to ensure the discussion is productive and that the learner feels safe and supported (i.e., punitive or accusatory comments are not tolerated).

1. Establish a sense of rapport amongst participants, set an empathetic tone for the meeting, and identify the purpose for the meeting. Assure the learner they are not in trouble.

    - Identify the purpose of the meeting: to help the learner understand what makes school difficult; to remove barriers that interfere with learning; to make school more fun; and to identify ways to achieve success.
    - Reassure the learner that everyone in attendance is there to support them and help make the meeting a success.
    - If this is a repeat Academic Intervention, ask the learner to recite their transformation narrative (a story about how they met goals that they had previously set).

2. Guide learner to identify and list problematic behaviors that interfere with academic development. List the behaviors on the Academic Contact. Involve participants in the discussion as needed.

3. Remind the learner of the Social Contract Talk (the Talk is described in Chapter 18 and is a prerequisite experience for the Intervention). Review the list of Student Rights and Responsibilities outlined in the school discipline code. Guide the learner to read aloud with you, in unison, Rights and Responsibilities that are relevant to academic performance (e.g., the responsibility to make *every effort to achieve in school*). Encourage the learner to breach with questions or comments.

4. In the process of reading, support the learner to take initiative to **identify which responsibilities they are currently meeting and which they are unable to meet due to problematic behaviors**. List problematic behaviors on the Academic Intervention Worksheet. In case the learner denies any problem, invite other participants to help the learner reflect on school scenarios that illustrate problematic behaviors (e.g., "Your teacher and I have noticed you've been having some trouble lately focusing in class and that you seem to spend most of work time talking with your friends"). Help the learner explain why or how the behavior interferes with responsibility to learn. Document their responses in #2 on the Academic Intervention Worksheet.

5. Discuss the *growth mindset* and *self-determination*. People who have a growth mindset understand how applied effort and a constant search for new strategies positively influences learning outcomes (Dweck, 2015). In other words, they understand that the harder they press on the gas, the faster the car goes, metaphorically speaking. The opposite of a growth mindset is an entity mindset. People with this way of thinking tend to believe either they are good at something or bad at it, but don't understand that they have control of their growth. They are more powerless than people with a growth mindset.

    Self-determination is a form of internal motivation. There are three main ingredients that result in being self-determined (Deci & Ryan, 2012). The first is sharing a sense of the importance with others about the thing that motivates you. That sense of relatedness boosts motivation. Next, we are motivated when we have autonomy or independence in doing the things we care about. Finally, we are motivated when we get competence feedback about how well we're doing the thing. Competence feedback is information about your performance.

People control their own development through their beliefs and conscious, willful action. In this meeting, we're going to help you understand how you can make goals for new behaviors that result in better learning outcomes.

To proceed with the **Behavior Intervention**, follow steps 6–11, directly below. To proceed with the **Academic Intervention**, skip the Behavior Intervention, below, and resume with the Academic Intervention, steps 6–13.

Behavior Intervention, Steps 6–10

6 Now reflect. Help the learner make sense of the Intervention experience thus far. Use one/some of these prompts:

    What do think of what we've talked about?
    What do you make of all this information?

    Allow the learner an opportunity to make a value statement about the nature of his/her behaviors in relation to personal aspirations.

7 Solicit a commitment to change. Tell the learner, *we can help you make new goals and a plan of action to meet them*. Ask the learner, *would you like to make changes in your behavior to meet new goals?* Let them respond. Of total, 99.9% of learners will say they want to change if the protocol has been implemented effectively. If not, engage the learner in a discussion about new goals and behaviors. If they say they want to change, now ask: *Do you want me to help you think through some possibilities?* Then review the behaviors that get in the way of learning and the responsibilities they violate.

8 Explain the importance of making a plan to develop new behaviors. Invite the learner to identify a course of action to take when she or he experiences a trigger to the problematic behavior before it begins to escalate. Participants offer their contributions to the conversation with strategies to help the learner self-regulate (e.g., remove self from situation; find a quite spot; count to three before I speak; talk to myself; shift attention by focusing on an object or new task). Invite the learner to make a *personal behavior plan* in the form of a contract. Use the Behavior Intervention Contract template, below.

    - Develop a list of goals in the form of new behaviors that will enable them to meet their responsibilities, achieve academically, and get along with others. This will be a preliminary list, intended to be the foundation for a plan that evolves in response to new patterns of effort, future Behavior Intervention meetings, and new goals.
    - Make a commitment to change in the form of a promise: "*I promise…*"
    - Enlist the learner to name conditions or consequences if the promise is broken.
    - Learner signs contract.

9 The student has made a promise. And it is the responsibility of the adults in the school to help the learner make sure the promise is kept and appropriate conditions are enforced if or when it is not. The facilitator laminates a copy of the Promise Card for the student to keep until the next meeting. Copies of the Contract are filed centrally and given to each of the learner's teachers.

10 Behavior Intervention meetings are re-scheduled every two weeks until maladaptive patterns are replaced with adaptive patterns of behavior.

Academic Intervention, Steps 6–13

6. Referring to Item #3 on the Academic Intervention Worksheet, explain the *bell curve* in relation to the distribution of levels of performance that normally occur in groups of people. The large number of people perform at an average rate, and outliers perform very well or poorly (illustrate using examples from different domains of performance, such as physical performance, memory, reading speed, artistic talent). Prompt the learner to identify 2–3 of their own competencies or talents. Ask them where on the curve they would plot their performance in each domain. Then prompt the learner to identify sources of effort that contributed to the development of the competency.

7. Now prompt the learner to identify the position on the bell curve that is predictive of their performance in the content subject(s) that is the primary focus of concern (e.g., math, reading, science, etc.). Prompt the learner to consider what behaviors interfere with growth. Then prompt the learner to speculate how growth would be impacted if they applied the same kind of effort to their weakness as they did to their area of strength.

8. Share curriculum-based measures in Math; Reading (Oral Reading Fluency); Reading Comprehension (MAZE); and Writing. For each data point, share the national norm as a reference. In schools where the Degrees of Reading Power® is administered, share data and help the learner discern patterns in performance. Share national norms as a reference. For each measure, provide a grade-level average and an end-of-year target.

    Help the learner identify how many points she or he would need to improve on a specified interval of time in order to meet end-of-year nationally normed grade-level targets.

9. Discuss the *growth mindset* and *self-determination*. People who have a growth mindset understand how applied effort and a constant search for new strategies positively influences learning outcomes (Dweck, 2015). In other words, they understand that the harder they press on the gas, the faster the car goes, metaphorically speaking. The opposite of a growth mindset is an entity mindset. People with this way of thinking tend to believe either they are good at something or bad at it, but don't understand that they have control of their growth. They are more powerless than people with a growth mindset.

    Self-determination is a form of internal motivation. There are three main ingredients that result in being self-determined (Deci & Ryan, 2012). The first is sharing with others a sense of importance about the things we do. That sense of relatedness boosts motivation. Next, having autonomy and independence to do the things we care about makes us motivated and self-determined. Finally, receiving feedback about how well we do something increases our motivation.

    People control their own development through their beliefs. In this meeting, we're going to help you understand how you can make goals for new behaviors that result in better learning outcomes.

10. Now reflect. Help the learner make sense of the Intervention experience thus far. Use one/some of these prompts:

    What do you think of what we've talked about?
    What do you make of all this information?

    Allow the learner an opportunity to make a value statement about the nature of his/her behaviors in relation to personal academic aspirations.

11 Solicit a commitment to change. Tell the learner, *we can help you make new goals and a plan of action to meet them.* Ask the learner, *would you like to make changes in your behavior to meet new goals? If you do, you need to make a commitment to new behaviors that will improve your academic progress. Do you want me to help you think through some possibilities?*

Most learners say they want to change. If not, engage the learner in a discussion about new goals and behaviors.

12 Invite the learner to make a *personal learning plan* in the form of a contract. Use the Academic Intervention. On the Contract,
Review and list behaviors that get in the way of learning;

- List the Social Contract or Format indicators that the behaviors violate.
- Develop a list of goals in the form of new behaviors that will enable them to meet their responsibilities and achieve academically. This will be a preliminary list, intended to be the foundation for a plan that evolves in response to new patterns of effort, future Academic Intervention meetings, and new goals.
- Make a commitment to change in the form of a promise: "*I promise...*"
- Identify conditions or consequences if the promise is broken.
- Learner signs contract.
- The student has made a promise. And it is the responsibility of the adults to help the learner make sure the promise is kept and appropriate conditions are enforced if or when it is not. The facilitator laminates a copy of the Promise Card for the student to keep until the next meeting. Copies of the Contract are filed centrally and given to each of the learner's teachers.

13 Academic Intervention meetings are re-scheduled every two weeks until disordered behavior patterns disappear and adaptive replace them.

Discussion

The McCallister Model is based on the logic that social norms underpin most forms of higher mental functioning. Within the McCallister program, students are Keepers of their Culture. They learn to appreciate their rights and to view their responsibilities as obligations to membership in the school community that they have a moral obligation to observe. The Formats Rubrics specify procedures that enable every learner to thrive and achieve, so the ability to regulate to these norms is a means through which learners can direct their own development.

Positive development depends on the learner's own sense of commitment to and responsibility for learning. In other words, a person can only learn what she or he takes responsibility for (Olson, 2007). From this perspective, chronic academic under-performance or behavior difficulties reflect a lack commitment to and responsibility for learning and personal behavior as opposed to the more typical view that these behaviors reflect a deficit in cognitive functioning. Thus, strategies to enlist the learner's commitment to and responsibility for productive behaviors are effective means to improve behavior, learning, and achievement. The Intervention Protocol stimulates the learner's natural capacities to exercise moral self-governance to shared social norms (Olson, 2007; Tomasello, 2016).

The theory-of-change of the Intervention Format is based on new evidence from neural science and genetics. Disorders, it is now understood, are quantitative results of a large range of genetic influences that each have small effects (Kandel, 2007; Plomin, 2018). The geneticist Robert Plomin (2018) points out that what we had once understood to be psychological disorders are really a spectra of behaviors that have been caused by a large range of genetic influences, each with a small effect. Instead of the traditional notion that one gene was responsible for one disorder (OGOD), Plomin explains that many DNA differences are each responsible for small effects. In other words, a disability—behavioral or cognitive—is a socially constructed idea, not a natural fact. We cannot cure or remediate a disorder, because they do not exist; but suffering can be alleviated through changes in behavior and thinking (Plomin, 2018).

This approach challenges traditional and still largely conventional practices in the treatment of learning and behavior disabilities that are found on nativist and modularity theories of the mind (Fodor, 1983) and behaviorist psychology (Skinner, 1974). The mind maps onto internal modules in the brain that are the locus of functioning. Disabilities are diagnosed on the assumption that they are structural abnormalities for which symptoms can be treated in standardized ways for any patient that is stricken with the disorder. Nomothetic interventions are developed to treat disorders, and are administered in standardized, "evidence-based" protocols (protocols in which the evidence standards that the positive outcome was a result of the intervention are high). This Intervention Protocol is based on the normal/abnormal dichotomy and the belief that abnormalities are qualitatively similar across populations. The new science of the mind and genetics shows that so-called abnormalities are really just extreme versions of normal—a spectra of behaviors that arise from a confluence of small effects that are a result of genetic differences and a reflection of human individuality (Plomin, 2018). Disability is more properly understood as maladaptive expressions of personal individuality that can be mediated in order to help the person self-organize in ways that enhance well-being. These insights cast doubt on the conventional ways we have supported learners with so-called disabilities and behavior disorders.

The Intervention Protocol relates to new paradigms in psychotherapy praxis. It was once thought that distorted thinking or behavior were symptoms of underlying abnormalities or disorders, and recognize that distorted behavior is not a symptom of underlying disorders, but an agent in the maladaptive development and continued suffering (Kandel, 2007). The emerging paradigm in psychotherapy, manifested in Cognitive Behavioral Therapy, for example, emphasizes the role of conscious thought in behavior (Beck in Kandel, 2007). Through a therapeutic course that involves identifying the problematic behavior and replacing it with more adaptive behaviors, suffering could be alleviated (Beck, 1996).

This paradigm has inspired the field of Interpersonal Neurobiology and the construct of mental integration (Siegel, 2020). Coherence between the continuous flow of self-states is defined as "integration" (Siegel, 2020). According to the psychiatrist Dan Siegel (2020), so-called disorders come into being when parts of the mind (e.g., consciousness, memory, narrative sense of self, cognitive states, and interpersonal relationships) become restricted in response to patterned maladaptive thoughts and behaviors. Differentiating these parts of the mind and cultivating and developing them, and then relinking them through mental integration is a means to achieve well-being.

The Intervention Protocols create opportunities to enlist the learner in identifying how disordered behaviors interfere with their personal obligations to their own learning, and possibly to others' learning, to help the learner make a new plan for productive behavior, and to make a commitment to change. The Academic and Behavior Interventions provide a scaffolded process whereby learners can be helped to take responsibility to change their own thoughts and behaviors in order to achieve an improved sense of well-being. They are helped to understand that doing so is a moral responsibility, articulated in the Social Contract (i.e., Discipline Code).

Academic Intervention Rubric

Rating Scale: (✓-) Needs Immediate Improvement (✓) Making Progress (✓+) Proficient (NA) No opportunity to observe

Procedures

1. Facilitator establishes positive rapport with the learner by explaining that the meeting is intended to improve their experience of school. Guides, teachers, significant peers and parents may be in attendance. Where schools have adopted the Keepers of the Culture program, trained peer mentors may facilitate meetings under supervision. If the Intervention is a repeat meeting, the learner recites a *transformation narrative* to relate the behavioral changes they have achieved.
2. Facilitator guides the learner to identify and list problematic behaviors that interfere with academic development. Attendees are involved in the discussion as needed.
3. Facilitator guides the learner to read the Social Contract (e.g., rights and responsibilities from the school Discipline Code) aloud and helps to clarify questions that arise.
4. In the process of reading, the learner identifies the behaviors that prevent them from meeting their responsibilities.
5. Facilitator presents a diagram of the normal curve, explains how it depicts a typical range of human performance.
6. Facilitator engages the learner in identifying competencies (e.g., list of things they are good at), and prompts learner to indicate where on a normal curve the learner positions him or herself with regard to their most proud competency. The learner is prompted to identify the sources of effort that contributed to the development of the competency.
7. Facilitator prompts the learner to predict where on the bell curve they would position themselves in relation to an academic competency that is the focus of the meeting (e.g., math, reading, science, etc.). The learner is prompted the learner to consider which behaviors interfere with growth. The learner is then prompted to speculate how growth would be impacted if they applied the same effort to their weakness as they did to their area of strength.
8. Facilitator shares competence data (e.g., class grades, Degrees of Reading Power scores, reading, writing or math fluency assessments). For each data point, the facilitator shares the national norm reference. The learner is helped to identify how many points they would need to improve in order to meet the nationally-normed end-of-year target or what they would need to do to achieve another goal.
9. Facilitator invites the learner to reflect on the meeting experience, then asks the learner if they want to change undesirable behaviors and solicits a commitment to change.
10. Facilitator supports learner to develop a list of new goals and behaviors that will enable them to meet their responsibilities and achieve academically.
11. Learner reads their new promises aloud, and signs the Intervention Contract.
12. Facilitator creates a 'Promise Card,' listing new goals and behaviors, which serves as a behavioral contract. Copies are given to the student and their teachers.
13. Academic Intervention meetings are re-scheduled as needed until adaptive patterns of behavior are established.

Primary Aims

1. To assist the learner in understanding their behavior in reference to objective norms for community conduct.
2. To gain insight about strategies for normative self-regulation.
3. To gain insight into distorted or maladaptive behaviors and to entertain possibilities for more adaptive behaviors.
4. To make the processes transparent that support successful participation with others in the routines and rituals of the community, particularly those of service to future academic achievement.
5. To promote an experience of positive emotional interdependence and shared empathy to enhance feelings of belonging and well-being.

6. To plan a self-directed personal growth plan centered on collectively informed strategies that align with normative community behavioral conduct and academic achievement.

1. Learner Rating

1a. Demonstrates a willingness to participate, demonstrated through cooperative verbal and nonverbal behaviors (e.g., eye contact and receptive physical positioning).

1b. Is able to identify personal behaviors that contribute to problematic experiences in school.

1c. Through a cooperative reading of the Social Contract, is able to identify instances where problematic behaviors interfere with responsibilities and prevent achievement.

1d. Signals moral identification with collective group norms in making a commitment to change problematic behaviors.

1e. Makes an earnest effort to identify positive behaviors as alternatives to problematic behaviors.

1f. Pledges their personal commitment to change by signing a "Promise Card."

1g. In repeat meetings, the learner is able to tell a 'transformation narrative' in which they relate their success in adopting new, generative behaviors.

2. Facilitator Rating

2a. Establishes positive rapport and a tone of reassurance.

2b. Is supportive and shows respect and empathy for learner.

2c. Skillfully facilitates a cooperative, problem-solving process in which the learner assumes responsibility to follow the Intervention procedures.

2d. Supports learner to identify problematic behaviors. If the learner is resistant or unsure, the facilitator engages other participants in a deliberative dialogue to identify and describe problematic behaviors. When those other than the learner identify problematic behaviors, the learner is asked whether they agree with the observation. The learner should state each problematic behavior in their own words.

2e. When a learner identifies an overly-general behavior or names a behavior that is not relevant, redirects the learner to more precisely describe relevant behavior and to elaborate on the context in which it occurs.

2f. Encourages the learner to identify appropriate alternative behaviors and to solicit suggestions from meeting participants.

3. Recordkeeping Rating

3a. Learner's progress monitoring assessment data and documented grade-level norms are available for reference.

3b. Problematic behaviors are described in specific terms. Records show evidence that learners fully understand how problematic behaviors interfere with responsibilities.

3c. Resolutions, suggestions and plans for improvement are described in specific terms.

3d. Records are kept centrally so that they are accessible to teachers and focus learners.

3e. Intervention follow-up meeting records show evidence of *transformation narratives*, in which the learner relates instances in which new behaviors replace previously problematic behavior.

4. Organization and School Procedures Rating

4a. A system is established for adult and/or learner facilitators to lead Academic interventions on a regular basis (e.g., within an existing course structure, after-school program, or advisory).

4b. A system is established for learners to sign up for Interventions at times that are not disruptive to their academic schedules.

Comments:

Copyright © 2015, 2016, 2018, 2020 Cynthia McCallister. All rights reserved. Reproduction and distribution are prohibited without permission from the author.   www.LearningCultures.net

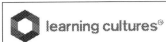

Behavior Intervention Rubric

Rating Scale: (✓-) Needs Immediate Improvement (✓) Making Progress (✓+) Proficient (NA) No opportunity to observe

Procedures

1. Facilitator establishes positive rapport with the learner by explaining that the meeting is intended to improve the experience of school. The learner's teachers, significant peers and parents may be in attendance. In schools that have adopted the Keepers of the Culture program, trained peer mentors may facilitate meetings under supervision. If the Intervention is a repeat meeting, the learner recites a *transformation narrative* to relate the behavioral changes they have achieved.
2. Facilitator guides the learner to identify and list problematic behaviors that interfere with a positive school experience. Attendees are involved in the discussion as needed.
3. Facilitator guides the learner to read the Social Contract (e.g., rights and responsibilities from the school discipline code) aloud and helps to clarify questions that arise.
4. In the process of reading, the learner identifies the behaviors that prevent them from meeting their responsibilities.
5. Facilitator asks the learner if they want to change undesirable behaviors and solicits a commitment to change.
6. Facilitator supports learner to develop a list of new behaviors that will enable them to meet their responsibilities.
7. Learner signs a 'Promise Card,' which serves as a behavioral contract, and which they bring to classes. Each teacher receives a copy of the card.
8. Intervention meetings are re-scheduled as needed until adaptive patterns of behavior are established.

Primary Aims

1. To assist the learner in understanding their behavior in reference to objective norms for community conduct.
2. To gain insight into strategies for normative self-regulation.
3. To gain insight about distorted or maladaptive behaviors and to entertain possibilities for more adaptive behaviors.
4. To make the processes transparent that support successful participation with others in the routines and rituals of the community.
5. To promote an experience of positive emotional interdependence and shared empathy to enhance feelings of belonging and well-being.
6. To plan a self-directed personal growth plan centered on collectively informed strategies that align with normative community behavioral conduct.

1. Learner	Rating
1a. Demonstrates a willingness to participate, demonstrated through cooperative verbal and nonverbal behaviors (e.g., eye contact and receptive physical positioning).	
1b. Is able to identify personal behaviors that contribute to problematic experiences in school.	
1c. Through a cooperative reading of the Social Contract, is able to identify instances where problematic behaviors interfere with responsibilities and contribute to behavior problems.	
1d. Signals moral identification with collective group norms in making a commitment to change problematic behaviors.	
1e. Makes an earnest effort to identify positive behaviors as alternatives to problematic behaviors.	
1f. Pledges their personal commitment to change by signing a "Promise Card."	
1g. In repeat meetings, the learner is able to tell a 'transformation narrative' in which they relate their success in adopting new, generative behaviors.	

2.	Facilitator	Rating

2a. Establishes positive rapport and a tone of reassurance.

2b. Is supportive and shows respect and empathy for learner.

2c. Skillfully facilitates a cooperative, problem-solving process in which the learner assumes responsibility to follow the intervention procedures.

2d. Supports learner to identify problematic behaviors. If the learner is resistant or unsure, the facilitator engages other participants in a deliberative dialogue to identify and describe problematic behaviors. When those other than the learner identify problematic behaviors, the learner is asked whether they agree with the observation. The learner should state each problematic behavior in their own words.

2e. When a learner identifies an overly-general behavior or names a behavior that is not relevant, redirects the child to more precisely describe relevant behavior and to elaborate on the context in which it occurs.

2f. Encourages the learner to identify appropriate alternative behaviors and to solicit suggestions from meeting participants.

3.	Recordkeeping	Rating

3a. Problematic behaviors are described in specific terms. Records show evidence that learners fully understand how problematic behaviors interfere with responsibilities.

3b. Resolutions, suggestions and plans for improvement are described in specific terms.

3c. Records are kept centrally so that they are accessible to teachers and focus learners.

3d. Intervention follow-up meeting records show evidence of *transformation narratives*, in which the learner relates instances in which new behaviors replace previously problematic behavior.

4.	Organization and School Procedures	Rating

4a. A system is established for adult and/or learner facilitators to lead Behavior Interventions on a regular basis (e.g., within an existing course structure, after-school program, or advisory).

4b. A system is established for learners to sign up for Interventions at times that are not disruptive to their academic schedules.

Comments:

Section V
The Ecosystem Curriculum

20 Whole-School Transformation
The Ecosystem Design

>...the representatives of the status quo have seldom, if ever, been able to preside over revolutionary processes.
>
> Edmund W. Gordon (2014a, pp. 293–294)

> The problem is that the complex educational changes demanded by current standards-based reform initiatives, combined with an increasingly heterogeneous student population largely composed of students whom schools have traditionally failed, have pushed the technology of schooling toward unprecedented levels of complexity.
>
> Borman et al. (2004, p. 55)

Introduction

This chapter outlines comprehensive second-level bureaucratic systems of the McCallister Model that are employed to implement a school-level infrastructure that builds teacher and leadership capacity, ensures skilled instruction, quality systems of assessment, coherent curricula, adequate professional development support, and a culture of professionalism and trust. They are simple to implement within the timeframe of less than a year. These relatively simple systems provide a means by which a competent school leader can preside over the revolutionary process of transforming an industrial school into a 21st-century learning organization.

The process begins with a firm commitment to change in the form of a Resolution (see Box 20.1).

The Ecosystem

The transformation of an industrial school into a learning organization is hindered by deeply entrenched problems core educational activities, such as shallow, fragmented, and incoherent instructional programs, low expectations for learners, and low quality professional development; as such, schools are challenged to design, enact and coordinate a functional infrastructure (Peurach & Neumerski, 2015). Leadership is challenging because, as Rowan, Camburn, and Barnes (2004) point out, "...the principal alone can't carry the day because problems of school reform are too large and complex for one individual" (p. 26).

The current egg-crate school, with its linear, incremental, subject-based curriculum, multitudes of classes, and fractured school schedule, makes instructional supervision all but impossible. In a hypothetical elementary school of 500 students and 28 teachers divided into 14 classes of five periods a day, two of which theoretically require

> **Box 20.1**
>
> **Resolution on improving the quality of elementary and secondary education**
>
> *Institutional facts create new institutional realities by redescribing the conditions of reality (Searle, 2010). To that end, this chapter begins with a resolution to be adopted by education leaders to dismantle and replace the obsolete systems of the current industrial school.*
>
> **Resolution to Improve the Quality and Intensity of Schooling**
>
> Whereas the current system of public schooling guarantees every child with a free, compulsory education;
>
> Whereas an education on equal terms is considered every child's right;
>
> Whereas current schooling systems have failed to significantly impact student achievement or to reduce social inequalities;
>
> Whereas the current system of schooling employs classical transmission pedagogical approaches to implement a linear, ability-based skills curriculum to transmit knowledge;
>
> Whereas it is known that learning is a self-directed process and that autonomous, self-selected experiences drawn from rich learning environments result in greater social opportunity; now, therefore, be it
>
> *Resolved*, that the school administration:
>
> 1. Replace the current function of teaching as the technical process of transmission prevailing in the traditional schooling system with the function of self-organized, self-directed learning activities;
> 2. Replace the incremental linear curriculum with a curriculum of self-directed, personalized learning;
> 3. Replace the traditional 'classroom' structure, designed for classical transmission pedagogy, with a cultural niche learning environment that supports self-organized learning and full and free forms of association;
> 4. Implement proven, learner-directed activities and protocols to support academic achievement;
> 5. Regulate inequality in achievement outcomes through a system of distributive justice, whereby the lowest achieving learners are provided supplementary opportunities to learn that are sufficient and adequate to support the achievement of potential; and
> 6. Reallocate resources from the of classical transmission instruction into the creation of diverse, rich, self-organizing learning environments.

multiple-level ability groups, a principal has responsibility to monitor the quality of 98 lessons a day. They are responsible for providing professional development support for teachers of every subject at every level. And, they are required to conduct formal evaluations. Given a teaching force of 28 teachers, with minimal requirement of two evaluations a year, a principal must conduct at least 56 evaluations every year.[1] The principal bears the duty to ensure that the rights of all teachers outlined in a 238-page contract are protected (United Federation of Teachers, 2018).

In Title I schools, the complexity is magnified. Since the enactment of the Elementary and Secondary Education Act (ESEA) of 1965, U.S. federal policy has sought to equalize educational opportunity by providing resources to schools that serve students from low-income families and by holding schools accountable to programs designed to raise achievement in marginalized student populations. In total, more than two dozen ESEA programs have been created to incentivize reforms for schools that serve disadvantaged populations.[2]

The McCallister system of distributed leadership alleviates the burden normally associated with the role of the principal in the industrial school by providing an integrated design for core educational activities (curriculum, instruction, learning, and assessment), and provides a detailed plan and step-by-step procedures for implementing it.

The McCallister school is designed to be an *ecosystem* as opposed to a factory. By employing a pedagogical paradigm that transfers responsibility to learners, and by creating learner-driven systems for self-regulation to academic and social norms, the McCallister Model transfers the mechanism of change in the industrial system from adult labor (teaching) to learner effort (learning). Since curriculum is now seen as rights that are enforced, as opposed to incremental curriculum content to be transmitted, the second-level changes exist to ensure learners' rights are enforced. This learner-driven ecosystem is supported by a school infrastructure that is managed by the school administrator and a cadre of staff leads who together secure and sustain first-level systems described in the previous chapters.

The second-level bureaucratic changes are organized into school-wide programs of *assessment, community education, civil rights, curriculum, school culture,* and *training*. These initiatives operate in synchrony to implement changes directly linked to improvements in learning, teaching, and curriculum and high achievement outcomes.

The school administration supervises the leads, who enact the school ecosystem infrastructure. The infrastructure consists of the following:

- Coherent curriculum organized around personalized learning and consistent implementation of the Formats;
- Distributed responsibility to student representatives to carry out activities to help peers self-regulate to positive academic and social norms;
- Ongoing collaborative professional development;
- Quality assessments that generate ongoing streams of progress feedback to stakeholders;
- Systems to develop a culture of trust amongst school stakeholders;
- A system of rapid-response behavioral and Academic Intervention support learners who have fallen behind.

Year-long Implementation Plan

The Ecosystem is enacted through a Yearlong Implementation Plan (McCallister, 2013a). Collectively, provided each leadership team member implements their responsibilities according to the Plan, transformation can be achieved in under a year (case studies in Chapters 27–30 provide existence proof of year-long transformations).

The Plan provides a solution to the current challenge in the field of rapid school turnaround because existing models require long periods of time to successfully implement. Current approaches to school transformation are seen to progress incrementally, through a number of levels of improvement. The school begins a process of *becoming familiar* with a new program (Level 1); then, the school *prepares* to implement (Level 2); next, teachers begin initial implementation (Level 3); over time, they achieve *stabilized teaching* (in which teachers see the connection between instruction and achievement) (Level 4); *skilled teaching* (Level 5); finally, the school refines cross-school *improvements in implementation* (Level 6) (Peurach & Neumerski, 2015). This progression is dependent upon teacher training and skilled labor and normally takes from three to seven years to achieve in a school (Peurach & Neumerski, 2015). Since the McCallister design is reliant upon self-regulation and responsibilities to obligations, and not labor (teaching), Levels 2–4 are effectively eliminated. Within the McCallister Model, Level 5, skilled teaching, is supplanted by *responsibility taking*, on the part of both learners and adults, which can be achieved across the entire ecosystem of learners and adults within a year. Change in the McCallister school is transformational, rather than incremental. The distributed leadership infrastructure of the Plan provides a system for continuous renewal when it is integrated into the school's bureaucratic systems (McCallister, 2013b, 2013c).

This chapter outlines the ecosystem design and the central administrative leadership responsibilities.

School Leader Responsibilities

The school leader assumes responsibility to execute second-level changes implemented through a system of distributed leadership. As leads execute their responsibilities, they activate leadership roles within a system that functions to (1) stage-planned institutional change; (2) engage the whole school community as participants in the change process; (3) actively monitor and adjust the course of change; and (4) maintain and sustain the momentum of change. Working together, the school leadership and the team of leads replace the school infrastructure in ways that optimize decentralized operations, power growth and renewal, and uphold the school's obligations to learners' rights. Direct responsibilities of the administration are much fewer in number than they are for the leads (see Table 20.1 in a later section). Ongoing responsibilities include the following:

- School triumph narrative
- Newsletter
- Supervise leads (weekly leadership team meetings with each other)
- Coordinate with McCallister project (learning cultures; sparks; keepers of the culture [KoC])
- Quality review preparation
- Maintain implementation plan and accountability deadlines
- Staff evaluation

Table 20.1 Year-long implementation plan: school administration

Calendar action	Calendar dates
Program the school schedule (aim for fewer but longer blocks than is typical in the factory school)	
Determine Instructional Days	B3
Learning Environment walk-throughs, with follow-up feedback	B1
Oversee the implementation of the Formats in all classrooms	Day 1
Give the annual Social Contract Talk	Week 1
Conduct Classroom Environment re-checks	Weeks 1, 8, 16, 24, and 32
Conduct informal observations of Work Time and Social Norms in all classrooms to identify points of need	Week 1
Monitor the implementation of Sparks in all classrooms in coordination with Curriculum Lead	Week 2
Meet with Leads	Weekly
Newsletter	Weekly
Identify teachers in need of improvement	By Week 2
Identify anchor classrooms	By Week 2
Daily classroom walkthroughs to identify disengagement "hot spots"	Weeks 1–4
Opportunity checks	Weeks 8, 16, 20, 24, 28, 32
Complete formal evaluations	By weeks 6, 15, 24, 33

Note: B3 means three weeks before school; B1 means one week before school.

- Instructional accounting system
- Proficiency in Learning Cultures Formats
- Manage coverage for in-house lab sites (hire and train subs to facilitate Formats)
- Purchasing
- State testing (prevent test preparation activities)

Distributed Leadership

The school leader's role within the distributed leadership initiative is to coordinate the leads' work and to monitor the timely execution of their responsibilities. This system works as a whole to create an infrastructure for effective site-based management. The McCallister distributed leadership model provides a tested plan for a collective leadership approach to school transformation that can be used by a capable school leader to succeed in leading a dramatic, rapid school transformation. The leadership projects function in an integrated and coordinated way to support classroom-level implementation of the Learning Cultures Formats, the Sparks curriculum, and the KoC curriculum (see Figure 20.1). Staff assume leadership responsibilities to implement the projects outlined below.

Assessment

Assessment plays an essential role in the educational infrastructure. A centralized assessment system provides continuous streams of competence feedback to learners and staff.

The school-wide assessment and progress monitoring program includes the following:

- Curriculum-based measures of reading, writing, and math fluency administered every six to eight weeks to document the development of academic background abilities.
- A criterion- and norm-reference reading comprehension assessment is administered three times annually in grades 2–12.
- Periodic standards-based assessments to state-aligned content.

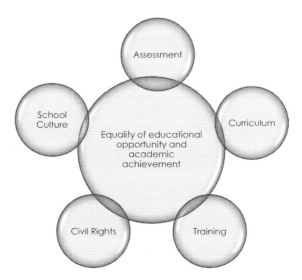

Figure 20.1 The synchronized system for equality of educational opportunity and academic achievement

Assessment Leads coordinate with the Civil Rights Lead and School Culture Lead to identify learners who require Academic or Behavior Interventions. The Assessment Lead works with the Professional Development Lead to coordinate trainings in assessment administration and data analysis.

The Assessment Lead also takes responsibility to share achievement data with teachers and learners as sources of competence feedback. Learners become highly motivated when they have proof that their efforts result in achievement gains. These assessment data provide learners with evidence of their growth, promoting self-determination; they identify learners who fail to make achievement in a timely enough way so as to inform immediate and responsive intervention; and they provide staff with competence feedback about their own teaching, which functions to enhance self-efficacy. The Assessment Program is described in Chapter 21.

Civil Rights

The Civil Rights Program provides means to monitor the extent to which the school is upholding its obligation to all learners' right to an education on equal terms. The Civil Rights Lead helps establish a system of additional support for learners whose behaviors, academic or social, are preventing the school from enforcing their right to an education on equal terms. Working with the Assessment Lead, the Civil Rights Lead identifies learners in need of academic or behavioral intervention support. The Civil Rights Program is described in Chapter 22.

Community Education

The Community Education Lead interfaces with the community to provide information about the school's education program, to recruit talent to serve as guides to support learners taking part in Sparks and Learning Cultures curriculum, and maintains the school's social media presence and website. The Community Education Lead also coordinates monthly school tours, which serve a dual purpose to showcase the school's educational innovations and to provide adults with opportunities to develop professionally by planning and presenting information sessions showcasing the school's education model. The Community Education Program is described in Chapter 23.

Curriculum

The Curriculum Lead maintains quality control of both the Sparks and Learning Cultures curriculum programs in all grades and content subject classes, ensuring opportunities to learn are being supported with the provision of rich, diverse, self-organized learning environments in all classrooms. They ensure learners have access to the Activity Inventory, a menu of personalized learning protocols within the Sparks curriculum. And they work with teachers to support learners in engaging with the Learning Cultures Formats to achieve their personal learning goals.

Teachers who have been trained traditionally often need support to hand over learning responsibilities to learners and to learn themselves how to use the protocols from Sparks and Learning Cultures to support learners to meet curriculum and learning standards. The Curriculum Lead takes responsibility to monitor learning opportunities and to respond proactively in cases where the systems fails, and instructional practices revert back to traditional teacher-directed activities. The Curriculum Program is described in Chapter 24.

School Culture

The School Cultures Lead assumes responsibility to ensure the successful implementation of the KoC program, the social norms curriculum of the McCallister Method (McCallister, 2013f). The KoC curriculum includes the annual Social Contract Talk, implementation of the Ladder of Self-regulation in every classroom, management of the On-call classroom support program, and advisement to the KoC Corps of peer-nominated learners who assist with Interventions and curriculum training. The School Culture Program is described in Chapter 25.

Training

Since the McCallister Model is a universal design for learning, programs in every classroom are structured around the same Formats. The training program (as opposed to professional development) is organized to support not only staff members' professional development but also extends to a training program for learners, since the curriculum presents in the form of social practices as opposed to knowledge transfer. Because the same Formats are used universally, the training program is universal as well.

Training support for staff (teachers and noncertified guides) is organized around the Framework for Professional Development (McCallister, 2008c, 2011d), a comprehensive, school-wide approach to professional change through action inquiry (Lewin, 1946). This practice-embedded approach to supports teachers and they undertake radical shifts in practice. The Framework includes the following components:

- Classroom lab sites, residencies, and intervisitation opportunities;
- Online learning from seven and half hours of explainer videos produced that cover McCallister Model components;
- Professional development and self-assessments using the Rubrics as a norming tool;
- Teacher evaluations by school leaders using the Rubric indicators as evaluative criteria;
- Teacher-to-teacher feedback using the Rubrics as a norming tool;
- Study groups that focus on the McCallister Method canon, a reading list of articles and papers that unpack the philosophical and theoretical ideas implicit in the model.

The Training Lead helps to identify staff in need of training support and the provision of effective professional learning opportunities. They also help to identify well-developed levels of professional practice and to work with those staff to develop classroom lab sites to support the building-wide training initiative.

Teachers' professional development needs are identified through a survey administered several times annually, described below (McCallister, 2013d). All staff are expected to be proactive in pursuing a course of self-determined professional learning based on administrative feedback and self-identified needs. Staff create their own professional development plan and take part in a self-initiated, self-directed professional development program that is linked to the teacher evaluation system. Highly competent teachers are identified to offer their classrooms as lab sites for their colleagues. The Training Program is described in Chapter 26.

Systems for Second-Level Transformation

In addition to supervising the distributed leadership systems of Civil Rights, Community Education, Curriculum, Training, the school leadership implements other programs to support innovation and permanent change.

278 *The Ecosystem Curriculum*

Transformative Evaluation

The observation-evaluation-feedback cycle is the engine school transformation and the priority leadership agenda. Competence feedback, autonomy to make improvements in practice, and opportunities to learn from others are factors that motivate improvements in performance (Deci & Ryan, 2012). The Rubrics provide standards for learning and teaching, and all staff are expected to adhere to their procedures. With concrete criteria for high performance, there is little room for surprise in the evaluation process since all parties are aware of expectations. The Learning Cultures Rubric criteria align with common frameworks for teacher performance (e.g., the Danielson Framework), so they provide a discourse that can inform the observation process and the evaluation write-up. They provide the language that is used to give concrete, corrective, actionable feedback.

The evaluation program is organized annually into four cycles.

Cycle 1: One week before school beings through Week 6
Cycle 2: Week 7 through 15
Cycle 3: Week 16 through 24
Cycle 4: Week 25 through 33

Cycle 1 begins prior to the first week of school when the administration observes classrooms against criteria outlined in the Learning Environment Rubric. Informal, formative observations of learning in every classroom are made in the first week of school to ensure the Formats are implemented with fidelity and social opportunities are adequate. By the end of the first week, the leadership should have a general idea of the quality of learning opportunities in every classroom and who needs immediate training support. By the second week of the Cycle, classrooms that support high levels of engagement and fidelity to the program are identified as the Anchor Classrooms for lab sites, and for the subsequent two weeks, these staff members receive McCallister program training support to be prepared to host trainings by Week 5. The evaluation process incentivizes participation in the school-wide training program.

The priority agenda of Cycle 1 is to instantiate an improvement agenda for the school that is percolated through action inquiry. The first round of formal evaluations is conducted during Cycle 1.

Observation Protocols

Observations are anchored to the Learning Cultures Rubrics. The Rubrics have a norming property, to create a new reality by describing it. It follows the "X, Y, C Rule," described in Chapter 3. Every observation is structured by a protocol designed by principles of narrative analysis (Bruner, 2004). One is quick, and easy. The other is more esoteric, and fun.

Every conscious experience we have is channeled through our *self*. The self is an expert story teller, so it is a handy tool to have at the ready when you are trying to make sense of experience. As you enter a classroom for an observation, set the stage for your narrative by getting into a *once-upon-a-time* mindset. The narrative you are starting to tell yourself about what you see is the basis of the observation. Your sense of the canonical—the way things should be or the way the story should go—is determined by the pedagogical aims of the curriculum (e.g., Rubric criteria). Be conscious of *your* canonical. What is the aim of your observation? What are you hoping to see? Here are some prompts to help develop your observation mindset:

- What do you notice that you *expected* (hoped) to see?
- What do you notice that makes the "performance" you are observing *unique*? In other words, what do you notice that you did not expect to see? How does this story challenge expected *conventions*?
- What are the *particulars* of this story that make it unique/exceptional/problematic?
- How do the characters' *intentions* influence the way the story is unfolding? How are adults or learners carrying out their own *intentions*? And what do you think about the way that they are?
- In what ways are you *interpreting* the "character's" actions? What *evaluative criteria* are you relying on to make your judgment?

The breach—the part of the story that breaks the canonical—is the story plot. The feedback you give is how the narrative influences the "character's" (teachers) actions.

> The protocol for this procedure is simple. Using the Rubric as a reference, state what you saw. It starts with an assertion: "In McCallister classrooms... [insert language from the Rubric that describes what teachers and students should be doing]." Then an observation: "In your classroom, I observed... [insert description of what was observed]." Then corrective feedback: "In order to achieve effectiveness... [insert a directive of necessary changes in practice]." The Rubrics are used instrumentally to unfreeze competing practices, secure new changes in practice, and freeze new practices into place. I demonstrated this practice as the basis for observations at Urban Assembly School for Green Careers and High School of Language and Innovation.

1 **Expectations** (Story conventions, and the sense of what *should* be):

   In an effective Work Time Format, we expect to see [every learner engaged in their own independent learning activities].

2 **Rising action** (Canonicality, or the way the particulars of the story breach or challenge conventions):

   During my observation, [I sensed that general learner engagement was low].

3 **Particulars** (The particulars of the setting):

   In my observation of your classroom during Work Time, I observed an average of 60% of learners engaged over a period of 10 minutes.

4 **Normativeness** (How agency is negotiated):

   In order to support [higher levels of learner engagement]…

5 **Intentionality** (How character's intentions are influenced):

   …I suggest you [observe Work Time and follow into disengaged learners to provide each with two concrete suggestions for engaging independent learning activities that will provide better opportunities to learn].

280 The Ecosystem Curriculum

6 **Outcomes** (Diachronicity, or the way the story unfolds through intentional improvement):

When I conduct a follow-up observation in two weeks, after disengaged learners have had the opportunity to engage with new content, I will expect to see at least 80% of learners engaged during work time over a period of 10 minutes.

Check In Conferences and Action Plans

Since staff receives evaluative feedback at least four times annually, they benefit from a constant stream of action-related feedback that can be assimilated into their pedagogical intentions. A brief, post-observation Check In conference provides an opportunity to review the evaluation and to discuss an action plan to support future development. The Professional Conference Record (McCallister, 2012d) creates an opportunity to discuss strengths, needs, and goals and to develop an action plan based on a menu of in-house training options (see Appendix 36, www.routledge.com/9780367458591). A target date for reevaluation is also discussed. Training options are discussed in the Training Program chapter in this section.

Observations are strategically planned to target high-impact Formats that support high engagement, cognitive control, and mentalizing, and to provide feedback on a specific area of need (e.g., management in chaotic classrooms; quality of perspective-shifting discourse in highly developed classrooms). Observations are also prioritized so that staff in need of immediate improvement get the support they need so as not to compromise opportunities to learn. Those who receive an unsatisfactory rating have a period of two weeks to make necessary immediate improvements before they are re-evaluated. A follow-up evaluation should be done within three weeks. (This is imperative as changes in behavior need immediate support in order to be secured.)

Maintaining the Ecosystem

The school as an ecosystem is like a closed-glass garden. Once the components are planted in a rich bed of soil and the lid is put on, it maintains its own ecosystem. By the beginning of Cycle 2, the distributed leadership systems are in place and the metaphorical water cycle is functioning on its own.

Cycle 2 Observations and Beyond

Cycle 2 observations are conducted beginning the first week of Cycle 2 (Week 7) after adequate opportunity to act on feedback and take advantage of training options. By that time, every staff member will have had six weeks to norm their practice to program expectations, they will have taken part in the professional development program, and results of the Professional Development Survey will have revealed patterns of need. By this time, it will also be apparent where pockets of disengagement exist in classrooms, and which staff members need training support.

The school leadership should observe evidence that the quality of learning opportunities are improving consistently across the school as per these trends:

- Formats are implemented in all classrooms with fidelity
- Quality of Learning Conferences is improving across the school, evidenced in quality of Content Shares

- Quality of Cooperative Unison Reading is improving across the school, evidenced by student investment, high-quality reading selections, high levels of breaching, robust perspective-shifting and cooperative reasoning discourse, and socially promotive behaviors;
- Work Time quality is improving, evidenced by higher ratios of students on-task;
- Learners' independent work initiatives are increasingly purposeful, independent, focused, intentional, and reasoned;
- Quality of written work is improving as evidenced in portfolio quality;
- Improved levels of social interdependence and cooperation are evidenced in classroom interactions;
- Learning Team unit post-test scores trend upward.

In each Cycle, priority attention is given to staff that had been previously identified to need improvement. If the second observation is unsatisfactory, another period of professional development should be required, followed by a second observation. Those who score low on the Holistic Assessment and whose classrooms reflect low levels of engagement and/or high levels of civil disorder will need bi-monthly observations and feedback. By requirement of the *fairness principle* (Rawls, 1985), it is imperative that every classroom reflect high levels of learning. Those who refuse to make change might need the opportunity to have a conversation to discuss the goodness of fit. Some otherwise competent teachers who might excel in a teacher-directed classroom can be a toxic asset in a McCallister classroom, where there is no room on the stage for the teacher and where proactive relational negativity can disrupt the responsibility cycle.

The cumulative record of formal observations should reflect what each member of the staff is capable of achieving with high levels of professional support and independent responsibility to make improvements in practice. The timelines for formal observation presented here are ideal and can be used as a reference. Local union contracts specify formal observation timelines and deadlines, and the timeline should be adapted to meet contractual terms.

"Opportunity Checks": Instructional Equity and Accounting

With a shift in definition of pedagogy from classical transmission to self-directed learning and social interaction, there is a parallel shift from a concern for oversight of instruction (monitoring lesson planning, developing instructional expertise, observing and evaluating instructional quality) to a concern for monitoring and enforcing every student's right to participate in prescribed learning situations (the Formats).

Since equality of educational opportunity for every learner depends on *sufficient* access to participation in the Formats, a system of Instructional Accounting is implemented to monitor and confirm opportunities to learn.

The administration implements classroom-based record-keeping systems that are transparent, in which records are kept in an orderly manner and accessible to all stakeholders. Records are archived by week. The Civil Rights Lead takes responsibility to conduct the Opportunity Checks and coordinates the process with the school administration. The school administration monitors this evidence once every two months in what are called Opportunity Checks. Beginning the second month of the school year, the administration conducts monthly Checks in each classroom to confirm learning opportunities in Cooperative Unison Reading and Conferences.[3]

To determine Opportunity Targets for each Format, the administration determines the number of Instructional Days per year. This is the total number of school days minus days in which instruction is suspended for events and activities like testing, field trips, etc. (while the latter are educational, they are not instructional from the standpoint that Format activities do not occur). For example, 165 Instructional Days in the year (total school days minus testing days, field trips, etc.), and two Learning Conferences take place in a classroom each day, so there should be 330 Learning Conference records on file by the last day of school. Each staff member is informed of the number of Opportunity Targets for each Format.

Sufficient evidence will confirm that the learner has had at least two hours weekly of Cooperative Unison Reading (four hours for those who score in the lowest quartile on reading CBM measures), or approximately 300 records per year minus non-instructional days. Evidence will confirm that each learner has had one Conference monthly in Math, Reading and, Writing. Lesson Logs and Standards Checklists should also be monitored for quality and quantity. Standards checklists in reading, language, and listening and speaking indicate requisite skills are being covered through large-group instruction at a pace that guarantees complete coverage by year's end (e.g., 25% coverage at the quarter year mark, 50% coverage at mid-year, etc.). Lesson logs show evidence of high-quality instruction (see Lesson Rubric for quality criteria). For example, if there are 160 instructional days, and two Conferences are scheduled four times per week, the teacher should have conducted 240 Conferences per year. With consistent participation, a sufficient number of opportunities for each learner will be confirmed in the predicable accumulation of assessment records.

The principle of instructional equity is practiced at the Tier I of instruction, or in the normal, day-to-day practices of the classroom. But based on the difference principle of justice as *fairness* (Rawls, 1985), records of those in the lowest performing quartile in reading and/or math should receive double the opportunities of others. The leadership should determine where these opportunities should arise and how to document them.

In the new era of voter fraud and outside interference in elections, handling of the long taken-for-granted paper ballot box has become a measure of the strength of our democracy. Assessment records are just about the same thing. Assessments within the McCallister Model confirm a right has been granted and the school has met its obligation. Every Conference Record or Cooperative Unison Reading Record confirms an opportunity to that experience.

Sufficiency Supplements

The McCallister Method Sufficiency Principle dictates that those who need the most get more. Learners who are identified through the Assessment Program to have "flat lined," or stopped making predictable achievement progress, and those who score in the bottom quartile on assessment measures are referred for Sufficiency Supplements. These are the high-impact Formats of Cooperative Unison Reading, Integrative Math, and Language Games that are scheduled after school, in the extended-day program, or throughout the day during the learners' Work Time blocks in classrooms. Participation in these programs continues until adequate progress is achieved (e.g., English learners have reached 2nd-grade language proficiency, learners in the bottom quartile on an assessment measure have demonstrated progress near the 50th percentile ranking). The Civil Rights Program Lead codirects this program with the support of the Curriculum Lead and the Curriculum Corps.

Keepers of the Culture Corps

Every school has a KoC Corps—a group of learners who have been nominated by their peers to represent them in the curriculum-based self-regulation program, "the Corps."

Twice annually, 10% of learners at every grade level are nominated by their peers for being fair-minded, compassionate, wise, and trustworthy. Keepers Corps support the Academic and Behavior Intervention Programs and are supervised by the Civil Rights Lead. Curriculum Corps members support the Learning Cultures and Sparks implementation and peer training program and are supervised by the Curriculum Lead. Each Corps body nominates a Director, who interfaces between assigned Leads and their Corps members.

Substitute Guides

The school administration cultivates a cadre of regular substitute guides to cover for mentor teachers while they are working in colleagues' classrooms. These subs are trained to implement the Formats and to adhere to the social norms curriculum.

Year-Long Implementation Plan

"Learning Cultures is a comprehensive school-wide reform model that we raised from the ground up in six months." Kerry Decker, former principal, Urban Assembly School for Green Careers (personal communication, March 17, 2014).[4]

To synchronize, stage, and carry out the ambitious change process with fidelity, the school leadership follows a Year-long Implementation Plan, which indicates the specific tasks that the administration and each lead will accomplish on a weekly basis (the action plan for each lead that is incorporated into the Year-long Implementation Guide is presented at the end of each chapter in this section). Working collaboratively, the school staff enact the Implementation Plan and restructure the bureaucracy of the school to decentralized institutional operations and power growth and renewal. When followed with relative fidelity, the administration can successfully transform a traditional school into a self-sustaining culture for learning within a period of a year. When the Plan is used on a yearly basis, a powerful culture of learning continues to grow.

Lead by Example

Since the administration is responsible for making judgments about practice, it is imperative that they are competent in the practices that they evaluate. It is recommended to push into a class every day or two to take part in a Cooperative Unison Reading Group or to do a Learning or Writing Conference. We only take advice when it comes from someone we deem justified in giving it. And advice that comes from an administrator who is perceived as being removed from practice can seem audacious. That's not good for anyone. To support the development of expertise, support through the McCallister Project is provided to train administrators and to connect them to other administrators who participate in the program.[5]

The fact that everyone in the school takes part in the same Formats that are "played" by the same rules creates a coherent world of familiar practices in which the school leader can routinely participate. Participatory involvement will provide direct evidence for how the program is working and will provide a way to get to know learners more personally. Giving them the chance to get to know you will give them reason to identify with the community as a *sacred moral commune* where even the most powerful leader wants to know who I am.

Support for the External Review Process

In order to support the administration successfully to stakeholders outside the school, the Quality Review Guide (McCallister, 2013i) presents a crosswalk between the criteria for school quality used in the NYC DOE Quality Review process with McCallister program components (see Appendix 38, www.routledge.com/9780367458591). This guide was used by leaders in the McCallister Initiative to prepare their Quality Review Self-studies, and the form can be adapted to any district school quality guide. The Quality Review Guide provides actionable recommendations that school leaders can follow to implement changes that result in high-quality review ratings.[6]

For the Record

Guiding institutional change is a perilous undertaking due largely to the fact that current educational systems are entrenched social orders dictated by the intentions of members of the establishment. At every turn, agents within the current system who benefit from the status quo will act to undermine the effort. Many of the documentary practices called for in second-order systems exist to generate evidence of the efficacy of the transformation initiative, which can be used in response to critique. They create a means to document positive changes that can be used to refute spurious or defamatory claims about the reform initiative. For example, to the objection that a curriculum designed to promote children's freedoms lacks rigor, the comprehensive school-wide assessment program captures achievement measures at short intervals across the school year that provide evidence of robust academic development across all learner groups. To counter negative rumors generated and perpetuated by disgruntled staff, a Staff Survey is administered every year in the Spring, which provides data that will affirm general agreement about the efficacy of the McCallister Model on both teacher and learner development.

It is also important for the administration to take responsibility to compose and keep its own triumph narrative of institutional transformation. The triumph narrative is useful in the sense that it can be used in formal reports and in public media. It is also useful to the development of an institutional identity that reflects collective intentionality and describes the identity of the collective moral commune.

Materials and Supplies

The procurement of institutional supplies for the ecosystem is as satisfying a task as making lists and buying ingredients for a Thanksgiving dinner. It represents an effort of affection and the anticipation of the joy that will be experienced in the celebration of living. Materials and supplies are sources of energy in the environment that learners can use to power their minds. Refer to the Resource List of suggested materials and supplies as an annual purchasing guide (see Appendix 34, refer to www.routledge.com/9780367458591).

Dimensions of Scale

The second-level systems of the McCallister Model are designed to support whole-school, full-scale implementation of model. But if prevailing conditions prevent full implementation and immediate implementation, the model can be scaled back accordingly. Follow these guidelines to implement in an incremental, one-subject-at-a-time design:[7]

1. Build awareness: Provide information about the McCallister Model to school staff. I suggest beginning with a Writing Activity Block since it is the most simple to implement, and learners are immediately engaged and motivated to write and share their

writing. Solicit teachers' interest. Hold an information session. Show videos on the Writing program components (Work Time, Writing Conference, Writing Share). Identify one teacher who is motivated to experiment with implementation.

2 Work with the teacher to schedule one hour per day for a Writing Activity Block to include the Formats, below. Schedule time each day for someone (perhaps yourself) to push into the teachers classroom to the implementation of Writing Activity Block Formats.

  a Lesson (five minutes)
  b Work Time (30 minutes)
  c Writing Conference (two, 10-minute Conferences during Work Time)
  d Writing Share (20 minutes)

3 Once the teacher and learners are accustomed to the Writing Program Formats, begin scheduling lab sites in the experienced teacher's classroom. Invite interested teachers to observe and debrief (use the Labsite Observation Protocol, Appendix 35, www.routledge.com/9780367458591).
4 Enlist the Curriculum and Training Lead to organize a study group for a set number of weeks to allow participating teachers to share experiences and provide support.
5 Identify teachers who have high potential to successfully implement the model, and plan to implement it in the largest possible number of classrooms where you can be confident of success.

  Provide short-term support to teachers as they begin to implement the Writing Activity Block in their classroom. Release experienced teachers to embed in experimenting teachers' classrooms for week-long residencies.
6 Continue Steps 3–5, above, until the intended scale is achieved (e.g., building-wide implementation of the Writing Activity Block).
7 Use this protocol to implement Activity Blocks in other curriculum areas as desired. Once the Writing program has been implemented building-wide, implement the Reading Activity Block curriculum, then the Math Activity Block curriculum.

Press for full-scale implementation in Writing, Reading, and Math, if possible. Substantive, broad-scale reform will yield greater gains in student achievement.

Title I School-wide Program Design

The McCallister Method school design, structured around inclusive, self-organized classroom learning environments, provides a simplified, comprehensive school reform (CSR) approach and meets the federal requirement for CSR under the Federal Title I program. Title I originated to close the achievement gap for educationally disadvantaged students, and provided financial assistance to school districts with high percentages of low-SES families. Initially, Title I was a targeted assistance program, providing funding to support academic remediation for children who qualified for the program. But in the 1990s, federal policy began to encourage comprehensive or whole-school reform, which is an integrated approach to the process that, according to Keltner (1998), "is based on the concept that the way to successfully improve school performance is to simultaneously change all elements of a school's operating environment so as to bring each element into alignment with a central, guiding vision" (p. 2). with the reasoning that better outcomes could be achieved through integrated programs that favorably impacted all students in a school and helped the school develop a stronger culture of learning (McChesney, 1998). Schools that choose the whole-school reform option can use Title I funding to support a broader range of programs than they are allowed through a targeted assistance approach. Table 20.2 outlines requirements

Table 20.2 Comprehensive school reform, local use of funds

Federal Title I requirements	McCallister Method program attributes
Employs proven methods and strategies based on scientifically based research	Educational methods incorporate principles from the new science of the mind and human development that emphasize learner agency and autonomy and social interaction in the service of powerful forms of learning
Integrates a comprehensive design with aligned components	The unique, rights-based methods that organize learning activities in the classroom are supported and reinforced by bureaucratic-level systems of professional development, curriculum, instructional intervention, community education, school culture, and professional training
Provides ongoing, high-quality professional development for teachers and staff	An integrated professional training program is specifically tailored to provide curriculum-embedded learning opportunities structured to support staff in developing and refining their skill
Includes measurable goals and benchmarks for student achievement	The integrated progress-monitoring assessment program provides continuous, ongoing data from curriculum-embedded measures in reading, writing, math, and content subjects
Is supported within the school by teachers, administrators and staff	The McCallister Method training program is designed to help staff learn about the conceptual and practical advantages of the model, providing a means to develop staff buy-in and program support
Provides support for teachers, administrators, and staff	Explicit procedures for curriculum and assessment combined with extensive training support facilitate adult mastery and self-competence in program practices
Provides for meaningful parent and community involvement in planning, implementing, and evaluating school improvement activities	An in-house staff member takes responsibility for implementing an extensive community education program that functions to involve the community in meaningful school activities and informs them of school operations
Uses high-quality external technical support and assistance from an external partner with experience and expertise in school-wide reform and improvement	The McCallister Group, led by Cynthia McCallister, provides ongoing training and program support to schools
Plans for the evaluation of strategies for the implementation of school reforms and for student results achieved	Incorporates on-going progress and achievement monitoring, the data for which is used to modify individual learner's academic plans. Annual staff surveys illuminate where program changes need to be made
Identifies resources to support and sustain the school's comprehensive reform effort	Incorporates strategies to procure resources necessary to support the program. Strategies are provided directly to learners to access high-quality resources to support their individualized learning plans, and guidance for resource procurement is provided at the leadership level to ensure academic and enrichment programs are adequately resourced
Has been found to significantly improve the academic achievement of students or demonstrates strong evidence that it will improve the academic achievement of students	Demonstrated effectiveness in multiple school implementations, resulting in gains in student achievement, improvements in student behavior, and the quality of school environments (see Section IV)

Source: United States Department of Education (2020a).

for the use of Title I funding under the whole-school option in a crosswalk with features of the McCallister Method (Title I, Part F, Section 1606).

Simplified Systems, Amplified Learning

The McCallister Model can be implemented in two possible ways. First, the existing egg-crate structure characteristic of the industrial school can be used to transform existing classrooms into self-organizing learning environments under the direction of teachers, retaining the existing educational establishment. Or, second, it can be used to transform the entire school into a new laterally organized learning ecosystem. Both the egg-crate and ecosystem applications transform the traditional teacher-directed curriculum into a curriculum of self-organizing social interactions that promote mental coordination and cognitive control. In both applications, the model shifts the focus of school administration and management from a concern for oversight of instruction (monitoring lesson planning, developing instructional expertise, observing and evaluating instructional quality) to a concern for monitoring and enforcing every learner's rights to participate in the Formats.

The shift away from teaching and instruction alleviates the intensive supervisory burdens required of the industrial school leader. A curriculum of rights emphasizes self-responsibility as opposed to teaching. Everyone across the school system takes part in meeting obligations to and enforcing rights, so the traditional function of "supervision" is eliminated. A rights-based educational approach is more cost-effective and sustainable than a traditional educational approach (United Nations Children's Fund/UNESCO, 2007). A rights-based approach also eliminates many structural inequalities that are (re)produced in the industrial school through testing, ranking, sorting, segregating, and differential treatment.

The Egg-Crate Design

The McCallister Model can be implemented as a transformation design in a traditional egg-crate (e.g., multiple subject- and grade-based classes). In elementary classrooms, subject-based periods are programmed as Activity Blocks that include a lesson, Work Time, group Formats, such as of Cooperative Unison Reading and Learning Teams, and a Share to conclude the block. Subject-based classes at the middle and high school level are similarly programmed. It is ideal if a longer block schedule of 75 minutes can be negotiated with the union. Otherwise, it is difficult to include all of the Formats, and learners do not have adequate time to pursue personal learning goals. Examples of five- and six-period programs are presented in Table 20.3. The egg-crate design application was used in all of the NYC whole-school transformation initiatives described in Section IV.

The diagram in Figure 20.2 illustrates the Activity Block in the egg-crate design. The large, light gray rectangle represents the Activity Block. In the egg-crate design, the first activity of the Block is the Lesson Format, which appears at the top of the Block. Work Time is represented by the light blue circle within the Block. During Work Time, other Formats take place. These are represented by the colored circles. At the end of class, learners move out of Work Time and into the Share Format. There are two types of Shares. The Learning Share is represented by the small circle at the bottom of the Block, which is 10 minutes in length. The large circle represents the Writing Share, which is 20 minutes in length. This diagram can be used as a teaching tool to help learners understand how time is organized in the classroom.

288 *The Ecosystem Curriculum*

Table 20.3 Six-period schedule

8:30–8:55 **READING**	Meeting: 5 minutes Reading Work Time Format (Cooperative Unison Reading Format [CUR], back-to-back sessions of 15 minutes, Monday–Thursday; Learning Conference Format, 2-per day) Learning Share Format: 10 minutes
8:55–9:50 **WRITING**	Meeting: 5 minutes Writing Work Time: 30 minutes Writing Share Format: 20 minutes
9:50–10:45 **MATH**	Meeting: 5 minutes Math Work Time: 40 minutes Share: 10 minutes
10:45–11:35 **LUNCH AND RECESS**	Lunch and recess
11:35–12:30 **CLUSTER CLASSES, SPECIALS AND ENRICHMENT**	Gym, music, art, chess, dance
12:30–1:25 **SCIENCE AND SOCIAL STUDIES**	Science Workshop, MW; Science Lab, F; Social Studies Workshop, TTh
1:25–2:20 **RECREATION**	Worktime Format: Choice of classroom activities (play) Learning Share Format: 10 minutes
2:20–2:50 **READ ALOUD WORKOUT PLAN**	

Figure 20.2 The Activity Block

The Ecosystem Design

The ecosystem application of the McCallister Model takes advantage of the potential for self-organized learning inherent in the Formats and applies them in a more radical reconceptualization of the systems of school. This *ecosystem* design reorganizes the school's time, space, scheduling, staff assignments, and grouping by creating two, two-and-half to three-hour Work Time blocks in the school day separated by lunch. What is normally considered after-school time is incorporated into the formal school day, when learners have opportunities to take part in Workshops of Possibility. Community space is supervised by a Floor Manager, who serves in a similar capacity to paraprofessionals who are assigned responsibility to supervise recess and lunch. Guides push into three, three and half-hour extended Work Time blocks to supervise Formats.

Sample ecosystem design schedules are presented in Table 20.4. A comparison of ecosystem design elements to a traditional application of five- and six-period school days is presented in Table 20.2. A visual comparison of these designs is presented in Table 20.3. The implications of the ecosystem design are described below.

The ecosystem design is ideally suited for remote education. Learners who are working from home follow the six-hour block schedule. They do Sparks curriculum activities independently, or asynchronously, and take part in synchronous Learning Cultures Formats remotely.

The diagram in Figure 20.3 illustrates the Activity Block in an open design. The blue space represents Work Time. It is a day-long, self-organizing learning environment. Learners adhere to individual programs that specify when and in which Formats they participate.

Altering the Landscape of Traditional Schooling

> The problem is that the complex educational changes demanded by current standards-based reform initiatives, combined with an increasingly heterogeneous student population largely composed of students whom schools have traditionally failed, have pushed the technology of schooling toward unprecedented levels of complexity.
> Borman et al. (2004, p. 55)

The McCallister Model is a unique ecosystem school design that can be used to dismantle the complex systems of factory schooling. By providing a universal design for learning that addresses the needs of all learners in the Tier I of response, it eliminates costs for multiple instructional programs in multiple subjects and in multiple grades targeted to meet the multiple needs of many subgroups. These reforms provide a possible way to reallocate resources into experiences that more directly benefit children.

A visual depiction of the Ecosystem school is presented in Figure 20.4, depicting the school leader centrally delegating responsibility to Leads, who manage and coordinate infrastructure systems and delegate responsibility to student representatives (i.e., "Keepers") and learners. Instead of the flow of knowledge through efficiently controlled labor (teaching), the ecosystem school is a metaphorical closed-glass garden whereby growth develops through the flow of responsibility as everyone meets their obligations. Contrast the ecosystem school design to the industrial school design depicted in Figure 20.5.

The Ecosystem School depicted presents an ideal. In reality, schools operate under legal constraints, such as union contracts and state seat time mandates, examples of which are described in Chapter 3. These directives freeze and secure traditional practices of the industrial school. All of the schools that implemented the McCallister Model in the Urban Assembly Initiative retained the egg-crate design.

Table 20.4 75-minute block schedule

Time	Monday	Tuesday	Wednesday	Thursday	Friday
8:30–9:40	**READING** Meeting: 5 minutes Reading Work Time 60 minutes (Cooperative Unison Reading Format [CUR], back-to-back sessions of 15 minutes, Monday–Thursday; Learning Conferences) Learning Share Format: 10 minutes	**READING** Meeting: 5 minutes Reading Work Time: 60 minutes (Cooperative Unison Reading Format [CUR], back-to-back sessions of 15 minutes, Monday–Thursday; Learning Conferences) Learning Share Format: 10 minutes	**READING** Meeting: 5 minutes Reading Work Time: 60 minutes (Cooperative Unison Reading Format [CUR], back-to-back sessions of 15 minutes, Monday–Thursday; Learning Conferences) Learning Share Format: 10 minutes	**READING** Meeting: 5 minutes Reading Work Time Format: 60 minutes (Cooperative Unison Reading Format [CUR], back-to-back sessions of 15 minutes, Monday–Thursday; Learning Conference Format, 2-per day) Learning Share Format: 10 minutes	**MATH** Meeting: 5 minutes Math Work Time Format: 60 minutes (Learning Conference Format, 2-per day) Math Learning Share Format: 10 minutes
9:40–10:50	**WRITING** Meeting: 5 minutes Writing Work Time Format: 50 minutes Writing Share Format: 20 minutes	**WRITING** Meeting: 5 minutes Writing Work Time Format: 50 minutes Writing Share Format: 20 minutes	**MATH** Meeting: 5 minutes Math Work Time Format: 60 minutes Math Learning Share Format: 10 minutes	**WRITING** Meeting: 5 minutes Writing Work Time Format: 50 minutes Writing Share Format: 20 minutes	**WRITING** Meeting: 5 minutes Writing Work Time Format: 50 minutes Writing Share Format: 20 minutes
10:50–12:00	**MATH** Meeting: 5 minutes Math Work Time Format: 60 minutes Math Learning Share Format: 10 minutes	RECREATION Work Time: 65 minutes Learning Share Format: 10 minutes	RECREATION Work Time: 65 minutes Learning Share Format: 10 minutes	WORK TIME	WORK TIME
12:06–12:47 Lunch					
12:50–2:05	SCIENCE WORKSHOP	SOCIAL STUDIES WORKSHOP	SCIENCE WORKSHOP	SOCIAL STUDIES WORKSHOP	SCIENCE LAB
2:08–3:23	GYM	ART	MUSIC	RE-CREATION Work Time: 65 minutes Learning Share Format: 10 minutes	RE-CREATION Work Time: 65 minutes Learning Share Format: 10 minutes

3:30–6:00 After School Enrichment: "Workshops of Possibility"

Figure 20.3 Activity Block, open design

Innovative Grouping Systems

Class and instructional groups sizes in the industrial school were determined by scientific management principles and a concern for labor efficiency. The typical class size of 30 is the upper limit to the number of learners a teacher can manage in terms of the requirements for ability-based group instruction. A new orientation for a curriculum of self-direction and social interaction creates a new set of considerations for social organization in schools. Absent the traditional concern for the labor of knowledge transfer, and based on theories of human social organization, the traditional social grouping practices of the industrial school can be reconceptualized.

The Niche replaces the traditional class from the standpoint that it is the number of individuals who share physical space. The Niche is inspired by Thomas Jefferson's Academical Village, the center of which is the Rotunda, that is the heart of the community and the symbol of learning (Jefferson, 1810). The Niche is 50 learners in size,[8] which is the optimal number of individuals to constitute an *active* or *close network*, and which is the upper limit of a group still able to retain democratic norms (Dunbar, 2010) and maximize the "fullness and freedom" of forms of association (Dewey, 1916/1944).[9] Contrary to

292 *The Ecosystem Curriculum*

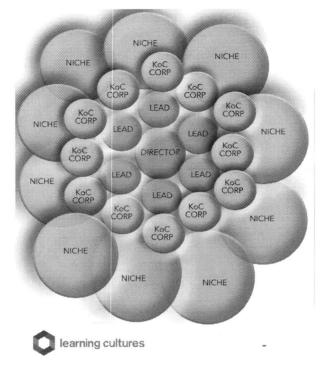

Figure 20.4 Ecosystem school design

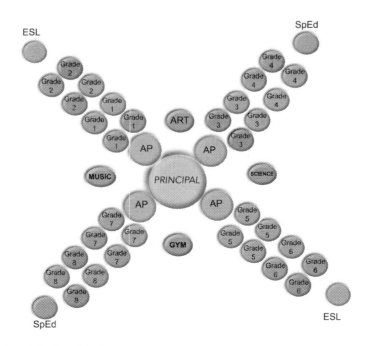

Figure 20.5 Industrial school design

the traditional concern for small class size and didact instruction, the Ecosystem is based on the Deweyian (1916/1944) idea that the fullness and freedom of association is a means by which democracy is understood, which is now substantiated with the recognition that large human groups provide optimal conditions in which knowledge can develop (Boyd, Richerson, & Henrich, 2011), simply because there are more possible people with whom one has opportunities on a continual basis to coordinate mental states. The Niche is like an Apple retail store, a studio, or a wing of a children's museum, with tables distributed across a large, carpeted, aesthetically appealing space.

Next, Clusters are the equivalent of learning squads, comprising 10–15 learners, which are the equivalent of school families, and remain permanent throughout the school year. These groups become socially interdependent "sympathy groups" (Dunbar & Spoors, 1995) that meet frequently to provide mutual guidance, moral support, and friendship. They conduct their agendas based on protocols established in the Sparks curriculum, a personalized curriculum, and therefore require only minimal adult guidance. Other flexible groups are formed on a daily and weekly basis through Format procedures. With no more than five members per groups, these small learning communities are the size of "support cliques" (Dunbar & Spoors, 1995) which promote emotional closeness, provide support in the context of challenge, and require a large proportion of the learner's "class time." The small-group configurations of the ecosystem design align with federal ESEA policy supporting initiatives to create small learning communities in schools.

Floor managers, who are paraprofessionals, supervise learner activity and hold them accountable to the Social Contract. As per most union contracts, teachers are relieved of study hall duties.[10] Clusters meet several times a week to coordinate and share information about goals and progress. Forty percent of their meetings are supervised by a guide. The group remains formally connected throughout the school year. Group Formats replace the traditional institutional unit of "class." The Format is the programmatic equivalent to a class from the standpoint of staff assignments. One teacher or guide is assigned responsibility for 25–30 Formats per week. The teacher-student ratio is between 5 and 25, bringing the average "class size" to no more than 15.

The ecosystem environment is akin to a studio or library. Figure 20.6 is a rendering of a niche floorplan, organized around the Rotunda that serves as the center of the *academical village*.

Minimized Labor, Maximized Learning: Self-organized Learning Environments

Learners spend the majority of their day in the Work Time Format, which requires autonomy, independence, and self-direction. Learners enjoy opportunities to exercise fundamental freedoms of movement, thought, expression, and social affiliation. The extended two and half-hour block design takes advantage of what we know about learners' capacities for self-organized, self-directed learning, and their need for prolonged periods of time to self-regulate their activities in order to achieve their goals.

Since learners self-regulate to Format procedures, these is no need for a classroom teacher to direct or supervise instructional activity. The space is supervised by a Community Manager, a paraprofessional, who oversees the floor, and guides/teachers push into classrooms to participate with learners in the Formats for a total of 35 hours/week. Most of the Formats require only minimal adult guidance. So, the ecosystem design enables the equivalent of one teacher or guide to meet the instructional needs of 50 learners. This model provides a way to structure the formal systems of school without dependence on trained teachers. This innovation can help reduce instructional costs in existing schooling systems but can also provide a means by which formal education can be provided to learners in remote or impoverished communities which lack access to trained teachers.

294 *The Ecosystem Curriculum*

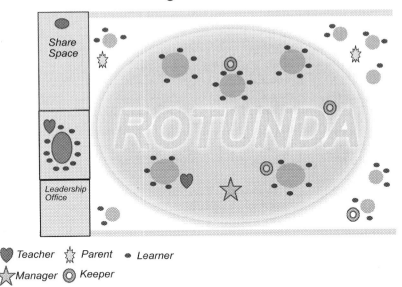

Figure 20.6 Academical Village

Promoting Every Learner's Native Ability

Since the McCallister Model rests on the assumption that competencies and dispositions are developed as "background" in social interactions, all learners are able to participate on equal terms. As discussed in the Positive Learning Paradigm, disordered patterns of behavior—what have traditionally been recognized as learning disabilities—are in reality a spectrum of behaviors caused by many genes, each with small effect (Plomin, 2018). IEP goals and recommendations are rewritten in terms of opportunities outlined in the Formats (e.g., student will have two additional hours of Cooperative Unison Reading each week). Over time, as learners take part in pro-adaptive situations, maladaptive behaviors tend to subside, which becomes verified in assessment data as it accumulates. Children with physical disabilities continue to receive additional support through programs that push into the ecosystem environment, as will those with visual impairments and some neurological disabilities. But learners with intellectual, learning, hearing, and some psychiatric disabilities (e.g., oppositional defiance) will quickly develop adequate social and academic competencies to participate independently. The same is the case for English learners. Since language is learned through social participation, and since the Formats support meaningful, authentic social participation in English, English learners quickly develop language competencies that will be substantiated in progress monitoring data.[11]

More Resources to Invest in Social Opportunity, Personalized Learning, and Talent Development

An educational system that eliminates or dramatically reduces dependence on the teaching function greatly reduces instructional costs. Substantially shrinking the instructional budget allows for resources to be reallocated to enrichment programs and funds the extension of the school day to 10 hours and the school year to 200 days (represented in Table 20.6). More available revenue allows for the development of a wide range of enrichment opportunities into the educational program, such as those outlined in the

Table 20.5 Extended block schedule within the ecosystem design

Time	Monday	Tuesday	Wednesday	Thursday	Friday
9:30–12:10 Work Time Format	Cooperative Unison Reading Format F(CUR): 30 minutes Workout Teams Format (60 minutes) Writing Share Format: 30 minutes	Cooperative Unison Reading Format (CUR): 30 minutes Writing Share: Format 30 minutes Math Learning Conference Format (60 minutes)	Cooperative Unison Reading Format (CUR): 30 minutes Writing Share Format: 30 minutes	Cooperative Unison Reading Format (CUR): 30 minutes Writing Share Format: 30 minutes	Integrative Math Format (60 minutes) Writing Share Format: 30 minutes
12:13–12:55 LUNCH					
1:00–2:30 Work Time Format	Learning Conference Format (60 minutes) Social Studies Learning Teams Format (60 minutes)	Gym (55 minutes) Science Learning Teams Format (60 minutes)	Art (55 minutes) Math Learning Conference Format (60 minutes)	Science Lab (55 minutes) Social Studies Learning Teams Format (60 minutes)	Music (55 minutes) Science Learning Teams Format (60 minutes)
2:30–3:30 RECREATION Work Time Format with recreation activity options	Learners select from Workshop of Possibility options. One hour per day is spent in physical education				
3:35–6:00 ENRICHMENT: WORKSHOPS OF POSSIBILITY Work Time Format					

curriculum of *Workshops of Possibility* (see Chapter 6). Workshops of Possibility support the development of learners passions, talents, interests, and aptitudes—experiences that have proven to be the most important factors in terms of social opportunity (Plomin, 2018). With input from the student body and the parent-teacher association, the school leadership (administration and Curriculum Lead) creates up to 10 Workshops of Possibility in the arts, music, dance, theater, green house/gardening, culinary arts, coding and technology, science lab, woodworking, and textiles. Artists- and craftspeople-in-residence are hired to manage Workshops in which activities are structured by the Worktime Format criteria. Learners who join the Workshop of Possibility form Guilds who take responsibility to maintain the Workshop spaces. Cost savings also free up funding for the Culinary Arts Program, a farm-to-table/nutrition initiative.

More Resources for More School Time

The school day can begin as early as 8:00 a.m. in elementary grades but should begin no earlier than 10:00 a.m. in middle and high schools, due to the fact that, generally, adolescents become night owls, and need more morning sleep time to avoid sleep disorders and to promote healthy brain development (American Academy of Pediatrics, 2014). The delayed school day ends at 4:30 p.m., but the Niche remains open until 6:00 p.m., providing a space for learners to continue working on self-selected projects or to take part in recreational activities.

Community-involved School Development and Governance

The ecosystem requires less dependence on teacher labor, and more dependence on non-instructional floor management, who can be recruited from the parent body and the community. This advantage helps change the culture of the school to reflect community values. Often, especially in schools in low-income neighborhoods, the teaching force lives outside the community, creating a cultural niche in which actors in the system who are foreign to the child's culture are regularly in a position to make evaluative judgments about the child which then translate into the provision of social opportunity. This option also provides a means through which financial capital from education funding can be used to more directly enrich the community, helping to address broader issues of structural/economic inequality.

Cost Implications

The cost to implement the McCallister Model is a fraction of the typical costs associated with whole-school reform.[12] Since the model offers a fully developed, universal design, there is no cost involved in planning a school-reform initiative.[13] Academic and behavioral support programs are integrated into the model's Tier I design, eliminating the costs associated with stand-alone programs targeted to meet the needs of subgroups of differing abilities.

Three transformation scenarios were presented above: the six-period egg-crate design featured in Table 20.5; the 75-minute design featured in Table 20.6; and the ecosystem design featured in Table 20.7. We will now explore cost implications for each application. To begin, we will establish the economic variables to be used in cost calculations. Table 20.7 presents the current 2020 salary scale for NYC UFT teachers as a point of reference: beginning and maximum salaries of New York City teachers at the current rate for a

Table 20.6 Ecosystem school design

Group unit	Ecosystem	Industrial school
School size	1 school director, 500 learners	1 principal, 2 assistant principals, 500 students
Class size and teacher: student ratio	2:50 Format activities take place in a *Rotunda*	2:30 Group instruction is provided in a classroom
Clusters	A group of 10 learners who remain formally connected through the year	
Learning groups	Five learners (Cooperative Unison Reading; Learning Teams; Integrative Math; Language Games) to 25 learners (Writing Share; Learning Share)	
Individual learning	Work Time takes place in a study hall environment supervised by a manager/paraprofessional	

36-week year and at a prorated rate for a 44-week year. In Table 20.7, Scenario One shows the cost in salaries (non-benefit wages) for a traditional curriculum in an egg-crate school design. Scenario Two represents an application of the McCallister Model to a traditional egg-crate design.[14] Each of these Scenarios project annual salary expenditures for 34 teachers at $3.483M. Scenarios Four and Five describe the ecosystem application of the McCallister design, which restructures traditional classroom systems into a self-directed learning environment with guides or teachers who push into learning spaces to participate in the Formats with learners. Scenario Four presents a 180-day ecosystem design at a total staffing cost of $1.519M, and Scenario Five presents a 220-day ecosystem design at a total staffing cost of $2.120M. The total savings of staff expenditures of the ecosystem designs in comparison to egg-crate designs are $1.964M and $1.363M, respectively. In a school of 500 implementing the Ecosystem design, 350 teaching hours in a month can satisfy what requires 1,020 teaching hours per month within an egg-crate design.

Current starting salary at 36 weeks per year	Starting salary prorated for a 44-week year	Current maximum salary at 44 weeks per year	Maximum salary prorated for a 44-week year
$76,231	$93,171	$128,657	$157,269

Staffing

The industrial school is like a factory that depends on laborers to dispense information. The ecosystem relies on adults to facilitate a wide range of social activities and to ensure learners' rights are upheld. This shift in emphasis has implications for the way a school is staffed.

The Lead role can be understood as a mid-level manager. They need to have the training to successfully carry out the complex responsibilities associated with their roles. Rather than the traditional notion of teacher, the Lead position is more like a Learning Specialist. They have academic preparation that enables them to understand the Positive Learning Paradigm (e.g., coursework in biology, chemistry, anthropology, social and cultural psychology and linguistics). They are activists, who have demonstrated their

298 *The Ecosystem Curriculum*

Table 20.7 NYC UFT beginning and maximum salaries with a master's degree or 30 additional credits beyond a bachelor's degree at current 36-week year and prorated for a 44-week year

	Pupils per school	Days per year	Hours per day	Classrooms	Staff per class[15]	Inst. hours per year	Staff and teacher costs	Savings
Scenario One: Traditional Egg-crate	500	180	6 hours, 20 minutes	17 (30 learners per class)	2 teachers	36,720[16]	$3.483 million	
Scenario Two: McCallister Method egg-crate	500	180	6 hours, 20 minutes	17 (30 learners per class)	2 teachers	36,720	$3.483 million[17]	
Scenario Three: Ecosystem Design on traditional 180-day calendar	500	180	6 hours, 20 minutes	10 (50 learners per community)	1 Mgr. hourly teachers	10,800[18] hours of staff supervision of self-directed, semi-supervised Formats 12,600[19,20] hours of teacher-supervised Formats	$324K staff costs $1.195M teacher costs[21,22] Total wages: $1.519M	$1.964M[23]
Scenario 4: Ecosystem extended, 200-day calendar	500	220	10 hours	10 (50 learners per Community)	1 Mgr. Hourly teachers	22,000[24] hours of staff supervision of self-directed, semi-supervised Formats 15,400[25] hours of teacher-supervised Formats	$660K[26] $1.460M[27] Total wages: $2.120M	$1.363M[28]

commitment to important social causes. They have a record of experience that enables them to effectively carry out responsibilities that impact participants in a large organization.

Guides can be understood as assistants. Unlike the traditional role of the teacher, who needed training in instructional methodologies and methods of instruction and assessment, the guide does not require such expertise. They assume their role on the floor of the Rotunda, in the cultural niche, to assist learners in taking responsibility to meet their obligations. Since guides do not need a teaching credential, the role is open to adults who are community minded, activist-oriented, well respected members of the local community.

Toward a Revolutionary Process that Is Simple, Effective, Inexpensive, and Fast

The McCallister school design challenges some of the conventional wisdom of the turn-around literature. It is a comprehensive transformation design that can be used in any school. It can be implemented in under a year, as opposed to the three-to-ten-year time-frame predicted in the school turnaround literature. It eliminates the need for a full planning year to develop a transformation design. Instead of the typical $1M annual price tag of the current school turnaround, it can be accomplished with existing federal funding earmarked for CSR. As an alternative to the assertion that a turnaround leader needs special training or a unique vision, the McCallister design can be implemented by any skilled administrator.

In the remaining chapters of Section III, proven methods to implement transformative and lasting changes within the complex systems of schools are laid out in a series of simple, actionable procedures that can accomplish planned change within the period of a year when led by a competent school leader. These systems provide a model to replace the industrial school.

Notes

1. These figures are based on minimum number of observations as per the NYC UFT contract.
2. Learning Cultures served as the school-wide Title I program in schools that participated in the McCallister-Learning Cultures Initiative.
3. The instructional equity practice was inspired by my mentor, Ed Gordon, and his ideas about sufficiency of education opportunity. It was also provoked by my own sense of injustice when each of my three kids were in classrooms of teachers who simply chose not to conduct the assessments that were expected programmatically, and there was, apparently, no effective means in place to hold them accountable. We expect physicians to keep accurate records as a matter of ethical practice. We should expect the same of teachers.
4. In the interest of transparency, in her role as principal at the Jacob Riis School in New York City from Fall 2007 to Fall 2011, Ms. Decker me to work in the school to provide weekly professional development in my methods.
5. Principals of schools in the McCallister Learning Cultures Initiative took part in monthly cross-school visitations in which they spent the day observing classrooms, discussing observations, and receiving training support from Dr. McCallister.
6. The Urban Assembly High School for Green Careers in NYC received an "F" on its 2013 report card with a graduation rate of 39% and a suspension rate of over 200. After seven months of implementation, the school received a quality review rating of 'proficient.' And after three years the school received a quality review rating of "well-developed," one of only a fraction citywide that do so every year.
7. The principal of The Family School in the South Bronx led her school in a similar implementation, beginning with the writing program in kindergarten, and within two years, scaled up to a full-scale implementation of the Writing and Reading programs inside of two years.

8. Niches in K-3 classrooms are 35 or fewer, managed by a classroom teacher.
9. The ecosystem is a scientifically based design alternative to the traditional classroom-level grouping of the "egg-crate" school.
10. Specified in NYC UFT contract Article 7(A)(5)(a).
11. See case studies of English learners in the Jacob Riis and High School of Language and Innovation implementation efforts featured in Section IV.
12. Positive Behavioral Interventions and Supports (PBIS) costs $50 per student per year. Success for All®, a 90-minute-a-day literacy intervention costs $100 per student per year. In 2010, the cost to implement a school transformation initiative in NYC ran from $750,000 to over $1.8 million per year per school. Between 2014 and 2019, the average cost of whole-school transformation in NYC was $430,000 per school per year (NYC School Renewal Program). The average cost for a school-wide reading intervention is $100 per student per year (Success for All). The McCallister Model is a whole-school model that can be implemented in every subject discipline, that can serve as integrated ESL and special education programs, that provides an integrated behavioral support program, and provides an integrated, universal system for teacher evaluation and professional development. As such, it is a very competitively-priced comprehensive school reform model.
13. The average cost to plan a school transformation initiative is $300,000 per year.
14. These are the implementation designs employed in the school transformation initiatives described in case studies in Section IV.
15. Salary costs included in this analysis include allocations to classroom instruction, special education support, and other instructional and behavioral support services.
16. 34 Teachers at a salary of $102,444 calculated as the mean of the starting and maximum UFT salaries for 2021.
17. This sum can be significantly lowered if IEPs are rewritten according to terms of full participation in the Learning Cultures Formats.
18. Ten managers at six hours per day, 180 days per year at a rate of $30/hour.
19. Required hours to supervise 350 hours of Formats per week (Unison @ 100 hours/week, Learning Conferences @ 50 hours/week, Math Conferences @ 50 hours/week, Workout Teams @ 50 hours/week, Learning Teams @ 50 hours/week, and Writing Share@ 50 hours/week) at 36 weeks per year.
20. Format activities do not require instruction by an adult and can be considered 'study activities' that, in some states, do not require supervision by a certified teacher, in which case paraprofessionals can serve the role of Format guides, significantly reducing staff costs.
21. Totally, 12,600 hours a year calculated at an hourly rate of $94.86.
22. Reported costs do not include non-wage benefits.
23. Difference in costs for traditional egg-crate system of formal instruction and McCallister ecosystem design.
24. Managers at 10 hours per day, 220 days per year.
25. Required hours to supervise 350 hours of Formats per week (Unison @ 100 hours/week, Learning Conferences @ 50 hours/week, Math Conferences @ 50 hours/week, Workout Teams @ 50 hours/week, Learning Teams @ 50 hours/week, and Writing Share @ 50 hours/week) at 44 weeks per year.
26. Managers at $30 per hour, 22,000 hours per year.
27. Totally, 13,200 hours a year calculated at an hourly rate of $94.86.
28. Difference between total staff costs of a 180-day year egg-crate design and a 220-day ecosystem design.

21 The Assessment Program

> There are some who are sympathetic to high standards and rigorous assessment, but insist that it is immoral to begin by measuring outcomes before we have seriously engaged in the equitable and sufficient distribution of inputs, that is, opportunities and resources essential to the development of intellect and competence.
>
> E. W. Gordon and Associates (1995, p. 755)

Introduction

If equality of educational opportunity is defined by the degree to which educational inputs are sufficient to enable all children to achieve equal outcomes, regardless of life conditions and social circumstances, the school's assessment system is a means through which opportunity can be tracked and measured. If the school has a moral responsibility to ensure learners meet their potential, it is important that they have access to opportunities that would let them develop cultural competencies so that they feel emotional consonance within the school commune and have opportunities to develop their personalities and talents.

Assessment systems within the McCallister Method track the background abilities that are necessary for grade-level academic engagement in order to ensure that learners are progressing as expected (see Box 21.1 for a description of academic background abilities and capacities). The assessment program measures and monitors each individual learner's educationally relevant cognitive functioning, such as basic math and literacy skills, allowing data-driven judgments to be made about the quality of interactions that the learner is having with others. Assessment data provide important competence feedback to learners, which they can assimilate into their intentions and drive their efforts. By collecting, analyzing, and disseminating data to all stakeholders regularly, it is possible for each actor to make better informed decisions relating to curriculum and learning. As improvements lead to increasingly higher outcomes, the assessment program plays a key role in fostering an ethos of accomplishment in the school culture.

The Assessment Lead is the manager of the school-wide assessment program.

Assessment Lead Responsibilities

Assessment and Evaluation Practices

- Manage classroom-level assessment systems. Provide support to staff to improve curriculum-embedded assessment practices and documentary systems, ensuring that records are accurate, orderly, and accessible.

302 *The Ecosystem Curriculum*

- Schedule school-wide assessments (Degrees of Reading Power® [DRP]; curriculum-based measures [CBM]; Learning Teams Assessments in state testing subjects).
- Distribute appropriate CBM measures to relevant staff for periodic scheduled administration.
- Conduct a survey of incoming students to ascertain the nature of students' prior school experiences.
- Coordinate state testing (ESL; grades 3–8 math and reading; high school tests in English, math, science, social studies).
- Coordinate with Special Education Team to make appropriate testing accommodations
- Monitor quality of school report cards.
- Maintain archives of course syllabi and report cards.
- Maintain archive of Learning Teams Program assessments (in coordination with Curriculum Lead).
- Coordinate with School Management Team to ensure coherence in grading practices. Consistent grading criteria are applied across subjects, courses, and departments. Grading reflects balanced weight across the domains of *content mastery, growth in background abilities and self-regulation dispositions, responsibility in meeting obligations to the Social Contract,* and *achievement of independent learning goals.*

Box 21.1

Academic background abilities and capacities

Background are the abilities, dispositions, and capabilities we rely on in order to carry out our intentions (Searle, 2010). Academic development unfolds along a trajectory of expanding competencies. Each new form of competence becomes internalized as new memory into the neural circuits of our brain. Once deeply internalized, these skills and competencies become automatic. We can perform complex mathematical operations because our knowledge of math computation has become Background, and we have internalized the cultural practices in which such knowledge is used. We can rapidly write our ideas and thoughts in a journal because our knowledge of spelling conventions has become Background.

Grade-level academic performance in reading, writing, math, or discipline-based subjects requires Background of grade-level competencies. In other words, Background competencies in math, reading, and writing are the foundation upon which higher levels of intellective capacities are built. So, in order to ensure Background develops, we continually assess it and monitor its development.

As learners develop literacy competencies in math, reading, and writing, their growth is documented using assessment systems whose scores can be referenced to national norms. These assessments enable judgments to be made about learners' progress in relation to national norms. By using norm-referenced assessments to measure learners' progress in math, reading, writing, and content subjects, we are able to make reliable judgments about whether and how the curriculum is supporting learners' educational needs. Norm-based assessments are conducted on a frequent basis so that dynamic progress can be closely measured and monitored.

Data Management and Analysis

- Manage school-wide achievement data systems;
- Compile new assessment data in usable Format;
- Maintain progress monitoring database;

- Monitor assessment databases to identify trends;
- Identify non-progressive learners;
- Share data with relevant stakeholders (learners, guides, Code Blue lead, and school administration);
- Coordinate with program leaders to make CBM and DRP assessment data available to learners;
- Report DRP and state assessment trends to school administration.

McCallister Group

- Member, Project Team—interface with McCallister Group and participate in network-wide professional development.

Resources

- Interface with assessment publishers and vendors to review commercial assessments (if they are used) and provide advisement to school administration;
- Create and maintain CBM measures (one-page display of random upper- and lower-case letters for Letter Name Fluency (LNF) CBM for kindergarten and 1st grade; writing prompts for each grade, 1st through 12th; six grade-level MAZE reading passages for each grade, 1st through 12th; six passages at grade-level complexity for every grade, 1st through 12th to be used for Oral Reading Fluency).

School Governance

- Member, School Management Team
- Chair, Assessment Committee

Training

- Oversee progress monitoring assessment training

Traditional Uses of Assessment

Traditionally, assessment has been used by teachers in the classroom for diagnostic purposes, to identify deficits in learners in order to appropriately group them for instructional intervention (Bobbit, 1918). The assessment-grouping-instruction components of the teaching function have all but defined the role of the classroom teacher for more than 100 years.

In a system tailored to meet the needs of the *norm*, those who speed ahead or fall behind present a challenge. It has been assumed that significant delays in developmental progress stem from deficits in learners. Those who fall too far behind were often retained or held back to repeat a grade in school in order to re-experience the curriculum when they are developmentally prepared to benefit from the curriculum and keep up with the *norm*. The traditional system neglected the needs of millions of children who did not receive appropriate educational services, who were excluded entirely from the public system and prevented from having opportunities to be educated with peers, whose families were encumbered by the need to find services outside the school system, and whose undiagnosed difficulties prevented them from having a successful school experience (Individuals with Disabilities Education Act, Subchapter I, Part A, §1400, 2004).

Schools were not legally required to make accommodations for those who fell behind until 1975, with the passage of the All Handicapped Children Act (1975), which guaranteed the right to an education on equal terms to people with disabilities. Standardized assessments of academic achievement were now needed to identify learners for special education services. A delay of two or more years relative to grade-level norms showed justification for referral to special education services. Within this model, learners had to be in at least the 3rd grade before determinations could be made that the learner was at least two years behind grade-level expectations and special services could be provided.

In 2004, with the passage of the Individuals with Disabilities Education Improvement Act (Individuals with Disabilities Education Act, 2004), Response to Intervention (RTI) was proposed as an alternative to the traditional ability-achievement discrepancy approach. RTI involves frequent progress monitoring in math, reading, spelling, and writing so that more immediate determinations can be made about how well the learner is responding to instructional intervention. RTI allows a more timely means to identify potential "disabilities." Frequent progress monitoring is a critical component of RTI. Within the RTI model, teachers use assessment data to make decisions about how to plan instruction to meet the needs of learners who fall behind through a three-tier model of instruction. Tier I involves whole-class instruction geared to the needs of the norm. Tier II involves small-group instruction differentiated to the needs of classroom subgroups. Tier III instruction is more individualized and intensive, usually in a one-to-one context. Those who require Tier III instruction to keep up with the curriculum are typically referred for special education services.

Reconceptualizing Assessment and Instruction

The McCallister Method rejects the assessment-grouping-teaching paradigm of the industrial school. Instead, the McCallister Method curriculum is based on guaranteed opportunities to take part in socially inclusive and educationally efficacious activities that harness innate learning capacities in ways that ensure expected academic progress without the need for teaching. McCallister Method grouping practices are democratic and self-organizing. Since the Format activities are not ability based, diagnostic assessment for the purposes of grouping is eliminated from the system.

The conventional three-tier model, in which the teacher identifies learners based on the deficit for ability-based instruction, is not only irrelevant within the McCallister Method but also undermines its principle of equality of educational opportunity. Learners have a right to take part in the social practices of the Formats on equal terms with all others, regardless of their ability status. Removal from Tier I activities is considered a violation of their rights according to the Keepers of the Culture Social Contract.

If learners are not provided tailored instruction by teachers in the classroom, how, then, does the McCallister Method propose to meet the civil rights imperative of IDEA? How are the special needs of learners provided within the program?

The new science of the mind has proven that self-direction is the primary mechanism of learning. Learning, rather than teaching, is the new focus of pedagogy. And self-responsibility is the means through which learners take an initiative to do what they need to do in order to develop along typical academic developmental pathways. The Tier II program within the McCallister Method is organized to ensure that learners with special needs have the support they need to take responsibility to do the things they wish to do to succeed on equal terms with their peers.

> "Learning, rather than teaching, is the focus of pedagogy within the McCallister Method."

Assessment is vitally important to this process. While assessment is not used to identify deficits as a means to group learners for tailored instruction, it *is* used to monitor learners' progress in the Tier I system of the Formats and identify those who require intervention. Learners who are not making expected progress in the first Tier I of the curriculum are referred for Tier II supports, which, in the McCallister Model, include an initial Academic Intervention with an adult and follow-up Academic Interventions with adults and/or Keepers of the Culture peers. Academic Interventions are situations that provide support to learners to take responsibility for learning what is necessary to catch up with grade-level norms.

The RTI system within the McCallister Model works like this: all learners take part in the Formats as the universal Tier I program. Assessments are used to monitor progress and identify those who fail to make progress. Pre-established progress benchmarks are referenced in order to determine intervention response. Those who appear to need additional support—who fail to make normal progress—are referred to the Tier II program, in which they take part in Academic Interventions until they have begun to make normal progress.

Assessment Systems within the McCallister Model

While assessments are not used within the McCallister Model for the purposes of grouping learners for instruction, or determining what kind of instruction to provide, they are nonetheless still of value in providing information about general patterns in learners' growth and achievement and how well background abilities are developing (see Box 21.1). To that end, assessment within the McCallister program plays two main functions. First, because it provides a means by which judgments can be made regarding how well the school is achieving its equal opportunity objective. The equity assertion of the McCallister Model is that every child can meet their highest potential when they are provided sufficient access to social experiences that enable them to coordinate and control their thinking relative to school expectations.

> "The equity assertion of the McCallister model is that every child can meet their highest potential when they are provided sufficient access to social experiences that enable them to coordinate and control their thinking relative to school expectations."

The second function of the school-wide assessment program is to provide everyone in the system with the competence feedback they need to continue meeting obligations to the Social Contract. Learners, guides, and school administrators have access to progress data, which serves as a form of competence feedback. Progress monitoring data are made available to students through Learning Conferences and Checkups and used to inform learner's Workout Plans. When data confirm that increased effort results in expected outcomes, one's sense of self-competence contributes to an overall sense of motivation and self-determination. The McCallister school-wide assessment program provides competence feedback to learners and guides, serving an important motivation function across the school system as a whole.

Assessment Program Agenda

The school-wide assessment program generates person-level data streams in grades K-1 in reading "subskills," and in grades 2–12 in reading, writing, and math fluency. These data allow the school leadership to monitor general achievement trends and identify learners who are failing to make expected progress in order to provide requisite intervention support. The McCallister assessment program is a centralized system whereby all learners are assessed and monitored according to the same, school-wide schedule. The program is designed to monitor the development of every learner's background abilities and competencies.

The Assessment Lead facilitates the work that needs to be done to implement the school-wide assessment program. The Assessment Lead takes responsibility for compiling and disseminating assessment data to relevant stakeholders. They share data with the Code Blue lead, who identifies learners who require Academic Intervention support, and the administration, which monitors system-wide progress. Data are also shared with reading, writing, and math teachers so that they can, in turn, provide individual learners with data they can use to understand their own academic progress. Data are shared with the school administration in order to monitor general trends in achievement. Baseline and progress monitoring data are made available to all learners so that they have a clear understanding of where their competencies lie in relation to learning targets.

Each type of assessment used in the school-wide assessment program is described below.

Curriculum-based Measures

CBM are informal assessments designed to measure skills needed for cognitive fluency in math, reading, and writing. They are administered in the McCallister program every six weeks for progress monitoring purposes, to provide information that is used formatively, to guide instruction.

CBMs are administered in math fluency, reading fluency, reading comprehension (unless the DRP assessment is used to assess reading comprehension), and writing fluency in grades 2–12 in **weeks 1, 6, 18, 24, 30, and 34**. All learners take part in the CBM program until they have achieved 8th-grade proficiency norms and test out of the CBM process. The Assessment Lead takes responsibility to identify learners who have achieved 8th-grade proficiency and remove them from the CBM program. CBMs are not used in kindergarten or 1st grade since most learners at these levels have not yet developed a level of literacy proficiency for which Background is a component. In other words, they do not yet have adequate levels of Background to measure.

CBMs are inexpensive and quick to administer. CBMs can be administered in several minutes. With the exception of the reading fluency CBM, they can be group administered. They can be created using grade-based curriculum material. In doing so, it is important to maintain consistency in terms of the complexity of assessment probes used. In other words, since CBMs track progress across six administrations over the course of the year, it is important that all of the CBMs administered reflect the same skill level. That way, the learner's progress in relation to the baseline score can be tracked over time. In other words, all of the reading fluency CBMs for the year need to reflect text complexity at the same Lexile or grade level. All of the math CBMs need to reflect the same math skills.

CBMs are also available through commercial publishers, such as Pearson's Aimsweb® Plus program, at a cost of $6.50 per student per year (Pearson, 2020). In a school of 400 students, a commercial CBM program would cost $2,600. Taking into consideration the time required to prepare the assessment probes, manage, and analyze data, it might make economic sense to use a commercial CBM program.

CBMs are easy to administer, but using them nonetheless requires training. With support of the Project Team, the Assessment Lead takes responsibility to learn and understand the CBM model in order to provide guidance and support to guides and the school leadership. The Assessment Lead works with the Professional Development Lead to coordinate training for staff who have been identified to administer CBMs. Responsibility to administer CBMs and collect data can be delegated to reading, writing, and math teachers or trained aides who can work in classrooms under supervision.

Math Fluency CBM

Math CBMs are two-minute timed computation worksheets administered to groups of students. Math CBMs are designed to measure speed and accuracy in addition, multiplication, and division. CBM math fluency assessments are designed to assess either computation or concepts and application and are scored by calculating the number of digits, which are correct (see Table 21.1) (Vanderbilt, 2020). To generate probes, select a task and use the same level and type of task throughout the academic year. Math sheets can be generated from websites such as webmathminute.com, themathworksheetsite.com, varsitytutors.com/aplusmath, easycbm.com, and InterventionCentral.org. For a summary overview of Math CBM procedures, see: https://my.vanderbilt.edu/specialeducationinduction/files/2013/07/IA.Math-CBM.pdf.

Table 21.1 Math fluency grade benchmarks

Grade	Computation probe benchmark (end of year)	Concepts and application probe benchmark
1	20 digits	NA
2	20 digits	20 blanks
3	30 digits	30 blanks
4	40 digits	30 blanks
5	30 digits	15 blanks
6	35 digits	15 blanks
7–12	Refer to 6th-grade norms	Refer to 6th-grade norms

Source: Vanderbilt (2020).

CBM Letter Name Fluency and Letter Sound Fluency

Letters and the sounds they make are the building blocks of our system of written language. Children's knowledge of letters and their sounds can provide reliable information about their developing awareness of literacy. Both LNF and Letter Sound Fluency (LSF) CBMs consist of a timed, one-minute probe (Table 21.2). For the LNF assessment, the learner is presented with a one-page display of random upper- and lower-case letters.

Table 21.2 Letter name fluency and letter sound fluency CBM grade norms

Grade	LNF Fall	LNF Winter	LNF Spring	LSF Fall	LSF Winter	LSF Spring
K	24	35	45	6	27	37
1	40	56	68	31	40	44

Source: EasyCBM (2014).

They are given one minute to name as many letters as they can. The LSF assessment presents the learner with a page of pictures. The examiner tells the word for the image in the picture and asks the learner to identify the first letter sound of the word. LNF and LSF measures can be downloaded from easycbm.com.

CBM-Maze

A cloze passage is a sample of text in which words have been eliminated, and where the learner selects among a choice of words to fill in the blank in a way that preserves the meaning of the text. Cloze passages have a long tradition in reading comprehension instruction, as they require a number of skills that are essential to text understanding, including reading accuracy, self-correction, and interpretive understanding. The CBM-Maze is a cloze passage in which the first sentence is left intact, and where the seventh word in the remainder of the text has been eliminated. The original word is compiled into a response item that includes the original word in addition to two more words that do not make sense (Wright, 2013). These words are randomly arranged and inserted back into the text. In a timed, three-minute reading of the Maze passage, the learner selects the best word options that preserve the meaning of the text (Wright, 2013). Maze passage fluency norms appear in Table 21.3. CBM-Maze passages can be generated from InterventionCentral.org at https://www.interventioncentral.org/teacher-resources/test-of-reading-comprehension.

Table 21.3 Maze passage fluency norms

Grade	Fall	Winter	Spring
2	6	NA	15
3	13	14	15
4	14	21	20
5	18	22	26
6	33	NA	39
7–12	Refer to 6th-grade norms	Refer to 6th-grade norms	Refer to 6th-grade norms

Source: Jenkins and Jewell (1993); Graney et al. (2009).

Oral Reading Fluency CBM

Reading speed and accuracy are predictable measures of reading ability. The reading fluency CBM is a one-minute timed oral reading of a grade-level text in which scores are determined by correctly read words (Table 21.4). The examiner marks as incorrect any errors or hesitations of more than three seconds (Wright, 2013). For a summary overview of Math CBM procedures, see: https://my.vanderbilt.edu/specialeducationinduction/files/2013/07/IA.Math-CBM.pdf. Oral Reading Fluency CBM passages can be generated from InterventionCentral.org at https://www.interventioncentral.org/teacher-resources/oral-reading-fluency-passages-generator.

Written Expression CBM

The Written Expression CBM is used to measure how many words the learner can spell correctly in a certain timeframe. The assessment Format is simple. Learners can be

Table 21.4 Oral reading fluency grade benchmarks

Grade	Correct words per minute, 50th percentile, Fall	Correct words per minute, 50th percentile, Winter	Correct words per minute, 50th percentile, Spring
1	NA	29	60
2	50	84	100
3	83	97	112
4	94	120	133
5	121	133	146
6	132	145	146
7	131	140	153
8	138	146	155
9–12	Refer to 8th-grade norms	Refer to 8th-grade norms	Refer to 8th-grade norms

Source: Hasbrouck and Tindal (2017); Hosp, Hosp, and Howell (2007).

assessed in a large group. The examiner provides each learner with a writing prompt on a lined sheet of paper, distributed face down on the table. Prompts are short story starters (e.g., I was looking through the telescope, when suddenly…). On cue, each learner turns the page on its face and reads the prompt. They are told to think about their response to the prompt for 30 seconds before beginning to write. After 30 seconds, learners are given the directive to begin writing. Writing is timed according to the table as shown in Tables 21.5 and 21.6. Norms are provided through grade six (Box 21.2). Written expression probes can be generated from InterventionCentral.org at https://www.interventioncentral.org/teacher-resources/curriculum-based-measurement-probes-writing.

Table 21.5 Writing fluency norms

Grade level	Fall average	Spring average
1	5	10
2	20	27
3	32	33
4	38	44
5	48	55
6	42	56
7	49	56
8–12	70	76

Source: Fuches & Fuches, Writing Fluency CBM.

Table 21.6 CBM written expression norms for Fall and Spring

Grade	Thinking time	Writing time	Fall	Spring
1	30 seconds	3 minutes	8	14
2	30 seconds	3 minutes	24	31
3	30 seconds	3 minutes	36	36
4	30 seconds	5 minutes	41	46
5	30 seconds	5 minutes	51	67
6	30 seconds	7 minutes	44	58
7	30 seconds	7 minutes	Refer to grade 6 norms	Refer to grade 6 norms
8	30 seconds	7 minutes	Refer to grade 6 norms	Refer to grade 6 norms
9	30 seconds	7 minutes	Refer to grade 6 norms	Refer to grade 6 norms
10	30 seconds	7 minutes	Refer to grade 6 norms	Refer to grade 6 norms

Source: Malecki and Jewell (2003).

> **Box 21.2**
>
> **Cynthia's reflection**
>
> I use the writing fluency norms in a calculating way. For example, one morning I was asked to have a Writing Conference with a 6th grader whose avoidant and challenging behavior, according to his teacher, interfered with his productivity. After chatting briefly about what he intended to write, and realizing he really didn't have any intention to write, I offered this challenge: "The average 6th grader can write about 44 words per minute. Do you think you can write a fourth of that? Like, do you think you could write 11 words a minute? (Of course, he responded that he could.) OK, I'm going to go to conference with someone else. Be sure to come and let me know if you managed to write a quarter of what the average 6th grader can write. (Note: this child came to find me later in the day in another classroom, showing me proof that he had written a total of 250 words.)

Interim Reading Comprehension Assessment

Reading is the linchpin of academic achievement, and it is critically important to monitor every learner's general progress throughout the year so that steps can be taken to intervene to correct delayed progress. The DRP is a holistic, criterion- and norm-referenced test of reading comprehension that can be group-administered in a single day, providing a precise way to track reading development over time. DRP scores on a scale of 1–100 are aligned to grade-level progress norms and provide a way to gauge how learners are progressing relative to typical patterns of reading achievement. The DRP score can be used as a measure of text complexity that can be compared to other norms such as Lexile or grade level (see Table 21.7). The DRP is administered in grades 2–12 in **weeks 2, 16, and 32**.

The first DRP assessment of the year serves as a baseline. Mid-year and end-of-year scores are compared to baseline scores to identify patterns of progress (e.g., not progressing, average progression, higher-than-average progression).

Table 21.7 Comparative reading-level metrics across grade levels

Grade level	DRP score range (end of year)	Lexile level (mid-year)	Common core state standards
1	NA	BR (Beginning Reading Measure) 120L–295L	190L–530L
2	42–49	170L–545L	420L–650L
3	48–54	415L–760L	520L–820L
4	52–57	635L–950L	740L–940L
5	55–60	770L–1080L	830L–1010L
6	57–62	855L–1165L	925L–1070L
7	60–64	925L–1235L	970L–1120L
8	62–67	985L–1295L	1010L–1185L
9	62–69	1040L–1350L	1050L–1260L
10	64–72	1085L–1400L	1080L–1335L
11	67–72	1130L–1440L	1185L–1385L
12	67–74	1130L–1440L	1185L–1385L
College and career ready	70		

Source: MetaMetrics, Inc. (2020); Questar (2016).

Table 21.8 Degrees of Reading Power focus of data analysis

Analysis timetable	Focus of analysis
Fall baseline	Average DRP score by class
	Average DRP score of lowest 20%
	Average DRP score of highest 20%
	Average DRP score for ELLs
	Average DRP score for SpEd
Mid-year	Average DRP score *and* average gains by class (from baseline to mid-year)
	Average DRP score *and* average gains of lowest 20% (from baseline to mid-year)
	Average DRP score *and* average gains of highest 20% (from baseline to mid-year)
	Average DRP score *and* average gains for ELLs (from baseline to mid-year)
	Average DRP score *and* average gains for SpEd (from baseline to mid-year)
End-of-year	Average DRP score *and* average gains by class (from baseline to end-of-year)
	Average DRP score *and* average gains of lowest 20% (from baseline to end-of-year)
	Average DRP score *and* average gains of highest 20% (from baseline to end-of-year)
	Average DRP score *and* average gains for ELLs (from baseline to end-of-year)
	Average DRP score *and* average gains for SpEd (from baseline to end-of-year)

Source: McCallister, C. (2011). Unison Reading: Socially Inclusive Group Instruction for Equity and Achievement.

Analysis of Data

DRP data are analyzed throughout the year to identify trends in individual learners, learner subgroups, and overall patterns of growth across the school. Fall DRP assessment data serve as the baseline for the year. Mid-year and end-of-year data are analyzed for comparative purposes. The summary analysis of each administration appears in Table 21.8.

The School Director/Principal makes reference to DRP data trends to confirm program efficacy. Data trends in schools where the McCallister Model is implemented routinely demonstrate DRP gains that are double the national norms (see McCallister, 2011a). Dips in DRP data trends in any one of the school's subgroups will alert the administration to interrogate program implementation in relevant classrooms. Unusually low scores, flat levels of achievement in the lowest 20% or among ELLs should alert the administration to investigate factors that might be compromising learning opportunities (e.g., low fidelity adherence to Rubric criteria in Cooperative Unison Reading, Learning Teams, Writing Conferences and Learning Conferences, or lack of evidence of sufficient numbers of these experiences) (Box 21.3).

Formal Assessments

Formal assessments come with high stakes. They are reality-creating instruments because they have the power to make something real by describing it as real (Searle, 2010). For example, a high score on an SAT exam creates a reality of expanded opportunity, just as a low score limits opportunity. For this reason, high-stakes assessments are handled with caution within the McCallister program.

Report Cards

Report cards are vetted each year to determine that their uses to make judgments about learners are balanced, fair, and consistent across classes and grades. Report cards are weighted across a range of values, including *attitudes and dispositions* (approach,

Box 21.3

Why we do not use informal reading inventories

Informal reading inventories (IRIs) have been a mainstay of reading literacy programs for decades. These assessments typically incorporate an oral reading component, in which the teacher takes a record of reading accuracy and analyzes mistakes. The IRI also includes reading comprehension questions, in which teachers read questions that have been written to probe existing understanding.

Within the old paradigm of teacher-directed instruction, it is necessary that the level of complexity of material being taught matches the level of the learner's development. IRIs are based on Goldilocks reasoning—the porridge, or lessons, cannot be too complex (too hot) or too easy (too cold) but need to be *just right* in order to provide the learner what they need to progress to the next level. In the old days of leveled reading groups, learners were typically assessed at the beginning of the year and assigned to high, medium, and low groups and usually remained in these groups for the entirety of the year. In recognition that these practices assigned the fate of readers irrespective of personal developmental patterns, a new innovation called *flexible grouping* was developed. The practice of flexible grouping requires more frequent assessment so that learners can move more fluidly between groups according to unique developmental trajectories. So, the Goldilocks process was made more complex. Instead of assigning each learner to one of three groups at the beginning of the year, and providing three different levels of instruction to each group, teachers now are responsible for using IRIs on a continual basis throughout the year to flexibly group learners in more fluid groupings that match their ability.

The problems with this model are several-fold. First, IRIs are costly due to the amount of time they take to administer. They can only be administered one learner at a time and can take as long as 30 minutes to complete (not counting extra time to analyze results). In a class of 24, it would take 12 hours of instructional time to administer IRIs to every student. In a daily hour-long reading program, it would take almost three weeks to identify every learner's reading level through the IRI assessment. And it would only be possible for a single teacher to administer three cycles of IRIs a year, leaving almost no time left for instruction. Moreover, with a strong reliance on children's *question-and-answer* discourse skills, the IRI's construct validity for comprehension is questionable since the ability to succeed depends on mastery of the Q&A discourse, a form of cultural knowledge acquired outside of school (Heath, 1983). Children experienced in Q&A practices will appear to have higher levels of comprehension. This is where the logic of the level-based reading curriculum falls apart. In relation to system inputs, its measurement is heavy and instruction is meager.

Second, the validity of the IRI is questionable. Most children find the assessment situation to be uncomfortable, thus the information they provide relates to behaviors in fight-flight-or-freeze learning contexts, not those that relate to behaviors of optimal functioning, which are arguably the more relevant sources of information needed to make judgments about educational progress. Last, the information is not useful. Next, the IRI results are not very useful. Scores indicate an instructional level, but, they do not provide information that is useful to inform instruction. Comprehension questions are either answered correctly or not but cannot offer insight into ways of thinking that support or mitigate achievement. Finally, from a systems' point of view, because they are so human resource heavy, they drain resources that are arguably better invested in instructional support rather than educational measurement. For all of these reasons, IRIs are not used in the McCallister program.

The Cooperative Unison Reading (CUR) program eliminates the need for leveled grouping. Learners are not assigned to leveled groups; instead, they choose their own groups based on personal preferences. The theory of learning implicit in CUR is that Background (i.e., reading skills) develops as an outcome of competent social participation in groups. If learners have sufficient opportunity to take part in CUR (at least 60 minutes a week), they make predictable, normative progress. Now that we have dispensed with the labor-intensive pedagogical project of continual assessment, adult resources can be allocated to instruction instead of assessment.

self-responsibility, work habits) as well as performance (improvements in progress monitoring scores and formal interim assessments, quality of participation in Formats, improvement in quality of writing).

Course Syllabi

Grading criteria for middle- and high school classes are consistent across classes and prominently outlined in the *course syllabus*. New syllabi are developed and submitted to the Curriculum Committee in the spring of the academic year prior to the academic year in which the course runs. The Assessment Lead works with the Curriculum Committee to ensure that grading practices are fair and balanced.

State Assessment Program

The Assessment Lead helps implement the school's formal assessment program and ensures that all learners are prepared to take the exam. The McCallister curriculum incorporates opportunities to use state assessment items as curriculum content in the context of the Formats (e.g., Learning Teams are organized around a championship competition in which teams compete to achieve the highest score; and learners in grades 3–8 have opportunities to read and respond to test items in Cooperative Unison Reading and Integrative Math). The Assessment Lead compiles a database in which these informal learning opportunities are recorded and monitored, ensuring that all learners have had the opportunity to take a practice version of the state exam that is required. Works with the school administration to plan the administration of state exams and to ensure proper accommodations are done (Table 21.9).

Year-long Implementation Plan: Assessment Lead

The Assessment Lead executes the agenda that is outlined in Table 21.10.

Table 21.9 Summary assessments

Assessment	Frequency	Type	Purpose
Math diagnostic assessment	Once, upon intake	Diagnostic	Measure of mathematical abilities
State English as a second language assessment	Once, upon intake	Diagnostic	Measure of English proficiency, to determine ESL support needed, if necessary
Degrees of Reading Power®	Three times annually (baseline, midline, end-of-year)	Diagnostic, interim	Measure of reading comprehension
Every six weeks	Curriculum-based measures (CBM): Math CBM; Oral Reading Fluency CBM; writing CBM	Progress monitoring/ formative	To determine growth in academic skills and to inform adjustment of Individual Learning Plans
Post-tests (created by staff and Curriculum and Assessment Leads)	Every four to six weeks, at the conclusion of academic units	Interim	To assess understanding of content gained in a unit of study, and to make curricular modifications for the next unit

(*Continued*)

Table 21.9 Summary assessments *(Continued)*

C-DEEP social assessment	One week into an academic unit and one week before its conclusion	Formative	Peer assessment of growth on social-emotional capacities
Mock state assessment	At the conclusion of each standards-aligned, credit-bearing course	Summative	To determine if academic goals are met and to assess college readiness
State ESL assessment	Annually, as applicable	Summative	To assess English language proficiency and growth
PSAT	Fall of sophomore and Junior years	Summative	To assess college readiness skills in math and ELA
SAT	Spring of Junior year and fall of senior year	Summative	To assess college readiness skills in math and ELA
State tests	Grades 3–12, as mandated	Summative	To assess academic development

Table 21.10 Year-long implementation plan: assessment

Calendar action	Calendar dates
Purchase commercial assessments (DRP; CBMs)	B3
Interface with McCallister Project Team to maintain up-to-date curriculum assessments and disseminate to guides/teachers	B3
Administer Degrees of Reading Power, grades 2–12; administer DIBELS in K-1	Weeks 2, 16, and 32
Administer state ELL placement assessment (refer those at beginner or emerging proficiency level to Civil Rights Lead for placement in Language Games Program)	As per state regulations
Report DRP and DIBELS results to School Director, Civil Rights Lead, Curriculum Lead, Classroom Teachers/Community Managers	Weeks 3, 17, and 33
Administer CBMs in math, reading and writing, grades 2–12	Weeks 1, 6, 18, 24, 30, and 34
Report CBM results to School Director, Civil Rights Lead, Curriculum Lead, Classroom Teachers/Community Managers	Weeks 2, 7, 19, 25, 30, and 35
Administer Learning Teams assessments in grades 6–8 in English language arts and math, and in grades 9–12 in algebra, geometry, global history, U.S. history, Earth science, living environment and physics one time during high school	Weeks 7, 13, 19, 25, and 31
Report Learning Teams post-assessment scores to Team Members and Curriculum Lead	Weeks 8, 14, 20, 25, and 31
Administer C-DEEP social assessments in Learning Teams	Weeks 3/6, 9/12, 14/18, 21/24, 25/30
Report C-Deep social assessment results to Learning Team members and Curriculum Lead	Weeks 4/7, 10/13, 15/19, 22/25, 26/31
Report Card and Syllabus review (in coordination with School Management Team)	Week 20
Update Learning Teams Assessment Archive	Week 21
Coordinate state testing in grades 3–8, ELA and math, ESL, and high school exams	By state/district
Maintain learner's writing portfolios	One piece, the last day of each month

Note: B3 means three weeks before school (week by which all resources are ordered).

22 The Civil Rights Program

Introduction

The McCallister Model conceives of the curriculum as a set of rights to rich learning experiences that are granted to all learners and enforced through pedagogical systems as opposed to the traditional approach to curriculum as skills to be taught and learned. Invariably, structural inequalities result in differential social opportunities, and these inequalities are then reflected in differential achievement outcomes. Traditionally, achievement gaps are addressed through targeted instruction focused on skills. Academically vulnerable populations within the school, such as students with special needs, English learners, and low-achieving students, are typically assigned to academic remediation programs based on missing competencies. Within the McCallister Model, achievement gaps are understood as a consequence of limited human capital of a certain kind, the development of which depends on opportunities to experiences to acquire these forms of capital. The Sparks, Learning Cultures, and Keepers of the Culture programs are the first Tier of response. They are universal designs for learning that provide opportunities for learners to develop educationally necessary forms of capital through experiences provided by the curriculum. But since opportunities can only be taken, not given (Plomin, 2018), these programs only succeed when learners take responsibility to adhere to curriculum expectations. In many cases, academically vulnerable learners lack the desire and motivation to do so, therefore compromising their own rights to equality of educational opportunity.

The Keepers of the Culture program employs the Academic and Behavior Intervention programs to ensure learners internalize and act on their responsibilities to learn and rise to their opportunity. Delayed academic development, therefore, is seen as a civil rights concern as opposed to a concern of deficits in skills. The student rosters of failing high schools are populated by a majority of learners who have been failed by the current system, one year after the next. In these cases, schools have, however unwittingly, betrayed their moral obligation to learners.

The Civil Rights Lead is responsible for implementing the Academic and Behavior Intervention programs as the Tier 2 response system of the McCallister Method. The Intervention Program is designed to ensure that learners take responsibility to acquire educationally necessary experiences. It is designed to support learners to enact a course of personal action that will enable them to rise to their opportunity.

Democratic Equality

The U.S. Supreme Court ruled in its historic *Brown v. Board of Education* ruling that school segregation was illegal, asserting that social exclusion violated the child's right to an *education on equal terms*. One decade prior to the Court's ruling, John Dewey published

Democracy and Education, which no doubt influenced the Court's decision. Several key comments from *Democracy and Education* are presented here, because they offer a clairvoyant articulation of the aims to which an equitable, socially inclusive, democratic education should aspire, and most aptly capture the spirit of the Court's aspirations.

> The two points selected by which to measure the worth of a form of social life are the extent in which the interests of a group are shared by all its members, and the fullness and freedom with which it interacts with other groups. An undesirable society, in other words, is one which internally and externally sets up barriers to free intercourse and communication of experience. A society which makes provision for the participation in its good of all its members on equal terms and which secures flexible readjustment of its institutions through interactions of the different forms of associated life is in so far democratic. Such a society must have a type of education which gives individuals a personal interest in social relationships and control, and the habits of mind which secure social changes without introducing disorder.
>
> John Dewey (1916/1944, p. 99)

> The extension in space of the number of individuals who participate in an interest so that each has to refer his own action to that of others, and to consider the action of others to give point and direction to his own, is equivalent to the breaking down of those barriers of class, race, and national territory which kept men from perceiving the full import of their activity.
>
> John Dewey (1916/1944, p. 87).

> In order to have a large number of values in common, all the members of the group must have an equable opportunity to receive and to take from others. There must be a large variety of shared understandings and experiences. Otherwise, the influences which educate some into master, educate others into slaves.
>
> John Dewey (1916/1944, p. 84).

Civil Rights Lead Responsibilities

Assessment

- Coordinate with Assessment Lead to identify non-progressing learners upon review of school-wide periodic progress-monitoring data;
- Identify emergent readers/writers in grades 2–12 for emergent reader's Daily To-do List Program;
- Create subgroups of non-progressing learners (reading, writing, behavior, language), and monitor progress to identify *flat-lining*, or failure to demonstrate progress toward grade- or age norms;
- Identify learners with Individual Education Programs (IEPs) who have demonstrated significant gains in progress monitoring assessments in order to re-evaluate them for possible declassification.

Instructional Accounting: Records and Reporting

- In coordination with school administration, calculate opportunity mandates that specify the required number of each Format that every teacher will implement through

the course of the year (for example, Cooperative Unison Reading groups meet four out of every five days. Over a total of 110 Instructional Days, Cooperative Unison Reading groups will meet 88 times, half of which are documented in Cooperative Unison Reading Records. Therefore, classroom assessment archives should reflect 44 documented opportunities by the end of the school year).
- Conduct quarterly opportunity checks through a review of assessment archives in every classroom to ensure opportunity targets for each Format are being met (e.g., Learning Conferences: 1–2 per month per learner; Writing Conferences: 1–2 per month per learner; and Cooperative Unison Reading groups: 12 per month per classroom).
- Conduct randomized Writing Portfolio checks (8 checks per 100 learners).

Intervention Coordinator

- Communicate weekly with School Director to identify learners' in need of Behavior Interventions (those who were referred through the School Culture Lead via the Ladder of Self-regulation process, those who are chronically late or absent identified through attendance records, or those who are identified through attendance records).
- Manage Academic and Behavior Intervention schedule and case load.
  Assign initial Interventions to Civil Rights Team (School Director, Special Education Director, School Counselor).
  Assign follow-up Interventions to Keepers of the Culture Corps.
- Maintain a central Intervention Records Database, which should include Intervention Records, the Promise Card database (Promise Cards are the end-products of Interventions in which learners indicate their commitment to changes in behavior), and the Transformation Narrative database (Transformation Narratives are conducted in follow-up Interventions to support learners to revise their academic self-identities).
- Identify learners to be discharged from Academic and Behavior Intervention Programs (monitor weekly).
- Manage the supplemental after-school Cooperative Unison Reading program for learners identified in need of academic, behavioral, or language support.
- Coordinate with Keepers of Curriculum to organize Daily Emergent Reader To-do List program for learners in grades 2–12. Learners are discharged from Emergent Readers Daily To-do Program once they have reached 2nd-grade reading proficiency (see Activity Inventory).
- Identify English as a second language (ESL) learners for Language Games Program (qualifying learners are those whose parents indicate they cannot speak or understand English or those identified through the state language assessment to be at an *entering* or *beginning* level of English language proficiency). Supervise Keepers Corps Members in implementing the program. ELLs take part in Language Games until they reach elementary language proficiency, at which time they are discharged from the program.

Advisement

- Adviser, Keepers Corps

McCallister Group

- Member, Project Team—interface with McCallister Group and participate in network-wide professional development

School Governance

- Member, School Management Team

Equity Practices

Code Blue

The first sign that a learner is failing to make achievement progress is considered an emergency that requires immediate intervention. The program applies the same urgency of a *code blue* response in medicine to the academic emergency of low achievement progress (Medicinenet.com, 2020). The Assessment Lead instantiates *code blue* when a learner is identified as failing to make expected academic progress, and they are referred to the Academic Intervention Program. Learners whose negative behaviors threaten to undermine their achievement and well-being are identified by the School Culture Lead and referred to the Behavior Intervention Program. Once referred, the learner enters the Intervention Program.

The Civil Rights Lead works with the Assessment Lead to monitor and identify learners who appear to be failing to make expected academic progress. They also work with the administration to identify learners whose negative behaviors threaten to undermine achievement and well-being. Once identified, the learner enters the Intervention Program, the Tier 2 level of response in the McCallister Method.

Full Inclusion: The Equity Imperative

The success of a rights-based education initiative can be judged, in large measure, by how successfully it supports learning for the most diverse, vulnerable, or hard-to-teach students and inclusively integrates them with the general education population. Reaching the ideal of full social inclusion in a school has been impossible within the rational-empirical, reductionist approach to teaching as transmission that dominates in the industrial school. These practices mandate that learners are grouped by need for instruction, thereby mandating a form of social segregation that further reinforces existing structural inequalities.

The more distal learners become within the cultural niche of school, the more likely they are to develop depressive symptoms and the more their well-being is threatened (Dressler, 2019). Remedial, pull-out programs, contrary to their intention to support so-called *normal* behaviors, really function, essentially, to abnormalize learners. This fact was observed nearly a century ago by the anthropologist, Ruth Benedict (1934), who warned, "…civilization in setting higher and possibly more worthwhile goals may increase the number of its abnormals" (p. 274). To have spent 13,000 hours in a place where you are supposed to learn something, only to be told that, even after all that time, you failed, must be utterly soul crushing. That is why we simply cannot allow children to fail.

Vulnerable learners stand to gain the most by taking part in forms of social participation that enable them to resolve disordered behaviors and access social information and innovative thinking, which are most abundant in large and diverse learning groups (see Derex & Boyd, 2015). Human beings evolved to thrive and survive in large, diverse, and inclusive social groups (Dunbar, 1998). Full inclusion within the least restrictive environment is educationally optimal, even for learners with significant developmental delays or for non-English speakers. It is only through participation in the social worlds in which competencies are used that they develop.

Full inclusion of these learners in the general education classroom also provides typically developing learners with opportunities to care for peers, providing them important opportunities to develop compassion, empathy, and tolerance for human diversity. The McCallister classroom attempts to achieve these adaptively suitable conditions in the classroom cultural niche for all learners.

Intervention Program

The Civil Rights Lead manages the Intervention Program. The Intervention is an effort to sensitize learners to their vested interests as citizens of the *demos* who have a stake in its privileged and entitlements, and to alert them to how their rights might be exercised. This program comprises any and all learners in the school who have been identified as not responding to the Tier 1 programs. Intake Interventions are typically facilitated by a trained staff member, and usually involve teachers and, if necessary, parents (training is provided by the McCallister Group, and training qualifications are determined by the school leadership in consultation with the McCallister Project Team). After the initial Intervention, if the learner demonstrates positive intentionality toward program goals, subsequent meetings are facilitated by Keepers or Curriculum Corp members on a bi-monthly basis until the Civil Rights Lead determines the program is no longer needed and the learner is discharged from the Tier 2 Intervention program.

The Intervention Program is an example of norm psychology applied to an effort to address the long-intractable social problem of low achievement through an intensive effort to help the learner begin to self-regulate to positive social and academic norms.

Opportunity Checks

The Civil Rights Lead takes responsibility to conduct monthly Opportunity Checks of assessment records in classrooms and communicates data to the school administration. The school administration monitors this evidence once every two months in what are called Opportunity Checks. Opportunity checks confirm learners' rights to Format experience have been met.

Keepers Corps

The Keepers of the Culture Corp, a group of learners nominated by their peers, is enlisted to help provide support in implementing the Intervention Program. The Civil Rights Lead advises and works with the Keepers Corp to push to conduct follow-up Interventions. The Corps also assists to plan and present the New Learner Orientation at the beginning of the year. Corps members assist in conducting Opportunity Checks every two months.

Special Learners

Democratic education is, by definition, inclusive (*Brown v. Board*, 1954; Dewey, 1916/1944). The success of a rights-based education initiative can be judged, in large measure, by how successfully it supports learning for the most diverse, vulnerable, or hard-to-teach students and inclusively integrates them with the general education population. Reaching the ideal of full social inclusion in a school has been impossible within the rational-empirical, reductionist approach to teaching as transmission due to the necessity of grouping learners together under the illusion they lacked in common certain skills.

Debunking Disability

The Positive Learning Paradigm asserts that all human psychological functions are stimulated by the skills and motivations of shared intentionality (Tomasello, 2019). These capacities are universal in human beings. Provided an environment in which they are adequately and appropriately stimulated, competencies will develop. That is why the Tier 1 experiences of the McCallister Method, which target key social and psychological processes, support development for all learners.

The Individuals with Disabilities Act (2004) identifies a disability as follows:

> Specific learning disability means a disorder in one or more of the psychological processes involved in understanding or in using language, spoken or written, that may manifest itself in the imperfect ability to listen, think, speak, read, write, spell, or to do mathematical calculations, including conditions such as perceptual disabilities, brain injury, minimal brain dysfunction, dyslexia, and developmental aphasia.... Specific learning disability does not include learning problems that are primarily the result of visual, hearing, or motor disabilities, of intellectual disability, of emotional disturbance, or of environmental, cultural, or economic disadvantage.

It goes on to explain that a disability can be identified by the determination of a discrepancy between "ability" and "achievement"; failure to respond to a scientifically based intervention; or alternative research-based procedures for identification of a specific learning disability (Individuals with Disabilities Education Act, 2004).

The first-level classroom practices of Learning Cultures are fully inclusive, non-restrictive social activities, which result in a learning environment that supports universal access. Students diagnosed with learning disabilities take part in the Tier 1 program on equal terms with their peers in the general education program. IEPs are rewritten to specify goals in terms of participation in the Tier I program. If additional services are required, special education teachers push into the general education classroom where they support students in the context of the Formats.

12:1:1

The Tier I and II programs of the McCallister Model provide a universal design for learning that addresses every learner's needs. Therefore, in schools transitioning to the McCallister Model, it will be necessary to phase out the highly restrictive environments of the 12:1:1 program. Learners currently assigned to these programs will have Interventions in order to help them begin to establish normative behaviors. As enfranchised members of the *demos*, these learners have a right to take part in the general education classroom on equal terms with their peers. They should be re-evaluated after sustained participation over several weeks in the general education program, by which time they will have sufficiently progressed to be de- or re-classified and placed into the less restrictive environment of the general education setting.

Individual Education Plans

It is required by law that learners with IEPs be formally evaluated each year. However, since learners make rapid developmental progress within the context of the McCallister

Methods, and these gains begin to appear in progress monitoring data relatively quickly, formal evaluations should be conducted at the first sign they have made significant progress (e.g., double the national average in reading comprehension) in order to track gains in reading comprehension evaluated every month based on progress monitoring and determine when they can be most quickly be declassified from the special education program.

Language Learning

Based upon these its unique universal design, the McCallister program also aligns with the aims of the English Language Acquisition, Language Enhancement, and Academic Achievement Act by providing limited English proficient learners of every level access to the general education curriculum and full inclusion in the general student population as means to develop high levels of attainment in English and meet the same challenging achievement standards as all children are expected to meet. Federal law does not require special language services if the learner is able to access the district curriculum through the general education program and if they are developing English language competencies at an acceptable rate. Because these two criteria are met in the context of the Tier 1 program of the McCallister Methods, ESL and bilingual programs are not only unnecessary, if they separate English learners from the demos, they are inequitable.

Sufficiency Supplements: The Double Down Principle

The Civil Rights Lead directs the Sufficiency Supplements Program. This program provides additional learning opportunities to those who have been identified as academically vulnerable. In coordination with the school administration, opportunities throughout the day should be made available for these learners to take part in additional opportunities in the "Me" Formats of Cooperative Unison Reading, Integrative Math, and Language Games. The Civil Rights Lead works with the Curriculum Lead, who monitors the quality of the curriculum. Participation in these programs continues until adequate progress is achieved (e.g., English learners have reached 2nd-grade language proficiency, learners in the bottom quartile on an assessment measure have demonstrated progress near the 50th percentile ranking). The Curriculum Corps help implement this program.

Year-long Implementation Plan: Civil Rights Lead

The Civil Rights Lead executes the agenda that is outlined in Table 22.1.

Table 22.1 Civil rights project calendar actions

Calendar action	Calendar dates
In coordination with school administration, determine monthly Instructional Days and calculate Opportunity Mandates in Cooperative Unison Reading, Learning Conference, Writing Conferences, and Workout Plans—communicate monthly targets to staff	B2 (two weeks before school begins)
Coordinate with school administration and Curriculum Lead to implement Sufficiency Supplements (Extended-day Program)	Week 1
With Training Lead, coordinate Intervention training for new Keepers of the Cultures Civil Rights Corps members	Week 3

(*Continued*)

Table 22.1 Civil rights project calendar actions *(Continued)*

Calendar action	Calendar dates
Co-plan the New Learner Curriculum Orientation with Training and Curriculum Lead	Week 1
Schedule weekly Interventions for new Tier 2 intakes who are referred for behavior and/or academic challenges	Week 2, and thereafter weekly
Implement supplemental/extended-day Cooperative Unison Reading Program for beginner ELLs, learners who scored a 1 or 2 on the state ELA exam, and those who are not meeting grade-level norms on Reading Fluency CBMs	Week 2
Monitor assessment and behavior data to identify	
Identify ELLs for referral to Language Games Program	Week 3
Conduct Instructional Opportunity Checks in each classroom of Cooperative Unison Reading Records, Learning Conference Records, Writing Conference Records, and Workout Plans	Week 4, 8, 12, 16, 20, 24, 28, and 32
Conduct random Writing Portfolio checks in K-12	Weeks 8, 16, 20, 24, 28, and 32
Convene bi-monthly Keepers Corps meetings (identify Corp Lead)	Weeks 4, 6, 8, 10, 12, 14, 16, 18, 20, 22, 24, 26, 28, 30, 32, and 34
Review and informally evaluate learners with IEPs to determine the need for re-evaluation and possible declassification (in coordination with school administration, Special Education Director, Curriculum and Assessment Leads)	Monthly
With Assessment Lead, review DRP, DIBELS, and CBM data to identify non-progressing learners	DRP & DIBELS: Weeks 3, 17, and 33 Math, Reading and Writing CBM: Weeks 2, 7, 19, 25, 30, and 35
Create/update subgroups based on progress monitoring data (discharge participants from Language Games, Academic Intervention, extended-day Cooperative Unison Reading programs when they have achieved grade-level standards on Reading Fluency CBM or DRP/DIBELS and discharge Daily To-do List Program participants when they have reached 2nd-grade standards on Reading Fluency CBM or DRP)	Weeks 3, 4, 8, 18, 20, 26, 31, and 34
Conduct initial Academic Interventions for learners newly identified in progress monitoring data	Weeks 4, 5, 9, 19, 21, 27, and 32
Identify Behavior Intervention referrals and discharge current participants of Behavior Intervention Program who have resolved maladaptive behaviors	Weekly

Note: B2 means two weeks before school begins.

23 The Community Education Program

Introduction

Practically everyone who has attended formal schooling has experienced teaching as telling and demonstrating, and learning as reciting or remembering. The industrial model of education is a legacy of history that is deeply embedded within cultural representations of what schooling is. The McCallister Method requires a much more active role for the learner and a much less dominant role for the teacher.

The radical changes brought about by the McCallister Model might be welcome by some learners and their families. But to others, they will be threatening. There will be groups of learners and parents who protest change, who insist that it is the teacher's proper role to teach in a more traditional way, and who perceive that the school is attempting to change the rules of a game that will put them at an unfair advantage. Parents who are concerned that their children receive an academically rigorous education are sometimes initially ill-at-ease with a curriculum that is not teacher directed. So, in addition to educating learners, the school also needs to educate families.

It is, therefore, essential that the school assumes a proactive stance in working to educate the community about the McCallister Model and all of the advantages it provides the learners. The Community Education Lead plays an important role in helping parents and caregivers understand the advantages of the new, learner-centered educational paradigm of the McCallister Model. This knowledge helps parents and caregivers provide the support their children need to make the most of the opportunities that the McCallister Model provides. Children whose parents understand and appreciate a curriculum that centers students as the agents of learning are more able to invest themselves in the curriculum. Establishing and maintaining strong connections to the community and taking initiative to educate them about the work of the school is a central focus of the school-wide leadership mission.

Community Education Lead Responsibilities

The primary responsibility of the Community Education Lead is to maintain strong connections to the community and to use these connections to educate and involve the community in the work of the school. The Community Lead plays an important role in sustaining the community ecosystem.

Events Coordinator

- Plan and host Monthly Open House
- Conduct school-wide Writing Portfolio Night (in coordination with McCallister Project Team and Curriculum Lead)
- Science and Technology Fair, hosted annually in Week 20

McCallister Group

- Member, Program Team—interface with McCallister Group and participate in network-wide professional development

School Newspaper

- Chair, School Newspaper Committee
- Conduct search, hire, and oversee part-time journalist to serve as School Newspaper Editor and Adviser (in coordination with school administration)
- Supervise Keepers of the Culture Curriculum Corps members to Advertise and recruit learners to become reporters/journalists

School Governance

- Chair, Community Education Committee
- Chair, Volunteer Committee and Adviser to the Volunteer Corps
- Adviser, School Assembly—implement and supervise the school-wide election process and meet monthly with the Assembly
- Member, School Management Team

Web Presence and Social Media

- Develops and implements school Communication Plan
- Updates school website (for events, curriculum content, and the school's unique content)

Community Education Lead Projects

Community Talent Recruitment

The McCallister Model opens up pedagogical space in the school for community members to become Guides (paraprofessionals can serve as Guides). The Community Education Lead is ideally positioned, through their extensive contact with the community, to assume leadership for the school-wide talent recruitment effort. The Community Education Lead conducts outreach initiatives to identify potential talent and makes recommendations to the school administration.

Monthly Open House

The Community Education Lead organizes and hosts monthly open house events, which include an information session, classroom tours, and debriefs with guides and learners. Information sessions are an hour in length. Each session features a description of a learning format, an explanation of the learning theory that is animated in the Format, and examples from classrooms. Classroom tours provide opportunities to see the Formats in action. A debrief provides opportunities to learn about the Format experience from the perspective of guides and learners. The Open House concludes with an informal opportunity to socialize with learners and school staff. The Community Education Lead will coordinate with the PD Lead to identify talented teachers/guides and to help them prepare to present at Open House events.

Monthly Talent Night

The Community Education Lead works with the Keepers of the Culture Corps to host the Monthly Talent Night. Each learner is expected to contribute their talent to at least one event. Talent is showcased in the form of stage performances (skits, stand-up comedy, poetry recitations, drama, musical performances), art and science exhibits, and video presentations.

School Newspaper

The Community Education Lead works with the Keepers of the Culture Curriculum Corps to recruit journalists from every grade to work on the Monthly School Newspaper. In an age of disinformation and biased media reporting, it is ever more necessary for the school curriculum to provide opportunities to learn to understand and value the role of a free, objective press in a democracy. The School Newspaper provides these important learning opportunities. The paper solicits feature stories, opinion columns, movie, music and game reviews, how-to articles, editorials, and news articles. The Community Education Lead works with the News Staff and Editor/Adviser to publish a monthly newspaper.

Science and Technology Fair

Learners from every grade have the opportunity to compete in teams to create a project made with technology. The Community Education Lead advertises and hosts the event and works in collaboration with the school's math and science teachers, who support and supervise learning teams.

Volunteer Corps

In addition to helping those in need and supporting worthwhile causes, the opportunity to volunteer in the community provides a powerful learning experience. Volunteering is often the first phase of a career, an opportunity to meet new people, and a chance to learn new skills. The Community Education Lead chairs the school-wide Volunteer Committee. All learners are invited to join the Volunteer Corps.

Web and Social Media Presence

The Community Education Lead is responsible for managing the school website. In coordination with the school director/principal, the Community Education Lead works with the web developer or a learner versed in web development technology to update and maintain the school website. The Community Education Lead interfaces with the McCallister Project Manager to provide content that is relevant to the McCallister curriculum.

The Community Education Lead manages the school's Communications Plan, which outlines the ways and means to deliver appropriate information to the school's stakeholders. It includes the messages to be delivered, the audience to be targeted, the media vehicle to be used, the frequency to be used, who has responsibility to execute, and the mechanism employed for feedback. The Community Education Lead will coordinate with school staff and students to successfully enact the Communications Plan.

Year-Long Implementation Plan: Community Education Lead

The Community Education Lead executes the agenda that is outlined in Table 23.1.

Table 23.1 Community education project calendar actions

Calendar action	Calendar dates
Community Education Committee	Monthly
Volunteer Corps meeting	Monthly
Talent Night	Monthly
Open House	Monthly
Newspaper publication	Monthly
Writing Portfolio Night	Weeks 16 and 32
Communications releases	As per Communications Plan

24 The Curriculum Program

Introduction

The Curriculum in the McCallister Method employs one universal personalized curriculum in all grades and subjects. The Sparks program informs learners about personal goals and activity plans to achieve them. The Learning Cultures Formats create the zones of proximal development (Vygotsky, 1978) that provide space for classroom activity. The Curriculum Lead is responsible for implementing these curricula (the School Culture and Civil Rights Lead are responsible for the Keepers of the Culture program).

The primary responsibility of the Curriculum Lead is to manage all facets of the Sparks and Learning Cultures curricula, and all of the program extensions that employ these curricula.

Curriculum Lead Responsibilities

In order for the Curriculum Lead to carry out their responsibilities, it is imperative that they have a deep understanding of both the Sparks and Learning Cultures curriculum programs. All of the responsibilities outlined in this chapter make reference to activities and procedures in these programs and will not be elaborated in this chapter.

Advisement

- Adviser, Keepers of the Curriculum Corps

Assessment, Evaluation, and Reporting

- Coordinate with school administration to review report cards and course syllabi to ensure consistency and content validity in grading
- Maintain archives of course syllabi and report cards
- Maintain learners' writing portfolios
- Maintain Learning Teams Assessment Archive
- Conduct Learning Environment assessments prior to school opening to ensure that environments are well-developed

Curriculum Practice

- Organize classroom environment preparation prior to school opening. Using the Learning Environment Rubric as a guide, advise staff to prepare classroom environments. Organize staff to work across collaboratively to systematize the process (e.g., photocopy forms, organize assessment systems).

- Conduct classroom environment observations with feedback on classrooms in need of improvement, then follow up with re-evaluation.
- Maintain Sparks Activity Inventory.
- Manage school-wide Sparks curriculum (genre collections, literary canon projects, discipline-based study guides, writing portfolios).
- Support teachers to create activity archives for Work Time options in their classrooms. (Ensure one-dozen activity options in each subject prior to school opening.)
- Supervise Learning Teams program implementation in middle and high school testing subjects.
- Supervise genre exposure curriculum. Ensure that learners in every classroom are exposed to a new writing genre every week.
- Supervise grade and/or Content Teams to systematize curriculum planning and implementation (Format sign-up procedures, Cooperative Unison Reading text archives, genre exposure archives, Work Time activity curriculum).
- Monitor curriculum quality (learner-selected Work Time activities aligned to learning standards, ample activity choices, high-quality Format interactions, availability of standards documents for learner reference).
- Monitor Cultural Capital Curriculum, ensuring classrooms are well-equipped with recreational and enrichment activities suited to learners' interests.
- Supervise Workshops of Possibility curriculum (in coordination with PTA and school administration).

Curriculum Training

- Serve as curriculum point person to the Training Lead, as needed, to support staff training in McCallister Methods curricula.
- Supervise implementation of New Learner Curriculum Orientation for learners who are new to the school (i.e., kindergarten learners in elementary, 6th-grade learners in middle school, and 9th-grade learners in high school) and learners who transfer into the school (see Box 24.1).
- Supervise McCallister assessments training (in coordination with McCallister Project Team and Training Lead) in Cooperative Unison Reading Records, Learning Conferences, Writing Conference, and Workout Plans.
- Provide training to staff in "grassroots lesson" development (lessons derived from curriculum and assessment data generated through informal observations).

McCallister Group

- Member, Project Team—interface with McCallister Group and participate in network-wide professional development.

Box 24.1

New student curriculum

Sparks curriculum overview
Learning Cultures curriculum overview
Keepers of the Culture curriculum overview
Watch explainer videos (Grades 2–12)

Programs and Events

- Organize cross-school academic rituals (book clubs, field trips, special guest visitors, movie nights for canonical documentaries and films)
- Coordinate school-wide Field Education Curriculum
- Co-direct the Sufficiency Supplements (supplemental/extended-day) program with Civil Rights Lead
- Organize, with Training Lead, summer professional development
- Classroom environment assessment
- New Learner Curriculum
- Coordinate school-wide Sparks and Learning Cultures program
- Supervise Cultural Capital and Workshops of Possibility program
- Manage the school-wide Writing Portfolio Program
- Co-direct monthly Assessment Workshops (with Training Lead)
- Supervise Learning Teams curriculum (maintain Curriculum Maps, Unit Question Guides, Unit Assessments)
- Manage emergent readers "Daily To-do" List program
- Supervise Test Genre Program

Resources

- Assist school administration in the procurement of quality resources and equipment used for curriculum purposes (see Resources List).
- Maintain Field Education Resources (list of local cultural institutions, parks, preserves, etc.).
- Lead in the development of Learning Teams assessments. Coordinate with staff to develop unit-based practice tests for state curriculum subjects. Provide updated Learning Teams assessments to Assessment Lead for archiving.

School Governance

- Chair, Curriculum Committee (monitor curriculum across grades and subjects for quality, consistency, and coherence)
- Member, School Management Team
- Adviser, Curriculum Corps

Test Genre Curriculum

- Monitor school-wide Test Genre Curriculum. Two weeks before the state tests in Math and English language arts (ELA) (grades 3–8), implement the Genre Practice Test Exposure program. Activities are restricted to genre exposure lessons that feature test items (no more than 10 days total throughout the year in any class); Cooperative Unison Reading cycles that feature text items (two week-long cycles prior to the state test); and Learning Teams (see discussion below).

Training

Quality of learning within the Formats depends on learners' self-regulation and their ability to control their thinking and self-regulate to norms. Staff are provided training support through the Training Program. The Curriculum Lead works with the Training

Lead to implement the Framework for Professional Development to support staff. But in most schools, staff professional development is not enough to achieve optimal levels of social functioning in the Formats. Invariably, there are staff who do not "buy in" to the program or lack skills to adequately coach learners to adhere to Rubric criteria. They eventually improve or leave the school. But in the meantime, learners in their class stand to lose invaluable learning opportunities. To that end, the Keepers of the Curriculum Corps, a group of learners nominated by their peers, is enlisted to help provide training support. The Curriculum Lead advises and works with the Curriculum Corps to push into classrooms to provide training. The Corps also assists to plan and present the New Learner Orientation at the beginning of the year. And they help to implement the emergent readers Daily To-do List curriculum (see Sparks, Chapter 5b).

Sufficiency Supplements

The Curriculum Lead coordinates with the Civil Rights Lead to co-direct the Sufficiency Supplements program to oversee curriculum quality (see Sufficiency Supplements in Chapter 22).

Year-Long Implementation Plan: Curriculum Lead

The Curriculum Lead executes the agenda that is outlined in Table 24.1.

Table 24.1 Curriculum project calendar actions

Calendar action	Calendar dates
Resource procurement (refer to Resources List, Appendix 34, www.routledge.com/9780367458591)	B3
Organize classroom environment preparation training session—delegate responsibility to department/grade teams to conduct classroom environment Rubric-based assessments	B1
Conduct Environment assessments of every classroom	B1
Calendar extracurricular rituals (book clubs, field trips, special guest visitors, movie nights)	B1
Coordinate Sparks, Learning Cultures and Keepers of the Culture orientation for new staff, in coordination with Training Lead	B1
Confirm all classrooms have Work Time/Sparks curricula prepared with a dozen standards-aligned activities per subject	B1
Co-plan the New Learner Curriculum Orientation with Training and Civil Rights Lead	Week 1
Organize New Learner Curriculum Orientation for kindergarten, Grade 3, Grade 6, Grade 9, and any learners who are new to the school community (curriculum covering Social Contract and Formats)	Week 1

(Continued)

Table 24.1 Curriculum project calendar actions *(Continued)*

Calendar action	Calendar dates
Coordinate with school administration and Curriculum Lead to implement Sufficiency Supplements (Extended-day Program)	Week 1
Maintain Sparks Activity Inventory	Ongoing
Implement Workout Plan protocol with bi-weekly Checkups for every learner	Week 2 and every two weeks thereafter
With Training Lead, coordinate Intervention training for new Keepers of the Curriculum Corps' members	Week 3
Convene bi-monthly Keepers of the Curriculum Corps meeting (identify Corps Lead)	Weeks 4, 6, 8, 10, 12, 14, 16, 18, 20, 22, 24, 26, 28, 30, 32, and 34
Calendar monthly Workshop of the Possible meetings with managers and PTA representatives	Weeks 2, 6, 10, 14, 18, 22, 26, 30, and 34
Collect writing portfolio pieces. Learner choice of topic/genre across CCSS domains of narrative, informative/explanatory, opinion (K–5)/argument (6–12) (two pieces from each domain by the end of the school year). Grades 4–8 include short research projects and grades 9–12 alternate short and sustained research projects	Week 2, 6, 10, 14, 18, 22, 26, 30, and 34
Oversee McCallister Assessments training (Cooperative Unison Reading Records, Portfolio Assessment, Learning Conference Record, Writing Conference Record, Workout Plan, Academic and Behavior Interventions)	One training per week, Weeks 1, 2, 3, 4, and 5
Supervise Learning Teams curriculum in grades 6–12 (calendar by tournament launch date/tournament finale date)	Weeks 2/7, 8/13, 14/19, 20/25, 26/31
Coordinate with Keepers of the Curriculum to organize meetings with emergent readers/writers in grades 2–12 for "Daily To-do List" training (see Sparks curriculum for instructions)	Week 3, and as needed for incoming students
Announce Learning Teams Champions	Weeks 8, 14, 20, 26, and 32
Create/update Learning Teams assessments in every state testing curriculum domain, grades 6–8 in English language arts and math, and in grades 9–12 in science, math, and history	Week 20
With School Management Team, review report cards and course syllabi for next academic year	Week 28
Update Field Education Archive	Week 30
Conduct Test Genre Curriculum Workshop	Three weeks prior to the state test
Cooperative Unison Reading Test Genre Curriculum, grades 3–5. Support staff to ensure that every learner has the opportunity to take part in the Test Genre Curriculum	Two weeks prior to state exams in English language arts and Math

Note: B3 means three weeks before school (week by which all resources are ordered).
B1 means one week before school (week by which all new staff are trained).

25 The School Culture Program

Introduction

The McCallister Model is structured around a Social Contract—the agreement among all of the members of the school community to forfeit some personal freedoms in order to benefit and be part of a larger group (Rousseau, 1920). Learners are free to exercise their fundamental freedoms of thought, movement, speech, and social affiliation so long as they conform to the norms specified in the Format Rubrics and responsibilities outlined in the school discipline code. As learners take part in the continuous and ongoing routines of the conventional practices of the Formats, strong classroom learning cultures develop around the shared values of liberty, equality, justice, and the common good.

Classroom cultures do not exist in isolation. They are elements within a layered organizational hierarchy that includes the school and the community beyond. In McCallister schools, the activities of classroom cultures are supported by the activities of the school culture, and vice versa. The objective of the school-wide social norms curriculum is to implement dual-level activity systems—those of the classroom and those of the school—that work reciprocally to cultivate the democratic values within the whole community.

School Culture Lead Responsibilities

The School Culture Lead, the school administration, and the Keepers of the Culture Corps are caretakers of the school-wide culture. They work collectively to implement activity systems designed to maintain healthy classroom-level cultures and to develop a coherent, egalitarian, and vibrant school culture. The School Culture Lead manages all of the systems of the Keepers of the Culture program, described in Chapter 18: the Social Contract Talk, the Ladder of Self-regulation, the 'On-call' Program, and the After-school Detention Program. The School Culture Lead should be thoroughly familiar with the Keepers of the Culture program.

Advisement

- Advise and provide leadership and oversight to the Keepers of the Culture Corps. Convene the first meeting of the year to delegate membership between Civil Rights Corps and Curriculum Corps and to establish bi-monthly meeting dates

Assessment and Data Monitoring

- Maintain Behavior Conference Records (look for behavioral outliers among learners and adults)
- Monitor attendance records to identify those who are chronically late or absent
- Maintain "On-call" database of staff requests to identify patterns in over-use, under-use, and submit monthly report to school administration
- Submit weekly report to school administration on Call Home and attendance records, and hallway citations

Behavior

- Plan the Social Contract Talk in coordination with the school administration, to be given on the first day of school. Take attendance and maintain records of those who have heard the Social Contract Talk
- Maintain updated Ladder of Self-regulation, modified annually after learner input from the Social Contract Talk
- Oversee After-school Detention Program
- Oversee "On-Call" System, providing continual staffing to provide classroom support in the event that back-up behavioral supports are needed in the classroom
- Oversee Hallway Curriculum (monitor hallway behavior; in coordination with school administration, assign Hallway Duty to staff; maintain Hallway Citation archive)

Governance

- Member, School Management Team
- Chair, School Culture Committee

McCallister Group

- Member, Project Team—interface with McCallister Group and participate in network-wide professional development

Training

- Oversee Keepers of the Culture curriculum training for learners and staff (in coordination with McCallister Group project team and Training Lead)

School Development

- Maintain the School Culture Office. The School Culture Office is a designated space in the school that serves as a base of operation for "On-call" services, Keepers of the Culture meetings, and Interventions
- Identify Keepers of the Culture Corps members who show potential to serve as Guides in the school upon graduation
- Manage Keepers of the Culture Corps nominations for both Keepers Corps and Curriculum Corps (Week 2). In the Fall, administer bi-annual Keepers of the Culture Survey to the full student body to nominate, in every age group, 10% of those who demonstrate leadership, compassion, responsibility, and wisdom. These learners will become the Keepers of the Culture Corps

334 *The Ecosystem Curriculum*

Table 25.1 School culture project calendar actions

Calendar action	Calendar dates
Organize Social Norms/Social Contract training to staff (coordinate with Training Lead)	B3
Organize School Culture Office	B1
Classroom environment checks to ensure signage is posted in every classroom: Ladder of Self-regulation, Students' Rights and Responsibilities, and Progressive Infraction and Response Levels	B1
Classroom environment checks for Rubric Binder, Share Protocols (posted on presentation podium or document camera), laminated Cooperative Unison Reading Rules and Rubrics (in every Cooperative Unison Reading Bin)	B1
Organize "On-call" system and notify staff of their responsibilities	B1
Organize Detention Program and notify staff of policy, procedures, and staffing	B1
Notify staff of Hallway Duty	B1
Organize the Social Contract Talk	Week 1
Analyze school-wide social norms data and submit report to school administration: Call Home records; Hallway Citations; attendance records, Behavior Conference Records; On-call records	Weekly
Administer Keepers of the Culture Survey and notify nominees	Week 1
Develop/update the Ladder of Self-regulation and distribute laminated copies to classrooms	Week 2
Civil Rights and Curriculum Director elections	Week 4
Keepers of the Culture Directors meeting	Weeks 5, 7, 9, 11, 13, 15, 17, 19, 21, 23, 25, 27, 29, 31, 33, and 35 (alternating schedule with Keepers Corps meeting)
Nominate graduating seniors for potential Guide position	Week 30

Note: B3 means three weeks before school.
B1 means one week before school.

Year-Long Implementation Plan: School Culture Lead

The School Culture Lead executes the agenda that is outlined in Table 25.1.

26 The Training Program

Introduction

Teacher professional development within the industrial school is typically approached in a topical fashion, targeting methods of content delivery, and neglecting to attend to the underlying beliefs and intentions that teachers bring to their work (McCallister, 2010). The curriculum in the McCallister Method is the cultural habitus of *practices*; therefore, training in the practices—for teachers as well as students—is the fulcrum of school transformation. Successful implementation of the method depends on learners and adults assuming responsibility to their roles as participants in the Formats. The Training Lead manages that initiative.

Training Lead Responsibilities

Assessment and Recordkeeping

- Maintain records of staff participation in training initiatives
- Maintain archive of Professional Development surveys and assessments

Learner Training

- Organize, with support from Civil Rights and Curriculum Lead, the New Student Curriculum Orientation
- Coordinate with Curriculum Lead to schedule Keepers of the Curriculum training
- Coordinate with Civil Rights Lead to schedule Keepers Corps training

McCallister Group

- Member, Project Team—interface with McCallister Group and participate in network-wide professional development.

Professional Development

- Director, Professional Development Committee (a team convened by the school administration to assist in the school-wide training initiative)
- Organize and manage two-day McCallister Professional Development Orientation before school opening
- Administer Professional Development Survey every eight weeks
- Analyze Survey results in a report to school administration with recommendations to address staff's perceived needs (planning in coordination with McCallister)

- Identify Anchor Classrooms (in coordination with school administration and Curriculum Lead)
- Organize professional development support to staff in immediate need of improvement (identified through first round of administrative evaluations)
- Plan and orchestrate training opportunities every eight weeks, informed by Professional Development Survey, in coordination with school administration and McCallister Project Team (Monthly Training Workshop; Lab Sites; Residencies; Assessment Workshops; Study Groups)
- Coordinate with school administration, Curriculum Lead, and McCallister Group project team to identify staff members who show promise of exemplary practice to receive training, serve as mentors, and host Lab Sites and Intervisitations
- Identify and recruit staff to present at monthly Open House presentations
- Facilitate Inquiry Team process to support required bi-monthly self-assessment (self-organized teams in which "you observe me, I observe you, and we debrief")
- Follow up with school administration after formal observation cycles to identify professional development needs as they arise
- Identify emerging expertise and provide professional development support to develop the next generation of coaches

School Governance

- Chair, Professional Development Team
- Member, School Management Team

The McCallister Framework for Professional Development

Professional development in schools is traditionally designed to support training in methods of knowledge transmission, which is targeted to meet the levels and needs of various subgroups in the school. The industrial design of schools makes it impossible to manage and fund consistent, ongoing professional development support for all of the programs in the school, so typically only reading and math instruction programs receive attention. Since unique design of the McCallister Model supports *human development*, rather than the development of *content knowledge*, and all staff adhere to the same procedures, it creates the possibility for a universal training program that spans across all programs in the school.

The Framework for Professional Development (FPD) (McCallister, 2009a, 2011a) is a one-of-a-kind, whole-school approach to improvements in professional practice. It provides a system of inter-related initiatives that are incorporated into the bureaucratic systems of the school and transform the industrial school into a learning organization. These initiatives provide an infrastructure that is used by staff to take part in clinical experiences that emphasize action-inquiry, self-reflection, and self-regulation. The FPD includes the following components:

- Online learning from seven and half hours of explainer videos produced by the author that cover each of the Learning Cultures Formats
- Inquiry groups
- Lab sites, in which new practices are demonstrated in anchor classrooms
- Collaborative peer residencies
- Formal evaluations that are linked to Rubric criteria and provide constructive and corrective feedback

- Teacher-to-teacher feedback using the Rubrics as a norming tool
- Study groups that focus on the McCallister Methods canon, a reading list of articles and papers that unpack the philosophical and theoretical ideas implicit in the model

The FPD is a child of necessity that I developed while working in a PK-8 school in Manhattan to implement the Genre Practice reading and writing programs, where the PD infrastructure was organized by grade-level teams, and where cliques had developed to varying degrees within them. The grade-level training infrastructure presented certain challenges. In some cases, resistance within the cliques limited the potential to secure changes in classroom practice. Also, each team was essentially its own subculture, and the prospect of securing change in two programs—reading and writing—across eight subcultures was unsustainable.

Sustainability

The FPD is a solution to a design challenge. It is a system that provides the same integrated system of support to teachers at all grades, transcending grade-level subcultures, and laterally and evenly distributing knowledge and expertise that is provided from within the PD infrastructure. Grade-level subcultures in schools are spaces of comfort and security, and invariably there is resistance by some to move outside them. Initially, when the principal at the PK-8 Jacob Riis School where my methods were implemented pitched the FPD to the school professional development committee, she related to me that they did not seem ready to embrace it because they were overwhelmed by it and felt they were not ready to collaborate and learn because the culture was not yet safe (Kerry Decker, personal communication, September 11, 2008). This concern mirrors a universal challenge in school turnaround, wherein the norms of the industrial school favor privacy and autonomy over collaboration and lack of trust amongst stakeholders (Peurach & Neumerski, 2015). We nonetheless began implementing the FPD to scale on a gradual basis throughout the course of the year, and the FPD itself was a catalyst that influenced the development of trust, collaboration, and a positive school culture. The FPD provided a way to break up the grade-team juggernaut and promoted a more democratic, egalitarian school learning culture characterized by the fluidity of knowledge and freer forms of association.

A universal approach to PD also has monetary advantages: it reduces the amount of external training support required to maintain quality instruction; and it reduces the amount of time and expense of administrative instructional supervision. At the Jacob Riis School, featured in Section III of this book, prior to implementation of the FPD, the school spent over $360K per year on professional development consultants who worked individually with teachers on a one-on-one basis in classrooms. In 2009–2010, after implementation of the FPD, these costs were reduced to $90K (See McCallister, 2011a). The FPD creates a sustainable professional development infrastructure that allows the school to become relatively independent of the need for support by external contract vendors.

Framework for Professional Development Components

Project Coaching

Seeding the McCallister Model in a new school always begins with classroom-based demonstrations and training in the model. Staff members are recruited who show interest in the model and have a positive orientation toward the opportunity to provide leadership in the school. Once trained in the practices, these teachers open their doors to others, who then open their doors to others. At the heart of the FPD is a "train the trainer" model of professional learning. In the schools featured in Section III where my model was implemented, I trained staff and principals, who then became the source of expertise within the training infrastructure to train others through lab sites, intervisitations, and residencies. Project expertise invested in staff becomes human capital within the infrastructure of the FPD.

At Urban Assembly School for Green Careers, High School of Language and Innovation, and the other schools where I worked to implement my model, I provided support to teachers by demonstrating them in the classroom, handing over responsibility, then coaching them existentially in the context of practice. My coaching support was targeted at teachers who had strong potential to quickly master the practices and share their knowledge, and their rooms then became Anchor Classrooms where we hosted lab sites.

Orientation

Prior to the school year, staff take part in a training orientation. The orientation agenda includes demonstrations of practices, opportunities for those new to the program to take part in the Formats, more than seven hours of explainer videos that describe each of the Formats, and other activities that help staff prepare for the upcoming year (see Box 26.1).

Box 26.1

McCallister orientation agenda

Read Rubrics in unison (identify work to be completed before school begins)
Review Sparks curriculum and the Activity Inventory
Learn the practices of the Keepers of the Culture program
Create Genre Collections
Organize Inquiry Teams
Prepare classroom learning environments
Discuss expectations of the Framework for Professional Development, teacher evaluation, and personal professional development plans (Teacher Workout Plans)
Watch training videos
View classroom slideshows
Review McCallister assessment forms

Evaluation

Traditionally, teacher evaluation is wholly evaluative. The administrator observes and, using a formal rating system, assigns a rating. The McCallister teacher evaluation system is designed to be formative, providing feedback to staff that supports the development of exemplary practice. The school's teacher evaluation system is based entirely upon the McCallister practices. School leaders, trained in the practices, use the Rubrics and their indicators as evaluative criteria. After each formal observation, the staff member meets with a school administrator during a brief *Check In* to complete a Staff Conference Record, which specifies a course of action to meet goals identified in the observation (see Appendix 36, www.routledge.com/9780367458591).

Over the course of four evaluation cycles throughout the year, staff are provided with a constant source of competence feedback that is actionable and can be used meaningfully to develop competence. Using this feedback, staff members create their own professional learning program based on a menu of in-house training options from the FPD. The observation-evaluation-feedback-learning cycle leverages improvements in professional practice, which results in positive achievement in learners.

Holistic Assessment of Professional Learning

In Week 8, staff take a self-assessment using the Holistic Assessment of Professional Learning (see Appendix 37, www.routledge.com/9780367458591). This measure assesses agency, intentionality, learning mindset, and understanding of human development. The evaluative discourse of this assessment is presented in Box 26.2. These assessments

---

Box 26.2

Holistic assessment of professional learning

- **Exemplary.** Teacher invites critical feedback as a means to constantly improve practice. Demonstrates sophisticated level of critical awareness of professional practice and continually develops by setting and meeting goals for improvement. Conveys understanding of and implications for the principle that students have the ability to carry out their own intentions as a means to reaching high learning standards, and strives to master practices that allow students to exercise agency and responsibility. Solid understanding of and demonstrated commitment to the theory and philosophy of the instructional model. Teacher's action plan for professional development is consistently ambitious, demonstrated by a willingness to participate in continuing education and peer-mentoring opportunities and to offer leadership to the community in the area of professional development.
- **Acceptable.** Teacher is mostly receptive to feedback and attempts to respond by making changes in practice. Demonstrates willingness to critically examine and identify areas of practice in need of improvement. Conveys appreciation that students have the ability to carry out their own intentions as a means to reaching high learning standards, and is willing to take initiative to learn practices that allow students to exercise agency and responsibility. Developing or limited understanding of and/or commitment to the theory and philosophy of the school's instructional model. Action plan for professional development generally demonstrates a commitment to growth.
- **Progressing.** Teacher is usually receptive to feedback but responds inconsistently and fails to successfully make changes in practice. Lacks willingness to critically examine and identify areas of practice in need of improvement. Conveys an appreciation that students have the ability to carry out their own intentions as a means to reaching high learning standards, but has difficulty implementing practices that allow students to exercise agency and responsibility. Minimal understanding of and/or commitment to the theory and philosophy of the schools' instructional model. Action plan for professional development lacks evidence of a commitment to growth.
- **Unsatisfactory.** Teacher is unreceptive to feedback. Limited changes in practice reflect an unwillingness to respond to feedback. Demonstrates lack of critical self-reflection and is unable to identify substantive areas of practice in need of improvement. Actions convey a lack of confidence in students' ability to carry out their own intentions as a means to reaching high learning standards and an unwillingness to learn practices that allow students to exercise agency and responsibility. Lacks understanding of and/or commitment to the theory and philosophy of the school's instructional model. Action plan for professional development is generally unambitious.

are an ideal topic of discussion in professional development meeting. The point is that the process adheres to the principles for how norms are internalized—by holding a rule in mind and then bending activity to incorporate the rule. Category 4 represents the norms we need to see in practice in order for learners to reach their potential.

Staff members discuss their ratings with the school administration in their Cycle 2 Check In. It is expected that administrative perceptions of strengths and needs align with those of the staff member him or herself, confirmation that expectations for high levels of professional practice are objectively shared and not biased or personal. Staff who are rated unsatisfactory are expected to correct areas of need at a swift rate of improvement, within two weeks.

Needs Assessment Survey

A Needs Assessment Survey is administered at the beginning of the year, which provides information about which aspects of McCallister practice should be emphasized in planning the training agenda (see Appendix 40, www.routledge.com/9780367458591). The Training Lead administers, analyzes data, and reports the results to the school leadership and the Professional Development Committee, who then establish an eight-week Phase I training plan to determine the first cycle of lab sites, residencies, and study groups. This process is repeated in each of the three subsequent evaluation cycles, continually revising FPD offerings.

Professional Personalized Learning Plan

Traditionally, PD is *given* in the same way that traditional lessons are *given*, as if expertise can be transmitted. The McCallister approach to professional learning is through the cultivation of intentions and supports to ensure they are carried out. Every staff member is responsible for designing their own professional learning plan based on their intentions using opportunities afforded in the FPD. The Staff Workout Plan provides an opportunity to explore personal values and intentions as they relate to the educational program and provide a way to think about goals for professional development as the expression of agency in carrying out intentions (see Appendix 41, www.routledge.com/9780367458591). Professional learning plans outline how staff assume their professional responsibilities outlined in Table 26.1.

Table 26.1 Staff expectations for professional learning

Obligation	Date
McCallister Project Orientation	Before school begins
Professional Development Survey	Quarterly
Holistic Assessment of Professional Learning	Week 8
Professional Portfolio	Ongoing
Study group participation	Voluntary
Self-assessment and Professional Action Plan	Quarterly
Presenter, Monthly Training Workshops	Voluntary
Presenter, Monthly Open House	Voluntary
Intervisitations, Lab Sites, and Study Groups	Optional
Residencies	As needed as per administration recommendation
Professional Development Improvement Survey	Ongoing, four times annually, in Professional Development Cycles

Inquiry Teams, Lab Sites, and Intervisitations

Inquiry teams and lab sites are the heart of the FPD. Staff members self-select into cross-grade/subject inquiry groups based on a dimension of McCallister practice that they want to improve. Inquiry teams remain together for a period of a month, during which time they participate together to take part in lab sites and other learning experiences.

The lab site follows a predictable Format in which the group visits the host classroom and takes part in a follow-up debrief session. The Labsite Observation Protocol is used to structure the Lab Site agenda (see Appendix 35 (www.routledge.com/9780367458591) and Figure 26.1). The Protocol is organized around a specific Format for observation. Participants review of the relevant Rubric and take part in observation and data gathering ("Circles of Evidence"). In the debrief, participants provide "Circles of Feedback," in which the observer provides constructive feedback using what's referred to as the X, Y, C Rule ("X counts as Y in context C," as proposed by John Searle, 2010) (see Box 26.3) (Searle, 2010). Those interested in participating in Lab Sites sign up on a voluntary basis

---

learning cultures

Observation Protocol

Teacher:_____ Date:_____

Overview:
Use this protocol as a tool to reflect on professional practice.

Roles:
Facilitator: Keeps time and facilitates the discussion, holding group members to agreed up norms.
Note taker: Takes responsibility for documenting discussion.
Observers: Follow protocol.

Protocol:

Establish the "unit of analysis": Determine what phenomenon (Format) will be the focus of observation. In a Lab Site, the focus of analysis will usually have been previously determined.

Establish Observation activity timeline (as per suggestions. below).

Review the Rubric(s) (5 minutes or less): Read relevant criteria from the focus Format Rubric.

Circles of Evidence (5-10 minutes): Observe Format activity. Reference observations to Rubric criteria. Take relevant notes.

Circles of Feedback (5-10 minutes): Provide constructive feedback to the staff member using an X, Y, C rule[1] ("X counts as Y in context C"). For example, in **C** (focus Format), **X** (behavior specified in the Rubric) counts as **Y** (desirable/competent/expected).

  For example, to be a proficient guide (Y) in the context of the Writing Share Format (C), according to rubric criteria, the presenter should *secure audience members' attention*, and the *audience should appear engaged and attentive* (X) in order to participate according to criteria outlined in the Share Rubric (Y). Guides (X) are proficient (Y) in Share contexts in which presenters manage their audience, and audience members are attentive. Give feedback in relation to the X, Y & C rule. For example, "In the Share Format (C), I noticed the presenter continued presenting even when there were side conversations in the audience. The quality of the Share would improve if presenters were taught strategies to manage audience attention and if the class were reminded of their responsibilities as audience members."

Strategy discussion (10 minutes): This is a free-form conversation to share ideas, apply insights from the observation activity, and discuss general "take-aways."

Commitments to Practice (3 minutes): Participants take turns sharing one new strategy they intend to commit to their practice.

Protocol Tuning (2 minutes): Briefly debrief the Observation process and make a commitment to improvement for next time.

---

[1] The X, Y, C Rule is inspired by the philosopher John Searle's explanation of the status function declaration as a reality-creating linguistic device. See *Making the Social World* (2010), published by Oxford University Press.
© 2012 2020 Cynthia McCallister All Rights Reserved

Figure 26.1 Learning Cultures Format Observation Protocol

> **Box 26.3**
>
> **The X, Y, C Rule**
>
> The "X, Y, C Rule" is inspired by John Searle's (2010) explanation for how status function declarations (SFDs) work. A SFD is a way of using speech that functions to create a reality by describing it. Laws, store coupons, insurance policies, marriage certificates are all examples of SFDs because they create a certain reality by describing it. Human civilization, as Searle points out, is built on SFDs.
>
> SFDs can be described using this shorthand: "X counts as Y in context C" (Searle, p. 101). The X, Y, C Rule can be useful for the purpose of transformative assessment. For example, to be a proficient guide (Y) in the context of the Writing Share Format (C), according to Rubric criteria, the presenter should secure audience members' attention, and the audience should appear engaged and attentive (X) in order to participate according to criteria outlined in the Share Rubric (Y). Guides (X) are proficient (Y) in Share contexts in which presenters manage their audience, and audience members are attentive. Give feedback in relation to the X, Y, C Rule. For example, "In the Share Format (C), I noticed the presenter continued presenting even when there were side conversations in the audience. The quality of the Share would improve if presenters were taught strategies to manage audience attention and if the class were reminded of their responsibilities as audience members."

during their preparation periods (substitute teacher coverage may be provided in special circumstances based on approval by the school administration). Four cycles of Lab Sites are scheduled each year (each cycle might include multiple Lab Sites offered on a staggered schedule). *Intervisitation* opportunities are more informal classroom learning opportunities, in which individual teachers select to voluntarily visit host classrooms to jointly participate in practices with the Host, be provided existential coaching support, and learn strategies to improve practice.

Curriculum in the McCallister Model derives from activity in the Formats. Formats *are* the curriculum, and the Rubrics are the *lesson plans*. Training in the practices of the Formats, therefore, replaces lesson planning. Since training is the equivalent of preparation, staff are expected to use their prep time to take part in lab sites. If union contracts present an obstacle to professional planning within the McCallister paradigm, subs are needed to provide coverage.

Assessment Workshops

Equality of educational opportunity is achieved in the McCallister program through a system that grants rights to learners to participate in the Formats to an extent that is sufficient to the development of their potential. Assessment records are used to document these opportunities. As means of accountability, the school administration issues opportunity targets, which specify how many of each assessment should be completed by the end of each year, and conducts periodic assessment reviews in order to ensure learners' rights are being met. The Training Lead works in coordination with the Curriculum Lead to offer training workshops to new staff and those who need support in using the McCallister assessments to make judgments about learners' development in the domains of math, reading, and writing.

Broadcast Professional Development

Broadly relevant professional development concerns are noted and addressed through the school director's weekly newsletter (issues are typically identified through observations, informal building walk-throughs, and communication from McCallister Project Team).

Monthly Training Workshops

The Training Lead recruits volunteers who have demonstrated exemplary levels of professional practice to present at the monthly Training Workshop. Workshops are an hour in length, and follow a protocol whereby the focus Format is identified, the relevant portion of the Format Rubric is examined, a profile of activity or a work sample is shared, and follow-up discussion is facilitated.

Support for New Staff and Staff in Need of Additional Support

New staff and staff identified to be in need of additional support (e.g., those rated "unsatisfactory") are matched with experienced mentors in order to receive consistent and frequent coaching. Working in teams, the team observes in one another's classrooms. New staff gain insight from observing experienced teacher's practice and is provided corrective feedback from the experienced teacher. New staff receive a month of informal mentoring prior to their first formal observation.

Professional Development Improvement Survey

Staff perceptions are a critical factor in determining the efficacy of the reform effort. At the end of each year, the Training Lead administers the Professional Development Improvement Survey to ascertain the degree to which the FPD met staff needs and how well they perceived the program supported growth in both learner and staff independence and competence. The Survey is analyzed to determine training program modifications for the future.

Residencies

Staff identified to be in need of significant levels of support have opportunities for classroom residencies in which a Project coach or fellow teacher embeds in the classroom to provide demonstrations and scaffolded support (e.g., those who have been observed and whose performance has been rated unsatisfactory or those who have difficulty securing necessary changes in practice).

Study Groups

Study Groups provide opportunities to deeply explore topics identified as necessary for further professional development. They are formed based on popular interest in addressing problems of practice or to conduct action inquiry. Staff are encouraged to initiate their own study groups.

Public Information Presentations

Staff are encouraged to volunteer to present at monthly school Open House events. When I worked with teachers at the Jacob Riis School, I regularly involved teachers in presentations that I organized at the school, the university where I work, and national education conferences. These dissemination opportunities were a way to cultivate expertise in the school. Public presentations as a strategy for professional learning is incorporated into the school's monthly

Improvement Survey

In the final month of school, a Professional Development Improvement Survey is administered (see Appendix 42, www.routledge.com/9780367458591) (McCallister, 2010). The Survey solicits information about the degree to which the McCallister curriculum and the FPD functioned for the previous year to support learning for adults and learners. The Training Lead administers, analyzes, and reports results to the school administration, and they meet to discuss results and implications for next year's professional development program.

Survey results serve two purposes. First, data are used formatively to identify aspects of the program that worked and those that need improvement. Second, they provide evidence for the School Narrative. Institutional change is fraught with politics and negative gossip generated by disgruntled staff that implicates a new initiative can achieve the status of objective knowledge unless it is countered. Data from the Survey, which are invariably overwhelmingly positive, become part of the School Narrative, confirming that planned change results in positive outcomes. These data also can be used as evidence to justify the change effort to stakeholders outside of the school, which is useful when outsiders are against the initiative.

Year-Long Implementation Plan: Training Lead

The Training Lead executes the agenda that is outlined in Table 26.4.

Table 26.4 Training project calendar actions

Calendar action	Calendar dates
Organize and manage two-day McCallister Professional Development Orientation for new staff	B2
Administer PD Survey Needs Assessment	Weeks 1, 9, 17, 25
In consultation with Curriculum Lead, Civil Rights Lead, Keepers Corps, and Keepers of the Curriculum Chairs, hold New Learner Curriculum Orientation for kindergarten, Grade 3, Grade 6, Grade 9, and any learners who are new to the school community (curriculum covering Social Contract and Formats), in coordination with Curriculum Lead (who manages Orientation content)	Week 1
Identify anchor classrooms	Week 2
Communicate with administration to create a training program for staff identified to be in need of immediate improvement and coordinate coaching support	Week 2
Organize Keepers of the Culture Corp and Keepers of the Curriculum Corp training (in coordination with Civil Rights and Curriculum Leads)	Week 3
Analyze Professional Development Survey results and submit a report of findings and recommendations to school administration and McCallister Project Team	Weeks 2, 10, 18, 26
Plan Professional Development Cycle (in coordination with school administration and McCallister Program Team) to include weekly lab sites, residencies, intervisitations, and study groups	To begin Weeks 3, 11, 19, 26
Co-plan Monthly Open House curriculum presentations with Community Education Lead	Monthly
Identify emerging professional talent in staff who show promise of exemplary practice (in coordination with school administration and McCallister Project Team)	Ongoing
Facilitate and support Inquiry Team process (monitor Portfolios and execution of bi-monthly assessment)	Ongoing
Recruit staff to present at Open House and Monthly Training Workshops	Ongoing
Administer end-of-year PD Improvement Survey	Week 30

Note: B2 means two weeks before school begins.

Section VI
Existence Proof

27 There *Are* Learning Cultures

Introduction

The McCallister Model is the culminating project of a three-decade action research program that began when I started my career as a new teacher in rural Maine and continued to work in more than 20 Title I schools in New York City. This chapter provides a summary of implementation efforts of the Model in six schools and reports student achievement outcomes.

The Research Problem

My research program grew from these assertions: (1) Education in a democracy should function to equalize social opportunity so that educational outcomes and life chances they afford are not determined by circumstances of birth; and, (2) Equality of educational opportunity inheres in the capacity of formal pedagogy to provide the learner with experiences that are sufficient to enable the achievement of their highest potential. As discussed in Chapter 2, our existing system of education is dedicated to a commitment of social equality but so far has failed to close achievement gaps due to social inequality. In my school-based research program, I have sought to develop an educational model that succeeds in closing the achievement gap. This chapter provides an account of my work in schools where the model succeeded in equalizing educational opportunity.

The Research Questions

The research questions that drove my inquiry were the following: (1) What is the nature of pedagogical practices that might function to equalize social opportunity? (2) How can equitable practices be implemented on a large enough scale to serve as a potential solution to the problem of social inequality in education? (3) What implications for the future of American educational reform can be wrought from this experiment?

The Research Design

Starting in 1996, I embedded as a practitioner in NYC public schools as a literacy staff developer and through the course of the next two-and-a-half decades worked with educators to improve educational practice and student achievement outcomes. This process unfolded over three decades, starting in my first year of classroom teaching, and extending through my work in 23 Title I schools in NYC. Through a Lewian-spiral (1946) of planning and designing educational methods and organizational systems to support them, taking action to implement new designs, analyzing outcomes, and refining and documenting the practices as they evolved, the McCallister Model was born.

My research was built on this logic: if higher mental functions are the outcome of social participation of a certain kind, it is possible to manipulate classroom environments and social activities so that they result in targeted forms of higher-level thinking (Vygotsky, 1978), and it is possible to restructure the bureaucratic systems of schools in ways that support targeted activities so that they are available to all in sufficient number and quality to maximize every child's learning potential. I came to understand that formal learning is most strongly influenced by the extent to which the learning person has an autonomy to select their own experiences and through opportunities to coordinate perspectives with others, and I refined practices to incorporate these opportunities.

As I became more enlightened about the self-directed nature of learning, I refined my research questions to consider how learning environments can be organized to enable learners to achieve intended learning outcomes through self-organized interactions with peers and minimal reliance on teachers.

Positionality

I am a teacher educator by profession. Since 1998, I have worked at New York University as a professor of literacy education, where I teach emerging teachers. Being a professor is my full-time job, but I am also an educational consultant. For most of the 25 years I have lived in NYC, I routinely consulted with schools at the request of principals to help them improve their school's literacy achievement outcomes. But action research is a project of pragmatism. I was recruited to work in these schools because educational leaders sought my expertise to achieve the outcomes they wanted.

I began my work in NYC public schools at the start of the comprehensive school reform movement in a school that was funded through New Visions for Public Schools, a private foundation that supports small schools in NYC. Later, under the administration of Mayor Bloomberg, when NYC DOE policy emphasized innovation, accountability, and high achievement, my services grew in demand. I provided a number of schools with literacy program supports that they wanted and needed in order to improve achievement in their schools. This chapter provides case reports of several schools where I worked to implement my model as both a literacy program intervention and a model for comprehensive school reform.

I am a mother of three. All of my children attended NYC public schools. In total, my children have spent 34 years in 11 different NYC public schools. Through this experience, I was faced with countless challenges to overcome the negative consequences of schooling on my children's development. With each new challenge, I had reason to improve my understanding of human development and cause to refine my model.

Setting the Research Stage: The New York City Department of Education

The NYC DOE is the largest, most diverse educational system in the United States. The NYC DOE became my educational laboratory when, in 1996, I moved with my family to Washington Heights. My children, then ages five and six, started school at P.S./I.S. 176, the W. Haywood Burns School, in the Inwood section of Manhattan. The school, named in honor of the late Haywood Burns, a human rights activist, housed three small schools. The Lower School included Muscota New School, founded in 1993, which served a population of students who were mostly White, from middle-class families. The Lower School also included Amistad, a dual-language school that served a population of mostly Spanish-speaking children from low-SES families of Dominican descent. My own children attended Amistad. The W. Haywood Burns campus also housed the W. Haywood Burns Middle School, which served a predominately Hispanic population from low-SES families.

Soon after the school year started, I was invited by the principal to work in a formal capacity to assist the administration and teachers of Amistad and the middle school to implement my school-wide literacy program. The program was an early version of the McCallister Model, consisting of Activity Blocks in both Reading and Writing. Blocks were centered around autonomously selected activity choices that enabled learners to enjoy maximal freedom of movement, expression, and social affiliation. The Blocks ended with a whole-group gathering in which one child shared their work. To support classroom change, I organized a standing teacher inquiry group. I devised a professional development model that combined inquiry-based learning with weekly classroom-based professional development support.

The W. Haywood Burns School initiative was funded by New Visions for Public Schools, a New York City-based school reform organization that began in 1989 to support innovation within the NYC public school system. The original aim of New Visions for Public Schools was to fund and support innovation in the public system, but it has since become a large service operator with a network of 71 public schools. My involvement with the Haywood Burns School lasted over a period of three years.

Part of my work on the Haywood Burns initiative was supported by a post-doctoral fellowship opportunity from the Spencer Foundation, which enabled me to take part in their Scholar Development Program. The Spencer Foundation is a non-profit organization that invests in research to cultivate learning and transform lives (SpencerFoundation.org). Through this fellowship, I had the opportunity to be mentored by the legendary civil rights activist and psychologist, Edmund W. Gordon, who became a thought partner and would, for the next two-and-a-half decades, help me sharpen the focus of my work to address concerns that had defined his own life's work: how can pedagogy be conceptualized in a way that enables teachers to respond to all manifestations of human diversity? How can systems of teaching, learning, and assessment—what Professor Gordon refers to as the *pedagogical troika*—be employed to create a schooling system that ensures every child's right to an education on equal terms? Equality can only be achieved, Gordon reasons, if inputs are sufficient to result in equal outputs. How can an educational system be designed in order to ensure inputs are sufficient to result in the equality of educational opportunity?

Professor Gordon visited the Haywood Burns School one day in 1998. In our debrief, he sagely reflected on what he had witnessed. He said, in essence, *It looked good. The students seemed engaged. You'll have something if you can show they have achieved.* His words have stayed with me over these long years. And through all my work in schools, I have made every effort to adjust my methods in ways that make a difference on educational outcomes.

The work at the Haywood Burns School was not impactful. While all of the teachers initially voiced support for the program and commitment to implement changes that had been agreed-upon, only a few implemented the new model with fidelity. Ultimately, the principal dismissed my suggestion to hold teachers accountable for implementing changes as a strategy for fidelity.

My initiative came to a halt in 1999 when the school's founding principal was replaced with a leader who was not committed to the program and was concerned with teaching methods that more explicitly focused on improving test scores. After ending my involvement with the Haywood Burns School, I spent the next few years developing the theoretical foundation of my emergent whole-school literacy education model and working toward tenure at New York University.[1,2]

NYC School Reform

In 2002, the NYC Board of Education was reorganized and placed under mayoral control. Community School Districts were eliminated and the system was centralized under the new Department of Education. These Bloomberg-era reforms included greater autonomy to principals for curriculum, professional development and hiring, stronger measures of school accountability, closure of large, under-performing high schools, and the creation of small high schools (O'Day, Bitter, & Gomez, 2011). At the beginning of 2007, I resumed work in the field, where I would again partner with schools but now within a new space for reform in the City that permitted principals to make decisions about curriculum, training, and teacher evaluation, all of which held potential to become instrumental in seeding and sustaining change.

Within the context of an NYC DOE space now open to outside innovation, I was recruited by an educational service provider to work with three NYC schools—P.S. 35 in Staten Island, the early childhood center of P.S. 235 in Canarsie, Brooklyn, and the Jacob Riis School, P.S./I.S. 126, in Lower Manhattan. In each school, I worked across all classrooms, helping the teachers to replace their existing literacy programs with the Formats of my model. The P.S. 35 and 235 collaborations extended through the 2007–2008 school year, but the Jacob Riis partnership would last through Spring 2011.

The Jacob Riis School: P.S./I.S. 126

The Jacob Riis School is a public Pre-K through 8th grade school in Lower Manhattan, comprising two school populations. The elementary school, Primary School 126 (P.S. 126), serves children from the local neighborhood, including those who live in public housing projects on the block surrounding the school and children from the surrounding neighborhood of Chinatown. The school also serves the homeless shelter adjacent to the school. The population of the middle school, called the Manhattan Academy of Technology (MAT), includes children who matriculate from the elementary school as well as those who apply for admission from other schools. MAT is more economically and culturally diverse (see Table 27.1 for school census data).

In 2007, the school received a "C" on its annual report card. While the school's overall proficiency rates in English language arts (ELA) and math were in the 60th percentiles in relation to other schools citywide, progress levels of the lowest third placed the school at 36% citywide in ELA and 24% in math. Since these school-wide averages conflate

Table 27.1 Jacob Riis school census data

Elementary School census data			
Poverty			
87.30% Free Meal	6.18% Reduced Meal	6.18% Full Meal	
Race			
57.60% Asian	29.00% Hispanic	10.50% Black	2.60% White
Middle School census data			
Poverty			
48.99% Free meal	8.41% Reduced meal	42.50% Full meal	
Race			
36.40% Asian	22.00% Hispanic	13.10% Black	29.00% White

Source: Unison Reading: Socially Inclusive Group Instruction for Equity and Achievement (McCallister, 2011a).

performance of students in the more affluent middle school with that of students in the lower SES elementary school, it could be inferred that achievement performance of elementary students was significantly lower. It seemed that the school's "inputs" of the units-of-study writing program and the leveled approach to group reading instruction were insufficient in the achievement of equitable outcomes.

In my initial meeting with the principal, Kerry Decker, I described the principles of my whole-school model. She hired me to implement the program in all K-5 classrooms and middle school ELA programs. Within two months, the program was implemented in most classrooms where every child was provided 45 minutes a day to write on topics of their choice, collaborate with peers, and share their writing. The program, which I called Genre Practice (McCallister, 2008a, 2011a, 2011b),[3] helped learners become more engaged, independent, and productive. Positive changes in achievement were reflected in the 2008 achievement data, where now the school's citywide ranking in overall ELA proficiency had climbed by 5 points to 72% and in math proficiency 15 points to 81%. The school rose from a ranking of 36th to 82nd citywide in ELA and from 47th to 82nd percentile citywide in ELA and from 47th to 69th percentile citywide in math. Even more dramatic gains in achievement were observed in the school's citywide ranking in measures of growth in academic performance of the lowest third, climbing 25% to a ranking of 61% citywide in ELA and climbing 38% to a ranking of 52% citywide in math. These dramatic gains reflected in the school report card were replicated in a comparative study of Jacob Riis student achievement gains through 2007–2012 to 5,000 students in 10 other schools.[4]

While my work during the first year in the school focused on the writing program implementation, the principal enlisted me to work with teachers to incorporate my methods into the school's reading program in 2008–2009. By April of 2009, I had introduced the Unison Reading (McCallister, 2011a) method and the other reading program Formats to all teachers in the school. Learners responded well to the reading program, demonstrating engagement, independence, and productivity. Most teachers adhered to the guidelines of my program, but there were pockets of teacher resistance, resulting in the practices not being implemented with fidelity.

In order to improve the use of evaluation to achieve the changes specified in my model, I devised a formal teacher evaluation system directly aligned with pedagogical practices from my model. The Danielson Framework for teacher effectiveness had been adopted by the teacher education program at NYU. The Framework offers descriptive criteria for teaching effectiveness but intentionally avoids recommendations linked to any single pedagogical model. In other words, the tool provides a language for what effective practice achieves without prescribing what should be done in order to achieve it. This limits the possibility of using evaluation as a tool to leverage specific changes in practice. I helped the principal create an evaluation tool adapted from Danielson that incorporated indicators of effectiveness described by the procedures and expectations from my model.

In April of 2009, the school administration mandated Formats from my reading and writing programs, including four weekly Unison Reading opportunities for each child at all grade levels (McCallister, 2011a) and two monthly Writing Shares. The administration also began to conduct formal evaluations using the new observation framework, enacting a system of accountability based on my application of Edmund Gordon's sufficiency of educational opportunity tenet.

When I was asked by the principal to work with all of the ELA teachers in the school to implement my model in the ELA program in all classrooms in the 2009–2010 school year, I accepted the challenge on two conditions: first, that a comprehensive assessment system should be implemented in order to document achievement trends; and second, that teachers would be accountable for implementing basic program components, including a Work

Time block in both reading and writing programs, four sessions of Unison Reading per week (two supervised by a teacher and two independent), a Writing Conference, a Reading Conference, and a Share at the conclusion of every Activity Block.[5,6] A number of teachers who were averse to the accountability expectations of the program opted to take positions in other schools, but most teachers approved of the program, as results of the school-wide survey of teachers indicated (McCallister, 2009a). I also proposed the school implement my school-wide Framework for Professional Development (FPD) (McCallister, 2009a) in order to more systematically support the training needs of all teachers.[7,8]

Achievement trends reported in the school's 2009 annual report card continued to confirm the efficacy of my model. Measures of achievement of the school's lowest third continued to grow. The school's citywide ranking for the average change in proficiency for students in the lowest third making at least one-year progress in ELA rose by 8 points to 69%; and the average change in proficiency for students in the lowest third making at least one-year progress in math rose by 37 points to 89%. Not only did the lowest achieving students appear to be flourishing in the curriculum, but also the high-performing students did. The average change in proficiency for Level 3 and 4 students grew from 83% citywide to 100% citywide in ELA.

The methods of my program, which guarantee sufficient opportunity to learn through socially inclusive activities, enabled the elimination of several existing programs in the school that had been geared toward targeted assistance based on ability levels. The school administration eliminated the Reading Recovery program. They modified the highly restrictive 12:1 program by integrating those learners into the general education classroom for most of their school day. ELLs were also fully integrated into the general education classrooms. The administration also eliminated the honors program.[9] My school-wide program, which incorporated systems for teacher development and accountability, created conditions for a sustainable model of school development, reducing the overall annual expenditures for remediation programs and professional development support by more than 75%.

Radical, school-wide changes can initiate instability within an institution,[10] which is why a comprehensive system of progress monitoring is critical. The ongoing flow of data generated through the progress monitoring systems that were established generated evidence of achievement, functioning to assure stakeholders that reforms were positively impacting achievement. The 2009–2010 administration of the Degrees of Reading Power assessment revealed that learners in grades 3, 6, and 7 doubled national average gains; learners in grade 5 quadrupled national average gains; and the learners in grade 8 outpaced national average gains by five times (see Table 27.2). Gains for the English learners

Table 27.2 Jacob Riis students' average gains in DRP units compared to national average, September 2009 through June 2010

Grade	Number of students	Average change in DRP units, September–June	National average gain in DRP units, September–June[a]
2nd	57	+14.3	10
3rd	53	+15.9	8
4th	54	+9.5	6
5th	60	+13.4	3
6th	112	+8.8	4
7th	102	+6.9	3
8th	108	+11.0	2

a Questar Assessment (formerly Touchstone Applied Science Associates). (2000) *DRP Norms: Primary & Standard DRP Test Forms*, Brewster, NY: Author

Table 27.3 Student's average gains in DRP units for lowest 20% and highest 20% subgroups compared to national average gains in DRP units, September through June 2010

Grade	Number of students	Average change in DRP units for lowest 20% subgroup, September–June	Average change in DRP units for highest 20% subgroup, September–June	National average gain in DRP units, September–June[a]
2nd	12	+16.8	+14.4	10
3rd	11	+16.8	+13.0	8
4th	11	+11.9	+8.6	6
5th	12	+16.3	+10.2	3
6th	23	+12.7	+9.1	4
7th	21	+7.1	+7.4	3
8th	22	+9.1	+12.6	2

a Questar Assessment (formerly Touchstone Applied Science Associates). (2000) *DRP Norms: Primary & Standard DRP Test Forms*, Brewster, NY: Author

and the lowest achieving learners were especially robust (see Tables 27.3–27.5). It is worth reiterating that these gains were accomplished within the context of a first-tier general education classroom, in the context of a 75% reduction in external professional development support, and without test preparation or increased emphasis.[11]

The school's 2010 NYC DOE report card indicated dramatic programmatic and bureaucratic changes impacted performance. Median levels of ELA and math proficiency dipped, while the performance of the bottom third academically remained robust. The data suggests that the number of top test scorers decreased as the population of lower test scorers secured patterns of growth. These changes, however, were not statistically significant in the comparative study of Jacob Riis students and 5,000 other students from 10 demographically similar schools (McCallister & Olson, under review). Based on the research hypothesis of the proposed intervention program, higher-order thinking is dependent on the quality of opportunities for learners to coordinate perspectives with others and control their thinking. Based on this premise, teachers who have been trained in classical transmission pedagogical traditions must alter their practice in ways that transfer responsibility for learning to students. It can be speculated that the system as a whole

Table 27.4 English language learners' gains on the Degrees of Reading Power assessment compared to national average gains in DRP units, September through January

Grade	Number of students	Average change in DRP units for ELL subgroup, September–June	National average gains in DRP units for ELLs, September–June[a]
2nd	23	12.1	Not available
3rd	16	15.2	Not available
4th	8	7.5	5
5th	11	14.6	2
6th	5	2.0	2
7th	5	9.2	2
8th	6	9.0	3

a Maculaitis (2001) *The MAC II Handbook with Norms Tables: A&B Forms*, Brewster, NY: Questar Assessment (formerly Touchstone Applied Science Associates)

Table 27.5 Jacob Riis School, progress report metrics, 2007–2012

Year	2007	2008	2009	2010	2011	2012
Overall score	48.5: C	76.4/100: A	92.1/100: A	75/100: A	67.8/100: A	71/100: A
Student performance	18/30	17.8/25	22.5/25	14.9/25	13.7/25	21.2/25
ELA proficiency (Level 3 or 4 on state ELA)	63.9% (66.3% relative to City)	71.8% (74.1% relative to City)	83.5% (90.3% relative to City)	62.7% (57.8% relative to City)	63.4% (57.6% relative to City)	
ELA median proficiency	3.1 (67.3% relative to City)	3.25 (72.0% relative to City)	3.35 (82.0% relative to City)	3.07 (55.9% relative to City)	3.06 (55.0% relative to City)	
Math proficiency (Level 3 or 4)	72.3% (63.0% relative to City)	81.3% (70.9% relative to City)	94.3% (91.1% relative to City)	80.1% (68.6% relative to City)	83.2% (77.3% relative to City)	
Math median proficiency	3.44 (64.4% relative to City)	3.73 (79.1% relative to City)	3.91 (91.2% relative to City)	3.84 (80.6% relative to City)	3.65 (73.3% relative to City)	
Student progress	21.4/55	42.7/60	54.9/60	44.9/60	41.1/60	36.8/60
ELA: percentage of students making one-year progress	53.8% (56.6% relative to City)	64.9% (76.3% relative to City)	68.4% (89.5% relative to City)			
Median-adjusted growth percentile				74.5 (69.8% relative to City)	74.0 (66.7% relative to City)	64.0 (53.9% relative to City)
ELA: average change in proficiency in lowest third students	0.22 (35.9% relative to City)					
ELA: percentage of students in lowest third making at least one-year progress		81.6% (60.8% relative to citywide)	83.7% (68.8% relative to citywide)			
Median growth percentile for school's lowest third				80.0 (64.5% relative to citywide)	82.5 (71.8% relative to citywide)	75.0 (64.1% relative to citywide)
ELA: average change in student proficiency for Level 1 and 2 students		0.35 (73.3% relative to citywide)	0.37 (80.0% relative to citywide)			
ELA: average change in student proficiency for Level 3 and 4 students		0.01 (83.3% relative to citywide)	0.06 (100.0% relative to citywide)			
ELA: percentage of ELLs who scored in the 75th growth percentile or higher					44.3% (ranks in top 40% citywide)	

(*Continued*)

Table 27.5 Jacob Riis School, progress report metrics, 2007–2012 (Continued)

Year	2007	2008	2009	2010	2011	2012
ELA: percentage of students in the lowest third students who scored in the 75th growth percentile or higher					71.1% (ranks in top 20% citywide)	
ELA: percentage of special education students who scored in the 75th growth percentile or higher					52.9%	
ELA: percentage of Black and Hispanic males who scored in the 75th growth percentile or higher					65.7% (ranks in top 20% citywide)	
Math: percentage of students making at least one-year progress	52.6% (56.6% relative to citywide)	72.2% (75.5% relative to citywide)	78.7% (90.5% relative to citywide)			Median-adjusted growth percentile: 74.0 (83.7% relative to citywide)
Math: average change in student proficiency	0.02 (38.4% relative to citywide)					
Math: average change in proficiency in school's lowest third students	0.13 (24.3% relative to citywide)					
Percentage of students in lowest third making at least one-year progress		69.2% (52% relative to citywide)	82.9% (88.7% relative to citywide)			
Median-adjusted growth percentile for school's lowest third				81.0% (84.4% relative to citywide)	73.0 (61.2% relative to citywide)	75.5 (75.7% relative to citywide)
Average change in student proficiency for Level 1 and 2 students		0.24 (34% relative to citywide)	0.71 (128.0% relative to citywide)			
Average change in student proficiency for Level 3 and Level 4 students		0.06 (75% relative to citywide)	0.06 (75% relative to citywide)			

The row "Median-adjusted growth percentile for school's lowest third" also shows for 2010: Median-adjusted growth percentile: 82.5% (90.8% relative to citywide) will function more effectively to hold learners accountable for high learning standards once new bureaucratic and classroom changes are better secured. This hypothesis would be confirmed in subsequent implementation initiatives in schools where program effects would be associated with robust achievement gains as described below.

The Genre Practice program implementation at the Jacob Riis School came to an official end when the principal moved out of state in Fall 2010 and a new principal took the helm in Fall 2011. But the Jacob Riis implementation was an important and significant social reform experiment. It demonstrated that a civil and human rights-based program is capable of achieving equality of educational opportunity through a democratic and egalitarian curriculum that transfers rights and responsibilities of learning to learners themselves. Sufficiency of educational opportunity is achieved through classroom systems that grant learners rights to fundamental freedoms to autonomously select rich learning experiences and create their own conditions to achieve their potential. These methods, when implemented school-wide, proved sufficient to bring about high levels of achievement, especially in historically vulnerable populations, and provided an economically sustainable model for school transformation. This experiment proved that dramatic school transformation could be achieved in three years at a fraction of the costs normally associated with transformation and school improvement.

The Jacob Riis implementation also provided a context to prove the stability of the ecosystem design. The principal who had implemented the my model left her position in Fall 2010. Within the context of an industrial school, in which instructional, assessment, and evaluation systems are implemented from a top-down agenda, mid-year changes in leadership can introduce significant disruptions to the system. The McCallister infrastructure of the universal Sparks curriculum, the Learning Cultures Formats, and the ecosystem projects of professional development, teacher evaluation, and assessment were sufficiently developed to enable a smooth transfer of leadership.

New, Small Schools as Incubators for Learning Cultures: Case Studies of Disruptive Innovation

By 2011, the small schools' movement was well underway in the NYC DOE, with an Office of New Schools, which functioned to support the development of new school proposals and implementation initiatives. This initiative was a centerpiece of Bloomberg-era reforms, which sought to close large, under-performing high schools and replaced them with small, themed schools. Small schools, which enroll fewer than 600 students, are thought to promote both academic rigor and close personal relationships between staff and students and have shown to be correlated with higher graduation rates, especially for Black males and low-income students (New Visions for Public Schools, 2020; Untermann & Haider, 2019). But as the practices and perspectives presented so far in this volume suggest, school success is less a matter of size than it is of substance of the curriculum. The next phase of the McCallister educational experiment would take place in the space of eight initiatives that took place in the schools that grew out of the DOE's small schools initiative.

In the wake of the success of the Jacob Riis intervention, in Spring 2011, I was invited to present information about my model to various educational organizations in NYC. By this time, I had begun to call my model by the name, Learning Cultures, to capture the idea that the properties of culture can be harnessed to create intentional learning cultures in which social practices function effectively to produce target outcomes. I was invited by the director of the NYC DOE Office of New Schools to present my model to a group of soon-to-be principals of new, small schools. The principal of the High School of Language and Innovation (HSLI), Julie Nariman, attended that meeting and within several months had adopted the McCallister as the school's education model. The director of the Urban Assembly school network, Jon Green, enlisted me to support the network's adoption of a McCallister-Learning Cultures program, and Pamela Lee, the principal of The Family School, a new K-5 elementary school in the South Bronx, enlisted me to help implement McCallister Methods in the school's reading and writing programs. In each collaborative project, I provided consultative advice to school leaders and teachers on how to implement the methods I created, on-site demonstrations of the practices and administrative, instructional, and assessment support, and ongoing, in-depth off-site remote support. Each of these initiatives is described below, with summaries of student achievement. The Family School reform is discussed below. And two NYC high schools that were part of the McCallister-Learning Cultures initiative and High School of Language and Innovation are discussed in Chapter 28.

The Family School: Comprehensive School Reform in a South Bronx Elementary School

Pamela Lee, the principal of The Family School, a K-5 Title I school located in the South Bronx, in the poorest Congressional district in the United States, brought McCallister Methods to the school in Fall 2011. The Family School serves a population of students who are mostly from Africa and the Caribbean and who live in the poorest Congressional House district in the United States. Through a collaboration that would last three years and extend through 350 email threads of conversation, we would collaborate to implement McCallister Methods in K-5 classrooms. We began by implementing the Writing Activity Block in the kindergarten classroom of a teacher who had familiarized herself with the Model. We also began implementing the Writing and Reading Activity Block components in a 4th-grade ESL classroom. We attempted to implement it in another ESL classroom, but classroom management was too problematic to warrant the investment of PD support in that classroom. The Keepers of the Cultures social norms curriculum was not yet a focus of elementary-level school implementation, which was described in Chapter 5, and which could otherwise have been employed as a means to address problematic student behaviors.

The Family School demographics	Result
Total students	546
Black	28%
Hispanic	66%
Asian	4%
White	1%
English learners	42.5%
IEP	18.5%
Free lunch	94%
Reduced lunch	2%

Within the space of two site visits, students in the kindergarten classroom demonstrated independence and engagement, and the teacher had mastered the lesson, Work Time,

Writing Conference, and Writing Share Formats. We opened the classroom as a lab site for other primary teachers to visit and invited them to join the implementation effort on a voluntary basis. Within a few short weeks, the Writing Activity Block was operational in all but a few primary classrooms. Shortly after launching writing professional development lab sites, I began working with several primary teachers and the 4th-grade ESL teacher to implement Formats of the Reading Activity Block. By the conclusion of the academic year, both the Writing and Reading Activity Blocks were fully operational in the primary grades of the Family School and upper elementary teachers were increasingly interested in implementing the model. All of the students who were exposed to the McCallister program responded enthusiastically.

In 2012–2013, the principal decided to implement McCallister Methods on a school-wide basis. To that end, the Formats of the Activity Block were mandated in all classrooms, and the administration began using the Rubrics as a norming tool for professional development and a framework for teacher evaluation. In total, five staff developers, including myself, worked a total of 63 days in the school (38 days in 2011–2012 and 25 days in 2012–2013). I provided site-based coaching in classrooms, and other staff developers, who provided support to the principals and teachers to help set up Format procedures and second-level bureaucratic systems. In the third year of implementation, the school continued to use components of the McCallister program, but without site-based support (see Table 27.6). The McCallister initiative at The Family School ended in 2014 when Principal Lee took a position in a different school.

A survey of achievement data from The Family School shows evidence of dramatic gains in achievement, particularly in the traditionally vulnerable subgroups of Black and Hispanic males, ELLs, and students with disabilities (see Table 27.6). The number of students scoring a proficient level of achievement in ELA grew consistently over time, from a rate of 1.5% relative to the citywide average in 2011 to 31% relative to the citywide average in 2014. The median-adjusted growth percentile for the lowest third relative to citywide averages jumped from 5.4% in 2012 to 68.6% in 2013. Growth trends in ELA were dramatic, beginning in 2011 with only 18% of all students scoring a level 3 or 4 to the majority of students in the "achievement gap" subgroups of ELLs, students with disabilities, the lowest third citywide, and Black and Hispanic males scoring in the top 75th growth percentile in 2013–2014. At 94.2%, the middle school-adjusted core course pass rate for former students placed the school in at 73% citywide. Their performance is remarkable given that their cohort began the 2011 school year with an average proficiency in ELA that placed the school at 4.9% citywide, that 43% of students at The Family School are ELLs, and that 94% of students in the school qualify for free lunch.

The school's 2013–2014 Quality Review describes how the Cooperative Unison Reading program aligns with quality indicators (see Table 27.7).

The story of The Family School demonstrates that an educational program that provides sufficient equality of educational opportunity can enable children to beat the typical odds of low achievement that result from social inequality and economic disadvantage.

Chapters 28–30 present the processes and outcomes of McCallister Model implementation in four other schools.

There Are Learning Cultures 359

Table 27.6 The Family School quality guide

Category	2010–2011	2011–2012	2012–2013	2013–2014	2014–2015
NYS ESL Achievement Test: Reading and Writing, grades K-1	Level I: 25% Level II: 46% Level III: 19% Level IV: 10%	Level I: 36% Level II: 20% Level III: 24% Level IV: 20%			
NYS ESL Achievement Test: Reading and Writing, grades 2–4	Level I: 20% Level II: 47 Level III: 33% Level IV: 0%	Level I: 13% Level II: 41% Level III: 35% Level IV: 11%			
ELA: percentage of students at level 3 or 4	18.3% (1.5% relative to citywide)	19.3% (10.2% relative to citywide)	6.4% (11.6% relative to citywide and 17% relative to comparison)	9.60 (17% relative to citywide and 31% relative to comparison)	16.4% (14.8% meeting target) (28% relative to citywide and 70% relative to comparison)
Average ELA proficiency	2.45 (4.9% relative to citywide)	2.43 (7.5% relative to citywide)	2.02 (11.4% relative to citywide and 8% relative to comparison)	2.09 (19% relative to citywide and 25% relative to comparison)	2.24 (2.24 meeting target) (30% relative to citywide and 59% relative to comparison)
ELA: median-adjusted growth percentile		50.5% (15.4% relative to citywide)	65.0 (52.7% relative to citywide and 45% relative to comparison)	79.0 (98% relative to citywide and 100% relative to comparison)	63.0 (63.9 meeting target) (48% relative to citywide and 50% relative to comparison)
ELA: median-adjusted growth percentile for school's lowest third		54.0% (5.4% relative to citywide)	82.0 (68.6% relative to citywide and 54% relative to comparison)	86.5 (86% relative to city and 82% relative to comparison)	77.5 (76.4 relative to citywide (63% relative to citywide and 65% relative to comparison)
ELA: early-grade progress		25.9% (19.7% relative to citywide)	1.24 (24.6% relative to citywide and 32% relative to comparison)	1.42 (32% relative to citywide and 40% relative to comparison)	2.40 (1.63 relative to citywide (59% relative to citywide and 67% relative to comparison)
Math: percentage of students at 3 or 4	14.2% (0.0% relative to citywide)	40.3% (24.7% relative to citywide)	10.7% (16.6% relative to citywide and 23% relative to comparison)	16.3 (23% relative to citywide and 40% relative to comparison)	13.0% (17% relative to citywide and 27% relative to comparison)
Math: average proficiency	2.44 (0.0% relative to citywide)	2.43 (25% relative to citywide)	2.19 (22% relative to citywide and 27% relative to comparison)	2.31 (28% relative to citywide and 42% relative to comparison)	2.22 (2.39 relative to citywide (21% relative to citywide and 27% relative to comparison)
Math: median-adjusted growth percentile		100.0% (86.4 relative to citywide)	59.5 (42.3% relative to citywide and 45% relative to comparison)	81.0 (93% relative to citywide and 100% relative to comparison)	57.0 (60.1 relative to citywide)
Math: adjusted growth percentile for school's lowest third		87.4% (89.5% relative to citywide)	76.5 (56.3% relative to citywide and 52% relative to comparison)	87.0 (89% relative to citywide and 86% relative to comparison)	61.0 (26% relative to citywide and 18% relative to comparison)
Math: early-grade progress		42.9% (34.5% relative to citywide)	1.77 (36.5% relative to citywide and 39% relative to comparison)	1.35 (26% relative to citywide and 22% relative to comparison)	2.13 (39% relative to citywide and 33% relative to comparison)

(Continued)

Table 27.6 The Family School quality guide (Continued)

Category	2010–2011	2011–2012	2012–2013	2013–2014	2014–2015
Middle school-adjusted core course pass rate of former students				87.7 (51% relative to citywide and 33% relative to comparison)	94.2 (73% relative to citywide and 71% relative to comparison)
ELA: percentage of students at 75th growth percentile ELLs		21.8%	42.3 (61% relative to citywide and 74% relative to comparison)	56.5 (77% relative to citywide and 92% relative to comparison)	38.7 (48% relative to citywide and 55% relative to comparison)
ELA: percentage of students at 75th growth percentile lowest third citywide		30.5%	48.2 (61% relative to citywide and 75% relative to comparison)	64.1 (78% relative to citywide and 88% relative to comparison)	46.3 (41% relative to citywide and 54% relative to comparison)
ELA: percentage of students at 75th growth percentile Black and Hispanic males		22.2%	50.5 (48% relative to citywide and 53% relative to comparison)	61.5 (70% relative to citywide and 78% relative to comparison)	51.2 (53% relative to citywide and 66% relative to comparison)
ELA: percentage of students at 75th growth percentile SC/ICT/SETTS		21.7%	62.5 (83% relative to citywide and 76% relative to comparison)	52.9 (56% relative to citywide and 47% relative to comparison)	50.0 (53% relative to citywide and 50% relative to city)
Math: percentage of students at 75th growth percentile ELLs		45.3%	37.9 (50% relative to citywide and 60% relative to comparison)	61.0 (85% relative to citywide and 100% relative to comparison)	28.2 (33% relative to citywide and 30% relative to comparison)
Math: percentage of students at 75th growth percentile lowest third citywide		53.7%	47.3 (67% relative to citywide and 74% relative to comparison)	69.6 (88% relative to citywide and 100% relative to comparison)	27.0 (16% relative to citywide and 17% relative to comparison)
Math: percentage of students at 75th growth percentile Black and Hispanic males		56.4%	45.7 (66% relative to citywide and 70% relative to comparison)	80.4 (100% relative to citywide and 100% relative to comparison)	34.8 (33% relative to citywide and 31% relative to comparison)
Math: percentage of students at 75th growth percentile SC/ICT/SETTS		44.0%	48.9 (70% relative to citywide and 71% relative to comparison)	62.9 (78% relative to citywide and 73% relative to comparison)	34.5 (34% relative to citywide and 17% relative to comparison)
ELL progress		47.2%	47.0 (28% relative to citywide and 38% relative to comparison)	46.1 (25% relative to citywide and 30% relative to comparison)	50.5 (33% relative to citywide and 40% relative to comparison)

Table 27.7 2013–2014 school quality review excerpt

2013–2014 Quality review	McCallister Model program component alignment
Findings	Cooperative Unison Reading Format.
Teaching strategies consistently provide multiple entry points and challenging tasks for students in all grades.	
Every week, students in all grades rotate in groups to participate in a Unison Reading book club in their English language arts classes. On alternate weeks, the students are in whole group or small reading groups. During the Unison Reading time, students meet in reading clubs according to a posted schedule. The teacher confers with one group of students while the others are in their assigned groups. Students keep reading logs in their class folders.	
Many lessons included strategies to encourage high-level discussion such as requiring students to outline their reasons for agreeing or disagreeing with each other. In one class, students discussed the definition of wealth and how it would be displayed through clothing and jewelry in different cultures around the world and in another they were predicting how an unfamiliar story might end.	

Notes

1. At NYU, I assumed leadership in my department (Teaching and Learning) to develop a new program in Literacy Education for launch in 2001. New York state had just revised its credentialing system for Reading Teachers. In keeping with the movement in national policy at the time to replace remedial reading instruction in compensatory programs with whole-school approaches to literacy program improvement, the credential for Reading Teacher was now replaced with the Literacy Specialist credential. Previously, as a professor at Hofstra University, I had led a similar effort. At NYU, the Reading MA program had been housed within the Department of Applied Psychology, reflecting the cognitive orientation of the field of reading education at the time. Now situated within the emerging field of literacy, with an expanded emphasis on the role of culture in learning, the new Literacy MA was moved into the Department of Teaching and Learning. The program I helped develop reflected my sensibilities as a practitioner, and included courses on Reading theories and methods, Writing theories and methods, a course on language and literacy development from a usage-based perspective, a course called Texts, Tools and Culture, which approached literacy learning from a cultural-historical/activity theory perspective, a course on the Administration of Literacy Programs, and course on literacy for special learners. While this textbook emphasizes my work in the field, my involvement in literacy research and teacher education was a venue for the development of expertise needed to inform applications of theory to practice.
2. I knew from my experience in classrooms that freedom is a fundamental condition of learning. But freedom alone could not explain the powerful forms of learning that it gives rise to. Some force of agency that I had not yet been able to identify or operationalize in my model was the key to explaining the true mechanisms of learning. One afternoon, in a meeting with my mentor, Ed Gordon, he asked me, *what is it that you think you need to study?* I paused, and responded as much with another question as an answer: *intentionality?* I had been grappling with the concept of intentionality in the literature of cultural psychology I was reading (e.g., Bruner, 1996; Shweder, 1990). But Ed cautioned me that it was not a construct that was prevalent in the psychological existing literature. In fact, it was mentioned only a couple dozen times in psychological papers in 1999 (Kornhuber & Deecke, 1965). I had a strong hunch it was important. But what, exactly, is intentionality? What form does it take? How can it be operationalized in pedagogy to achieve sufficiency in opportunity, especially for vulnerable learners? And once operationalized in practice, how might school infrastructures be organized to enforce accountability in ways that protect every learner's right to these

opportunities? My NYU colleague, Jerry Bruner, was sympathetic with my cause and gave me a tip that would shape the course of my research agenda. He urged me, "Watch Tomasello." I devoured every book that Tomasello would write over the next two decades and followed along as he developed a theory about how the skills and intentions of shared intentionality define human psychological functioning.

3. I coined my program, "Genre Practice" to capture the notion that literacy is largely a process of learning that texts are forms of social action, and literacy competence develops through increasing facility to use texts to perform intended goals. I later coined the term "Learning Cultures" to describe the potential to achieve systemic change through the deliberate creation of school and classroom cultures that support learning.
4. McCallister & Olson (under review).
5. I recommended the comprehensive progress monitoring system outlined in Chapter 21, which I had incorporated into the course I developed at NYU on the administration and supervision of literacy programs.
6. Reading instruction is politically controversial in many schools. I could foresee potential backlash by teachers and parents averse to the social-constructivist methods I proposed and wanted to ensure adequate evidence of the efficacy of our reforms.
7. In 2008–2009, almost a dozen professional development coaches worked a total of 11 days per week in the school to support Pk-5 classroom teachers and middle school ELA teachers. The Framework for Professional Development (FPD) plan that I developed was organized to harness peer learning and to seed a self-sustaining PD system in the school. Initially, the school's Inquiry Team rejected my proposal. They were overwhelmed by it and felt the need to first build community (Kerry Decker, personal communication, September 11, 2008). But most FPD components were in place mid-year.
8. In 2008–2009, the school hired a half-dozen coaches to provide a total of 11 full days of training support to teachers. In addition, the school implemented Reading Recovery, the reading intervention program for first low-achieving first graders. These programs cost in total more than $350,000 a year. In 2009–2010, the FPD, together with two days of site-based support, reduced the professional development budget by more than 75%. The school's Comprehensive Educational Plan and annual budgets confirm these expenditures.
9. The flat trends in growth for the highest achieving students were probably limited by the elimination of the program. In future implementations of Learning Cultures model in other schools, I would strengthen the personalized learning curriculum used by learners in Work Time by incorporating intellectually rigorous activities that provide opportunities for high-achieving students to be sufficiently challenged.
10. I once overheard a Jacob Riis elementary teacher in a meeting with the principal literally sobbing in protest that the practices I was advocating were changing the culture of the school, which was clearly an upsetting experience for her.
11. Test preparation is a non-instructional activity, discouraged in the Learning Cultures model. Homework is also discouraged, as learners are provided adequate time for independent work in order to finish study activities within the hours of the school day.

28 Transforming a Large NYC High School

Introduction

High School of Language and Innovation (HSLI) is one of the small schools that was created after Columbus High School, in the Bronx, was closed due to chronic low performance. HSLI serves a population of 354 students, 95% of whom qualify for free lunch and 81% of whom are English learners. Approximately 55% of the HSLI population speaks Spanish, and another 45% speak Bengali, Arabic, Albanian, French, English, and Chinese. The school serves several challenging populations: a relatively large population of Students with Interrupted Formal Education (SIFE) who as a group lack formal literacy in their native language and English and have poor background knowledge in content subjects; English learners who enter school reading below a third-grade comprehension level; and Hispanic males who, as a group, have historically experienced lower graduation rates than overall graduation averages (HSLI, Comprehensive Educational Plan, 2018–2019). The school also serves a sizable population of children who live in temporary housing.

In Fall 2011, I had begun a collaboration with principal Julie Nariman that lasted for four years, with more than 40 visits to the school, and through more than 600 email threads of dialogue and coaching support. Through this collaboration, the McCallister Model was used as the comprehensive school design for HSLI.

HSLI began with a small class of under 100 freshman and added one new class each year. Over the course of four years, I worked in the school on average one day per month (more frequently in the earlier years of implementation and less so in the latter). The school staff, led by Principal Julie Nariman, were new to the McCallister Model in 2011, and I spent the first year demonstrating new practices, helping teachers understand their rationale, and gaining teacher buy-in. By the second year, the staff were invested in the model and committed to implementing the model in all grades and subjects. New teachers were hired with a conditional commitment to the program. In the third and fourth years, the school implemented the second-order changes with fidelity. In addition to implementing the Formats of the Reading and Writing program that were implemented in the Jacob Riis reform, I worked with teachers in history, math, and science to implement a personalized curriculum of autonomously selected activities that aligned with formal learning standards as well as the Formats of Learning Conferences, the Learning Share, and Cooperative Unison Reading.

In adopting the McCallister Model, HSLI chose a course of dramatic departure from the traditional formalist, skills-based approaches approach to teaching language learners. The McCallister Model is a usage-based approach to language and literacy education, which is based on a philosophy of pragmatism and the assumption that language is learned as an outcome of its functional use in the achievement of cooperative social goals (Tomasello, 2003). Language instruction was fully integrated into the general education classroom and curricula through the inclusive practices of the Formats. In my work with the teachers, I demonstrated how to help learners use language to communicate, solve problems that arose from the curriculum, and accomplish collective goals in the context of the Formats. Through coaching and demonstrations, I helped teachers learn a usage-based approach to language and literacy instruction. In this way, English learners acquired both English competence and subject competence through full participation in the general education classroom. This innovative approach functioned to both reduce the social isolation normally associated with programs that segregate and group language learners for instruction and rely on the increased complexity and expense of add-on language programs.

During the first year, I worked in classrooms alongside the founding team of teachers to demonstrate McCallister practices and support teachers in learning how to implement them. The school's original curriculum included in HSLI's new school proposal consisted of an amalgam of traditional teacher-centered practices. Teachers were committed to these practices, and my work at HSLI during the first year revolved around helping them transition from a mostly teacher-directed curriculum to the McCallister Model. By the end of the first year, most of the teachers had come to believe in the learner-centered tenets of the McCallister Model and were proficient in the Formats. During the second year, my work at HSLI focused on helping teachers refine their expertise in the Formats and develop self-directed learning activities for each of the Regents-aligned content courses that could be used by learners during Work Time. By the second year, several of the founding teachers had become skilled in the McCallister Model practices. During the second year of implementation, I also helped to develop a training infrastructure within the school so that teachers experienced in the McCallister Model could successfully onboard new teachers and to coach them in Learning Cultures Format practices.

In the third year of implementation, HSLI joined a team of other schools in the Urban Assembly McCallister-Learning Cultures Initiative, which was a consortium of five schools that collaborated to implement the McCallister Model as a whole-school transformation approach. This Initiative is discussed below. It provided a context in which the HSLI staff could learn and receive support to implement the second-level changes of the McCallister program, including a school-wide school culture and behavior program that helped teachers address increasingly challenging learner behaviors as the school population expanded. The Initiative also offered the opportunity for HSLI teachers to learn the curriculum of Learning Teams, which provided a means through which learners could master standards-based curriculum expectations across the disciplines.

In 2013, HSLI was the only high school in which the McCallister Model had been implemented with high fidelity in all classes and disciplinary subjects. Realizing her teachers were the "pioneers" of The McCallister Model at the high school level, and that there was no existing training infrastructure for high school application, and that it was important for teachers to hear directly from me during my visits to the school, Principal Nariman created a "Cynthia walkthrough" protocol to improve the impact of my visits. Rather than having me work one-on-one with the principal or a teacher, the protocol required teachers sign up for a time during the day to shadow me in classrooms, hear my reasoning, reason cooperatively with me, and form joint intentions about how to improve practice. Ms. Nariman made a schedule for my monthly visit and posted it in the teachers' work room with instructions to sign up for a time to shadow me during my visit. The teachers were expected to take part in one classroom intervisitation for the week, so shadowing me on the day of my visit counted for that week's intervisitation. We determined ahead of time the Format and theory we would examine in practice and decided together once we entered the classroom which activities looked most promising to examine (personal communication, Julie Nariman, February 28, 2013).

The McCallister Model initiative at HSLI stood out as a stellar example of high-fidelity implementation. The principal demonstrated incomparable leadership in ensuring teachers adhered to program guidelines and followed recommendations for programmatic improvement. The principal and two teachers on the school's founding team were pioneers in implementing the McCallister Model in high school discipline-based courses. They were also pioneers in using the McCallister curriculum as a context for full inclusion of ELLs and special education students. HSLI students were never grouped by ability for instruction or segregated from their peers for the purpose of targeted teaching. HSLI staff emerged as leaders in the cross-network McCallister Initiative, sharing their expertise with other principals and teacher leads during school intervisitations.

The HSLI graduating class of 2015 would be the only cohort of a school which implemented the McCallister Initiative for the entirety of their high school program over a span of all four years of high school. Consistent and ongoing exposure to first-level changes in classroom practice, such as the high-impact Formats of Cooperative Unison Reading, Learning Teams, the Share, Work Time, and Conferences, most of which support higher thinking through active forms of mentalizing and cognitive control in relation to formal learning standards, supported high levels of academic achievement. Due to capable leadership by the principal and teacher leads in enacting second-level changes, the McCallister program was implemented consistently and with fidelity across classrooms. Programmatic consistency and coherence appeared to have a significant impact on measures of rigorous academic success and college and career preparation. The impact of the curriculum on student achievement and school performance will be examined below.

Reform Success

As data from Table 28.1 indicate, the 2015 HSLI graduation rate of 83.3% outpaced the 2012 Columbus High School graduation rate of 50% for the class of 2012 by 30.3%. In comparison to the Columbus class of 2012, 52% more of HSLI's graduating class of 2015 earned the academically rigorous Regents high school diploma (as opposed to the less rigorous Local Diploma). But a simple comparison of graduation rates between the two cohorts deflates the relative success of HSLI in supporting English language learners, whose citywide graduation rate in 2012 was a mere 30.8% and only 40.5% in 2015. If graduation rates of 40.5% had applied to the HSLI class of 2015, 115 less students would have graduated. Simple comparisons of graduation rates between HSLI and Columbus also deflate the efficacy of HSLI's educational program to overcome the predictive correlation between poverty and low achievement (Lacour & Tissington, 2011). The rate of poverty among HSLI students was 30 points higher than that of Columbus students.

Academic Development

The McCallister program appears to have provided a strong foundation for the development of academic competence. For example, students demonstrated strong initial footing in high school, with a population of 87.7% first-year students earning 10+ credits (relative to the comparison group at 76.4%) (see Table 28.2). General rates of literacy proficiency were higher in HSLI students in 2015 compared to Columbus students in 2015 (70% of HSLI students scored at the proficiency in ELA compared to 45% of Columbus students; and 92% of HSLI students scored proficient in math compared to 61% of Columbus students) (see Table 28.1). The 2015 graduating cohort's ratings on the index of college and career preparation (credit for advanced diplomas associated with greater proficiency and for diplomas obtained by students with higher need demographic characteristics) was dramatically higher than the comparison group, at 63.6% and 3.7%, respectively. And overall the HSLI program appears to have been extraordinarily beneficial to ELLs in the school.

Table 28.1 Comparison of Columbus High School 2012 NY State Report Card metrics and HSLI 2015 NYC DOE School Quality Report metrics and NY State Report Card metrics

Category	Columbus High School (2012)	High School of Language and Innovation (2015)
Total students	749	354
Graduates	167	
Free lunch	72%	95%
Reduced lunch	4%	1%
Temporary housing		21%
Overage, under-credit		25%
Limited English proficient/English language learners	19%	74%
Black	36%	15%
Hispanic	47%	58%
White	10%	11%
Asian	6%	16%
Average incoming eighth-grade ELA		1.91 (out of 4)
Average incoming eighth-grade math		1.97 (out of 4)
Attendance	69%	91%
Suspensions	189 @ 13% (2010–2011 reported)	1 @ 0%
Dropped out	136 @ 19%	13 @ 4%
Graduation rate	62% (N = 167)	83.3% (N = 56)
Regents diplomas	104 students (62% of grads)	91%
Advanced Regents	0%	
ELA proficiency	All: 48%	All: 70%
	Black: 53%	Black: 91%
	Hispanic: 45%	Hispanic: 61%
	Disabilities: 7%	Disabilities: not reported
	ELLs: 20%	ELLs: 61%
ELA state exam score level 1	44%	7%
ELA level 2	8%	10%
ELA level 3	43%	55%
ELA level 4	5%	15%
Math proficiency	All: 60%	All: 92%
	Black: 57%	Black: 100%
	Hispanic: 57%	Hispanic: 88%
	Disabilities: 26%	Disabilities: not reported
		ELLs: 89%
Math level 1	29%	1%
Math level 2	10%	4%
Math level 3	60%	85%
Math level 4	1%	7%

Closing the Achievement Gap

Perhaps the most remarkable characteristic of the academic performance of the 2015 HSLI graduating cohort is their astonishing pattern of achievement amongst the "achievement gap" populations, or subgroups identified by the NYC DOE who are particularly vulnerable in the current educational system—students who perform academically in the lowest third citywide, Black and Hispanic males, English language learners, and students with IEPs. Performance of the lowest third citywide and Black and Hispanic boys in the HSLI 2015 cohort was exceptional. The four-year weighted diploma rate, which gives greater credit for advanced diplomas associated with greater proficiency and

Table 28.2 HSLI School Quality Guide 2015

Category	High school of language and innovation	Comparison group	Metric score (out of 4.99)
Earned 10+ credits in their first year	87.7%	73 % (72% citywide)	4.02
Lowest third in the school to earn 10+ credits in their first year	86.7%	75% (80% citywide)	4.28
Weighted pass rate for English Regents	110.0%	60% (69% citywide)	3.90
Weighted pass rate for math Regents	1.22	51% (67% citywide)	3.68
Weighted pass rate for science Regents	0.87	22% (38% citywide)	2.51
Weighted pass rate for global history	0.59	20% (30% citywide)	2.25
Average pass rate for U.S. history	1.0	36% (59% citywide)	3.55
Average 4-year graduation rate	72.7%	65% (55% citywide)	3.26
4-year weighted diploma[1]	297.7%	100% (100% citywide)	4.99
College/career preparatory course index[2]	63.6%	100% (80% citywide)	4.37
4-year non-remediation index	52.3%	19.3%	
4-year college readiness index[3]	52.3%	100% (99% citywide)	4.99
4-year weighted diploma rate—English language learners	301.3%	87% comparison (88% citywide)	4.80
4-year weighted diploma rate lowest third citywide	310.2%	95% comparison (100% citywide)	4.99
4-year weighted diploma rate—Black/Hispanic males	319.2%	100% comparison (99% citywide)	4.99
Lowest third citywide, college, and career preparatory index	63.6%	97% comparison (100% citywide)	4.99
Lowest third citywide, 4-year college readiness index	50.0%	100% (100% citywide)	4.99

Source: https://tools.nycenet.edu/; School Quality Guide https://tools.nycenet.edu/guide/2015/#dbn=03M402&report_type=HS

for diplomas obtained by students with higher need demographic characteristics, gave the school values of 310% for the lowest their citywide and 319% for Black and Hispanic males, placing the school in the 100th percentile citywide in performance of both groups and giving the school and metric ratings of 4.99 for both subgroups (see Table 28.2). The four-year weighted diploma rate for ELLs was 301%, placing the school in the 88th percentile citywide and giving it a metric rating of 4.80 for the ELL subgroup.

HSLI and the Achievement of Equality of Educational Opportunity

The demographic characteristics of the HSLI 9th-grade cohort of 2011–2012, who graduated in 2015, bore a composite of demographic characteristic that have been, in the literature on student achievement, predictable indicators of poor academic achievement. A total of 84% of the class had limited English proficiency and more than 90% qualified for free lunch (See Table 28.1). And almost three-quarters of the children were Black or Hispanic. Most students had failed their 8th-grade ELA exam. And only 32% of students scored at a level 2 or 3 on their NY State English as a second language achievement test in 9th grade.

Existence Proof

But these children had access to an educational program designed to achieve equality of educational opportunity through experiences that were sufficient to enable them to acquire the social and cultural capital that would assist them to be highly successful in high school. It allowed them to beat the normal educational odds that have long been stubbornly associated with disadvantage. The graduating class of 2015 proved both of the original assertions of my career-long educational experiment: education in a democracy can function to equalize social opportunity so that educational outcomes and life chances are not determined by social circumstance; and equality of educational opportunity can be achieved through experiences that enable the achievement of students' highest potential.

School Culture

The HSLI faculty also succeeded in improving the school culture in measurable ways. Dropout rates in HSLI were dramatically lower than those in Columbus High School in 2012 (4% in HSLI compared to 19% in Columbus); attendance rates were dramatically higher (91% in HSLI compared to 69% in Columbus); and suspensions were dramatically lower (1% in HSLI compared to 13% in Columbus) (see Table 28.1). HSLI bettered city-wide ratings on all measures of school quality, except that of "supportive environment," in which citywide ratings and HSLI's were equal. On overall measures of school quality in 2014–2015, HSLI met or exceeded standards in all categories (see Tables 28.3 and 28.4).

Rigorous Academic Preparation

HSLI's 2015 graduating cohort achieved an average four-year college readiness[4] index of 52.2%, indicating the percentage of students who graduated with a Regents diploma and met CUNY's standards for college readiness in English and math within four years (see Table 28.5). HSLI's metric score for its four-year college and career readiness was 4.99, equal to that of both the Bronx High School of Science and Stuyvesant High School, NYC's highly selective public magnet schools. The school's four-year weighted diploma value of 297.7%, which reflects the diplomas received within four years and provides greater credit for advanced diplomas associated with greater proficiency and for diplomas obtained by students with higher need demographic characteristics, gave the school a metric score of 4.99 (on a scale of 4.99), outpacing both Bronx Science and Stuyvesant in this category. There is no way to compare HSLI's rate of performance in this academically vulnerable population to that of similar students in the City's magnet schools, because those schools are segregated by high achievement status and do not accept low-achieving students. The HSLI cohort's college and career preparatory course index, which relates the percentage of students who competed approved rigorous courses and assessments within the first four years of high school after entering 9th grade in 2011–2012, placed them in the 80th percentile citywide and in the 100th percentile in relation to comparison schools, giving it a metric score of 4.37 (on a scale of 4.99).

Table 28.3 HSLI school quality ratings, 2014–2015

Category	Rating	Score out of 4.99
Collaborative teachers	Exceeding target	4.68
Supportive environment	Meeting target	3.04
Effective school leadership	Exceeding target	4.20
Strong family-community ties	Exceeding target	4.20
Trust	Meeting target	3.76
Student achievement	Meeting target	3.85

Table 28.4 School Quality 2014–2015 School Quality Guide

Measure	HSLI	Borough	City
Rigorous Instruction	90% of survey takers responded positively to questions about Rigorous Instruction	84%	85%
Collaborative Teachers	95% of survey takers responded positively to questions about Collaborative Teachers	85%	86%
Supportive Environment	80% of survey takers responded positively to questions about Supportive Environment	82%	80%
Effective School Leadership (School leadership inspires the school community with a clear instructional vision and effectively distributes leadership to realize this vision)	92% of survey takers responded positively to questions about Effective School Leadership	81%	82%
Trust (Relationships between administrators, educators, students, and families are based on trust and respect)	92% of survey takers responded positively to questions about Trust	88%	89%

Education and Economics

Education is the great equalizer and is a significant factor in projected lifetime earnings. To compare the relative economic opportunities provided through the provision of a more equitable education, we will compare the projected life earnings of the graduating class of 2012 cohort of Columbus with that of HSLI. These figures are calculated by taking the total number of students in the grade (graduates plus non-graduates) and adding the number of students who dropped out. Using this figure as the hypothetical class size, we assign values for projected lifetime earning in four different educational attainment groups (dropouts are calculated to earn $0.89M; non-graduates/sill enrolled predicted to earn $1.0K; high school graduates with local diplomas predicted to earn $1.12; high school graduates with Regents diplomas predicted to finish college and earn $1.76K; and advanced Regents predicted to earn $2.19). Based on these projections, 2015 HSLI graduates will earn an average of $500,000 more over their lifetimes than 2012 Columbus graduates (see Table 28.6).

External Evaluations of School Quality

HSLI school quality review documents from 2014, 2015, and 2017 outline the range of ways that external reviewers from the NYC DOE determined the McCallister Model related to school-wide educational program and their determinations about the effectiveness of program components. Excerpts from the quality reviews are featured in Tables 28.7 and 28.8 together with aligning McCallister program components.[5]

Table 28.5 College and career readiness metrics of HSLI, Bronx High School for Science and Stuyvesant High School

Metric	Bronx Science	HSLI	Stuyvesant
College and career preparatory course index	4.99	4.37	4.99
4-year college readiness index	4.99	4.99	4.99
4-year weighted diploma rate	4.66	4.99	4.75

Table 28.6 Comparative projected life earnings for 2012 Columbus graduates and 2015 HSLI graduates

School	Total students	Projected income for non-completers (136 dropouts + 9 GED)	Projected income for high school graduates (number of local diploma) with no college	Projected income for college graduates (number of grads with Regents)	Projected income for advanced Regents	Projected income for non-graduates of cohort with a predicted 50/50 high school graduation rate	Average life earnings for cohort
Colum-bus	318	N = 145 × $885K = $128.31M	N = 63 × $1.12M = $70.56M	N = 104 × $1.76M = $183.04M	0	N = 6 × $1.01M = $6.06M	$387.97M/318 = **$1.22M**
HSLI	93	N = 11 × $885 = $9.74M	N = 7 × $1.12M = $7.84M	N = 51 @ $1.76M = $89.76M	22 × $2.19 = $48.07	N = 5 @ $1M = $5M	$160.41M/93 = **$1.72M**

Source: Social Security Administration (2020).

Table 28.7 HSLI quality review report, 2013–2014 (March 11–12, 2015, lead reviewer: Ariledya A. Ureña)

2013–2014 quality review	McCallister Model program component alignment
What the school does well: The administration makes organizational decisions to create supports aligned to the school's instructional goals to improve staff and student performance. (1.3) To address the school's priority and overarching goals of increasing the school's safety and academic performance, the administration allocated funds to provide additional professional development to teachers on classroom management and how to conference with students regarding social-emotional and academic matters. Additional resources support the behavioral intervention program, such as JumpRope, an online standard-based grading system that is used to help students, parents, and teachers monitor student progress on specific work habits and content standards. Per-session funds enable teachers to meet with students after school, and consultants from the Learning Cultures program provide professional development to teachers to further support the school's goals and students' performance. Furthermore, aside from having teacher leaders as coaches and teacher mentors, the school administration made the decision to develop an additional position to include the director of the behavior intervention team to support the school's goal for safety. The school's schedule also affords teachers opportunities to meet on a daily basis with options for planning time, record and share, looking at student work and data, for updating classroom environments, and for whole-staff professional development. For example, during the classroom environment updates, teachers can either choose to focus the meeting on using the learning cultures classroom environment Rubric to make one positive change to a classroom, replenish missing materials, or reorganize/re-labeled classroom libraries and resources, thus ensuring that teachers engage in professional work that supports the school's instructional goals to improve instruction at the classroom level, thereby increasing student engagement of challenging academic tasks.	Keepers of the Culture social norms curriculum and second-level distributed leadership systems that enlist Training and School Culture Leads to help enact the school-wide discipline and classroom management programs. Learning Cultures Classroom Environment system outlined in the Learning Environment Rubric.
What the school does well: A collaborative school culture promotes the adoption of self-regulating academic and personal behaviors for students and adults. (1.4)	Keepers of the Culture curriculum and Behavior and Academic Intervention protocols.

(Continued)

Table 28.7 HSLI quality review report, 2013–2014 (March 11–12, 2015, lead reviewer: Ariledya A. Ureña) *(Continued)*

2013–2014 quality review	McCallister Model program component alignment
A school-wide initiative to address students' social-emotional growth by developing systems to track and professionally develop teachers on how to support students' with behavioral issues has been initiated by the principal. For example, the behavior intervention team conferences with students regarding behavior issues, thus allowing opportunities for students to reflect and make a plan to improve their behavior. This team, headed by a lead teacher, meets one period per week to discuss students' social-emotional progress and next steps. Teachers are also provided with professional development to learn how to guide conversations related to behavior issues. In addition, the Ladder of Consequences, a tool that was developed by the behavior intervention team, includes feedback from students and teachers to set clear expectations for academic and personal behavior. This initiative has contributed to improved attendance for some students in the target population, and a decreased of infractions. Students, in the meeting, shared how the Ladder of Consequences gives them clear guidance of "how teachers and the principal expect them to behave." Alike, in the teacher meeting, teachers shared how everyone collaborates and respects each other's work, thus creating a supportive school culture and tone.	
School leadership is a developing a system of accountability that communicates high expectations among staff, parents, and students, to ensure progress toward those expectations. (3.4) The school leadership supports teachers in developing strategies for improving student learning by scheduling ongoing professional development around the Danielson Framework for Teaching and classroom management techniques for conducting effective conferences with students. For example, every summer since the school's inception, the administration, with support from teachers, organizes professional development to communicate the school's goals, expectations for teaching and learning aligned to the Danielson Framework, and the Learning Cultures curricula framework. In the teacher team meetings, a first-year teacher, new to the profession, shared that he was thrilled to have had a head start in understanding the school's expectations for teaching and "not wait until for September to prepare for his students." Furthermore, the staff is held accountable through observation cycles, scheduled meetings, and ongoing discussions about meeting the school's instructional goals.	McCallister professional development systems incorporate norming of pedagogical practice through reference to the Danielson-aligned Learning Cultures Rubrics. The Rubrics continue to serve as a tool for norming in ongoing professional development.

(Continued)

Table 28.7 HSLI quality review report, 2013–2014 (March 11–12, 2015, lead reviewer: Ariledya A. Ureña) *(Continued)*

2013–2014 quality review	McCallister Model program component alignment
Strengthen pedagogical practices to provide all students access to the curricula and ensure consistent student engagement. (1.2) Across classrooms, teachers use the Learning Cultures "formats" for planning and teaching. In all classrooms visited, students engage in any one of prescribed activities. Students work either in groups for Unison Reading, or are reviewing of a test, preparing for a post-test, individually using a book or a laptop to get information about the content topic, completing a test reflect sheet (Analyzing Regents Multiple Choice Questions) with a partner, or meeting with the teacher for a scheduled conference. When students were asked what they were working on, some were able to respond relative to the specific activity, but others were not able to answer at the moment as he/she was still deciding what to do for the class period. In other classrooms, the class periods end with a 5-minute share by having the student, with whom the teacher had the individual conference, present to the rest of the class her/his challenge in the test, how to answer that particular question, and asked the other students if they had any questions.	The Learning Cultures curriculum of Formats is used in all classrooms to structure activity routines and practices.
Refine school practices so that teachers consistently implement assessment practices that inform planning, lesson adjustments, and provide students with feedback to support learning and progress. (2.2) Departmental assessments are common across math, literacy, history, and recently for science, are administered before a unit, at checkpoints, post-test, and at the end of the unit to inform additional Academic Intervention supports in preparing students for the Regents' exams.	The Learning Team (formerly called Responsibility Team) protocol is used in all content-based courses to structure a standards-based learning experience that promotes learning.

Table 28.8 HSLI quality review report, 2014–2015 (January 9, 2015, lead reviewer: Carron Staple)

Teacher teams and leadership (well developed) Findings The vast majority of teachers are engaged in structured, inquiry-based collaborations that promote the Common Core Learning Standards and have key leadership roles that focus on improved student learning and pedagogy through systematic analysis of instruction, data, and student work. Impact Inquiry work and distributed leadership has strengthened teacher collaborations resulting in school-wide instructional coherence, effective teacher leadership, and improvement in teacher pedagogy and student achievement. Supporting Evidence	The McCallister Model provides the school's educational program and structures the focus of professional inquiry, professional development, and teacher evaluation systems aligned to the Danielson Framework criteria.

(Continued)

Table 28.8 HSLI quality review report, 2014–2015 (January 9, 2015, lead reviewer: Carron Staple) *(Continued)*

All teacher teams are involved in structured, inquiry-based collaborations. Teachers meet weekly in their respective teams to work on their practice, analyze student work, and discuss specific instructional strategies within the Learning Cultures' model of this English Language Learners school, and to ensure collaborations improve their practice and progress toward student goals. Some teachers stated that because of meeting regularly, they have seen growth in their own planning, especially to align curricula and instruction with instructional shifts and Common Core Learning Standards, plus in the areas of differentiation and introducing elements of the Learning Cultures model. Additionally, the principal provided Advance-tracker data to show evidence of teachers improving in competencies of the Danielson Framework for Learning, specifically around questioning (3b), engagement of students (3c), and assessment (3d).

Pedagogy

Findings

In all classrooms visited, it is clear that most teachers plan well and engage in pedagogy aligned to the Danielson Framework, have adopted the Learning Cultures model, and use elements of it, such as unison reading, responsibility groups, the share, and learning conferences. These Learning Culture elements promote higher-order thinking skills and help students master the English language as they learn skills and content necessary to pass classes and Regents exams. Clear evidence that this model is working with some students can be seen in the Measures of Student Learning (MOSL) data from 2013 to 2014, teacher ratings, and student growth from New York State English as a Second Language Assessment Test (NYSESLAT) scores, and Regents exam results.

The reviewer makes reference to the aims of McCallister practices to support higher-order thinking, but asserts a concern in evidence that teachers inconsistently demonstrate proficiency in model implementation. This finding, with examples from classrooms of teachers demonstrating inability to successfully use McCallister protocols to hold learners responsible for higher-order thinking, suggests a need for increased professional development support to staff to enable them to more successfully implement McCallister Model components.

While the Learning Cultures model specifically creates strategies for teachers to use with students, there were some classes where student engagement and participation was low and where questioning remained at a low level. In one Earth Science class, the teacher stated, "Today we are going to learn how slope affects runoff." The teacher then showed a rock and stated, "It's a flow of water on what? Fill in the blank." "What does slope mean?" Students remained silent and only one student raised his hand to answer. Students were not collaborating in writing, taking notes, or having discussions even though they were sitting together at tables, they worked independently. In a Living Environment class, the teacher showed a PowerPoint about photosynthesis. No notes were distributed nor did students take notes or have a discussion. When a student asked, "What happens when we eat lettuce?" the teacher stated, "We get energy." The teacher answered the question directly and the student missed the opportunity to discuss it with his peers or try to answer himself based on the PowerPoint he just viewed. Consequently, students in both classes were not challenged to either demonstrate their knowledge in their discussions or work products, which is contrary to the goal of the Learning Cultures model.

(Continued)

Table 28.8 HSLI quality review report, 2014–2015 (January 9, 2015, lead reviewer: Carron Staple) *(Continued)*

Teachers check-in individually with students and provide one-to-one support. Yet, in some classes observed, teachers spent the bulk of their time conferencing without any direct instruction or extensions offered to the whole class, where some early-finishers had to wait for further directions as the teacher concentrated on other students. Additionally, student-centered unison reading activities had all the students in the responsibility groups reading aloud with no one person leading the pace of the readers, the pronunciation of words, or the comprehension of text. While this student-centered activity is meant to support fluency and communication, group check-ins with the teacher were minimal, resulting in missed opportunities for students to achieve the session's reading goals.

Pedagogy

Findings

Curricula across grades and subject are aligned to the Common Core Learning Standards and integrate the instructional shifts. Curricular and instructional refinements are made using student work and data.

McCallister practices and curriculum development protocols provide an educational infrastructure that builds pedagogical coherence in the school.

Impact

Findings

The school's purposeful curricular decisions build coherence and promote cognitive engagement and college and career readiness for a variety of learners.

Supporting Evidence

A review of curricula shows evidence of coherence in planning across all grades and subjects. All teachers incorporate some aspect of the Learning Cultures model as part of their daily planning and almost all teachers utilize Cooperative Unison Reading, where small groups of students read aloud in sync to help support language fluency and comprehension. Further, the principal provided curricula maps, unit plans, and lesson plans that have been revised based on student work and data.

Curricula across grades reflect the use of the Learning Cultures model, which frames and includes tasks that support all students learning via language that is not native to them. Learning Cultures is a curriculum development model based on the idea that all students can succeed in college and careers if they learn to take responsibility for their own learning. Tasks include daily discussions, reading a variety of texts in every class, building knowledge with peers, and accessing a rich variety of resources and materials. For example, all unit plans include collaborative learning where students are required to engage in either role-play, debates, presentations, or discussions of their reflections and enduring understandings.

A review of teacher lesson plans shows evidence that teachers are planning summative tasks where students have opportunities to show mastery of skills and content that emphasize higher-order thinking skills, such as developing logical arguments and using text-based evidence to defend claims or counterclaims. Teacher plans also incorporate various literacy Formats of the Learning Cultures model. For example, some lesson plans for literacy block instruction provide opportunities for direct and small group instruction, and independent work or student-generated research. The curricula provide opportunities for students to choose topics and genres for some of their writing pieces, and independent texts they wish to read for enrichment, based on their ability or interest

(Continued)

Table 28.8 HSLI quality review report, 2014–2015 (January 9, 2015, lead reviewer: Carron Staple) *(Continued)*

Assessment	
Findings Across classrooms, teachers create common assessments and rubrics aligned to the school's curricula to determine student progress toward goals across grades and subjects. Teachers' assessment practices consistently utilize ongoing checks for understanding and students engage in peer and self-assessment. Supporting Evidence Teachers' assessment practices provide timely and actionable feedback to students, to make effective adjustments to curricula and instruction, and to meet the students' varying learning needs. Impact Across classrooms all teachers use rubrics to provide assessment criteria for student work. For example, in a geometry class students were asked to solve various dilations of figures. Initially, they worked alone to try to solve the problems and then moved into responsibility groups, where they worked as a team to discuss their answers, ultimately solving the problems collectively. The teacher then pushed them further to find even more solutions using a geometry assessment Rubric as a guide. After bringing the whole class together, the teacher listened carefully as students shared their thinking with the class as to how they problem-solved, then she made on-the-spot assessments using their Rubric to support students with any breakdown within the problem-solving process. In most classrooms, teachers share the same Rubric for student presentations and argumentative writing. However, across the school common assessments include pre- and post-tests, learning conferences, whole class share, peer assessment, and self-assessment. Current school data as compared to last year reveals that more students are engaged in the Learning Culture strategies and have improved their skills in reading, writing, and speaking as evidenced by NYSESLAT scores, teacher assessments, scholarship reports, and Regents data. Formative assessments for checking for understanding and learning are embedded throughout lessons and happen in a variety of ways. For example, the responsibility group is one strategy observed that provides students an opportunity for peer assessment and to discuss and share their work using a set Rubric. Another strategy observed is one-to-one check-ins by the teacher, where students receive feedback on work submitted, are working on, or something the teacher observed during the responsibility groups. These assessment strategies allow for immediate teacher support and feedback to students, resulting in better work products that meet or exceed Rubric standards. Additionally, teachers have revised their instruction by assessing students to support the development of communicative skills, specifically the five major components of language: vocabulary, syntax, morphological, pragmatic, and phonological skill. Students are assessed on understanding the meaning of words, how to appropriately use these components of language, the awareness of syllables and sounds, and the social rules of using certain words when communicating. This revised instructional support helps English Language Learners in mastering these skills to meet the challenges of responding orally and in writing when taking school and state exams.	Learning Cultures Format assessments provide an ongoing stream of process data used by teachers to inform instruction. They provide actionable forms of feedback tailored to learners' individual needs. Learning Cultures Formats provide scaffolded contexts in which learners take responsibility to work with others to solve challenges that arise in the curriculum. The Format procedures and assessments are used across the curriculum, providing a means through which to embed assessment to inform learning and teaching.

Substance More than Size

In the case of HSLI, it would appear that the small school reform strategy succeeded. The HSLI educational program succeeded in significantly raising student achievement, improving the school culture, and improving the life chances of students. Size, no doubt, was an important factor. A smaller size made it easier for the administration to grow a new school culture, roll out a new curriculum, and evaluate and develop expertise in teachers. But the substance of the curriculum, and not school size, was the primary causal factor of the success of school reform at HSLI. This hypothesis will be tested, below, when we examine the case study of The McCallister Model implementation at Urban Assembly School for Green Careers.

Notes

1. On a scale of 0–4.99, this metric reflects the diplomas received within four years by the students who entered 9th grade in 2011–2012 and provides greater credit for advanced diplomas associated with greater proficiency and for diplomas obtained by students with higher need demographic characteristics.
2. The percentage of students who successfully completed approved courses and assessments within the first four years of high school, after entering 9th grade in 2011–2012.
3. On a scale of 0–4.99, this metric shows the percentage of students who graduated with a Regents diploma and met CUNY's standards for college readiness in English and math within four years, after entering 9th grade in 2011–2012.
4. The NYC DOE definition for college readiness is the percentile of students who were able to pass out of remedial coursework in accordance with City University of New York (CUNY) standards by: 1) graduating with a Regents diploma; 2) either a) earning a 75 or higher on the ELA Regents or b) scoring 480 or higher on the Critical Reading SAT, and 3) either a) earning an 90 or higher on one math Regents exam and completing coursework in Algebra II/Trigonometry or a higher-level math subject, or b) scoring 480 or higher on the Math SAT. The comparison group is all district high schools, except transfer high schools, weighted by progress report sample size for this metric (New York City Charter School Center, 2020).
5. Interestingly, even while the first cohort to graduate provided evidence that the school leadership and faculty provided learners with an education that was exceptional according to almost every means by which judgments are made, the external reviewers' relatively low ratings seem to suggest subjective bias and/or a lack of capacity in the evaluation system to identify the most powerful mechanisms of educational opportunity.

29 The Urban Assembly's McCallister-Learning Cultures Initiative

Introduction

The Urban Assembly (UA) network, founded in 1990 by Richard Kahan, a leader in urban redevelopment in NYC, was established to address poverty issues through urban development initiatives. In 1997, the network established a partnership with the NYC Board of Education and New Visions for Public Schools to open its first high school in the Bronx and over the ensuing years built a network of more than 20 middle and high schools with the aim of partnering with public, private, and nonprofit partners to increase educational opportunities and close the opportunity gap for thousands of low-income children in NYC (Urbanassembly.org). The mission of UA—to advance students' economic and social mobility through public education—aligned closely with the aims of my model.

Jon Green, the former Director of UA, was responsible for bringing the "McCallister-Learning Cultures Initiative" to the network in Spring 2011. Over the next two years, in over 300 email threads and multiple meetings, Jon and I planned and executed the implementation Initiative in three phases, described in Table 29.1. In summary, the Initiative would be implemented in three phases, which can be summarized as Exploratory, Pilot, and High-fidelity Implementation. In the Exploratory Phase, Emily Jarrell, a teacher I had previously coached at the Jacob Riis School for four years, joined the staff of UA and worked as a coach in several participating schools. In the Pilot Phase, several additional coaches were hired, all of whom I had coached at Jacob Riis (former principal Kerry Decker, and teachers Sabina McNamara and Tara Silva). In the High-fidelity Implementation Phase, the role of Learning Cultures network coach was eliminated. Those who had been network coaches now embedded as staff members in schools to assist in the High-fidelity Implementation Phase of the Initiative.

The McCallister-Learning Cultures Initiative at UA also included an initiative to create a new Learning Cultures middle school. I worked with the planning team to develop a proposal and participate in the selection process through the NYC DOE's Office of New Schools. The new school, christened as the *Urban Assembly Unison School* in recognition of the spirit of collective intentionality expressed in the practice of Cooperative Unison Reading, opened in the Clinton Hill neighborhood of Brooklyn in Fall 2012.

In May 2012, the UA received a commitment from the Petrie Foundation for a $1.185 million grant to support the McCallister Initiative for three years (Jon Green, personal communication, May 9, 2012; Jeremy Gough, personal communication, July 3, 2013).

With the infusion of generous support from the Petrie Foundation, the network hired two coaches who had previously been trained by me, Kerry Decker and Emily Jarrell, and provided funds to cover new school startup expenses, in-kind network expenses, and visits to participating schools by me.

Table 29.1 The Urban Assembly McCallister-Learning Cultures Initiative implementation

Phase	Participating schools	Intervention description
Phase I: AY 2011–2012	Brooklyn Academy of Arts and Letters; Bronx Academy of Letters; Urban Assembly Institute of Math and Science for Young Women; Urban Assembly School for Civic Engagement; Urban Assembly School for Green Careers	**Exploratory.** Trial implementation of Reading and Writing Activity Blocks in Pilot classrooms; school-based training support from a network achievement coach who was previously trained by Cynthia in Genre Practice methods; public relations plan to coordinate project efforts with NYC DOE central administration; development of a training infrastructure and plan to bring the model to scale in schools in AY 2012–2013. Occasional school visits by Cynthia to provide feedback to UA coaches and network leaders.
Phase II: AY 2012–2013	Bronx Academy of Letters; Urban Assembly Institute of Math and Science for Young Women; Urban Assembly School for Civic Engagement; Urban Assembly School for Green Careers; Urban Assembly School for New Technologies	**Pilot Implementation.** Principals at participating schools work with Cynthia and UA network Learning Cultures coach to implement Learning Cultures bureaucratic systems (e.g., progress monitoring; instructional accounting; social norms and behavioral supports; Rubric-based teacher evaluation; implement Framework for Professional Development; develop internal by training anchor teachers whose classrooms serve as lab sites). UA coaches, trained by Cynthia in Genre Practice, embed in participating schools to provide support to teachers and school leaders.
Phase III: AY 2013–2015	High School of Language and Innovation; Urban Assembly Institute of Math and Science for Young Women; Urban Assembly School for Green Careers; Urban Assembly Unison School	**High-fidelity implementation.** Build Learning Cultures leadership capacity at schools; develop Rubric-based teacher evaluation systems; improve fidelity of implementation through the implementation of bureaucratic systems; improve Work Time curriculum across schools; improve progress monitoring and assessment practices to track progress and achievement; implement Cynthia's distributed leadership system and bureaucratic changes through work with appointed leads from each school for assessment, "code blue," curriculum, community education, professional development, and social norms. Schools follow an implementation timeline similar to that outlined in Chapter 7. Cynthia visits schools for full days of embedded PD (principal shadows for a whole day, with pre- and post-visit meetings). Teacher leads take part in cross-network, school-based teacher-led PD with Cynthia. Principals participate in cross-network, school-based leadership PD with Cynthia.

Academic Year 2012–2013

With growing political and financial support, the UA/McCallister Initiative was transformed from a Pilot trial in 2011–2012 into a full-scale implementation and replication project for AY 2012–2013 which continued through AY 2014–2015. I developed an implementation plan for the 2012–2013 school year that emphasized support to principals to implement second-level bureaucratic changes in five participating schools (see Table 29.1). The plan was organized around a "leadership apprenticeship," in which I worked more directly with principals to help them learn and implement the second-level bureaucratic systems of the McCallister Model (see Box 29.1). I collaborated with the principals to plan my site visits based on an agreed-upon agenda aligned with the implementation plan. During visits, I demonstrated practices in classrooms and advised principals to help them develop and execute implementation plans tailored to the needs of their schools.

In my work in schools, I continued to emphasize improvements in Learning Cultures Formats, but universally, across schools, challenging student behaviors continued to impede successful program implementation. Or, rather, successful program implementation depended on the degree to which school leaders could successfully implement the Keepers of the Culture curriculum. During my site visits, I continued to conduct classroom demonstrations of the Formats, and I also provided training in the Keepers curriculum, demonstrating the Social Contract Talk, use of the Ladder of Self-regulation, and Behavior Interventions, and coaching principals and teachers on how to effectively use these strategies. The plan also specified my continued support for the McCallister Initiative achievement coaches, Ms. Decker and Ms. Jarrell, who embedded in schools to provide support to classroom teachers. The coaches also supervised the school-wide assessment and progress monitoring systems.

Academic Year 2013–2014

Achievement trends from the 2012–2013 year across schools were impressive, and participating principals remained strongly committed. Based on a collective interest in improving the quality of implementation and expanding the scale of the model in schools, I developed a new implementation plan for the 2013–2014 school year organized around a distributed leadership design. The plan was designed to support the implementation of the Formats and other first-level classroom changes, build internal capacity in schools to faithfully implement the McCallister program, and provide technical support to principals and teachers tailored to the specific needs of each school through routine site visits. Though not specified in the formal plan, support to principal and teacher leads involved a substantial level of remote coaching, and program implementation was largely coordinated through my involvement in sustained, ongoing email communication with principals and teacher leads. The plan also provided schools free access to my program

---

Box 29.1

McCallister-Learning Cultures Initiative Schools, 2013–2014

High School of Language and Innovation (high school)
　Urban Assembly Institute of Math and Science for Young Women (middle and high school)
　　Urban Assembly High School for Green Careers
　　Urban Assembly Unison School (grades 6 and 7)

manuals and materials, in which I described how the first- and second-level systems should be carried out.

Participating schools agreed to the following terms: Learning Cultures would serve as the curriculum model in all classrooms in every disciplinary subject; the Learning Cultures Social Norms Curriculum would serve as the school-wide behavioral support program; the Framework for Professional Development would be used to structure teacher evaluation and training in the Learning Cultures model; the McCallister Year-long Implementation Plan would be followed with fidelity; and teacher leads would be appointed to work with me to implement the Learning Cultures programs. Leads worked with me on a monthly basis to implement the responsibilities associated with each lead position. Leads from participating schools rotated to join me at the appointed school during my weekly visit. I provided guidance to help them implement their lead position responsibilities (outlined in Chapter 20), and they shadowed me in classroom lab sites to refine their expertise in McCallister Model practices. Leads learned to refine practice in classroom lab sites.

In order to stage and activate curricular reforms, I developed a systems-based bureaucratic program design organized around projects in *assessment*, "*code blue*" (now called "Civil Rights," an intervention program for non-achieving students), *community education*, *curriculum*, *professional development* (now called Training), and *school culture*. Teacher leads were selected in each school to take responsibility to implement changes outlined in their job descriptions. Leads participated in school intervisitations, joining me in my site visits to receive guidance and support and share knowledge. For example, assessment leads met at School A in September and curriculum leads met at School B in September, and so on.

Principals convened regularly to take part in leadership meetings, which rotated across schools, providing opportunities for knowledge sharing, troubleshooting, and planning. Leadership meetings included school walk-throughs and opportunities for me to provide demonstrations of the practices and technical support. In order to stage and activate planned change, I developed a three-phase implementation timeline, which was the basis for the second-level systems described in Chapter 7.

Staffing changes at the UA affected the course of the Initiative. Jon Green, UA's champion of the McCallister Initiative, took a position at New Visions for public schools, and Shannon Curran assumed the position of Director of UA. Kerry Decker, UA's 2012–2013 Learning Cultures project manager, assumed the principalship at UA High School for Green Careers. Sarah Dennis, one of my former students at NYU was hired by UA to be the new program manager. The school-based Learning Cultures achievement coach positions were eliminated, and those individuals were appointed to positions in the participating schools. Participating schools for the 2013–2014 school year appear in Box 29.1.

Schools continued to adhere to the Year-long Implementation Plan through 2015, and I worked with teachers and principals to refine and improve first- and second-level systems in participating schools.

Academic Years 2015–2019

The McCallister Initiative came to an end in Spring 2015 when the UA ended support for the program, and principals of participating schools chose not to continue to participate in the Initiative. The UA School for Green Careers (UAGC) was the exception. While UAGC ceased participation in the Initiative, they nonetheless elected to continue attempting to implement McCallister Model practices independently with minimal external technical support from Fall 2015 through Spring 2019.

382   *Existence Proof*

The remainder of this chapter recounts the implementation of the McCallister Initiative in two middle schools—one in Harlem and one in the Bronx. The next chapter details the transformation of UAGC.

Urban Assembly Institute for New Technologies: Transforming a Failing Harlem Middle School

UA Institute for New Technologies (New Tech) is a small middle school located in Harlem. Jeff Chetirko was recruited by the UA to assume the principalship of New Tech in Spring 2012 when the former principal left the school mid-year. Despite being a new school, New Tech had already established a pattern of low student achievement and negative school culture. On his second day on the job, a melee erupted in the cafeteria, requiring police intervention and a number of suspensions, signaling an indication of level of behavior challenges that lay ahead for Jeff and the teachers (Jeff Chetirko, personal communication, June 11, 2013). I began working with the school in Fall 2012, after UA determined that New Tech would be included in the McCallister-Learning Cultures Initiative.

Metric	*2011–2012*
Free lunch	79%
Reduced lunch	4%
Limited English proficiency	9%
Black	77%
Hispanic	23%
Asian	1%

On my first visit to "New Tech," it was clear that the school culture was marred by deeply secured norms of incivility and disrespect. Almost constant and continual eruptions of interpersonal conflict in classrooms generated a general tone of negative emotions across the school. My attempts to conduct classroom demonstrations of the Formats were prevented by the need to address problematic behaviors as they arose. It was easy to see why achievement trends were so low in the school, since the school culture prevented learning. The nature of the behavioral challenges at New Tech was no different than any kind I had seen in any other school in which low-achieving children express feelings of frustration, disengagement, and anger. But while they were no different in nature, there were many more of them. As a cultural niche, New Tech was an institution that positioned most of its inhabitants as culturally incompetent, and being positioned in such a way causes symptoms of depression and other disordered patterns of behavior (Dressler, 2019). Only 17% of learners scored at a level of proficiency on the state English language arts test in 2012, and only 10% of Black and Hispanic males, or 5% of the total school population, scored at the 75th growth percentile on the ELA exam.

The human being yearns to be connected to a larger social collective and conforms to group norms, whatever they may be. In toxic school cultures, poisoned patterns of culture have left children few options but to self-regulate to negative norms through means such as rebellion, passivity, or avoidance. When they have no way to function, children fight, flee, or freeze. Due to the fractionated nature of the culture of middle and high schools, where students travel from one class to the next, and where the responsibility falls upon individual teachers to establish their own rules, it is virtually impossible to change a toxic school culture because doing so requires changing every culture of every classroom in the "egg-crate." The sheer scale of behavior challenges at New Tech required a whole-school, programmatic strategy.

The strategy I used to help the principal correct the toxic culture at New Tech followed a three-point strategy. First, I demonstrated the Social Contract Talk in a classroom, and Jeff took responsibility for giving the talk as many times as needed in order for every learner to hear it. Jeff developed a New Tech Ladder that outlined "distractions" and "responses," which was posted in every classroom. Next, I demonstrated the Behavior Intervention to Jeff, then coached him in conducting one himself. I also demonstrated how to use the Ladder as a response in the context of challenging behaviors in the classroom. One afternoon, while facilitating the Writing Share in a classroom, a boy remained seated with his head down in the back of the room. The child scheduled to Share stood waiting. I cued the Sharer to call his classmates to the Share area. He did, but the boy in the back remained seated, with his head down. Several minutes elapsed. I persisted. Jeff, who was sitting at the side of the room, told me later that he had been watching in fear as I went to battle, wishing I would back down (Jeff Chetirko, personal communication, June 11, 2013). But the book of rules does not permit adults to back away from holding children accountable to the collective code of conduct or the enforcement of their rights. I had a moral obligation to "go to battle" if I was unwilling to allow the negative behavior to be secured as a norm.

Finally, probably out of frustration and discomfort at the awkwardness, the students in the audience began to prompt the resister: "just come to the Share!" The bell rang, and the kids started to get up from their seats. "No, you have to stay here until the Share is finished," I asserted. The paraprofessional who co-taught the class slid a child's desk in front of the door and sat on it, blocking the children from leaving. His peers urged him to comply. After a few directives ("Yo, come on!"), the resister finally came to join the Share. The author read his piece, the audience clapped, and away they all went, out the door and on to their next class. With that, this class, with a previously with a dysfunctional Share Format, now has the kernel of a new norm to carry them forward.

The work in the school from the beginning of the year until December was a challenge. One conference, Jeff reported, lasted a full two hours with his teachers and the dean in attendance. But it was worth the investment because, by the end of the meeting, the child had created his own contract holding himself responsible for adhering to Format rules (Jeff Chetirko, personal communication, June 11, 2013). With consistency by all teachers in using the Ladder (non-verbal warning; verbal warning; move seat; behavior conference with the teacher; assigned seat; call home; behavior conference with dean; parent conference; and then, possibly, suspension), the culture shifted.

Of course, it is only in the context of the Formats, as behavior challenges arise and are corrected, that the classroom and school culture changes. And while it is undergoing change, the children become more and more competent in the Formats. So that, by the time the culture transforms, learners have already built up considerable competence in the intellective competencies the Formats promote. That is why the mid-year reading comprehension assessments at New Tech were so impressive. Table 29.2 shows 2.6 points in 6th grade, 1.4 points in 7th grade, and 4 points in 8th grade.

Table 29.2 Degrees of Reading Power scores from Fall 2012 to Spring 2013

Grade	Fall to Winter gains	Winter to Spring gains	Fall to Spring gains	Nationally normed annual growth
6	2.6	4.24	6.64	4
7	1.4	3.32	4.72	3
8	4	1.73	5.73	2 points

The phenomenal growth in comprehension achievement trends across grades was confirmed in the 2013 annual student achievement results and school environment data. The marked improvement in school culture was represented in a 2/3 decrease in suspensions, from 18% in 2011–2012 to 5% in 2012–2013. Performance in ELA by academically vulnerable subgroups was astonishing. The ELA median-adjusted growth percentile for the school's lowest third rose from 74.0% in 2012 to 94.0% in 2013, catapulting the school from the 56th percentile citywide to the 100th percentile. The percentage of ELLs in the school who scored at the 75th growth percentile in ELA improved the school's citywide ranking from 23.1% in 2012 to 81.8% in 2013, placing the school in the 100th percentile citywide. The lowest-performing third in the school who scored at the 75th percentile increased from 43.2% in 2012 to 68.9% in 2013, placing the school in the top 100% citywide. Black and Hispanic males in the school scored at the 75th percentile citywide. Special education students in the school who scored at the 75th percentile increased from 44.4% in 2012 to 79.1% in 2013, placing the school in the 100th percentile citywide.

Mr. Chetirko summed up the success of the McCallister Model at New Tech when he pointed out that the school embodied the spirit of the Learning Cultures curriculum, having succeeded at both improving learning and improving the culture (Jeff Chetirko, personal communication, June 11, 2013). Under the strong and capable leadership of Jeff Chetirko, the McCallister program was successfully used to turn around the school and close the achievement gap.

New Tech was part of the McCallister Initiative through part of the 2013–2014 school year, and, in 2014–2015, ended its participation in the program as the network brought the McCallister project to a conclusion. Patterns in student achievement declined to a remarkable extent from 2013 to 2015. For example, the median-adjusted growth percentile for the school's lowest third in ELA declined from 94.0% in 2013 to 77.5% in 2015, dropping the school from the 100th percentile citywide in 2013 and the 76th percentile in 2014 to the 56th percentile citywide in 2015. Similar patterns of decline are observed in other categories of student achievement. The citywide ranking of the school in the number of ELLs performing in the 75th growth percentile in ELA dropped a staggering 88% from a high in 2013 of 81.8% to 22.2% in 2015. The citywide ranking of the school in the number of students in the lowest third demonstrating growth at the 75th percentile in ELA dropped from the 100th percentile in 2013, at 68.9%, to the 57th percentile in 2015, at 53.8%. The citywide ranking of the school in the number of Black and Hispanic males performing in the 75th growth percentile in ELA dropped 46% from 65.9% in 2013 to 50.0% in 2015. And citywide ranking of the school in the number of special education students performing in the 75th growth percentile in ELA dropped a staggering 50% from 2013 to 2015, from 79.1 to 53.3%.

Urban Assembly Academy of Civic Engagement

The UA Academy of Civic Engagement is a middle school in the Throggs Neck neighborhood of the Bronx. In 2011, it was identified as a persistently failing school when the network recruited me to provide program support for the McCallister Model implementation. Throughout the 2011–2012 school year, the principal and teachers explored and experimented with the model, and in 2012–2013, under the leadership of a new principal, Mary Anne Sheppard, the school took on a full-scale implementation of the model in reading and writing programs.

In Spring 2013, data from the Degrees of Reading Power assessment administered three times throughout the year indicated strong patterns of achievement. The percentage of students school-wide who performed at or above grade level in measures of reading comprehension rose from 21.3% in September 2012 to 47.6% in May 2013 (Mary Anne Sheppard, personal communication, June 7, 2013). Students in grade 6 outperformed the national average gains reported by Questar, the maker of the Degrees of Reading Power, by more than 50%; students in grade 7 outperformed the national norm by almost double, and students in grade 8 outperformed the national norm by more than three times. These dramatic gains in reading comprehension were a harbinger of the student achievement outcomes reported in the school's NYC DOE school quality report for 2012–2013, where the median-adjusted growth percentile for the school's lowest third catapulted the school from a citywide ranking of 9.9% in 2012 to 70.3% in 2013. Achievement trends for the school's most vulnerable students indicated strong growth across subgroups. The percentage of ELLs who performed in the top 75th percentile in ELA climbed from 17.4% in 2013 to 44.4% in 2013. The percentage of Black and Hispanic males who performed in the top 75% in ELA almost doubled, from 29.1% in 2012 to 58.3% in 2013. Growth trends in math across most of these subgroups were even higher. For example, the percentage of learners with IEPs who scored in the top 75% in math shot up from 20.4% in 2012 to 60.4% in 2013 (Table 29.3).

Table 29.3 Urban Assembly Institute for New Technologies student achievement data (annual NYC DOE report cards and school quality guide)

	2011–2012	*2012–2013*	*2013–2014*	*2014–2015*
Suspensions	18% (21)	5% (8)	7% (8)	13% (12)
ELA: median-adjusted growth percentile	63.0 (53.3% relative to citywide and 57.9% relative to comparison)	78.0 (95.3% relative to citywide and 84.0% relative to comparison)	76.5 (97% relative to citywide and 96% relative to comparison)	67.0 (64% relative to citywide and 54% relative to comparison)
ELA: median-adjusted growth percentile for school's lowest third	74.0% (55.6% relative to citywide and 41.3% relative to comparison)	94.0 (100.0% relative to citywide and 86.1% relative to comparison)	84.0 (76% relative to city and 60% relative to comparison)	77.5 (56% relative to citywide and 27% relative to comparison)
Math: median-adjusted growth percentile	49.0% (29.5% relative to city and 34.2% relative to comparison)	61.5 (49.0% relative to citywide and 51.4% relative to comparison)	60.5 (48% relative to citywide and 48% relative to comparison)	62.0 (52% relative to citywide and 45% relative to comparison)
Math: adjusted growth percentile for school's lowest third	64% (45.3% relative to citywide and 45.3% relative to comparison)	69.0 (32.6% relative to citywide and 27.9% relative to comparison)	77.0 (62% relative to citywide and 54% relative to comparison)	76.0 (60% relative to citywide and 44% relative to comparison)
Ninth grade-adjusted credit accumulation of former eighth graders		77.0 (34% relative to citywide and 57% relative to comparison)	70.0 (23% relative to citywide and 46% relative to comparison)	55.0 (6% relative to citywide and 0% relative to comparison)

(*Continued*)

Table 29.3 Urban Assembly Institute for New Technologies student achievement data (annual NYC DOE report cards and school quality guide) *(Continued)*

	2011–2012	2012–2013	2013–2014	2014–2015
ELA percentage at 75th growth percentile ELLs	23.1%	81.8 (100% relative to citywide and 100% relative to comparison)	90.9 (100% relative to citywide and 100% relative to comparison)	22.2 (12% relative to citywide and 2% relative to comparison)
ELA percentage at 75th growth percentile lowest third citywide	43.2%	68.9 (100% relative to citywide and 100% relative to comparison)	63.6 (78% relative to citywide and 87% relative to comparison)	53.8 (57% relative to citywide and 59% relative to comparison)
ELA percentage at 75th growth percentile Black and Hispanic males	44.4%	65.9 (100% relative to citywide and 100% relative to comparison)	66.7 (85% relative to citywide and 88% relative to comparison)	50.0 (54% relative to citywide and 54% relative to comparison)
ELA percentage at 75th growth percentile SC/ICT/SETTS	44.4%	79.1 (100% relative to citywide and 100% relative to comparison)	69.4 (83% relative to citywide and 79% relative to comparison)	53.3 (50% relative to citywide and 47% relative to city)
Math percentage at 75th growth percentile ELLs	23.5%	41.7 (59% relative to citywide and 66% relative to comparison)	Not reported	27.3 (27% relative to citywide and 33% relative to comparison)
Math percentage at 75th growth percentile lowest third citywide	20.8%	43.5 (60% relative to citywide and 70% relative to comparison)	46.6 (44% relative to citywide and 52% relative to comparison)	51.1 (55% relative to citywide and 61% relative to comparison)
Math percentage at 75th growth percentile Black and Hispanic males	10.0%	47.6 (69% relative to citywide and 78% relative to comparison)	50.0 (50% relative to citywide and 56% relative to comparison)	50.0 (54% relative to citywide and 54% relative to comparison)
Math percentage at 75th growth percentile SC/ICT/SETTS	27.3%	50.0 (77% relative to citywide and 87% relative to comparison)	48.6 (50% relative to citywide and 48% relative to comparison)	60.0 (79% relative to citywide and 77% relative to comparison)

Civic was part of the McCallister Initiative through part of the 2013–2014 school year, and, like New Tech, ended its participation in the program in 2014–2015 as the network brought the McCallister project to a conclusion. Patterns in student achievement at Civic, like New Tech, also declined from 2013 to 2015. For example, the median-adjusted growth percentile for the school's lowest third in ELA declined from 63.0% in 2013 to 58.0% in 2015. Similar patterns of decline are observed in other categories of student achievement. The citywide ranking of the school in the number of ELLs performing in the 75th growth percentile in ELA dropped from 44.4% in 2013 to 42.1% in 2015. The citywide ranking of the school in the number of students in the lowest third demonstrating growth at the 75th percentile in ELA dropped from 51.9% in 2013 to 46.5% in 2015. The citywide ranking of the school in the number of Black and Hispanic males performing in the 75th growth percentile in ELA dropped from 58.3% in 2013 to 44.7% in 2015. And citywide ranking of the school in the number of special education students performing in the 75th growth percentile in ELA dropped from 59.3% in 2013 to 50.0% in 2015 (Table 29.4).

Table 29.4 Urban Assembly Academy of Civic Engagement student achievement results

Civic Engagement	2011–2012	2012–2013	2014–2015
Student progress	8.5 out of 60	33.3 out of 60	
Student performance	13 out of 25	7.4 out of 25	
School environment	6.2 out of 15	9.0 out of 15	
Closing the achievement gap	3.3 out of 17	4.9 out of 17	
Overall score	31.0 out of 100	54.7 out of 100	
ELA median-adjusted growth percentile	55.0 (27.1% relative to citywide)	63.0 (44.6% relative to citywide)	58.0%
ELA median-adjusted growth for school's lowest third	61.0 (9.9% relative to citywide)	85.0 (70.3% relative to citywide)	76.0%
Math median-adjusted growth percentile	40.0 (9.7% relative to citywide)	62.0 (50.3% relative to citywide)	63.0%
Math median-adjusted growth percentile for school's lowest third	52.0 (14.1% relative to citywide)	81.5 (71.4% relative to citywide)	77.0%
ELA percentage at 75th growth percentile or higher: ELLs (%)	17.4	44.4	42.1
ELA percentage at 75th growth percentile or higher: lowest third citywide (%)	33.0	51.9	46.5
ELA percentage at 75th growth percentile or higher: Black and Hispanic Males in lowest third citywide (%)	29.1	58.3	44.7
ELA percentage at 75th growth percentile or higher: Self-contained/ICT/SETTS (%)	50.0	59.3	50.0
Math percentage at 75th growth percentile or higher: ELLs (%)	15.4	55.6	30.0
Math percentage at 75th growth percentile or higher: lowest third citywide (%)	22.5	53.8	48.7
Math percentage at 75th growth percentile or higher: Black and Hispanic Males in lowest third citywide (%)	23.8	51.9	52.0
Math percentage at 75th growth percentile or higher: Self-contained/ICT/SETTS (%)	20.4	60.4	52.3

Source: NYC DOE 2011–2012 and 2012–2013 progress reports.

30 The "Rise of the Phoenix"

Introduction

In 2013, the Urban Assembly High School for Green Careers (UAGC) was a microcosm of the universe of 5,000 or more failing schools nationwide. It is an urban school serving majority of students who are Hispanic and Black and who live in poverty. In 2013, of 375 students, 88% received free lunch, 21% were students with disabilities, 24% were of limited proficiency in English, 30% were Black, and 67% were Hispanic (see Table 30.5).

UAGC is one of the small schools housed on the Brandies campus on the Upper West Side of Manhattan. Built in 1965 and once serving over 2,200 students, Brandies High School was a chronically low performing school with a four-year graduation rate in 2012 of 38.9%. Brandies was one of the large NYC high schools closed under the leadership of Mayor Bloomberg, and the school was broken into several smaller schools (Hernandez, 2009). UAGC is the only one of the small schools to be created that would be "unscreened," meaning that students are accepted without regard to their academic record or other admissions criteria. The small school reform strategy was a failure at UAGC, where, in 2013, the school graduated its first class at a rate of only 29.8%, only 1% above the failing school it replaced. That year the school received an "F" on its annual NYC DOE report card, scoring in the lowest 5% of schools citywide on measures of school quality (see Table 30.1). In 2013, the average ELA and math proficiency rates of UAGC students were lower than they were for Brandies students in 2012 (see Table 30.5).

Despite its small size, in many respects, UAGC was performing more poorly than the failing school it was created to replace. According to parents, teachers, and students who took part in the 2012–2013 Learning Environment Survey, the school ranked below the citywide average in safety and respect, engagement, communication, and academic expectations (see Table 30.2). In 2012–2013, 39% of the staff reported feeling unsafe working at the school; 100% of teachers disagreed that order and discipline were maintained at the school; 84% disagreed that most students treated adults with respect; 91% felt they did not receive the help needed to address student behavior issues; and 42% reported there being gang activity at the school. Academic expectations at the school were low. A total of 60% of teachers disagreed that the school set high learning standards for work in classes; 78% disagreed that the school provides students with the best courses and supports to achieve postsecondary goals; and 94% disagreed that the school supported students who were at risk for dropping out (see 2012–2013 school survey results, Table 30.2).

Table 30.1 2012–2013 report card overview

Category	Score	Grade	Citywide ranking	Description
School progress	18.2 out of 55	D	Among lowest 6–12% of schools	Student Progress measures the annual progress students make toward meeting the state's graduation requirements by earning course credits and passing state Regents exams.
School performance	2.4 out of 20	F	Among lowest 1–5% of schools	Student Performance measures how many students graduated within 4 and 6 years of starting high school, and the types of diplomas they earned.
School environment	3.3 out of 15	F	Among lowest 1–5% of schools	School Environment measures student attendance and a survey of the school community rating academic expectations, safety and respect, communication, and engagement.
College and career readiness	2.0 out of 10	F	Among lowest 1–5% of schools	College and Career Readiness measures how well students are prepared for life after high school on the basis of passing advanced courses, meeting English and math standards, and enrolling in a postsecondary institution.
Closing the achievement gap	3.8 out of 16	F	Among lowest 1–5% of schools	Schools receive additional credit for exceptional graduation and college/career readiness outcomes of students with disabilities, English Language Learners, and students who enter high school at a low performance level.
Overall score	29.8 out of 100	F	Overall percentile rank: 1	The overall grade is based on the total of all scores above. Category scores may not add up to total score because of rounding.

Implementation Timeline

The Learning Cultures Initiative at UAGC began in Fall 2013, when Kerry Decker, the former principal of the Jacob Riis School and UA coach in the McCallister-Learning Cultures Initiative from 2012 to 2013, took the helm as principal, bringing considerable experience with the Learning Cultures model to lead a whole-school transformation. From Fall 2013 to Spring 2015, when the McCallister-Learning Cultures Initiative ended, the first- and second-level Learning Cultures systems were implemented at UAGC with high levels of fidelity according to standards I developed. The Initiative provided UAGC and other schools with technical support to implement the Year-long Implementation Plan in recursive annual cycles and provided a training infrastructure that enabled me to work with school leads and principals to carry out both first- and second-level changes of the McCallister Model with fidelity. Through our collaboration, over more than 40 site visits by me, and in over 400 email threads of cooperative communication and remote coaching, I collaborated with Ms. Decker and the UAGC staff to transform the school into a high-performance learning organization.

Table 30.2 UAGC school environment survey results, 2012–2013

Category	Results
Safety and Respect School Score: 6.2 out of 10 compared to 7.5 citywide average for high schools	39% of teachers disagreed with the statement: *At my school, I am safe* 100% of teachers disagree that order and discipline are maintained at the school 51% of teacher report that students are often bullied at the school 67% of teachers report that crime and violence are a problem at the school 84% of teachers disagreed that most students treat adults with respect 76% of teachers report that gang activity is a problem in school 62% of students disagree that most students at my school treat adults with respect 42% of parents report there being gang activity at their child's school 67% of teachers disagree that they felt respected by the principal 60% of teachers disagree that the school is kept clean 91% of teachers disagree to the statement: *I can get the help I need at my school to address student behavior issues*
Engagement School Score: 6.0 out of 10 compared to 7.7 citywide average for high schools	97% of teachers disagree with the statement that they wouldn't want to work in any other school 97% of teachers say they wouldn't recommend the school to parents seeking a place for their child 75% of teacher say they disagree with the statement: *I usually look forward to each working day at my school* 75% of teachers disagree that the school offers a wide enough variety of programs, classes, and activities to keep students engaged 39% of teacher disagree that the school educates students with disabilities in the least restrictive environment appropriate 67% of teachers disagree that the principal understands how children learn 56% of teachers disagree that the principal knows what's going on in their classroom 66% of teachers disagree that they were provided with content support in their subject area 56% of teachers disagree that professional development has been sustained and coherently focused, rather than short-term and unrelated
Communication School Score: 6.1 out of 10 compared to 7.8 citywide average for high schools	88% of teachers disagree that the principal communicates a clear vision for the school 76% of teachers disagree that the principal encourages open communication on important school issues 66% of teachers disagree that the school communicates effectively with parents regarding students' behavior 66% of teacher disagree that the school communicates effectively with parents about their child's progress 69% of teachers disagree that school leaders give regular and helpful feedback about teaching 94% of teachers disagree that the principal is an effective manager who makes the school run smoothly 70% of teachers disagree that the principal makes clear to the staff expectations for meeting instructional goals

(Continued)

Table 30.2 UAGC school environment survey results, 2012–2013 *(Continued)*

Category	Results
Academic Expectations School Score: 6.4 out of 10 compared to 8.0 citywide average for high schools	79% of teachers disagree that the principal places the learning needs of children ahead of personal and political interests 57% of teachers disagree that the school leaders place a high priority on the quality of teaching 60% of teachers disagree that the school sets high standards for work in their classes 54% of teacher disagree that the school helps students reach targets for mastery of important skills and content 63% of teachers disagree that the school ensures ELLs receive the same curriculum as their no-English language learner peers with appropriate supports 57% of teachers disagree that the school uses assessments that re relevant to daily instruction 66% of teachers disagree that the school supports students who aspire to go on to a 2- or 4-year college, career or technical training, or enter the workforce by helping them develop a plan to achieve those goals 94% of teachers disagree that the school supports students who are at risk for dropping out 54% of teachers disagree that the school uses assessments that are relevant to daily instruction say the school disagree that the school uses 78% of teachers disagree that the school provides students with the best courses and supports to achieve their postsecondary goals

After the McCallister Initiative ended in Spring 2015, the UAGC leadership elected to implement Learning Cultures independently through Spring 2019 with declining levels of technical support. After the conclusion of the Initiative, when the school was no longer accountable to project implementation standards, it was not possible to make judgments about program implementation fidelity. In Spring 2016, UAGC underwent a change in leadership when Ms. Decker moved abroad, and Assistant Principal, Madeline Young, took the helm as principal. Under Young's leadership, UAGC elected to continue to implement Learning Cultures independently, with very minimal levels of project support from Spring 2015 through Spring 2019. In Summer 2019, the UAGC leadership elected to formally end the McCallister program. See Table 30.3 for an overview of the six-year McCallister Model implementation program.

The UAGC McCallister Model implementation case study demonstrates what is possible after a two-year full-scale implementation with site-based technical support followed by a three-year period of independent implementation which appears to continue until the time of this report (Decker, 2019; LaBua, 2020).

In the sections that follow, I will outline salient aspects of the implementation of the McCallister program in the first two years of high-fidelity implementation. I will indicate how and in what order of pacing the principal utilized implementation support from the McCallister Group.

UAGC in Fall 2013: An Unhealthy Ecosystem

Human beings depend on the cultural niche for survival, and the extent to which one is supported by culture determines the state of well-being. In Fall 2013, the culture of UAGC could only be described as toxic, chaotic, hostile, hopeless, and disordered.

Table 30.3 Learning cultures implementation timeline at Urban Assembly School for Green careers

Time period	Implementation scale	Implementation support and program fidelity	Principal
Fall 2013 to Spring 2015	Full-scale, high-fidelity implementation.	Strong technical support provided through the McCallister-Learning Cultures Initiative. School accountability to implementation standards yielded strong program fidelity.	Kerry Decker
Fall 2015 to Spring 2016	Independent implementation. Unknown scale of implementation.	Independent implementation with minimal technical support. Absent accountability to program standards or means to assess implementation, fidelity of implementation could not be determined.	Kerry Decker
Fall 2016 to Spring 2018	Independent implementation. Unknown scale of implementation.	Independent implementation with minimal technical support. Absent accountability to program standards or means to assess implementation, fidelity of implementation could not be determined.	Madeline Young
Fall 2018 to Spring 2019	Independent implementation. Unknown scale of implementation.	Independent implementation. No technical support.	Madeline Young

Students exhibited high levels of irritation, anger, resentment, hopelessness, and frustration. Children were uncooperative and uncaring toward peers, and disrespectful and cynical toward adults. The School Environment rating of 3.3 out of 15 on the 2012–2013 Progress Report suggest that UAGC suffered from a dismal school culture (see Table 30.2).

It was easy to understand UAGC students' feelings of frustration and hopelessness. A nationally norm-referenced assessment of reading comprehension administered in Fall 2013 indicated the average score of students at every grade in the school was below the third-grade level. More than half of the incoming children had failed either their ELA or math state assessment in 8th grade and, given the low performance track record of the school, had little hope for future success. UAGC presented a unique set of challenges. UAGC, which ranked in the bottom 1% of schools citywide, was a full-scale high school turnaround, with a deeply established culture of failure, and the Learning Cultures classroom-level Formats needed to be implemented in all disciplinary departments and the Social Norms curriculum had to be implemented across the school. For the next few months, during my visits to the school, I supported the principal and teacher leads in implementing the first- and second-level changes of the McCallister Model that have been outlined in earlier chapters of this book.[1]

Social norms and school culture. The most significant challenge at UAGC was the extremely toxic school culture and the staggering magnitude of disruptive student behaviors that interfered with normal social interchange. The first order of business was to shift the school culture, and the only way to do that was to seed and sustain positive behavioral changes across the entire community of learners and teachers. I provided all the principals in the Initiative with the Social Norms Curriculum, which would be used in the upcoming year to transform the school culture. The first order of business was to give the Social Contract Talk to all learners, establish a Ladder of Self-regulation in each class, and implement the On-call system of classroom behavioral support. I conducted classroom demonstrations to show teachers and the principal how to use the Ladder to address problematic behaviors.

The Ladder could be used by teachers inside the classroom. But school hallways are the arteries that connect classroom organs. They, too, had to be orderly and safe. In a previous visit to the school under the former principal, I was struck by the chaos and disorder in hallways and suggested that correcting them should be a first order of business. In fact, feeling safe in the hallways is a formal indicator of a positive school culture as indicated on the NYC DOE school environment survey. Now, in Fall 2013, the problem of chaos in the hallways persisted. Learners were using the hallway passes and trips to the bathroom or the guidance counselor as opportunities to escape the classroom and to kill time. In one of my early school visits, the principal and I did a hallway walkthrough in which I demonstrated how to secure hallways by using the Ladder to address problematic behaviors of students as they passed between classes. In one particularly memorable incident, two students, walking arm-in-arm, turned the corner to approach us. As they did, one of two students, a female, screamed a profanity. Her friend, a male, laughed in response. I advised the principal to let the female student, who was visibly energized in the situation, to pass and enter the classroom. But I urged the principal to intervene with the male student to address his behavior. Responsibility #23 of the NYC Discipline Code requires every student to encourage peers to adhere to school procedures. By laughing aloud at a behavior prohibited in the Code, the male student was not only encouraging the behavior, but failing to assume the responsibility required of him to encourage his peer to adhere to school procedures. The strategy used to transform the toxic culture of UAGC was to demonstrate to teachers how they can hold students responsible for holding their peers accountable to norms of civility. The male student protested initially but accepted the fact that his behavior was, in fact, an infringement of the Code. This demonstration illustrates a tenet of the Keepers of the Culture curriculum. The school culture belongs to everyone, and everyone shares responsibility to uphold shared values.

Violent and disruptive incidents were more than frequent the first several months of the school year. In my classroom demonstrations of the Formats for the first three months of the school year, I spent almost all of my time and effort devoted to addressing negative/maladaptive behaviors. In other words, I used the context of the Formats to demonstrate to teachers and children how to hold others accountable to norms of civility, specified in the Rubrics, the Ladder of Self-regulation, and the Discipline Code. Some teachers protested that too much time was spent on social norms, and not enough on academics. But, as I have mentioned, every infraction must be addressed or else the infraction will create and strengthen the very norm that teachers are trying so hard to change. Permitting maladaptive behaviors to go unaddressed functions to secure them into the culture.

The excess of problematic behavior infractions, extreme the first two years of the Initiative, required intervention responses outlined in the NYC Discipline Code. For example, it was not uncommon for as many as two-dozen students to be assigned to after-school detention due to misbehavior on any given day. Suspensions were also high in number the first two years until a positive culture was securely established. In 2013–2014, there were 166 Principal Suspensions and 13 Superintendent Suspensions; in 2014–2015, there were 169 Principal Suspensions and 16 Superintendent Suspensions; and in 2015–2016, there were 48 Principal Suspensions and 4 Superintendent Suspensions (Kerry Decker, personal communication January 6, 2016). With continued implementation of the Social Norms Curriculum after Ms. Decker's departure from the school mid-year in 2016, suspensions continued to decline, with only 13 in 2016–2017 (NY State School Report Card).

The school culture also became more positive as a result of the McCallister Initiative. The 2016 school survey indicated that 88% students felt positive about school safety; 98% felt positive about social-emotional learning in the school; 91% strongly agreed the school encourages them to continue their education past high school; 85% strongly agree that adults in the school help them plan to meet their future goals.

The Behavior Intervention protocol is used in cases in which a child is persistently uncooperative, noncompliant, disobedient, oppositional, and aggressive. When implemented effectively in a toxic school culture, classroom-level execution of the Ladder generates a steady stream of Behavior Intervention referrals. It would be necessary to conduct numerous Interventions every week in order to address highly problematic behaviors as they arose. I demonstrated the Behavior Intervention at UAGC in early September, 2013, after which point the principal assumed responsibility for conducting multiple Interventions each week.[2]

I had previously suggested that the principal, as arbiter of justice in the school, should be the person in the school to conduct the Intervention. But it soon became apparent at UAGC that this responsibility was unsustainable, and it appeared to me that the Social Norms Curriculum, as implemented in the school, was requiring too much of the principal's time. I therefore recommended that schools implement the "Keepers of the Culture" program in which several students from each grade, nominated by their peers to, be charged with keeping the culture of the school by providing support to peers through the Intervention Format. I was encouraged that the principals were on board and endorsed the idea. Ms. Decker expressed strong approval of the program and said her school was ready to go to this next level (Kerry Decker, personal communication, April 16, 2014).

With support from the principals, I worked with the School Culture Leads to administer survey nomination, and trained Keepers at each school in the Intervention Protocol. I recommended the Keepers run interventions in regularly scheduled time blocks, which was accomplished programmatically in different ways at each school. "Keepers" eventually became a stand-alone program at UAGC.

Professional Development, Curriculum, and Teacher Evaluation

The Framework for Professional Development (FPD) (McCallister 2009a), as described in Chapter 26, is a comprehensive school-wide system of support for teachers to learn how to undertake radical shifts in practice. The FPD is used in conjunction with the McCallister teacher evaluation system, which is based on judgments of professional practice that align to Format Rubric criteria.

I worked with the principal and Professional Development Lead to implement components of the FPD, including the organization of lab sites and intervisitation opportunities, teacher self-assessment using Rubrics as a norming tool, school-wide professional development surveys, and teacher inquiry activities. In the second year of implementation, schools had access to over seven hours of training videos that explain the foundations of McCallister Model and Format procedures and theoretical rationale. The school followed the FPD with fidelity. Ms. Decker had employed my FPD (McCallister, 2009) as principal at Jacob Riis and had served as a coach to help implement the Framework at New Tech and Civic the previous year to develop anchor classrooms, which served as school-wide lab sites.

The FPD was instrumental in building relevant teaching capacity necessary to support school-wide professional learning. As per the Implementation Plan, through the first round of teacher evaluations, those who demonstrate promise in implementing McCallister practices are identified as candidates for support from me. In the Fall of 2013, I worked with four teachers to develop their practice so that theirs could become anchor classrooms and the system of professional development lab sites could begin. Once lab sites were functional, I began conducting classroom demonstrations in anchor classrooms and the lab site component of the FPD was made available to teachers on a school-wide basis.

The Implementation Plan also specifies that first-round observations will allow the identification of teachers in need of improvement (TINIs). Once anchor classrooms were established, TINIs could begin to visit their colleagues' classrooms in order to satisfy professional development goals they established in their own professional improvement plans.

Teacher evaluation: The Implementation Plan calls for the teacher evaluation process to begin before school begins with classroom environment observations, and to continue in the early weeks of school to identify both high-potential teachers and those in need of improvement. In school walkthroughs, the principal and I normed our observations in relation to the Rubrics. After first phase of informal observations, I began working with the principal to conduct formal observations using the Rubrics as the evaluative framework, musing procedures described in Chapter 26. I continued to provide ongoing support to the principal to utilize the McCallister teacher evaluation system in response to her requests to do teacher observations together, to examine teacher artifacts, and to write up and give feedback on formal teacher evaluation reports (Kerry Decker, personal communication, May 2, 2014 & September 9, 2014).

Curriculum

The structure of the curriculum was an impediment to learning at UAGC that required immediate attention in early Fall 2013. The school had experimented with a number of different curriculum programs throughout the previous four years, and teachers had "piled on" layers of curriculum. The principal asked me to advise her what content to incorporate into standards-based grading systems and student-facing work plans (Kerry Decker, personal communication, September 1, 2013). As a stop-gap measure, I advised that grades be divided into categories: *participation and responsibility taking* (e.g., completing homework and using Formats wisely, but not grading Format participation); *projects* (papers and portfolio items, graded by criteria); *growth of competencies* (based on progress monitoring assessments); and *labs* (if applicable). Behavior indicators in each category should all be actionable and described in terms that could be observed and assigned a value. During a follow-up visit, I asked to see sample syllabi from a range of courses from all departments. Upon examination, I saw that the curriculum in most courses consisted of a large battery of isolated activities, each of which aligned to a different learning standard. These teacher-directed, skills-oriented activities lacked depth and purpose, and the curriculum as a whole was devoid of opportunities for learners to exercise fundamental freedoms in the context of curriculum and to develop self-responsibility, autonomy, and independence. There was little wonder that the course pass rates at the school were low. I told the principal, if I were a student in any one of these classes, I would probably fail the class too. I recommended a radical overhaul of course syllabi and provided a sample syllabus exemplar, with contents from the Sparks Activity Inventory as a template. The sample syllabus provided a menu of activity options that learners could pursue independently, giving them an opportunity to personalize the curriculum and to structure their activity during Work Time in Activity Blocks in courses across the curriculum.

I continued to provide support on improving the curriculum through work with the Curriculum Lead. The primary aim was to support teachers to create self-directed activities for learners to pursue during the Work Time Format that would ensure they could identify discipline-based learning targets and make and execute action plans to meet standards. Rather than assigning activities, the teacher's responsibility within the McCallister curriculum would be to identify a range of activity options that aligned with standards-based competencies, and to broadcast them to learners. As curriculum guide, it was now necessary for the teacher to help the learner identify where they stood in relation to learning expectations, where they needed to get at the end of a given period of time, and how to map a course of activities that would ensure they met their own goals. The school would continue to refine the learner-centered curriculum through the following two years. In September 2015, the principal expressed interest in implementing the Sparks curriculum into the department teams' curriculum maps and into the schools' Keepers of the Culture curriculum (Kerry Decker, personal communication, September 7, 2015).

The Activity Block in UAGC classrooms was initially structured around Work Time, inclusive of Cooperative Unison Reading and Conferences. However, it had become apparent in my work at HSLI and UAGC that learners would need more proleptically powerful learning experiences that aligned directly to the canonical forms of knowledge, such as that on the formal state curriculum, tested in Regents examination. To that end, I introduced the Responsibility Teams Format (now called Learning Teams).[3] Learning Teams are an incredibly powerful context for learning because they employ interdependence and group norms as sources of motivation independent of personal desire. Learners take responsibility to learn what they need to learn out of an obligation to their group. I introduced Learning Teams to the teachers at HSLI and UAGC in November, 2013. Within weeks, they were implemented in all classes across all departments in the school. With pre- and post-tests of social-emotional capacities and content knowledge, learners were able to track their group's progress. And at the conclusion of the Learning Teams tournaments, the dramatic growth that could be observed across groups became a strong source of motivation, even for the most resistant learners.[4] With the implementation of Learning Teams, I was confident we would see improvements in Regents pass rates the upcoming spring.

Throughout the next three years, I would work with the staff at UAGC to develop the "Code Blue" component (now referred to as the Civil Rights Project) of the model, incorporating systems to ensure that those learners who failed to make academic progress received an Academic Intervention and follow-ups, and that all learners developed personal Workout Plans to ensure they achieve academic goals.

Integrating the McCallister Methods into the DNA of the School

UAGC incorporated the McCallister Methods and procedures into formal school policy. In UAGC's second year of participation in the McCallister Initiative, Ms. Decker requested written documents describing the McCallister assessment systems, social norms curriculum, professional development, *code blue* systems, and other distributed leadership systems in order to incorporate them into the school's online handbook in order to adopt them as the schools' official policy (Kerry Decker, personal communication, August 29 and August 30, 2014). As procedures are incorporated into the policy DNA of the school, they become internalized bureaucratic systems that function to strengthen patterns of culture in the school and contribute to the momentum for the achievement of success.

School self-reported implementation accomplishments. The extent to which the school leadership perceived how the components of the McCallister Model were employed as a whole-school design is reflected in school Self Evaluation Reports submitted to the NYC DOE prior to the formal Quality Review process. I participated in the preparation of the School Self Evaluations, providing feedback to principals in the process in 2014, 2015 and 2016. Probably the best summary of UAGC's adherence to the McCallister program implementation criteria are Quality Review Self Evaluations submitted by principals in advance of Quality Reviews in 2014, 2015, 2016, and 2018. A synthesis of content reported in the UAGC Self Evaluation Reports for 2014 and 2016 appear in Boxes 30.1 and 30.2.

Box 30.1

2014 School quality review self evaluation summary of its use of Learning Cultures program components

The school endorses the tenets of the Learning Cultures model—that students learn only what they take responsibility for and that learning is most successful when it is rooted in the social process. It states, "To support this belief across all classrooms, the school reported it implements a leadership, instructional and behavioral school-wide reform model called Learning Cultures developed by Cynthia McCallister Ed.D. at New York University."

Programming. Every classroom is organized into three segments—the Lesson, Work Time, and The Share. All teachers use a uniform conference Format, and teachers and students are provided the following: Cooperative Unison Reading in every subject for 15–20 minutes a day; Learning Conferences weekly for ELLs and students with disabilities, and twice monthly for general education students; The Share in all content and writing classes twice monthly.

Curriculum. Responsibility Teams (now called Learning Teams) were piloted in three classes in Fall 2013 and school-wide in Spring 2014. Student-facing curricula were developed in all classes, including standards targets, personal academic resources, and personal learning plans. Students met periodically to develop learning action plans.

Assessment. Multiple streams of data are assessed continuously. The Degrees of Reading Power are administered in Fall, Winter, and Spring. Data is used in goal-setting conferences with students. Curriculum-based measures are administered every six weeks. Mock Regents were administered through the Responsibility Team program. Monthly opportunity checks are conducted for Cooperative Unison Reading and Conference Records across all classrooms. Frequent informal observations are conducted to assess student discourse quality within high-impact Formats.

Teacher evaluation and professional development. The school utilizes the Learning Cultures Framework for Professional Development (FPD) to embed principal, network coaches and UAGC lead teachers into classrooms to facilitate residencies, modeling a fully implemented curriculum, supporting teachers to develop within the Formats, and ultimately creating professional lab sites. Lab sites are programmed for intervisitation of model classrooms. (1–2 lab sites per week attended by 10 teachers with follow-up debrief.) The principal conducted six lab sites and four residencies, and McCallister conducted more than 10 lab sites in Fall 2013 (supporting social norms, Unison Reading, Responsibility Groups, and conducted five residencies with high-potential teachers). The Professional Development committee coordinates weekly PD schedules through data generated from (Learning Cultures) PD surveys, leadership insights, and teacher learning plans. Frequent teacher observations are conducted with Danielson-aligned Learning Cultures Rubrics, which inform specific feedback. The PD structures emphasize Danielson-aligned Learning Cultures Rubrics and their provision of actionable, evidence-based feedback to teachers. The impact of the PD program resulted in 18 teachers rated Developing and 13 rated Effective by February 2014, confirming all staff were progressing toward Effective.

Bureaucratic systems. The school's identified structures for improvement are described in terms of the Learning Cultures infrastructures of the second-level bureaucratic systems of distributed leadership. The school organizes its bureaucratic infrastructure around the Learning Cultures system of distributed leadership, identifying outcomes of project-related goals as follows:

- Behavior Leads (e.g., School Culture Leads) to implement social norms curriculum
- Professional Development Leads to implement the Learning Cultures Framework for *Professional Development
- Assessment Leads to implement the progress monitoring systems (CBMs, DRPs, mock Regents)
- Code Blue Team to develop Academic Interventions

The school's action plan outlines how the Leads work together to enact the school's educational program. The Leads meet weekly to target instructional improvement.

Participation in the Learning Cultures Initiative. Citywide PD days are coordinated with other schools participating in the Learning Cultures Initiative.

School culture. The school's initiative to improve the school culture is organized around the implementation of Responsibility Based Cognitive Discipline (sic) model (McCallister, 2013f) and the social norms curriculum. The school's goal in implementing McCallister's Model is to routinize the teacher culture, secure common structures to create coherent environments with common social norms that support positive student behaviors, and to enforce social norms that enable promotive and responsible learning environments.

The school reported its action plan in relation to school climate was to adhere to the Learning Cultures Classroom Environment criteria in preparing uniform classroom environments across the school. They did this by working in department teams prior to the school year to prepare classrooms according to classroom environment criteria (established in the Classroom Environment Rubric). The school implemented the social norms curriculum, including the Social Contract Talk, and "On-call" system.

Confirmation of a Successful School Transformation

Close implementation of the McCallister program through two-year-long recursive iterations of the Year-long Implementation Plan[7] enabled UAGC to be transformed into a successful learning organization. The 2017 UAGC graduation rate more than doubled the 2012 Brandeis and 2013 UAGC graduation rates (see Table 30.5).

In March 2014, less than a year after receiving an "F" on its report card, the school earned a rating of "Proficient" on its quality review, which assesses Instruction, School Culture, and Systems for Improvement within the school. The quality review process results in one of four scores: UD (Underdeveloped); D (Developing); P (Proficient); WD

Box 30.2

2016 School quality review self evaluation summary of Learning Cultures program components

The school reported that 100% of teachers took part in the Learning Cultures Framework for Professional Development in 2015–2016.

Instructional Core: Curriculum

The school reported that its curriculum is aligned to the common Core Learning Standards and/or content standards in the following ways: students breach and ask their own questions of the curriculum (as per Cooperative Unison Reading); they research information and write "briefs" to argue, inform, or explain concepts to members of Responsibility Teams (now called Learning Teams); teachers keep lesson inventories and standards checklists as per the instructional accounting protocols; students take part in monthly Learning Conferences in each subject; students develop Individual Academic Plans (aka Workout Plans) and develop Behavior Contracts with the UAGC Keepers of the Culture group.

The school reported that it refined academic tasks to provide students access to the Common Core Standards in the following ways: Unison Reading and the conference records ensure alignment to the Common Core. Staff use these records with students, along with writing pieces, in department teams to plan instruction and curriculum modification; Grassroots Lessons are drawn from student work and experiences in Conferences, Cooperative Unison Reading, and Research Briefs; and students are presented with learning standards, which they use to map their learning.

The school reported the powerful impact of its work as follows: improved graduation rates from 39% in 2013, to 49% in 2014, to 68% in 2015; and higher levels of performance on ELA Regents performance, with Regents ELA pass rate in 2013 of 32.7% to a 74.3% pass rate in 2015 in a student cohort in which only 17.1% of students passed their 8th-grade ELA exam. The school also reported higher levels of Regents pass rates in Living Environment from 26.8% in 2013 to 59% in 2015, and in U.S. History from 18.3% in 2013 to 54% in 2014. The number of students receiving the more rigorous Regents Diploma (compared to the Local Diploma) increased from 28.4% in 2014 to 48.8% in 2015. College enrollment increased from 73.1% in 2015 to 84.6% in 2015.

Instructional Core: Pedagogy

The school reported its instructional focus and the use of the Danielson Framework for Teaching relate to the coherent teaching practices of the Learning Cultures Formats. Every classroom program includes the Formats of Unison Reading, Responsibility Teams, the Learning Conference, Work Time, and the Share. In its self-evaluation report, the school provided a summary of each Format and aligning standards from the Common Core State Standards and the Danielson Framework, below:

"The Lesson – A venue for teachers to present competencies drawn from grassroots student experiences (from the Formats below) for skills and strategies for learning and perspective-shifting discourse (Danielson 1a, 3d).

Unison Reading – Students participate in a group dialogue about a text. To practice perspectives and reasoning cooperatively. To access new knowledge and to develop literacy skills. (CCLSR.1–10, Danielson 1a, 1e, 2a, 3b, 3c, 3d).

Responsibility Teams – The purpose is to meet objectives outlined in the formal curriculum and learning standards. Students collaborate to learn concepts by taking collective responsibility for research and then preparing information summaries in the form of a written 'brief' in order to share concepts they were responsible for learning in Unison Reading (CCLSR. 7,8, CCSLR.SL. 1,2,3,4,6, CCRA.L.1,2,3,4, CCRA.W.1,2,4,5,6,7,8,9,10, Danielson 1e, 2a, 3c, 3d).

The Learning Conference – Develops cognitive control and strengthens a growth mindset by allowing students an opportunity to dissect a challenge, resolve it and retell the process. Develops strategic thinking by allowing students to make goals that can be applied to novel situations. (CCLSR. 2,4,6, CCSLR.SL. 1,6, CCRA.1, CCRA.W8, Danielson 1a, 2a, 2d, 3b, 3d).

Work Time – Provides an opportunity to practice autonomy, agency, and independence in meeting learning goals. Supports motivation and engagement by offering maximal freedom of movement, speech, and activity within the constraints of the Work Time Format criteria, providing an opportunity to work cooperatively and develop interdependence and collaboration skills (CCLS, Danielson Domains 1–4).

The Share – Provides opportunity to receive feedback to inform the processes of writing and revision. To provide all participants with opportunities to develop critical insights about the dynamics of written genres (CCRA.R.1,7,8, CCRA.SL.1, 2,3,5,6, CCRA.L.1,3,CCRA.W.1,5,6,7,8,9, Danielson 1e,2a,2d,3b,3c,3d)."

The school reported that its teaching practices provide multiple entry points, supports, and extensions to all students. In this regard, they report the following: "a) The Learning Cultures pedagogy is based upon students being agents of their own learning and learning the soft skills necessary for success in life: As students breach, formulate their own questions and units of study, the different Formats enable them to activate new and unique strategies to push beyond their current limits. Presented on the top of every Unison tracker are the cooperative literacy strategies that students are pushed to understand and regularly utilize. The teacher facilitates the students activating these processes organically, centered on their need, rather than pushing it upon them at a time when there may be no clear application. The collaborative elements of Unison, Work Time, & Share, as well as the heterogeneous groupings, ensure that students, no matter their designation, get support for their specific need. b) These structures motivate students to participate and give voice to their confusions. English Language Learners and students with disabilities are fully integrated into these groups. Therefore, it's the student, not the teacher, who differentiates instruction to student needs. c) Extensions to all students take the form of students changing groups frequently so that they have access to all kinds of learners and group dynamics. Students who need extra time or support have more frequent access to small-group learning (Unison Reading and Learning Groups) or One-One Learning Conferences. All of our classrooms have two teachers (co-teachers or teacher assist 2/3 classes) so that more students can be supported in small group and one-one Learning Conferences."

The school offered an explanation for how instructional practices promote high levels of student thinking and participation as follows: "a) Perspective-shifting discourse through student-initiated breaches fosters a discursive, collaborative approach to learning. b) In all of our Learning Cultures classrooms, students collaborate with peers in heterogeneous groups to access new knowledge and to develop literacy skills through discourse. The primary aim of the Learning Cultures pedagogy is to develop perspective-shifting discourse and cooperative reasoning abilities. The process of socially referenced thinking (ToM) is what is referred to in our curriculum as *triangulation, the highest form of higher-order thinking*. For example, across all content classrooms student academic tasks include reading complex texts in a Unison Reading group, and then preparing information summaries in the form of a written 'brief' in order to share concepts they were responsible for learning in Unison Reading. Brief summaries are meant to be comprehensive and accessible to all learners (ELL and Sped) to permit a fuller understanding of the target concept. Each student must demonstrate their thinking with others in a Large Group or Table Share and be open to feedback to revise their summaries."

The school indicated the impact of its work to date as follows:

a We cross-check instructional content against standards in the instructional points section of the Unison records. These records showcase that students consistently use skills and strategies aligned to the CCLS when shifting perspectives to achieve full understanding of texts and ideas. For example, in one breach, a group reading very complex texts with ELL and SPED students had 17 turns of conversation, the teacher had only one conversational turn, and they used 8 different strategies and skills to understand how the author intended to use the word irascible.

b Growth model for grading and outcomes (aligned to the CCLS) allows every student to hit growth goals that will achieve college readiness by graduation as measured by the DRP growth (% at grade level and college career readiness). For example, Graduating class 2016, Cohort R (consistent growth, despite serious drops over the summer). This class entered 9th grade with only 15% passing the 8th grade ELA exam. The DRP score in the fall of 2012 demonstrated the same results with only 12.5% of the cohort reaching national grade level standards for reading comprehension. Over the last three years, the class has grown steadily from 12.5% to 30% passing grade level standards in reading comprehension in the spring of 2015.

   1 Year 1: 12.5% to 25%
   2 Year 2: 19.2% to 24.4%
   3 Year 3: 22.7% to 30%

c The Learning Cultures rubrics articulate teacher and student responsibilities in each of the Formats, leading to higher performance in the Formats by teachers (ratings) and students (leading to literacy growth outlined below):

Advance Teacher Ratings SY 2014–2015 to SY 2015–2016

- Highly Effective: 19% to 33%
- Effective: 60% to 56%
- Developing: 20% to 11%
- Ineffective: 1% to 0%

Instructional Core: Assessment

The school reported how it aligns assessments to curricula and analyzes data to improve student learning, and indicates its impact of this work, below:

Students grades are made up of 25% summative assessments and 75% formative assessments. Students have numerous opportunities to track their progress through formative assessments through Unison Reading debriefs and records, Learning Conference Records, Responsibility Team Social Survey (aka C-DEEP within the Learning Cultures model), Responsibility Team Briefs, Genre Practice writing, Grassroots Lessons, Promise Cards, and Workout Plans. Students are provided clear "next steps" for each assessment though Format Rubrics. Rubrics are consistent across departments. The Common Core and Regents-based standards-aligned assessments,[5] associated with the Responsibility Teams Format, include monthly study guides and tests and student-generated weekly inquiry questions.

The school reported how it uses assessment data to adjust curriculum and instruction as follows: the school uses the Learning Cultures Progress monitoring systems, including (a) the Degrees of Reading Power administered three times annually to measure students' literacy growth; (b) monthly Curriculum-based Measure in writing fluency; (c) monthly Responsibility Team Self-Survey (aka, C-DEEP) to provide peers with social-emotional feedback. Students who struggle socially or emotionally create and keep a Promise Card that is created in meetings with the Keepers of the Culture group, and which includes a change narrative (aka, Transformation Narrative). Promise Cards and Workout Plans are considered an integral part of curriculum.

The impact of the curriculum-aligned assessment work was reported by the school as follows: there was consistent, school-wide growth indicated in Degrees of Reading Power results. For example, 25% of students who were three or more grade levels below national reading standards in the fall of 2015 are now on or above grade level standards in January 2016. The graduating class of 2017 entered 9th grade with only 10% passing the eighth-grade ELA exam. Their 9th-grade Fall DRP scores showed a similar national reading level with only 10.5% testing at grade level. Within two years, this cohort of students grew to 30% passing the DRP in May 2015. The Degrees of Reading Power results give students and teachers a point of conversation to track literacy growth and college/career readiness, and to set growth goals in the context of Academic Interventions. Data from the Curriculum-based Measures show an increase in student fluency across time. For example, Writing Fluency scores in one class rose from below the 10% nationally to above the 50th percentile in one year. Trends in credit accumulation improved across the school. In 2013, the 9th-grade pass rate was 60% compared to a 93.2% pass rate in 2015. Student suspensions dropped by 41% from January 2015 to January 2016.

School Culture

The school reported it makes effort to communicate high expectations to all students in the following ways; (a) The Learning Cultures rubrics, aligned to the Danielson Framework, are used by school leaders and teachers to frame both instructional expectations and student learning outcomes; (b) The school Website provides transparent access to the curriculum, pedagogical methods, assessment practices, and school-wide policies, and publishes student writing; (c) The school principal reviews students' rights and responsibilities through the Social Contract Talk, which is given in each classroom. The Talk provides a collaborative context in which the principal, with input from students, develops the Classroom Responsibility Ladder.

Academic and Behavior Interventions are employed as a strategy, in partnership with families, to support students' progress toward college and career readiness. In school-wide Academic Interventions, teachers, administrators, and guidance counselors engage students and families to create a Workout Plan for each student, a minimum of four times a year, which is determined based on analysis of performance data, including transcripts, attendance records, credit accumulation, Degrees of Reading Power, and Curriculum-based Measures data. Some students take part in Behavior Interventions, a product of which is the Promise Card. This process affords them the opportunity to reflect on social and academic behaviors that may be getting in the way of their full participation and achievement.

The impact of the school culture work is reflected in increases in college enrollment, from 61.5% of graduates of 2013 to 84.6% for 2015 graduates. From Spring 2013 to Spring 2015, Principal Decker facilitated Behavior Interventions with students and parents, resulting in 50 Promise Cards. In Spring 2015, the process of the creation of Promise Cards was handed over to students in the Keepers of the Culture program, who manage a growing caseload of over 70 Promise Cards and 12 weekly Intervention meetings. The Principal Suspension rate dropped by 41% once the Keepers of the Culture program began in January 2015.

Structures for Improvement (Teacher Teams)

Teachers take part in weekly professional development lab sites based on self-determined learning needs. All PD practices and observations are linked to Learning Cultures Rubrics. PD offerings are based on the Framework for Professional Development (McCallister, 2009a, 2010) and involve lab sites, intervisitations, and study groups. Weekly department meetings are a context for teachers to examine CBM results, pre- and post-test results from Responsibility Team units, breach resolvers, and students' research syntheses. The school's Steering Committee incorporates the second-level distributed leadership responsibilities outlined in the Learning Cultures model, including leads in Code Blue, Curriculum, Behavior, Community Education, and Professional Development. The principal meets weekly with each lead.

The school reports a significant impact of the school culture structures. Specifically, the school reports the creation of the Keepers of the Culture program in 2015,[6] which resulted in a 300% increase in the number of students who receive Behavior Interventions and a 41% decrease in School Suspensions. The school reported being on track for reducing the suspension rate for students with disabilities by 50% and that the suspension rate of students with disabilities was lower than that of the General Education population as a direct result of the Behavior Interventions provided by the Keepers of the Culture program. The school also implemented a Keepers of Unison program, to which they attributed rapid gains in Degrees of Reading Power scores. The school also implemented the Learning Cultures' teacher On-call program, to which they attributed reduced suspension rates, increased attendance, reduced tardiness, and reduced classroom removals. Only 7 of 84 incidents reported at the time of the self-evaluation report occurred in the hallways. And attendance increased steadily over four years from 79% in 2013 to 84.7% by January 2016.

Teacher evaluation and professional development. A total of 100% of teachers participate in the McCallister Framework for Professional Development activities.

Curriculum. Students engage directly with CCLS and content standards through the McCallister personalized curriculum components. Students ask their own questions through the Cooperative Unison Reading process of breaching, or posing their own questions. Teachers employ Learning Cultures Lesson Inventories and Standards Checklists in relation to CCLS. All students take part in daily Unison Reading. Students write "briefs" (as per Learning Team protocol) that they share with teammates to develop collaborative understanding. The classroom environment is employed as an aspect of curriculum (Classroom Environment Rubrics specify environmental criteria). Students take part in both a reading course and a writing course every year (structured by the Learning Cultures Activity Block Formats). Students are active participants in pursuing their own goals through Behavior Contracts developed four times annually with peers through the Keepers of the Culture program and monthly Learning Conferences in each subject, in which students have opportunity to dissect a challenge, resolve it, retell the process, and retell their triumph narrative. The curriculum continues to emphasize the process of breaching, in which the learner exercises their own intentions, asking their own questions of the texts they read, and developing higher-order thinking by exchanging perspectives with others. The school recognizes the value of mental coordination in using and developing Theory of Mind and social cognition. The Formats are recognized as contexts in which learners have opportunities to develop CCLS-aligned competencies.

Impact. The school recognizes that, with full implementation of the McCallister Model, students' literacy levels increased dramatically in both Math and ELA.

(Well Developed). In a period of seven months, UAGC improved its rating by two full rating levels. The principal sent the school staff a congratulatory post Review email that confirmed that the school had succeeded in using Learning Cultures as a school-wide reform model that implemented fully in six months (Kerry Decker, personal communication, March 17, 2014). See Table 30.4 for an explanation of the alignment between school quality criteria used in the 2014 Quality Review process and McCallister Model program components. The external quality review rating was substantiated by improving trends in student achievement. The average pass rate on the annual Regents exam in ELA after the first year of implementation rose from 50% in 2013 to 68% in 2014. The graduation rate increased from 39.8% in 2014 to 49.3% in 2014 (see Table 30.5).

Table 30.4 A crosswalk of 2013–2014 School Quality Criteria and UAGC Quality Review ratings that align with Learning Cultures program components

School Quality Category	School Quality Criteria used in the 2013–2014 Quality Review	Learning Cultures program features that align with School Quality Criteria
Instructional Core	1.1: Ensure engaging, rigorous, and coherent curricula in all subjects, accessible for a variety of learners and aligned to Common Core Learning Standards and/or content standards (Rating: Proficient). 1.2: Develop teacher pedagogy from a coherent set of beliefs about how students learn best that is informed by the instructional shifts and Danielson Framework for Teaching, aligned to the curricula, engaging, and meets the needs of all learners so that all students produce meaningful work products (Rating: Proficient). 2.2: Align assessments to curricula, use ongoing assessment and grading practices, and analyze information on student learning outcomes to adjust instructional decisions at the team and classroom levels (Rating: Proficient).	1.1: Learning Cultures curriculum of Format Rubrics; Learning Cultures personalized curriculum. 1.2: Learning Cultures Rubrics outline a comprehensive set of pedagogical methods that were developed by Dr. McCallister to reflect what is currently known about how all people learn and a personalized curriculum that is personally meaningful for all students and promotes high levels of engagement. 2.2: Learning Cultures Format assessments provide ongoing opportunities, within the context of daily classroom practice, to generate information about student learning that can be used to plan instruction.
School Culture	1.4: Maintain a culture of mutual trust and positive attitudes that supports the academic and personal growth of students and adults (Rating: Developing). 3.4: Establish a culture for learning that communicates high expectations to staff, students and families, and provide supports to achieve those expectations (Rating: Proficient).	1.4: The Learning Cultures Social Norms Curriculum provides an actionable plan that can be used by students, teachers, and school leaders to develop a positive school culture. 3.4: The Learning Cultures Format Rubrics establish explicit expectations that are catalyzed through practice, as learners and teachers self-regulate and conform to norms.
Systems for Improvement	1.3: Make strategic organizational decisions to support the school's instructional goals and meet student learning needs, as evidenced by meaningful student work products (Rating: Proficient). 3.1: Establish a coherent vision of school improvement that is reflected in a short list of focused, data-based goals that are tracked for progress and are understood and supported by the entire school community (Rating: Proficient).	1.3: The Learning Cultures Year-long Implementation Plan outlines a comprehensive set of directives to be executed through a system of distributed leadership to ensure the school meets student learning needs and universal goals for instruction to ensure all children are provided opportunities to learn that are sufficient to enable them to meet their potential.

(Continued)

Table 30.4 A crosswalk of 2013–2014 School Quality Criteria and UAGC Quality Review ratings that align with Learning Cultures program components *(Continued)*

School Quality Category	School Quality Criteria used in the 2013–2014 Quality Review	Learning Cultures program features that align with School Quality Criteria
	4.1: Observe teachers using the Danielson Framework for Teaching along with the analysis of learning outcomes to elevate school-wide instructional practices and implement strategies that promote professional growth and reflection (Rating: Proficient). 4.2: Engage in structured professional collaborations on teams using an inquiry approach that promotes shared leadership and focuses on improved student learning (Rating: Proficient). 4.3: Evaluate the quality of school-level decisions, making adjustments as needed to increase coherence of policies and practices across the school, with particular attention to CCLS (Rating: Proficient).	3.1: The Learning Cultures model embodies a coherent vision of school improvement that is reflected in prescribed, data-based goals, staged through a school-wide progress monitoring assessment system, which is used by the entire school community to track success. 4.1: Teachers are observed and evaluated using the Learning Cultures Format Rubrics, which are aligned to Danielson Framework criteria. McCallister's Framework for Professional Development prescribes training and professional learning experiences that are integrated into the bureaucratic systems of the school, which teachers employ to engage in self-directed professional learning. 4.2: The Framework for Professional Development specifies that teachers collaborate in teacher-led teams to employ an inquiry approach to professional learning focused on classroom practice. 4.3: Judgments about the quality of school-level decisions are made in reference to criteria for first- and second-level systems specified in the Learning Cultures design.

The Implementation Plan was followed with fidelity through AY 2014–2015.[8] Graduation rates rose again between 2014 and 2015 to 68% and increase of 19%. A year-and-a-half into the McCallister turnaround at UAGC, 100% of teachers reported feeling safe in the school. In 2015–2016, the school received a "well developed" on its quality review, one of only 7% of schools citywide to receive that high rating. In 2017, the first cohort to have had exposure to the McCallister program for four years in every grade and subject graduated at a rate of 83%, more than doubling its 2013 graduation rate of 39.8% in 2013 (see Table 30.5). A total of 76% of all students were deemed proficient in ELA in 2017 compared to 54% in 2013; and 59% of students were deemed proficient in math compared to 48% in 2013. The percentage of students who received the more rigorous Regents high school diploma (as opposed to the Local diploma) doubled between 2013 and 2017. Measures of academic rigor also improved. In 2017, 29.0% of UAGC graduates were deemed to be ready for college compared to 0.0% in 2013 UAGC. The school culture of UAGC improved dramatically from 2013 to 2017. In its School Quality Report of 2017, UAGC received top metrics in the categories of Rigorous Instruction (4.61 out of 4.99), Collaborative Teachers (4.45 out of 4.99), Supportive Environment (3.81 out of 4.99), and Effective School Leadership (3.91 out of 4.99) (see Table 30.6, 30.7, and 30.8 for data indicators of school quality in 2016–2017).[9]

Table 30.5 Comparative demographic and achievement data for Brandeis High School and Urban Assembly School for Green Careers, 2012–2017

Metric	Brandeis High School 2012	UAGC 2013	UAGC 2014	UAGC 2015	UAGC 2016	UAGC 2017
Total students	288	375				313
Free lunch (%)	56	88				86
Reduced lunch (%)	4	5				5
Limited English proficient/English language learners (%)	28	24				14
Disabilities (%)	19	21				28
Black (%)	30	25				27
Hispanic (%)	67	71				64
White (%)	1	2				4
Asian (%)	2	2				2
Suspensions	67 @ 8%	12 @ 4%				13 @ 4%
Dropout	109 @ 35%	12 @ 4%				9 @ 10%
Graduation rate (four-year, August)	38.9%	39.8% (7% citywide)		66.3%		82.8% (57% citywide)
Regents (%)	66	30				65
Local diploma (%)	23	18				20
College readiness		0.0% (0.0% relative to citywide and 0.0% relative to peer)		10%		29.0% (57% relative to city and 35% relative to peer)
College and career preparatory course index		12.2% (15.9% relative to citywide and 35.1% relative to peer)		2.5%		18% (51% relative to citywide and 27% relative to peer)
ELA proficiency	All: 56% Black: 65% Hispanic: 51% Disabilities: 15%	All: 54% Black: Not reported Hispanic: 53% Disabilities: 24%	–	–	–	All: 76% Black: 64% Hispanic: 80% Disabilities: 55%
ELA state exam score level 1 (%)	39	14	–	–	–	2
ELA level 2 (%)	5	33	–	–	–	9
ELA level 3 (%)	47	48	–	–	–	30
ELA level 4 (%)	9	0	–	–	–	46
Math proficiency	All: 57% Black: 68% Hispanic: 53% Disabilities: 19%	All: 48% Black: Not reported Hispanic: 51% Disabilities: 10%	–	–	–	All: 59% Black: 52% Hispanic: 59% Disabilities: 17%
Math level 1 (%)	8	14	–	–	–	6
Math level 2 (%)	9	33	–	–	–	32
Math level 3 (%)	54	48	–	–	–	55
Math level 4 (%)	3	0	–	–	–	0

Source: NYC DOE School Progress Reports and NY State Education Department for Brandeis High School 2011–2012; UAGC 2012–2013; and UAGC 2016–2017.

Table 30.6 UAGC 2016–2017 school quality data

Category	Descriptor (score)	Score out of 4.99
Rigorous Instruction	Academic Press (2.50) Common Core shifts in literacy instruction (4.64) Common Core shifts in math instruction (4.38) Course clarity (1.57) Quality of student discussion (4.15) Level of interest and challenge in the curriculum (4.99) Effectiveness of teaching and learning (4.99) How well the school assesses what students are learning (4.99)	**4.61**
Collaborative Teachers	Cultural awareness and Inclusive Classroom Instruction: 1.67 out of 4.99 Quality of Professional Development: 3.24 out of 4.99 School Commitment (how committed teachers are to the school): 2.56 out of 4.99 Innovation and Collective Responsibility: 4.45 out of 4.99 Peer Collaboration: 4.73 out of 4.99 Quality of Professional Development: 3.79 out of 4.99 School Commitment: 4.02 out of 4.99 How well teachers work with each other: 4.99	**4.45**
Supportive Environment	Classroom Behavior: 2.52 out of 4.99 Guidance: 3.15 out of 4.99 Peer support for academic work: 2.57 out of 4.99 Personal attention and support: 2.60 out of 4.99 Safety: 4.0 out of 4.99 Social-emotional: 4.79 out of 4.99 Clarity of expectations to students and staff: 4.99	**3.81**
Effective School Leadership	Inclusive leadership: 2.11 out of 4.99 Instructional leadership: 4.53 out of 4.99 Program coherence: 4.50 out of 4.99 Teacher influence: 4.51 out of 4.99	**3.91**
Strong Family-Community	Outreach to parents: 3.00 out of 4.99 Parental involvement in school: 1.31 out of 4.99 Trust: 3.71 out of 4.99 Parent-principal trust: 2.56 out of 4.99 Parent-teacher trust: 2.00 Student-teacher trust: 2.54 Teacher-principal trust: 4.60 Teacher-teacher trust: 4.17	**2.58**

The McCallister Model at UAGC: A Retrospective Analysis

The McCallister school transformation initiative at UAGC was a success according to conventional school turnaround standards (Duncan, 2009; Kutash et al., 2010). Graduation rates were on an upward trajectory through 2016–2017, when the graduation rate of 83% placed the school in the 57th percentile citywide (Table 30.5). But then graduation rates began to decline. In 2018, the four-year graduation rate of 78.8% placed the school in the 41st percentile citywide, and in 2017–2018, the graduation rate of 77.1% placed the school in the 29th percentile citywide. The school culture also improved dramatically throughout the period of implementation. Apart from achievement and school culture metrics, the UAGC implementation offers other insights about the potential of the McCallister Model to impact children's opportunity to learn.

Table 30.7 UAGC progress report data, 2016–2017

Measure	Green careers	Borough	City
4-year graduation (%)	83	75	74
College readiness (%)	29	35 (peer schools)	57
CCPCI (Advanced courses) (%)	18	27 (peer schools)	51
Progress Toward Graduation: percent of ninth graders earned enough credits to be on track for graduation (%)	100	85	85
Progress Toward Graduation: percent of tenth graders earned enough credits to be on track for graduation (%)	87	84	82
College readiness (%)	29	50	46
Rigorous Instruction (How interesting and challenging is the curriculum? How effective is the teaching and learning? How well does the school assess what students are learning?) (%)	81	80	79
Collaborative Teachers (How well teachers work with each other and are developed and evaluated.) (%)	90	81	83
Supportive Environment (How clearly are high expectations communicated to students and staff? How safe and inclusive is the school? Movement of students with special needs to less restrictive environments.)			
Effective School Leadership (How well are resources aligned to instructional goals? How well does school meet its goals? How well does the school make decision?) (%)	93	84	85
Trust (Trust in principal; teachers trust in each other; parents trust of teachers; students' perceptions about how respectfully they are treated by teachers.) (%)	89	87	87
Percent of students agreed or strongly agreed that their teachers use examples of students' different cultures/backgrounds/families in their lessons to make learning more meaningful for them (%)	87	88	88
Percent of students agreed or strongly agreed that they see people of many races, ethnicities, cultures, and backgrounds represented in the curriculum (%)	87	88	88
Percent of students agreed or strongly agreed that, in general, their teachers treat students from different cultures or backgrounds equally (%)	85	89	90
Percent of students agreed or strongly agreed that their teachers respect their culture/background (%)	92	92	94
Percent of students agreed or strongly agreed that, in general, their teachers make the lessons relevant to their everyday life experiences (%)	70	77	74
Percent of students agreed or strongly agreed that, in general, their teachers present positive images of people from a variety of races, ethnicities, cultures, and backgrounds (%)	90	91	91

(Continued)

Table 30.7 UAGC progress report data, 2016–2017

Measure	Green careers	Borough	City
Percent of teachers agreed or strongly agreed that they are able to receive support around how to incorporate students' cultural and linguistic backgrounds in their practice (%)	87	80	81
Percent of teachers agreed or strongly agreed that they are able to use their students' prior knowledge to make their lessons relevant to their everyday life (%)	100	96	96
Percent of teachers agreed or strongly agreed that they are able to modify instructional activities and materials to meet the development needs and learning interests of all their students (%)	100	96	95
Percent of teachers agreed or strongly agreed that they are able to adapt instruction to ensure it represents all cultures/backgrounds positively (%)	98	95	94
Percent of teachers agreed or strongly agreed that they are able to design appropriate instruction that is matched to students' need (e.g., English language learners (ELL) proficiency and students with disabilities) (%)	97	89	92
Percent of teachers agreed or strongly agreed that they are able to apply their knowledge of parents' various cultural backgrounds when collaborating with them regarding their child's educational progress (%)	97	92	88
Percent of teachers agreed or strongly agreed that they are able to develop appropriate Individual Education Programs for their students with disabilities (%)	97	88	89
Teachers agreed or strongly agreed that they are able to distinguish linguistic/cultural differences from learning disabilities (%)	100	92	91

While the graduation rates at UAGC climbed significantly over the four-year implementation of the model, ratings for college, and career readiness ratings remained relatively flat. For example, graduates performed on measures of academic excellence well below those of HSLI according to published NYC DOE achievement metrics. The College and Career Preparatory Course Index was over three times higher in the 2015 HSLI cohort compared to the 2017 UAGC cohort. HSLI's 4-year College Readiness Index was more than 20% higher than that of UAGC, and the 4-year College Readiness Index for the HSLI's lowest third was 63% higher than that of UAGC, at 0.0%. In other words, of all students in the school's lowest third academically, none were deemed prepared for college. These differences might be explained by several factors. HSLI grew a grade at a time, securing positive academic and social norms each year as it grew, whereas UAGC had the additional burden of a toxic culture that that required human capital in the form of energy and attention to correct, which might have otherwise been invested into the educational infrastructure. Differences might also be due to a disruption in leadership at the departure of the principal in the third year of implementation. Also, the Urban Assembly network ended the Learning Cultures Initiative after the second year of implementation, and the school all but eliminated site-based training support for teachers at that time.

Education and economics. In order to understand relationship between education reform and economic opportunity, we will compare the projected life earnings of the graduating

Table 30.8 UAGC 2017 school quality report metrics

Category	Results	Metric score (out of 4.99)
ELA Average student proficiency	2.64	3.44
ELA Average student proficiency school's lowest third	2.12	3.50
ELA percentage of students at Level 3 or 4	32.1%	3.76
Math average student proficiency	2.25	1.65
Math average student proficiency of school's lowest third	1.82	1.94
Math percentage of students at Level 3 or 4	14.8%	1.90
ELA course pass rate	95.5%	3.68
Math course pass rate	92.9%	3.35
Science course pass rate	97.4%	4.13
Social Studies course pass rate	92.9%	3.01
ELA Integrated co-teaching	2.35	4.95
ELA Self-contained	2.12	4.85
ELA-ELLs	2.17	Not reported
ELA Lowest third citywide	2.20	4.73
ELA Black and Hispanic males in lowest third citywide	Not reported	
Math Integrated co-teaching	1.79	1.67
Math ELLs	2.10	Not reported
Math lowest third citywide	1.87	1.93
Math Black and Hispanic Males in lowest third	Not reported	Not reported
ELL progress	57.1%	
Earned 10+ credits in their first year	100.0%	4.99
Lowest third in the school to earn 10+ credits in their first year	100.0%	4.99
Average completion rate for English Regents	68.8%	2.84
Average completion rate for algebra I Regents	60.9%	2.42
Average completion rate for living environment Regents	63.6%	2.69
Average completion rate for global history Regents	54.1%	1.87
Average completion rate for U.S. history Regents	63.6%	2.33
Average 4-year graduation rate	82.8%	4.14
6-year graduation rate	80.0%	3.72
College/career preparatory course index[10]	8.0%	1.74
4-year high school persistence	83.9%	2.59
6-year high school persistence	80.0%	3.23
4-year readiness index[11]	31.0%	4.80
6-year college readiness index	10.0%	4.80
Postsecondary enrollment rate—6 months	10.0%	3.62
Postsecondary enrollment rate—18 months	61.3%	4.35
4-year graduation rate English language learners	75%	–
4-year graduation rate self-contained/ICT/SETTS	73.3%	3.73
4-year graduation rate lowest third citywide	65.8%	3.83
4-year graduation rate Black/Hispanic males	65.2%	4.05
College and career readiness of students in lowest third citywide, college, and career preparatory course index	0.0%	1.00
College and career readiness of students in lowest third citywide, 4-year college readiness index	7.9%	4.99
College and career readiness of students in lowest third citywide, postsecondary enrollment rate—6 months	25.5%	3.19

Source: NYC DOE School Performance Dashboard https://tools.nycenet.edu/dashboard/#dbn=03M402&report_type=HS&view=City.

Table 30.9 Comparative projected life earnings for 2012 Columbus graduates and 2015 HSLI graduates

School	Total students	Projected income for dropouts	Projected income for still enrolled	Projected income for high school graduates (number of local diploma) with no college	Projected income for college graduates (number of grads with Regents)	Projected income for advanced Regents	Average life earnings for cohort
Brandeis 2012 graduates	293 total 144 grads	N = 99 × $885K = $87.62M	N = 68 × $1M = $68M	N = 8 × $1.12M = $8.96M	N = 84 × $1.76M = $147.84M	N = 22 × 2.19 = $48.18M	$360.56M/ 293 = **$1.23M**
UAGC 2013 graduates	98 total 39 grads	N = 10 × $885K = $8.85M	N = 49 × $1M = $49M	N = 8 × $1.12M = $8.96M	N = 31 × $1.76M = $54.56M	0	$121.37M/98 = **$1.24M**
UAGC 2015 graduates	87 total 72 grads	N = 9 × $885 = $7.97M	N = 4 × $1M = $4M	N = 19 × $1.12M = $21.28M	N=53 @ $1.76M = $93.28M	0	$126.53M/87 = **$1.45M**

Source: Social Security Administration (2020).

class of 2012 of Brandeis High School with the UAGC graduating class of 2013, when the school ranked in the bottom 1% of schools citywide, and the UAGC class of 2017, the first cohort to have had the Learning Cultures curriculum for four years. These figures are calculated by taking the total number of students in the grade (graduates plus non-graduates) and adding the number of students who dropped out. Using this figure as the hypothetical class size, we assign values for projected lifetime earning in four different educational attainment groups (dropouts are calculated to earn $0.89M; non-graduates or those still enrolled are predicted to earn $1.0K; high school graduates with local diplomas predicted to earn $1.12; high school graduates with Regents diplomas predicted to finish college and earn $1.76K; and advanced Regents predicted to earn $2.19). Based on these projections, 2017 UAGC graduates will earn an average of $220K more over their lifetimes than 2012 Brandeis graduates and $210K more than UAGC 2013 graduates. However, compared to the HSLI graduating class of 2015 who had four years of the Learning Cultures curriculum in full implementation, who will earn an average of $1.72M over their lifetimes, UAGC 2017 graduates will earn $270K less over their lifetimes. If 30% of UAGC graduates had earned advanced diplomas, as was the case with the HSLI graduating class of 2015, 16 students would have been projected to earn an additional $430K over their lifetimes, bringing the mean projected lifetime income of the UAGC 2017 graduating cohort to $1.53M, an average of $80K more in lifetime earnings than was the case (Table 30.9).

"The Rise of the Phoenix" and the Rebirth of Failing Public Schools

The principal of Green Careers from 2013 to 2016 described the transformation of Green Careers as *the Rise of the Phoenix* (Decker, 2019). The phoenix, a mythological bird that was said to have risen from the ashes is, perhaps, an apt metaphor for a failing school that was transformed in the astonishing pace of a single year. A transformation so dramatic and rapid has not been documented in the school reform literature (Backstrom, 2019; Dragoset et al., 2017). Perhaps the reform stories of UAGC and the other case studies reported here have the makings of good mythology. But characterizing it in this way would be inaccurate. The transformations of UAGC and the other schools recounted in this chapter are outcomes of a scientifically based experiment in social reform through comprehensive school reform. Reports of these transformations are not myths but evidence that a theoretically and scientifically informed intervention implemented with fidelity can be replicated multiple times as a means to provide large populations of children with opportunities to learn that are sufficient to enable them to achieve their potential. The principals of these schools, as public servants invested with the public trust to ensure children in their schools have access to an education on equal terms, bravely embraced a radical innovation that upturned conventional practices pervasive not only in NYC DOE schools, but in schools everywhere. Their courage paid off. And their stories offer hope that their successes can be replicated by other schools where more children can benefit.

Lessons Learned

The case studies presented in this chapter offer important lessons that can guide future comprehensive school reform efforts. What are the important lessons that their stories have to tell?

Surpassing the bar for school turnaround. The McCallister intervention in each of the school implementations described above surpasses the existing bar set for school turnarounds. Each school saw significant gains in student achievement within one year, where the existing literature reports that school culture improves only after two years and student achievement gains are typically not seen in a school until the second or third year of the turnaround implementation (Kutash, et al., 2010). The school turnaround literature also reports a standard planning period of at least a year (Duncan, 2009), typically costing an average of $300K. The McCallister Model, a fully developed design, was used directly 'off the shelf,' so to speak, with no need for prior planning, yielding savings in the six-school McCallister Initiative that would have otherwise cost $1.8M.

Deconstructing program efficacy: comparative achievement outcomes in two McCallister Model high schools. HSLI and UAGC offer an opportunity to examine outcomes in two different populations of students who were also differentially exposed to the McCallister intervention (see Table 30.10 for HSLI and UAGC comparative data referred to in this section). The HSLI graduating class of 2015 is the only cohort to have been exposed to a true-fidelity implementation of the McCallister program for four years. It provides a point of comparison to the UAGC graduating cohort of 2017, who were exposed to two years of a true-fidelity program and two years of partial implementation.

The 2017 UAGC and 2015 HSLI graduation rates were similar, at 83%. But among graduates, indicators of academic rigor were much lower in UAGC. The College and Career Preparatory Course Index was over three times higher in the 2015 HSLI cohort compared to the 2017 UAGC cohort. HSLI's 4-year College Readiness Index was more than 20 points higher than that of UAGC, and the 4-year College Readiness Index for the HSLI's lowest third was 63% higher than that of UAGC, at 0.0%. In other words, of all students in the school's lowest third academically, none were deemed prepared for college. Graduation rates amongst each school's most vulnerable subgroups—ELLs, special education students, the lowest third, and Black and Hispanic males in the city's lowest third in each school—were similar.

Differences in achievement performance could be explained by the fact that each school serves different populations. The majority of 2015 HSLI graduates were from immigrant families, and no doubt their educational attainment was influenced by the various forms of cultural and social that are particular to the immigrant experience (see Ogbu & Simons, 1998). But students of HSLI also came from higher levels of poverty (95% at HSLI and 86% at UAGC), and HSLI served a much higher number of ELLs (74% at HSLI and 14% at UAGC). Moreover, the majority of students in the 2015 HSLI cohort began high school not knowing English, and their secondary education experience was made all the more challenging by the need to learn the English language in addition to the district curricula. A more sophisticated analysis of the variation of population characteristics on achievement outcomes is beyond the scope of this analysis. However, based on the theory-of-change operating in the McCallister Model, UAGC students would have performed on a par with HSLI students had they been provided a sufficient cultural niche in which to learn the formal curriculum.

Variable achievement between schools can also be explained by differences between the level of implementation fidelity of the McCallister program. Since I was only able to work with UAGC for the first two years to support implementation according to standards I developed, it is impossible to systematically analyze where the program failed to achieve standards. Anecdotally, during my occasional visits to UAGC between 2016 and 2018, it was not uncommon to encounter learners who were unaware of Format procedures and expectations for their participation. Also, the Learning Teams Format, which is the most powerful mechanism in the Learning Cultures curriculum to develop academic competencies relating to state curriculum content in the disciplines, was not implemented at UAGC with fidelity. Since conformity to procedures and participatory norms ensure high-quality opportunities to engage in mental coordination and cognitive control, it is likely that learners generally lacked access to opportunities that might have otherwise enhanced academic achievement.

The McCallister comprehensive school design employs second-level bureaucratic systems of distributed leadership to ensure quality of implementation of the classroom-level curriculum of the Formats. After its initial two years of implementation, UAGC had incorporated the McCallister bureaucratic systems into its formal policies, but I was not involved in the operations of these systems and did not have opportunities to coach leads to perform their roles according to established standards. In other words, the relatively low metrics for the 2017 UAGC cohort in measures of college and career readiness, particularly for the lowest third citywide, and average Regents pass rates are probably due, in part, to the fact that UAGC only participated in the McCallister Initiative for the first two years of the turnaround, thereafter using the program independently with diminishing levels of technical support. Lacking sufficient technical support to implement the first- and second-level changes with fidelity, the UAGC was unable to achieve the high levels of academic achievement across all school subgroups, particularly the most academically vulnerable.

Student achievement after discontinued treatment. I have asserted that the McCallister Model as a whole-school reform intervention results in improved achievement trends. Examination of achievement trends in two schools in which the program was implemented for four years and then discontinued provides the opportunity to assess program efficacy. In both HSLI and UAGC, graduation rates achieved their height in graduating cohorts who had the program for four full years, and then, in both schools, graduation rates and/or measures of college and career readiness declined upon discontinuation of the program (see Table 30.10).

Graduation rates at HSLI dipped the year after the conclusion of the Initiative. While graduation rates rose again in 2017 to the 2015 level, college and career metrics in all categories declined from 2015 to 2017, except the graduation rate for ELLs, which dipped and then rebounded in 2017. Declines in achievement at HSLI were steep. The College and Career Preparatory Course (CCPC) Index declined 26 points between 2015 to 2017. The CCPC declined 45 points for the school's lowest third from 2015 to 2019. The College Readiness Index for the school's lowest third decreased during this time by 38 points.

Table 30.10 School quality metrics of UAGC and HSLI of graduating cohorts in final implementation year of McCallister Model implementation and two subsequent years

Achievement and college-readiness metrics in phase-out years at HSLI and UAGC	2015 HSLI	2016 HSLI	2017 HSLI	2017 UAGC	2018 UAGC	2019 UAGC
Number of years of cohort's 4-year program that school participated in McCallister Initiative (full-scale implementation vs. partial implementation)	Four full	Three full	Two full	Two full and two partial	One full and three partial	Four partial
NYC DOE Impact Score	NA	0.41	0.69	0.64	0.52	0.59
NYC DOE Performance Score	NA	0.37	0.48	0.44	0.38	0.45
4-year graduation rate (%)	72.7	65.1	72.7	82.2	78.8	77.1
College and Career Preparatory Course Index (%)	63.6	26.6	37.7	8.0	1.2	18.1
4-year College Readiness Index (%)	52.3	17.4	42.9	31.0	25.9	28.9
College and Career Preparatory Course Index- Lowest Third (%)	63.3	12.0	18.8	0.0	2.0	5.3
4-year College Readiness Index- Lowest Third (%)	50.0	6.0	12.5	7.9	12.2	5.3
Graduation rate ELLs (%)	71.8	64.6	72.1	75.0	44.4	70.0
Graduation rate Special Ed (%)	NA	28.6	NA	73.3	85.0	70.8
Graduation rate Lowest Third (%)	70.5	42.0	50.0	65.8	67.3	17.1
Graduation rate Black/Hispanic Males in Lowest Third (%)	69.2	28.0	24.4	65.2	72.0	80.0

The graduation rate for the school's lowest third declined by 21 points. And the graduation rate for Black and Hispanic males in the school's lowest third declined by 45 points, a tragic backslide given the relationship between education and economic mobility and the broader historic context of depressed levels of African American male social mobility, which has increased by only 35% in 150 years (Collins & Wanamaker, 2017).

At UAGC, graduation rates increased from 2017 to 2019 in each successive year relative to the number of years of the graduating cohort took part in the Initiative. The school's overall impact score also declined between 2017 and 2019, as did the College Readiness Index. Graduation rates for ELLs, the school's lowest third, and special education students declined between 2017 and 2019 (though graduation rates for Black and Hispanic males in the lowest third increased 15 points during that time). Declines in rates of graduation in the school's lowest third were steep, falling from 65.8% in 2017 by 49 points to 17.1% in 2019. But overall declines in achievement, especially for the school's most vulnerable populations, were less steep at UAGC than HSLI. This is likely due to the higher level of leadership training in the second-level bureaucratic systems of the McCallister Model at UAGC and the fact that HSLI students as a whole reflect higher levels of poverty and linguistic diversity.[12] These diminishing trends in achievement were observed in other schools that took part in the Learning Cultures Initiative described in previous chapters.

The mythical, incomparable leader. The existing literature on school turnaround rests on the assumption that a successful turnaround initiative hinges on the capacity of a school leader to guide a team to develop a uniquely tailored, comprehensive school design, presumably based on evidence-based practices. Is it realistic to expect principals, trained in educational leadership, to lead teams of educators, trained as knowledge-transmission technicians, in developing successful, scientifically based school designs? Is it practical to expect such teams to possess the deep multidisciplinary expertise in the learning sciences, developmental and social psychology, social philosophy, psychometrics, organizational systems theory, literacy theory, instructional theory, curriculum theory, educational policy, and a host of other relevant bodies of knowledge together with extensive expertise in pedagogical practice that are necessary to develop successful school designs? The McCallister school design is an outcome of a three-decade process by someone with doctoral-level training in literacy learning theory and practice, and involved extensive theoretical research and iterative cycles of experimental trial and improvement. It is completely unrealistic to expect a school administrator, trained in educational leadership, to possess adequate technical expertise to design an effective school-wide intervention.

The McCallister experiment at UAGC and the other schools that participated in the Initiative suggest that successful school transformation might be better achieved in cases where educators have access to fully developed, scientifically based, comprehensive school reform designs and support to implement them. With such a plan, any capable administrator can lead a capable team of teachers to successfully transform a school. Indeed, the principal at HSLI and the principal of UAGC from 2016 to present were both new to the position of principalship when they took on McCallister Model program implementation, or new to the principal role at the high school level. The principal at UAGC from 2013 to 2016 was new to the high school principalship. Thus, successful school transformation in schools participating in the McCallister Initiative were not dependent on principal expertise.

The current emphasis on the incomparable school leader is an unrealistic expectation and an unsustainable solution to the massive scale of failing schools nationwide that need to be transformed. It is much more realistic and sustainable to identify competent leaders who are capable of leading a school to implement a fully developed, scientifically based, comprehensive school design. This was the approach used in all of the accounts presented in this chapter. The case studies recounted here provide evidence that highly capable leaders, albeit those with little to no previous experience, can successfully implement a scientifically based CSR model to transform the culture of the school and dramatically raise student achievement. Evidence of the importance of a theoretically sound school design is further proven by the declines in student achievement once the intervention was removed.

Consistent leadership. The story of UAGC also offers another interesting twist to the conventional wisdom of school transformation, which emphasizes the importance of consistent leadership. It is worth noting again that UAGC underwent a change in leadership mid-year in Spring 2016, when left the school mid-year, at which point the Assistant Principal took the helm as principal. With the McCallister Model incorporated into the DNA of the school's official infrastructure, the new principal was able to continue to implement the program relatively successfully.[13] A mid-year leadership transition, which in most cases is highly disruptive to the various systems of the school that support student achievement and a positive school environment, occurred without impact. UAGC's story of leadership transition proves that success can be achieved with a strong school design in the hands of a capable leadership, even in a leadership transition.

Prior planning. The CSR literature suggests that school transformation initiatives typically require a planning period of a year. The McCallister implementations reported in this chapter required no prior planning. Because the McCallister CSR design is fully developed, and can be implemented with none-to-little prior planning, the extensive costs that are typically associated with turnaround and transformation initiatives are eliminated.[14]

Substance vs. size. Some suggest that the creation of small schools is a proven strategy for successful school transformation. Bloom and Unterman (2014) assert that large-scale transformation of NYC's high school landscape occurred between 2002 and 2010 in a combination of a system-wide high school choice program and the option to attend one of 68 new "small schools of choice," and increased graduation rates over this period at a rate of 9% (p. 741). This assertion is misleading. The definition of a school transformation established in the school turnaround literature is a school that significantly raises achievement *rapidly* within two years (e.g., Duncan, 2009; Kutash et al., 2010). A 9% increase over a period of eight years—less than 2% per year—is not a transformation according to these criteria. And, as our case study of UAGC suggests, small size does not necessarily result in school success. The first graduating cohort of UAGC, one of the small schools created to replace Brandeis High School, actually underperformed its predecessor in many respects. The case studies presented here suggest that it is more the substance of the activities that occur within a school as opposed to its size that account for student achievement.

Political entrenchment. Despite its proven power to support students to become more successful, the McCallister-Learning Cultures Initiative came to an end in NYC DOE schools in 2015, coinciding with the appointment of a new schools chancellor, Carmen Farina. Farina systematically dismantled Bloomberg-era reforms, centralized the NYC DOE bureaucracy, restricted principal autonomy, and embraced a reform strategy grounded in her own intuition and folk wisdom (Taylor, February, 2015 & January, 2015). It is reported that Ms. Farina, early in her tenure as Chancellor, interrupted a meeting of NYC DOE officials who were scrutinizing achievement data to identify high-impact schools to serve as models of reform, to suggest the irrelevance of data in relation to her own expertise. She is alleged to have made the assertion: "I know a good quality school when I'm in the building" (Taylor, February, 2015).

One can speculate about whether the significant declines in student achievement demonstrated across all of the schools presented in the cases above might have been averted if school leaders had been encouraged by the NYC DOE central administration to embrace innovations that evidence in student achievement data suggested were working to close the achievement gap.

It is also tempting to speculate why school and network leaders elected to end an experimental trial of an education model that appeared to demonstrate strong efficacy in closing the long-intractable achievement gap at a fraction of the cost of the average school transformation. These questions raise concerns about the political context in which reforms are pursued. They are questions that cannot be answered in this report. So rather than look backward to interrogate the past, it is more productive to look forward to envision conditions of possibility for the future. In future implementation efforts of the McCallister school design, it will be important to specify more ideal political conditions to ensure every child's right to an education on equal terms, regardless of the interests of the establishments that broker opportunities to learn.

Conclusion

Some suggest that the public schools we have no longer meet society's needs and that they will soon become redundant. The cases I've shared recount stories of transformation in persistently failing industrial schools. Maybe *the Rise of the Phoenix* could be a fitting metaphor for American education generally if every school now has the potential to rise from the ashes of obsolescence and transform itself into a 21st-century learning organization.

Notes

1. All of the schools that participated in the Initiative followed the Year-long Implementation Plan used at UAGC and participated in the network-sponsored, cross-school training program.
2. I first demonstrated the Intervention Protocol to Kerry Decker when she was principal of the Jacob Riis School (see McCallister, 2011a).
3. Learning Teams had their genesis in the context of homeschooling my youngest son during his 5th-grade year. With his older sister, he took part in a daily Work Time, during which time he and she did Cooperative Unison Reading, independent reading, and writing. As a solution to a curriculum in content subjects, I directed him to the NY State standards for social studies and science. I showed him how to turn each standard indicator into a question, and from there, to engage in his own inquiry (Google search) to find research the questions he couldn't answer. The following year, this protocol would become Responsibility Teams at HSLI and UAGC.
4. One day, visiting HSLI, I observed that a notorious mischief-maker at HSLI and his usual side-kick sitting in the back row, as usual, during a Lesson in which the teacher was announcing Learning Teams Tournament winners. To my surprise, these two were announced to be the top scores in the competition. This was evidence to me that the Learning Teams intervention was working to support achievement of some of the most vulnerable students.
5. As described in the Learning Teams protocol, this volume.
6. I first proposed the idea of the Keepers program to principals in an email of April 14, 2014, when I suggested that we develop a leadership council of students nominated by peers to be "keepers of the culture" to meet with peers to read and discuss responsibilities and to address behavioral challenges and to develop a sense of "we-ness" described by Tomasello. Ms. Decker responded in an email of April 16 that "We are ready to go to this next level. This is great!" (personal communication, April 16, 2020). I thereafter initiated the Keepers of the Culture program at UAGC when I worked with the School Culture Lead to conduct a student survey to identify peer-nominated Keepers members. I then trained the first Keepers cohort in the procedures of the Behavior Intervention.
7. The Year-long Implementation Plan was the blueprint schools used to enact the model of rapid school transformation that I engineered.
8. Official NYC DOE Quality Review and school Self-Evaluation documents for the school from the period of implementation provide evidence of the comprehensive extent to which the McCallister program was implemented.
9. School quality metrics are derived from surveys of students, parents, and teachers and student performance data.
10. The percentage of students who successfully completed approved courses and assessments within the first four years of high school, after entering 9th grade in 2011–2012.
11. Percent of students who graduated with a Regents diploma and met City University of New York's standards for college readiness in English and math within four years, after entering 9th grade in 2011–2012.
12. I coached the principal of UAGC from 2013 to 2016 to implement the second-level bureaucratic systems of Learning Cultures in her role as principal of Jacob Riis and Learning Cultures coach at The Urban Assembly. The UAGC implementation was no doubt facilitated by the additional human capital of a leader with extensive prior Learning Cultures training.
13. Declining achievement patterns under the new leadership were probably due to lack of technical support in implementing the Learning Cultures model as opposed to lack of leadership capacity as school environment metrics continued on an upward trend after the leadership transition.
14. Turnaround and transformation planning typically involved direct costs between $250K and $350K per year. These costs do not reflect the human opportunity costs to children whose futures are negatively impacted by additional time required for the system to plan how to achieve success.

31 Conclusion
Shapes

> Lovers and madmen have such seething brains,
> Such shaping fantasies, that apprehend
> More than cool reason ever comprehends.
> The lunatic, the lover, and the poet
> Are of imagination all compact.
> One sees more devils than vast hell can hold—
> That is the madman. The lover, all as frantic,
> Sees Helen's beauty in a brow of Egypt.
> The poet's eye, in fine frenzy rolling,
> Doth glance from heaven to Earth, from Earth to heaven.
> And as imagination bodies forth
> The forms of things unknown, the poet's pen
> Turns them to shapes and gives to airy nothing
> A local habitation and a name.
>
> William Shakespeare, A Midsummer's Night Dream

Introduction

In this book, I have given shape to forms from my own imagination of what school could be. They are simple forms—spheres of space that contain the freedom for learners to think, move, speak, and relate to others—defined by rules that provide the grammar for norms of civility, cooperation, aspiration, and learning.

The forms took years to materialize in my imagination. Thirty years ago, when I was a kindergarten teacher, I gave my students time and space each day to exercise their fundamental freedoms of thought, movement, expression, and association. But these freedoms were conditional. They could have the run of the room as long as they wrote during writing time, read during reading time, and did math during math time, and did all of these things with ascendent intentions—to strive to become a better version of themselves. At the beginning of each school year, the children displayed an infinite kaleidoscope of individuality and diversity in expressions of human competence. But despite their differences, they found common ground as they shared their minds with one another to do the things they needed to do to carry out their intentions.

In my second year of teaching, one of my kindergarten students, a precocious, somewhat neurotic, small-for-his-age boy called Andy, who could, in a savant-like manner, read literally anything, led Scott, still a scribbler, in a game of Batman. The two dashed around the room hiding cards that they had made with messages in code:

"YDNA is Batman" (in case you can't break the code, it is "YDNA" is "ANDY" written backward).

I was taking an ethnography course at the university at the time, and for my research, I had chosen to study Scott, Andy, and two of their peers in order to try to understand how the activity of writing, set in the context of freedom of choice to do the things they wanted, through playful social interaction with others, gives rise to literacy competencies. I picked my topic out of passion and curiosity. I had enjoyed the affordances of fundamental freedom in my own education as a child in a progressive university laboratory school. And when I decided to become a teacher, I had the opportunity to be mentored by a teacher who conferred these freedoms to her own students. As a new teacher, I was captivated by the mysterious alchemy of play and its power as a context to support the emergence of human competence.

In my study findings, I made the assertion, backed with evidence, that play, and the freedom it provides, creates conditions for literacy learning. Space and freedom seemed to me, back then, to be such simple and obvious criteria. But what I learned by spending time in hundreds of classrooms over the ensuing years, working with teachers to help them grant learners the same freedoms I gave my students, is that there was something significant hidden in the generous space of freedom that shaped development. Through years of theory building from insights from the behavioral sciences and philosophy, I eventually got a grasp of the criteria that makes freedom generative.

Over time, I came to appreciate three essential conditions of freedom for learning that would anchor my model: the need for learners to have access to diverse, rich environmental experiences; the need for them to enjoy fundamental freedom and autonomy to direct their own learning; and the need to access full and free forms of association. Over time I more tightly coupled freedoms with certain conditions I spelled out in pedagogical procedures, or 'rules.' Under conditions of absolute freedom, the self erodes into disorder (Csikszentmihalyi, 1993). But forms of freedom that are bound by rules that motivate compliance to generative norms can promote higher levels of being. In fact, ascendent forms of being in humans are only possible in the context of normative freedom.

John Dewey wrote, "The conception of education as a social process and function has no definite meaning until we define the kind of society we have in mind" (1916/1944, p. 97). Testing them in classrooms, year after year, I pinched and stretched the language of my 'rules' until they resulted in optimal conditions to enable learners to coordinate their minds with others, to develop their identities, personalities, and talents, and to contribute collectively to the creation of a microcosm of the democratic society our nation's founders had in mind. After each alteration, I tested them again in classrooms. This cycle of action and inquiry eventually resulted in the *big book of rules* that I have shared in this book.

As researchers, we are obligated to test our hypotheses. As I watched the children, year after year, listening to what they said and seeing what they did, they helped confirm my findings. I could finally say that my 'rules' were finally a *well-wrought urn*—a container for a certain existential capaciousness that is crucial for learning and a vessel for the mysterious alchemy of play-cum-human competence.

To close, I would like to take you on a tour of classrooms so that you can listen in and hear for yourself the answers to my questions. Read vignettes from the classroom to see yourself what lessons the children choose to take from the *book of rules*.

James is a first grader who has just joined a Unison group for the first time. The kids have gotten stuck on the word *shark*. In Unison groups, kids take turns using the marker and the white board to write unknown words and break them into familiar "chunks." James asserts that it is his turn to use the marker. But his peers disagree. "You had a turn, but Lee hasn't had one yet. It's his turn." With every passing second, he appears more annoyed, and the scowl on his face is more pronounced. Finally, he bolts out of his seat and leaves the table. By doing so, he has broken two of the Unison Reading Rules: read aloud in sync (the other kids can't read unless everyone is at the table); and be promotive (be nice to others). The teacher informs the remaining three at the table that they need to give James a reminder. Tayla takes after James, trying to corner him in the hallway. She directs him back to the table. He ignores her and darts across the room. She tries and appeals to him a few more times until she had no choice but to give him an ultimatum: "James, you have to come back to the table. Santa won't come…You won't get presents.…Your family won't love you." Within the next few minutes, with a little more convincing (and a warning from the teacher), James returns to the table.

The presumed academic objectives of the "breach" on the table were word reading and decoding. But James used the *book of rules* to take his learning to a much higher level by exercising emotional self-regulation and exchanging mental states with others to understand moral norms for turn taking and fairness.

In a high school writing classroom where I have been asked to demonstrate a writing conference, I am directed toward a young woman who sits alone at a table in the back of the room. The teacher informs me, "She never writes anything." I approach Ayalla, who sits with her pen in hand, but is not writing. I notice she wears a jacket over a T-shirt with silver-sequined lettering. Her long nails are brightly painted with airbrush decorations, and she's wearing eyelash extensions. These particulars of her appearance make me think she is older than the others in the class, who are primarily freshman and sophomore classmates. "Could I have a conference with you?" I ask as I approach her. She shakes her head firmly and looks away from me. Her intentional stance is negative-reactive. My immediate goal is to provoke more positive intentions. "Is it ok if I sit here next to you anyway?" I ask. She reluctantly looks at me and nods her head without expression, then looks away. "I know you don't want to have a conference with me. But do you mind telling me what you're writing?" She pushes her notebook toward me, telling me it is an invitation for her upcoming birthday party when I ask what it's about. A group of a half dozen teachers is sitting alongside me, waiting for my demonstration. "Sorry. Again, I know you don't want to have a conference, but do you mind if I stand in, kind of like the fictive you, and read your writing to the group so they can give feedback? They're here to watch me, and if you don't mind, I'll help them learn how to do a conference by sharing your writing."

Ayalla pauses a second or two to consider, then nods her approval. I whisper to her what I'm guessing is her writing purpose—to get people to want to come to my party. She nods approval. I inform the teachers and proceed to read the dozen or so words she has written on the page. The group claps when I finish. I offer my insights about how I think the piece worked, and so do the teachers. Ayalla, the student, is warming to us, even breaking the occasional partial smile. Then I say how I could have made it better, and so do the teachers. I ask the group of teachers to share their opinions. By this time, they are directing their comments to Ayalla, and she's engaged with them: make it a theme party; entice would-be partygoers by telling them what kind of music and food you'll have; link the invitation to a website; and say more about why this particular birthday is significant. Ayalla is receptive. By the end of the conference, she is in charge. And when we say goodbye, Ayalla begins writing.

Ayalla practiced writing fluency and spelling and explored a form of informational writing that had practical value. But the larger lesson she drew from the big *book of rules* was the will to exercise more forceful intentions to be open to new experience, to use the written word in ways that could effectively expand her social world, and to develop a stronger sense of self-competence and confidence.

Teresa, a 2nd grader in a South Bronx public elementary school, sits before her classmates to share her newest piece of writing entitled *Friends*. In it, she outlines the positive qualities of her friends. The piece goes something like this: *Friends are helpful. Friends are nice. Friends play with you.* When she's finished, hands go up, and she calls on classmates, one after another, who offer predictable feedback: "I like how you said such-and-such." I like the part where you said "so-and-so." But there's suddenly a wave of a disturbance in the audience. "Ralique, don't interrupt!" one child shouts. Teresa continues to call on classmates to hear their comments. But Ralique continues to mumble something disagreeable. And again, a few of the children object: *"Ralique!"*

Finally, Ralique decides to play by the rules. He raises his hand, and Teresa calls on him. "It's all wrong!" he protests. "These girls are not your friends! They are mean to you in the cafeteria. They don't play with you at recess. Meesha makes fun of you. These girls are not your friends!" Members of the audience protest loudly. "Ralique, it's her story!" "Ralique, you shouldn't use people's names!" (a directive from Meesha, who, by the way, *does* make fun of Teresa and who is well practiced in the art of relational aggression). The commotion rises to a pitch with about half the class weighing in with the issue at hand, and then finally subsides when Teresa points to Ralique and says, "Please continue sayin' what you were sayin' Ralique." She seems satisfied for her peers to hear Ralique voice a truth in the group forum.

Two weeks later, I visit the same class. As it happens, Ralique, whose father is a pastor, is sharing his writing, a poem called *Friends*. The poem offers some evidence that the issue of friendship has been on his mind recently, that reality isn't always what it seems, and that friendships are complicated. The poem goes something like this:

Friends are nice
Friends are mean
Friends are truthful
Friends are dishonest
Friends are helpful
Friends are hurtful

Ralique used the *book of rules* to wrestle with a universal moral dilemma concerning the relational contradictions and ambiguities that are part of navigating friendships. And he practiced courage and compassion by standing up for a peer by speaking truth to power and calling out her aggressors.

In "Ms. M's" 2nd-grade classroom Lower Manhattan, this week, *knock-knock jokes* are the current rage at writing time. Today it's Maya's turn to share her work. She is seated before her classmates and reads her piece:
Maya: Knock-knock.

Peers: Who's there?
Maya: Banana peel.
Peers: Banana peel who?
Maya: Banana peel partied with strawberry and apple!

The 2nd graders peal with laughter (get it?)—some clutch their tummies, others fall backward and roll from side to side—Maya laughs along with her audience. After Maya collects herself, she begins to call on members of the audience who are eager to share comments. Like most seven-year olds, Maya and her classmates can't yet create knock-knock jokes with a proper pun. They have not yet learned the *rules* for what we call two-faced texts, like pun, when something can mean two different things at once. For Maya and her classmates, it seems, a pun requires only the familiar "knock-knock" set up in order to provide listeners an excuse to laugh. The attempted pun *works* in this situation, and the laughter is contagious. I giggle along with them.

Maya used the *book of rules* as an opportunity not only to explore a new writing genre, but to use her own psychic energy generously to create a social space for the purpose of sharing joy and experiencing happiness and laughter with others.

Four high school boys are sitting in their Learning Team group, reviewing the briefs they were each supposed to write and share at their meeting today. James, apparently, had not done his part. David calls him out, asking his peer to please say why he didn't do the work. The wrongdoer explains he was doing other things. David asks why. Raymond joins in, saying he saw James on Facebook. David says he saw him on Chat. Quinton asks if James could do it now, but David says there's no time. James, now showing some inclination to consider doing the work, asserts that there is. David, attempting to prove that there is not, holds his notebook up for James to see, showing him three pages he had written the night before and adding that he even skipped basketball practice and stayed up till midnight to do it.

Their Learning Teams meeting provided an opportunity to study the formal curriculum and prepare for the state history test. But the larger lesson from the *book of rules* on this day concerned the importance of personal accountability and self-responsibility, interdependence and mutuality, and conscientiousness.

Tayquan, a 6th grader, is a new transfer to the school. His body language conveys, in no uncertain terms, that he is not happy being here. In Unison Reading, he slouches back in his seat to pull as far from the table as he is physically able. The score he got on his reading comprehension assessment put him in the 8th percentile nationally. I hear him explaining some weeks later to his teacher that in his last school, his teacher wouldn't let him read Percy Jackson because she said it was too hard. He seemed incensed at the assault to his dignity. Through the weeks, I notice Tayquan's disposition has transformed. He's now intensely engaged in Unison sessions and seems especially energized by mentalizing. I notice in his reading folder that he has a copy of Machiavelli's, *The Prince*. I noted my observation to the

> teacher, who told me he was writing a paper on the book. In a conversation with his teacher I overheard, he commented that he uses Unison Reading group as a way of learning how other people think. His curriculum is Machiavelli, mind reading, and strategic use of social capital. I have the idea that he'll be a politician one day.
>
> Tayquan used the *big book of rules* to exercise his intellect in ways that affirmed his own sense of pride and dignity. He used his freedom to explore political philosophy to understand the world and made effort at every turn to find opportunities to expand his thinking through the exchange of mental states with others.

> Shiang is a first grader who lives with his father, mother, and brother in a Chinatown apartment. He shared his story about the day his dad brought home a monkey and how he and his brother were so excited to have an exotic pet monkey. The story took a sudden and tragic turn when Shiang realizes his father's intention to kill the monkey and cook it for dinner. Both terrified and invested with the elder brother's protective responsibility, the two boys hide under the kitchen table. The picture accompanying Shiang's story illustrates two stick figures—a large one and a little one—next to what appears to be a stove, with a large pot on top, out of which peered the eyes of a monkey.
>
> What is a young child to do when their father brings home an exotic animal and their mother cooks it for dinner? There is no option to call the A.S.P.C.A., or to schedule a session of psychotherapy. Shiang used the book of rules to write about and share one of life's most intense experiences. He used this space to adjudicate a moral contradiction stemming from his primary family experience and to learn, through the responses of others, possible ways to manage his emotions, navigate his identity, and regain mental integration.

Closing

Michael Cole (2005) wrote that the alternative to the current industrial school, if it comes into being, will be,

> a hybrid of new and old forms, of the standardized and the locally adapted. It will eschew the notion of human education as the preparation of children to triumph over nature and teach us how to live within, as part of nature, including nature's multicolored, multicultural, enormously heterogeneous forms of society. If society is to become re-integrated, it will not be by returning to the past but by creating a new kind of future in which central values of the past combine with the amazing accomplishments of the present to enable us to live in a sustainable garden, for and with our children.
>
> (p. 213)

I have learned from children that, when they are given the freedom to exercise their will in compliance with a book of carefully written rules that hold them accountable to the values we hold dear in our democratic society, they respond in ways that give reason to believe that our future civilization could eventually become a sustainable garden.

References

Advise. (June 11, 2020). In https://www.lexico.com/en/definition/advise.
Aladjem, D. K. & Borman, K. M. (Eds.). (2006). *Examining comprehensive school reform*. Washington, DC: The Urban Institute Press.
All Handicapped Children Act. P.S. 94–142. U.S.C. § 1401 et. Seq. (1975).
American Academy of Pediatrics. (2014). School start time for adolescents. Adolescent Sleep Working Group, Committee on Adolescence and Council on School Health. *Pediatrics*, 134(3), 642–648.
American Pet Products Association. (2020). Pet industry market size and ownership statistics. Retrieved from https://www.americanpetproducts.org/press_industrytrends.asp.
Ananiadou, K. & Claro, M. (2008). 21st century skills and competencies for new millennium learners in OECD countries. EDU working paper no. 41. Organisation for Economic Co-operation and Development. Paris.
Artsy. (2020). The global art market reached $67.4 billion in 2018, up 6%. Retrieved from https://www.artsy.net/article/artsy-editorial-global-art-market-reached-674-billion-2018-6.
Ashton-Warner, S. (1986). *Teacher*. New York, NY: Simon & Schuster.
Audubon. (2020). *Birding*. Retrieved from https://www.audubon.org/birding.
Backstrom, B. (2019). *School turnaround efforts: What's been tried, why those efforts failed, and what to do now*. Albany, NY: Rockefeller Institute of Government.
Bakhtin, M. M. (1987). *Speech genres and other late essays*. In C. Emerson & M. Holquist (Eds.). Trans. V. W. McGee. Austin, TX: University of Texas Press.
Banich, M. T. & Compton, R. J. (2018). *Cognitive neuroscience*. (4th ed.). Cambridge: Cambridge University Press.
Battelle for Kids. (2019). *Framework for 21st century learning definitions*. Columbus, OH. Retrieved from http://static.battelleforkids.org/documents/p21/P21_Framework_DefinitionsBFK.pdf.
Beck, A. T. (2019). A 60-year evolution of cognitive theory and therapy. *Perspectives on Psychological Science*, 14(1), 16–20.
Beck, A. (1996). The past and future of cognitive therapy. *Journal of Psychotherapy Practice and Research*, 6(4), 276–284.
Benedict, R. (1934). *Patterns of culture*. Boston, MA: Houthton Mifflin Company.
Berends, M., Bodilly, S. J., & Kirby, S. N. (2002) *Facing the challenges of whole-school reform*. New American schools after a decade. Santa Monica, CA: RAND Corporation.
Bicchieri, C. (2017). *Norms in the wild: How to diagnose, measure, and change social norms*. New York, NY: Oxford University Press.
Bicchieri, C. & Mercier, H. (2014). Norms and beliefs: How change occurs. *Iyyun: The Jerusalem Philosophical Quarterly*, 63, 60–82.
Bloom, H. S., Unterman, R., Zhu, P. & Reardon, S. (2020). Lessons from New York City's small schools of choice about high school features that promote graduation for disadvantaged students. *Journal of Policy Analysis and Management*, 39(3), 740–771.
Bloom, H. S. & Unterman, R. (2014). Can small high schools of choice improve educational prospects for disadvantaged students? *Journal of Policy Analysis and Management*, 33(2), 290–319.
Bobbitt, F. (1918). *The curriculum*. Cambridge, MA: The Riverside Press.

Borman, G. D., Hewes, G. M., Overman, L. T., & Brown, S. (2004). Comprehensive school reform and achievement: A meta-analysis. In C. T. Cross (Ed.). *Putting the pieces together: Lessons from comprehensive school reform research*). Washington, DC: The National Clearinghouse for Comprehensive School Reform, 53–108.

Bouchard, T. J. & McGue, M. (1981). Familial studies of intelligence: A review. *Science*, 212, 1055–1059.

Bourdieu, P. (1986). The forms of capital. In J. Richardson (Ed.). *Handbook of theory and research for the sociology of education*. Westport, CT: Greenwood, 241–258.

Bourdieu, P. (1977). *Outline of a theory of practice*. New York, NY: Cambridge University Press.

Boyd, R., Richerson, P. J., & Henrich, J. (2011). The cultural niche: Why social learning is essential for human adaptation. *Proceedings of the National Academy of Sciences of the United States of America*, 108, 10918–10925.

Brown v. Board of Education, 347 U.S. 483 (1954).

Bruner, J. (2004). Life as narrative. *Social Research*, 71(3), 691–710.

Bruner, J. (1996). *The culture of education*. Cambridge, MA: Cambridge University Press.

Bruner, J. (1983). *Child's talk*. New York, NY: W. W. Norton & Company.

Bruner, J. S. (1966). *Toward a theory of instruction*. Cambridge. MA: Harvard University Press.

Bruner, J. S. (May, 1963). Needed: A theory of instruction. *Educational leadership*. Washington, DC: Association for Supervision and Curriculum Development.

Bruner, J. S. (1960). *The process of education*. Cambridge, MA: Harvard University Press.

Calkins, A., Guenther, W., Belfiore, G., & Lash, D. (2007). *The turnaround challenge: Why America's best opportunity to improve student achievement lies in our worst-performing schools*. Boston, MA: Mass Insights Education & Research Institute.

Callahan, R. E. (1962). *Education and the cult of efficiency*. Chicago, IL: University of Chicago Press.

Cascone, S. (2018). Arts industries add $764 billion per year to the U.S. economy, says a landmark new study. Art World. Retrieved from https://news.artnet.com/art-world/arts-contribute-764-billion-us-economy-1254170.

Centers for Disease Control and Prevention. (2020). About pets and people. Retrieved from https://www.cdc.gov/healthypets/health-benefits/index.html.

Cherry, K. (2020). The big five personality traits. Verywellmind.com. Retrieved from https://www.verywellmind.com/the-big-five-personality-dimensions-2795422.

Cheung, E.O, Gardner, W. L., & Anderson, J. F. (2015). Emotionships: Examining people's emotion-regulation relationships and their consequences for well-being. *Social Psychological and Personality Science*, 6(4), 407–414.

Chomsky, N. (1965). *Aspects of the theory of syntax*. Cambridge, MA: MIT Press.

Chomsky, N. (1957). *Syntactic structures*. The Hague: Mouton & Co.

Chudek, M. & Henrich, J. (2011). Culture-gene coevolution, norm-psychology and the emergence of human prosociality. *Trends in Cognitive Science*, 15(5), 218–226.

Civil Rights Act of 1964, 42 U.S.C. § 2000e et seq (1964).

Cole, M. (2015, December 5). Mike Cole on the ZOPD. Retrieved from https://www.youtube.com/watch?v=h3H4qQcfYUo.

Cole, M. (2005). Cross-cultural and historical perspectives on the developmental consequences of education. *Human Development*, 48, 195–216.

Cole, M. (1996). *Cultural psychology: A once and future discipline*. Cambridge, MA: Harvard University Press.

Coleman, J. S., United States, & National Center for Education Statistics. (1966). *Equality of educational opportunity* [summary report]. Washington, DC: U.S. Dept.

Coleman, J. S. (1967). The concept of equality of educational opportunity (Report No. ED 015 157). U. S. Office of Education, report on Equality of Educational Opportunity.

Collins, W. J. & Wanamaker, M. H. (2017). *African American intergenerational economic mobility since 1880*. Cambridge, MA: National Bureau of Economic Research. Working paper 23395. http://www.nber.org/papers/w23395.

Cornman, S. Q., Zhou, L., Howell, M. R., & Young, J. (2018). *Revenues and expenditures for public elementary and secondary education: School year 2015–16 (fiscal year 2016): First look (NCES 2019-301)*. U.S. Department of Education. Washington, DC: National Center for Education Statistics. Retrieved [April 16, 2021] from https://nces.ed.gov/pubs2019/2019301.pdf.

Courtis, S. A. (1925). Ability-grouping in Detroit schools. In G. M. Whipple (Ed.). *The ability grouping of pupils, 35th yearbook of the national society for the study of education.* Bloomington, IL: Public school Publishing, 44–47.

Cruz, E. & Zonneveld, J. (2019). Alternatives to restorative justice: A student-centered approach to discipline. *2019 innovative schools network national conference on educational innovation.* Wisconsin Dells, WI.

Csikszentmihalyi, M. (1993). *The evolving self: A psychology for the third millennium.* New York: Harper Perennial.

Csikszentmihalyi, M. (1990). *Flow: The psychology of optimal experience.* New York, NY: Harper & Row.

Cummings, S., Bridgman, T., & Brown, K. G. (2016). Unfreezing change as three steps: Rethinking Kurt Lewin's legacy for change management. *Human Relations,* 69(1), 33–60.

Curtainly. (July 14, 2020). Why Shakespeare's brain is better than yours. [Blog post]. Retrieved from https://curtainly.wordpress.com/2014/05/07/why-shakespeares-brain-is-better-than-yours/.

Danielson, C. (2008). *The handbook for enhancing professional practice: Using the framework for teaching in your school.* Alexandria, VA: Association for Supervision and Curriculum Development.

David-Barrett, T. & Dunbar, R. I. M. (2013). Processing power limits social group size: Computational evidence for the cognitive costs of sociality. *Proceedings of the Royal Society of London,* 280: 20131151. Retrieved from http://dx.doi.org/10.1098/rspb.2013.1151.

Davis, J. L. (2020). 5 ways pets can improve your health. WebMD. Retrieved from https://www.webmd.com/hypertension-high-blood-pressure/features/health-benefits-of-pets#1.

Decker, K. (2019). Employ the "Five Principles of Freedom" as a practical and theoretical framework to create a thriving teacher leadership culture in your school. *Presentation at innovative schools network.* Wisconsin Dells, WI. Retrieved from: https://www.innovativeschoolsnetwork.com/event/show/5ae1df1c26bb0c9e548b4567.

Deci, E. L. & Ryan, R. M. (2017). *Self-determination theory: Basic psychological needs in motivation, development, and wellness.* New York: Guilford Press.

Deci, E. L. & Ryan, R. M. (2012). Self-determination theory. In P. A. M. Van Lange, A. W. Kruglanski, & E. T. Higgins (Eds.). *Handbook of theories of social psychology.* Thousand Oaks, CA: Sage Publications Ltd., 416–436.

Deci, E. & Ryan, R. (Eds.). (2002). *Handbook of self-determination research.* Rochester, NY: University of Rochester Press.

Deci, E. L. & Ryan, R. M. (1985). *Intrinsic motivation and self-determination in human behavior.* New York, NY: Plenum.

Decker, K. (2019). Employ the "Five Principles of Freedom" as a practical and theoretical framework to create a thriving teacher leadership culture in your school. *2019 innovative schools network national conference on educational innovation.* Wisconsin Dells, WI.

Delnero, P. (2012). Memorization and the transmission of Sumerian literary compositions. *Journal of Near Eastern Studies,* 71(2), 189–208.

Delpit, L. (1986). Skills and other dilemmas of a progressive Black educator. *Harvard Educational Review,* 56(4), 379–385.

Dennett, D. (1983). Intentional systems in cognitive ethology: The "Panglossian paradigm" defended. *Behavioral and Brain Sciences,* 6, 343–390.

Derex, M. & Boyd, R. (2015). The foundations of the human cultural niche. *Nature Communications.* 6:8398. Retrieved from https://doi.org/10.1038/ncomms9398.

Dewey, J. (1976). The child and the curriculum. In J. A. Boydston (Ed.). *John Dewey: The middle works, volume 2: 1902–1903.* Carbondale, IL: Southern Illinois University Press, 271–291.

Dewey, J. (1916/1944). *Democracy and education: An introduction to the philosophy of education.* Toronto: Collier-Macmillan.

Dewey, J. (1938). *Experience and education.* Indianapolis, IN: Kappa Delta Pi.

Douglass, F. (1882). *The life and times of Frederick Douglass: From 1817 to 1882, written by himself; with an introduction by the Right Hon. John Bright,* ed. John Lobb. London: Christina Age Office.

Douglass, F. (2005). *Narrative of the life of Frederick Douglass.* New York: Signet Classics.

Dragoset, L., Thomas, J., Herrmann, M., Deke, J., James-Burdumy, S., Graczewski, C., Boyle, A., Upton, R., Tanenbaum, C., & Giffin, J. (2017). *School improvement grants: Implementation and effectiveness: Executive summary (NCEE 2017-4012).* Washington, DC: National Center for Education

Evaluation and Regional Assistance, Institute of Education Sciences, U.S. Department of Education.

Draper, S. W. (2009). Catalytic assessment: Understanding how MCQs and EVS can foster deep learning. *British Journal of Educational Technology*, 40(2), 285–293.

Dressler, W. W. (2019). The construction of the cultural niche: A biocultural model. *American Journal of Human Biology*, 1–11. doi:10.1002/ajhb.23311.

DuBois, W. E. B. (1903). *The souls of black folk*. Chicago, IL: A. C. McClurg & Co.

Dunbar. R. I. M. (October 27, 2020). *Personal communication*.

Dunbar, R. I. M. (2010). *How many friends does one person need?* Cambridge, MA: Harvard University Press.

Dunbar, R. I. M. (2004). Gossip in evolutionary perspective. *Review of General Psychology*, 8(2), 100–110.

Dunbar R. I. M. (1998). The social brain hypothesis. *Evolutionary Anthropology: Issues, News, and Reviews*, 6(5), 178–190. doi:10.1002/(SICI)1520-6505(1998)6:5<178::AID-EVAN5>3.0.CO;2-8.

Dunbar, R. (1998). *Grooming, gossip, and the evolution language*. Cambridge, MA: Harvard University Press.

Dunbar, R. I. M. (1993). Coevolution of neocortical size, group size and language in humans. *Behavioral and Brain Sciences*, 16(4), 681–735.

Dunbar, R. I. M. & Spoors, M. (1995). Social networks, support cliques, and kinship. *Human Nature*, 6(3), 273–290.

Duncan, A. (2009). Turning around the bottom 5 percent: Address by the secretary of education at the national alliance for public charter schools conference. Retrieved December 27, 2013 from http://www2.ed.gov/news/speeches/2009/06/06222009.pdf.

Dweck, C. (2013). *Mindset: The new psychology of success*. New York: Ballantine Books.

Dweck, C. (2015). Carol Dweck revisits the "growth mindset." *Education Week*. Retrieved June 2, 2020 from https://www.edweek.org/ew/articles/2015/09/23/carol-dweck-revisits-the-growth-mindset.html.

Dynarski, M. & Kainz, K. (2015). Why federal spending on disadvantaged students (Title I) doesn't work. *Evidence Speaks Reports*, 1(7). Economic Studies at Brookings. Retrieved from https://www.brookings.edu/research/why-federal-spending-on-disadvantaged-students-title-i-doesnt-work/.

EasyCBM. (2014). easyCBM: Detailed percentile lookup table. Author. Retrieved from https://app.easycbm.com/static/files/pdfs/info/easyddddcbm_percentile_lookup_table.pdf.

Editorial Projects in Education Research Center. (2004, September 21). Low-performing schools. *Education Week*. Retrieved from http://www.edweek.org/ew/issues/low-performing-schools/index.html.

Education Reimagined. (2015). *A transformational vision for education in the U.S.* Washington, DC: Education Reimagined.

Education Week. (2004). *Low-performing schools*. Williamsport, PA: Education Week. Retrieved from https://www.edweek.org/leadership/low-performing-schools/2004/09.

Elementary and Secondary Education Act of 1965, P.L. 89–10, U.S.C. § 6301 (1965).

Elmore, R. (2018, November 12). TEACH keynote address: Dr. Richard Elmore. Retrieved from https://www.youtube.com/watch?v=nuiju6pEa4o.

Elmore, R. (2017, July 15). Richard Elmore on school reform. Retrieved from https://youtu.be/gE7zAsafmEo.

Erneling, C. (2010). *Towards discursive education: Philosophy, technology, and modern education*. Cambridge, UK: Cambridge University Press.

Feinberg, M., Willer, R., & Schultz, M. (2014). Gossip and ostracism promote cooperation in groups. *Psychological Science*. doi:10.1177/0956797613510184.

Fodor, J. A. (1983). *Modularity of mind: An essay on faculty psychology*. Cambridge, MA: MIT Press.

Foucault, M. (1995). *Discipline and punish: The birth of the prison*. New York, NY: Vintage Books.

Foucault, M. (1980). *Power/knowledge: Selected interviews and other writings, 1972–1977*. New York, NY: Pantheon Books.

Friere, P. (1970). *Pedagogy of the oppressed*. New York: Seabury Press.

Frow, J. (2006). *Genre: The new critical idiom*. New York, NY: Routledge.

Fuches, L. & Fuches, D. *Using CBM for progress monitoring*. Washington, DC: U.S. Office of Special Education.

Fuches, L. S. & Fuches, D. *Using CBM for progress monitoring in written expression and spelling*. Washington, DC: U.S. Office of Special Education.

Fullan, M. (2005). *Leadership and sustainability: System thinkers in action*. Thousand Oaks, CA: Corwin Press.

Gamble, O., Gowlett, J., & Dunbar, R. (2014). *Thinking big: How the evolution of social life shaped the human mind*. London: Thames & Hudson.

Garvey, M. (2014). *Philosophy and opinions of Marcus Garvey, Vol. I & II*. Amy Jacques Garvey (Ed.). Eastford, CT: Martino Fine Books.

Genre. (August 19, 2020). In https://www.merriam-webster.com/dictionary/genre.

Gergen, K. J. (1990). Social understanding and the inscription of self. In Stigler, J. W., Schweder, R. A., & Herdt, G. (Eds.). *Cultural psychology: Essays on comparative human development*. Cambridge: Cambridge University Press.

Gergen, K. J. (2021). *An invitation to social construction*. Los Angeles, CA: Sage.

Gordon, E. W. (May 23, 2020). Personal communication.

Gordon, E. W. (2014a). *Pedagogical imagination: A conceptual memoir, volume I*. Chicago, IL: Third World Press.

Gordon, E. W. (2014b). *Pedagogical imagination: A conceptual memoir, volume II*. Chicago, IL: Third World Press.

Gordon, E. W. (2004). *Inaugural Brown lecture in educational research*. Washington, DC: American Educational Research Association. Retrieved from https://www.youtube.com/watch?v=4lAF2e9imek.

Gordon, E. W. (1999). *Education and justice: A view from the back of the bus*. New York, NY: Teachers College Press.

Gordon, E. W. (1990). Coping with communicentric bias in knowledge production in the social sciences. *Educational Researcher*, 19(3), 14–19.

Gordon, E. W. (1972). Toward defining equality of educational opportunity. In F. Mosteller & D. P. Moynihan (Eds.). *On equality of educational opportunity: Papers deriving from the Harvard University faculty seminar on the Coleman report*. New York, NY: Random House, Inc.

Gordon, E. W. (1968). "Relevance or revolt." April 30, 1969, Teachers College, New York, NY.

Gordon, E. W., & Associates. (1995). *The evaluative review of the performance assessment collaboratives in education (PACE)*. New York City: Rockefeller Foundation.

Gordon, E. W. & Associates. (1988). Human diversity and pedagogy. New Haven: Center in Research on Education, Culture and Ethnicity, Institution for Social and Policy Studies. New Haven: Yale University.

Gordon, E. W. & Bridglall, B. L. (Eds.). (2007). *Affirmative development: Cultivating academic ability*. Lanham, MD: Rowman & Littlefield Publishers.

Gordon, E. W., Bridglall, B. L., & Meroe, A. S. (Eds.). (2004). *Supplemental education: The hidden curriculum of high achievement*. Lanham, MD: Rowman & Littlefield Publishers.

Gordon, E. W. & Nigro, G. (1988). Human diversity and pedagogy. New Haven, CT: Yale University, Center in Research on Education, Culture and Ethnicity, Institution for Social and Policy Studies.

Gordon, E. W. & Shipman, S. (1979) (1988). Human diversity, pedagogy and educational equity. *American Psychologist*, 34(10), 1030–1036.

Graney, S. B., Martinez, R. S., Missall, K. N., & Aricak, O. T. (2009). Universal screening of reading in late elementary school: R-CBM versus CBM Maze. Remedial and Special Education, 31(5), 368–377. DOI: 10.1177/0741932509338371.

Grice, H. P. (1989). *Studies in the way of words*. Cambridge, MA: Harvard University Press.

Guide. (June 10, 2020). https://www.lexico.com/en/definition/guide.

Hanushek, E. A. (2016). What matters for student achievement. *Education Next*, 16(2), 22–30. Retrieved from http://hanushek.stanford.edu/publications/what-matters-achievement-updating-coleman-influence-families-and-schools.

Hasbrouck, J. & Tindal, G. (2017). An update to compiled ORF norms (Technical report no. 1702). Eugene, OR, Behavioral Research and Teaching, University of Oregon.

Heath, S. B. (1983). *Ways with words*. New York: Cambridge University Press.

Heidegger, M. (1968). *What is called thinking?* Trans. J. Glenn Gray. New York: Harper and Row.

Herculano-Houzel, S. (2012). The remarkable, yet not extraordinary, human brain as a scaled-up primate brain and its associated cost. *Proceedings of the National Academy of Sciences of the United States of America*, 109, 10661–10668. Retrieved from https://doi.org/10.1073/pnas.1201895109.

Herman, R., Dawson, P., Dee, T., Greene, J., Maynard, R., Redding, S., & Darwin, M. (2008). *Turning around chronically low-performing schools: A practice guide* (NCEE #2008-4020). Washington, DC: National Center for Education Evaluation and Regional Assistance, Institute of Education Sciences, U.S. Department of Education. Retrieved from http://ies.ed.gov/ncee/wwc/publications/practiceguides.

Hernandez, J. C. (2009). Giant Manhattan school to be broken up to further smaller-is-better policy. *New York Times*. Retrieved from https://www.nytimes.com/2009/02/04/education/04brandeis.html?_r=0.

Hosp, M. K, Hosp, J. L., & Howell, K. W. (2007). *The ABCs of CBM*. New York, NY: Guilford.

Incorvaia, J. & Katz, J. (2019). Literacy practices in a struggling NYC school. *2019 innovative schools network national conference on educational innovation*. Wisconsin Dells, WI.

Individuals with Disabilities Education Act, 20 U.S.C. § 1400 (2004).

Institute of Education Sciences. (2020). *Revenues and expenditures for public elementary and secondary education: FY 17*. Washington, DC: U.S. Department of Education, Institute of Education Sciences, National Center for Education Statistics. Retrieved from https://nces.ed.gov/pubs2020/2020301.pdf.

Institute of Educational Sciences. (2012). *Schools and staffing survey (SASS). Table 7. Average class size in public primary schools, middle schools, high schools, and schools with combined grades, by classroom type and state: 2011–12*. Washington, DC: U.S. Department of Education, Institute of Education Sciences, National Center for Education Statistics. Retrieved from https://nces.ed.gov/surveys/sass/tables/sass1112_2013314_t1s_007.asp.

International Health, Racquet and Sportsclub Association. (2020). IHRSA 2018 global report: Health club industry revenue totaled $87.2 billion in 2017. Retrieved from https://www.ihrsa.org/about/media-center/press-releases/ihrsa-2018-global-report-club-industry-revenue-totaled-87-2-billion-in-2017/.

Itard, Jean-Marc-Gaspard (1962). *The wild boy of Aveyron*. New York, NY: Meredith Company.

Jacob, F. (1988). *The statue within: An autobiography*. Trans. F. Philip. New York: Basic Books.

Jefferson, T. (1943). *The complete Jefferson: Containing his major writings, published and unpublished, except his letters*. In S. Padover (ed.). New York: Duell, Sloan & Pearce, Inc.

Jefferson, T. (1810). Thomas Jefferson to the Trustees of the Lottery for East Tennessee College, May 6, 1810. Transcription available at Founders Online. Retrieved from https://founders.archives.gov/documents/Jefferson/03-02-02-0322.

Jenkins, J. R. & Jewell, M. (1993). Examining the validity of two measures for formative teaching: Reading aloud and maze. *Exceptional Children*, 59, 421–432.

Johnson, S. L., Alfonso, N., Player, D., & Bradshaw, C. (2018). Understanding and estimating the true costs associated with PBIS implementation and scale up. *Paper presentation at the society for prevention research annual meeting*. Washington, DC.

Kabat-Zinn, J. (1991). *Full catastrophe living: Using the wisdom of your body and mind to face stress, pain, and illness*. New York, NY: Delta Trade Paperbacks.

Kandel, E. R. (2007). *In search of memory: The emergence of a new science of mind*. New York, NY: W. W. Norton & Co.

Kandel, E. R., Schwartz, J. H., & Jessell, T. M. (Eds.) (2000). *Principles of neural science*. (4th ed). New York, NY: McGraw-Hill Health Professions Division.

Kelly, A. (1 June 2016). 46 million people living as slaves, latest global index reveals. *The Guardian*. Retrieved May 20, 2020. https://www.theguardian.com/global-development/2016/jun/01/46-million-people-living-as-slaves-latest-global-index-reveals-russell-crowe.

Kelly, D. R. & Davis, T. (2018). Social norms and human normative psychology. *Social Philosophy and Policy*. 35(1): 54–76. DOI:10.1017/S0265052518000122.

King, M. L. Jr. (1998). *The autobiography of Martin Luther King, Jr.*, ed. Clayborne Carson. New York: Warner Books, Inc.

Klinzing, J. G., Niethard, N., & Born, J. (2019). Mechanisms of systems memory consolidation during sleep. *Nature Neuroscience*, 22, 1598–1610.

Kordsmeyer, T., Mac Carron, P., & Dunbar, R. I. M. (2017). Sizes of permanent campsite communities reflect constraints on natural human communities. *Current Anthropology*, 58(2), 289–294.

Kornhuber H.H. & Deecke L. (1965). Changes in the brain potential in voluntary movements and passive movements in man: Readiness potential and reafferent potentials. *Pflügers Archiv fur die gesamte Physiologie des Menschen und der Tiere*, 284, 1–17.

Kulik, J. A. (2004). Grouping, tracking, and de-tracking. In H. J. Walberg, A. J. Reynolds, & M. C. Wang (Eds.). *Can unlike students learn together? Grade retention, tracking, and grouping.* Greenwich, CT: Information Age Publishing. 157–182.

Kutash, J., Nico, E., Gorin, E., Rahmatullah, S., & Tallant, K. (2010). *The school turnaround field guide.* Boston, MA: FSG Social Impact Advisors.

LAB at Brown University. (1998). *Block scheduling: Innovations with time.* Providence, RI: LAB Northeast Islands Regional Educational Laboratory. A Program of The Educational Alliance at Brown University.

LaBua, D. (2020, November 25). *UAGC family orientation, Fall 2020.* http://uagreencareers.org/remote-learning.

Lacour, M. & Tissington, L. D. (2011). The effects of poverty on academic achievement. *Educational Research and Reviews*, 6(7), 522–527.

Lagemann, E. C. (1989). The plural worlds of educational research. *History of Education Quarterly*, 29(2 Summer), 185–214.

Laland, K. N., Boogert, N., & Evans, C. (2014). Niche construction, innovation and complexity. *Environmental Innovation and Societal Transitions*, 11, 71–86.

Lamov, D. (2015). *Teach like a champion, 2.0: 62 techniques that put students in college.* San Francisco, CA: Jossey-Bass.

Law. (April 17, 2021). In https://www.merriam-webster.com/dictionary/law.

Learning Metrics Task Force (LMFT). (2013). *Toward universal learning: A global framework for measuring learning.* Report No. 2 of the Learning Metrics Task Force. Montreal and Washington: UNESCO Institute for Statistics and Center for Universal Education at the Brookings Institute.

Lee, C. D., White, G. & Dong, D. (Eds.). (2021). *Educating for civic reasoning and discourse.* Washington, DC: National Academy of Education.

Lewin, K. (1951). *Field theory in social science.* New York, NY: Harper.

Lewin, K. (1946). Action research and minority problems. *Journal of Social Issues*, 2(4), 34–46.

Lewin, K. (1943). Defining fining the "field at a given time." *Psychological Review*, 50, 292–310.

Lewin, K. (1936). *Principles of topological psychology.* New York, NY: McGraw-Hill.

Lewis, P., Birch, A., Hall, A., & Dunbar, R. I. M. (2017). Higher order intentionality tasks are cognitively more demanding. *Social Cognitive and Affective Neuroscience*, 12(7), 1063–1071. Retrieved from https://doi.org/10.1093/scan/nsx034.

Lohman, H. & Tomasello, M. (January, 2003). The role of language in the development of false belief understanding: A training study. *Child Development*, 74(4), 1130–1144.

Lleras, C. & Rangel, C. (2009). Ability grouping practices in elementary school and African American/Hispanic achievement. *American Journal of Education*, 115(2), 279–304.

Lortie, D. (1975). *Schoolteacher: A sociological study.* Chicago, IL: University of Chicago Press.

Makerspaces.com. (2020). *27 makerspace materials and supplies.* Retrieved from https://www.makerspaces.com/27-makerspace-materials-supplies/.

Malecki, C. K. & Jewell, J. (2003). Developmental, gender, and practical considerations in scoring curriculum- based measurement writing probes. *Psychology in the Schools*, 40, 379–390.

Mass Insight. (2007). *The turnaround challenge.* Retrieved December 3, 2020 from https://files.eric.ed.gov/fulltext/ED538298.pdf.

McCallister, C. (2017). Catalytic assessment. In E. W. Gordon & C. McCallister (Eds.) (May, 2017). *Diversity, equity and excellence in achievement and assessment in science, technology, engineering and mathematics education.* A Report Submitted to the National Science Foundation.

McCallister, C. (2014a). *School-wide leadership systems and job descriptions.* Unpublished manual.
McCallister, C. (2014b). *Genre collection probes.* Unpublished assessment.
McCallister, C. (2013a). *Learning cultures year-long implementation guide.* Unpublished manual.
McCallister, C. (2013b). *Network implementation plan.* Unpublished manuscript.
McCallister, C. (2013c). *Wide-scale implementation of learning cultures.* Unpublished proposal.
McCallister, C. (2013d). *Professional development survey.* Unpublished survey.
McCallister, C. (2013e). *School-wide leadership systems and job descriptions 2013.* Unpublished manual.
McCallister, C. (2013f). *Social norms.* Unpublished manuscript.
McCallister, C. (2013g). *Workout plan.* Unpublished assessment.
McCallister, C. (2013h). *Uses of genre.* Unpublished assessment.
McCallister, C. (2013i). *School-wide quality review crosswalk.* Unpublished assessment.
McCallister, C. (2012a). *Writing prompts.* Unpublished assessment.
McCallister, C. (2012b). *Learning cultures implementation rubric.* Unpublished assessment.
McCallister, C. (2012c). *Genre collection probes.* Unpublished assessment.
McCallister, C. (2012d). *Professional conference record.* Unpublished assessment.
McCallister, C. (2011a). *Unison reading: Socially inclusive group instruction for equity and achievement.* Thousand Oaks, CA: Corwin.
McCallister, C. (2011b). *Genre practice.* Unpublished manuscript.
McCallister, C. (2011c). *Teacher evaluation protocol.* Unpublished assessment.
McCallister, C. (2011d). *A framework for professional development: Culture, coherence, and capacity.* Unpublished manuscript.
McCallister, C. (2011e). *The activity arc: A tool for independent learning.* Unpublished manuscript.
McCallister, C. (2010). *A framework for professional development: Culture, coherence, and capacity.* Unpublished manuscript.
McCallister, C. (2009a). *A framework for professional development.* Unpublished manuscript.
McCallister, C. (2009b). *Genre practice.* An unpublished essay.
McCallister, C. (2009c). *Curriculum reform/professional development survey.* Unpublished survey.
McCallister, C. (2008a). The author's chair revisited. *Curriculum Inquiry, 38*(4), 455–472.
McCallister, C. (2008b). *Genre practice.* Unpublished manuscript.
McCallister, C. (2008c). *Professional development framework.* Unpublished proposal.
McCallister, C. (1998). *Reconceptualizing literacy methods instruction: To build a house that remembers its forest.* New York, NY: Peter Lang.
McCallister, C. & Olson, D. R. (under review). *Learning cultures: A new pedagogical model for enhancing literacy learning.*
McChesney, J. (1998). *Whole-school reform.* ERIC Digest, Number 124. Portland, OR: Educational Resources information Center (ED427388).
McCullough, D. (1995). *John Adams.* New York: Simon & Schuster.
Mead, G. H. (1934/1972). *George Herbert Mead on social psychology.* Chicago, IL: University of Chicago Press.
Medicinenet.com. (June 15, 2020. Retrieved from https://www.medicinenet.com/script/main/art.asp?articlekey=59953#:~:text=Code%20blue%3A%20An%20emergency%20situation,and%20begin%20immediate%20resuscitative%20efforts.
Mehan, H. (1979). *Learning lessons: Social organization in the classroom.* Cambridge, MA: Harvard University Press.
MetaMetrics, Inc. (2020). Lexile® measures and grade levels. MetaMetrics, Inc. Retrieved from https://lexile.com/wp-content/uploads/2017/08/T1.4.FAQ_LM-and-Grade-Levels.pdf.
Meyer, A., Rose, D. H., & Gordon, D. (2013). *Universal design for learning: Theory and practice.* Wakefield, MA: CAST, Inc.
Mitra, S. (2015). Knowing stuff? No, thanks. That's so last century... The Times Educational Supplement. *London Iss.* 5173, 20–21.
Mitra, S. (2014). The future of schooling: Children and learning at the edge of chaos. *Prospects, 44*(4), 547–558.
Mitra, S. (2003). Minimally invasive education: A progress report on the "hole-in-the-wall" experiments. *British Journal of Educational Technology, 34*(3), 367–371.

Mitra, S. & Dangwal, R. (2010). Limits to self-organizing systems of learning—The Kalikuppam experiment. *British Journal of Educational Technology*, 41(5), 72–688.

Mitra, S. & Rana, V. (2001). Children and the internet: Experiments with minimally invasive education in India. *British Journal of educational Technology*, 32(2), 221–232.

Montessori, M. (1965). *Dr. Montessori's own handbook: A short guide*. New York: Schocken Books Inc.

Montessori, M. (1912). *The Montessori method*. New York, NY: Frederick A Stokes Company.

Mosteller, F. & Moynihan, D. P. (1972). On equality of educational opportunity. *Papers deriving from the Harvard University faculty seminar on the Coleman Report*. New York, NY: Random House, Inc.

National Center for Education Statistics. (2021). Dropout rates. Retrieved from https://nces.ed.gov/fastfacts/display.asp?id=16.

National Center for Education Statistics. (2020). Expenditures. Retrieved from https://nces.ed.gov/fastfacts/display.asp?id=66.

National Center for Education Statistics. (2019). *National assessment of educational progress: An overview of **NAEP***. Washington, DC: National Center for Education Statistics, Institute of Education Sciences, U.S. Dept.

National Center for Education Statistics. (2012). *National assessment of educational progress: An overview of **NAEP***. Washington, DC: National Center for Education Statistics, Institute of Education Sciences, U.S. Dept.

National Center for Educational Statistics. (2012). Schools and staffing survey (SASS).

National Commission on Excellence in Education. (1983). A nation at risk: The imperative for educational reform. A report to the Nation and the Secretary of Education, United States Department of Education. Washington, DC: The Commission (Supt of Docs., U.S. G. P.O. distributor).

National Governors Association Center for Best Practices, Council of Chief State School Officers (2010). *Common core state standards*. Washington, DC. National Governors Association Center for Best Practices, Council of Chief State School Officers.

National Reading Panel (U.S.), & National Institute of Child Health and Human Development (U.S.) (2000). *Report of the National Reading Panel: Teaching children to read: An evidence-based assessment of the scientific research literature on reading and its implications for reading instruction*. Bethesda, MD: U.S. Dept. of Health and Human Services, Public Health Service, National Institutes of Health, National Institute of Child Health and Human Development.

National Study Group for the Affirmative Development of Academic Ability. (2004). *All students reaching the top: Strategies for closing the achievement gaps*. Naperville, IL: Learning Point Associates.

National Retail Federation. (2019). Record spending expected for school and college supplies. Retrieved from https://nrf.com/media-center/press-releases/record-spending-expected-school-and-college-supplies.

New Visions for Public Schools. (2020). Small schools study. Retrieved from https://www.newvisions.org/pages/small-schools-study#:~:text=Small%20Schools%20Approach&text=New%20Visions'%20work%20over%20the,scale%20in%20urban%20education%20today.

New York City Charter School Center. (2020). Charter school data dashboards back up. Retrieved from https://www.nyccharterschools.org/content/detailed-notes-bak#7.

New York City Department of Education. (2019a). Citywide behavioral expectations to support student learning Grades K-5. Retrieved from https://www.schools.nyc.gov/docs/default-source/default-document-library/discipline-code-kindergarten-grade-5-english.

New York City Department of Education. (2019b). Citywide behavioral expectations to support student learning Grades 6–12. Retrieved from https://www.schools.nyc.gov/school-life/know-your-rights/discipline-code.

No Child Left Behind (NCLB) Act of 2001, P. L. 107–110, U.S.C. § 6319 (2002).

O'Day, J., Bitter, C., & Gomez, L. (Eds.). (2011). *Education reform in New York City: Ambitious change in the nation's most complex school system*. Cambridge, MA: Harvard Education Press.

OECD (Organisation for Economic Co-operation and Development). (2019). *Education at a glance 2019: OECD indicators*. Paris: OECD Publishing.

OECD (Organisation for Economic Co-operation and Development). (2018). *Preparing our youth for an inclusive and sustainable world: The OECD PISA global competence framework*. Paris: OECD.

OECD. (2008). 21st century skills and competencies for new millennium learners in OECD countries. EDU working paper no. 41. Paris: Organisation for Economic Co-operation and Development.
Ogbu, J. U. & Simons, H. D. (1998). Voluntary and involuntary minorities: A cultural-ecological theory of school performance with some implications for education. *Anthropology & Education Quarterly*, 29(2), 155–188.
Olson, D. R. (2007). Self-ascription of intention: Responsibility, obligation and self-control. *Synthese* 159(2), 297–314. doi:10.1007/s11229-007-9209-2.
Olson, D. R. (2003). *Psychological theory and educational reform: How schools remake mind and society*. Cambridge: Cambridge University Press.
Olson, D. R. (1994). *The world on paper: The conceptual and cognitive implications of writing and reading*. Cambridge: Cambridge University Press.
Olson, D. R. & Bruner, J. (1996). Folk psychology and fold pedagogy. In D. R. Olson & N. Torrance (Eds.), *Handbook of education and human development* (pp. 9–27). Oxford: Blackwell.
Parker, F. W. (1900). The Quincy method. *American Journal of Sociology*, 6, 114–120.
Partnership for 21st Century Learning. (2019). https://education-reimagined.org/resources/partnership-for-21st-century-learning/.
Pearson. (2020). aimswebPlus. Retrieved from https://www.pearsonassessments.com/store/usassessments/en/Store/Professional-Assessments/Academic-Learning/Brief/aimsweb-Plus/p/100000519.html?tab=product-details.
Peurach, D. J. & Neumerski, C. M. (2015). Mixing metaphors: Building infrastructure for large scale school turnaround. *Journal of Educational Change*, 16, 379–420.
Pianta, R. C., Belsky, J., Houts, R., & Morrison, F. (2007). Opportunities to learn in America's elementary classrooms. *Science*, 315(5820), 1795–1796.
Plomin, R. (2018). *Blueprint: How DNA makes us who we are*. Boston, MA: MIT Press.
Questar. (2021). *Degrees of reading power®*. Apple Valley, MN: Questar Assessment Inc.
Questar. (2016). *Degrees of reading power®: Report interpretation guide*. Questar, Inc. Retrieved from https://www.questarai.com/drp-docs/Degrees-of-Reading-Power-Report-Interpretation-Guide.pdf.
Rakoczy, H., Brosche, N., Warneken, F., & Tomasello, M. (2009). Young children's understanding of the context-relativity of normative rules in conventional games. *British Journal of Developmental Psychology*, 27, 445–456.
RAND. (2002). *A decade of whole-school reform: The new American schools experience*. Santa Monica, CA: RAND Corporation. Retrieved from https://www.rand.org/pubs/research_briefs/RB8019.html.
Rawls, J. (1985). Justice as fairness: Political not metaphysical. *Philosophy and Public Affairs*, 14, 223–251.
Raymond, L., Weldon, S. L., Kelly, D., Arriaga, X. B., & Clark, A. M. (2013). Making change: Norm-based strategies for institutional change to address intractable problems. *Political Research Quarterly*, 67(1), 197–211.
Rebell, M. A. (2018). *Flunking democracy: Schools, courts, and civic participation*. New York: Teachers College Press.
Roccas, S., Sagiv, L., Schwartz, S. H., & Knafo, A. (2002). The big five personality factors and personal values. *Personality and Social Psychology Bulletin*, 28(6), 789–801. doi:10.1177/0146167202289008.
Rousseau, J. (1979). *Emile: Or on education*. Trans. A. Bloom. New York, NY: Basic Books.
Rousseau, J. J. (1920). *The social contract & discourses*. London & Toronto: J. M. Dent & Sons.
Rowan, B., Camburn, E., & Barnes, C. (2004). Benefiting from comprehensive school reform: A review of research on CSR implementation. In C. T. Cross (Ed.). *Putting the pieces together: Lessons from comprehensive school reform research* (pp. 1–52). Washington, DC: The National Clearinghouse for Comprehensive School Reform.
RTI Action Network. (2020). Tiered instruction and intervention in a response-to-intervention model. Retrieved from http://www.rtinetwork.org/essential/tieredinstruction/tiered-instruction-and-intervention-rti-model.
Ryan, R. M. & Deci, E. L. (2000). Self-determination theory and the facilitation of intrinsic motivation, social development, and well-being. *American Psychologist*, 55, 68–78.

Salz, J. B., Geiger, A. P., Anderson, R., Johnson, BB, & Marren, R. (2016). What, if anything, is a social niche? *Evolutionary Ecology*, 30, 349–364.

Science Daily. (June 26, 2020). Comprehending comprehension. Retrieved from https://www.sciencedaily.com/releases/2013/11/131106101610.htm.

Science Daily. (June 26, 2020). Sound and vision: Visual cortex processes information auditory information, too. Retrieved from https://www.sciencedaily.com/releases/2014/05/140525155316.htm.

Science Daily. (June 26, 2020). More challenging content in kindergarten boosts later performance. Retrieved from https://www.sciencedaily.com/releases/2014/03/140319093753.htm.

Science Daily. (June 26, 2020). Researchers show power of mirror neuron system in learning, language understanding. Retrieved from https://www.sciencedaily.com/releases/2013/12/131219142317.htm.

Science Daily. (June 26, 2020). Study shows 'readability' scores largely inaccurate. Retrieved from https://www.sciencedaily.com/releases/2014/01/140108102449.htm.

Scribner, S. & Cole, M. (1973). Cognitive consequences of formal and informal education. *Science*, 182(4112), 553–559.

Searle, J. (2010). *Making the social world*. New York, NY: Oxford University Press.

Searle, J. R. (1983). *Intentionality: An essay in the philosophy of mind*. Cambridge: Cambridge University Press.

Searle, J. (1969). *Speech acts: An essay in the philosophy of language*. Cambridge: Cambridge University Press.

SelectUSA. (2020). Media and entertainment spotlight. Retrieved from https://www.selectusa.gov/media-entertainment-industry-united-states.

Self-identity (June 10, 2020). In Lexico. Retrieved from https://www.lexico.com/en/definition/self-identity.

Senge, P. M. (2006). *The fifth discipline: The art and practice of the learning organization*. New York, NY: Doubleday.

Shweder, R. A. (1990). Cultural psychology: What is it? In Stigler, J. W., Shweder, R. A., & Herdt, G. (Eds.). *Cultural psychology: Essays on comparative human development* (pp. 1–46). Cambridge, UK: Cambridge University Press.

Siegel, D. (2020). *The developing mind: How relationships and the brain interact to shape who we are*. (3rd ed.). New York, NY: The Guilford Press.

Siegel, D. (2014). The science and art of presence: How being open and receptive to life cultivates well-being. *Mindsight Digital Journal*. Mindsight Institute.

Siegel, D. (2010). *Mindsight: The new science of personal transformation*. New York, NY: Bantam Books Trade Paperbacks.

Skinner, B. F. (1974). *About behaviorism*. New York, NY: Alfred Knopf, Inc.

Skinner, B. F. (1965). Science and human behavior.

Skinner, B. F. (1957). *Verbal learning*. New York, NY: Appleton-Century-Croft.

Social Security Administration. (2020). Education and lifetime earnings. Retrieved from https://www.ssa.gov/policy/docs/research-summaries/education-earnings.html#:~:text=Men%20with%20bachelor's%20degrees%20earn,earnings%20than%20high%20school%20graduates.

Sousa, S. & Armor, D. (2016). The effectiveness of title I: Synthesis of national-level evidence from 1966-2013. *Universal Journal of Educational Research*, 4(1), 205–311.

Southwood, N. & Eriksson, L. (2011). Norms and conventions. *Philosophical Explorations*, 14(2), 195–2017.

Stigler, J. W. & Hiebert, J. (1999). *The teaching gap*. New York, NY: Free Press.

Stiller, J. & Dunbar, R. I. M. (2007). Perspective-taking and memory capacity predict social network size. *Social Networks*, 29(1), 93–104.

Study. (June 4, 2020). In Lexico.com. Retrieved from https://www.lexico.com/definition/study.

Tamborini, C. R., Kim, C, & Sakamoto, A. (2015). Education and lifetime earnings in the United States. *Demography*, 52, 1383–1407.

Taylor, K. (January 21, 2015). Chancellor set to centralize management of New York City schools. *New York Times*. https://www.nytimes.com/2015/02/08/nyregion/chancellor-carmen-farina-changes-new-york-city-schools-course.html?searchResultPosition=4.

Taylor, K. (February 6, 2015). Chancellor Carmen Farina changes New York City schools' course. *New York Times*. https://www.nytimes.com/2015/01/22/nyregion/new-york-city-school-superintendents-authority-over-principals.html?action=click&module=RelatedCoverage&pgtype=Article&region=Footer.

Taylor, F. W. (1911). *The principles of scientific management*. New York, NY: Harper & Brothers.
Taylor, F. W. (1912). *Shop management*. New York, NY: Harper & Brothers Publishers.
Teach. (June 10, 2020). In https://www.lexico.com/en/definition/teach.
Teaching. (June 10, 2020). In https://www.lexico.com/en/definition/teaching.
The Center for civil Rights Remedies. (2016, June 2). School suspensions cost taxpayers billions. Retrieved from https://www.civilrightsproject.ucla.edu/news/press-releases/featured-research-2016/school-suspensions-cost-taxpayers-billions.
The Members of the Established Church. (1843). *Christian observer*. London: Hatchard and Company.
The World Bank. (2018). Decline of global extreme poverty continues but has slowed: World Bank. Press Release No: 2019/030/DEC-GPV. Retrieved from https://www.worldbank.org/en/news/press-release/2018/09/19/decline-of-global-extreme-poverty-continues-but-has-slowed-world-bank.
Thorndike, E. L. (1898). Animal intelligence: An experimental study of the associative processes in animals. *Psychological Monographs: General and Applied*, 2(4), i–109.
Tippett, K. (Host). (2009, November 19). On being. *Adele Diamond: The science of attention*. Retrieved from https://onbeing.org/programs/adele-diamond-the-science-of-attention/.
Toe the Line. (July 7, 2020). In Lexico. Retrieved from https://www.lexico.com/en/definition/toe.
Tomasello, M. (2019). *Becoming human: A theory of ontogeny*. Cambridge, MA: Belknap Press: An imprint of Harvard University Press.
Tomasello, M. (2016). *A natural history of human morality*. Cambridge, MA: Harvard University Press.
Tomasello, M. (2014). *A natural history of human thinking*. Cambridge, MA: Harvard University Press.
Tomasello, M. (2009). *Why we cooperate*. Boston, MA: MIT Press.
Tomasello, M. (2008). *Origins of human communication*. Boston, MA: MIT Press.
Tomasello, M (2003) *Constructing a language: A usage-based theory of language acquisition*. Boston, MA: Harvard University Press.
Tomasello, M. (1999). *The cultural origins of human cognition*. Cambridge, MA: Harvard University Press.
Tomasello, M. & Farrar, M. J. (1986). Joint attention and early language. *Child Development*, 57(6): 1454–1463.
Tomasello, M. & Rakoczy, H. (April, 2003). What makes human cognition unique? From individual to shared to collective intentionality. *Mind & Language*, 18(2), 121–147.
Tocqueville, A. (1900). *Democracy in America*. London and New York: Colonial (trans. Henry Reeve).
Tucker-Drob, E. M., Briley, D. A., & Harden, K. P. (2013). Genetic and environmental influences on cognition across development and context. *Current Directions in Psychological Science*, 22(5), 349–355. doi:10.1177/0963721413485087.
Tyack. (1974). *The one best system*. Cambridge, MA: Harvard University Press.
Tyler, R. W. (1949). *Basic principles of curriculum and instruction*. Chicago, IL: University of Chicago Press.
United Federation of Teachers. (2018). Teachers salary schedule—2018–2020. Retrieved from https://www.uft.org/sites/default/files/attachments/Teachers%20Salary%20Schedule%20-%202018%20to%202021.pdf.
United Federation of Teachers. (2018). Joint intentions and commitments. Retrieved from https://www.uft.org/files/attachments/teachers-contract-2009-2018.pdf.
UNESCO (United Nations Educational, Scientific and Cultural Organization) & UNICEF. (2017). Accountability in education: Meeting our commitments. Global education monitoring report. Available from https://unesdoc.unesco.org/ark:/48223/pf0000259338.
United Nations Children's Fund/UNESCO. (2007). *A human rights-based approach to education for all*. New York, NY: UNESCO.
United Nations General Assembly. (1948). *Universal declaration of human rights (217 [III] A)*. Paris. Retrieved from https://www.un.org/en/about-us/universal-declaration-of-human-rights.
United States Bureau of Economic Analysis. (2020). Outdoor recreation. Retrieved from https://www.bea.gov/data/special-topics/outdoor-recreation#:~:text=The%20U.S.%20outdoor%20recreation%20economy,product%20(GDP)%20in%202017.

United States Bureau of Labor Statistics. (2020). Food and beverage serving and related workers. Retrieved from https://www.bls.gov/ooh/food-preparation-and-serving/food-and-beverage-serving-and-related-workers.htm.

United States Bureau of Labor Statistics. (2020). Recreation workers. Retrieved from https://www.bls.gov/ooh/personal-care-and-service/recreation-workers.htm.

United States Census. (2020). U.S. school spending per pupil increased for fifth consecutive year, U.S. Census Bureau reports. Retrieved from https://www.census.gov/newsroom/press-releases/2019/school-spending.html.

United States Department of Agriculture. (2020). Food service industry market segments. Retrieved from https://www.ers.usda.gov/topics/food-markets-prices/food-service-industry/market-segments/#:~:text=A%20Large%20and%20Growing%20Market,was%20supplied%20by%20foodservice%20facilities.

United States Department of Agriculture. (2016). U.S. horticulture in 2014. Retrieved from https://www.nass.usda.gov/Publications/Highlights/2016/Census_of_Horticulture_Highlights.pdf.

United States Department of Education (2020a). Part F: Comprehensive school reform. Retrieved August 10, 2020 from https://www2.ed.gov/policy/elsec/leg/esea02/pg13.html.

United States Department of Education (2020b). Race to the Top Fund. Retrieved from https://www2.ed.gov/programs/racetothetop/index.html.

United States Department of Labor Statistics. (2020). Food and beverage serving and related workers. Retrieved from https://www.bls.gov/ooh/food-preparation-and-serving/food-and-beverage-serving-and-related-workers.htm.

Unterman, R. & Haider, Z. (2019). *New York City's small schools of choice: A first look at effects on postsecondary persistence and labor market outcomes.* New York, NY: MDRC.

Urban Assembly School for Green Careers. (December 6, 2020). Retrieved from https://uagreencareers.org/remote-learning.

Urbinati, N. (2015). *The tyranny of the moderns.* New Haven, CT: Yale University Press.

Valsiner, J. (1997). *Culture and the development of children's actions: A theory of human development* (2nd ed.). Chichester: John Wiley & Sons.

Vanderbilt. (2020). Math curriculum based measures. Retrieved from https://my.vanderbilt.edu/specialeducationinduction/files/2013/07/IA.Math-CBM.pdf.

Vygotsky, L. S. (1978). *Mind in society: The development of higher psychological processes.* In M. Cole, et al. (Eds.). Cambridge, MA: Harvard University Press.

Walz, M. (2010, November 4). City receives $19.8 mill. For 11 schools it hopes to "transform." Chalkbeat. https://ny.chalkbeat.org/2010/11/4/21087417/city-receives-19-8-mill-for-11-schools-it-hopes-to-transform.

Wimmer, H. & Peerner, J. (1983). Beliefs about beliefs: Representation and constraining function of wrong beliefs in young children's understanding of deception. *Cognition,* 13, 103–128.

World Health Organization. (2020, May). UN-Water global analysis and assessment of sanitation and drinking-water (GLAAS). Retrieved from https://www.who.int/water_sanitation_health/monitoring/investments/glaas/en/.

Wright, J. (2013). How to: Assess reading comprehension with DBM: Maze passages. Retrieved from http://www.jimwrightonline.com/mixed_files/lansing_IL/_Lansing_IL_Aug_2013/3_CBA_Maze_Directions.pdf.

Wright, J. (2013). How to: Assess reading speed with DBM: Oral reading fluency passages. Retrieved from http://www.jimwrightonline.com/mixed_files/lansing_IL/_Lansing_IL_Aug_2013/2_CBA_ORF_Directions.pdf.

Wylie, R. E. & Durrell, D. D. (1970). Teaching vowels through phonograms. *Elementary English,* 47, 787–791.

Zimmerman, A. (2019). New York City ends controversial renewal turnaround program—But the approach is here to stay. Chalkbeat. https://ny.chalkbeat.org/2019/2/26/21106894/new-york-city-ends-controversial-renewal-turnaround-program-but-the-approach-is-here-to-stay.

Zittoun, T., Valsiner, J., Vedeler, D. Salgado, J., Goncalves, M. M., & Ferring, D. (2013). *Human development in the life course: Melodies of living.* New York: Cambridge University Press.

Index

Note: *Italicized* page numbers refer to figures, **bold** page numbers refer to tables

Academic and Behavior Intervention Formats **8**
Academic Intervention Format 246, 257–265; materials 258; need for 257; overview 257; participants 258; primary aims 257; procedures 259–262; Rubric 264–265
Academical Village 291, *294*
achievement gap 21, 22, 38, 43, 285, 315, 347, 366–367, 416
action plans 280
actions 49
Activity Arc 51, *51*, 134
activity blocks 11–12, *12*, 79–80; egg-crate design *80*; open design *81*
Adams, John 27
African Americans 30–31
agency 45, 187
agreeableness 54
All Handicapped Children Act (1975) 304
anxiety disorder 69
Aristotle 42, 233
arts and crafts 119–120; *see also* Cultural Capital Curriculum
assessment program 301–314; academic background abilities and capacities 302; agenda 305–313; assessment lead **313–314**; course syllabi 313; curriculum-based measures 306–309; data management and analysis 302–303; evaluation practices 302–303; formal assessments 311; interim reading comprehension 309–311, **311**; lead responsibilities 301–304; letter name fluency CBM 307–308; letter sound fluency CBM 307–308; math fluency CBM 307; within McAllister model 305; oral reading fluency CBM 308, *309*; overview 301; reconceptualizing 304–305; report cards 311–313; resources 303; school governance 303; state 313; traditional uses 303–304; training 303; written expression CBMs 308–309, **309–310**; year-long implementation plan **313–314**
assessment workshop 342

atelier 78
Atlanta Compromise 30–31, 33
attention deficit and hyperactivity disorder (ADHD) 69
audio books 112
audio files 114
autobiographical memory 47, 49, 155, 159, 187

Background 50
back-up/on-call 245
banking approach 32
basic actions 50
BBC Wordmaster 109
behavior conference 244–245
behavior intervention 246
behavior reflection 244–245
behavioral disorders 69
Behavioral Intervention Format 257–267; materials 258; need for 257–258; overview 257; participants 258; primary aims 257–258; procedures 259–260; Rubric 266–267
behaviorism 28, 35
Benedict, Ruth 15, 25, 46, 137, 318
Bentham, Jeremy 27, 72
Big 5 personality traits 54
Binet, Alfred 28–29
birding 118; *see also* natural world curriculum
blank canvas curriculum 120–121; *see also* Cultural Capital Curriculum
Blue Book 240
Bobbitt, Franklin 28
boxing club 125–126; *see also* physical education program
Brandies High School **406–407**
broadcast professional development 343
Brookings Institute 70
Brown v. Board of Education (1954) 20, 33, 43, 239
Bruner, Jerome 6, 35, 62, 63, 83, 221–222
Burns, Haywood 348

Carranza, Richard 22
Center for Civil Rights Remedies 238

438 *Index*

check in conferences 280
Chetirko, Jeff 382–383
childhood, social worlds of 58
Chomsky, Noam 62
Christopher Columbus High School 17–20
cingulate 135
circle of freedom 241
citizen science 118; *see also* natural world curriculum
civic competencies 45
civic skills 45
civil rights 16, 32–33, 276
Civil Rights Act (1964) 21, 33, 34
Civil Rights movement 239
Civil Rights program 315–322; 12:1:1 program 320; assessment in 316; code blue 318; democratic equality 315–316; and disability 320; double down principle 321; equity imperative 318–319; equity practices 318–319; individualized education programs 320–321; instructional accounting 316–317; intervention coordinator 317; intervention programs 319; keepers corps 319; language learning 321; lead responsibilities 316–318; opportunity checks 319; overview 315; school governance 318; special learners 319–321; sufficiently supplements 321; year-long implementation plan **321–322**
code blue 381
Cole, Michael 41, 65, 73, 423
Coleman Report 21, 34, 43–44
collaborative art 120; *see also* blank canvas curriculum
collective intentionality 57, 62, 72, 235, 284, 378
Columbus High School 18, 363, 365, **366**, 368
Common Core State Standards (CCSS) 36, 70, 95
Community Education program 276, 323–326, 381; community talent recruitment 324; events coordinator 323; lead projects 324–326; lead responsibilities 323–324; monthly open house 324–325; school governance 324; school newspaper 324, 325; science and technology fair 325; social media 324, 325–326; volunteer corps 325; web presence 324, 325–326
community talent recruitment 324
community-involved school development and governance 296
competence feedback 12
complex actions 50
Comprehensive School Reform (CSR) program 21
compulsory education 26–27
conscientiousness 54
conscious awareness 48–52
conscious intentions 49
construction-based language acquisition 63

Content Share Format **8**
conventional liberties 3, 240
cooperation 187
Cooperative Unison Reading Format **8**, 12, 84, 190–207; activities 204; assessment 197–198; coordinating mental states 201; deep learning 200–201; democracy in 199; description of 190; dismantling curricular segregation 202–203; distributed leadership in 192; embracing confusion and uncertainty 202; even participation in 192; executive regulation 199; genre practice 200; group cohesion in 192; group schedules in 196–197; grouping in 195–196; identity building 201–202; log 198; materials 191; mindful reading 202; power of discourse 203; primary aims 191; procedures 191–195; process check 192–193; productive breaching in 192; program procedures 195–198; relational adjudication 199; resources 192; role of the guide in 193; Rubric 204–207; as a rule game 192; rules 193–195; self-responsibility 199–200; social capital 202; social grooming 203; social plane 200; text preparation in 196; text selection in 196; transfer 203
creative expression 116
critical consciousness 32
crossword puzzles 109
Csikszentmihalyi, Mihaly 47, 53, 105
culinary arts 126; *see also* Cultural Capital Curriculum
cultural capital 14, 68
Cultural Capital Curriculum 5–6, 115–128; annual gala 127; arts and crafts 119–120; blank canvas curriculum 120–121; citizen science 118; collaborative art 120; culinary arts 126; curation of music 121; dance time 121; domains 116–117; electronic piano 121; entrepreneur program 124–125; games 118–119; horticulture 117–118; makers space 123–124; media lab 126; miniature paintings 121; music and dance 121; natural world 117–118; open mic 121; overview 115–116; pets 117; physical education program 126; playlists 121; programmatic priorities 127; school hires 126; school uniforms 120; workshops of possibility 122–123; writing gallery 121
cultural expression 116
cultural niche 5, 7, 25, 65–67, 68, 69, 70, 72, 77, 122, 296
cultural respon-civility 234
curation of music 121; *see also* music and dance
Curran, Shannon 381
curriculum 6; linear/incremental 28; reform 35–36
Curriculum Program 327–331; advertisements 327; assessment 327; Cultural Capital Curriculum 6; evaluation 327; lead

responsibilities 327–329; Learning Cultures 6–14; practice 327–328; programs and events 329; reporting 327; resources 329; school governance 329; Sparks 5–6; sufficiently supplements 330; test genre curriculum 329; training 328, 329–330; year-long implementation plan **330–331**
curriculum-based measures (CBMs) 306–309; description of 306–307; letter name fluency 307–308; letter sound fluency 307–308; math fluency 307; maze 308; oral reading fluency 308, **309**; written expression 308–309, **309–310**
cycle 2 observations 280–281

dance time 121
Danielson Framework for teacher effectiveness 351
De Blasio, Bill 21
De Tocqueville, Alexis 43
Deci, E.L. 159
Decker, Kerry 283, 351, 378, 381, 389, 391, 394
deep learning 200–201
Degrees of Reading Power (DRP) 309–311, **311**
deliberation skills 45
Delpit, Lisa 139
democratic education 45
democratic individualism 234
Dennis, Sarah 381
desegregation 14, 20, 33–35, 43
Dewey, John 29, 31–32, 33, 53, 54, 67, 68, 115, 127, 131, 134, 155, 199, 202, 315–316, 419
Dilemmas of a Progressive Black Educator (Delpit) 139
disability 320
discipline 237–238; code 238, 252–253; costs of 238; hallway 245; punitive 238
disequilibrium 159
dispositions 106–107
distractions 106–107
diversity 68–69
documentaries 112
dorsolateral prefrontal cortex 135
double down principle 321
Douglass, Frederick 190
dropouts 238
DuBois, W.E.B. 31, 33, 71
Dunbar, Robin 26–27, 55, 67
Dunbar's Number 67
Dweck, Carol 160
dyslexia 69, 202

E. W. Gordon and Associates 301
Ecosystem Curriculum 79
ecosystem design 289, **290**, *292*, **295**
Edinburgh Enlightenment 27
education: and rights 71–72; sustaining innovations in 73–74

education reform 32–38; adequacy of opportunity 34–35; and civil rights 32–33; curriculum reform 35–36; equality of educational opportunity (EEO) 33–35
egalitarianism 15–17
egg-crate design 287, *288*
electronic piano 121; *see also* music and dance
Elementary and Secondary Education Act (1965) 34, 38, 43, 240, 272
Emancipation Proclamation (1863) 239
emotionships 61
empiricism 45, 68
English language arts (ELA) 350–353, 358, 384, 385–387
English Language learners (ELLs) 215, 358, 384, 385
entrepreneur program 124–125
entrepreneurship 116–117
epistemic vigilance 59, 60
Equality Act 240
equality of educational opportunity (EEO) 21, 33–35, 42, 43–45; adequacy-based definition of 44–45; criteria for 43–44; and framework for learning 47–70
equilibration 60, 199
Etsy 125
evaluative discourses 60
events coordinator 323
evolutionary self 105
extroversion 54

fairness principle 281, 282
Family Educational Rights and Privacy Act (FERPA) 251–252
fascism, defeat of 32
feedback 159
first folk pedagogy 86
Fiverr 125
Foucault, Michel 27
Fourteenth Amendment 14, 21
fourth pedagogy 86
Framework for Professional Development (FPD) 336–344, 394–395; assessment workshop 342; broadcast professional development 343; evaluation 338–339; holistic assessment of professional learning 339–340; improvement survey 344; inquiry teams 341–342; intervisitations 341–342; lab sites 341–342; monthly training workshops 343; needs assessment survey 340; new staff 343; orientation 338; professional development improvement survey 343; professional personalized learning plan **340**, 340; project coaching in 337–338; public information presentations 343; staff in need of additional support 343; study groups 343; sustainability 337; year-long implementation plan **345**
free will 50
freedom 53

Freire, Paolo 30–31
functionalist language acquisition 63

games 118–119; *see also* Cultural Capital Curriculum
genre 110
genre collections 110
genre practice 64–65, 83–85, 99–100; Cooperative Unison Reading 200; learning through use and activity 84; mentalizing 85; prolepsis 84–85; texts as forms of actions 83–84
Gergen, Kenneth 59
gig economy 125
gist 110–111
Gordon, Edmund W. 20, 32, 34, 44–45, 85, 349
gossips 136
grassroots lesson 148–150
gratitude list 107
Green, Jon 378, 381
group identity 233
group teaching 28–29
guides 86

hallway discipline 245
Hanushek, Eric 22
happiness 105–106
Harvard Seminar On Equality of Educational Opportunity (1972) 44
hate 49
Haywood Burns initiative 348–349
High School of Language and Innovation (HSLI) 17–20, 356, 363–377; academic development 365; academic preparation 368; achievement gap 366–367; achievement of equality of educational opportunity 367–368; education and economics 369; external evaluations of school quality 369, **371–376**; graduation rates 365; McCallister Model initiative 363–365; populations 363; projected life earnings for graduates **370**; quality review report **371–376**; reform success 365; report card metrics **366**; school culture 368; school quality guide **367**, **369**; school quality metrics **410**; school quality ratings **368**
holistic assessment of professional learning 339–340
horticulture 117–118; *see also* natural world curriculum
human capital 67–68, 114
hunter-gatherer societies 68

identity 160
identity building 201–202
imaginary rights 72
improvement survey 344
In *Rodriguez v. San Antonio ISD* 20–21
individual expression 116
individualism 30–31

individualized education programs (IEPs) 320–321
Individuals with Disabilities Act (2004) 320
Individuals with Disabilities Education Improvement Act 304
industrial schools 27, *30*
informal reading inventories (IRIs) 312
inquiry teams 341–342
instructional accounting 17, 160–161
instructional equity and accounting 281–282
Integrative Math Format 219–223; description of 219; integration 222; materials 220; primary aims 219; procedures 220–221; Rubric 223; zones of proximal development 222
intention 49–50
intentions-in-actions 49–50
intervisitations 341–342
intrinsic motivation 159–160
I-R-E discourse 29, 147
I-self 4, 13, 48, 60

Jacob, Francois 122–123
Jacob Riis School 19, 350–356, **355–356**
James, William 48
Jarrell, Emily 378
Jefferson, T. 27
Jim Crow laws 239
Johnson, Lyndon B. 43
joint intentionality 56–57, **57**
Jung, Richard 89

K-12 Student Bill of Rights and Responsibilities: addition rights of students age 18 and over 251–252; right to due process 251; right to free, public school education 249–250; right to freedom of expression and person 250–251; student responsibilities 252
Kahan, Richard 378
Keepers of the Culture 6, 79, 233–256; academic and behavior intervention 246; activities 249; background 235–236; back-up/on-call 245; behavior conference 244–245; behavior regulation 244–245; classroom social norms rubric 254–256; cultural respon-civility 234; curriculum practices 238–246; democratic individualism in 234; discipline in 237–238; freedom's paradox 247–249; hallway discipline 245; K-12 Student Bill of Rights and Responsibilities 249–253; keepers corps 246, 282–283; ladder of self-regulation 242–244; responsibility-based self-control 237; social contract talk 239–242; social norms 234–237, 247, **248**; social norms onboarding 238; status function declarations 235; teaching norms 236–237; tiers of 246–247, **247**; we-ness principle 233–234

KhanAcademy.org 94
Kornhuber, Hans 89

lab sites 341–342
LaBua, Daphne 198
ladder of self-regulation 242–244, 393
Lagemann, Ellen 29
language, acquisition of 61–63
language acquisition device (LAD) 62
language acquisition support system (LASS) 6, 62
Language Games Format 225–229; description of 225; integration 227; materials 225; primary aims 225; procedures 226; Rubric 228–229; social contract 234; as usage-based alternative 227
lateness 151–152
Lau v. Nichols decision 240
learning: domains of 90; self-organized 86–87
Learning Conference Format **8**, 155–163; activities 161; calendar 156; classroom systems 160–161; concrete feedback 159; description 155; disequilibrium 159; identity 160; intrinsic motivation 159–160; materials 156; primary aims 155; procedures 156–158; record 156; recordkeeping 161; rights and opportunities to learn 160–161; Rubric 162–163; self-direction 159; self-perceptions 160; Sparks 111, 114
Learning Cultures Formats 6–14, 78–79, 91, **92**; architecture 11–12; description of **8**; Lesson in 147–148; observation protocol *341*; rubrics 7–11; and self-identity 12–13
learning disorders 69
Learning Environment 137–144; activities 137–138, 139; environmental print displays 141; organizing 137–138; primary aims 140; records 141–142; resources and equipment 141; Rubric 140–142; space 140
Learning Metrics Task Force (LMTF) 70
Learning Share Format 164–175; cultural learning 166; description 164; materials 164; primary aims 164; procedures 164–165; responsibility 165; Rubric 166–167; speaking and listening 166; vicarious learning 165
Learning Teams Format **8**, 208–218, 396; activities 215; C-DEEP Survey 212; check-in quiz 212; critical consciousness 214; curriculum extensions and integration 214; description of 208; drafts 209–210; English Language learners 215; evidence record 210; framework 214; GIST study guide 210; ground rules 211; group goal setting 212; materials 209; moral self-governance 215; motivation of shared intentionality 212; peer accountability 214; peer assessment 212; personal learning form 211; pre-test 210; primary aims 208–209; procedures 209–213; prolepsis 214; research archive 211; research process 210–211; Rubric 215–218;

social assessment 212; social cognition 215; students with special needs 215; technology in 215; unit questions guide 210
learning zones 79–82
Lee, Pamela 357
Lesson Format **8**, 145–155; description 145; disruptions from lateness 151–152; grassroots lesson 148–150; in Learning Cultures model 147–148; materials 145; norming 150–151; planning and lesson content 148; primary aims 145; procedures 145–147; Rubric 153–154; Small-group Instruction Format 152
letter name fluency 307–308; *see also* curriculum-based measures (CBMs)
letter sound fluency 307–308; *see also* curriculum-based measures (CBMs)
Lewin, Kurt 52
library card 112
life spaces 52
Lincoln Logs 139
literacy: acquisition of 61–63; learning as genre practice 64–65
literacy hypothesis 83
Locke, John 45

Machiavelli, Niccolò 3, 25
makers space 123–124; *see also* Cultural Capital Curriculum
Manhattan Academy of Technology (MAT) 350
math fluency 307; *see also* curriculum-based measures (CBMs)
math skills 108
McCallister Learning Cultures Initiative 19
McCallister Model 3–4, 77–87; curriculum programs 5–14, 78–79; genre practice 83–85; learning zones 79–82; role of guides in 85–87; rubrics 82; as a studio for the self 78; as universal design for learning 13–14
McNamara, Sabina 378
Mead, George Herbert 4, 48
Media Lab 126; *see also* Cultural Capital Curriculum
mediational triangle 73, *73*
meditation 106
memorization 26
mentalizing 55, 85
Me-self 4, 13, 48–52, 60
Mesopotamia 26
meta language 179
mind reading 111
mindful reading 202
mindreading 55, 85
miniature paintings 121; *see also* blank canvas curriculum
Mitra, Sugata 87
modes of representation 221–222
Montessori, M. 149
monthly open house 324–325

monthly training workshops 343
moral self-governance 215
morphemes 108
music and dance 121; curation of music 121; dance time 121; electronic piano 121; open mic 121; personal play lists 121; *see also* Cultural Capital Curriculum

Nariman, Julie 357, 363, 364
narratives 111
National Association for the Advancement of Colored People (NAACP) 33
nativism 35, 45
natural world 116
natural world curriculum: birding 118; citizen science 118; horticulture 117–118; pets 117; *see also* Cultural Capital Curriculum
needs assessment survey 340
negative rights 72, 241
neuroticism 54
neurotransmitters 49
New Hope Charter School 243
New Visions for Public Schools 349
New York City Code of Discipline 240, 393
New York City Department of Education 348–349
norm psychology 55, 72, 237, 319
norms 57–58

Obama, Barack 22
objective morality 57, 234
OGOD (one gene, one disorder) hypothesis 69, 263
Olson, David 57, 236
on-call 245
open mic 121; *see also* music and dance
openness 54
operant conditioning 237
opportunity checks 281–282
oppositional defiance disorder 69
oral reading fluency 113–114, 308, **309**; *see also* curriculum-based measures (CBMs)
Othello 55
outliers 15–17
over-justification 238

panopticon 27
Parker, Francis 115
pedagogy: first folk 86; fourth 86; role of adults in 85–87; second folk 86; third folk 86
personality 53–54
person-environment relationship **52**, 52–53
perspective-shifting discourse 60, 61, 201, 203, 213, 400
Petrie Foundation 378
pets 117; *see also* natural world curriculum
phonemes 108
phonograms **98**
physical education program 125–126; *see also* Cultural Capital Curriculum

Piaget, Jean 60, 199
Pianta, R.C. 36
plans 49
playlists 121; *see also* music and dance
pleiotropy 69
Plessy v. Ferguson (1896) 33
Plomin, Robert 53–54, 69
positionality 348
Positive Behavioral Support System (PBIS) 238
positive learning paradigm 4, 42–74; cultural niche 65–67, 68, 69, 70, 72, 77; and equality of educational opportunity (EEO) 43–45; freedom 53; human capital 67–68; I-self 48; language acquisition 61–63; literacy learning 64–65; Me-self 48–52; overview 42–43; paradigm shift in learning 45–47; personality 53–54; person-environment relationship 52–53; prolepsis 69–70; shared intentionality 55–59; social construction 59–61; zones of proximal development 65–67
positive rights 71, 72, 241
Pretend Play Format 186–189; agency 187; autobiographical memory 187; cooperation in 187; description of 186; management 188; materials 186; primary aims 186; problem solving in 188; procedures 186–187; recreation in 188; Rubric 188–189
problem solving 188
professional development improvement survey 343
professional personalized learning plan **340**, 340
project coaching 337–338
prolepsis 69–70, 84–85, 101
proleptic activities 5
psychic energy 52–53
psychological force field 52
public education 29–32
public information presentations 343

quantum of education 21, 35

Race to the Top school turnaround initiative 22
rationalism 45, 68
readiness potential 48, 50, 89, 135
recreation 116, 188
reification 47
relational adjudication 59–60, 199, 201
remote learning 81–82
Renewal Schools Program 21
rereading 114
research design 347–348
research problem 347
research questions 347
respon-civility 234
response to intervention (RTI) 304
responsibility-based self-control 72, 237
rights 11; and education 71–72; imaginary 72; negative 72; positive 71

ritual 11
Rousseau, Jean-Jacques 3, 53, 57, 115, 234
Rubrics 7–11, 78–79, 82; Cooperative Unison Reading Format 204–207; Integrative Math Format 223; Language Games Format 228–229; as laws 82; Learning Conference Format 162–163; Learning Environment 140–142; Learning Share Format 166–167; Learning Teams Format 215–218; Lesson Format 153–154; Pretend Play Format 188–189; rights 11; ritual 11; Work Time Format 143–144; Writing Conference Format 174–175; Writing Share Format 181–184
Ryan, R.M.159, 180

San Antonio School District v. Rodriguez (1972) 35
scaffold 7
school culture 381
School Culture program 331–334; advertisements 332; assessment 333; behavior 333; governance 333; lead responsibilities 332–334; school development 333; training 333; year-long implementation plan **334**
school governance 324
school hires 126
school newspaper 324, 325
school uniforms 120; *see also* blank canvas curriculum
schools 25–41; civilization's first schools 26–29; and compulsory education 26–27; curriculum 28; discipline and control in 27; group teaching 28–29; as history's relic 26–29; industrial 27, *30*; overview 24; standardized testing 28–29
science and technology fair 325
Searle, John 50, 61, 62–63, 64, 71, 134, 235, 342
second folk pedagogy 86
second-level transformation 277–283; action plans 280; check in conferences 280; cycle 2 observations 280–281; ecosystem maintenance 280; instructional equity and accounting 281–282; Keepers of the Culture Corps 282–283; opportunity checks 281–282; substitute guides 283; sufficiency supplements 282; transformative evaluation 277–283
second-person morality 57
segregation *14*, 14
selective attention 46, 48–49
self-actualizing 47–70; cultural niche 67; freedom 53; human capital 67–68; I-self 48; language acquisition 61–63; literacy learning 64–65; Me-self 48–52; personality 53–54; person-environment relationship 52–53; prolepsis 69–70; shared intentionality 55–59; social construction 59–61; zones of proximal development 65–67

self-awareness 77
self-direction 159
self-identity 4, 12–13, 135; levels of *4*
self-organized learning 86–87
self-organized learning environments 293
self-perceptions 160
self-regulation 135–137
self-responsibility 91, 199–200
Shakespeare, William 55, 418
shared intentionality 55–59
Shweder, Richard 52
Siegel, Dan 61, 221, 263
sight word recognition 109
Silva, Tara 378
Skinner, B.F. 237
Small-group Instruction Format 152
Small-group Lesson Format **8**
social assessment 212
social brain 46, 56
social capital 68, 190, 202
social cognition 215
social construction 59–61
social contract 234
social contract talk 239–242; impact of 242; protocol 239–241; talk logistics 242
social grooming 136, 203
social learning 179
social media 324, 325–326
social norms 234–237, **248**; background 235–236; on-boarding 238; responsibility-based self-control 237; rubric 247; status function declarations 235; teaching norms 236–237
social opportunities 67–68
social plane 200
social worlds 58
socio-economic status (SES) 5–6, 21, 115
Sparks 5–6, 78, 88–114, 108–109; activity inventory 106–114; activity plan 91–105; benefits of 89–90; commitment 114; curriculum 90–91; curriculum map 93–94; daily learning regimen 95–101; discipline 114; dispositions 106–107; genre practice 99–100, 109–111; and happiness 105–106; learning 111–113; Learning Cultures 91, **92**; learning identity development 92–93; long-term academic goals 93; overview 88–89; personal development timeline 91–92, **92**; prolepsis 101; reading regimen for emergent readers 97; reading regimen for fluent readers 96–97; remote applications/plans 104–105; self-responsibility 91; synchronized thinking 113–114; vocabulary 109; weekly workout plan for short-term goals 102–104; writing regimen 98–99
special needs 29
spelling 109
Spencer Foundation 349
standardized testing 28–29

status function declarations (SFD) 8, 40, 72, 82, 235, 342
Students with Interrupted Formal Education (SIFE) 363
students with special needs 215
studio 78
study groups 343
substitute guides 283
sufficiency supplements 282
sufficiently supplements 321
Sumer 26
suspensions 238, 393–394

tabula rasa approach 45
talent 136
talk logistics 242
teachers in need of improvement (TINIs) 395
The Family School 357–358, **359–360**
the Individuals with Disabilities Education Act (IDEA) 251
The Urban Assembly 19
theory of mind 55, 58–59, 85
third folk pedagogy 86
Thorndike, Edward 28
Title I programs 21
Title I school-wide program design 285–287
Tomasello, Michael 46, 56–61, 63, 213, 233, 235
Training program: assessment and recordkeeping 335; framework for professional development 336–344; lead responsibilities 335–336; professional development 335–336; school governance 336; year-long implementation plan 335–345
transactional assessments 82
transactive paradigm 131
triumph narrative 155
turnaround 37–38
two-faced texts 110
Tyler, Ralph 28

UA Unison School 378
unconscious intentions 50
UNESCO 70
United Nations 32
United Nations Declaration of Human Rights 116, 244
Universal Declaration of Human Rights (1948) 32
Universal Declaration of Human Rights (UDHR) 239
universal education 26–27
Upanishads 42
Urban Assembly Academy of Civic Engagement 384–387, **387**
Urban Assembly High School for Green Careers (UAGC) 388–417; assessment 401–402; confirmation of successful transformation 398–405; culture 401–402; curriculum 395–396, 399; demographic and achievement data **406–407**; in fall 2013 391–394; graduation rate 388; instructional core 399–402, **404**; integration of McCallister Methods 396–397; Learning Cultures implementation timeline 389–394, **392**; lessons learned 412–416; pedagogy 399–401; professional development 394–395; progress report data 2016–2017 **408–409**; projected life earnings for graduates **411**, 411; and rebirth of public schools 411–412; report card overview 2012–2013 **389**, **390–391**; retrospective analysis of McAllister Model 407–411; school culture **404**; school environment survey results 388; school quality criteria 2013–2014 404–405; school quality metrics **410**; self-evaluations 397–403; social norms and culture in 392–394; student population 388; systems for improvement **404–405**; teacher evaluation 395; teacher teams 402–403
Urban Assembly Institute for New Technologies 382–384, **385–386**
Urban Assembly McCallister-Learning Cultures Initiative 364, 378–387; academic year 2012–2013 380; academic year 2013–2014 380–381; academic year 2015–2019 381–382; implementation of **380**; overview 378; phases **380**; suspensions 393–394; Urban Assembly Academy of Civic Engagement 384–387, **387**; Urban Assembly Institute for New Technologies 382–384, **385–386**
Urban Assembly School for Green Careers (UAGC) 17–20
usage-based theory of language acquisition 63, 225, 227

Valsiner, Jaan 66–67
volunteer corps 325
Vygotskian social plane 179
Vygotsky, L.S. 54–55, 65–66, 138, 200

W. Haywood Burns School 348–349
War on Poverty 21, 43
Warner, Sylvia Ashton 88
Washington, Booker T. 30, 33
"We" self 4, 13
web presence 324, 325–326
we-ness principle 233–234
We-self 54–55
whole-group teaching 29
whole-school transformation 15–17, 271–299; assessment 16, 275–276; civil rights 16, 276; community education 276; community-involved school development and governance 296; costs 296–297; curriculum 16, 276; dimensions of scale 284–285; distributed leadership in **274**, 275–277; ecosystem 271–273; ecosystem design 289, **290**, *292*, **295**; egg-crate design

287, *288*; innovative grouping systems 291–293; instructional accounting 17; lateral school training 17; school culture 16, 277; school leader responsibilities 274–275; self-organized learning environments 293; staffing 297–299; systems for second-level transformation 277–283; teacher evaluation 17; Title I school-wide program design 285–287; training 17, 277; year-long implementation plan 273–274, **274**, 283–284

Woods Hole conference 35–36

word chunking 108

work, dignity of 116

Work Time Format **8**, 11, 131–137; activity arc 134; contextualized instruction and guidance 137; curriculum 134–135; development 134–135; guide 143; learner 143; materials and learning environment 133; overview 131–132; potential 136; primary aims of 132–133, 143; procedures 133–137; Rubric 143–144; self-identity 135; self-regulation 135–136, 136–137; set up 133–134; social grooming 136; talent 136; time frame 132

workshops of possibility 122–123; *see also* Cultural Capital Curriculum

Writing Conference Format **8**, 85, 169–175; classroom systems 171–172; description 169; executive functions 171; materials 169; mental coordination 171; primary aims 169; procedures 169–171; record 173; recordkeeping 172–173; rights and opportunities to learn in 172; Rubric 174–175; social plane 171

writing fluency 113–114

writing gallery 121; *see also* Cultural Capital Curriculum

Writing Share Format **8**, *9–10*, 12, 176–184; classroom systems 180–181; materials 176; motivation 180; primary aims 176; procedures 176–178; rights and opportunities to learn in 180; Rubric 181–184; sharing as responsibility in 179–180; social learning 179; space in 180–181; writing instruction 179

written expression CBMs 308–309, **309–310**; *see also* curriculum-based measures (CBMs)

X,Y,C rule 341

XYZ Plan 29

yoga 126; *see also* physical education program

Young, Madeline 391

zone of free movement (ZFM) 66, 138

zone of possible action (ZPA) 66, 67, 138

Zone Theory 66

zones of proximal development (ZPDs) 65–67, 138

Printed in the United States
by Baker & Taylor Publisher Services